MW01121546

DATE DUE	RETURNED

STUDIES IN NATIONALISM AND ETHNIC CONFLICT

General Editors: Sid Noel, Richard Vernon

Studies in Nationalism and Ethnic Conflict examines the political dimensions of nationality in the contemporary world. The series includes both scholarly monographs and edited volumes that consider the varied sources and political expressions of national identities, the politics of multiple loyalty, the domestic and international effects of competing identities within a single state, and the causes of – and political responses to – conflict between ethnic and religious groups. The books are designed for use by university students, scholars, and interested general readers.

The editors welcome inquiries from authors. If you are in the process of completing a manuscript that you think might fit into the series, you are invited to contact them.

Parallel Paths

The Development of Nationalism in Ireland and Quebec

GARTH STEVENSON

McGill-Queen's University Press

Montreal & Kingston • London • Ithaca

ISBN 13 978-0-7735-3029-4   ISBN 10 0-7735-3029-0 (cloth)
ISBN 13 978-0-7735-3073-7   ISBN 10 0-7735-3073-8 (paper)

Legal deposit second quarter 2006
Bibliothèque nationale du Quebec

Printed in Canada on acid-free paper that is 100% ancient forest free
(100% post-consumer recycled), processed chlorine free

McGill-Queen's University Press acknowledges the support of the
Canada Council for the Arts for our publishing program. We also
acknowledge the financial support of the Government of Canada
through the Book Publishing Industry Development Program (BPIDP)
for our publishing activities.

Library and Archives Canada Cataloguing in Publication

Stevenson, Garth, 1943–
   Parallel paths : the development of nationalism in Ireland and
Quebec / Garth Stevenson.

Includes bibliographical references and index.
ISBN 13: 978-0-7735-3029-4   ISBN 10: 0-7735-3029-0 (bnd)
ISBN 13: 978-0-7735-3073-7   ISBN 10: 0-7735-3073-8 (pbk)

1. Nationalism–Québec (Province)–History. 2. Nationalism–Ireland–
History. 3. Québec (Province)–History–Autonomy and independence
movements. 4. Ireland–History–Autonomy and independence
movements. I. Title.

JC311.S827 2006   320.54'09714   C2005-907238-5

Typeset by Jay Tee Graphics in 10/12.5 New Baskerville

Contents

Acknowledgments

This book, like most academic publications, is the result of several years of reflection and (sometimes unconscious) preparation, several more years of research, several months of intensive writing, and a lengthy period of waiting for the comments of readers on the (more or less) finished product. During each stage, a number of obligations were incurred.

First and foremost, I am grateful to the Social Sciences and Humanities Research Council of Canada for funding this research under grant no. 410-99-0519. Its support enabled me to make several visits to Ireland, a country of which I had no previous experience, between 1999 and 2003, as well as shorter visits to archives in Ottawa and Quebec, and to hire student research assistants for three years.

I am grateful also to the Irish academics who took an interest in this project and provided me with hospitality and advice, including Tom Garvin and John Coakley of University College Dublin, Michael Marsh of Trinity College Dublin, and Richard English of Queen's University Belfast. They helped to make my visits to their great country both enjoyable and productive: so much so that I am now planning to embark on a second Irish research project once the present one is published.

Brock University in St Catharines, Ontario, which has transformed itself in recent years from a small, primarily undergraduate teaching institution to a medium-sized, research-oriented university, has provided me with a congenial working environment since 1987, and specifically during the period in which I worked on this book. In particular, I would like to thank my student research assistants at Brock: Richard Delano, Kristi Plett, and

Graham Howell. My colleagues in the Department of Political Science and the university community more broadly have also been supportive, while my students in various courses have contributed more ideas and insights to my understanding of nationalism than they probably realize.

I would like also to thank McGill-Queen's University Press and its two senior editors, Philip Cercone, with whom I have now worked on three books, and Donald H. Akenson, who is himself a distinguished scholar in the field of Irish history. I wish also to thank the two anonymous reviewers for the Press for their kind comments and useful suggestions regarding the manuscript. Finally, I thank Elizabeth Hulse for performing the sometimes tedious task of a freelance copy editor with patience, diligence, and erudition.

PARALLEL PATHS

CHAPTER ONE

Quebec, Ireland, and the Study of Nationalism

The end of the Cold War and the apparent collapse of Marxism as an influential system of ideological thought have rekindled academic interest in nationalism, which seems to be the only surviving thought system, apart from religion, with the capacity to inspire people and mobilize them for collective action. Nationalism, however, continues to have a bad press, possibly because of the excesses committed in its name by the Axis powers during the Second World War and the lasting after-effect of the propaganda generated in those days by the ultimately victorious (and allegedly non-nationalist) powers. Even an excessive interest in the subject of nationalism, let alone sympathy for it, can render a person suspect in some quarters. The British historian Eric Hobsbawm has actually suggested that "no serious historian of nations and nationalism can be a convinced political nationalist," although he would presumably not apply a similar caveat to the study of Marxism by Marxists.[1] The ease with which the populations of normally peaceful democracies could be mobilized in support of illegal wars of aggression against the nationalist regimes of Serbia and Iraq in recent years suggests that the phobia about nationalism is not confined to academic circles. Conversely, it might suggest that those populations, particularly in the United States, are not immune from their own form of nationalism, even if it is a nationalism that dares not speak its name.

There seems to be no universally accepted definition of nationalism, or even of the term "nation," from which it is derived. In the careless usage favoured by some English-speaking people and implicitly endorsed by the global organization called the "United Nations," any organized political community is a nation. At the other extreme, the precise and narrow definition of the term used by Joseph Stalin still carries some authority, despite its author's failings as a statesman. In Stalin's words, "A nation is an historically evolved, stable community of language, territory, economic life, and psychological makeup manifested in a community of culture ... It must be emphasized that none of the above characteristics is by itself sufficient to define a nation. On the other hand, it is sufficient for a single one of these characteristics to be absent and the nation ceases to be a nation."[2]

Stalin's definition, requiring the nation to pass many tests before its authenticity can be certified, seems excessively rigid. Nonetheless, many nationalists have selected one or more of the criteria listed by Stalin as indicators of who belongs to the nation and who is excluded. Common ancestry, or "race," for example, was once widely considered synonymous with nationality. Early in the twentieth century the French geographer André Siegfried entitled his book about the relations between anglophone and francophone Canadians *Le Canada: Les deux races*. However, ancestry is an involuntary and predetermined characteristic that cannot be changed. Definitions of the nation based on this characteristic, real or imagined, thus tend to be exclusive and intolerant, and have helped to give nationalism a bad name, particularly after the experience of Nazi Germany. (In fact, ethnicity as a qualification for German citizenship predated the Nazis and was not actually removed from German law until the 1990s.)[3] They have also been discredited by research demonstrating that "purity" of racial or ethnic origin is a myth in virtually all cases. This is particularly so in central Europe, where this form of nationalism has been most influential but where the population was formed by repeated waves of migration from different sources prior to the emergence of the modern state system. The same is also true of England, Scotland, and Ireland, despite their more insular locations.

An even more influential, and more plausible, criterion of nationality is language. Admittedly, this criterion owes some of its popularity to the myth that language is a reliable indicator of common origin or that people with similar languages must be genetically related. (We still refer to peoples speaking Slavic languages as Slavs, implying that in some way they must be of common ancestry.) However, it is possible to learn a new language and even to forget one's original language; so a linguistic definition of nationalism is not necessarily exclusive as a definition in terms of ancestry. Using language as a criterion of nationality also has a pragmatic justification since language is a means of communication, and those who share a language can more easily communicate with one another to form a political and social community. Democracy, which must be based on a shared discourse, made a common language more important than it was in dynastic states or empires. Particularly in Europe, the names of languages tend to correspond with the names of states: French in France, Swedish in Sweden, Polish in Poland, and so forth. On the other hand, closer investigation reveals that many of these languages were given their standard form, or in some cases virtually invented, by the nation-state with which they are identified or by a nationalist movement prior to the formation of the state. In France for example, as late as 1789 only a minority could speak any language recognizable as French. National schools and media imposed a standard language, based on the Parisian dialect, and a government agency, the Académie française, is still responsible for maintaining the purity of the language. French, in other words, was created by the French state, not vice versa. Modern Hebrew was virtually the creation of the state of Israel, few of whose Jewish settlers were really fluent in it when they arrived. Some languages, such as Norwegian and Slovakian, were regarded as mere dialects of other languages (Danish and Czech respectively) until after nationalist movements emerged in the nineteenth century. Some nations, such as Switzerland, still lack a common language. Some languages, particularly English, Arabic, and Spanish, are used by a number of different nations. There are thus major difficulties with making linguistic definitions of nationality fit the facts.

A completely different approach to defining the nation is to see it as an essentially subjective phenomenon, a product of the human imagination. A group of people who wish to be a nation and consider themselves as such are a nation This view is associated with the nineteenth-century French writer Ernest Renan, who used it in a celebrated public lecture to argue that Alsace-Lorraine was really a part of the French nation, which had annexed it before the French Revolution, despite its cultural affinities with Germany. (The new united German state had recently reclaimed the territory at the time when Renan spoke, but France was not reconciled to its loss.) Renan described a nation as "a great solidarity, based on the consciousness of the sacrifices that have been made and of those that there is a willingness to make again."[4] His point, made more concisely in his more familiar description of a nation as "un plébiscite de tous les jours," was that the nation is a subjective entity. The people of Alsace-Lorraine had become French by sharing in the memories and ideals of 1789, regardless of their ethnic origins. This view has become widely, although not universally, accepted, particularly by social scientists and historians. Ernest Gellner, one of the most influential students of nationalism in modern times, appeared uncertain whether the nation was an objective fact or a subjective construct, offering two possible definitions of the nation so as to avoid making a choice.[5] However, Benedict Anderson, in a widely cited book, agrees in effect with Renan by defining a nation as "an imagined political community."[6] It is imagined because no one can actually know all the other members of the group with which he or she claims to have the common bond of nationality. Walker Connor recognizes the subjective element by suggesting that a nation is a group of people who believe they are ancestrally related.[7] His definition is too narrow, however, since it would exclude nations that are divided by informal barriers of race or that have absorbed large numbers of immigrants since they were established; the United States of America would be disqualified on both counts. A definition that excludes the most important example of the phenomenon that it purports to define must be found wanting.

As a subjective entity, a nation does not depend on a list of objective characteristics so much as on the belief of a group of people that they constitute a community with common memories and aspirations. Renan rejected race, language, religion, and geography as essential criteria of nationhood, although it is a known fact that some self-described nations claim to be based on race (Japan), language (numerous European examples), religion (Pakistan), or geography (Australia). Renan might also have considered and rejected common institutions, which have brought about a sense of national solidarity among people of different origins in some instances (Switzerland or the United States) but have failed to do so in others (the Austrian Habsburg empire or, apparently, the USSR). This is not to deny that any of these criteria might contribute to the sense of solidarity with one another and differentiation from the rest of humankind that makes a group of people a nation, but none of them will necessarily do so, and all of them together may not suffice to do so. Both the fact that Hawaii is part of the United States and the fact that Ontario is not seem illogical to most people, apart from Canadians and Americans, but if the people of Hawaii consider themselves Americans and the people of Ontario do not, as is apparently the case, why should someone else's judgment be substituted for their own?

The question of whether states create nations or nations create states does not have a simple answer. In some cases, the sense of constituting a nation may include the aspiration to create a national state that has never existed, as with the Palestinians today. If a Palestinian state comes into existence, we may say that it was created by the Palestinian nation. In other cases, the sense of nationhood may persist for long periods after the disappearance of the state, as with partitioned Poland, and may eventually be rewarded with the establishment of a new state. Yet many states were created without benefit of nation or nationalism, through the ambitions of dynasties, the arbitrary boundary-setting of colonial empires, or even, as in the case of Belgium, as a result of agreement among their neighbours. In such cases, the sense of being a nation may (or may not) develop after the formation of the state, partly stimulated by the many ways in which states can influence the minds of the people who live in them. (As we have noted, a state can even create a language in its own image.) A state called England probably existed before the English nation, but few would doubt the reality of the English nation subsequently. On the other hand, a state may never create any real sense of nationhood among its people, although some states have survived into modern times without it. (It is doubtful whether Belarus, Kuwait, Macedonia, Moldova, Panama, or Singapore are nations in any meaningful sense, although all are members in good standing of the United Nations.) A more common situation is when a state develops a sense of nationhood among some, but not all, of its people. This may happen deliberately, if some of the people in the state are deemed by the dominant group to lack some of the criteria by which membership in the nation is defined. It may also happen, without deliberate intent by the dominant group, because one group of people believes itself to be either symbolically or materially disadvantaged by the nation/state and begins to form an "imagined community" of its own. If the deliberately or accidentally excluded group predominates on a particular part of the state's territory and is largely concentrated there, the chances are very high that it will contemplate seceding to form its own territorial nation-state. In theory, this outcome might be prevented by transforming the existing state into a multinational state, but that is a remedy that is rarely considered until it is too late, and in the best of circumstances, either creating or maintaining such a state is an extremely difficult endeavour.

Our discussion of the relationship between nation and state leads us from defining the nation to defining nationalism. Definitions of nationalism, like those of the root word from which it is derived, vary from narrow to broad. Ernest Gellner's definition, which Hobsbawm also accepts, describes nationalism as "a political principle, which holds that the political and the national unit should be congruent."[8] This is fairly specific, and it ignores the fact that some nationalists have been primarily concerned with cultural issues and have not demanded a sovereign state corresponding to their nation. Anthony Smith is perhaps somewhat less specific when he refers to nationalism as "an ideological movement, for the attainment and maintenance of self-government on behalf of a group, some of whose members conceive it to constitute an actual or potential 'nation' like the others."[9] Michael Hechter's definition of nationalism as collective action to make the governance unit correspond with the nation is almost identical with Smith's.[10] Elie Kedourie, in his influential anti-nationalist polemic published more than forty years ago, called nationalism "the doctrine [which] holds that humanity is naturally divided into nations, that nations are known

by certain characteristics which can be ascertained, and that the only legitimate type of government is national self-government."[11] At the broader end
of the spectrum, Walker Connor defines nationalism as identification with
and loyalty to one's nation, but as we have seen, his definition of "nation" is
somewhat narrow.[12] Perhaps the broadest, and most satisfactory, definition
of nationalism, is that of Louis Balthazar. In his classic history of Quebec
nationalism, Balthazar defines nationalism as "a movement that consists of
giving priority to national affiliation and to the struggle for a better recognition of the nation to which one belongs."[13] This definition has the merit of
encompassing nationalists whose demands do not include a fully sovereign
state or even a territorial "governance unit" corresponding to their nation.

Related to, but distinct from, the question of defining nationalism is the
issue of deciding when it was invented. Some scholars still see it as a phenomenon that recurs in many times and places throughout history, so that
certain passages of the Hebrew scriptures, the funeral oration of Pericles, or
the historical plays of Shakespeare might stand as evidence of its existence at
the time and place when they were written. Anthony Smith is perhaps the
leading exponent of this view, particularly in his later work. Smith argues
that the modernist theories are flawed because they "fail to account for the
historical depth and spatial reach of the ties that underpin modern
nations."[14] Adrian Hastings, in a book intended as a rebuttal to Hobsbawm's,
also adopts this position. He says that the Israel of the Old Testament provided the Western world with its original model of a nation, and that both
English and Scottish nationalism have existed since medieval times.[15] Liah
Greenfeld takes a middle-of-the-road position by suggesting that nationalism developed in the sixteenth century in England, but much later in most
other parts of the world.[16]

What is still the most influential academic view of nationalism nowadays,
however, sees it, like the steam engine, as an invention dating from near the
end of the eighteenth century. The pioneering work in this regard was perhaps that of Kedourie, a critic of nationalism who viewed it as a product of
Immanuel Kant's philosophy. Others attribute it to the French Revolution.
(The American Revolution, which preceded the French one by several
years, is less often cited, although the American sociologist Seymour Martin
Lipset referred to the United States as "the first new nation.")[17] This influential school of thought, known as the "modernists," includes Gellner, Anderson, Hobsbawm, and John Breuilly, among others. Anderson states that the
emergence of nationalism was only made possible by "the convergence of
capitalism and print technology on the fatal diversity of human language."[18]
Gellner associates it with the transition from agrarian to industrial society,
and Hobsbawm with the emergence of a lower middle class. Those who see

nationalism as a more universal phenomenon, or at least as predating these various factors, are sometimes called the "perennialists," as opposed to the modernists. Modernists logically have to regard the nation as subjective, a product of the imagination. Perennialists may or may not do so, but most of them nowadays in fact do so.

Apart from efforts to define and explain nationalism, there have been many attempts to classify particular examples of nationalism into categories. For example, nationalism may be classified as political nationalism, economic nationalism, or cultural nationalism, depending on the objectives emphasized by the nationalists. While political nationalism stresses the establishment of a national state, economic nationalism, often found in nations that already possess a state, focuses on industrialization, economic growth, and the lessening of dependence on external markets or sources of capital. Cultural nationalism, which at times may appear indifferent to both economics and politics, emphasizes objectives such as the preservation or revival of a distinct national language or an allegedly distinctive "way of life." The Irish historian John Hutchinson has even asserted that "cultural nationalism is a movement quite independent of political nationalism," although his book on cultural nationalism in Ireland actually suggests a certain degree of interdependence.[19]

Within the broad categories of political, economic, and cultural nationalism, further subclassifications are also possible; some political nationalists want to secede from an existing state, others to gain more autonomy within an existing state, still others to combine several existing states into a single new one. Some economic nationalists emphasize tariffs and self-sufficiency, while others are more concerned with restricting foreign ownership of economic assets. Some cultural nationalists wish to protect or to revive a language, while for others (such as anglophone Canadians who worry about the cultural influence of the United States), language is not really an issue.

Other kinds of classifications are also possible, such as Anthony Smith's distinction between ethnocentric and polycentric nationalism.[20] Ethnocentric nationalists, as defined by Smith, regard their own nation as superior to all others and are indifferent or hostile to nationalisms other than their own. This kind of nationalism is associated with imperialism and the desire to dominate other nations, although the relationship between cause and effect is not entirely clear. Some would say that the nationalism of Victorian England and of the present-day United States are cases in point. The examples of Germany and Japan in the 1930s and early 1940s hardly need to be emphasized. Less-powerful national groups are not immune to the tendency, as when some Canadian nationalists are reluctant to recognize the legitimacy of Quebec nationalism.

Polycentric nationalism, which, according to Smith, emerged after the French Revolution, is different in that it tends to approve of nationalism in general and does not regard its own nation as superior, or at least does not regard it as entitled to dominate others. Polycentric nationalists have a romantic sympathy for nations other than their own and are inclined to draw parallels between their own aspirations and those of other nationalists. Their ideal is a world of free and equal nations peacefully coexisting. The French (and later Russian) revolutionaries believed in this ideal in theory, although their actual treatment of less-powerful neighbours fell far short of it in practice. The young United States, Lipset's "first new nation," encouraged anti-colonial rebellions in Spanish America, but it too fell short of its ideals a generation later when it invaded Mexico. In the early twentieth century, Indian, Irish, and Egyptian polycentric nationalists observed one another's struggles against the British Empire with mutual interest and sympathy. In our own time, polycentric nationalists in several parts of the world, including Ireland and Quebec, seem to identify with the Palestinians. Commenting on the death of President Yasser Arafat in November 2004, Sinn Fein leader Gerry Adams observed, "There is a close affinity and affection between the Irish and Palestinian people and his death this evening will be a cause of much sorrow." Taoiseach Bertie Ahern, leader of the moderately nationalist Fianna Fail party, described Arafat as "a friend of Ireland and, indeed, a personal friend."[21]

A more familiar, although possibly less clear, distinction is that between "ethnic" and "civic" nationalism. The former is said to be exclusive, defining the national community in terms of some ascriptive criterion such as language, race, or religion and excluding those who do not share the characteristic. Civic nationalism, in contrast, is deemed to be inclusive, regarding all, or nearly all, persons residing permanently on the national territory as part of the nation and making no ascriptive distinctions between them.[22] At the risk of some oversimplification, we may say that ethnic nationalists reject, while civic nationalists accept, Renan's view of the nation as a voluntary association of individuals who share the same memories and aspirations.

The origins of the distinction between ethnic and civic nationalism can be traced back to the pioneering work of Hans Kohn, who used the labels "eastern" and "western" respectively for what would later be called ethnic and civic nationalism.[23] Kohn identified "western" (or civic) nationalism with France after the revolution and with democracy and liberalism. "Eastern" (or ethnic) nationalism arose in central Europe out of the reaction against the French invasion that followed the revolution. Nationalists there emphasized ascriptive inherited characteristics that allegedly defined their nations and distinguished them from the French. This type of nationalism, according to Kohn, later spread into eastern and southeastern Europe and what is now called the Middle East. Allegedly, it also rejected the democracy and liberalism associated with the French Revolution, as well as the tendency of the French revolutionaries to impose those ideals on their neighbours. Writing during the Second World War as a refugee from the latest manifestation of German ethnic nationalism, Kohn hardly needed to emphasize his conviction that the civic or French version was preferable to the ethnic or German version. The view that civic nationalism is morally superior to ethnic nationalism has characterized virtually all subsequent writing on the subject.

Most subsequent writers on nationalism, particularly those of the modernist school, have continued to make the distinction between these two types of nationalism, however labelled. Some, such as Kedourie and Connor, confuse the issue by using the label of "nationalism" to mean the "ethnic" type only. Kedourie, whose book on nationalism influenced Pierre Elliott Trudeau, regarded nationalism (thus narrowly defined) as evil. Yet, like Trudeau, he saw nothing necessarily reprehensible in giving loyalty or allegiance to the state. Connor distinguishes loyalty to the ethnic nation (nationalism) from loyalty to the state (patriotism). Implicitly, the former is viewed with suspicion, while the latter is acceptable and even praiseworthy. However, the power of ethnic nationalism is recognized. Connor even suggests that the Germans and Japanese fought more effectively than their opponents in the Second World War because Germany and Japan were real nation-states that could inspire nationalist loyalty, while their principal opponents were not.[24] Non-national states could inspire only patriotism, which is a less-powerful emotion.

We will encounter this distinction between ethnic and civic nationalism later in the present study, but will try to reserve moral judgment where it is not clearly warranted. The distinction between the two types is not as clear-cut as it is sometimes alleged to be, and is in large part the product of circumstances. Civic nationalism – or patriotism, if that term is preferred – comes easily to those who are fortunate enough to live under a state whose boundaries correspond at least approximately to their nation, however defined. In these happy circumstances, no clear distinction between nationalism and patriotism, or between nation and state, is necessary or even possible. Although the state may include a few people who are not recognized as co-nationals, and although a few people who are so recognized may be located outside the state, the congruence between state and nation is close enough that allegiance to the state is a way of showing loyalty to the nation. The territorial state itself, by its very nature, tends to distribute many benefits (such as law and order) impartially to all who are located under its jurisdiction. Even more divisible and discretionary benefits (such as free education) may be distributed that way, out of some sense of justice or perhaps only for the sake of convenience. Thus the state's policies appear to be motivated by civic rather than ethnic, criteria.

People who have no state corresponding even roughly with their sense of national identity are in a different situation. Loyalty to their nation and allegiance to the state under whose jurisdiction they find themselves will not coincide. The imagined community that they recognize as their nation may be a minority within the population of a powerful state or empire, a minority within more than one state (like the Kurds divided between Turkey, Syria, and Iraq), or divided among several jurisdictions without being a minority in any (like the Germans before 1871). Particularly in the first situation and particularly if the members of the nation are economically, socially, or politfoically disadvantaged in relation to the state's population as a whole, it is natural for a movement to arise which is dedicated to pursuing the interests of the nation and of people who belong to the nation, interests that may be defined to include achieving a state of their own or at least some kind of national self-determination. Such a national movement will naturally distinguish between people on the basis of whether or not they belong to the national community, rather than on some impersonal criterion such as residence or citizenship. This will be particularly so if the nation lacks a clearly defined territory, and to a somewhat lesser extent if it has a defined territory but is still denied self-government within that territory. It is easy for those who do not belong to the national community in question, particularly if they perceive benefits to themselves from denying it the right of self-determination or if they view its aspirations as a threat to order and stability, to stigmatize its demands as "ethnic nationalism." Yet the chances are that as the nation in question moves towards equality and self-determination, its nationalism will, not instantly but gradually, take on a more civic character. Once it has a state of its own, that state will, like other states, probably find it convenient to treat its residents more or less impartially, all things being equal.

All things of course are not always equal. Minorities may be discriminated against, or at least viewed with suspicion, particularly if they are identified with an external threat to the security of the state. Estonia, Latvia, and Lithuania are suspicious of their Russian minorities today, just as the Czechoslovakia of the 1930s was suspicious of its German (actually Austrian) minority. When Catholic Spain was England's enemy in the reign of Elizabeth I, all Catholics in England were considered potentially subversive, as some of them actually were. Even Canada and the United States discriminated against their citizens of Japanese ancestry when they were at war with Japan.

Of course, such fears can be self-fulfilling. Stigmatizing Catholics or Freemasons or Jews or Arabs as potentially subversive makes them far more likely to become so, as history demonstrates.

Even before it achieves statehood, the nationalism of a national group struggling for self-determination and independence may be more or less civic in character, depending on circumstances. Nationalism arises, or at least intensifies, as a result of a perception that one's own national group is mistreated, threatened, or discriminated against by some other group of people. If the other group is located somewhere else, the relationship between it and one's own nation is easily perceived in geographical terms, so that everyone on the national territory appears to be a victim, and therefore to be part of the imagined national community. The nationalism of the American War of Independence, in which all residents of the Thirteen Colonies were viewed as victims of the tyranny of George III and his Tory government in England, is an example of this type. Scottish nationalism also tends to be civic because its opponents are external to Scottish territory; there is no privileged minority of English settlers in Scotland as there was in Ireland, Kenya, or Zimbabwe.

On the other hand, if the victims and their oppressors are geographically mingled on the same territory, geography cannot be the criterion that distinguishes the imagined national community from its opponents. For example, if white settlers oppress Africans in the same country, or Protestants oppress Catholics in the same country, or people who speak one language in a country oppress their neighbours who speak another language, the nationalism that arises in response will tend to define the imagined national community in terms of race, religion, or language as the case may be. During the struggle for national self-determination, and probably for some time afterwards, this nationalism will have an exclusive and ethnic character, since members of the previously dominant group will not be viewed as part of the nation. Thus ethnic, as opposed to civic, nationalism tends to arise when there is an unequal relationship between groups distinguished by some ascriptive characteristic and sharing the same territory.

Another, although perhaps related, distinction may be made between different instances of nationalism depending on whether or not there exist political or administrative institutions with jurisdiction over a clearly defined territory that can be credibly identified with the nation. In the former situation, nationalism is more likely to have civic characteristics, viewing everyone within the territory as part of the nation. The nationalism of the French Revolution, which could identify with a territorial unit called "France" that had existed for centuries, was viewed by Hans Kohn as the prototypical example. Even a territorial administrative entity that is not fully sovereign, such as Scotland, may have this effect. On the other hand, if there is no territorial political or administrative entity corresponding to the national community, it is difficult to envisage the nation in territorial terms, and a more ethnic definition of the nation may result. The Germans in the early nineteenth century, like the Kurds and Palestinians today, were in this situation. Zionism is a classic example of a non-territorial, and therefore unavoidably ethnic, nationalism. The ethnic nationalism of aboriginal "First Nations" in Canada also comes to mind in this connection. Civic nationalism requires a state, but ethnic nationalism does not, and it may be more vigorous in the absence of a state.

Ethnic nationalists are not therefore bad people; they are merely people who find themselves in different, and often more unpleasant, circumstances from those experienced by civic nationalists. The study of nationalism should seek to understand, rather than to condemn, the phenomenon that it addresses, something that it has not always in fact done. In some of the most recent writings on nationalism, however, there seems to be some recognition of this issue, and also of the fact that ethnic and civic nationalism are only ideal types, rather than totally distinct phenomena with precise empirical referents.[25] A particular instance of nationalism may display ethnic and civic characteristics in varying proportions at different times. Ethnic nationalists may be humane and polycentric (as defined above), viewing nationalities other than their own with sympathy and respect. Civic nationalists may be intolerant and violent, as Canadian descendants of refugees from the American Revolution will attest.

The present work is a comparative study of how nationalism has developed and evolved over time in two different settings: Ireland and Quebec. The origins of the study may be attributed to the author's curiosity about Quebec nationalism, formerly known as French Canadian nationalism, a phenomenon that more than any other has decisively influenced Canadian politics, particularly since the Quiet Revolution of the 1960s. About forty years have passed since the independence of Quebec began to be widely discussed as a serious option. Particularly after the Parti québécois was formed under the leadership of René Lévesque in 1968, it seemed reasonable to anticipate that Quebec, with a strong and growing sense of national identity and with all the attributes needed to form a viable sovereign state, would eventually become one, as about one hundred other political entities have done since the end of the Second World War. The referendum of 1980, the outcome of which had probably been decided by the astute and forceful intervention of Prime Minister Trudeau, clearly set back the timetable, but the author was not among those who thought that it had settled the issue for all time. In fact, those who proclaimed the demise of Quebec nationalism enjoyed only a few years of satisfaction, as unresolved controversies over language policy and the Canadian constitution again rose to the surface. By the early 1990s, Quebec's independence seemed to be only a matter of time. Opinion in Quebec had been profoundly disturbed by anglophone Canada's rejection of the Meech Lake Accord. Free trade with the United States and the trend towards economic laissez-faire in Ottawa had lessened both the risks of sovereignty and the advantages of federalism. The peaceful disintegration of Czechoslovakia and the Soviet Union and the somewhat less peaceful demise of Yugoslavia had provided fresh precedents for the emergence of a new sovereign state in the industrialized world. When the Parti québécois took office for the second time in 1994, not long after the Bloc québécois had won most of Quebec's ridings at the federal level, it seemed almost certain that Quebec would be a sovereign state by the end of the millennium. The lacklustre campaign against sovereignty waged by the Canadian federal government, under a prime minister who was notoriously unpopular in his own province and a party whose electoral support in Quebec consisted mainly of anglophones and immigrants, was apparently the last piece of evidence needed to confirm this estimate of the situation.

When the option of sovereignty was rejected again in the referendum of October 1995, Canadian federalists were relieved and Quebec nationalists were disappointed. While appreciating and understanding the sentiments of both sides, the author was more concerned, as a political scientist, to ask why events had produced such an unexpected outcome. Why had four decades of political controversy and political mobilization, the hopes and aspirations of so many people, fizzled out so ignominiously in October 1995? Was "money and ethnic votes" really an adequate explanation, as a disappointed Premier Jacques Parizeau had memorably asserted on the night of the referendum? Even Nova Scotia and Western Australia had once voted to secede from their respective federations (long ago and admittedly to no avail), although no sensible argument could be made, or had been made, that either was a distinct nation. Why was Quebec practically the only nation, apart from Scotland and Puerto Rico, that continued to reject independence despite having a clearly defined territory, institutions, and national identity? Would a comparative study, comparing Quebec with a somewhat similar national entity that had actually achieved independence, help to cast some light on this question?

Much has been written on the subject of Quebec nationalism in both of Canada's official languages, and much of it is useful and informative. Contrary to what Eric Hobsbawm has written, as quoted above, some of the most interesting contributions to the literature have come from writers who could themselves be described as Quebec nationalists. Some works on the subject have taken a historical approach, as does the present study. Very few, however, have taken a comparative approach.[26] The reason is probably related to the way in which academic disciplines are organized in Canada, whereby Canadian or Québécois politics and history are conventionally regarded as separate "fields" from the politics or history of foreign countries. Robert Frost's view that good fences make good neighbours is widely accepted in academia, and venturing outside one's field tends to be viewed with disfavour, both by those within it and by those in the other field on which the scholar may be tempted to trespass.

This by-product of academic specialization is unfortunate, for the comparative approach to the study of political and historical phenomena such as nationalism can provide great benefits. Observing the similarities between two cases of the same phenomenon can point the way towards a common explanation or can even lead one to predict that what has already happened in one case may subsequently happen in another, if the necessary conditions that preceded the first event are already becoming apparent somewhere else. Observing the differences between two cases can be even more rewarding, because it draws the scholar's attention to a feature of the more familiar case that may simply have been taken for granted, and it also encourages one to seek an explanation for the difference.

As noted above, the present study is not only comparative but historical, although it also includes a consideration of some very recent events. The belief that political science is only intellectually serious if written in the present tense has fortunately never been as powerful in Canadian political science as in that of some other countries. In any event, it seems to be losing popularity even in its former strongholds, as suggested by the emergence of an active "Politics and History" subgroup within the American Political Science Association. History has several merits for political scientists. It opens the door to a far larger universe of events, personalities, and political phenomena than we can discover by focusing exclusively on the present, it allows us to make comparisons and to observe both similarities and contrasts, across time as well as across space, and it contributes to an understanding of the present, which is really nothing more than the product of everything that has gone before. Historical narratives, viewed comparatively, can provide data with which to study the ways in which one event leads to another or closes off alternative possibilities, as well as the ways in which the absence of a particular event affects the future development of a society.[27] Even where events in two societies are broadly similar, differences of timing and sequence can lead them to have different and possibly contrasting consequences.[28]

Historical political science or comparative history seems particularly appropriate to the study of nationalism, because nationalism itself tends to be preoccupied with history. Benedict Anderson has suggested that nationalism resembles religion, and differs from secular political ideologies, in its concern with death and immortality, subjects that cannot be considered without recognizing the temporal dimension of existence.[29] His description of a nation as an imagined community suggests that members of the community are linked not only across space but across time. The nation, according to Edmund Burke, is a community of the dead, the living, and those who are not yet born. The writings of historians and the historical writings of non-historians such as William Shakespeare and Walter Scott have played a large part in the development of nationalism. Remembrance of the honoured dead has inspired much nationalist oratory, from Pericles to Abraham Lincoln to Patrick Pearse. Quebec's official motto, *Je me souviens,* makes the point succinctly.

Having decided to undertake a comparative and historical study, I wondered what other example of nationalism could be compared with Quebec. Stéphane Dion, a distinguished Quebec political scientist who became Canada's minister of intergovernmental affairs soon after the 1995 referendum, asserted just prior to the referendum that no political entity had ever seceded from a well-established democratic state, which he defined as a state where universal suffrage had existed for at least ten years.[30] The examples of Quebec, Scotland, and Puerto Rico and perhaps even Western Australia, whose separatist movement had quickly collapsed after winning almost two-thirds of the votes cast in a referendum, gave some credence to his view. However, another case that came to mind, and that seemed to refute Dion's observation, was Ireland, a small island that has greatly influenced the history of the North Atlantic world. Ireland, or most of it, won its independence from the United Kingdom early in the twentieth century. Although, technically, British democracy was not then "well established" by Dion's definition, the suffrage approached universality by 1918, and parliamentary responsible government had existed since the early nineteenth century.

The comparison between Ireland and Quebec was one that seemed likely to be fruitful, given the similarities, as well as the historical ties, between the two. Ireland, even more than Quebec, is a society that appears fascinated with its history, and understandably so. Almost every village and crossroads in Ireland seems associated with a remembered historical event, and the richness of its historical scholarship is astonishing for so small a country. The more the author explored Irish history, the more the parallels between Ireland and Quebec became apparent.

Both Ireland and Quebec are relatively small, predominantly Catholic, North Atlantic societies that were conquered and then colonized by the English/British. (The English state became the British state in 1707, about midway in time between the conquest of Ireland and that of French Canada, but the essential continuity of that state was not fundamentally altered by its change of name and extension of boundaries.) In both cases, colonization by settlers from Great Britain was not complete enough to reduce the pre-conquest population to the status of a small minority, as happened in Britain's other North American colonies and in Australia and New Zealand; but it was not demographically insignificant, as was the case in Asia and most of Africa. Conflict between "new" settlers and the descendants of pre-conquest inhabitants helped to shape the politics of both societies. In both Ireland and Quebec a dependent post-conquest state was built that was subordinated to the British Empire and disproportionately influenced by the British settler minority. In both cases an anti-colonial rebellion, partly influenced by the successful example of the thirteen colonies that became the United States, took place but was rather easily suppressed. In both cases this setback was followed by a British decision to dilute the rebellious tendencies of the country by merging it politically and administratively with one that was deemed to be more reliable: the United Kingdom itself in the case of Ireland and neighbouring Upper Canada (subsequently Ontario) in the case of Lower Canada (subsequently Quebec). In both cases these events were followed by a transformation of nationalism into a form that was more conservative, more peaceful in its methods, more concerned with cultural issues, and more influenced by Catholicism. Indeed, it is in this post-rebellion period that the stereotype of the "priest-ridden society" was invented and became relatively credible in both places.

There are also many differences between Ireland and Quebec, which will also be explored in the pages that follow. Ireland was conquered when English anti-Catholicism was at its height, Quebec when it was already beginning to abate. Ireland's population was much larger than Quebec's at the outset but subsequently declined, largely through massive emigration, although there were other causes as well. Quebec's population grew rapidly, even though it too lost many of its people through emigration, and finally surpassed that of Ireland around the middle of the twentieth century. Ireland was geographically much closer to Great Britain, a fact that increased the British incentive to colonize it and to keep it under tight control. It was also geographically small and thickly populated, while Quebec was large and thinly populated. The struggle over the ownership of agricultural land was a major theme in Ireland's history but a relatively minor one in Quebec's. These circumstances contributed to the fact that the Irish experiences of conquest, colonization, and subsequent subordination to British rule were much harsher and more traumatic than those of Quebec, and as a result, the Irish response was relatively more violent and hostile. Ireland virtually lost its indigenous language under colonial rule, while Quebec did not. During the Victorian era, Quebec was granted a degree of self-government or "home rule" within a Canadian federation that was itself a dominion of the British crown. Ireland failed to achieve even that limited degree of autonomy a few years later, despite two attempts by a British prime minister to bring it about.

In the twentieth century the destinies of the two countries continued to diverge. Ireland developed a "separatist" movement, a term that later entered the discourse of Canadian politics, seeking independence rather than merely home rule. After the First World War it achieved virtual independence through armed struggle, but at the price of a partition that deprived the Irish state of almost a third of its population and almost a quarter of its territory, including the city (Belfast) that was then its industrial metropolis. Quebec, in contrast, failed to develop a serious movement for independence until half a century later. As we know, that movement had not, by the end of the twentieth century, been successful, despite four decades of effort to mobilize the population. On the other hand, there was an intriguing parallel between Quebec and the part of Ireland that had not seceded from the United Kingdom: the six counties that constituted Northern Ireland. Like Quebec, although in a far less peaceful manner, Northern Ireland has been frequently in the news since the 1960s. Although the demographic balance was different, the "Troubles" there seemed to suggest some parallels with the cultural and political conflict within Quebec between anglophones and francophones. In Northern Ireland, as in Quebec, a seemingly powerful nationalist movement has achieved some successes, particularly with regard to the internal distribution of social and economic power between communities, but so far it has failed to achieve its ultimate objective of changing the province's political status.

Although few political studies have explicitly compared Ireland and Quebec, the parallels and affinities between these two North Atlantic neighbours have not gone entirely unnoticed.[31] This is particularly so in Quebec, which received massive immigration from Ireland in the nineteenth century and perhaps even earlier. Although the descendants of most of the Irish immigrants who arrived on the St Lawrence have moved on to other parts of North America, "Irish" is still the third most popular ethnic ancestry claimed by Quebecers, after "Canadian" and "French." Many prominent francophone Quebecers have recognizably Irish family names, and other Quebec names appear to be of Irish origin, although the spelling and pronunciation have been modified.[32] Quebec's National Assembly annually commemorates St Patrick's Day if it happens to be sitting on that day, with party leaders discussing their own Irish roots, praising the Irish contribution to Quebec's history, or drawing parallels between the two countries. In earlier times French Canadian nationalists such as Honoré Mercier and Henri Bourassa expressed sympathy for Ireland's struggle for national self-determination. Jacques Ferron, a Quebec nationalist writer and medical doctor best known as the founder of the satirical Rhinoceros Party, wrote a novel about a Quebecer of mixed origins whose Irish father tells him that "the salvation of Ireland" is a metaphor for the hopes of oppressed people everywhere; the son eventually joins the terrorist Front de libération du Québec.[33] Another novel inspired by Quebec's October Crisis, and perhaps the most insightful book ever written about that event, was the work of an immigrant from Belfast, Brian Moore.[34] Quebec's oldest nationalist organization, the Societé Saint-Jean-Baptiste de Montréal, helped to establish a "Quebec-Ireland committee," which was active in the 1980s, proclaiming the solidarity of Quebec nationalists with Irish republicans.[35] The Irish civil rights activist Bernadette Devlin McAliskey visited Montreal in 1984, as Charles Stewart Parnell had done more than a century earlier, in an effort to win support for the Irish cause.[36]

The present work is arranged chronologically, apart from the first and last chapters; each of the intervening chapters compares and contrastes parallel developments in Ireland and Quebec. Chapter 2 examines the nature, impact, and legacy of British conquest on the two countries, a formative event, or perhaps one should say a process, which had a lasting and decisive impact on the development of nationalism. Chapter 3 considers two parallel events that occurred four decades apart: the unsuccessful rebellions against British rule in Ireland and Lower Canada, which were partly inspired by the examples of the American and French Revolutions. Chapter 4 looks at the developments that followed the defeat of the rebellions and the subsequent abolition of both the Irish parliament and the Lower Canadian legislature: a more conservative, constitutional, but also ethnically exclusive nationalism that pursued limited goals within a new institutional framework. Chapter 5 describes how and why Quebec achieved a limited form of "home rule" under Confederation in 1867, while Ireland twice failed to achieve home rule during the next generation, despite the support of a British prime minister. It also describes the downfall and disgrace of charismatic nationalist leaders in the early 1890s and some of the political, social, and economic trends in the two societies in the latter part of the nineteenth century.

With chapter 6 we enter the twentieth century, examining the development of both Irish and French Canadian nationalism prior to the First

World War and the dramatic events that followed. While the conscription crisis in Quebec was a dramatic event by Canadian standards, Ireland at the same time experienced unionist mobilization against the threat of home rule, the formation of paramilitary forces by both unionists and nationalists, the Easter rising, partition, the war of independence, and finally the achievement of dominion status within the British Empire for a truncated twenty-six-county state. Chapter 7 describes the heyday of conservative and Catholic nationalism from the 1920s through the 1950s, a period during which Ireland gradually moved from the status of a dominion to that of a republic, albeit still economically dependent on the United Kingdom, while Quebec attempted to maximize its autonomy within the Canadian federation.

The remaining chapters focus on more recent events. Chapter 8 considers the important developments of the 1960s and early 1970s: Quebec's Quiet Revolution and the rise of the independence movement, the less-dramatic but still significant changes that ended the era of conservative nationalism in southern Ireland, and the outbreak and early course of the Troubles in Northern Ireland. Chapter 9 continues the story, examining the efforts to detach Quebec from the Canadian federation and Northern Ireland from the United Kingdom, as well as the British and Canadian efforts to accommodate at least the less-radical wing of Irish and Quebec nationalism through constitutional change. The final chapter looks backwards and forwards in an effort to explain the limited success of nationalists in achieving their goals and to assess their prospects in the future.

CHAPTER TWO

The Legacy of Conquest

It was suggested in the first chapter that nationalism on the part of a people, defined by location, culture, ethnicity, or whatever, develops in opposition to another people or peoples with which the nation-envisaging people contrasts itself. If one could imagine a group of human beings so isolated that it was unaware of the existence of any other group of human beings, that group could not develop national consciousness, and in fact would have no reason to do so. The nature of the relationship between the people envisaging itself as a nation and the other people or peoples may vary, but it usually involves an element of conflict. An important category of group-group relationships, although by no means the only one, is that which exists when the nation-envisaging people has been conquered and subsequently dominated by another identifiable group. Sometimes, although not always, this phenomenon of conquest is followed by the associated phenomenon of colonization, by which is meant a situation in which members of the conquering people settle more or less permanently among the conquered, on the territory that was occupied by the conquered prior to the conquest. Of course, the general categories of conquest and colonization include a wide range of possible situations, and the specific nature of the experience is likely to have an important impact on the kind of the nationalism that results.

As noted in chapter 1, both Ireland and Quebec were conquered and partially colonized, and in both cases the conquering/colonizing group were the English or, as they began to style themselves after 1707, the British. In both Ireland and Quebec the English/British conquest is viewed, at least by nationalists, as a major formative event whose significance for the subsequent history of the country is profound and far-reaching. In both cases the precise nature and significance of the conquest and its consequences for the history that followed are subjects of historical controversy. Without entering, at least for the moment, into these controversies, we can, however, note that there were important and obvious differences, as well as similarities, between the English/British conquests experienced by Ireland and Quebec. These differences can be illustrated by sketching the relevant history, first in Ireland and then in Quebec.

THE NATURE OF TWO CONQUESTS

In the Irish case much of the ambiguity about the conquest is chronological. If the English conquest of Ireland is viewed as an event, when did it take place, when did it begin, and when did it end? The answers to these questions are not immediately obvious, and this lack of certainty is related to uncertainty over another question: what exactly was the status of Ireland before the conquest, whenever that was? Did a political entity called "Ireland" even exist? Perhaps we can approach the problem by suggesting that there were three successive conquests of Ireland, or at least a conquest in three stages.

Traditionally, Irish nationalists have referred to "seven hundred years" of Irish resistance to the English. Since references of this kind began in the latter part of the nineteenth century, they suggest that English encroachments on Ireland's independence began in the latter part of the twelfth century, specifically during the reign of King Henry II of England (1154–89); so we may take this period as our starting point. The history of Ireland prior to this date is complex and not easily summarized, but it is generally agreed that no Irish state capable of administering the whole island had emerged prior to this date, a fact that is not surprising since most of Europe at this time lacked states which met the Weberian criterion of a monopoly over the legitimate use of force within clearly defined territorial boundaries. The island of Ireland was divided into kingdoms that claimed and at times exercised jurisdiction over portions of the island, as well as sub-kingdoms whose leaders owed formal allegiance to one or other of the kingdoms but retained significant military capabilities of their own. This lack of unity enabled the Vikings to descend on the coasts of Ireland from time to time with relative impunity, beginning in the year 795 and continuing for two centuries thereafter. It was the Vikings rather than the Irish themselves who founded most of the coastal settlements that became Ireland's major cities.

Towards the end of this period the idea, if not the reality, of political unity for the whole of Ireland was beginning to emerge. Some historians consider that a sense of national consciousness may have been developing also. In the tenth century a northern-based dynasty, the Ui Neill, asserted a claim to the high kingship of all Ireland. This largely symbolic office was associated with the Hill of Tara in County Meath, a landmark where evidence of human settlement dates back to the neolithic era. It was, however, a king from the south of Ireland, Brian Boru, who came closest to realizing the project of political unity between 1005, when he set out to conquer the whole island, and 1014, when he was killed at the battle of Clontarf near Dublin, a battle actually won by his own forces. Like the modern Irish state, Brian never managed to extend his authority over the northeastern part of the island. Part of the reason that his memory has been cherished is because he provides evidence that some semblance of an Irish state existed, however briefly. The notion of high kingship survived him and was claimed during the eleventh and twelfth centuries by a number of aspirants who enjoyed varying degrees of success. (An appropriate parallel would be the office of holy Roman emperor, which existed for a thousand years, although its occupant rarely ruled the entire "empire" in any meaningful sense.) Terry Golway, a historian sympathetic to Irish nationalism, concedes, "In its political life Ireland, unlike England, had yet to develop a strong, centralized monarchy, although there was no shortage of kings."[1] However, Irish nationalists can credibly claim that some notion of an Irish political community existed and that the English conquest can thus be regarded as an act of aggression against a neighbour, not a spontaneous expansion into a territory where political authority was previously lacking.

The first conquest of Ireland by the better-organized English state is customarily dated from 1171, when King Henry II landed at Waterford, although it had actually begun a few years earlier. In 1155 the pope, somewhat ironically, gave his blessing to Henry's ambitions with regard to Ireland. (As Irish nationalists point out, it is probably not coincidental that this pope, Adrian IV, was the only Englishman ever to hold the office; both he and Henry had ascended their respective thrones in 1154.) Since the Norman conquest of England in 1066 the Norman English state had developed administrative and military capabilities that were quite impressive by contemporary standards, and by the early thirteenth century the Normans militarily dominated most of Ireland. Henry named his second son, John, "Lord of Ireland" in 1177. (Interestingly, this event predates by more than a century the better-known title of Prince of Wales, conferred on the heir to the English throne after 1301.) After John also became king of England in 1199, the lordship of Ireland and the kingship of England were permanently associated.[2] In practice, an official appointed by the king exercised the royal authority in Ireland. At various times this official was known as justiciar, king's deputy, lord deputy, and lord lieutenant, with the last of these titles always being used from the seventeenth century onwards. The conquest was followed by colonization as Norman English feudal lords seized much of the land in Ireland and populated some of it with their own tenants and retainers. An Irish parliament, similar to its English prototype, met at least intermittently in Dublin from 1297 onwards. Essentially it represented the Norman English overlords of the country, not the indigenous Irish.

Yet in practice, English rule over the island was not firmly established, perhaps because there had been no pre-existing state structure through which the English could exercise control.[3] An invasion from Scotland, then a completely separate kingdom, came close to expelling the English between 1315 and 1318. Famine and bubonic plague weakened English control, and local warlords challenged English military and administrative supremacy on the peripheries of the island. By the fifteenth century the effective power of the colonial state was confined to a small area on the east coast known as the Pale, centred around the city of Dublin, even though the English monarchy still claimed sovereignty over all of Ireland.[4] Outside the Pale, English settlers were too few to exercise much influence, and English authority existed in form but not in fact. At most, the English could govern indirectly through alliances with local chieftains such as the Fitzgeralds, whose hereditary title was Earl of Kildare.[5]

A more insidious threat to English rule was the tendency of English settlers or their descendants to "go native" by assimilating into the local population, becoming more Irish than English. Many family names now regarded as typically Irish are in fact of Anglo-Norman origin and were borne by the English settlers who arrived during the first conquest. The Statute of Kilkenny (1366) attempted to halt this process of assimilation by reducing contact between natives and settlers to a minimum. Its provisions included the prohibition of intermarriage with the native Irish and of the use of the Irish language and Irish customs by settlers, but it came too late and its effect was limited.[6] Although the distinction between the Anglo-Norman settlers and the indigenous population, a distinction of class as well as one of language and culture, did not entirely disappear, it was becoming weaker. After a few generations, the Anglo-Normans had no meaningful ties with England, given the difficulty of transportation and communication in those days between the two islands, and regarded themselves as Irish. So they must have seemed to visitors from England.

Despite their allegiance to a common king, England and Ireland were two distinct countries for all practical purposes at the end of the fifteenth century. English rule was tenuous, possessing no obvious legitimacy, and with

the consolidation of absolutist states in western Europe and the improvement of oceanic transportation, the possibility existed that one of England's
rivals would gain a foothold in Ireland and outflank England on the west.
The latter point was to become a preoccupation, and at times an obsession,
of English policy-makers, lasting well into the twentieth century. It was reinforced by well-founded uncertainty about the degree to which the Irish
population accepted English rule.

These circumstances paved the way for the second and perhaps more significant English conquest of Ireland, which was accomplished by the modernizing and state-building Tudor dynasty that ruled England after 1485.
Poyning's Law, introduced in 1494, attempted to curtail the autonomy of
the lord deputy and to assert direct royal control over Ireland.[7] However, it
was not until 1541 that Henry VIII, the second Tudor monarch, proclaimed
himself king (rather than lord) of Ireland. The actual conquest, or
reconquest, was mainly accomplished in a series of military campaigns
under Elizabeth I, the last Tudor monarch, who reigned from 1558 until
1603.

While the success of the Tudor monarchs in modernizing the English
state made this second conquest possible, it must also be seen in the context
of relations between states in the developing European state system, as well
as the religious schism in western Christianity, which gave interstate relations an ideological character somewhat analogous to the Cold War in the
second half of the twentieth century. The foreign policy of Henry VIII, as
well as his repudiation of papal authority, contributed to hostility between
England and its powerful neighbours, France and Spain. Anglo-Spanish
hostility grew particularly intense during the reign of Henry's Protestant
daughter, Elizabeth I. In the 1570s both France and Spain supported the
claim of Mary of Scotland, a Catholic, to the English throne, although neither intervened openly for fear of driving England into the arms of the
other. (The pope did attempt to intervene with a small expeditionary force
in 1578–79.)[8] English fear that Ireland would drift into the orbit of one of
these hostile powers, or even that it would be used a base from which to
launch an invasion of England itself, became a powerful and lasting motive
to reinforce English control over the neighbouring island. Indeed, such
concerns, which were not entirely without foundation, motivated English
policy towards Ireland as late as the first half of the twentieth century, when
a united Germany had become the major threat to the security of England.

Events within Ireland tempted continental powers to intervene and thus
contributed to the timing and progress of the Tudor conquest. Henry's
proclamation of himself as king of Ireland was in part a response to the
unsuccessful rebellion led by the Kildare (Fitzgerald) dynasty, which had

previously served as an important bulwark of English indirect rule. The rebels requested help from the pope and from Charles v of Spain, but were decisively defeated in 1535, an event that contributed to the reinforcement of English authority over Ireland. Two generations later, the last and most serious resistance to the Elizabethan conquest was led by Hugh O'Neill, Earl of Tyrone, beginning in 1592. O'Neill and his supporters sought help from Spain, whose armada had been defeated by the English in 1588 but which had not abandoned hope of turning the tables on its rival. A Spanish expeditionary force allied with O'Neill landed at Kinsale in 1601, but the combined Spanish and Irish force was soon defeated by the English. According to one historian, this battle marked "the failure of the Spanish effort, the collapse of the Ulster resistance, the completion of the Tudor conquest, and the eclipse of Gaelic Ireland."[9] O'Neill formally submitted to the English in 1603, the year of Elizabeth's death. Four years later he and some other opponents of English rule left the country in what is known as the Flight of the Earls. The significance of these events as a watershed in Irish history is suggested by the fact that two leading historians, J.C. Beckett and Roy Foster, begin their histories of "modern Ireland" at 1603 and 1600 respectively.

This second English conquest left a far deeper imprint on Ireland than the first. English common law was imposed on Ireland for the first time. Colonization by settlers from England (and also from Scotland, whose king, James, had acquired the English throne at Elizabeth's death) began on a small scale under Elizabeth and was massive during the seventeenth century, far greater than the colonization during the Norman period. After 1603 it was largely, although not entirely, concentrated in the northern province of Ulster, the former stronghold of Hugh O'Neill, which had hitherto been the part of Ireland most isolated from English influences.[10] This combination of volume and geographical concentration, as well as the religious differences between natives and settlers, a factor not present in Norman times, ensured that the settlers this time would not be absorbed into the indigenous population. The vast improvement in the administrative capabilities of the English state, a major and lasting achievement of Henry VIII and his chancellor, Thomas Cromwell, also ensured that English rule would be more firmly established henceforth than it had been after the first conquest.

Most significantly of all, there was now a religious cleavage between the English and the Irish that would cast a long shadow over Irish history. Henry VIII had broken with the Roman Catholic Church in 1534, proclaiming himself the head of an independent Church of England. From that date onwards, England was militantly Protestant, except during the brief reign of Henry's Catholic daughter, Mary (1553–58), who attempted to reverse the religious revolution wrought by her father. The "New English" and Scottish settlers who went to Ireland after 1603 were Protestants. The native Irish remained Roman Catholic, as did the remnants of the "Old English" settlers, whose roots in Ireland dated back to the era of the first conquest.

A Protestant "Church of Ireland" in communion with the Church of England was established under the Tudor dynasty, and like its English counterpart, it took over the buildings and other property previously owned by the Catholic Church. However, it would never gain the allegiance of more than a small minority of the people in Ireland. The vast majority of its adherents would always be the descendants of settlers who arrived in Ireland after it was established. In northeastern Ireland, extensively settled by people from Scotland, a more radical (Presbyterian) form of Protestantism enjoyed a large following. The native Irish and the Old English remained Catholic. With the English, and later British, national identity largely based on Protestantism and resistance to the transnational Catholic Church, Catholics were implicitly excluded from that identity. Because England's external enemies tended to be Catholic, Catholics were viewed as potentially subversive, in much the same way that American Marxists were considered "un-American" and potentially subversive during the Cold War. This situation had particularly serious consequences in Ireland, the only part of the English-dominated realm where Catholics remained a majority of the population. Marcus Tanner has argued in a recent book that the English effort to impose Protestantism on Ireland lies at the root of the conflict between English and Irish that has lasted almost up to the present day.[11]

Catholicism continued for a while to be tolerated in Ireland more than in England itself, where it retained only an illegal and clandestine existence after the accession of Elizabeth. Catholics, mainly Old English, still sat in the Irish parliament, but that body did not meet from 1586 until 1613, and after the latter date it had a Protestant majority.[12] Catholics owned 60 per cent of Irish land as late as the 1640s.[13] Nonetheless, the English after 1603 governed Ireland indirectly through a Protestant elite, shunning the Old English as well as the natives. And the worst, for Irish Catholics, was still to come.

The Scottish Stuart dynasty, which reigned in England after the death of Queen Elizabeth, never achieved complete legitimacy in its adopted country, whose political culture the Stuarts seemed to have some difficulty in understanding. Political unrest in England was reinforced by religious tensions between the ecclesiastical establishment, supported by the Crown, and the increasing number of Englishmen, known as Puritans, who preferred a less-hierarchical church and a simpler form of worship. The civil wars that resulted soon spread from England into Ireland, which endured a series of events in the seventeenth century so traumatic as to almost constitute a third conquest. Even more than in England, the resulting struggles in Ireland linked politics with religion.

There were signs of dissatisfaction with English rule among the Irish, perhaps more on religious than on secular grounds. In the 1630s a Catholic priest, Geoffrey Keating, wrote a history of Ireland in the Irish language, arguing that because the Irish had been Christians since long before the Anglo-Norman conquest, their conquest by England was illegitimate. Keating's work was not published, but was circulated in manuscript form, much like the writings of political dissidents in the last days of Soviet Russia.[14] Violent resistance began in 1641 when Catholics in Ulster, taking advantage of the civil war that had recently begun in England, killed at least 2,000 of the Protestant settlers.[15] The rising spread to Catholics further south, including the Old English, and culminated in the establishment of a Catholic Confederacy with a government based at Kilkenny, in opposition to the English-dominated government at Dublin. The Confederacy was loosely allied with King Charles I, whom it considered a lesser evil than the Puritan-dominated English parliament.

In 1649, responding to these events, Oliver Cromwell arrived in Ireland, having been given the title of lord lieutenant by Parliament, and subdued the country in a series of campaigns lasting only nine months. His visit would be largely remembered for the siege and subsequent massacre of Drogheda, a mainly Old English town within what had been the Pale. About 3,500 were killed at Drogheda, including 1,000 civilians.[16] Cromwell hoped to remove the entire Catholic population of Ireland to the province of Connacht, west of the river Shannon. While this relocation did not happen and was probably not feasible, Catholic ownership of land was virtually ended outside Connacht and fell from 60 to 9 per cent of the acreage in Ireland as a whole. Confiscated land was granted to army officers and other prominent Englishmen, not all of whom chose to reside on their new estates. This massive transfer of ownership created the "Anglo-Irish" Protestant elite that dominated the country economically and politically until the twentieth century.[17] The few bands of outlaws who resisted the new order in Ireland were known by the Irish term *toraidhe*.[18] (Subsequently, the word "Tory," derived from this term, would be applied to all supporters of the Stuart dynasty and, by extension, to opponents of political progress and reform in both Britain and North America.)

Cromwell's death in 1658 and the restoration of the monarchy two years later changed the situation in conquered Ireland only slightly, since the new English governing class accepted the monarchy on condition that most of their gains from the revolution be preserved. King Charles II confirmed eight thousand beneficiaries of the Cromwellian land settlement, most of them veterans of Cromwell's army, in possession of their lands. The percentage of Irish land owned by Catholics increased only modestly to 20 per cent during his reign.[19] However, Catholics began to regain influence and to benefit from royal patronage under Charles's Catholic brother, King James II, who succeeded him in 1685. James's preference for those of his own faith aroused Protestant suspicions and ensured that his reign would be a brief one. The so-called Glorious Revolution of 1688 replaced James with his Protestant daughter Mary and her husband, William of Orange, provided that no Catholic could ever again occupy the British throne, and effectively subordinated the Crown to the Protestant oligarchy represented by the parliament at Westminster.

After James lost the English throne and fled from England, he astutely decided to make his last stand in Ireland, where much of the Catholic population rallied to his cause. He landed in Ireland in March 1689 and remained there until July 1690. Patrick Sarsfield, an Old English Catholic, led an Irish army that won victories against William's forces. However, the defeat of James at the Boyne (near Drogheda) in 1690 and that of Sarsfield at Aughrim a year later really completed the third English (and Protestant) conquest of Ireland. The Treaty of Limerick, negotiated by Sarsfield in 1691, allowed soldiers on the losing side to leave Ireland for France, an option of which Sarsfield himself took advantage, and promised religious freedom for Catholics. However, it was followed by a series of penal laws that deprived Irish Catholics of most of their political and civil rights, such as they were.

The conquest of Canada, which began after that of Ireland was completed, occurred within a much shorter period of time and can thus be summarized more briefly. It also differed from the conquest of Ireland in important ways, as will be discussed below. The two conquests were, however, not unrelated and can be viewed as successive stages in the expansion of the English state and people to a position of global pre-eminence. The victories of Cromwell and William in Ireland, the union between the kingdoms of England and Scotland in 1707, and the final defeat of the Scottish Highlanders in 1746 transformed the English state into a British state that could draw upon the manpower and resources of both islands for purposes of further expansion. This was so even though Ireland, but not Scotland, retained its own, exclusively Protestant, parliament and a limited degree of autonomy.

The Whig merchants and politicians who had subdued the Celtic fringes of the British archipelago in the aftermath of their Glorious Revolution now followed the course of empire to further fields. Since Spain was no longer a power of the first rank, France was their only significant rival in the struggle for empire and commercial supremacy. It was also their ideological *bête*

noire, as it had been for William of Orange. Thus the defeat of the Highlanders at Culloden, which removed the only significant internal threat to the
British state, was followed almost immediately by a program of military
expansion in North America, culminating in the expulsion of France from
that continent and the British occupation of Canada. In contrast to the cen-
turies-long English assault on Ireland, this entire process was completed by
1763.

At first sight it seems anomalous that the conquest of a relatively small and
nearby island should be protracted over more than five centuries, while that
of a country many times larger and located three thousand miles from England should be accomplished in less than fifteen years. The obvious difference is the disparity in size of the populations. Canada had no more than
80,000 inhabitants when it was ceded to the British in 1763.[20] Ireland probably had more than 1 million inhabitants in the time of Cromwell and possibly more than 2 million during the Williamite war.[21] In addition, of course,
British economic, demographic, military, and especially naval power continued to grow, not least because Ireland's human and natural resources were
added to those of England, and had made enormous advances in the seven
decades that separated the battle of Aughrim from that of Quebec.

Offsetting these advantages to some extent was perhaps the most significant difference between the two conquests, at least in the way in which they
were understood by the British themselves. In conquering Ireland, England
expanded into an area that it had never regarded as belonging to any legitimate state other than itself. In fact, as we have seen, Henry ii had rather
casually granted Ireland to his son John long before it was effectively subdued by English arms, and on the apparent assumption that it was in some
sense *terra nullius*. Apart from the fact that legal norms about the relations
between states hardly existed at this time, Ireland gave some credence to
Henry's interpretation by its lack of a state or recognized sovereign prior to
the English invasion. In many ways the English expansion into Ireland
resembled that of England and other European powers into North and
South America and Australia, where the "natives" were not deemed by Euro-
peans to be worthy of serious consideration.

In the case of Canada, on the other hand, the British conquered a territory that already belonged to another recognized European state and in fact
to the most formidable of all their European neighbours: France. The conquered Canadians were French and could not plausibly be regarded as
racial or cultural inferiors or as enjoying a lower state of civilization than the
English themselves. Even more to the point, they were the subjects of a recognized sovereign, the king of France, with whom England had to negotiate
on equal terms, regardless of its successes on the battlefields. The formal

transfer of sovereignty was the result of a treaty between equals, signed in 1763, and did not officially take place until three years after the physical occupation of the territory.

The British conquest of Canada is thus part of the history of European expansion in the Western Hemisphere; but more significantly, it was a relatively late episode in a long history of rivalry and conflict between two European neighbours, a history that had begun almost as soon as the English and French dynastic states emerged in recognizable form at the dawn of the second millennium and only ended, at least in a military sense, with the battle of Waterloo in 1815. As such, the conquest of Canada was conducted more or less in accordance with rules of war and diplomacy that were fairly well established after the Treaty of Westphalia in 1648.

The English preceded the French in launching the exploration of North America, since John (Giovanni) Cabot sailed across the North Atlantic in 1497 and Jacques Cartier in 1534. However, the beginnings of permanent settlement by the two powers were almost simultaneous, with the foundation of Jamestown (Virginia) in 1607 preceding that of Quebec by only one year. The English founded a series of colonies on the long and fertile coastline hemmed in by the Appalachian Mountains and concentrated on agriculture. The French, having access to the interior of the continent through the St Lawrence River and the Great Lakes, devoted more attention to exploration and the fur trade. This orientation also gave the French the advantage of closer, and on the whole friendlier, relations with the aboriginal North Americans, whose methods of warfare and transportation they adopted. (The Iroquois, opponents of France's Native allies, were a conspicuous exception.) Some intermarriage between French and aboriginals took place as well, a phenomenon that was rare among the English.[22]

From the Great Lakes it was a short jump to North America's other great river system, the Mississippi, which the French from their Canadian base explored down to its mouth in the Gulf of Mexico. By 1713 France controlled, at least nominally, a gigantic empire extending from Acadia (Nova Scotia) to Louisiana and incorporating what are today the central heartlands of both Canada and the United States. Canada (New France) and its fortress-capital of Quebec were the heart of this extensive empire. The twelve English colonies on the eastern seaboard (Georgia, the thirteenth, was not settled until 1733) occupied a far more compact territory, but their population of European settlers and, in the southern colonies, African slaves was many times larger than the non-aboriginal population of the more extensive French possessions. It is estimated that only 30,000 persons migrated from France to Canada before 1763 and that only 12,000 of them founded families in Canada.[23]

Rivalries between the two powers in Europe and between their respective colonists in North America contributed to a series of wars, against a backdrop of British economic and military power that was gradually increasing relative to that of France, in spite of France's larger population. As early as 1627, the English had captured the tiny French outposts at Quebec and Port-Royal, temporarily dislodging the French from North America, only to lose their winnings at the negotiating table two years later. The lengthy War of the Spanish Succession (1701–14) produced a standoff in North America, while the War of the Austrian Succession (1740–48) included the temporary capture by English colonists of France's eastern outpost at Louisbourg, which was restored to France by the Treaty of Aix-la-Chapelle. The British did, however, establish a naval base of their own some two hundred miles to the southwest at the harbour which they called Halifax and which is the real birthplace of English-speaking Canada.

Few expected the latest declaration of "peace" between the two powers to be permanent.[24] The British colonists were outraged by the return of Louisbourg, and the British commercial community in England, hoping to monopolize the Atlantic trade at France's expense, wanted to renew the war as soon as possible. Meanwhile, the French prepared for what proved to be the decisive round by strengthening the fortifications at Louisbourg, improving their relations with the aboriginal tribes in the Ohio Valley, and building a military road from Lake Ontario to the upper Ohio, where they established a new outpost called Fort Duquesne (now Pittsburgh) in 1754. Almost immediately, clashes around this strategic point ignited a major war, subsequently known as the Seven Years War, even before it was formally declared in Europe. Most modern historians, in contrast to nineteenth-century proponents of "Anglo-Saxon" and Protestant superiority, agree that the result was not foreordained and could have gone either way. Britain had far more settlers in North America, but France had a larger population in Europe; Britain had a larger navy, but France had a larger army; Britain devoted a larger share of its military resources to the North American theatre, but France received more support from the aboriginal peoples and had largely adopted their military tactics, better suited than those of Europe to the North American environment.

As the war commenced, the British expelled the French settlers from Acadia (the area around the Bay of Fundy) in an early instance of what would much later be called "ethnic cleansing." This was a somewhat ruthless action by eighteenth-century standards and resembled Oliver Cromwell's attempt a century earlier to drive the native Irish "to hell or Connacht." Its motive, however, was primarily strategic rather than economic or religious; the Acadians, given their presumed sympathy for France, were viewed as a threat to

Halifax and a hindrance to the planned attack on Louisbourg. The main effect of the expulsion, apart from giving Louisiana the "Cajun" element in its population, was probably to make the French Canadians in the St Lawrence valley fight harder, since they could reasonably although, as it turned out, erroneously anticipate a similar fate to that of the Acadians if they were defeated.

At first the war went well for the French, aided by their aboriginal allies. A British attempt to capture Fort Duquesne resulted in the annihilation of the British force, while the French captured two important British outposts in what is now upstate New York, Oswego and Fort William Henry. In 1758 the tide turned, as the British devoted a much larger share of their military and naval forces to North America. The French, perhaps unwisely, shifted from the offensive strategy that had served them well to the defensive strategy preferred by their new supreme commander, the Marquis de Montcalm, who saw no hope of holding the western hinterlands and wished to concentrate his efforts on the St Lawrence valley. Montcalm, whose military career had been spent in Europe, also disdained the "savages," as he called the native North Americans, and had no interest in their unconventional but highly effective methods of warfare.[25]

Fort Duquesne fell to the British in 1758, as did Fort Frontenac (now Kingston, Ontario) and, for the second and last time, Louisbourg. The following spring the British took Fort Niagara (now in Youngstown, New York, where the original fort still stands). French Canada was now hemmed in on all sides. The British sent an amphibious expedition up the St Lawrence to capture the city of Quebec, considered the most formidable fortress in North America and the centre of French power on the continent. During the siege that followed, the British commander, James Wolfe, made war on the civilian population in the vicinity, destroying at least 1,400 farms, and also bombarded the city, 80 per cent of which was destroyed. Finally Quebec fell on 13 September 1759 after the brief battle of the Plains of Abraham, in which both Wolfe and Montcalm were killed. A French effort to retake it in the following year was terminated by the arrival of a British fleet in the St Lawrence with the spring thaw. A few months later a British army advancing from the south took Montreal, the second largest city in Canada and the principal base of the fur trade.

All of Canada was now in British hands, but the formal transfer of sovereignty was delayed until 1763, when the Treaty of Paris ended the Seven Years War. Conceivably, the French could have won it back at the bargaining table, but they had apparently had enough of North America and chose instead to keep the more profitable, and less vulnerable, tropical island of Guadeloupe, with its extensive sugar plantations. Voltaire's celebrated and cynical dismissal of Canada as "quelques arpents de neige" may serve as the epitaph for the North American empire which the French had explored and, for a time, defended with such brilliance but had conspicuously failed to colonize or develop to its full potential. At the time of the transfer, about one-fifth of the English-speaking people on the planet already lived in North America, compared with less than 1 per cent of the (much larger) population who spoke French.

The Treaty of Paris provided that subjects of the king of France living in Canada would be free to sell their real estate to British subjects and return to France with their movable property, provided they did so within eighteen months. Most of the officials, merchants, and professional soldiers took advantage of this offer, but most of the clergy did not. Those who remained – the vast majority of the population – were promised the right to practise their Catholic religion "as far as the laws of Great Britain permit."[26] Both promises were reiterated in the instructions given to the British governor later in the year. Probably because they were made to the recognized sovereign of a great power, rather than to a population viewed as rebels and outlaws, these promises were kept, unlike those made in the Treaty of Limerick.

JE ME SOUVIENS: TWO CONQUESTS IN HISTORICAL MEMORY

Despite their differences, both conquests have loomed large in the historical memories of the conquered. In both Ireland and Quebec the significance of the conquest has been interpreted in more than one way and is still a subject of controversy. In both cases the significance attributed to the conquest depends in part on perceptions of what the country was like, politically, economically, and socially, before it was conquered.. In both cases, too, the conflicting interpretations of the conquest continue to have implications for political orientations and allegiances.

In Irish nationalist historiography the traditional interpretation of the English conquest views it as a sustained assault by England, extending over a period of several centuries, against its smaller and weaker neighbour, which resisted against overwhelming odds until eventually it succumbed to superior force. The Irish, according to this perception, already shared a national identity prior to the conquest, even if they lacked an effective national state, and their incipient nationalism inspired and sustained their long struggle against the invaders.[27] Although eventually they were defeated, their nationalism and their spirit of resistance did not die, as suggested by subsequent risings against British rule, culminating in the war of independence (1919–21) or, some would say, the struggles of the Provisional IRA in the

1970s. Those who view Irish history in this way will tend to have strongly nationalist or republican political views and perhaps a certain degree of anglophobia.

According to an alternative and more skeptical view, sometimes described as "revisionist," this traditional interpretation suggests more coherence and continuity on the part of the conquest, and on the part of the struggle against it, than actually existed.[28] While not denying the rich cultural and religious heritage of pre-conquest Ireland and its distinctiveness in relation to English culture, the revisionist view suggests that a national identity and consciousness did not really exist in pre-conquest Ireland. Irish fought against Irish, and some groups, factions, and leaders formed alliances with the English, much as aboriginal nations in North America formed alliances with the European powers that invaded their continent. Irish national consciousness and political unity, according to this view, were products of the period of English rule rather than preceding it. Those who take this view may view English rule in Ireland as a more positive experience since it at least had the merit of creating national unity. Revisionists tend to be somewhat less nationalist in their political views than non-revisionists. The contrast between these two interpretations of Irish history recalls, and in fact is merely a specific example of, the contrast between the two schools of thought discussed in the preceding chapter. On the one hand are those who see nationalism as universal in time and space, and on the one are those "modernists" who see it as essentially a modern phenomenon associated with literacy, mass communications, and the impact of the French Revolution.

Apart from the question of national identity and sentiment, some of the latter school would even question whether the Irish or, for that matter, the English peoples existed as social and cultural entities during at least the first stage of the English conquest of Ireland. The pre-conquest Irish were of disparate origins, according to this view, and their culture was marked by regional variations. The "English" of the first conquest were in some cases Welsh and in most others could be viewed as Normans, bearing in mind that England itself had been conquered by the Normans barely a century before Henry II invaded Ireland and that Norman French was still the language of administration in England. In the case of the second and third conquests, the Old English, whose presence was a consequence of the first conquest, had come to be regarded as Irish for most purposes, particularly given their continuing adherence to the Catholic Church.

The conquest of Ireland was a process extending over several centuries, whether it is viewed as continuous or as a series of episodes, and the recounting of it constitutes much of the substance of Irish history. On the other hand, the British conquest of French Canada is more appropriately viewed as a single event located at a particular point in time. Indeed, it is sometimes, erroneously, narrowed down to the single battle on the Plains of Abraham, which lasted less than an hour. Partly because the British conquest of Canada was a less complex and a much more time-specific event than the conquest of Ireland, as well as taking place more recently, the historiographical controversy that surrounds it is of a somewhat different kind to that between the Irish traditionalists and revisionists. This controversy too, however, is largely based on different perceptions of what stage of development the country had achieved before the conquest. [29]

The more nationalist view of the Canadian conquest is sometimes referred to as that of the Montreal school, because it was most fully developed by a group of historians who taught at the Université de Montréal around the middle of the twentieth century. According to this view, French Canada before the conquest was a flourishing, viable, and (using an adjective much favoured by Quebec nationalists) normal society. It had its own economic elite, partly based on the fur trade but also on other sectors of the economy, and thus was somewhat more than an appendage of the metropolitan French economy. Its people had developed a national consciousness, viewing themselves not only as a cohesive community but as distinct from the French who lived in France, a country that most of their ancestors had left almost a century before the battle on the Plains of Abraham. If the conquest had not taken place, according to this view, Canada would eventually have declared its independence from France, just as the English, Spanish, and Portuguese colonies in North and South America did between 1776 and 1825.

The conquest, according to this view, was a major setback for French Canada's development and thus a uniquely tragic event in its history.[30] Canada was "decapitated" when its elites returned to France, taking advantage of the opportunity to do so provided by the Treaty of Paris. Its economy, apart from subsistence agriculture, was taken over by English-speaking people who arrived during and after the conquest, giving rise to an ethnic division of labour that lasted for two centuries and to a myth that French Canadians were culturally unsuited for commerce and industry. Its language was exposed to the continuous threat of being lost to the predominance of English. Its political life was forced into the mould of British institutions and subordinated to the needs and wishes of English-speaking people, who eventually became the majority in Canada as a whole. Deprived of its self-confidence and of its natural leaders, French Canada missed, or at the very least postponed for two centuries, its opportunity to join the long list of independent republics in the Western Hemisphere. Understandably, those who agree with the preceding interpretation of French Canada's fate tend to be nationalists and supporters of political independence for the province of Quebec, the only place where French Canadians comprise the majority.

The alternative interpretation of the British conquest of Canada is much less alarming. Its proponents are sometimes called the Laval school because it predominated among historians at Université Laval in Quebec City at the time when their counterparts at Montreal espoused the nationalist view.[31] According to this interpretation, French Canada was socially and economically underdeveloped under the French regime, it was economically as well as politically subordinated to France, and it lagged far behind the English colonies in North America. The seigneurial system of land tenure, which actually survived the conquest by almost a century, is often cited as evidence of its backwardness.

Far from being a catastrophe that set back Canada's development, the conquest, according to this view, merely transferred the colony from one European empire to another, with little or no structural change in its economy or its external commerce. If anything, French Canada benefited from the transfer since Britain after its seventeenth-century revolution, as French writers such as Voltaire and Montesquieu conceded, was more tolerant, liberal, and politically advanced than the France of the *ancien régime*. Under British rule, French Canada acquired printing presses, religious toleration, trial by jury, and a legislative assembly, all assets that it (and, apart from the printing presses, France) had lacked before the conquest. Furthermore, Britain's industrial revolution was already beginning in 1760, and it would soon become the leading economic power in the world, a situation that conferred some potential benefits on its colonies. If French Canada failed to participate fully in the economic development that followed, this fact is said to have reflected its own social and cultural disadvantages, the results of French absolutism and feudalism and perhaps, following Max Weber, of its Catholic religion. Understandably, those who agree with the argument of the preceding sentences in this paragraph tend, in Canadian parlance, to be federalists. In other words, they believe that Quebec would be well advised to remain a part of the Canadian federation rather than seeking independence.

NATIVES AND SETTLERS: THE DEMOGRAPHICS OF CONQUEST

Conquest was not merely a transfer of political sovereignty and administrative control but an event that altered, over the long term at least, the composition of the population in terms of language, ethnicity, and, perhaps most importantly, religion. Sovereignty over a territory includes the authority to determine who is entitled to enter the territory and reside there. In many areas conquered by the British, such as India, the number of persons from Britain who chose to reside permanently was so small, relative to the large indigenous population, that conquest had virtually no impact on the composition of the population, either long-term or short-term. In others, such as the Caribbean colonies, the indigenous population was eliminated and replaced mainly by African slaves or by indentured servants from other parts of the empire. In still others, including Australia, the indigenous population was small relative to the size of the territory, colonial settlement took place on a large scale, and the ethnic composition of the conquered land became predominantly British.

Ireland and Quebec do not really fall into any of these categories, or rather, they occupy an intermediate position between the two categories represented by India and Australia. Both experienced enough British immigration to be demographically significant but not enough to reduce the pre-conquest population to minority status. In both cases this partial, but not complete, process of colonial settlement introduced ethnocultural, religious, and political cleavages that had a lasting impact on the countries concerned.

As already noted, an undetermined number of persons from England and Wales migrated to Ireland during and after the first (twelfth-century) conquest, but these "Old English," as they came to be called much later, were gradually absorbed into the Irish population through intermarriage and assimilation. The process seems to have been well advanced at the time of the Statute of Kilkenny, which attempted, unsuccessfully, to prevent it from going any further. Unlike the English of England, these Old English did not adopt the Protestant form of religion when it appeared in the sixteenth century, a fact that reinforced their affinity with the native Irish.

The Tudors developed and, to a small extent, implemented the idea of "planting" English settlers in Ireland, particularly on lands confiscated from rebellious Irish families. Typically, a large area of land was allotted in the first instance to an English "undertaker," who was expected to find English settlers to occupy it. The major settlements were in central Ireland (King's and Queen's counties, restored after independence to their original names of Offaly and Laois) and in the southwest (Limerick and Kerry). From the English point of view, the results were disappointing; few English people actually settled in Ireland during the sixteenth century, and it is estimated that in 1600 only 2 per cent of the inhabitants of Ireland were of English ancestry.[32]

The accession of James VI of Scotland to the throne of England (where he was known as James I) in 1603 and the Flight of the Earls in 1607 gave a massive impetus to the colonization movement. Henceforth colonial settlement focused primarily on the province of Ulster, where the Flight of the Earls had created a power vacuum and also an abundance of confiscated land. James contemplated what he called the "removal of natives" to make way for the settlers, but little progress was made in this direction.[33] In the northeastern counties of Antrim and Down, which had historic ties with Scotland and are separated from that country by a fairly narrow body of water, most of the new settlers were Scottish Presbyterians. Scottish settlers had begun to arrive in Antrim and Down even before 1603, and they continued to do so until the end of the century. Most of them came independently without benefit of "undertakers."[34] By the early 1620s the number of adult settlers in the two counties is estimated to have been about 7,500.[35] The largest influx of Scottish settlement into these two counties, however, did not take place until the 1680s and 1690s.

In the remaining counties of Ulster, settlement was planned rather than spontaneous. A detailed scheme of colonization was prepared in London in 1608–9 and put into practice from 1610 onwards. English and Scottish undertakers were responsible for recruiting settlers in England or Scotland and transporting them to Ulster. By 1622 about 13,000 adult settlers, of which about half were from England and half from Scotland, were living in the counties of Armagh, Cavan, Derry, Donegal, Fermanagh, and Tyrone as a result of this project.[36] The "New English" settlers, unlike the Scots or the native Irish, mainly adhered to the established Church of Ireland, since it was in communion with the Church of England. While the Scots in most parts of Antrim and Down virtually overwhelmed the indigenous population, the settlers farther west were less successful in doing so, since the indigenous population was much larger. It had originally been intended to remove much of the native population, but the undertakers generally found this neither desirable nor feasible. The use of the native Irish as cheap labour was more profitable than sending them away. A deadline for the removal of the natives was extended and in practice was largely ignored. Some of the native Irish even retained ownership of land, although it was usually the less-desirable land at higher altitudes than that occupied by the settlers. The introduction of English property law also left many of the native Irish with no valid title to the lands they occupied.[37] In most of Ulster a characteristic pattern developed of settlers and natives living in unfriendly proximity to one another, with the new settlers occupying the best land and the native Irish the less-desirable land.

In 1641 the native and Catholic Irish of Ulster, joined by some of the Catholic Old English, rose in rebellion against these incursions on their land by Protestant settlers from across the sea. Large numbers of Protestant settlers, perhaps as many as 12,000, died as a result.[38] This event became entangled with the English Civil War and eventually helped to precipitate the military intervention of Oliver Cromwell, which followed the execution of King Charles I in 1649. The relatively brief military campaign was followed by the Act of Settlement (1652), which confiscated much land in southern and central Ireland from its Catholic owners and distributed it among officers of Cromwell's army and other English persons; these became the new governing class, a position that they retained for two and a half centuries. The proportion of Irish land owned by Catholics fell from 60 per cent in 1641 to about 9 per cent in 1660; it rose to about 20 per cent after the restoration of the monarchy.[39] Many of the dispossessed Catholics were displaced to new and poorer land farther west, contributing to the severe overpopulation of Connacht, a region rather poorly suited to agriculture. Although some zealous Puritans may have hoped to send the entire native population "to hell or Connacht," this removal was not actually achieved. The new Protestant landlords who owed their position to the Act of Settlement allowed most of the indigenous population to remain as tenants or farm labourers on their estates. Apart from the new owners themselves, there was no significant influx of settlers from England in the Cromwellian era. An Irish Catholic labour force that could be excluded from political and economic power on religious grounds suited the interests of the landlord class better than a fresh influx of English settlers, who might have been influenced by the egalitarian ideas that were circulating during the English revolution. Most of the new governing class were presumably Puritans to begin with, but after the restoration of the monarchy in 1660, they conformed to the established Church of Ireland, with its bishops appointed by the Crown and its liturgy dating back to the sixteenth century. The Presbyterians of Ulster, on the other hand, successfully resisted pressure to force them into the established church. In that province, where colonization had been much more intensive than in the south, many tenants as well as landlords were Protestants. This was particularly true in Antrim and Down, where the Catholic population was very small and Presbyterian settlers predominated.

Although Catholics regained some land and some political influence after the Restoration, particularly during the brief reign of James II (1685–88), the outcome of the Williamite war decisively entrenched the Protestant ascendancy that had been established in the first half of the seventeenth century. In the words of one historian, "The war decided the balance of power in Ireland for over two centuries, and its effect is still to be seen in the six counties of the north-east."[40]

The result of all these developments was that by the early eighteenth century, persons of British ancestry were estimated to comprise 27 per cent of

Ireland's population.[41] This figure did not include owners of Irish land who actually resided in England and were thus not counted as part of the population. Because of the official discrimination against Catholics, to be discussed below, this substantial minority totally dominated Irish politics, administration, the law, the professions, and, to a large extent, the economy. The British government relied on the minority that adhered to the established Church of Ireland to rule the conquered kingdom on its behalf. That church, having abandoned any effort to convert the natives, was content to represent the privileged minority.[42] The Presbyterians (or Dissenters, as they were known in England) suffered some discrimination, although not as severe as that experienced by the Catholic Irish, and occupied a sort of intermediate position; they were heavily concentrated in the two northeastern counties where they comprised the majority of the population. In Ireland as a whole, they may have been as numerous as the adherents of the established church during the early 1700s.[43]

In the province of Quebec, as in Ireland, conquest eventually produced a significant change in the composition of the population. A number of camp followers and entrepreneurs followed the invading army into the conquered province; many of them had previously resided in the British colony of New York, the base from which Jeffery Amherst's army advanced to capture Montreal in 1760. The number of new arrivals was quite small at the outset. One estimate suggests that there were little more than five hundred residents of British origin, comprising less than 1 per cent of the population, in 1766.[44] Governor Guy Carleton, testifying before the British House of Commons, estimated in 1774 that there were only 360 Protestants in the province, and this category would have included virtually all of the English-speaking population, although Carleton may have deliberately underestimated the number to strengthen the case for his view that a legislative assembly should not be established.[45]

The real change came after the American War of Independence, which caused an influx of Loyalist refugees into Quebec as well as into Britain's other remaining North American colony of Nova Scotia. By 1792 the non-French population of Quebec reached 10,000, or 6 per cent of the population, even though the western part of the colony (the future province of Ontario) had been separated from it a year previously.[46] The influx of American settlers continued, although after the first few years their motivations were less likely to be political than a desire for unoccupied land on which to settle. The boundary drawn between Quebec and New York by the treaty that recognized the independence of the United States left to Quebec a large area south of the St Lawrence River valley which had never been occupied by the French. This area came to be known as the Eastern Townships because it was surveyed and divided in the English manner, rather than according to the French practice used in other parts of Quebec. As it was gradually opened up to settlement, it became, and for many years remained, predominantly English-speaking, with many of its settlers being attracted from the nearby United States.

British inhabitants also become relatively numerous in the two major cities of the colony, Quebec and Montreal. Quebec City was the administrative capital and the site of the major garrison, while Montreal was the principal centre of business and commerce, including the fur trade, which continued to flourish for sixty years after the conquest. The economic elite, concentrated in these two cities, was predominantly English-speaking, a large proportion of the entrepreneurs having been born in either Scotland or the United States. After the conclusion of the Napoleonic Wars, the United Kingdom, rather than the United States, became the major source of immigration, and most new arrivals landed at Quebec City after their transatlantic voyage. By 1827 the non-French population was estimated at 80,000, or 16 per cent, and by 1844, when a precise census was taken, it stood at 172,840, or 25 per cent of the total. (By the latter year a significant number of these were Irish.)[47] Thus in both Ireland and Quebec the post-conquest settler element comprised about one-quarter of the total population less than a century after the British established a firm control over the country. In both cases there was one important region – the northeastern counties in Ireland and the Eastern Townships in Quebec – where persons of British ancestry had become the largest element in the population.

There was, however, one very significant difference between the situation in the two countries. In Quebec there were no confiscations of land, no forced removals of the pre-conquest population, and no legal barriers to the ownership of land by the ethnic and religious group that had predominated before the conquest. In fact, the French system of seigneurial land tenure was left intact in the areas, particularly the St Lawrence valley, where it had existed under the French regime. (It was not abolished until nearly a century after the conquest.) Most of the landlords (seigneurs) continued to be French Canadians; some important seigneuries in fact were held by religious orders of the Catholic Church, a situation that, needless to say, would have been unthinkable in post-Cromwellian Ireland. English-speaking people did acquire some seigneuries, particularly in the area immediately south of Montreal, but they did so by paying a fair price to the previous owners. In the Eastern Townships, where seigneurial tenure had never existed, much land was granted by the Crown to land companies in the first instance, a decision that probably delayed settlement of the region. As late as 1840 only about a quarter of the surveyed land in the townships had been occupied.[48]

Eventually, however, most land there was owned in freehold by the farmers who occupied and worked it. Except to a limited extent in the area near Montreal, the situation of indigenous Catholic tenants and British Protestant landlords, which predominated over most of Ireland until the twentieth century, never existed in Quebec. In fact, landlordism of any kind disappeared from Quebec with the abolition of seigneurial tenure, and even before that date it had not imposed much of a burden, by European standards, on the tenants (*censitaires*).

BRITISH POLICY AFTER THE CONQUESTS

In conquering first Ireland and then Quebec, the British presented themselves with two situations that have obvious parallels, each of which required a response in terms of policy from the British government. In both cases the newly acquired territory was thinly populated enough and attractive enough, in terms of climate and suitability for cultivation, to attract substantial numbers of British settlers. As their numbers grew, these settlers would become an interest that would attempt to influence British policy. In both cases, however, the conquered country also contained an indigenous European (Caucasian) population that spoke a different language and practised a different form of Christian worship from that of the invaders. The Catholicism of both the Irish and the French Canadians is particularly significant because anti-Catholicism had been a core element of English nationalism since the time of Henry VIII's break with the Catholic Church. English people regarded Catholicism not only as a superstition but as a global conspiracy directed against the English state and its established church. After the union with Scotland in 1707, as Linda Colley has suggested, anti-Catholicism continued as a core element of the new synthetic "British" nationalism that sought to merge the national identities of the two kingdoms.[49]

This is not to say that British policy in either country was or could have been dominated exclusively by religious considerations. Colonies were usually conquered for the economic and strategic benefits that they were expected to confer on the imperial power and its people. The mercantilist doctrines of the day, attacked by Adam Smith in 1776 but not abandoned by the British state until seven decades later, proclaimed that colonies were an economic asset which could and should be exploited for the benefit of the state that possessed them. Colonies were also strategically significant insofar as they might provide bases, labour, or economic resources useful in war; at the very least one would try to prevent them from falling into the hands of a hostile power. These general considerations, applicable to both situations, might be expected to produce similarities between British policies in Ireland and Quebec.

In fact, there were very significant differences in the policies that the British pursued in the two situations, as well as some parallels. The differences and similarities will be explored by outlining the development of British policy after the two conquests, first in Ireland and then in Quebec. The starting point will be the Treaty of Limerick (1691) in the case of Ireland and the Treaty of Paris (1763) in the case of Quebec. In both cases the chronology will terminate prior to the beginning of the revolutionary crisis that ended colonial rule in its original form, a topic that is discussed in the next chapter. To conclude the present chapter, some reasons will be suggested for the differences between the policies pursued by the British state in the two cases.

British control of Ireland after 1691 was essentially based on a policy of indirect rule, a technique of government that would characterize British colonial policy in many parts of the world until the final disappearance of the colonial empire. As suggested by biblical references to King Herod and other dignitaries in the Roman Empire, the idea was not invented by the British, although few if any have practised it with greater success than they. The basic idea is to use a local elite within the colony as an intermediary between the colonial power and the population. The elite knows the local situation, is accustomed to exercising authority there, and may have a certain degree of legitimacy, or at least familiarity, which the newly arrived colonial power and its army do not have. By governing the colony on behalf of the colonial power, they spare it some administrative costs and difficulties, as well as preserving some continuity with the patterns of authority that existed before the conquest. In return for their services, they may demand and receive certain recognition of their own privileges and attention to their demands from the colonial power. Yet the colonial power, in the last analysis, holds the ultimate power, based on military force.

Indirect rule through the Anglo-Norman elite had been practised in Ireland after the first conquest, but as George Boyce has suggested, that elite were discarded by the English as partners during the reign of Elizabeth I.[50] Their failure to subdue the country effectively, as well as their refusal to embrace Protestantism, had made them unsuitable. The elite through whom indirect rule was exercised in Ireland after 1691 were the Protestant landlords of English origin, who were present in Ireland as a result of developments in the Cromwellian period. In later years they would come to be known as the Ascendancy. Unlike the Old English, these New English tended to view the native Irish as an inferior people, an attitude that privileged groups often develop as a rationale for their own privileges. They regarded themselves, on the other hand, as a natural governing class with both the right and the duty to rule the country.

The New English elite possessed economic power, since after the confiscations, they owned most of the land that was Ireland's major economic resource. They also possessed political power through their control of local government, such as it was, in the countryside and through their control of the Irish parliament, voting for which required a substantial property qualification and from which Catholics were, after the defeat of James II, totally excluded. Presbyterians, who comprised about half of Ireland's non-Catholic population in the early 1700s, were also excluded from the parliament as "dissenters."[51] As early as the reign of William of Orange and for more than a century thereafter, Ireland's Protestant parliament proved to be more militantly anti-Catholic than the government in England. (William himself was relatively moderate.)[52]

William may have been sincere in promising religious freedom to Catholics in the Treaty of Limerick, but the Protestant Irish parliament had other ideas and began almost immediately to limit Catholic rights in a series of penal laws. The principal target of these measures, apart from the Catholic Church itself, was the diminished, but not yet entirely extinct, class of the Catholic gentry and aristocracy, who had supported King James, some of whom had managed to retain ownership of their lands.[53]

The first penal laws, enacted in 1695, prohibited Catholics not specifically covered by the Treaty of Limerick from owning or bearing weapons and barred Catholics from teaching in any school or from travelling overseas for educational purposes. Another, in 1697, required all Catholic bishops and all members of monastic orders to leave the country. In 1704 Catholic priests were limited to one in each parish and required to register with the government, while additional priests were prohibited from entering Ireland. In the same year, Catholics were prohibited from buying land, inheriting land from Protestants, or leasing land for a term longer than thirty-one years. The law also required that the estates of a deceased Catholic be divided among his sons rather than inherited by the oldest, as was the rule for Protestants. Other laws prohibited Catholics from holding any political office, practising law, enlisting in the armed forces, or serving on municipal corporations or grand juries. Even the value of horses that could be owned by Catholics was restricted. Those few Catholics who still managed to vote in elections for the Irish parliament despite the property qualification were formally disenfranchised in 1728.[54]

It has been argued by revisionist historians that not all these laws were fully observed or scrupulously enforced.[55] For example, the laws pertaining to the Catholic clergy, if taken literally, would have caused the clergy to die out, since there was no seminary for training new priests in Ireland. A Catholic Church without bishops, as the law seemed to envisage, would have been an oxymoron. Nonetheless, the Catholic Church did not disappear; after lying low for a time, it existed more or less openly from about 1730, conducting its services in modest buildings that were known as "chapels," since the word "church" was officially reserved for the places of worship used by the established Protestant church. Restrictions on the ownership of land by Catholics may have benefited some Catholics by directing their attention to other sectors of the economy, as suggested by the growth of a Catholic middle class.[56] On the other hand, the Penal Laws were certainly invidious and reminded Irish Catholics of their status as a conquered people.

Presbyterians did not fare much better. The Toleration Act of 1719 allowed them to practise their form of worship in Ireland but gave them none of the other concessions that they had demanded and might have expected, given the fact that Scotland and England were now united in one kingdom.[57] Furthermore, everyone in Ireland, regardless of religion, had to pay tithes for the support of the established Church of Ireland, even in parts of the country where it scarcely existed.[58]

The Protestant elite, despite their privileges, had their own grievances against British policy towards Ireland. Although the Irish parliament could legislate, it had no real control over the executive government, which was not responsible to it. Even its legislative powers could be overriden, since the Declaratory Act, adopted by the British parliament in 1720, stated that Westminster could still legislate for Ireland if and when it wished to do so. Other British statutes restricted Ireland's trade, and thus its economic development, making it practically impossible to export anything other than agricultural commodities. Enactments such as this contributed to the rise of a distinctive sort of Protestant Irish nationalism, which appeared as early as the 1690s.[59] Despite their minority status and their ignorance of both the language and the religion shared by most Irish people, the Ascendancy saw themselves as the Irish nation, or at least as entitled to speak on its behalf, a plausible assumption in an age when politics everywhere was the monopoly of a small and unrepresentative elite. Those who criticized England's treatment of Ireland were known as Patriots, a term later adopted by those who resisted British rule in the North American colonies. In the 1720s the writings of Jonathan Swift, including his celebrated tongue-in-cheek proposal that the Irish should overcome their poverty by eating their own children, gave expression to Irish Protestant resentment against Britain's economic policies. Some of the Ascendancy, conveniently ignoring the fact that they owed their power and social status to an English conquest, began to claim that the two kingdoms should be equal in status, although sharing an allegiance to the Crown.[60]

Apart from its political, religious, and economic aspects, another component of English/British policy in Ireland was the gradual imposition of the

English language. As noted above, the effort to substitute English for the Irish language can be traced back as far as the Statute of Kilkenny in 1366, although the impact of that measure was very limited. From Tudor times onward, the growing effectiveness of the Dublin-based administration and courts, which functioned in English, tended further to undermine the importance of the Irish language, even though it was still spoken by the majority of the population. The effort to impose Protestantism, unsuccessful though it was in winning the hearts and minds of the population, had the same effect. R.F. Foster suggests that English was the usual language spoken in Leinster by 1600.[61] As early as 1612 a Catholic priest, Father Richard Conway, complained that the prohibition of Catholic schools was accompanied by insistence that children be taught in English and the punishment of Irish children who were caught speaking their native language in school.[62] The substantial number of settlers who arrived from England and Scotland in the seventeenth century had no reason to adopt the Irish language and continued to speak English, reinforcing the pre-eminence of that language. According to Douglas Hyde, one of the leaders in the movement to revive the Irish language and subsequently president of Ireland, "It is from the middle of the eighteenth century onward that the Irish language begins to die out."[63] It must be said that this trend was resented more in retrospect than it seems to have been at the time. However, the gradual adoption by the Irish people of the English language certainly did not bring about their assimilation into the British nation; nor did it reconcile them to British rule over their country.

English/British policy in Ireland after 1691 thus contributed to several different kinds of dissatisfaction, with the result that it failed to establish a fully legitimate political order. Members of the Protestant Ascendancy, although their power depended on the link with England, viewed themselves as "Ireland" and resented both the economic and the political constraints imposed on them. The Catholic middle class, and to some extent the Presbyterian middle class, resented the discrimination imposed against them on religious grounds. The Catholic Church itself, the most important and influential institution in Ireland that did not owe its existence to the English presence, naturally resented the obstacles that restricted its ability to function normally in a country where the vast majority of the population were baptized Catholics. The tenants and farm labourers who comprised most of the population seemed to have little political awareness until late in the eighteenth century, but they had economic grievances against the landlords and against the state that manifested themselves in sporadic outbursts of agrarian violence. Organized agrarian violence emerged with the formation of a secret society, the Whiteboys, beginning in Tipperary and

Waterford in 1761. In the north the Oakboy movement, which included Protestants as well as Catholics, arose at about the same time. Other movements of violent protest flared up in later decades.[64] As long as these different types of discontent, and the different groups of people that they represented, remained separate from one another, they posed no immediate threat to the established order, but their existence indicated that the status quo did not rest on solid foundations.

British policy in French Canada after 1763 differed substantially from the policy that the British state had earlier pursued, and largely continued to pursue, in Ireland. A policy of indirect rule was followed in French Canada as well, but the essential difference was that the group selected to serve as the intermediaries between the occupying power and the population was not the British settler minority in French Canada but the French-speaking Catholic clergy.[65] This policy was not foreordained or inevitable, and it was neither adopted immediately nor pursued with complete consistency, but on the whole it prevailed. In contrast to what might have been expected, given the precedents set by British policies in Ireland and in the Scottish Highlands, not to mention the expulsion of the French settlers in Acadia only a few years before, British policies in the St Lawrence valley proved to be at least relatively benign.

Like the conquest itself, the development by trial and error of a British policy towards French Canada was compressed into a brief period of time. Important decisions, sometimes contradictory, succeeded one another in fairly rapid succession. Because of the extreme distance and difficulty of communication between London and Quebec, the British governor on the spot had to enjoy more autonomy and exercise more initiative than the lord lieutenant in Dublin. So the individual holding the position of governor was an important variable.

The British military occupation of what was still, until formally ceded by the Treaty of Paris, French territory was followed by a brief period of provisional military rule. The military governor, James Murray, continued after 1763 as governor of the civil administration. He was recalled to London two years later because his policies had antagonized the English-speaking merchants in the colony and their allies in the United Kingdom, although he was not formally relieved of his office until 1767.[66] He was succeeded by Guy Carleton, a member of the Irish Ascendancy, who held office until 1778 and returned in 1786 for a second term of office with a new title as Lord Dorchester. These two governors were the decisive actors in the early development of British policy.

A problem which did not arise in Ireland but which the British faced in Canada was that of defining the territorial boundaries of their new acquisition. This problem affected, and was affected by, British policy towards two groups other than the French Canadians: the aboriginal peoples of North America and the Anglo-American settlers in the British colonies to the south. Initially, the Canada ceded by France to Great Britain included what are now the provinces of Quebec and Ontario, apart from the far northern portions of those provinces, where the rivers drain into Hudson Bay. By the royal proclamation of 1763, most of present-day Ontario, apart from the Ottawa Valley, was separated from Canada, which officially became the Province of Quebec, and reserved for the aboriginal peoples.[67] The Quebec Act of 1774 returned this area to the Province of Quebec and added a large area south of the Great Lakes, to the great consternation of Anglo-Americans in the Thirteen Colonies. The latter area was then ceded to the newly independent United States in 1783. Finally, in 1791 the Province of Quebec was divided into Lower Canada (later Quebec) and Upper Canada (later Ontario) along essentially their present boundary. Throughout all these changes, however, the French Canadians comprised the majority of the province's population, and the last change ensured that they would do so for the foreseeable future.

A more familiar problem for the British, and one for which Ireland provided an unhappy precedent, was what to do about the Catholic Church. Virtually all French Canadians were Catholic, although the level of piety and religious observance does not seem to have been particularly high. At the time of the conquest there were about 160 priests, roughly a tenth of whom returned to France after 1763.[68] There was also a bishop, Mgr Pontbriand, but he died in the summer of 1760, leaving his post, which had previously been filled by agreement between the king of France and the pope, vacant. The church's affairs were administered for the time being by three grand vicars, Jean-Olivier Briand in Quebec City, Étienne Montgolfier in Montreal, and Joseph-François Perrault in Trois-Rivières. Governor Murray's instructions, issued in 1763, envisaged establishing the Anglican church in the colony, just as it had been established in Ireland, and even, if possible, converting the people. Murray, a Presbyterian Scot, doubted the wisdom of this policy, although even he hoped that the Canadians would voluntarily embrace Protestantism in due course.[69]

It was obviously unthinkable for the vehemently anti-Catholic George III to nominate a successor to the deceased bishop, and the Canadian clergy elected their preferred candidate, Montgolfier, in 1763, a procedure not recognized as legitimate by either London or Rome, or by Governor Murray. Most of the British governing class would have preferred to leave the office vacant, but Murray disagreed. The governor favoured the candidacy of Briand, who had ingratiated himself by promptly offering prayers for

King George as soon as the conquest was accomplished. The clergy endorsed Briand in a second election a year after the first. After the law officers of the Crown in London had ruled that the Penal Laws did not apply to Quebec, this choice was endorsed in 1766 by the British government and by the pope. In 1772 Briand was allowed to name a coadjutor bishop, ensuring that on his death there would be no interregnum such as had followed the death of Pontbriand.[70]

The British still had some doubts about this experiment in religious toleration and did not formally recognize the existence of a Catholic bishop in Quebec until 1818.[71] Governor Carleton's instructions directed him to forbid correspondence between the new bishop and the pope, to review the appointments of all clergy, and to restrict Briand's authority as narrowly as possible. In practice, Carleton and most of his successors did not take these instructions too seriously.[72] As Philip Lawson has argued, the appointment of Bishop Briand was a seminal event, and his return to Quebec from Rome after his investiture was greeted with public rejoicing. "After this step had been taken, a Protestant ascendancy in the province was out of the question."[73] Although an Anglican bishop was also eventually appointed, the Catholic Church remained the most influential and important religious organization in the province.

The de facto recognition of Catholicism largely ensured that the Protestant minority, consisting essentially of the Anglo-American merchants who had followed the invading armies into Canada, would not obtain the monopoly of political power and influence enjoyed by their counterparts in Ireland. An additional consideration was that these English-speaking Protestants were very few in number for two decades after the conquest and appeared likely to remain so. In any event, neither Murray nor Carleton viewed the merchants with great sympathy; Murray described them as "Licentious Fanaticks" and accused them of wanting to expel the French Canadians.[74] The merchants' Whiggish demands for representative institutions (albeit ones in which only Protestants could participate) were also somewhat out of fashion in the political climate that followed the accession of George III. Carleton worried in 1768 that an assembly would "give a strong bias to Republican principles," and he argued that what he called the better elements among the French Canadians did not want one.[75] (If such an assembly were to be dominated by the Protestant merchants, this attitude on the part of the French Canadians was certainly understandable.)

Given this lack of enthusiasm for the English-speaking merchants, both Murray and Carleton looked for influential allies among the French Canadians who could serve as instruments of indirect rule. Apart from the Catholic clergy, whom most British people still tended to view with suspicion, the most obvious candidates for this role were the captains of militia and the seigneurs. The militia was a long-established institution in Canada, the most important pillar of the French regime, according to the historian A.L. Burt, and had proved useful to France in the wars against the British. Its captains were given new commissions by the British crown soon after the Treaty of Paris, but their failure to mount a serious defence against the American invasion of Quebec in 1775 cast some doubt on their usefulness and reliability. Carleton, who was even more sympathetic to the French Canadians than Murray, pinned his hopes to a large extent on the seigneurs, whom he imagined to be feudal landlords on the European model and thus the natural leaders of the community.[76]

In actual fact, Canadian feudalism had always been a pale shadow of its European prototype. The seigneurs were not socially exclusive and did not really constitute a distinct class.[77] The scarcity of labour and the perennial option of joining the fur traders in the northwest if life on the farm became too onerous gave the Canadian peasantry a bargaining power not enjoyed by their European counterparts. As a result, the seigneurs lacked the power and influence enjoyed by large landowners in England, Ireland, or France.[78] Many were also in financial difficulties and sold their holdings either to English-speaking merchants and speculators or to the Catholic Church. Carleton's hopes for the seigneurial class proved illusory, and this fact increased the influence and importance of the clergy, who increasingly became the main pillar of the British regime.

These complexities were related to the other major problem of British policy: the establishment or otherwise of a representative assembly. In 1763 all of Britain's North American and Caribbean colonies had assemblies, although the newest such body, that of Nova Scotia, was only four years old. Quebec, on the other hand, had never had one under the French regime; in France itself the Estates General had not met since 1614. Although the Anglo-American merchants in Quebec began to demand an assembly almost as soon as they arrived, and although Murray's first instructions directed him to establish one, both Murray and Carleton considered an assembly inappropriate in a colony where practically all of the population were Catholics and thus ineligible, under British law, to vote or hold office. So initially there was no assembly, although Murray appointed a council to advise him on local issues. French Canadians were to bear arms, a right denied to Catholics in Ireland. They were also allowed to practise law and serve on juries.[79]

The existing thrust of British policy in Quebec was reinforced, and to some extent extended, by the Quebec Act of 1774. Although some historians, such as Mason Wade and Hilda Neatby, discount its importance, this measure is generally regarded as one of the most important milestones in Canadian and Quebec history. On the other hand, it was unpopular with the people of the Thirteen Colonies, who denounced it in their Declaration of Independence two years later and viewed it as a prime exhibit in their case against George III and his Tory advisers. This notoriety in turn has contributed to a myth, once accepted by most historians, that its purpose was to enlist French Canadian support for the British in a prospective war against the Thirteen Colonies. Philip Lawson's research indicates, however, that the Quebec Act was planned over a period of several years and that the decisive shift in British policy occurred about 1770, well before there was any credible threat that the Thirteen Colonies would seek their independence.[80] Although the Quebec Act broke new ground in some respects, it also ratified what was already the evolving practice of British policy in Quebec under both Murray and Carleton.

As mentioned earlier, the act greatly extended Quebec's boundaries, mainly into territory that would become part of the United States less than a decade later. Its other provisions, however, were of more lasting significance. Freedom to practise the Catholic religion in Quebec was henceforth to be restricted only by "the King's Supremacy," rather than the more restrictive "laws of England." The Catholic Church was allowed to collect tithes (as the established Protestant church did in Ireland) but only from its own adherents. The oath of allegiance was revised so that Catholics could take it in good conscience. The French law related to "property and civil rights" was restored, although criminal law would continue to follow the English model. The act also declared that it was "inexpedient" to establish a legislative assembly, but in place of one there would be an appointed legislative council with limited powers.[81]

Lord North, the British prime minister, defended the bill in the House of Commons by arguing that it was not fair to have an assembly elected only by the Protestant minority, that it was "more humane" to give Canadians the civil law to which they were accustomed, and that there were no British settlers in the annexed territory. The House heard arguments in support of the bill from Governor Carleton, who had returned to England temporarily to lobby on its behalf, but not from General Murray, although opponents of the bill tried to call him as a witness. Several Whig members of both houses criticized the bill. Edmund Burke asked why it was needed when Quebec had existed without it since the conquest. Lord Chatham, who had been prime minister at the time of the conquest, described it as "cruel, oppressive, and odious" and claimed that it would establish "a despotic government."[82] The opposition's complaints including the lack of an assembly, the extension of Quebec's boundaries, the restoration of French civil law, the privileges given to the Catholic Church, and the modification of the oath, although most of them emphasized only one or two of these concerns. The vote in the House of Commons was 105 to 29 on second reading and 56 to 20 on third reading, numbers that do not suggest a high level of interest or participation.[83] A motion to repeal the Quebec Act four years after the event, on the grounds that it had contributed to the rebellion in the Thirteen Colonies, was defeated by a vote of 96 to 54 after a debate in which religious issues were hardly mentioned.[84]

The Quebec Act was possible because the English governing class were beginning to lose their traditional fear and hatred of the Catholic Church, even if they still viewed its theology with disdain. The church appeared weaker and less threatening in the skeptical age of Voltaire than it had earlier, the Jesuit order had been dissolved by the pope a year before the Quebec Act was adopted, and the threat that the Catholic Stuart dynasty would reclaim the British throne had ended with the death of the most plausible claimant in 1766. In any event, the Tories, who were now in office, had always been less fanatical on this topic than the Whigs. Even in Ireland, where a Catholic Committee had been formed to lobby peacefully against the Penal Laws in 1761, there were signs of change. Under pressure from the British government, which wanted to enlist Irish Catholics as soldiers, the Ascendancy parliament adopted a series of Catholic Relief Acts. Irish Catholics were allowed to take a modified oath of allegiance, similar to the one used henceforth in Quebec, in 1774, the same year that the Quebec Act was adopted. Four years later those Irish Catholics who had taken the oath were allowed to lease land for up to 999 years and to bequeath land to a single heir. The bill that made these concessions had bipartisan support and passed both houses at Westminster without a division. In 1782 most of the remaining restrictions on Catholic landownership, Catholic education, and the activities of the Catholic clergy were eliminated in Ireland.[85] But, in contrast to Quebec, where the British had begun with a clean slate, these measures did not erase the memories of what had happened before.

The Quebec Act permanently entrenched the Catholic religion and civil law on the French model as part of Quebec's heritage. By accepting Catholicism and civil law, it also implicitly accepted and even promoted the French language, though language was not explicitly mentioned anywhere in the act itself. The clear message of the act was that Quebec would remain a French and Catholic society, albeit under British rule. However, the Quebec Act's other main provisions, regarding territorial boundaries and the absence of a legislative assembly, proved to be of shorter duration.

The act came into effect early in 1775. A few months later Quebec was invaded by the Americans, who were already in rebellion, although they had not officially declared their independence. Most of the Catholic clergy, led by Bishop Briand, and the seigneurs rallied to the British cause. Briand issued a pastoral letter proclaiming that Catholics had a duty to defend both their country and King George, who had recently given them their civil law, the freedom to practise their religion, and all the privileges of British subjects.[86] The clergy were instructed to deny the sacraments to those who aided the invaders.

Despite the bishop's appeal, the French Canadian peasantry, persuaded by American propaganda that the Quebec Act would burden them with tithes and taxes, displayed little or no commitment to the British cause.[87] The Richelieu valley, through which the American army advanced on its way to Montreal, was openly pro-American, the first sign of a radical tradition that it would display even more dramatically in 1837. About five hundred Canadians actually joined the American army, a respectable number from a population of only about ninety thousand. Carleton had less than a thousand regulars and could raise no more than two thousand volunteers for the militia.[88] The English merchants also showed no interest in fighting the invaders. Although eventually forced to withdraw, the Americans occupied a large part of the province, including Montreal, until the summer of 1776. By the time they left, they had lost much of their popularity, largely because they paid for supplies in depreciated currency, or not at all. Three hundred of their Canadian supporters followed the retreating army as it fled to the south. Bishop Briand announced that Canadians who had aided the invaders would continue to be denied the sacraments until they publicly repented of their sins.[89]

Carleton, whose complacency in failing to organize an effective defence had contributed to the invasion, was disillusioned that the Quebec Act had done little to secure the loyalty of the population and that the clergy and seigneurs had proved to have less influence than he had expected of them. He concluded that the act might have been more effective had it been adopted several years earlier, as he had urged. However, his faith in the Canadians never fully recovered from the shock of the invasion.[90] The entry of France into the war in 1778 raised some hopes in Quebec that French rule might be restored. In fact, the Americans had insisted on a secret clause in their treaty of alliance with France whereby France renounced any interest in regaining its former North American possessions.[91]

The treaty of peace that ended the war established the international boundary that still exists in the eastern part of North America. The areas that remained under British rule received an influx of Loyalist refugees from the new republic. The refugees had no wish to live under the French civil law that had been restored by the Quebec Act, and their arrival contrib-

uted to a decision to partition the Province of Quebec more or less on ethnic lines. This decision was announced in the Constitutional Act, which the
government led by William Pitt, Lord Chatham's Tory son, introduced at
Westminster in 1791, and was implemented by an order-in-council later that
year.[92] The western and southern part of the old province, where a European population had scarcely existed before the influx of refugees, became
Upper Canada, the present Ontario. The northern and eastern part became
Lower Canada, the present province of Quebec.

By the Constitutional Act, English common law was established in Upper
Canada, but French civil law and the seigneurial system of land tenure were
retained in Lower Canada. To counterbalance the fact that more than a
quarter of all seigneurial land was controlled by the Catholic Church, areas
of land known as clergy reserves were to be set aside in both provinces for
the support of the Anglican church.[93] Both provinces would have elected
assemblies, and Catholics would be allowed to vote and be elected, even
though the most enthusiastic advocates of an assembly had been the English-speaking Protestants. As in the Quebec Act, most of whose provisions
continued to apply to Lower Canada, the French language was not explicitly
mentioned, but in practice the debates of the Lower Canadian assembly
would be conducted mainly in that language.[94]

Although Lower Canada was overwhelmingly French-speaking, it had
received some of the Loyalist refugees, mainly in the area that came to be
called the Eastern Townships and on the Quebec side of the Ottawa Valley.
Together with the Anglo-American merchants in Quebec City and Montreal, the new arrivals comprised a substantial English-speaking and
Protestant minority in the French and Catholic province, most of whose
non-agricultural economy was controlled by the minority. Although somewhat mollified by the decision to establish a legislative assembly and by the
fact that the English system of land tenure and survey would be used in the
Eastern Townships, the Loyalist settlers in Lower Canada had little regard
for the French Canadians and were not pleased to find themselves on the
wrong side of a boundary that had been ostensibly drawn to partition the old
province on ethnic and religious lines.

Acting on their behalf, some Whigs at Westminster opposed the partition.
The radical Charles James Fox, anticipating a theme that another radical,
Lord Durham, would pursue half a century later, argued against it on the
grounds that the "most desirable circumstance was that the French and English inhabitants of Canada should unite and coalesce, as it were, into one
body, and that the different distinctions of the people might be extinguished for ever." Pitt replied by agreeing that unity in support of English
laws and constitutional principles would be desirable, but said that partition

would make this more likely "since, by so doing, the French subjects would be sensible that the British government had no intention of forcing the English laws upon them." [95]

In the House of Lords the colonial secretary and sponsor of the bill, Lord Grenville, reminded the peers that Canada was not a colony originally settled by the British but "a province conquered from another nation, a colony already in possession of settled laws, much agriculture, and an extensive commerce."[96] Thus he argued that it was appropriate to divide the area settled by the French from the settlements on the upper river and around the Great Lakes, which were predominantly English. This was in fact a more credible argument than that of his cousin Pitt. The Constitutional Act was the real beginning of the province of Quebec that still exists today, with a territory centred around Quebec City, a predominantly French population, and an elected assembly that would increasingly serve as a forum for the expression of popular nationalism. Fox's hopes for Canada would never be realized.

The emergence of the United States of America as a viable entity under the federal constitution of 1787 made it expedient for the British to try to satisfy the demands of potentially disaffected subjects, and the outbreak of the French Revolution soon afterwards reinforced this impetus, at least initially. The two great revolutions in the North Atlantic world had placed democratic ideas on the agenda, like it or not. Tolerance of Catholicism was also made more respectable by the revolutionary danger, which the Catholic Church and the British governing class both opposed.[97] But where two distinct groups of disaffected subjects, divided by religion and language, coexisted uneasily on the same territory, satisfying both of them was easier said than done.

The Irish Protestants, comprising a quarter of Ireland's population, owning almost all the land, and with an existing parliament through which they expressed their own form of nationalism, had far more power to impose their wishes on the British government than their counterparts in Quebec. In fact, they represented a more serious immediate threat of dissatisfaction than did the Catholics. Many Irish Protestants, particularly the Presbyterians in County Down and County Antrim, had sympathized with the American Declaration of Independence, partly because many of them had relatives in America.[98] Some of them perceived parallels between their own economic and political grievances against Westminster and those of the Americans, even though Irish Protestants insisted that Ireland was not a colony. In 1778 they formed an unofficial part-time militia called the Volunteers, ostensibly to defend Ireland against an American or French attack but with the additional advantage that it enabled them to put pressure on the British government. By 1782, when the Volunteers held a national convention at Dungannon, County Tyrone, there were sixty thousand members.[99]

In response to Irish Protestant dissatisfaction and the pressure represented by the Volunteers, Ireland in 1780 was granted complete freedom to trade with England, a privilege that Scotland had enjoyed since 1707.[100] Two years later, following the Dungannon convention, the Declaratory Act of 1720 was repealed and Poyning's Law of 1494 was modified so that Irish bills could not be amended by the British Privy Council. They could still be refused royal assent, but this power was used only three times between 1782 and 1800, all with regard to issues of minor importance.[101] An Irish parliamentary leader, Henry Grattan, then drew up a declaration of independence which proclaimed that Ireland and England were united only by a common allegiance to the Crown. The Whigs, traditionally sympathetic to the Protestant interest in Ireland, were enjoying a brief interlude in office; so the British government accepted this declaration, no doubt aware that it could continue to influence the Irish parliament through the use of patronage.[102] By a further act of 1783, Westminster renounced the right to legislate for Ireland "forever," even though a basic principle of the unwritten British constitution states that Parliament cannot prohibit action that might be taken by a subsequent parliament.

These events inaugurated the era of "Grattan's parliament," during which the Irish Ascendancy enjoyed almost total independence until the turn of the century. However, this development did nothing for the Catholics, who comprised three-quarters of Ireland's population. Although Grattan personally favoured full civil and political rights for Catholics, most of his colleagues in the Dublin parliament did not, and Grattan himself was not a member of the government. In practice, the autonomy conceded to the Ascendancy parliament probably made reform on behalf of the Catholics less, rather than more, likely.[103]

Following the outbreak of the French Revolution, the British government, now led by William Pitt, became more sympathetic to Catholics, who were perceived as ideological allies, at least potentially. At any rate they seemed less dangerous than radical Presbyterians. The Catholic Committee continued its peaceful campaign for civil and political rights. In 1792, British pressure and patronage finally persuaded the Dublin parliament to allow Catholics to practise law. The following year they won the right to vote, but they could not sit in the Irish parliament or on the bench and were barred from holding a number of high offices in the administration. They could also not hold any rank higher than colonel in the British army.[104] In an even more dramatic development, Pitt's government allowed a seminary for the training of Catholic priests to open at Maynooth, near Dublin, in 1795.

Further relief for Irish Catholics, however, would not come until 1829, long after the Irish parliament had ceased to exist. For the few remaining years of its existence, that parliament would be the instrument of the Protestant minority. While Lower Canadian Catholics could express their sentiments in an elected assembly after 1791, Catholics in Ireland could not.

Our survey of British policies in the two conquered countries has suggested that there were some similarities, both in the situations that the British policy-makers faced and in their responses to them. Furthermore, the fate of neither conquered country can be fully understood in its larger context without reference to what was going on in the other. However, there were important differences as well, both in situations and outcomes. British policies towards the Catholic Church and towards the interests and sentiments of the indigenous Catholic population, more generally, were more favourable in Quebec than in Ireland, even though by the end of the eighteenth century, policy towards Ireland was evolving in the direction of greater tolerance. What were the reasons for this contrast?

The first difference is one of timing. However one dates the beginning and end of the British conquest of Ireland, it clearly preceded the conquest of Quebec chronologically. Furthermore, much of the process of conquering Ireland – or all of it, if we exclude the Anglo-Norman conquest of the twelfth century from consideration – occurred at a time when English fear and hatred of Catholicism were intense. The conquest of Quebec, by contrast, occurred in the more tolerant eighteenth century, when religious passions had abated, when England was stronger and felt more secure, and when liberal ideas of religious tolerance were beginning to have some influence. Another consideration related to timing is that England may have learned, to some extent, from its unhappy experience with Ireland and may have applied the lessons learned to Quebec. There are certainly many statements in the parliamentary debates that explicitly compare the two situations.

The second difference concerns the large and influential Protestant settler minority in Ireland. The lengthy process of conquering Ireland, extending over several generations, meant that by the time the conquest was accomplished, this minority was already present, entrenched in the country and in its political institutions, and comprised a very substantial share of its population. Furthermore, after Cromwell the Protestants in Ireland owned virtually all the land, at a time when ownership of land was the recognized criterion for political power and influence. Again there is a contrast with Quebec, where British settlement entirely followed the completion of the conquest, rather than preceding it, and where there were very few British settlers at the time when the fundamental decisions were made. Furthermore, the earliest British arrivals were merchants rather than landowners and thus tended to be looked down upon by aristocratic and Tory policy-makers such as Murray and Carleton. Clearly, they were not viewed as suitable instruments for indirect rule.

The third contrast concerns economic interests, which were more important in the Irish case, although not entirely negligible in the case of Quebec. As a close neighbour with a relatively large population, Ireland was an important market for English goods, while Quebec was a relatively minor one; so there was a much greater incentive to restrict Ireland's freedom to trade and its freedom to develop its economy. Furthermore, many of the English governing class owned Irish land or had relatives who did, as a result of the various confiscations in the seventeenth century. Concessions to the Catholics might threaten their interests directly.

A fourth contrast concerns the geographic and strategic situation of the two countries. Ireland was close to England and relatively large in population and resources. (It may have had two to three million inhabitants in the early seventeenth century, compared to about six million in England and Wales.) If occupied by another European power, particularly a Catholic power that might attract the sympathy of the indigenous Catholic population, it could be a critical threat to English security. Quebec could be invaded more easily than Ireland, as the Americans demonstrated in 1775, but it would not threaten England in a serious way, even if it were occupied by a foreign power. At most, it might threaten England's other North American colonies.

A final contrast concerns the different English views of the Irish and French Canadian people. This was not merely a question of attitudes towards the Catholic religion, although they certainly had an influence. The Irish, speaking a language that was spoken nowhere else and lacking a central government or a recognized sovereign prior to the conquest, were viewed as inferiors and barbarians, even thought they were white and Christian. These invidious attitudes of course served the interests of Protestant Irish landowners, just as racist attitudes towards Africans served the interests of those who owned or traded in slaves, but this does not mean that they were not sincerely believed by many people or that they were not an independent variable influencing policy. The French Canadians, on the other hand, were an offshoot of a powerful European nation that possessed a well-developed absolutist state and was viewed with respect, although not with affection, by most English people. French was the language of diplomacy and high culture, and many educated people in England and Scotland could read or speak it. Moreover, the French Canadians had come under British control through a solemn treaty between sovereign states of equal status. While not everyone went as far as Murray in claiming that they were "the best and bravest Race upon this Globe," it was difficult to regard them as inferiors.[105]

These various contrasts would continue and would have a lasting influence on policy, particularly towards Ireland, where direct British responsibility became more complete after 1800 and lasted much longer. The continuing impact of British policy will appear from time to time in subsequent chapters. But even if their direct impact had ended with the eighteenth century, they would have had important consequences, because the policies adopted prior to that date would have a lasting and decisive influence on later developments.

CHAPTER THREE

The Birth of Anti-colonial Nationalism

In the first chapter of this book, reference was made to the concept of a formative event in the development of nationalist politics and of the nation itself. Regardless of whether one views the nation as a collective actor in history or as an imagined community that exists only in the minds of the individuals who make history, it seems in many cases that the nation becomes a reality at a particular time and as a result of a particular episode.

In the histories of Ireland and of Quebec, two episodes stand out both for their importance as formative events in the development of national consciousness and for the many parallels between them. Ireland in 1798 and Lower Canada in 1837–38 experienced rebellions against British rule that followed long periods of growing tension and conflict in the colonial relationship. In each case the risings mobilized relatively large numbers of people and may have been tacitly supported by many more. However, the rebellions were not well-organized and revealed significant divisions among the population. The Catholic clergy, with scattered individual exceptions, advised submission to the Protestant British monarch. Foreign aid was hoped for by the rebels, but was limited and ineffectual in the Irish case and virtually non-existent in the Lower Canadian case. In contrast to the American War of Independence, which served as a prototype for both the Irish and Lower Canadian efforts to win independence by force of arms, both rebellions were rather easily suppressed by British troops. Apart from the usual reprisals, the British responded in both cases by abolishing the local parliament, apparently hoping that absorption into a larger administrative unit would douse the fires of nationalism. Nationalism, of course, did not die in either case, but when it re-emerged from temporary eclipse, it differed substantially in form and content from the nationalism of 1798 and 1837–38. Ultimately, the new form of nationalism proved to be more durable and more successful, although in some ways more divisive, than the old. Despite their defeats, the rebellions of 1798 and 1837–38 have survived as powerful myths to the present day. Both of these unsuccessful rebellions were the cause as much as the consequence of the development of national sentiment, although their significance is still disputed.

BACKGROUND TO THE REBELLIONS

Ireland in 1798 had a population that was probably between 3 and 5 million.[1] Thus its population was almost certainly larger than the combined population of the thirteen American colonies had been in 1776 and not much smaller than the population of the United States in 1800. Although estimates of the Irish population become less reliable and vary more widely as one moves backwards in time, it appears likely that it had grown rapidly, probably doubling in size, over the preceding century. The Protestant minority, concentrated mainly in the northern province of Ulster but existing throughout the country, was still very substantial, but as a proportion of the total it may have declined slightly from its peak of 27 per cent in the early part of the century. Contemporary observers spoke of Ireland as three-quarters Catholic and one-quarter Protestant, an estimate that is probably fairly accurate. In addition to its religious division, which corresponded roughly although not exactly to the distinction between those whose ancestors had lived there prior to the reign of Elizabeth I and those whose presence resulted from the various plantations and confiscations, Ireland was also divided by language. Although the Irish language was already in decline, it may have been the primary language for more than 1 million people and the only language spoken by more than half that number. Virtually all of those who used the Irish language would have been Catholics.

As discussed in chapter 2, ownership of land by Catholics had been permitted in Ireland only since 1778 and only on condition that they took an oath of allegiance to the Crown. In 1798 most landlords, obviously, were Protestant, with many residing for part or all of the time in Great Britain rather than in Ireland itself. Some landlords rented part of their land to middlemen, who in turn sub-rented to small tenants. Conspicuous consumption, rather than improvement of their estates, seems to have been the highest priority for the Irish landlord class at the end of the eighteenth century.[2] Tenants had few rights and could be evicted for nonpayment of rent or for any other cause, although in Ulster, where many tenants were Protestants, they enjoyed more customary rights than elsewhere.

Differences of religion, origin, and language, as well as differences of social status and economic class, made it difficult to mobilize the entire population behind a political cause and no doubt contributed to the ultimate failure of the rebellion. Tactics of divide and rule could be used with some success by the authorities. On the other hand, the divisions in Irish society also were reflected in the existence of several different kinds of discontent and dissatisfaction, which the authorities might have difficulty in satisfying simultaneously. The Ascendancy, represented in Grattan's parliament, were the most privileged group, but also the most articulate in expounding their grievances. Their complaints about both the economic and political restrictions imposed on Ireland by Great Britain had been appeased to some extent by the concessions made to them in the latter part of the eighteenth century, particularly by the autonomy given to the Irish parliament itself, but some dissatisfaction remained.

English observers, including a future prime minister, George Canning, commented on the relative absence of a middle class in Ireland as compared to England.[3] However, a middle class was in fact gradually emerging, particularly in Ulster but also in urban centres throughout the country. It included elements from all three of the major religious communities in Ireland: Catholics, Church of Ireland, and Presbyterian.[4] Middle-class Catholics and Presbyterians, particularly, resented the privileges enjoyed by the established Church of Ireland and the more extensive political and civil rights enjoyed by its adherents. The Catholic Committee, a peaceful interest group representing the Catholic middle class, had enjoyed some success, as noted in the previous chapter, although Catholics could still not sit in the Irish parliament.

Even among middle-class persons who belonged to the Church of Ireland, however, there was some discontent and restlessness, sometimes expressed in support for the American and French Revolutions. Theobald Wolfe Tone, the leader who more than any other is associated with historical memories of 1798, was a classic illustration of this type of person. Admiration for revolutionary principles such as democracy, republicanism, self-determination, and the separation of church and state transcended the religious boundaries that normally divided the middle classes of Ireland.

Finally, of course, there were the peasants, tenant farmers, and farm labourers, by far the most numerous, although not yet a very articulate, element of the population. Still largely illiterate, divided by religion and language, and isolated from one another by distance and the difficulties of transportation and communication, they remained politically inert to a large extent. However, the emergence in 1761 of the Whiteboys as a radical and clandestine movement of agrarian discontent was a warning to the authorities that they would not remain so indefinitely, even though the Whiteboys expressed no interest in separating Ireland from the British crown.

The real task of those seeking radical political change, a task that had not been achieved previously, was to unite these disparate elements of the population and their various discontents into a single movement. This task would be attempted, and to a limited extent achieved, by the rebels of 1798.

The state of the Irish economy in the latter part of the eighteenth century has been viewed differently by different historians, but the most widely accepted view today is that it was reasonably prosperous and growing, despite the restrictions which British policy for much of the eighteenth century had placed on its development.[5] This relative prosperity, as well as the absence of invasion or indigenous warfare, distinguished the eighteenth century from the seventeenth, and these two factors together probably explain the much more rapid growth of the population after the Treaty of Limerick than before it. Relative prosperity also suggests that economic hardship was not a significant short-term or even long-term cause of the revolutionary events of 1798. It is interesting to note, however, that Wexford, the county in which by far the most significant and violent revolutionary outbreak took place, was an exception to the rule. In that county the staple crop was barley, and a new malt tax had caused a significant decline in its price in 1798.[6] It is possible that this factor contributed to the mobilization of the peasantry for revolutionary action in Wexford, although admittedly, peasant "outrages" had occurred there in 1797.

As discussed in the preceding chapter, the British government had responded to Irish discontent and pressure by implementing a number of reforms and changes in its Irish policy in the latter part of the eighteenth century. Restrictions on Ireland's freedom to trade with Great Britain, a major grievance with Protestant "Patriots," had been lifted. The Penal Laws had for the most part been repealed, beginning in 1778. A very large degree of autonomy had been conceded to Ireland's parliament in 1782, largely as a result of the potential power represented by thousands of armed Volunteers. However, Ireland still lacked responsible government, so that the parliament could not really control the administration Catholics and Presbyterians who met the necessary property qualifications had been given the right to vote, but Catholics could still not sit in the Irish parliament. These limited reforms did nothing directly for the peasants, who comprised the overwhelming majority of the population, and they did not entirely allay the discontent among the middle classes or the impact of events in America and France on Irish aspirations. A revolutionary crisis was building up dur-

ing the years of Grattan's parliament and would explode spectacularly in
1798.

In the case of Quebec, which was officially known as Lower Canada after
1791, a revolutionary crisis also came eventually, but it was delayed until
almost forty years after its Irish counterpart. When it did arrive, it was on a
smaller scale and much less violent. The loss of human lives in Ireland as a
result of the revolutionary outbreak in 1798 has been estimated at 30,000,
a number far exceeding the losses in the American War of Independence,
which lasted for eight years.[7] In Lower Canada the losses among the local
population have been estimated at 300, and among the British soldiers
who quelled the rebellion, about 20.[8] Admittedly, the much smaller population in Lower Canada (about 220,000 at the turn of the century and
about 600,000 by 1837)[9] explains some of the contrast between the death
toll in the two countries, but by no means all of it. The British conquest had
been less traumatic, and British policy more benign, in Quebec than in Ireland, for reasons discussed in chapter 2. Lower Canada was also less influenced by the French Revolution than was Ireland, despite the fact that
most of its people spoke the French language. The width of the Atlantic
Ocean, at a time when an ocean crossing was a perilous venture taking several weeks or even months, proved as effective as any language barrier. In
any event, the France of the 1830s, under King Louis Philippe, was no longer the revolutionary country that Wolfe Tone had visited. Perhaps even
more significant was the weakness and slow development of the French
Canadian middle class. By 1837 that class had become quite significant,
but in the last decade of the eighteenth century it was not. The works of
such writers as Voltaire and Rousseau were available in Lower Canada at
the time of the French Revolution, but very few French Canadians at that
time could read them.

Yet although political discontent took longer to build up in Lower Canada than in Ireland, it undeniably still existed. In many ways the establishment of an elected legislative assembly in 1791 proved to be the beginning,
rather than the end, of the province's political troubles. The demand for
the assembly had come more from the English-speaking minority, who had
been complaining of its absence for thirty years, than from the French Canadians. However, once it was established, the assembly consisted mainly of
French Canadians, conducted its debates mainly in French, and served primarily as a vehicle for the expression of French Canadian wishes and concerns. This tendency was reinforced by the fact that the percentage of the
population entitled to vote in both Lower and Upper Canada was very high
by eighteenth-century standards, and probably exceeded only by the percentage that could vote in the northern parts of the United States.[10]

The Legislative Assembly of Lower Canada was thus far more representative of the totality of the population than Grattan's parliament, although neither could control the administration or the representative of the Crown. The existence of the assembly perhaps served as a safety valve for discontent which helped to postpone the revolutionary outbreak and to make it less violent when it did occur than its Irish counterpart. On the other hand, the assembly still lacked real political power or responsibility. Certainly, no one could have believed that it enjoyed the relative independence claimed by Grattan's parliament, either in theory or in practice. The governor general in Lower Canada, even after 1791, monopolized power to a greater extent than did the lord lieutenant in Ireland. His advisers, selected by himself, were drawn from the English-speaking minority or from the seigneurs, while his regime also relied on the support of the Catholic clergy. Despite its broad suffrage, religious toleration, and absence of rigid class distinctions, the regime was absolutist in many respects, as Bernier and Salée have argued.[11] The contrast with the United States was particularly obvious.

Nonetheless, a predominantly French Canadian assembly, elected by a suffrage that was very broad by eighteenth-century standards, did exist. The somewhat ironic result of this situation was that much of the English-speaking element in Lower Canada, including the merchant elite who had been most insistent on the need for a legislative assembly, came to view the assembly that they had wanted for so long as an opponent and an obstacle. To counterbalance it, they sought to exercise political power through the Legislative Council, appointed by the British governor; through the courts, the judges of which were also appointed; and through the governor himself. In the absence of responsible government, a stalemate developed between the assembly, representing the democratic and largely French element in the population, and the other organs of government, representing the oligarchic and largely English element. The latter group resisted political reform and sought to promote their own economic and political interests by defying the will of the majority.

The historiography of the Lower Canadian rebellion, in contrast to that of its Irish counterpart, has given more emphasis to economic circumstances as an explanatory factor. In the seigneuries around Montreal, where the revolutionary outbreaks took place, wheat was the staple crop and principal source of food for the French Canadian peasantry, although English-speaking farmers were beginning to abandon it in favour of other crops such as oats and potatoes. The leading economic historian of the period, Fernand Ouellet, has accumulated evidence that the wheat economy was in crisis, with both the quantity and the quality of the crop declining in the 1830s. The price of wheat also fell sharply in 1832, and although it rose slightly over the next few years, "The year 1832 marked the beginning of the decisive breakdown of wheat production in Lower Canada."[12] In 1834, 1835, and 1836 the wheat harvest was largely destroyed by insects, and wheat had to be imported.[13] Coincidentally, a crisis in the banking system spread over much of the Western world. The American banks suspended cash payments in May 1837 to avert disaster, an action imitated almost immediately by their Canadian counterparts.[14] Economic circumstances thus probably affected the timing of the rebellion, although they were not the main cause of it.[15]

DISSATISFACTION AND PROTEST

In both Ireland and Lower Canada the outbreak of armed struggle was preceded by many years of agitation that expressed the deep divisions in the society and the tensions between different groups. In Lower Canada the existence of an assembly that was reasonably representative of the entire population at least brought discontent out into the open. In Ireland discontent was more likely to take the form of pressure groups or secret societies, while in Lower Canada it was expressed through political parties.

The American War of Independence enjoyed considerable support among Irish Protestants, some of whom viewed it as a continuation of the Glorious Revolution of 1688.[16] Protestant Ireland, especially the Presbyterian community in Ulster, had contributed many settlers to the Thirteen Colonies, particularly the Appalachian highlands of Virginia and North Carolina. The decentralized and somewhat democratic structure of the Presbyterian church, with its emphasis on literacy, also predisposed its adherents to revolutionary and subversive ideas.

The outbreak of the French Revolution in 1789 had an even more profound effect on the stability of the status quo in Ireland, which had already been shaken by the American War of Independence a few years earlier. There was a strong sympathy for France in Catholic Ireland, which predated the revolution and survives to the present day. The revolution was initially welcomed by virtually all classes and religious groups in Ireland.[17] For middle-class reformers such as Wolfe Tone, most of whom were Protestants, the secular and non-sectarian ideology of the revolution offered hope that Ireland's different religious traditions could be united in a common cause. Thomas Paine's book *The Rights of Man*, a rebuttal of Burke's attack on the French Revolution, was widely read in Ireland.[18] It contributed to the formation in 1791 of the United Irishmen, a non-sectarian, although in practice mainly Protestant, middle-class liberal group which sympathized with revolutionary France. By 1793, as the French Revolution became more radical and the revolutionary government more authoritarian, some early adherents of the United Irishmen were having second thoughts. Those who remained faithful were convinced republicans who, in Marianne Elliott's words, viewed the struggle between reaction and revolution as "an ideological war which knew no national boundaries."[19] Given its potentially subversive nature at a time when Britain was at war with France, it is not surprising that the organization was extensively penetrated by informers working for the government.[20]

The greatest strength of the United Irishmen initially was in the predominantly Presbyterian counties of Down and Antrim, which had also been the part of Ireland most sympathetic to the American War of Independence. Presbyterians had suffered enough discrimination at the hands of the Church of Ireland and the British government to be radical, but they were more likely than Catholics to belong to the educated middle class. As noted earlier, their decentralized form of church government also inclined them in a radical and republican direction, both in Ireland and in North America.

Although they were not generally sympathetic towards the Catholic Church, and although some of them feared the possibility of sectarian violence instigated by the Catholic peasantry, the United Irishmen realized that an effective national movement in Ireland must be open to members of the Catholic majority. The oath sworn by each United Irishman expressed this aspiration: "I will endeavour, so much as lies in my ability, to forward a brotherhood of affection, an identity of interest, a communion of rights, and a union of power, among Irishmen of all religious persuasions."[21] (The administration of this oath, incidentally, was punishable by the death penalty in eighteenth-century Ireland.)

Enlisting Catholics in a radical cause, however, faced certain obstacles. As discussed in the previous chapter, the British government, led by William Pitt, had been astute enough to make some concessions to the Catholics, following the successful example of the Quebec Act almost two decades previously. These concessions earned it the gratitude of the higher clergy in Catholic Ireland, if not always of Catholics in general. Even more important was the fact that the anticlericalism, and at times outright atheism, of the French revolutionary leaders, followed by the military occupation of Rome and the virtual kidnapping of the pope, antagonized Catholics throughout the world, Ireland being no exception. It would not be inappropriate to draw a parallel with Catholic attitudes towards the Russian Revolution more than a century later.

Not everyone in Ireland, however, lost faith in the French experiment. One who did not was Lord Edward Fitzgerald, younger brother of the Duke of Leinster and a member of one of Ireland's most prominent aristocratic families. (The building now occupied by the Oireachtas, the parliament of independent Ireland, was originally the family's townhouse in Dublin.) The Fitzgeralds were Anglo-Norman "Old English" but, in contrast to most of that group, had converted to Protestantism during the Reformation. As a very young man, Lord Edward served in the army fighting against the Americans from 1781 to 1783, even though he was related to many of the Whig statesmen who disapproved of Lord North's anti-American policies. Later he regretted having fought on the wrong side, but he served in North America again as a British officer from 1788 to 1790. (On that second tour of duty he travelled extensively in Canada and met Joseph Brant, the pro-British chief of the Mohawks.)[22]

In contrast to other Whig aristocrats, Fitzgerald was not satisfied with the politics of Grattan's parliament, since he advocated electoral reform and the extension of full political rights to Catholics. He became a supporter first of American independence and then of the French Revolution. He was also an early supporter of the United Irishmen, although he did not formally join the organization until 1796. He visited France, whose language he spoke fluently, in 1792 and met some of the Irish radicals who lived there, as well as his hero, Tom Paine. Returning to Ireland, he began to learn the Irish language, believing that a successful revolution would require the support of the Irish-speaking peasantry.[23] He also urged the United Irishmen to seek military help from France, a policy to which they agreed in 1795. In pursuit of this objective, they sent Wolfe Tone to France to explore the possibilities. Fitzgerald himself met with French agents in Germany and Switzerland the following year.

Theobald Wolfe Tone, a middle-class Dublin Protestant and graduate of Trinity College, also emerged as a leading figure in the revolutionary movement. In his youth he had been pro-British, but he claimed to have changed his mind by 1789, if not sooner. Unimpressed with Grattan's parliament, he vowed to "subvert the tyranny of our execrable Government, to break the connection with England, the never-failing source of our political evils, and to assert the independence of my country-these were my objects."[24]

Although a member, like Fitzgerald, of the established Protestant church, Tone wished to "unite the whole people of Ireland, to abolish the memory of all past dissensions, and to substitute the common name of Irishman in place of the denominations of Protestant, Catholic, and Dissenter."[25] He wrote a pamphlet on this theme in 1791, although he was pessimistic about converting his fellow members of the established church. In 1793 Tone went to London as part of a delegation sent by the Catholic Committee to argue for the civil and political rights of Irish Catholics. They were partly successful, and the British government soon afterwards gave Catholics the right to vote.

In 1794 the United Irishmen initiated contacts with the Defenders, a revolutionary movement that enjoyed support among the Catholic peasantry but even more among the Catholic working class and lower middle class in the towns. The Defenders had actually been founded around 1785 in response to anti-Catholic sectarian attacks in Ulster. The Catholic Relief Act of 1793, which allowed some Catholics to vote but inconsistently prevented them from sitting in the Irish parliament, was viewed as invidious and insulting.[26] Since Catholic Ireland was traditionally pro-French, it was not difficult in 1793 for discontented Catholics to become republican in sentiment and then to hope for a French invasion as a solution to Ireland's problems. Not all the Defenders were convinced republicans; nor were all of the United Irishmen. But the two organizations were moving towards an alliance, despite the divisions of religion, region, ideology, and class. This was a decisive development in the progress towards a revolutionary crisis.[27]

In 1795 the Defenders and the United Irishmen merged, and the organization formally committed itself to pursue Wolfe Tone's objective: a complete separation of Ireland from the British Empire. These initiatives were largely a response to the dismissal by the British government of the popular and liberal lord lieutenant, Earl Fitzwilliam, who was considered sympathetic to the Catholics.[28] Fitzwilliam had accepted Grattan as his chief adviser and had dismissed many Protestant office-holders in an effort to give Catholics a share of the patronage.[29] His successor, Earl Camden, was almost as suspicious of Catholics as he was of French revolutionaries; his unpopularity and lack of judgment contributed to the crisis that followed.

In response to the growth of the Defenders and their increasing contacts with the United Irishmen, Protestant landlords in the northern county of Armagh encouraged the formation in 1795 of the Orange Order, which was destined to destabilize Irish politics for more than two centuries. In doing so, they made use of an existing sectarian organization known as the Peep of Day Boys, which had existed since about 1779. The Orange Order was (and still is) a right-wing and at times violent sectarian movement based on opposition both to Catholicism and to Irish nationalism. It also represented the idea of solidarity among all Protestants regardless of class, in contrast to the anti-elitist Peep of Day Boys. Its name recalled the victory, more than a century before, of William of Orange over James II. Originally its membership was confined to adherents of the established (Anglican) church, but in later years Presbyterians and other Protestants were also admitted. Its purpose was, by appealing to Irish Protestants on religious and ethnic grounds, to discourage them from supporting either Irish independence or the principles of the American and French Revolutions, and particularly from forming any alliance with Irish Catholics who were similarly inclined. (The order was subsequently introduced to Canada by Irish Protestant immigrants and became extremely influential in that country during the nineteenth century, combining Protestant sectarianism with anti-Americanism and Conservative politics.) In Ireland the Orangemen were influential within the Yeomanry, a semi-official and mainly Protestant counter-revolutionary militia that Lord Camden authorized because he distrusted the largely Catholic militia. By 1797 the Yeomanry numbered about 30,000 armed men.[30]

In Lower Canada also, the French Revolution caused some stresses and strains, although its direct impact was much less than in Ireland. Its chief consequence, particularly after Britain entered the war against revolutionary France in 1793, was to reinforce the francophobic sentiments of the English-speaking minority in Lower Canada.. Fear and hatred of republican France affected their attitudes towards the French Canadians and led to increasingly arbitrary actions by the administration and a deterioration in civil liberties.[31]

The English-speaking minority in Lower Canada already numbered about 10,000 and was continuing to grow rapidly in size.[32] In 1793 its members unsuccessfully tried to make English the only official language of the colony. They also offended the French Canadians by giving English names to the counties of Lower Canada, an innovation that had been inflicted on Ireland to only a limited extent and was happily abandoned after a few years.[33] In the same year an Anglican bishop of Quebec was appointed for the first time, raising the possibility that the Anglican church would be officially established, like the Church of Ireland. The new bishop, Jacob Mountain, hoped for this outcome and resented the quasi-official status of the Catholic Church in Lower Canada. He did his best, during his long incumbency, to undermine the position of his Catholic counterpart, Joseph-Octave Plessis.[34] This effort threatened to destroy the cooperation between the Catholic Church and the British authorities that had lasted since 1774, but Mountain's machinations were not successful.

By the early 1800s the English-speaking minority in Lower Canada had grown to about 30,000 and controlled most of the economy, including the already moribund fur trade.[35] Despite its rapid increase in numbers, its garrison mentality remained as strong as ever, reinforced by the ongoing war against France and deteriorating relations between Britain and the United States. Governor James Craig, an elderly soldier who held office in Lower Canada from 1808 to 1811, became particularly notorious for his suspicion of the French Canadians, who referred to his regime as "the Reign of Terror." He also tried to interfere in the appointment of Catholic parish priests, an initiative that was successfully resisted by the pro-British Bishop Plessis.[36]

In 1812, not long after Craig's departure, war broke out between Britain and the United States, and the following year the Americans invaded Lower Canada. Once again, as in 1775, the Catholic bishop called on the people to resist the invaders. Despite the provocations of the Craig regime, Bishop Plessis was more successful in this regard than Bishop Briand had been on the earlier occasion. The Americans were defeated at the battle of Châteauguay by a force that consisted largely of French Canadian volunteers, led by a French Canadian regular officer, Michel de Salaberry. They soon abandoned the effort to take Montreal and concentrated their attention on Upper Canada, where they enjoyed somewhat greater success, and on the war at sea. In 1818, as a reward for French Canada's loyalty in the war, the British government gave formal and official recognition to the Catholic bishop of Quebec, whose office had existed in a state of semi-legality for half a century. This move ended any threat of an established Anglican church serving a small minority of the population, like the Church of Ireland. As an additional reward for his services to the crown, Bishop Plessis was appointed to the Legislative Council.[37]

Despite this reinforcement of the alliance between the British colonial regime and the Catholic Church, Lower Canada remained politically unstable. The politics of the early nineteenth century revolved around the conflict between the governor general and the Legislative Assembly. The former tended to represent the interests of the mainly, but not exclusively, English-speaking economic elite of merchants, entrepreneurs, and seigneurs, who interacted with him socially and were frequently appointed by him to the Legislative Council or to judicial and other offices. The latter, led by a middle class of smaller entrepreneurs and self-employed professionals, tended to represent the interests of the mainly, but not exclusively, French Canadian farmers who made up most of the electorate.

Early in the nineteenth century the anti-establishment political party that dominated the assembly became organized and began to refer to itself as the Parti canadien. The smaller group of members who supported the executive government were often called the English party. The term "Canadien" was at that time usually understood to mean a person of French ancestry and mother tongue, but the Parti canadien did not exclude anyone on grounds of ethnicity or language. In fact, it had many English-speaking supporters and prominent members, including the Nelson brothers, Wolfred and Robert, and the Irish-born editor E.B. O'Callaghan. In 1827 the Parti canadien changed its name to the Parti patriote, thus reinforcing the message that it was open to anyone supporting political reform. The new name, which recalled the supporters of American independence in the eighteenth cen-

tury, as well as the Irish Protestants who had protested against British policies in the same era, began to be widely used about five years later.[38]

The most prominent figure in the Parti patriote for much of its history was
Louis-Joseph Papineau, who was elected to the assembly in 1809 and
became its speaker for the first time only six years later. By about 1828 he
was the unchallenged leader of the party, having led a successful campaign
against a plan by the Montreal merchants to unite Lower and Upper Canada
into a single colony. Papineau was a member of the professional middle
class, which was challenging the predominance of the traditional mer-
chant-seigneur elite. He was also, untypically for that class, the owner of a
seigneury, which he had purchased from his father in 1818. His support for
the seigneurial system, like Thomas Jefferson's acceptance of slavery, was
rather incongruous with his other political beliefs. It was not shared by most
of his followers.

The radicalization of the Parti patriote was a gradual process, but one
contributing factor was the shooting of three persons by British troops who
were called out to maintain order during a by-election in West Montreal in
1832. Two years later the Legislative Assembly, by a vote of 56 to 23,
adopted a list of demands known as the Ninety-Two Resolutions.[39] The
demands included an elected Legislative Council, control of public revenue and Crown lands by the assembly, and responsible government.[40] In
the election of 1834 the Parti patriote, which was committed to the resolutions, won 78 out of 89 seats. A Patriote banquet in Montreal on 24 June of
the same year, organized by the editor Ludger Duvernay, is sometimes considered the beginning of a process that would lead to the foundation of the
Societé Saint-Jean-Baptiste, a nationalist organization that still exists today.
Toasts were drunk to the Irish nationalist leader Daniel O'Connell, then at
the height of his fame, and to the government of the United States of
America.[41]

In Britain the Melbourne-Russell government, which took office in 1835,
initially seemed to accept at least some of the Ninety-Two Resolutions, but it
eventually rejected them categorically by adopting the Russell resolutions in
March 1837. The debate at Westminster on the Russell resolutions included
a notable speech by Daniel O'Connell, who had entered the House of Commons eight years earlier. He praised Papineau's party as the representatives
of the people of Canada and compared Papineau's opponents, the English
party, with the Orange Order. While admitting that religion was not really
the issue in Lower Canada, at least so far, he had this to say about the Russell
resolutions: "They involved principles that had been the fruitful source of
civil war, and dissension, and distraction in Ireland for centuries. The analogy between Canada and Ireland was greater than the honourable Gentle-

man was willing to admit. In fact it was complete; and if they came to names, when they spoke of Papineau they had only to substitute another name with an O at the beginning. The cases were precisely similar."[42]

The Russell resolutions seem to have impelled the Parti patriote to adopt an overtly separatist position, just as the dismissal of Fitzwilliam had for the United Irishmen. Only six months later, civil war, as O'Connell had predicted, was a reality in Lower Canada. Meanwhile, the other side had also begun to mobilize, using ethnic appeals to detach English-speaking supporters from the Parti patriote much as sectarian appeals had been used by the Orange Order to detach Protestants from the United Irishmen. The governor general, Lord Aylmer, predicted in March 1835 that the English party would soon "take the Law into their own hands." In December of that year they did so by forming an armed counter-revolutionary militia, the British Rifle Corps. When Aylmer's successor, Lord Gosford, ordered the dissolution of the corps, it re-formed under a new name.[43] Another and more serious armed counter-revolutionary group was the Doric Club, formed in 1837. Thus in Lower Canada, as in Ireland four decades earlier, an armed clash was probably inevitable, although its timing would depend on subsequent events.

THE INTERNATIONAL CONTEXT

Both the Irish rebellion of 1798 and the Canadian rebellion of 1837–38 were part of a global movement in the direction of democracy and liberalism that began with the American War of Independence. Their leaders were what Anthony Smith has called "polycentric nationalists," meaning that they regarded all humans as basically equal, sympathized with national movements of liberation other than their own, and looked forward to a peaceful world of independent nations that would treat one another with mutual respect.[44] Their nationalism had little in common with the ethnocentric and xenophobic variety that caused such misery in the twentieth century.

Both the United Irishmen and the Patriotes were inspired by the ideals of the American and French Revolutions. Both looked to their republican neighbours for assistance, which proved in the end to be disappointingly weak and ineffective, insofar as it existed at all. The successful American struggle for independence from British rule may also have caused both the Irish and the Lower Canadian rebels to underestimate the difficulty of the task that they undertook. It is fair to say that neither rebellion would have taken place had the American and French Revolutions not existed as prototypes.

There was considerable sympathy in Ireland for the American War of Independence, particularly, although not only, among northern Presbyterians, many of whom had relatives in the Thirteen Colonies. Soon afterwards, the outbreak of revolution in France inspired another and apparently more widespread wave of sympathy in Ireland. The war between Britain and revolutionary France, beginning in 1793, stimulated Irish hopes and British fears of French intervention in Ireland. French agents were certainly active in the country and made contact with the United Irishmen. British informers uncovered a variety of French contacts and plots. Lord Edward Fitzgerald, as already noted, became an admirer and associate of Thomas Paine and a convinced republican. While visiting France in 1792, he declared his sympathy for the French revolution and was dismissed from the army as a result. Four years later he joined the United Irishmen and in that capacity made a second visit to the continent, where he urged the revolutionary government to invade Ireland and assist in its liberation from the British.[45]

Wolfe Tone also had connections with both the American and French republics. He had considered emigrating to the United States in 1793 and finally did so two years later, after the government offered him a choice between exile and prosecution. After several months in New Jersey, he tired of the rustic atmosphere and made his way to Paris as agent of the United Irishmen, where he too urged the French government to undertake an Irish expedition, promising the support of the United Irishmen.[46] The French government initially had little enthusiasm for helping foreign revolutionaries, but it gradually became interested in the possibilities of Ireland, partly in response to the British intervention on behalf of French counter-revolutionaries in La Vendée.[47] In December 1796 a French armada led by General Hoche actually set sail for Ireland, with Tone aboard one of the ships, but it was unable to land because of the weather. Tone returned to France with the expedition and remained there, continuing his appeals for French assistance. He even met with Napoleon Bonaparte, but could not persuade him to take Ireland seriously.[48] Hoche, the most pro-Irish of the French generals, had died in 1797. Nonetheless, the hope of French intervention in 1798 was expressed in one of the best of Ireland's many political ballads:

> Oh, the French are on the sea, says the Shan van vocht
> The French are on the sea, says the Shan van vocht
> Oh, the French are in the bay
> They'll be here without delay
> And the Orange will decay
> Says the Shan van vocht.

In spite of these hopes, the French contribution to 1798, when it came, was late, half-hearted, and ineffective.

The Lower Canadian rebellion took place in a somewhat different geographical and historical context. Despite the common language, distance discouraged much contact between France and its former colony. More to the point, France's revolutionary image, still intact in 1798, had been tarnished during the next four decades by the Bonapartist dictatorship and then by the restoration of the monarchy. The second revolution of 1830 overthrew the Bourbon dynasty but did not make France either a republic or an opponent of the British Empire.

The United States was both, at least in theory. Since its border was only thirty-five miles from Montreal, a city that the Americans had occupied in 1775 and had tried to capture again in 1813, that country naturally loomed large in the consciousness of the Patriotes, both as an inspiration and as a potential source of assistance. The practice of refusing to buy British goods, or goods on which taxes were paid to the colonial regime, was used extensively by the Patriotes prior to 1837 and was drawn directly from American experience before the War of Independence.[49] Papineau, although he had served in the militia against the Americans during the War of 1812, became increasingly republican, pro-American, and anti-British in the late 1820s, and even more so after the rejection of the Ninety-Two Resolutions. As early as 1834, he expressed the hope that republicanism would spread in both America and Europe.[50] By 1836 he advised the British government to recognize that Canadian conditions required political institutions similar to those of the United States, an opinion that he seems to have retained until the end of his life.[51]

Papineau was not alone in the evolution of his views towards the neighbouring republic. There was much pro-American rhetoric at the Patriote banquet on 24 June 1834, the first observance of what would become Quebec's national holiday. There was more at the protest meetings held in the spring, summer, and fall of 1837. The first of these, held at Saint-Ours in May, adopted a resolution describing the Americans as "our natural friends and allies."[52] Although the Patriotes probably did not favour the annexation of Canada by the United States, as some of their enemies alleged, their enthusiasm for that country naturally grew as their disillusionment with Great Britain increased.

Actual help from the United States, however, was not forthcoming in 1837. As soon as hostilities broke out, President Martin Van Buren issued a declaration of neutrality and forebade any assistance to the rebels by employees of the US government. Papineau and other Patriote leaders did escape to the United States after the rebellion was suppressed. Some of them, although not Papineau, continued to hope for assistance from the United States when they reopened the struggle the following year. Although some individual Americans were sympathetic, such hopes were in vain: 1837 was not 1812, the United States and Britain were at peace, and the United States government would not risk fighting a war without allies against the most powerful empire in the world for the sake of its republican ideals.

1798 AND 1837–38: THE COURSE OF EVENTS

The timing of rebellion was not premeditated by the rebels in either Ireland or Lower Canada. One could even say, particularly in the case of Lower Canada, that rebellion was provoked by actions of the authorities. Although in both cases there was some organization and planning in advance of the events, it was not enough to give the organizers any realistic hope of success.

In Ireland the authorities had grown increasingly nervous since the French expedition of December 1796. In April the following year they arrested a large number of political dissidents in Belfast. Throughout 1797 there were numerous prosecutions for political offenses, although juries frequently refused to convict the suspects. The atmosphere in the countryside grew increasingly tense.[53] The event that precipitated armed struggle was the arrest of most of the Leinster Directory of the United Irishmen in Dublin on 12 March 1798, followed by the proclamation of martial law on 30 March. These measures and those that followed greatly damaged the effectiveness of the rebel movement. Nonetheless, on 17 May the rebel leaders made the decision to launch the rising on the 23rd. Two days after this decision, the authorities arrested Lord Edward Fitzgerald, who had narrowly escaped the roundup of United Irishmen in March. As a member of the governing class and a former military officer, he would have been the obvious leader of the planned rising, as George Washington had been in the United States. Instead he was captured and died in captivity soon afterwards from wounds suffered during his arrest.

In the next few days rebellion spread rapidly through the country. By the end of the summer there would be significant actions in seventeen of the thirty-two counties.[54] In most areas the rising was quickly contained by the authorities, most significantly in Kildare, just west of Dublin. By 26 May, Kildare was occupied by an army of 30,000 rebels.[55] However, the rising there was effectively over by the end of the month. In County Meath, immediately north of Kildare, the rising began on 23 May but was ended by a rebel defeat near the historic hill of Tara only three days later.

In the southeastern county of Wexford the rising began on the same day as the defeat at Tara. There, as noted above, the rebellion succeeded in mobilizing much of the Catholic peasantry and became much more serious, more prolonged, and more costly in human life than it was anywhere else in

Ireland. It also took on the character of a religious, as well as a class, war and was marked by anti-Protestant excesses, which in turn brought bloody reprisals from the government forces. The Wexford rebels captured the towns of Enniscorthy and Wexford before the end of the month. Although defeated with heavy losses in the battle of New Ross on 5 June, they held their stronghold at Vinegar Hill, near Enniscorthy, until the 21st. Wexford town was recaptured by the government forces on the same day, three weeks and a day after its capture by the insurgents. Part of the rebel force, led by a Catholic priest, Father John Murphy, escaped into neighbouring Carlow, where it was decisively defeated on the 26th. Another detachment made a long march to the north, hoping to link up with Presbyterian rebels in Ulster, and was not finally defeated until 14 July.[56]

Meanwhile, the mainly Presbyterian counties of Antrim and Down, in northeastern Ireland, had indeed seen risings in early June, but both were quickly suppressed. The Antrim rebels were led by a Presbyterian United Irishman, Henry Joy McCracken. They were defeated within two days, just as their counterparts in Down were preparing to rise under the leadership of Henry Monroe, a Presbyterian from Scotland. The rebellion in Down lasted for four days, ending on 13 June.[57]

The last act in the drama, too late to have any real impact on the outcome, was the long-awaited intervention by revolutionary France. A French expedition led by General Humbert landed at Killala Bay, County Mayo, on 23 August. Unfortunately it was three months too late, too small to be very effective, and in the wrong part of the country. The eastern counties, where rebel strength had been greatest, were too close to Great Britain for the inferior French navy to undertake an amphibious landing, even if the prevailing winds had facilitated such an operation. Humbert's army had some initial success and attracted some local support, but finally surrendered to the British on 8 September. Its Irish allies were massacred. Two weeks later the final major rebel force was defeated at Killala in what has been called "the last significant pitched battle in Irish history."[58] (The tragic fiasco of Humbert's campaign is memorably portrayed in Thomas Flanagan's great novel *The Year of the French,* which emphasizes the tensions between Catholic and Protestant rebels and between the French and their Irish allies.) Unaware of these events, a second French expedition, with Wolfe Tone on board, had sailed from Brest on 16 September. The entire force was captured by the British soon after it arrived, and Tone was placed on trial for treason.[59]

In Lower Canada, as in Ireland, the immediate cause that precipitated the rebellion was a series of arrests by the authorities. In both cases, however, tension had been building up for several months prior to the precipitating event. Following the news that the British parliament had adopted the Rus-

sell resolutions, a series of mass meetings were held in the counties around
Montreal. They were organized by the permanent central committee of the
Patriotes, which had been formed in 1834 at the time of the Ninety-Two Resolutions. The Saint-Ours meeting on 7 May 1837, referred to above, was the
first of these events, which continued through the summer and early fall.
The crowds heard speeches by Papineau and other Patriote leaders and
elected delegates to a national convention that was planned for later in the
year. Attendance at twelve of the largest meetings totalled about 25,000
according to Fernand Ouellet, a not very sympathetic historian.[60] The meetings were only the most visible sign of a broader movement to organize and
mobilize the rural population. In the county of Deux-Montagnes the
Patriotes formed what was virtually a provisional government with its own
executive, courts, and armed militia, as well as local committees in each parish.[61]

The county meetings culminated in a meeting of delegates from six counties at Saint-Charles-sur-Richelieu on 23 October 1837, attended by a crowd
variously estimated at from one to five thousand.[62] The meeting approved
an "Address from the confederation of six counties to the people of Canada," consciously modelled on the American Declaration of Independence,
to which it paid tribute, and apparently written by Papineau.[63] At this meeting a number of Patriote leaders, including Dr Wolfred Nelson, Amury
Girod, Thomas Brown, and Cyrille Côté, proclaimed that armed resistance
to the government had become inevitable. Papineau appeared reluctant to
take the final step, but events were now moving out of control. On 6 November a street fight between Patriotes and supporters of the government in
Montreal led to the reading of the Riot Act. A few days later the governor
general received an anonymous letter warning him that "the rebels" were
planning to attack Montreal with an army of from fifteen to twenty thousand
men.[64] On the 16th the government issued warrants for the arrest of the
Patriote leaders.

Anticipating the government's action, Papineau and other leaders had
already left Montreal for the Richelieu valley, a Patriote stronghold, where
they were guarded by armed supporters. On 23 November the Patriotes won
their first and only victory against British troops, at Saint-Denis. Wolfred
Nelson, the community's doctor and a former surgeon in the British army,
led the Patriote forces and directed the battle from his own house. Papineau
left Saint-Denis before the battle and subsequently escaped to the United
States, a course of action that he later claimed was agreed upon by the other
Patriote leaders, although Nelson suggested otherwise. Two days later there
was another battle at the nearby community of Saint-Charles, the site of the
six-county meeting in October. This time the Patriotes were defeated and

their ineffectual commander, Thomas Brown, escaped into the United States. Dr Nelson was captured, and his house in Saint-Denis, along with most of the other buildings in that community, was destroyed by the British soldiers.

News of these developments did not take long to reach the English-speaking and Protestant colony of Upper Canada, which had also experienced conflict between a reform-minded legislative assembly and the colonial regime. Inspired by the events in Lower Canada, the radical editor William Lyon Mackenzie, who had been elected as Toronto's first mayor in 1834, led a rather pathetic insurrection that lasted only three days, from the 4th to the 7th of December. Like the risings in Antrim and Down in 1798, Mackenzie's effort was too late and too small to help the more serious rebellions proceeding elsewhere.

With the Richelieu valley now subdued and with Upper Canada posing no real threat to the colonial regime, attention shifted to the other major Patriote stronghold in Deux-Montagnes, just west of Montreal. Papineau had designated Amury Girod, a Swiss immigrant who claimed to have fought with Bolivar in South America, the military commander in this county. The decisive battle was fought at Saint-Eustache on 13–14 December. As at Saint-Denis, the most effective leadership was provided by a local physician, in this case Dr Jean-Olivier Chénier, who died heroically in the ruins of the parish church as the British troops stormed the village. Girod was captured some distance from the scene and committed suicide. The British destroyed not only Saint-Eustache but the nearby village of Saint-Benoît, where they also desecrated the Catholic church and committed other atrocities.

With this battle the rebellion of 1837, strictly speaking, was at an end, but hostilities were renewed in the following year under the leadership of Dr Nelson's younger brother, Robert Nelson. The Patriotes regrouped in the United States, where they enjoyed considerable sympathy from the local population. No longer led by Papineau, they were now free to adopt a more radical program, including the abolition of seigneurial tenure.

In February 1838, armed with weapons stolen from a New York state armoury, a group of Patriotes crossed the border for long enough to proclaim Robert Nelson president of the republic of Lower Canada. They then prudently retired and devoted their energies to organizing a secret society, the Frères-chasseurs or Hunters' Lodges, which included both Canadians and Americans dedicated to liberating Canada from the British Empire. The last hurrah came in November 1838, when a group of Frères-chasseurs crossed the border into Lower Canada and fought two small battles at Napierville and Odelltown, both of which they lost. Another detachment occupied the Beauharnois manor house of Edward Ellice, a much-hated anglophone seigneur who was also a member of the British House of Commons. They were defeated by Natives from the nearby Mohawk reserve and by Glengarry Highlanders from Upper Canada.

Donald Creighton has described 1837–38 as "a rebellion without a plan of operations and without a chance of success."[65] The same could probably be said of 1798, in the absence of a serious and effective intervention by France on behalf of the rebels. Inspired by the American example, both groups of rebels probably underestimated the probability of defeat. The achievement of independence by the Americans in 1783 may seem inevitable with hindsight, but it was certainly not considered so while their war was in progress. Furthermore, the Americans, during their war of independence, received massive and sustained foreign military assistance, particularly from France, and had many prominent sympathizers in Great Britain itself.[66] They had a navy that could challenge Britain's control of the seas. Their country was also too large to be effectively occupied by British forces. Neither the Irish nor the Lower Canadians enjoyed any of these advantages.

As well, neither the Irish nor the Lower Canadians rebels were really able to determine the timing of their respective risings, which were precipitated when the authorities decided to arrest the principal leaders. This pattern seems fairly clear in the Irish case. In the Lower Canadian case, Lord Durham actually admitted, although not in his celebrated report, that the rebellion was "precipitated by the British from an instinctive sense of the danger of allowing the Canadians full time for preparation."[67]

Although both rebellions were nominally directed from the centre, neither of the central agencies of control functioned effectively, and in practice the rebellions degenerated into an uncoordinated series of local and regional struggles. Neither country was entirely behind the anti-colonial struggle: the Irish rebellion was largely confined to the eastern counties, while the Lower Canadian rebellion was entirely within a thirty-mile radius of Montreal. These were the most obvious reasons for defeat, but there were other reasons as well.

Both Ireland and Lower Canada were predominantly, but not exclusively, Catholic societies. Both were rebelling against a monarch and an empire that were officially Protestant. As was noted in the previous chapter, the nationalism of England (and after 1707 that of Great Britain) was strongly associated with Protestantism and anti-Catholicism. In the light of later developments in both Irish and French Canadian nationalism, it might be supposed that Catholicism had something to do with the rebellions. However, the facts are somewhat more complex. Most of the leading United Irishmen, in contrast to most of their followers who died on the battlefields, were Protestants. Wolfe Tone, although he championed civil and political rights for Irish Catholics, had little use for the Catholic Church itself, which he considered to be corrupt and superstitious. He was delighted when Napoleon Bonaparte occupied Rome and drove the pope out of that city.[68] Even in Wexford, where the rebellion was more influenced by Catholic sectarianism than elsewhere, the first commander of the rebel army, Bagenal Harvey, was a Protestant.

In Lower Canada also, some of the leading rebels were Protestants, including the Nelson brothers and Thomas Brown. Papineau, although raised Catholic, abandoned his faith while still in his teens and never regained it; he attended church largely to set a good example for his *censitaires*.[69] Like Wolfe Tone and Thomas Jefferson, he favoured toleration for all religions and special privileges for none, supporting the right of Jews to sit in the Legislative Assembly.

As we have seen, the British state had in practice begun to soften its official anti-Catholicism as early as the Quebec Act of 1774. This path-breaking measure had been followed by relaxation or abandonment of most of the restrictions on the civil and political rights of Catholics in Ireland. The Catholic Church, which had virtually been driven underground in Ireland during the seventeenth century, was increasingly tolerated by the authorities in the eighteenth. British policies of hostility towards Catholicism had been softened by the disappearance of any serious threat of a Stuart restoration, the increasing number of Catholics in the empire after 1763, and the desire to enlist Catholic soldiers to fight against the Americans and the French. In addition, some British Tories, the dominant party after 1770, saw Catholics as possible allies against the democratic and liberal ideologies associated with the American and French Revolutions.

If this was in fact the motive for concessions to Catholicism, the British strategy paid off in 1798 and 1837–38, as it did when the Americans invaded Lower Canada in 1813. In both rebellions a few parish priests joined the rebels. Father John Murphy, Father Michael Murphy, and Father Philip Roche in Wexford had their counterparts in Father Lagorce at Saint-Denis, Father Augustin-Magloire Blanchet at Saint-Charles, and Father Étienne Chartier at Saint-Benoît.[70] These patriotic priests were the exceptions, however. The Catholic Church as a whole supported the colonial authorities in both Ireland and Lower Canada and opposed both rebellions.

In the Irish case the Catholic archbishop of Dublin, John Thomas Troy, issued a pastoral letter in late May 1798, after the rebellion had already begun. In the letter, which was ordered to be read from every pulpit in the diocese, he condemned the rebellion and urged submission to lawful authority. Subsequently a group of prominent Catholics, including three archbishops, signed a declaration that opposed the rebellion and deplored the anti-Protestant outrages that had been reported in Wexford. Even in Wexford itself the majority of parish priests urged submission to the lawful authorities.[71]

Events followed a similar course in Lower Canada, where Papineau had complained to his wife about clerical hostility to the Patriotes two years before the outbreak of hostilities. Bishop Jean-Jacques Lartigue of Montreal, who ironically was Papineau's cousin, warned against rebellion in July 1837 in a speech at a banquet attended by 150 priests. On 24 October, the day after the six-county meeting at Saint-Charles, he repeated the warning in a pastoral letter similar to that issued by Archbishop Troy in 1798. In some churches, parishioners walked out in protest when this letter was read from the pulpit. In February 1838, prematurely as it turned out, Lartigue proclaimed a day of thanksgiving for the restoration of order in the province. During the rebellion, Patriotes who bore arms were denied the sacraments, and those killed were refused the privilege of burial in consecrated ground.[72] (Jean-Olivier Chénier was finally granted this privilege in 1987, a century and a half after his death.)

Both the United Irishmen and the Patriotes hoped to unite all opponents of the colonial regime behind their cause, regardless of ethnicity or religion. As noted above, Wolfe Tone insisted on the necessity of uniting the three main religious groups in Ireland – Catholics, Anglicans, and Dissenters – behind the common cause. Lord Edward Fitzgerald, a member of the Protestant ruling class, was equally committed to Catholic emancipation. The United Irishmen were founded in Belfast, and the Presbyterians of Antrim and Down appeared in the 1790s to be at least as disaffected towards the regime as the Catholics in the south, if not more so. In the end there were significant revolutionary outbreaks in both of those counties, even if neither came close to achieving success.

The situation was somewhat analogous in Lower Canada, where the three significant groups were French Canadian Catholics, Irish Catholics, and British Protestants. Like the United Irishmen, the Patriotes wished to unite members of all three groups on the basis of ideology and class, rather than ethnicity or religion. It is certainly misleading to view them as representing the kind of exclusively French Canadian ethnic nationalism that developed after their defeat. In fact, it was their opponents in the English party who deliberately appealed to narrow ethnic pride and solidarity, much as the Orangemen did in Ireland. Such appeals reduced the support that the Patriotes received from English-speaking Lower Canadians, but did not cause it to disappear entirely. The Nelson brothers, after all, were British Protestants. Five of the sixteen Lower Canadian Patriotes sentenced to death in absentia after 1837–38 were anglophones of British or Irish ancestry. So were 31 of the 501 suspicious characters rounded up by the authorities in Montreal and its environs.[73] There was some coordination, and much mutual sympathy, between the Patriotes and their exclusively English-speaking counterparts in Upper Canada. The second Lower Canadian rebellion in 1838 also involved English-speaking sympathizers in the United States.

These efforts to transcend religious and ethnic boundaries arose naturally from the liberal and democratic ideals of both the United Irishmen and the Patriotes and were consistent with their enthusiasm for the American and French Revolutions, both of which proclaimed their commitment to the liberation of all humanity. However, this is not to say that they were entirely successful. In both cases there is evidence of increasing ethnic polarization, encouraged and promoted by supporters of the colonial regime, in the period leading up to the revolutionary crisis. Using ethnic and religious appeals to persuade the minorities to rally around the government divided and weakened the forces seeking reform, while reinforcing the ranks of those opposing it. In turn, the success of "divide and rule" tactics gave credence to the argument that the United Irishmen and the Patriotes were exclusive movements of sectarian or ethnic nationalism.

Such tactics had an effect not only on the dominant Protestant groups most closely associated with the colonial establishment but on the more socially disadvantaged groups, Presbyterians in Ireland and Irish Catholics in Lower Canada, who in a sense held the balance of power. Belfast, which had long been a centre of discontent, remained unexpectedly quiet during Henry Joy McCracken's rising in Antrim after its newspapers carried accounts of anti-Protestant atrocities by the rebels in Wexford.[74] In Lower Canada, Irish Catholic immigrants had originally played a prominent part in the Patriote movement, but by 1837 the majority of them, although by no means all, were supporters of the colonial regime.[75] The hostility of some Patriotes to immigration, much of which came from Ireland, probably contributed to this shift.

The charge that the rebellions of 1798 and 1837–38 were actually manifestations of ethnic nationalism is most famously represented in the Lower Canadian case by Lord Durham's description of the rebellion as "two nations warring in the bosom of a single state." To understand the plausibility of this interpretation, it is necessary to consider the ambiguous and divided character of both the Irish and Lower Canadian rebellions.

In both 1798 and 1837–38 most of the most prominent leaders could be described as educated members of the middle class, often practising professions such as law or medicine. In most countries, and not just in Ireland and Lower Canada, movements for political reform and for national self-determination have tended to find their earliest and most articulate supporters among persons of this type. Such people were inspired by the liberal and universalistic ideals of the American and French Revolutions. They felt a sense of kinship with similar people in other countries and with movements of national liberation around the world. Although some of them were religious, they tended to be at least mildly anticlerical. They were not interested in promoting a sectarian or ethnic agenda. They believed in liberty and democracy, ideas that were radical in the context of their times, but on economic and class issues they might be relatively conservative, as in the case of Papineau's support for the seigneurial system.

To succeed in their objectives, however, it was necessary for these middle-class revolutionaries to mobilize a much larger sector of the population, particularly given the intransigent resistance of the colonial regimes to serious political reform. In both cases this meant mobilizing the discontent of the countryside, where peasants resented their exploitation by Irish landlords or by Lower Canadian seigneurs. Rural discontent was intensified and given an obvious target by the fact that in most of Ireland and in many of the seigneuries around Montreal the landlords or seigneurs differed in ethnicity and religion from the peasants. Xenophobia and, in Wexford, religious fanaticism reinforced economic discontent and resentment that had both long-term and immediate causes.

Exploited and resentful peasants are not interested in disquisitions on the thoughts of Jefferson or Voltaire. Theirs was a different kind of revolution from that envisaged by the middle-class radicals such as Wolfe Tone or Louis-Joseph Papineau. Far from being a product of the Age of Reason, it had antecedents going back to the *jacqueries* of the Middle Ages. Peasant insurrections tend to be violent; perhaps because the violent death of animals is a routine event in the countryside, the violent death of human beings does not seem particularly shocking.[76] People lacking formal education also tend to be xenophobic, narrow-minded, and suspicious of those who differ from them in religion, culture, or physical appearance. Thus peasant movements may be associated with an intolerant, exclusive ethnic nationalism, particularly when, as is often the case, the landlords do not share the culture or religion of the peasants. Tom Nairn has suggested, "Ethnic nationalism is in essence a peasantry transmuted, at least in ideal terms, into a nation."[77]

In both Ireland and Lower Canada it is fair to say that two different kinds of rebellions were taking place simultaneously: that of a liberal, cosmopolitian

middle class and that of an exploited and not particularly enlightened peasantry. Neither could have any hope of success without the other, but understandably they sometimes operated at cross-purposes.[78] In Ireland,
particularly in Wexford, the peasant insurrection led to excesses that tended
to discredit the rising of 1798 as a whole and led to equally savage and excessive reprisals by the government. The French expeditionary force that
landed in Mayo, inspired by the non-sectarian ideals of the revolution, was
horrified by the sectarian violence of the Irish peasantry, with whose cause
they quickly became disillusioned.

In Lower Canada the peasant insurrection was much less violent than its
Irish counterpart had been, probably because the seigneurial system,
although not particularly pleasant for those on the receiving end, was far
less oppressive than the rule of the Protestant landlords in southern Ireland.
Yet even in Lower Canada there were incidents, not always of an overtly
political character, which a sympathetic historian, Allan Greer, has
described as "terrorism."[79] Particularly in the county of Deux-Montagnes,
where English and French lived in close proximity to one another, there was
considerable harassment and intimidation of English-speaking neighbours
by some of the Patriotes, even though the Patriote committee included
anglophone representatives.[80] Reports of such incidents naturally turned
many English-speaking Lower Canadians into supporters of the government, just as reports of the excesses in Wexford had a similar impact on
many Irish Protestants.

In general, however, the increasing polarization along religious lines in
Ireland and along ethno-linguistic lines in Lower Canada should be blamed
on the "divide and rule" tactics of the authorities more than on the excesses
of the rebels. The humane and cosmopolitan ideals of the United Irishmen
and the Patriotes, and their efforts to create inclusive and liberal movements of national liberation failed to overcome the effects of such tactics,
with results that are still visible in both countries today.

AFTERMATH AND CONSEQUENCES

The British reprisals that followed the rebellions were much more severe in
Ireland, partly because the rebellion itself had been much more extensive
and more violent in that country and partly because Britain was at war with
France in 1798; civil liberties and due process tend to be forgotten in wartime. Altogether there were eighty-one executions from 22 June onwards,
including most of the main leaders.[81] In both houses of the British parliament, some opposition members criticized the use of torture, the burning
of houses, and other atrocities committed by the government forces.[82]

Wolfe Tone, who held an officer's commission in the French army, initially hoped to be traded for some British prisoners of war held by the French. He corresponded with both the British and French authorities with this end in view, but to no avail.[83] Instead, he was sentenced to be hanged as a traitor. He succeeded in committing suicide by stabbing himself with a knife after his request for a soldier's death by firing squad was refused.

Despite the defeat of the rebellion and the severity of the reprisals, the United Irishmen made one last effort five years later. In the summer of 1803 a rising led by Robert Emmet and confined to the city of Dublin was easily suppressed by the British, and twenty-two more executions followed. Emmet's speech at his trial would become one of the classic texts of Irish nationalism. After this episode the United Irishmen effectively ceased to exist.

In Lower Canada the thinly populated and almost unguarded border with the United States enabled many Patriotes to escape into that country. Sixteen of them were sentenced to death in absentia without trial, including Papineau, Robert Nelson, Thomas Brown, E.B. O'Callaghan, and George-Étienne Cartier.[84] Eight other Patriotes, including Wolfred Nelson, were transported to Bermuda, also without trial, on the orders of Lord Durham, who took office as governor general in May 1838. The British government's overturning of these arbitrary decisions led to Durham's resignation after six months in office. Following the second outbreak of rebellion, twelve Patriotes, none of whom was particularly prominent, were hanged in 1839, and fifty-eight were transported to Australia.[85] Papineau, Wolfred Nelson, Brown, and Cartier returned to Lower Canada within a few years, but Robert Nelson and O'Callaghan chose to stay in the United States.

Both the Irish parliament and the Legislative Assembly of Lower Canada were abolished by Westminster within three years of the rebellions. By the Act of Union of 1800, Ireland became part of the "United Kingdom of Great Britain and Ireland" and sent its own representatives to Westminster, but was still governed, rather anomalously, by a lord lieutenant. Although Irish Catholics were promised the right to sit at Westminster, a right they had not had in the Irish parliament, this was not achieved until 1829. Lower Canada was combined with Upper Canada into a single United Province of Canada by the Canada Union Act in 1840.[86] Although Lower Canada was by far the more populous of the two colonies, at least initially, they were given equal representation in the new assembly so as to ensure an English-speaking majority.

The idea of a legislative union between Great Britain and Ireland had been gaining favour in England for decades before 1798, largely because of the belief that it would contribute to national security. The events of that year, particularly the belated French invasion, appeared to lend more urgency to the project. Prime Minister Pitt argued that it would bring economic advantages to Ireland, lessen the danger of French intervention, and make the granting of full political rights to Catholics more feasible.[87] The Catholic bishops supported the idea. Nonetheless, it was rejected by the Irish parliament in 1799 and only accepted a year later after considerable use of patronage and the expenditure of almost £33,000 sterling from a secret fund on direct bribes to the members.[88]

Pitt had hoped that achievement of the union would be accompanied by, or at least shortly followed by, Catholic emancipation, meaning the right of Catholics to sit in Parliament and hold any public office under the Crown. He believed that Catholics would accept union if it included emancipation and that Protestants, fearful of the Catholic majority, would accept emancipation only if it included union. However, he refrained from openly promising emancipation to the Catholics, since he needed the consent of the Protestant Irish parliament to bring about the union. Although there was some opposition to Catholic emancipation within Pitt's party and government, the most serious obstacle to the project proved to be George III. The king's adamant refusal to accept Catholic emancipation, which he claimed would violate the oath he had taken at his coronation, led to Pitt's resignation as prime minister in 1801.[89] Pitt's failure to couple union with emancipation ensured that the Act of Union would never be accepted as legitimate by Irish Catholics.

Lower Canada's Legislative Assembly, unlike the Irish parliament, did not have to agree to its own disappearance; it was suspended during the rebellion and never met again. Lord John Russell, the government leader in the British House of Commons, introduced a bill to make the suspension permanent in January 1838, leading to a lengthy debate on "the affairs of Canada." Both Russell and Robert Peel, the leader of the opposition, agreed that Britain had treated the French Canadians generously, although each made some effort to blame the other's party for what Russell called "the horrors and misfortunes of civil war."[90] The measure had bipartisan support, but a number of radical or Irish members opposed it, and some of them drew explicit parallels between Ireland and Lower Canada. The Duke of Wellington, on the other hand, told the House of Lords that Canada's problems were caused by an excess of democracy.[91]

Two years after this debate, Russell introduced another proposal, to unite the two Canadas and thus undo the partition of 1791. Union of the two Canadas had been ardently desired by the Montreal merchants for years, but resisted by the Patriotes. A bill to that effect had been discussed by the British parliament in 1822, and the matter came up again in 1828, at which time Papineau travelled to London to oppose it. E.B. O'Callaghan charged that the English party had deliberately instigated the outbreak of violence in

1837 to facilitate its unification project, and he drew an explicit parallel with Ireland in 1798.[92] Be that as it may, the rebellion and the exile of its leading opponents certainly facilitated the project, as did its endorsement in Lord Durham's report. Only a few British MPs, of whom Daniel O'Connell was the most prominent, spoke against it in 1840. O'Connell, while deploring the violence of 1837–38, blamed the rebellion partly on the British and said that union on the terms provided by the bill was unfair to the French Canadians, whose wishes had not been consulted or considered.[93]

As the next chapter will describe, an important consequence of the rebellions was a change, at least for a time, in the character of both Irish and French Canadian nationalism; the change was more gradual in the Irish case and more abrupt in the French Canadian. In both cases the use of force to achieve political goals had failed disastrously, and this outcome reinforced the authority of the Catholic Church, which had argued against it in the first place. The abolition of indigenous political institutions by the two acts of union also created vacuums that the church was able to fill, at least in part. The church everywhere opposed the legacy of the French Revolution, and in Lower Canada it was almost equally hostile to the United States, as it had been since the American invasion of 1775. Nationalism in both countries therefore acquired, at least for a time, a more conservative, inward-looking, and Catholic orientation after the defeat of the rebellions, in contrast to the eighteenth-century liberalism of the United Irishmen and the Patriotes, to the point where it explicitly repudiated their legacy. In its new form, it became less inclusive, tending to divide both countries against themselves, rather than uniting them, as Tone and Papineau had hoped.

In the Irish case, however, a distinctly republican tradition, based on the universalistic ideals and principles of the French Revolution, remained as a lasting legacy of 1798. Part of this legacy was a determination to sever any political ties between Ireland and the United Kingdom, and for some republicans at least, the use of political violence for this purpose would henceforth be considered legitimate. More positively, perhaps, Irish republicanism included the aspiration to create a non-sectarian, inclusive national community in which no distinctions would be made on the basis of religion. In the twentieth century, this aspiration was manifested in a steadfast opposition to the partition of Ireland and to the creation of a sectarian Protestant state in the northeast, a development that many Irish nationalists, in both north and south, at least implicitly accepted. Some republicans would accept the legitimacy of the predominantly Catholic southern state that resulted from the partition, while others would oppose it, at times by violent means, and deny that it constituted "the republic" of their dreams, even after it formally designated itself a republic.

HISTORICAL MEMORY AND THE REBELLIONS

Both rebellions and their immediate consequences were important for the paths of national development that they closed off and those that they left open. Both were traumatic defeats, but defeats from which lessons were learned and which created new, and largely unforeseen, opportunities. However, they were also important not as concrete events but as collective memories and symbols. The different ways in which 1798 and 1837–38 have been imagined over the years may be almost as significant as the events themselves.

Daniel O'Connell, the charismatic and resolutely non-violent leader of Catholic Ireland in the first half of the nineteenth century, repudiated the legacy of the United Irishmen, whom he depicted as a largely Protestant organization. The movement known as Young Ireland, a radical offshoot of O'Connell's organization in the 1840s, was much more sympathetic to the legacy of 1798, and members of Young Ireland composed many of the ballads now associated with the great rebellion.[94] O'Connell's tradition of non-violent Catholic nationalism never entirely eradicated the other Irish tradition of republicanism and violent protest, which manifested itself again, on a small scale, in 1803, 1848, and 1867. The custom of annual pilgrimages to Wolfe Tone's grave in Bodenstown, County Kildare, was begun by Thomas Davis, the leader of Young Ireland, in 1844.[95] The Sunday closest to 20 June, the date of Tone's birth, became an opportunity to remember the legacy of 1798. The Irish Republican Brotherhood revived the tradition of an annual commemoration at the grave in 1891.[96]

The centennial of the rising in 1898 contributed to a resurgence of Irish nationalism, which had been deflated by the fall of Parnell in 1891, but it also indicated the deep divisions in the country.[97] The IRB played a large part in the commemoration, which considerably increased its membership. The celebrations also helped to reunite the various factions in the Irish Parliamentary Party. While the IRB emphasized the non-sectarian character of the United Irishmen and downplayed the anti-Protestant excesses of Wexford, some of the Catholic clergy who tried to co-opt the celebrations preferred to interpret 1798 as a Catholic struggle against Protestant domination.[98] The centennial was largely ignored by the Protestants in the northeastern counties, despite the significant role that their ancestors had played in the original events. William Butler Yeats was among the few Protestants who joined in the commemoration.

Wolfe Tone, although he had not managed to return to Ireland from France until the rising was over, became the central figure in the centennial celebrations. His message of unity between the Irish of all religious traditions seemed particularly apropos given the growing polarization between Catholics and non-Catholics, which the British Conservative Party had begun to stimulate for its own partisan purposes. Contributions were solicited for a Wolfe Tone monument in Dublin, and the project received, rather incongruously, a generous contribution from the Catholic archbishop, W.J. Walsh. However, the monument was not actually built until 1967 and was blown up by loyalist terrorists from Northern Ireland four years later.[99] It has since been restored.

In 1913 Patrick Pearse, who would himself give his life for Ireland three years later, spoke at the annual Wolfe Tone commemoration at Bodenstown. In his speech he compared Tone with St Patrick and declared the anticlerical patriot's grave in the Protestant churchyard to be "the holiest spot in Ireland," a rather odd statement for a devout Catholic.[100] The Irish Republican Army continued the annual commemorations at Tone's grave after the Irish Free State was established in 1922. Eamon de Valera's Fianna Fail government, although it claimed to embody the Irish republican tradition, banned all demonstrations at Bodenstown during the "emergency" of 1939–45, but they were revived after the war ended. Beginning in 1948, an official annual commemoration at Bodenstown was instituted, providing mainstream politicians an opportunity to declare their republican credentials and to denounce the partition of Ireland.[101] Sinn Fein, representing the more radical side of the Irish republican tradition, continues to hold a separate commemoration at the site each June.

In the last third of the twentieth century, the "revisionist" school, which opposed the traditional glorification of violent rebellion against the British, began to reassess the writing of Irish history. A Jesuit historian, Father Francis Shaw, wrote a lengthy and influential critique of Irish revolutionary nationalism in 1966, which was published four years later. In it he criticized Wolfe Tone, whom he called "the founder of separatism," for his hostility to the Catholic Church and his lack of contact with ordinary Irish people. Father Shaw also described Tone's political philosophy as "a synthesis of a personal London-born hatred of England and a rationalist's enthusiasm for the French revolution. Very little nourishment from Irish soil had gone to this curious growth."[102]

Tone's liberal and non-sectarian ideals, although perhaps not his methods, regained popularity, however, as the political influence of the Irish Catholic clergy declined. The two hundredth anniversary of the rebellion in 1998, coinciding with the Good Friday Agreement in British-occupied Northern Ireland, was celebrated on a massive scale, with speeches, conferences, television documentaries, commemorative postage stamps, and publications. Prior to the event, the Irish government had appointed a "1798 commemoration committee," which was instructed to emphasize the forward-looking, democratic, pluralistic, and internationalist aspects of the rebellion, as well as the contribution of Ulster Presbyterians.[103] An impressive National 1798 Museum was opened at Enniscorthy, near Vinegar Hill, where the "boys of Wexford" had camped two centuries before. Earlier in the year Gerry Adams, the leader of Sinn Fein, had addressed a crowd of five thousand persons on Vinegar Hill. Taoiseach Bertie Ahern described the rebellion of 1798 as "the birth of democracy in Ireland under very difficult conditions" and paid tribute to "the ideal of uniting Irishmen and Irishwomen of different traditions and in the rejection of sectarian bigotry." He also noted "the tremendous contribution of the Irish Presbyterian tradition, with its dignified pursuit of civil and religious liberties for all."[104] A hopeful sign, to which Ahern also referred, was that the Ulster Museum in Belfast had sponsored a commemorative exhibition entitled "Up in Arms." Visitors to the museum at Enniscorthy are told that a peaceful democratic Europe, embodied in the European Union, fulfills the dreams of those who died in 1798.

In Quebec, as in Ireland, the memory of rebellion was overshadowed for a century afterwards by the association of mainstream nationalism with Catholicism and non-violence. In 1858, when the Societé Saint-Jean-Baptiste, an organization founded by former Patriotes, considered erecting a monument to the rebels of 1837–38, the project was abandoned because of clerical disapproval.[105] This reflected the new alliance between nationalism and religion and the church's acceptance of the political status quo after 1841, an acceptance that was more complete in Quebec than it ever became in Ireland. In any event, Papineau and the Nelson brothers could not be martyrs because their lives had been spared, and Papineau's political activities after his return to Canada added little to his reputation.

The rehabilitation of the Patriote tradition perhaps began in 1921, when Father Lionel Groulx, already emerging as the principal proponent of conservative Catholic French Canadian nationalism, wrote a cautiously favourable essay on Papineau. In it he praised Papineau as a great leader and orator who had awakened French Canadians from their passivity, although he described Papineau's republicanism and admiration for the United States as "deplorable."[106] In the centennial year of 1937 Gérard Filteau published his *Histoire des Patriotes*, in which he admitted that he had not initially admired the Patriotes but had become more favourable towards them. He insisted that they had not really been American-style republicans, but had wanted a French-speaking state within the British Empire.[107] A monument to Dr Chénier was built at Saint-Eustache in the same year. Soon afterwards a Liberal MP from near Montreal, Vital Mallette, noted proudly in the Canadian House of Commons that his grandfather had been jailed as a Patriote a century earlier. He said that his grandfather had fought to obtain the representative institutions that Canadians enjoyed a century later, and he implicitly criticized his party leader, who ironically was the grandson of William Lyon Mackenzie, for ignoring the centennial.[108]

With the Quiet Revolution of the 1960s and the rise of the independence movement in Quebec, the reputation of the Patriotes improved. Secular, left-of-centre Quebec nationalism replaced the conservative and Catholic French Canadian ethnic nationalism that had dominated since 1841. The Patriote colours of red, white, and green were sometimes displayed at nationalist demonstrations. A drawing of a determined-looking Patriote, striding forward with his musket at the ready and a clay pipe (rather improbably) clenched in his teeth, became a nationalist icon at this time, although it had actually been drawn by Henri Julien, an artist who died in 1908. A rough version of it appeared on communiqués of the Front de liberation du Québec during the October Crisis, and it has since turned up on a Web site, apparently based in France, devoted to the independence of Quebec. The FLQ cell that kidnapped the British trade commissioner in October 1970 was named after Dr Chénier, the hero of Saint-Eustache. Yet mainstream Quebec nationalism, which was firmly committed to seeking sovereignty by peaceful means, remained cautious about the Patriotes, even though their pro-Americanism and secularism were once again in favour. Ironically, the National Archives of Canada, a federal agency, was less cautious. In 1986–87 it held an exhibition on Papineau, coinciding with the sesquicentennial of the rebellion. The bilingual souvenir booklet issued for this event described Papineau as "this great Canadian patriot." It was not until 2002 that Premier Bernard Landry of Quebec designated a province-wide official holiday in honour of the Patriotes.[109] The occasion was first celebrated on 19 May 2003, shortly after Landry and his Parti québécois left office. The new Liberal premier, Jean Charest, a federalist, chose to soft-pedal the celebrations. Anglophone Quebecers, oblivious to a significant part of their heritage, continue to refer to the statutory holiday in May as Victoria Day, the name it bears in Canada's other provinces.[110]

The rebellions of 1798 and 1837–38 thus continue to resonate, however ambiguously, in historical memory. In the narrow sense, both rebellions failed, unlike their American prototype. Yet they helped to create a sense of national identity and solidarity that endured in both Ireland and Quebec. Both were formative events and decisive turning points in the development of their respective nations, even if the particular type of nationalism that they represented was at least temporarily replaced by a nationalism that was quite different in content. The development of that different kind of nationalism in the years after the rebellions is the subject of the next chapter.

CHAPTER FOUR

New Regimes and a New Kind of Politics

The joining of Ireland to Great Britain in 1801 and the joining of Lower Canada to Upper Canada forty years later have a number of interesting parallels. Both initiatives by the British government were in part responses to the rebellions that had recently occurred in the countries concerned. Neither initiative, however, was an entirely new idea. Both had been considered, and in some quarters advocated, prior to the rebellions, in part for economic reasons, although there were other considerations as well. Both unions had consequences that were not foreseen either by the British or by the peoples of the countries directly involved. Both failed in their objectives if the objectives were, at least in part, to destroy the indigenous nationalism that had led to the outbreak of violence. Both inaugurated periods of change that transformed the nature of nationalism, the nature of politics, the relations between church and state, and the relations between the different ethnic and religious groups that inhabited the two countries. These were also periods of significant economic and social change. In comparing these parallel phases in the history of Ireland and Quebec, it is appropriate to begin with the respective acts of union and to end both narratives in the 1850s, when new political developments again transformed the face of nationalist politics in the two countries.

THE NATURE AND IMPLICATIONS OF UNION

The union of Ireland with Great Britain in 1801 established a British state coterminous with what geographers, or at least British geographers, call the

British Isles. Formally known as the United Kingdom of Great Britain and Ireland, that state was symbolized by the Union Jack flag incorporating the crosses of St Patrick, St Andrew, and St George, a symbol that would outlast the secession of most of Ireland from the union in 1922. Within the new United Kingdom, Ireland comprised, at the outset, about one-third of the entire population, a proportion that would decline precipitously in later years. In 1801 Ireland was far larger than Scotland in terms of population and almost two-thirds as large as England. This fact no doubt explains in part why British policy-makers took decisions about Ireland so seriously; the stakes for them and for their country were very high. On the other hand, Ireland's power and influence within the united state of which it was formally a part were much smaller than its demographic weight would suggest.

As far as Ireland was concerned, the most visible and obvious consequence of the union was the disappearance, ostensibly at its own request, of the Irish parliament. As we have seen, that parliament had existed since medieval times and had claimed, from 1782 until the termination of its existence, to be coequal in status with the British parliament at Westminster. After 1801 those (relatively few) Irish people who met the legal qualifications for the franchise sent their elected representatives to Westminster, not to Dublin. At Westminster, Ireland was allocated only a hundred seats, about half the number that would have corresponded to its share of the population. The building on College Green, Dublin, that had housed the two chambers of the Irish parliament for most of the eighteenth century became in due course the head office of a bank. It remains even today one of Dublin's most conspicuous landmarks, but its association with representative politics came to an end in 1801.

After 1801, decisions about the society and economy of Ireland would be made at Westminster, not in Dublin. Economic policies would be adopted with the objective of benefiting the United Kingdom as a whole, not Ireland as a part of the whole. A customs union and a common market between the two islands were envisaged, although for a transitional period of twenty years Irish manufactures would be shielded from British competition by protective tariffs. Ireland would pay British taxes and would be required to contribute a fixed proportion (two-seventeenths) of United Kingdom expenditures. The exchequers, and the debts, of the two countries were amalgamated in 1817, after a brief period of transition.

Yet in spite of these changes, the union between Ireland and Great Britain was not complete, either in the formal terms of law and institutions or in the less formal terms of culture and sentiment. Ireland remained a special case with its own administrative apparatus, separate from that of England and administering, for the most part, different laws. It also continued to be governed, as it had been for many centuries, by a lord lieutenant representing the interests of the British state, which appointed him. There was also a chief secretary for Ireland, who after 1801 spent most of his time in England and was appointed by the government, rather than by the lord lieutenant, as had earlier been the case. Another innovation in 1801 was the Irish Office, located in London, which assisted the chief secretary.

These arrangements drew attention both to Ireland's continuing distinctiveness and to its political subordination, which was now considerably more complete than it had been in the era of Grattan's parliament. It was a combination that, with hindsight at least, would seem likely to cause resentment and to keep the cause of nationalism alive. On the other hand, as Roy Foster has pointed out, the Act of Union ensured that Ireland would not be allowed to follow the same incremental progress towards self-government that would be experienced by some other parts of the British Empire.[1] Formally, the English had declared that their oldest colony was not a colony but an integral part of the metropolitan state. In doing so, they implicitly declared that separation was unthinkable and that even progress towards greater autonomy would be difficult and complicated, raising constitutional issues that might involve a redefinition and reconstruction of the metropolitan state itself.

Formally, the Irish were made "British" by the Act of Union, perhaps in anticipation of Walter Bagehot's comment later in the century that the Westminster parliament can do anything but turn a man into a woman. The idea that the Irish were British would have a long life; among other evidence of this, we may note that it would be perpetuated in the classification of ethnic data collected by the Canadian census as late as 1991. Yet the Irish remained a distinct people in their own estimation and indeed in that of the people of Great Britain also – separate but unequal. Unlike the Scots or the Welsh, most of them would never be content to be considered British. Perhaps the fact that they lived on a separate island contributed to this attitude. But a more important reason why they, or most of them, could not easily be British was because the "British" identity, itself less than a century old in 1801, was largely based on Protestantism. Although the English and the Scots professed quite different forms of Protestantism, this was an aspect of identity they could share. The Catholic Irish, or three-quarters of Ireland's total population, could not. To add insult to injury, Ireland was still required to support an established Protestant church on the English model whose adherents were a small minority within a mainly Catholic population. In fact, members of the Church of Ireland, as of 1801, were probably still less numerous than another Protestant minority, the Irish Presbyterians. Under the terms of the Act of Union, the Church of Ireland also ceased to exist as a separate body; it was formally merged into the Church of England, whose liturgy it shared.[2] The contrast with the treatment of religious issues under the union between England and Scotland in 1707 could not have been greater. In Scotland the Presbyterian church, whose adherents comprised the majority of the population, retained its freedom from English control and also enjoyed the status of an established church.

As was noted in the previous chapter, Prime Minister William Pitt had hoped to accompany the Act of Union with Catholic emancipation, entitling Catholics to sit in the Westminster parliament and to hold virtually any office under the Crown. This would have meant the elimination of the existing oath required of office-holders, which in effect denounced the Catholic faith as idolatrous and superstitious. Although no formal promise to Catholics had been made, the expectation that this change would happen had helped to bring about a situation in which the Irish Catholic hierarchy had supported the Act of Union while a great many influential Irish Protestants, in the College Green parliament and elsewhere, had opposed it. As it turned out, however, Catholic emancipation could not be achieved, since it was opposed by King George III and by many members of Pitt's party. When it was finally brought about in 1829, largely through the efforts of Daniel O'Connell and the movement that he founded, nearly three decades had passed.

During that long interval between 1801 and 1829, Irish Protestants continued to enjoy the virtual monopoly of the patronage of the Crown, just as they had done before the union. The opportunity was missed to give at least a portion of the Catholics – and more specifically, the Catholic middle class – a stake in the existing regime and a vested interest in its continuation.[3] Some historians have even suggested that the achievement of Catholic emancipation in 1801, as Pitt had envisaged, would have reconciled Irish Catholics to their status in the United Kingdom, just as Irish Protestants became unionists, thus making Ireland in effect another Scotland.[4] One need not go that far to recognize that the British missed an opportunity to give the Act of Union greater legitimacy than it ever actually enjoyed among Irish Catholics. The invidious political status of Catholics during the formative years of the post-union regime would appear seem a breach of promise and would undermine the substantial Catholic support for union that had existed in 1801.

In the long run, though, the Act of Union also led to a deterioration in the political status of Irish Protestants, perhaps particularly those who belonged to the upper or at least the middle class and to the established church. In the eighteenth century these people had viewed themselves as the Irish nation, perhaps a plausible assumption since they were the only Irish people who could vote (until 1792) or participate in politics. The autonomy achieved by Grattan's parliament in 1782 had been their victory, the realization of aspirations that they had held since the early decades of the century. After 1801, however, the bicameral parliament that had been their forum abruptly disappeared. Although they were represented at Westminster, it was as a minority within a larger British nation, not as the political manifestation of a distinctly Irish nation.[5] They were also forced into the mould of the British two-party system. In a somewhat more subtle way, their position would continue to deteriorate as Great Britain industrialized and as Ireland declined economically and demographically in relation to its larger neighbour. Instead of reinforcing their peculiar form of nationalism, however, these misfortunes led the Protestants to an increasingly vociferous support for the union. This was so because they feared the political mobilization of the Catholic masses, and the implications of their own situation as a religious and ethnic minority in their own country, more than they resented their subordination to Westminster.[6]

The union of the two Canadas in 1841 had some similarities with, but also some differences from, the union of Ireland with Great Britain forty years earlier. The Canadian union was primarily the work of Lord Durham, who had served briefly as governor general in 1838 and had recommended the union of the two colonies in his celebrated report. Somewhat ironically, the Whig Lord Durham, in bringing about the union of the Canadas, undid some of the work of the Tory William Pitt, who had been responsible for the Irish Act of Union, since it was also Pitt who had divided Canada into two separate provinces in 1791.

As we saw in chapter 2, Pitt and other Tories had sought, by preserving the religion, culture, and institutions of the French Canadians, to secure their loyalty to the empire and to immunize them against radical ideas originating in the United States. Although apparently successful for a time, this strategy had not been consistently pursued, thanks largely to the influence of Lower Canada's English-speaking merchant elite. The result, in the end, was a rebellion in 1837–38 inspired by and largely modelled upon the American War of Independence.

Lord Durham, a radical by the standards of the day, took an entirely different approach. Ignoring the prominent role played by English-speaking persons in the recent rebellion, he attributed that event to what he called "the vain endeavour to preserve a French Canadian nationality in the midst of Anglo-American colonies and states."[7] Rather than preserving the distinctiveness of the French Canadians, whom he described as "an old and stationary society, in a new and progressive world,"[8] he sought to assimilate them into English ways and thus to prepare them for full participation in the new world of responsible government and free market economics. He was encouraged by the example of Louisiana, where he noted that the use of the

French language had declined since the territory's purchase by the United States, and he hoped for a similar outcome in Lower Canada.[9] Abolishing French as an official language, encouraging French Canadians to participate in business, which was conducted mainly in English, and more intermarriage between English settlers and French Canadians were all suggested as means to this end. Believing that a predominantly French Canadian legislative assembly would inevitably seek to obstruct the implementation of his objectives, he had recommended reuniting Lower and Upper Canada and reducing the French Canadians to the status of a minority.

Pitt's Tory policy had not been consistently or systematically pursued and had been followed by exactly what it sought to prevent: an American-inspired rebellion. In a similar irony, Durham's radical policy would not be consistently or systematically pursued and would be followed by exactly what it sought to prevent: the preservation of the French language, French Canadian ethnic nationalism, and a century of clerical conservatism.

At the time of the union, Lower Canada had a population of about 650,000, of whom about 500,000 were French Canadians. Upper Canada had a population of about 450,000, almost entirely English-speaking, who, when added to the 150,000 English-speaking people in Lower Canada, produced an English-speaking majority in the united province. It was confidently assumed that immigration from the British Isles would reinforce this majority, gradually overwhelming the French Canadians and facilitating their assimilation.

The most obvious similarity between the Canadian union and its Irish prototype was the disappearance of a representative body, in this case the Legislative Assembly of Lower Canada. (The appointed Legislative Council of Lower Canada also disappeared, but this was considered less significant.) In fact, however, the Legislative Assembly had been suspended three years earlier; so there had been a hiatus with no representative institutions at all before Lower and Upper Canadians received new institutions, the Legislative Assembly and Legislative Council of the United Province of Canada.

Lower Canada would still be governed by a governor general, but he was henceforth the governor general of the united province, and he resided in Montreal, a city dominated by English-speaking merchants, not in the old colonial capital of Quebec City. The two former provinces became administrative divisions of a single province, to be known officially as Canada East and Canada West. The public services and administrative institutions of the two provinces, still fairly rudimentary in both cases, were united more completely than the Irish administration was ever united with the British. The economic union was also more complete and prompt than that of the

United Kingdom, with no provision for transitional tariffs. English was made the only official language.

Although it had much less than half the population, Canada West (Upper Canada) was given a fixed quota of half the seats in the Legislative Assembly, in order to ensure that an overwhelming majority of the members would be English-speaking. This provision could only be altered by a two-thirds majority vote in the assembly.[10] Despite this precaution, responsible government was not granted immediately. For the time being, Canada East (Lower Canada) retained its civil law, contrasting with the English common law of Canada West, and its system of seigneurial tenure, somewhat to the disappointment of the English-speaking business community. The special position of the Catholic Church in Lower Canada, the advantages of which even Lord Durham had recognized, was not affected by the reunification of the two colonies. In contrast to Irish Catholics before 1829, French Canadians could also anticipate receiving a reasonable share of the patronage, part of Lord Durham's prescription for weaning them away from nationalism.

ECONOMIC AND SOCIAL CONDITIONS AFTER UNION

Ireland after 1801 remained, as it had been, an overwhelmingly agricultural country in which most people were either tenants or landless labourers: 71.8 per cent of the male labour force was still employed in agriculture in 1841.[11] Despite the removal of the restrictions on the ownership of land by Catholics, most land was still owned by Protestants and would remain so for generations to come. Population continued to grow rapidly, although at a diminishing rate, until the famine of 1845–47. It exceeded 8 million by 1841, making Ireland one of the most densely populated countries in the world. (France, with about six times as much land, had only about four times as many people in 1840.) Nonetheless, Irish living standards were probably close to the European average, although considerably lower than in England.

There were still many subsistence farmers, growing potatoes on small plots for their own consumption; agriculture was becoming commercial in character, however, and oriented towards the English market. This focus made it subject to fluctuations in market prices and thus to periods of depression. Until 1846 the Corn Laws, which imposed tariffs on grain if its price fell below a certain level, protected Irish agriculture, as they did British agriculture, from foreign competition. Nonetheless, conditions for the landless poor were probably deteriorating, even before the famine. According to Cecil Woodham-Smith, the British government and parliament sponsored no less than 175 official inquiries into Irish problems between 1801 and 1845, all of which warned of impending disaster.[12]

Agrarian violence, a tradition that predated 1798, continued after the union, with major outbreaks in 1813–16, 1819–23, and 1831–34, all periods of falling prices. The greatest incidence of violent episodes was in the Munster counties of Clare, Tipperary, and Limerick, a relatively prosperous area. Agrarian movements of protest went by various names, with Whiteboys, Ribbonmen, and Rockites among the labels most frequently used in this period. The Whiteboys had existed in the eighteenth century, while the Ribbonmen, who seem to have been more political than the others and to have included the remnants of the United Irishmen, were first heard from in 1811. The Rockite movement apparently dated from 1821. In northern areas, where many tenants and farm labourers were Protestants, the Orange Order also contributed its share of agrarian violence. No longer regarded as an asset by the British government, the Orangemen were suppressed as an illegal organization in 1825 and theoretically disbanded in 1836, but neither event brought about their disappearance. Coercive emergency legislation was the government's usual response to outbursts of agrarian violence, especially when the Tories were in office.

Recent historians have suggested that, for the most part, agrarian violence in the early nineteenth century was not really political in character, the Ribbonmen being a partial exception. They view it rather as a defensive response to changing economic circumstances such as falling prices and the transition from traditional subsistence agriculture to commercial agriculture. It seems to have been particularly prevalent in times and places where this transition, with its associated disruption of tradition and routine, was taking place. Most agrarian movements seem also to have involved landless labourers more than tenant farmers; the tenants themselves were often the targets of violent protest rather than its instigators.[13]

One important response to the pressure of increasing population on the land was emigration. Data on emigration to North America exist from the 1820s onwards; they suggest that about 900,000 persons may have left Ireland for that continent in the twenty years prior to the famine. The largest numbers of departures during this period were in 1831 and 1832, which, as already noted, were years of depression in the rural economy. The majority sailed to the British North American colonies, particularly the port of Quebec, rather than to the United States, since the distance was shorter and the fare cheaper. Many of these moved on to the United States as soon as possible, but it will be recalled that immigration, much of it from Ireland, was resented by many Lower Canadians prior to 1837. Irish emigration to Great Britain, where industrialization produced a shortage of labour, was also very considerable and is not included in the data given above. One estimate of the numbers leaving Ireland to reside in that country in the early nineteenth century is 500,000.[14]

Although Irish manufacturing was given some protection against British competition for a transitional period of twenty years after the Act of Union, it failed to grow as rapidly during the nineteenth century as its English and Scottish counterparts. The industrial revolution, which had begun during the eighteenth century in England, progressed rapidly there and in Scotland during the nineteenth. While England and Scotland industrialized, Ireland continued to specialize in agriculture. The economic historian Cormac O'Grada attributes this contrast largely to Ireland's lack of coal and its proximity to England.[15] As time went on, a pronounced phenomenon of uneven development within the British Isles became apparent, with Ireland falling farther and farther behind the neighbouring island in industry, wealth, and even population. Insofar as Ireland experienced industrialization, it was largely concentrated in Ulster, particularly in the counties of Antrim and Down, with their large Presbyterian populations and historic affinities with Scotland.[16] The growing contrast in terms of economics between the northeast and the rest of Ireland reinforced the effect of the differences in terms of ethnicity and religion, with implications for Irish unity that would not become fully apparent until much later.

No discussion of the Irish economy and society in the early part of the nineteenth century, of course, can avoid the great famine of 1845–47, one of the major turning points in Irish history.[17] Although famines had occurred previously in Ireland, none compared with this one in severity, in its lasting economic, social, and political impact, or in the extent to which it shaped the collective memories of the nation. The famine originated in a blight that struck the potato crop, first in the fall of 1845 and again, with increased severity, in the following year. Not grown for export, the potato had become the staple diet of the rural Irish population because of its unique ability to produce a large amount of food from a small amount of land. The failure of the crop was thus devastating to the people, threatening them with actual starvation and fatally lowering their resistance to infectious diseases such as typhus, dysentery, relapsing fever, and cholera.

The British government's response to this catastrophe was totally inadequate, both before and after the Whigs under Lord John Russell replaced the Tories, led by Sir Robert Peel, in June 1846. Neither party seemed to realize the extent of the disaster or to take it as seriously as they presumably would have done had it occurred in England. Neither prevented the export of food from Ireland, which continued throughout the famine, and Peel's repeal of the Corn Laws, a reform adopted primarily for reasons unrelated to the Irish situation, had no immediate effect on the availability of food to those affected. His government responded mainly by authorizing relief works, which paid the destitute a small wage in return for their labour. Emergency imports of American corn (maize), a food unfamiliar to the Irish, were not greatly appreciated. After these remedies failed to relieve the suffering, Russell's government replaced them with soup kitchens, which were somewhat more succcessful. At their peak they were feeding 3 million people in a total population of about 8 million.[18] No one occupying more than a quarter-acre of land could benefit from either form of relief, a fact that encouraged many to abandon their holdings or their landlords to evict them. The Whigs also adopted legislation in June 1847 which provided that the entire burden of poor relief would be paid by Irish landowners through their rates, with no net contribution from England. This obviously encouraged landlords to evict starving tenants from the land rather than pay the cost of supporting them, and it thus greatly increased the flow of emigration to North America.

The effect of the famine on Ireland was so profound that it is difficult to put in a few words. Over 1 million Irish people died as a result of the famine, with infectious disease accounting for far more of the deaths than actual starvation. More than 1 million emigrated in a period of five years. The shortfall of births over what might have been expected in the absence of the famine has been estimated at 416,000.[19] The eviction of people from rural Ireland to make way for more profitable livestock, a process already underway before the famine, was vastly accelerated. Subsistence farming was replaced by commercial agriculture, so that the effect was to modernize the Irish economy, albeit at a terrible price. The famine also accelerated the decline of the Irish language, since the areas where it was still widely spoken suffered the highest toll of death and emigration.

The famine drastically reduced the population of rural Ireland, especially in the poorest and most overpopulated areas. The number of persons living in Connacht, Oliver Cromwell's old reservation for the displaced natives, was 28.81 per cent lower in 1851 than a decade earlier, a figure that understates the impact of the famine because the number had probably continued to grow until 1845. In Munster it had fallen in the same period by 22.47 per cent, in Ulster by 15.69 per cent, and in Leinster by 15.25 per cent.[20] Overall, the famine began a long period of continuous depopulation, unparalleled in any other country, which saw the population of Ireland reduced from over 8 million in 1841 to just over 4 million by 1926. The population of Connacht continued to fall until the 1970s. At the beginning of the twenty-first century, Leinster, as a result of urban growth in Dublin and its environs, was the only province with more residents than it had prior to the famine.

The famine also left a legacy of bitterness and resentment against the British among those who remained in Ireland and, to a perhaps even greater extent, among those who left for North America and elsewhere. This would have a lasting impact on Irish politics and the growth of popular nationalism, not to mention the domestic politics and foreign policy of the United States. Part of the effect on Irish politics will be discussed in this and later chapters. The British historian Cecil Woodham-Smith asserted in her book on the famine that "all hope of assimilation with England was then lost, and bitterness without parallel took possession of the Irish mind."[21] More than a century and a half after the event, freshly painted wall murals could still be seen on houses in Catholic neighbourhoods of Belfast depicting the famine and referring to it as "The Irish Holocaust." Although the implication of this label – that the British deliberately sought to exterminate the population – is not accepted by scholarly historians, there is certainly evidence of British callousness and indifference. (There is also some evidence of British generosity and compassion, particularly among the Quakers.) The British response to the famine exposed the fallacy of the Act of Union by revealing that the British did not really regard Ireland as part of their own nation.

Having ended our survey of Irish social and economic developments on this unhappy note, we may turn to the situation in Canada East after its union with Canada West in 1841. In Canada East, as in Ireland, most people lived and worked on the land, but subsistence farming, rather than commercial farming for export, still predominated in 1841. Agriculture was gradually changing from the traditional emphasis on wheat to a variety of crops and livestock. The production of wheat was shifting towards Canada West, which was better suited by geology and climate for its cultivation. The major export staple of Canada East was wood, most of it destined for the British market, where it was used in shipbuilding and for other purposes. In 1841 British commercial policy still gave preference to Canadian timber over that from countries outside the empire, but this would change within a few years when Britain adopted free trade, an event that caused a major economic and political crisis in Canada. Montreal's English-speaking business community responded to the abolition of British mercantilism with a manifesto in 1849 demanding annexation of Canada by the United States. In response to such sentiments, the British government negotiated an agreement with the United States that allowed free trade in natural products between the United States and Canada, beginning in 1854.

The population of Canada East continued to increase after the Union Act, from 697,084 in 1844 to 890,261 in 1851 and to 1,111,566 in 1861. The exceptionally high rate of increase between the first two dates was partly due to Irish immigration during and after the famine, but many of these immigrants eventually moved to the United States or to Canada West. Natural increase was also high, so that the French Canadian proportion of the population in Canada East remained stable at about 75 per cent. The area of land that was occupied for agricultural purposes was steadily expanding down the St Lawrence valley and into the still mainly English Eastern Townships. In the united province as a whole, the percentage of the population who spoke English and the percentage who lived in Canada West both increased rapidly as a result of immigration from the British Isles. Louis-Joseph Papineau predicted in 1848, "In a few years we shall be to Upper Canada as Ireland is to England."[22] Canada East had slightly less than half the total population by 1851, making its fixed quota of half the seats in the Legislative Assembly an asset rather than a liability. In Canada West, of course, the fixed quota became a target of resentment as soon as it began to work to that region's disadvantage.

Seigneurial tenure continued to be a controversial subject in Canada East until it was finally abolished in 1854. Louis-Hippolyte LaFontaine, the most influential French Canadian politician in the decade after the union of the Canadas, was in favour of abolition. On the other hand, Papineau, after his return to Canada, continued to support the institution to the end, and many French Canadians viewed it as a cherished part of their national heritage, even though Robert Nelson's declaration of independence had demanded its abolition in 1838. *Censitaires* were the owners of their land for most practical purposes, despite their not very onerous obligations to the seigneurs. The most determined supporters of abolition after 1841 were English-speaking entrepreneurs influenced by the ideas of laissez-faire that were gaining popularity in Great Britain. They viewed seigneurial rights and obligations as obstacles in the way of transforming land into a commercial commodity that could be bought and sold freely or settled by immigrants.[23] It was also an obstacle to expropriating land for the construction of railways, Lower Canada's first railway having opened for business in 1836.

Legislation adopted at Westminster in 1822 and 1825 had tried to abolish the system gradually and on a voluntary basis, but without success. An official report commissioned by the governor general recommended abolition, with compensation for the seigneurs, in 1843 but admitted that most of the *censitaires* were content with the seigneurial system. Over the next ten years French Canadian opinion seems to have moved in favour of abolition. The measure adopted in 1854 provided funds to compensate the seigneurs and allowed *censitaires* either to purchase outright ownership of their holdings by paying a small sum to the former seigneur or to occupy them as rent-paying tenants.[24]

Like rural Ireland, rural Canada East was becoming overpopulated, for most of the land in the province was not really suitable for agriculture, and much of the land that was suitable was remote and inaccessible. Large families meant that many farmers' sons had no prospect of inheriting the farm. Living standards in the countryside appear to have been declining after, as well as before, 1841. These conditions, however, as well as the harsh climate, preserved the French Canadian character of Canada East by discouraging settlers from the British Isles, most of whom settled in the cities if they stayed in Canada East at all. Canada West and the United States were far more attractive options for immigrants from Great Britain or Ireland. On the other hand, French Canadians themselves were beginning to emigrate to the United States, particularly to the industrial cities. This phenomenon was causing some concern by mid-century, when the legislature conducted an inquiry into its causes. The report recommended the encouragement of manufacturing.[25]

In response to the agricultural crisis, some French Canadians were perceptive enough to recognize that the future of their province and their people lay in industry rather than agriculture. Étienne Parent, who had been a Patriote prior to 1837, blamed French Canada's traditional elites for the economic predominance of the English-speaking element, and in 1846 he urged his compatriots to study political economy.[26] However, agriculture and forestry in Canada East were revitalized by free trade in natural products with the United States between 1854 and 1866, which probably delayed the necessary structural changes in the economy. Urbanization progressed hardly at all, and by 1861 only a sixth of the population of Canada East lived in towns with a population of more than one thousand.[27] If only the French Canadian population had been counted, the proportion would have been even lower.

POLITICAL MOBILIZATION IN IRELAND AFTER THE ACT OF UNION

Irish political history in the first half of the nineteenth century is largely the story of Daniel O'Connell, one of the most remarkable personalities in the history of the English-speaking world. David Thornley has called O'Connell "arguably the first modern politician in Western Europe."[28] Tom Garvin suggests that he was the only truly charismatic leader, in Max Weber's original sense of that often misused expression, in the modern history of Ireland.[29] Strangely enough in a predominantly Catholic country, O'Connell was the only Catholic among the prominent leaders and heroes of Irish nationalism in the eighteenth and nineteenth centuries. The pervasive, although not entirely accurate, modern perception that Irish nationalism is an essentially Catholic phenomenon owes more to the life and legacy of O'Connell than to any other person. Although radical republicans, in his own lifetime and afterwards, have viewed the O'Connell phenomenon with decidedly mixed feelings, his prominent place in the Irish imagination seems to be secure. Dublin's most famous street bears his name, his towering mausoleum in Glasnevin Cemetery is the most conspicuous structure in the city's north end, and Derrynane House, his home in County Kerry, occupies somewhat the same position in Ireland that Mount Vernon or Monticello does in the United States.

Daniel O'Connell, the nephew and eventual heir of a Catholic landlord in County Kerry, was born in 1775 and thus lived through the era of the French Revolution, which seems to have had a profound effect on his career and political thought. As a student in France, he observed part of the revolution at first hand and developed a lifelong aversion to extremism and political violence. Leaving France to escape the revolution, he studied law in London and qualified for the Irish bar. He opposed the rebellion in 1798, presumably as a result of his French experience, but two years later he also opposed the Act of Union, which the Catholic clergy and most of the Catholic middle class supported at the time. This was the first issue that brought him widespread attention.

His greatest success, however, came over the issue of Catholic emancipation, which seemed to enjoy wider support at the time than repeal of the union. Claiming that the existing oath disqualified Catholics from holding some thirty thousand offices in the British Isles, O'Connell began his campaign against it in 1805. Some supporters of Catholic emancipation, including Henry Grattan, wished to couple it with a provision whereby the British monarch would be able to veto the appointment of bishops, and perhaps even of parish priests, in order to ensure that clerical power remained in safe hands. As we have seen with reference to Quebec, the king of France had enjoyed such a power before the revolution. It was revealed in 1808 that the Irish bishops had secretly agreed to this provision in 1799 in return for Pitt's efforts on behalf of Catholic emancipation, a revelation that was embarrassing for the Catholic Church. O'Connell resolutely opposed the veto, arguing that since the abolition of the Irish parliament, the Catholic Church was the only major institution in the country that was not controlled by the British and that it should not risk losing its independence. He mobilized public opinion in support of this view, and by 1815 the clergy had changed their position. The conflict over this issue brought the clergy directly into politics for the first time, albeit unsuccessfully, and made O'Connell's reputation as an Irish Catholic leader.[30]

In 1821 the British House of Commons finally voted for Catholic emancipation on a free vote, but the king and the House of Lords still refused to
accept it. O'Connell's response was to form the Catholic Association, which
borrowed its name from a group formed in 1761 but since defunct. Unlike
the earlier association, O'Connell's was a genuine mass movement financed
by small contributions from its followers and mobilizing the peasants as well
as the middle class. He enlisted the help of parish priests in drumming up
support and collecting contributions, known as the "Catholic rent," from
their parishioners. Public meetings to support the cause were held in more
than half the parishes in Ireland, usually inside the parish church. The government suppressed O'Connell's association in 1825 but allowed it to reappear a few months later. Lacking representation in Parliament, since most
of them could not vote because of the property qualifications, O'Connell's
peasant followers used the Catholic Association as the vehicle for all their
discontents. By 1828 the association claimed 3 million "associates," more
than half of all the Catholics in Ireland, and an active membership of
15,000, many of whom were priests.[31] No one else had ever mobilized so
large a group of followers for a political purpose anywhere in the world. The
popular vote for Andrew Jackson in the presidential election of that year,
usually considered the beginning of mass politics in the United States, was
only 647,000.

In the general election of 1826, several Protestant supporters of Catholic
emancipation were elected in Irish ridings, largely through the intervention
of Catholic priests. Two years later O'Connell himself was a candidate in a
by-election in County Clare, the first Catholic to run for Parliament in the
British Isles since the Reformation. He was elected with more than
two-thirds of the vote but could not take his seat because of the objectionable oath. In the throne speech the following year, the British Tory government announced its intention to bring about Catholic emancipation at last.
Robert Peel, the home secretary and future prime minister, admitted in a
four-hour speech that he had earlier opposed the idea, but he asserted that
there was no way to suppress the Catholic Association and that further resistance to its demands would "add fuel to the flame in Ireland" and reinforce
clerical influence over the peasantry.[32] The Duke of Wellington, prime minister, hero of Waterloo, and a native of Dublin, warned that Catholic emancipation was the only alternative to civil war and reminded the House of
Lords that the Irish parliament had been abolished in 1801 "for the principle purpose of proposing this very measure."[33] Catholic emancipation
passed both houses of Parliament by margins of about two to one. At the
same time, however, the property qualification for the franchise in Ireland
was significantly raised, disenfranchising more than four-fifths of the rural

voters. O'Connell accepted this change because he believed that the votes of the poorer farmers would be influenced by their landlords.[34] Fewer than half those disenfranchised would regain their votes through the Reform Act of 1832. The only immediate beneficiaries of Catholic emancipation were the Catholic middle class, people like O'Connell himself.

This outcome raised the question of what was to become of the Catholic Association, now that its original purpose had been achieved, and with most of those who had made it possible unable to vote. Coincidentally or not, there was an outbreak of agrarian violence beginning in 1830. O'Connell, now a landlord himself, was as dismayed by this as was the government, for he feared social and economic revolution. However, he opposed the Coercion Bill, which was the government's immediate response.

By the time of the next general election, held in the winter of 1832–33, O'Connell had transformed his association into a third party dedicated to a different cause: the restoration of the Irish parliament through repeal of the Act of Union. In an address to the people of Ireland, he admitted that emancipation had benefited only the more affluent Catholics and proclaimed that repeal was a more important cause because it would also benefit the labourers, the workmen, and the poor. As usual, he urged his followers to avoid violence and warned that "the enemies of Ireland" would try to provoke them into committing violent acts.[35] O'Connell's party presented candidates in most of the Irish ridings outside Ulster and elected thirty-nine, more than either of the traditional parties. Several of the members elected were relatives of O'Connell, including three of his sons. In the twenty-six-county area that became the independent Irish state in 1922, O'Connell's supporters won a narrow majority of the seats. One-third of the members elected under O'Connell's banner were Protestants, although all represented mainly Catholic ridings.[36]

As leader of a third party in the House of Commons, O'Connell lent his support to a number of good causes, including the abolition of slavery throughout the British Empire, which took place in 1833. He also espoused municipal and educational reform, opposed coercive legislation to deal with agrarian disorders in Ireland, and sought relief for Irish farmers from the tithes that they still paid to support the established Protestant church. In 1834 he introduced a parliamentary motion for the repeal of the Act of Union, which was put to a vote in the House of Commons but gained no support outside of his own party. The debate allowed him an opportunity to make his case that Ireland was a distinct nation under the Crown, recognized as such in 1782 but unconstitutionally deprived of its independence by the Act of Union. He alleged that the rebellion of 1798 had been started by northern Presbyterians, not by Catholics, and that the government of the day had allowed it to happen so as to provide a pretext for abolishing the Irish parliament.[37]

After 1835, O'Connell's party held the balance of power and sustained the Whig government led by Lord Melbourne. This choice of alliance reflected O'Connell's liberalism but was not obviously appropriate, since it was the Tories who had brought about Catholic emancipation, while the Whigs were the party of William III and the Glorious Revolution of 1688. The Whigs distributed some patronage to O'Connell's followers, in return for which O'Connell soft-pedalled the issue of repeal, which was ostensibly the main reason for his party's existence. In response to the Whig-O'Connell alliance, the Tories, although traditionally less hostile to Irish Catholicism than the Whigs, began to propagate a form of British nationalism heavily seasoned with anti-Catholic rhetoric.[38] Earl Grey, a Whig of the old school and Melbourne's predecessor, was amused by the inconsistency between the government's alliance with O'Connell and its lack of sympathy for Papineau; Grey considered O'Connell a "scoundrel" and Papineau "the lesser villain of the two."[39] O'Connell opposed, as we have seen, the Russell resolutions, which helped to bring about the rebellion in Lower Canada, but he also criticized the Canadians for resorting to violence, a position consistent with the one he had taken towards Ireland's rebellion in 1798.

It is appropriate at this point to examine the nature of O'Connell's nationalism, both in theory and in practice. O'Connell was a sincere liberal, far ahead of his time, and a cosmopolitan supporter of oppressed or misgoverned peoples throughout the world, including French Canadians, Latin Americans, Jews, and African slaves. On the other hand, he opposed violent social revolutions on the French model, such as Ireland had experienced in 1798. In fact, he seemed to oppose political violence under almost any circumstances. He was not a republican, and the Ireland that he envisaged following the achievement of repeal was merely the restoration of Grattan's parliament, with the significant difference that Catholics would be allowed to sit in it. His economic views were those that were called liberal in his day and, less appropriately, conservative in ours. He opposed the adoption of an Irish poor law (which admittedly proved to be useless during the famine), even though the Irish Catholic clergy and both British parties were in favour of it.[40] He also supported repeal of the Corn Laws, which many of his followers did not.

O'Connell was not a cultural nationalist. In the words of one biographer, "he had no time for a nationalism based on the old Gaelic traditions and culture."[41] He cared little for the Irish language, although he could speak it himself, and neither did nor said anything to halt its decline, which continued throughout his lifetime. In this regard he had more in common with eighteenth-century patriots such as Wolfe Tone than with the romantic nationalists of later generations, in Ireland and elsewhere.

The religious cleavages in his own country were a problem that O'Connell never fully resolved. Like many people growing up in the eighteenth century, he was not particularly pious in his youth, but he became more so in middle age. He was prepared to disagree with the clergy over the veto controversy. Membership in his Catholic Association and in the Repeal Association, which he formed much later, was open to non-Catholics, and as we have seen, many of his followers in the House of Commons were Protestants. In principle, he accepted the idea that Ireland was a country of more than one faith and that it should not be divided by sectarian controversies. In the early 1830s he even tried to interest the Orangemen in his anti-unionist campaign, although without success.

Nevertheless, the effect of his long political career was to develop and reinforce a close association between Catholicism and Irish nationalism that led eventually to the partition of the country and that continues, to a somewhat lesser extent, even in the twenty-first century. As Michael Gallagher has suggested, "After O'Connell Irish nationalism and Roman Catholicism were inextricably linked," and this association made it difficult for Protestants to be Irish nationalists.[42] It occurred largely because the non-violent constitutional form of Irish nationalism that O'Connell pioneered, and on behalf of which he mobilized a mass movement more successfully than any Irishman has ever done, grew out of the movement for Catholic emancipation. If the rebels of 1798 had succeeded in establishing a non-sectarian republic with French assistance, or if the Act of Union had been accompanied by Catholic emancipation as Pitt intended, or even if Catholic emancipation had been adopted at the turn of the century without the abolition of the Irish parliament, it would not have happened.

None of these things occurred, however. In the aftermath of 1798 and 1801, there was more popular support for Catholic emancipation than for repeal, as well as a more credible prospect of achieving it. The only way to achieve Catholic emancipation was to persuade the British that denying it would pose a greater threat to law and order than allowing it. That required a mass movement, and the easiest way to build a mass movement was through the Catholic Church, the only institution that extended throughout the country, that had great influence over public opinion, and that was not under British control. Once Catholic emancipation was achieved, and once O'Connell returned to his original objective of repeal, this organization became the basis of his new campaign, but its dependence on the Catholic parishes continued, a fact that made it difficult to attract mass support among non-Catholics. O'Connell's party after 1832 and the Repeal Association, which he formed in 1841, had little support in the sectors of the population that had not supported his Catholic Association. This fact was most conspicuous in the northern counties, where Protestants were a significant part, or even a majority, of the population and where none of O'Connell's campaigns made any headway.

Partly in response to his mobilization of the Catholic population, there was a growing tendency after 1829 for Irish Protestants to regard themselves as a single sectarian group, whether they were Presbyterians or members of the established church. Imitating O'Connell's own methods, his Tory and Orange opponents in 1834 launched an anti-Catholic campaign that sought to unite Presbyterians with members of the established Church of Ireland. A series of mass meetings took place, beginning in Dublin, where 5,000 Protestants attended, and culminating in a rally that attracted 60,000 in County Down.[43] These developments were facilitated by the activities of Henry Cooke, an extremely influential Presbyterian clergyman in County Down, who was elected as moderator of the Ulster Synod in 1824. Both a theological and a political conservative, Cooke led the struggle against the more unitarian and liberal tendency in his church, which had earlier provided many recruits for the United Irishmen and whose ablest spokesman was his contemporary Henry Montgomery.[44] Cooke's form of Presbyterianism tended to reinforce the similarities, rather than the differences, between the Presbyterians and the Church of Ireland. However, politics and economics, as well as theology, were bringing adherents of the two Protestant churches closer together.

Cooke had given qualified support to Catholic emancipation in 1829, but he strongly opposed O'Connell's subsequent campaign to revive the Irish parliament. He recognized that Presbyterian Belfast, with its growing industrial economy, had economic reasons to support the Act of Union.[45] The "economic miracle" of Belfast, as Ian McBride has called it, seemed to confirm a link between Protestantism and prosperity, long before Max Weber arrived at the same conclusion.[46] In his challenge to O'Connell, Cooke used the credible argument that the wealth and industrialization of Belfast had resulted from closer union with Great Britain and would be threatened by repeal. He urged Presbyterians, who in pre-industrial days had been the most radical group in Ireland, to support the Tory party, since O'Connell was supporting the Whigs.[47] Although a significant number of Ulster Presbyterians continued to be Liberals until the 1880s, almost two decades after Cooke's death, the polarization of the country between Catholic nationalists and Protestant unionists eventually doomed the Liberal party in Ireland and pushed most Protestants of both varieties into the Conservative camp.

If sectarianism is the negative, albeit unintended, part of O'Connell's legacy to his country, there is a more positive side that deserves equal emphasis. His insistence on peaceful and constitutional forms of political struggle and his skill in constructing a mass movement that mobilized ordinary people behind a political cause had an important impact on Irish political culture. They helped to ensure that Ireland, unlike most of the countries that won their independence during the twentieth century, became a stable democracy soon after independence.[48] Admittedly, the liberal tendency in British political culture, with which Ireland was closely associated after the Act of Union, deserves some of the credit for this, but the achievement was largely O'Connell's.

The election of 1841, which brought the Tories to power under Robert Peel, reduced the number of O'Connell's followers in the House of Commons by more than half. The shift from popular agitation to parliamentary politics, with its inevitable compromises, had undermined his popularity and the vitality of the movement that he led. O'Connell was elected lord mayor of Dublin in the same year, but with his movement in decline and his Whig allies in opposition, he had to change his political strategy. He also came under pressure from his younger and more radical followers, who argued correctly that Ireland had gained little benefit from O'Connell's alliance with the Whigs. This group came to be known as Young Ireland and were associated with a radical newspaper founded in 1842, the *Nation*. Many of them were Protestants and graduates of Dublin's Trinity College, which had been established in the sixteenth century as a Protestant institution. (Very few Irish Catholics had the opportunity of receiving higher education at that time.) Thus they understandably favoured a non-sectarian kind of nationalism, although in other respects they differed from revolutionary radicals of the 1790s.

O'Connell's response to these developments was to return to extra-parliamentary agitation, although he remained a member of Parliament. He formed the Repeal Association, a reincarnation of the old Catholic Association, which had won Catholic emancipation. Like its predecessor, the new group was closely associated with the Catholic clergy, and its organization was based on the Catholic parishes, although O'Connell proclaimed its non-sectarian character and his desire to win the support of what he called the Protestant gentry. One member of that class, William Smith O'Brien, a former Tory MP, joined the movement and became second in influence only to O'Connell himself. The mass membership was overwhelmingly Catholic, however. Most of the Catholic bishops also backed the cause, despite the support of their predecessors for union in 1801.

Between March and October 1843 the Repeal Association organized a series of what were called "monster meetings." These meetings, of which twenty-five took place before the government put an end to them, were out-door assemblies at which O'Connell addressed crowds numbering upwards of a hundred thousand. The total attendance may have approached seven million, although obviously many people attended more than one.[49] Per-haps the largest and most successful took place on 15 August at the Hill of Tara, the neolithic site in County Meath associated with traditions of Irish kingship. O'Connell's opponents alleged that the priests coerced people into taking part in the demonstrations. The Peel government and many of the landlords became alarmed, fearing that popular nationalism might combine with smouldering agrarian discontent to produce a repetition of 1798. The government prohibited a scheduled monster meeting at Clon-tarf, the site where Brian Boru had been killed fighting the Vikings in 1014, and O'Connell obligingly cancelled it. A few months later he was nonethe-less convicted of "conspiracy" and imprisoned for several months. The can-cellation of the meeting suggested that the government had nothing to fear from O'Connell and his monster meetings; in effect, they had called his bluff. O'Connell's popularity suffered a severe setback as a result, although proba-bly less than it would have done had he not been imprisoned.

In 1845 the Peel government sharply increased the annual subsidy to the Catholic seminary at Maynooth, a measure that offended the growing anti-Catholic element in the Tory party and foreshadowed the split in the following year between moderate and right-wing Tories over the Corn Laws. By increasing the subsidy, Peel hoped to wean the clergy away from the Repeal Association and to discourage any alliance between the clergy and the movements of agrarian discontent.[50] Soon afterwards the British govern-ment recognized the pope as temporal ruler of the papal territories in cen-tral Italy; its reward in 1847 was an instruction by the pope to the Irish bishops to refrain from assisting any anti-British rebellion.[51]

Meanwhile, the group known as Young Ireland had been growing within O'Connell's movement. This was largely an urban intellectual movement that had little contact with ordinary Irish people. Its leading writer and thinker, until his premature death in 1845, was Thomas Davis, who had joined the Repeal Association in 1841 at the age of twenty-seven. Like Wolfe Tone, Davis was a middle-class Protestant and a graduate of Trinity College. His father was English. Despite, or perhaps because of, his mixed origins, he was a convinced cultural nationalist, an attribute that would be shared much later in Ireland's history by another Protestant, Douglas Hyde, and another Englishman's son, Patrick Pearse. Like Wolfe Tone, Davis was non-sectarian and anticlerical, but his nationalism had more to do with the romantic nine-teenth-century reaction against the French Revolution than with the revolu-tion itself, which had been Tone's inspiration.[52] Nonetheless, Davis and the

Young Irelanders, as was noted in the previous chapter, regarded themselves as inheritors of the republican tradition of 1798, which they sought to
commemorate and perpetuate in various ways.

J.C. Beckett has called the Young Irelanders "typical doctrinaire nationalists of the Romantic era."[53] The description seems unfair, but they were certainly nationalists as well as romantic. Davis's writings reveal his affinity with
the romantic cultural nationalist movements that arose in Germany as a
reaction to the Napoleonic invasion and spread to many parts of Europe
during the nineteenth century. Davis actually visited Germany in 1839–40,
when he was twenty-five years old, and the experience caused him to reject
English liberalism.[54] Rather than the universal principles based on reason
that had inspired Jefferson, Paine, and Wolfe Tone, he drew his inspiration
from the cultural heritage and imagined past of the country and people with
which he identified. He romanticized Ireland before the English conquest
as a land of learning and piety, whose people were virtuous and loved music
and poetry, despite their lack of material goods. He regretted the decline of
traditional handicrafts as a result of English influence and the reluctance of
middle- and upper-class Irish people to take vacations in their own country,
where the scenery was at least as good as anywhere else. He believed that
schools should place more emphasis on Ireland's history, geography, and
culture, even at the expense of science.

Like romantic nationalists in other lands, he was also preoccupied with
language, a subject to which earlier Irish nationalists had given little attention. In a lengthy essay on "our national language," he wrote that language
was an essential part of national identity and asserted, "A people without a
language of its own is only half a nation."[55] He described English, his own
mother tongue, as "a medley of Teutonic dialects" imposed on Ireland by
the conquerors. Since only recently had a majority of Irish people begun to
speak English, he was hopeful that the Irish language could be revived,
although he was not fluent in it himself. A modern historian, John Hutchinson, estimates that half the Irish people, or about 4 million persons, still had
Irish as their mother tongue in 1845, the year of Davis's death. Davis himself
estimated, more conservatively, that it was spoken by half the people west of
a line from Derry to Waterford. It lacked words for many modern concepts,
but it could borrow these from other languages. Davis urged middle- and
upper-class persons to teach Irish to their children as a second language
instead of French, advice that Wolfe Tone would probably not have appreciated. He advocated translating textbooks into Irish, founding an Irish-language newspaper, and requiring teachers in Irish-speaking districts to know
the language. Although he was a cultural nationalist, Davis's nationalism,
understandably in view of his own background, was not ethnically or reli-

giously exclusive. In an essay that praised County Wexford for its role in 1798, he noted that the people of Wexford were of mixed ancestry, English, Welsh, Danish, and Gaelic, "yet they are Irish in thought and feeling."[56] In his essay on the Irish language, quoted above, he conceded that only three-fourths, or at most five-sixths, of the Irish people were of "Celtic blood."

Davis also believed that Ireland should come to terms with the modern world if it was to flourish. He deplored illiteracy and emphasized the need for mass education, as well as praising the establishment of reading rooms by the Repeal Association. Prussia had made itself into a major power, while Ireland was "a farm," because Prussia educated its people.[57] He was also indignant that the peasants lived in poverty while landlords grew rich by exploiting them. Ireland could flourish, according to Davis, by developing its natural resources and by educating its people. Its aristocracy had sold the country in 1800 and been useless ever since, but the ordinary people of Ireland were the real wealth of the country.

O'Connell personally liked Davis, but there were many differences on issues of policy between the Young Irelanders and O'Connell. William S. O'Brien, who had a foot in both camps, used his influence in an effort to preserve the unity of the movement. In 1844 O'Connell unwisely endorsed "federalism," at that time the usual label for what would later be called "home rule." He insisted that this would preserve all the advantages of repeal while also giving Ireland some influence over British foreign and commercial policy.[58] Young Ireland interpreted this approach, not unreasonably, as a retreat from O'Connell's original position. The Young Irelanders were also somewhat anticlerical and supported the Peel government's proposal to establish non-sectarian colleges in Ireland, which O'Connell and the bishops opposed. (In the end, the only college established was in Protestant Belfast, where it became Queen's University.) As well, the Young Irelanders were discontented with O'Connell's laissez-faire economics and his lack of interest in the Irish language and cultural nationalism.

The year 1845 was marked by two disasters for the movement, the unexpected death of Davis, the only person who might have bridged the gap between O'Connell and the young radicals, and the beginning of the famine. O'Connell had been in poor health since his imprisonment and could no longer exercise effective leadership, probably because he was already suffering from the brain tumour that would kill him two years later. Understandably preoccupied with the struggle to survive the famine, people were losing interest in the repeal movement. O'Connell could not persuade all of his parliamentary party to support abolition of the Corn Laws. W.S. O'Brien, the recognized leader of Young Ireland since the death of Davis, argued that

Irish members should abstain from attendance at Westminster, a view that Davis had advocated. O'Connell's son John at first expressed agreement but then changed his mind, causing O'Brien to resign his seat.

The break finally came soon afterwards, when the Whigs returned to power and the O'Connells proposed reviving their old alliance with that party. The Young Ireland faction refused to accept this suggestion and were then read out of the repeal movement by John O'Connell, ostensibly because they refused unconditionally to renounce the use of violence. Soon afterwards, Daniel O'Connell, who had unsuccessfully tried to prevent the split, died while on a pilgrimage to Rome. The Young Irelanders formed a new party called the Irish Confederation but could elect no members other than O'Brien in the general election of 1847. By this time, however, they were falling under the influence of radicals such as James Fintan Lalor and John Mitchel, who had little interest in electoral politics. The famine and the misery in the countryside had undermined the legitimacy of the social and economic order, as well as that of the political regime.

Lalor, the son of a Catholic farmer, was one of the first Irish radicals to think and write seriously about economic issues. He believed, like the physiocrats in France, that agriculture was the ultimate source of all wealth and progress. He had no use for O'Connell's kind of politics and never joined the repeal movement, contending that solving the economic and social issues in the countryside was more important than restoring an Irish parliament. In a series of articles for the *Nation*, he argued that the Irish peoples were the real owners of the land but that they had been dispossessed by the conquest, which had led to control of the land by eight thousand landlords. The national question and the social question were inseparable.[59] Lalor does not seem to have envisaged collective ownership of the land, although he said that since land was created by God, property rights in land were valid only if based on the consent of the community. He called for a social revolution, by force if necessary, which would make Ireland a country of small peasant proprietors.

Mitchel, a solicitor educated at Trinity College and the son of a Unitarian minister in Ulster, had joined the repeal movement in 1843. He replaced Davis as the leading editorialist on the *Nation* after Davis died. In contrast to Davis, he was less concerned with cultural issues and more with the exploitation and deprivation of the rural people of Ireland, particularly after the impact of the famine became apparent. It was not always clear from his writings whether he hated the British because they supported the landlords or the landlords because they supported the British, but his feelings about both were clear enough. In 1847 he left the Irish Confederation when it refused to accept his demands for an armed insurrection and resigned from the *Nation*. Soon afterwards he founded his own paper, the *United Irishman*, whose name was an obvious reminder of 1798. It was suppressed by the government after three months of publication. In it Mitchel argued that the British and the landlords were deliberately seeking to reduce Ireland's population by starvation and emigration. He called on the rural tenants to resist, by force if necessary, any export of Irish food while the country was starving. In the longer term, he favoured a peasant-led revolution that would establish an Irish republic.

As a northern Protestant himself, Mitchel also confronted the issue of sectarianism. He urged northern Protestant farmers, labourers, and artisans in 1848 to think in terms of their class interests and to have "fraternal respect for your countrymen of the south." The religious issue, he wrote, was used by the British, the landlords, and the Orange Order to divide and rule the oppressed people of Ireland.[60] Earlier he had warned John O'Connell, at the time when the latter was driving the Young Irelanders out of the repeal movement, that Ireland's freedom could not be won without the Protestants. "And let me tell you, friends, this is our country as well as yours. You need not expect to free it from the mighty power of England by yourselves. Drive the Ulster Protestants away from your movement by needless tests, and you perpetuate the degradation both of yourselves and them."[61]

The writings of people such as Lalor and Mitchel made the authorities nervous, but the Irish people were too desperate, too afflicted, and too demoralized by the famine to launch a revolution at that time, a fact that Mitchel seems not to have appreciated. Those who retained enough vitality to save themselves were more interested in emigrating, and well over a million of them did so in the years 1847 through 1851, perhaps the greatest exodus in proportion to its size that any country has ever experienced.[62] Unlike their predecessors in 1798, the revolutionaries had no hope of foreign assistance, and they had no organization comparable to that of the United Irishmen in the 1790s, let alone the one O'Connell had at the peak of his influence.

The European revolutions that broke out in 1848 nonetheless persuaded Mitchel, and even some of the more moderate nationalists in the Irish Confederation, that some fundamental change in Ireland might be possible. At the urging of W.S. O'Brien, the Confederation adopted a motion calling for the creation of a national guard, similar to the Volunteers of the eighteenth century. Somewhat later it elected a five-member council to plan an insurrection. The rebels hoped for some support from the Catholic clergy, but reports of the anticlericalism of French and Italian revolutionaries, as well as the instructions the pope had sent to the Irish bishops a year earlier, prevented this from materializing.

A plan was formulated to seize and hold the Rock of Cashel, a prominent geological and historic landmark in County Tipperary, in the naive hope that Irish policemen and soldiers would join the insurrection once it was proclaimed. In the end all the rebels could achieve was to trap some policemen in a farmhouse at Ballingarry, about eighteen miles east of their objective. The "rebellion," if such it could be called, ended ignominiously with the bloodless capture of the few participants. Fifty years after 1798, Ireland had given some credence to what Karl Marx would write a few years later about great tragedies repeating themselves as farce.

Mitchel had already been sentenced to fourteen years of penal servitude in Australia and took no part in these events. He served only five years of his term before escaping to the United States. During his captivity he wrote his lengthy *Jail Journal,* one of the most celebrated texts of Irish republicanism, in which he denounced the British, the landlords, the Catholic Church, and Daniel O'Connell. He later, and somewhat incongruously, became a supporter of slavery during the American Civil War.[63] In Ireland four of the conspirators were sentenced to death, but Lord John Russell's government wisely decided to create no martyrs and commuted the sentences to various terms of imprisonment. The attempted rebellion of 1848 left no legacy to Ireland apart from the invention of the tricolour flag, obviously modelled after the French flag, which the state would eventually adopt after independence.[64] The tricolour, which incorporated orange as a well-intentioned but futile gesture to the northern Protestants, gradually replaced the old green flag of 1798 as a nationalist symbol.

With the collapse of the repeal movement and the anticlimax of 1848, Irish parliamentary politics returned for the time being to the British two-party system. In Ireland the choice of party was largely based on religion. Most Catholic voters were Whigs or, as they were known after 1855, Liberals, despite Peel's efforts to conciliate them in the 1840s. Most Protestants, at least in their stronghold of Ulster, were Conservatives. Catholics received much of the patronage distributed in Ireland by the Liberals but less from the Conservatives. The electorate was still very small; legislation in 1850 more than doubled the number of qualified voters, but there were still fewer than there had been prior to 1829.[65] For the vast majority of the population, who could not vote, economic and social relations between landlords and tenants were probably a more immediate concern than parliamentary politics or nationalism. The famine had largely eliminated the class of landless farm labourers, leaving the countryside polarized between landlords and tenants. As the country recovered from the famine, the issue of land reform would increasingly dominate the stage of Irish, and British, politics in the second half of the nineteenth century.

NATIONALISM AND POLITICS IN CANADA EAST

In Ireland many Catholics, and certainly the Catholic bishops, had supported the Irish Act of Union in 1801, if only because they expected Catholic emancipation to follow it. French Canadians, in contrast, opposed the Canada Union Act almost unanimously, including the Catholic clergy. The events of 1837–41 appeared to most French Canadians to be a collective disaster without any compensating advantages and one from which there was no hope of escape. The total rejection of the Patriote program by the Russell resolutions, the provocations of the merchant oligarchy in Montreal, the ill-considered and poorly planned resorts to violence in 1837 and 1838, the suspension of the Legislative Assembly, the reprisals against civilians and suspected Patriotes, and finally the union of the two colonies seemed to have wiped out all the progress that they had made since the conquest. Lord Durham's report created a lasting conviction that the aim of British policy, abetted by the most influential elements of the English-speaking minority in Lower Canada, was to eliminate every trace of the French language, culture, and nationality from British North America.

Some appeared to consider their nationality a lost cause, at least initially. Étienne Parent, who had been briefly imprisoned as a Patriote in 1838 and whose newspaper, *Le Canadien*, was the first to translate Lord Durham's report into French, accepted Durham's recommendation that Upper and Lower Canada be united. Parent suggested that since the British were determined to assimilate the French Canadians, the latter should abandon any effort to maintain their language or nationality. Assimilation was inevitable, and although regrettable, it would not be too high a price to pay for the achievement of responsible government.[66]

Few French Canadians were prepared to go that far, and even Parent soon moderated his views about assimilation. The more characteristic response to the Durham report was the emergence of a new type of nationalism which differed substantially from that of the Patriotes, even though many former Patriotes espoused it. Patriote nationalism, as we have seen, had been a movement for political and social reform that included many English-speaking residents of Lower Canada and borrowed many of its ideas and principles from the United States. It was not ethnically exclusive; nor was it primarily concerned with cultural issues. The type of nationalism that emerged among French-speaking Canadians after 1841 was in part a reaction against the Durham report, the union of the two Canadas, and the threat of assimilation that these things represented. However, it was also in part a product of larger trends in the western world. We have already seen that Irish nationalism in the 1840s was developing an interest in cultural issues and particularly in the preservation of the native language. French Canada was also influenced by the romantic cultural nationalism of that era, as were a number of European countries.

The new type of nationalism was French Canadian rather than Canadian, with emphasis on the adjective. At the time of the conquest, and for many years thereafter, the adjective had not often been used and had not really been necessary. Canada was a predominantly French-speaking society and a Canadien meant a French-speaking person; other persons who lived there were described, and described themselves, as English or British. However, as English-speaking settlers became more numerous, as the second and third generations developed roots in the country, and as the two colonies were united in 1841 to make the English-speaking people a majority in a new political unit, they too began to call themselves Canadians, making the adjective "French" necessary to distinguish the French-speaking people, who had now become a minority

The watchword of the new type of nationalism among the French Canadians was *la survivance*. Its proponents saw French Canadians as a minority ethnic group within a political system that they could not hope to control, rather than as a potentially independent nation. The Legislative Assembly that had provided Papineau and his colleagues with their platform was gone, and so was the colony of Lower Canada, which the Patriotes had hoped to transform into a democratic republic. The newly united colony of Canada was already predominantly English-speaking and destined to become more so with the passage of time. However it was reformed, it could not represent the aspirations of the French Canadian people. Rather than pursuing political reform, French Canadians should concentrate on protecting their ethnic group, their language, and their culture against the forces that were threatening to dissolve them in a sea of English-speaking North Americans. Louis Balthazar, in his history of Quebec nationalism, has described the kind of nationalism that began to emerge in the 1840s as religious, apolitical, and non-territorial.[67]

The conclusion drawn by the nationalists from an analysis of their situation was to separate nationalism, viewed as a cultural and even spiritual set of aspirations, from politics, which was seen as essentially concerned with more mundane material issues such as the building of roads and the distribution of patronage. While politics, defined in this limited sense, and the political order had their place, nationalism and the survival of the cultural community were more important. Étienne Parent, the former Patriote who had accepted assimilation and welcomed the promise of responsible government in 1839 but soon changed his mind, did not return to political activism. Instead he abandoned electoral politics and political journalism only three years later to concentrate on pursuing the goal of *la survivance* through his writings and speeches.[68]

The nationalists saw themselves as outnumbered and threatened in what was now a predominantly English-speaking colony, on an English-speaking continent, in an English-speaking empire. The survival of their cultural community was threatened by the English-speaking people who lived among them in Canada East, by the rapidly growing English-speaking population of Canada West, by the imperial government in London, and by their increasingly powerful neighbour, the United States. Faced with all these opponents, French Canadians could rely only on themselves, since no one else was interested in their goal of cultural survival. France was far away and could do little to help them, although any signs of French interest or sympathy, such as the visit of a French warship to Quebec in 1855, were welcomed.

In defining what was unique and worth preserving about the French Canadian cultural community, the nationalists naturally emphasized the French language, which Lord Durham had considered as an obstacle to progress, and the French civil law, including, for some although not all nationalists, the increasingly controversial system of seigneurial tenure. They also turned back to their history for inspiration. Lord Durham had ignorantly described the French Canadians as "a people with no history and no literature." He was proved wrong by a young notary, François-Xavier Garneau, who between 1845 and 1848 published a three-volume history of Canada from its origins to the establishment of Lower Canada as a separate colony in 1791. In a revised edition, published in 1852, he continued the story down to 1840. He is generally recognized as Canada's first scientific historian.

Garneau's great work was not, as is often believed, written solely to refute Lord Durham's opinion. He had already conceived the idea of writing a history of Canada a decade before Durham arrived, apparently in response to an English-speaking acquaintance who expressed scorn for the French Canadians as a conquered people with no history.[69] Garneau prepared for his project by spending two years (1831–33) in France and Great Britain, where he studied the liberal politics of the time. He was an active supporter of the Patriotes, although he did not participate in the armed insurrection. When he finally began his researches in 1841, he was given access to documents by E.B. O'Callaghan, who in his exile had become the archivist of the state of New York, and by Papineau, who owned an extensive library. In preparing the revised edition, he had similar help from the Catholic bishop of Quebec and also from Lord Elgin, the liberal governor general under whose administration the French language regained its official status and Canada won responsible government. Garneau's history described a long struggle to survive, against heavy odds, by a people whose shared language, laws, and customs made them a nation. It was thus an important milestone in the definition of *la survivance* as a collective project. However, the ideology of *la survivance* would evolve somewhat differently from what Garneau intended.

As time went on, proponents of *la survivance*, while continuing to assert the importance of language, laws, and customs, increasingly added religion as an essential defining characteristic of their nation, in much the same way as O'Connell had done in Ireland. Garneau, who was not particularly devout, had placed little emphasis on religion in his history and had been accused of anticlericalism after the publication of his first two volumes. In his third volume, however, he proclaimed the solidarity of religion and nationality in French Canada. Reflecting the changing ideological climate of the times, as well as the access to the diocesan archives given to Garneau by the bishop of Quebec, each subsequent edition of the history (there were four in all) placed greater emphasis than its predecessor on the importance of the church.[70]

The alliance between cultural nationalism and religion was facilitated by the growing prestige and influence of the church after the middle of the nineteenth century, a phenomenon that was not unique to French Canada and that is discussed in the last part of this chapter. It was a natural alliance for more than one reason. The new kind of nationalism was much more acceptable to the clergy than the nationalism of the Patriotes had been, precisely because, in Balthazar's words, it was apolitical and non-territorial. It carried no threat of armed rebellion, a phenomenon that the church traditionally deplored, or even of creating a liberal state, a phenomenon that the church had distrusted since the French Revolution. Placing politics and the state to one side almost automatically put greater emphasis on the church, the one major institution that was independent of politics and not directly affected by the Canada Union Act. In addition, the church, through its archives and its influence over education, was the guardian of French Canada's collective memory and of much of its culture. Finally, the church had opposed both the insurrection and the union of the two Canadas; so it could not be blamed for either of those events or for their consequences.

In its full-fledged version, which developed gradually after the middle of the nineteenth century and continued into the early part of the twentieth, French Canadian cultural nationalism began to give the Catholic religion pride of place among the defining characteristics of the nation. Furthermore it assigned to French Canada the divinely ordained mission of establishing and preserving the Catholic faith in a predominantly Protestant North America, an idea that Étienne Parent expressed in his last public speech in 1868.[71] Eventually, the history of French Canada would be rewritten to suggest that this missionary enterprise had been its primary vocation from the outset.

An organization that would play an important part in propagating the nationalism of *la survivance* was the Societé Saint-Jean-Baptiste. The custom of holding a patriotic banquet and celebration on 24 June had been started by the Patriote editor Ludger Duvernay in 1834, as discussed in the preceding chapter. However, the banquet of 1837 was not followed by another until 1843, after Duvernay and his friend George-Étienne Cartier had returned from exile. It was in that year that the society was actually organized. The banquet of 1834 had been hosted by an English-speaking Patriote named John McDonnell, but the organization that was formed almost a decade later was exclusively French Canadian and devoted to cultural nationalism. It also rejected the anticlericalism of the Patriotes and welcomed the Catholic clergy as members. Prayers were said at its meetings, and the annual event from 1843 onwards included the celebration of a mass, as well as a parade through the streets of Montreal.[72] Although the founding members were former Patriotes, the organization aimed to unite all French Canadians without regard to political distinctions. By the 1860s persons who had opposed the Ninety-two Resolutions a generation earlier were elected presidents of the society.

Some cultural nationalists were genuinely uninterested in politics and gave it as little attention as possible. Others could divide their attention between culture and politics in various ways, if we bear in mind that the two spheres of thought and activity were considered separate and distinct. Just as a Christian could render unto Caesar the things that were Caesar's, so a cultural nationalist could combine the pursuit of cultural survival, a semi-sacred vocation sought in common with other French Canadian Catholics, and legislative politics, a mundane activity that might be shared with neighbours and colleagues who were neither French nor Catholic. When political activity recommenced in a new context in 1841, following several years without representative institutions, this became a viable option.

Daniel O'Connell and Louis-Joseph Papineau were often compared during their lifetimes, but the French Canadian politician who perhaps provides a closer parallel with O'Connell is Louis-Hippolyte LaFontaine. LaFontaine opposed armed rebellion in 1837, as O'Connell did in 1798. After the union of the two Canadas in 1841, he became, and remained for a decade, the most influential politician in Canada East. Although he was not a charismatic leader like O'Connell, his achievements on behalf of his people – responsible government, the recognition of the French language, and compensation for property destroyed by British soldiers in 1837–38 – bear comparison with O'Connell's achievement of Catholic emancipation. Lafontaine also established a style and pattern of politics that endured for many decades in Quebec, and to some extent still does today. His impact on the political culture of his country was perhaps as lasting and significant as that of O'Connell on his.

LaFontaine, who was a generation younger than Papineau, had been a Patriote prior to the rebellion but opposed the resort to violence, even though he recognized that it had been largely provoked by the Patriotes' opponents. While the rebellion of 1837 was still in progress, he twice wrote to the governor general urging him to call the Legislative Assembly into session, but his representations were ignored.[73] During the second outbreak in 1838, he was arrested and questioned, an indignity that probably did his subsequent political career no harm. His response, along with another lawyer arrested at the same time, was to petition the British parliament, protesting against his own imprisonment but also against the behaviour of British troops, the suspension of civil liberties, and the capital sentences imposed on some of the Patriotes. The petition added that the French Canadian people understandably viewed the recent events as a deliberate plot to destroy their identity, language, and laws, in violation of the treaty by which the British had acquired Canada in 1763.[74]

For many French Canadians, Lord Durham's report and the subsequent unification of Upper and Lower Canada represented the realization of precisely that objective. LaFontaine, although originally opposed to the union of the two provinces, seems to have decided that the threat of assimilation could still be avoided by establishing responsible government as soon as possible. In the long term, he believed that responsible government would do more to ensure *la survivance* than agitating for the repeal of the Union Act. If government was made responsible to a majority in the Legislative Assembly, a minority as large in numbers as the French Canadians could not be disregarded by any politicians hoping to remain in office. By an alliance with reform-minded politicians in the upper province, LaFontaine hoped to form a liberal party committed to responsible government and drawing support from both sections of Canada. Since such a party would need French Canadian support to win a majority and form a responsible administration, it would have to reject Lord Durham's project of assimilation, accept the civil law and the French language of the lower province, and grant French Canadians a fair share of the patronage.

Beginning even before the Union Act was adopted by the British parliament, LaFontaine pursued his strategy with unexpected success, largely as a result of the emergence in Canada West of a Reform party leader committed to responsible government and sympathetic to the French Canadians, Robert Baldwin. By September 1842 LaFontaine was in office as attorney general for Canada East, sharing the leadership of the government with Baldwin, who served as attorney general for Canada West. Little more than a year after the formation of the united province, Governor General Sir Charles Bagot had concluded, contrary to British policy and the recommendations of the Durham report, that Canada could not be governed without the support of the French Canadians. Bagot's death the following year, however, led to a setback. The new governor general, Sir Charles Metcalfe, attempted to control patronage without consulting Baldwin or Lafontaine, who accordingly resigned in November 1843. The principle of responsible government was not fully established until February 1848, when Metcalfe's successor, Lord Elgin, called upon LaFontaine and Baldwin, whose followers had recently won a majority of seats in a general election, to form a government for the second time. On hearing of this event, the colonial secretary, Earl Grey, congratulated Elgin that a government enjoying the confidence of "the French party" had been formed before the news of the revolution in France reached Canada.[75]

Simultaneously with his campaign for responsible government, LaFontaine pursued a campaign to re-establish the official status of the French language. The Union Act made English the only language of official documents, but it did not explicitly prohibit the use of French in the Legislative Assembly. During the debate that preceded the formation of the first Baldwin-LaFontaine government, LaFontaine spoke in French, despite the heckling of some English-speaking members, and protested the cruel injustice of the Union Act for seeking to prohibit the mother tongue of half Canada's population.[76] In 1843, at LaFontaine's request, the governor general asked the British government to consider repealing the section of the Union Act that made English the only official language. This request was refused by Sir Robert Peel's government, but Lafontaine persisted in his campaign, even after the resignation of his government. In 1845 the Legislative Assembly of the united province unanimously voted to renew the request. The requirement that official documents be in English only was finally repealed in 1848 by the government led by Lord John Russell.[77] Lord Stanley, who had been colonial secretary at the time of the first request, regretted the change on the grounds that "a permanent barrier would be raised up between the two portions of the country, whose amalgamation was essential to the welfare of both." His successor, Earl Grey, conceded that a single official language would be more convenient, but stated that he attached even more importance to the principle of governing Canada according to the wishes of its inhabitants.[78] LaFontaine's faith in the link between responsible government and French Canadian rights was thus vindicated. In the following year, Lord Elgin read the speech from the throne in both languages.

Meanwhile, the French Canadians were dividing into two distinct political parties, both of which could claim descent from the Patriotes of 1837–38. Some of the politicians who had been Patriotes did not share LaFontaine's conviction that achieving responsible government was more important, and more feasible, than seeking repeal of the Union Act. Still preferring the American system of government to the British, they were not comfortable with the fusion of legislative and executive power that responsible government implied. Some of them also distrusted the Reformers of Canada West and argued that the French Canadian members should form a bloc that would hold the balance of power between the two English-speaking parties in the assembly, rather than making a permanent alliance with the Reformers. Initially, the principal representatives of this viewpoint were Denis-Benjamin Viger and Denis-Benjamin Papineau, respectively the cousin and the brother of the exiled Louis-Joseph Papineau. Both accepted office under Governor General Metcalfe after LaFontaine and Baldwin resigned. In 1845 Louis-Joseph himself was allowed to return to Canada, and he became LaFontaine's leading opponent. *L'Avenir*, a newspaper founded by J.B.E. Dorion in 1847, was the principal journalistic voice of Papineau's followers.

By this time the Catholic Church, which had originally disapproved of LaFontaine's acceptance of the Union Act, had become tacitly sympathetic to LaFontaine, who was careful to take the church's interests into account.[79] The anticlericalism and pro-Americanism of Papineau and his followers made this a natural alliance, as did the realization that responsible government would increase the political influence of the clergy. The European revolutions of 1848, which were welcomed by Papineau and deplored by the church, accentuated the contrast between the more conservative and the more radical wings of French Canadian nationalism. Although the issues that divided Papineau and LaFontaine were not the same as those on which the Young Irelanders disagreed with O'Connell, certain parallels are evident.

The Papineau group continued to insist that the most important objective was to repeal the Union Act. They criticized LaFontaine for his close ties with the reformers of Canada West and for accepting the spoils of office under what they considered an illegitimate regime. They retained the pro-American enthusiasm of the original Patriotes, which some of them carried to the point of believing that French Canada would be better off as part of the United States than as part of the British Empire. In 1848 *L'Avenir* alleged that the Cajuns of Louisiana had retained their French language and laws and that there was thus no reason to fear annexation by the United States.[80] The editors had apparently forgotten Lord Durham's more realistic comments on the same subject in his report.

The legislative session of 1849 began with a celebrated debate between Papineau and LaFontaine. Papineau gave LaFontaine and Lord Elgin due credit for restoring the status of the French language but was otherwise almost entirely critical of the speech from the throne. He continued to denounce LaFontaine for accepting the union of the Canadas after originally opposing it, and he maintained that the union was contrary to common sense and harmful to both sections of Canada. Papineau also attacked the principle of responsible government on the grounds that it made the executive power too strong in relation to the legislature. LaFontaine, in reply, pointed out that French Canadians had not been assimilated under the Union Act and that his policy of working within the system had proved the best guarantee of *la survivance*. He denounced Papineau as a friend of Parisian revolutionaries and a supporter of annexation by the United States.[81]

The session that followed was marked by the adoption of the Rebellion Losses Act, a highly controversial measure which LaFontaine had sought for several years and to which Lord Elgin gave royal assent. It provided compensation to Canadians whose property had been destroyed or damaged by British soldiers in 1837–38 and was thus anathema to the English-speaking Tories of Montreal, who still regarded the rebellions as treason and the British reprisals as well deserved. Already disgruntled by Britain's abandonment of mercantilism, which threatened the interests of merchant capital in the colonies, this element responded to the latest outrage by pelting the governor general's carriage with horse droppings, burning down the parliament buildings, and sponsoring a manifesto that demanded the annexation of Canada by the United States. The riot cost Montreal its position as the seat of government, a status it was never to regain. The manifesto, since it was signed mainly by English-speaking Tories and francophobes, helped to discredit Papineau and the pro-American type of nationalism that he represented. It thus contributed to a reorientation of French Canadian politics that was already in progress and would be completed by LaFontaine's retirement, at the early age of forty-four, less than two years later. Baldwin had also retired, and the new leaders of the Reform party in Canada West had little in common with LaFontaine's approach to politics.

In the 1850s French Canadian politics settled into a pattern that would last for many decades, and the forces of French Canadian nationalism were divided between two political parties that would prove equally durable. On one side were the heirs of LaFontaine, moderate conservatives, admirers of

British parliamentary government, defenders of, and supported by, the
Catholic Church, firmly committed to *la survivance,* and opponents of radical republican democracy in both its European and its American forms.
They were known as Bleus, and would find their natural allies among moderate
Upper Canadian conservatives such as John A. Macdonald. On the other
side were the heirs of Papineau, known as Rouges, a colour already associated by 1848 with political radicalism. Although they discarded Papineau's
distaste for responsible government and took over from the LaFontaine
group as partners with Upper Canadian Reformers in a sometimes precarious alliance, the Rouges retained some of Papineau's anticlericalism,
pro-Americanism, and political radicalism. For this reason they were distrusted by the Catholic Church, a fact that placed them at a serious disadvantage in elections that were heavily influenced by the clergy.

The distinction between these two groups can be compared with the distinction between the heirs of O'Connell and the heirs of Young Ireland that
would persist in Irish politics to the end of the nineteenth century and
beyond. The issues and the situations were not identical, but in both countries the less radical tendency predominated, largely because it enjoyed the
support of the Catholic Church. British concessions to Catholicism, most of
them granted by Tory governments, had given the colonial regimes a powerful ally in both Ireland and Canada. On the other hand, the church never
surrendered its independence and thus retained its credentials as the
embodiment of a certain kind of nationalism. Its support for the status quo
was cautious and conditional, based as much on its fear of radicalism as on
real enthusiasm for the British.

The reasons why the British strategy was more successful in French Canada than in Ireland will be explored in the chapters that follow. Before we
pursue that line of inquiry, however, it will be useful to examine the position
that the Catholic Church occupied in both countries around the middle
decades of the nineteenth century and the influence that it would exert over
the subsequent development of both societies.

CHURCH, STATE, AND CIVIL SOCIETY

The term "civil society" originated during the Scottish Enlightenment in the
eighteenth century, the age of Adam Smith and David Hume. It has recently
become more popular than ever before among social scientists. It refers to
those collective institutions and associations, such as organized religion,
that are independent of the state and that give shape and character to a society even in the absence of a state. The Scottish state disappeared in 1707,
but Scotland continued to be different from England because of its differ-

ent civil institutions, among which its Presbyterian church occupied a very significant place.

In both Ireland and French Canada the Catholic Church, although its influence is currently only a shadow of what it once was, has done more than any other institution to give civil society its distinct shape and character. In so doing, it has helped to provide an environment in which nationalism could flourish, for nationalism must be based on a belief that one is part of a distinct civil society and not merely a subject or citizen of a particular state. Powerful myths have emphasized the role of Christianity in the founding of both societies. However, it is not always realized how much the institutional church, in both Ireland and Quebec, is a product of the nineteenth century. Even a casual visitor to Ireland or Quebec notices the impressive Catholic parish churches in every village, town, and city. A closer examination of the buildings reveals that they too, with very rare exceptions, are products of the nineteenth century. Why is this so?

The reasons are in part specific to the two societies with which we are concerned but in part of a more general nature. The nineteenth century was a period of revival for the Catholic Church throughout the Western world after the long decline of the eighteenth century and the trauma of the French Revolution and its aftermath. This revival began quite early in the century but became particularly significant during the long and controversial reign of Pope Pius IX (1846–78). In Ireland and French Canada, decades after the French Revolution, the church endured its own specific traumas. The successful end of the long struggle for acceptance and recognition by the British conquerors was closely followed by two catastrophes: the famine of 1845–47 in Ireland and the rebellion of 1837–38 in Lower Canada. These events stimulated, or at least accelerated, the revival of the Catholic Church. The revival was associated in particular with two clerical leaders who emerged immediately after the catastrophes and who were contemporaries, almost precisely, of Pius IX. Paul Cullen was archbishop of Armagh from 1849 to 1852 and then of Dublin to 1878. Ignace Bourget was bishop of Montreal from 1840 until 1876.

The Catholic revival in Ireland and French Canada was also assisted by a number of other circumstances. In both cases the absence of a national state made civil society, particularly the church, more influential than it would have been otherwise. In both societies the British conquerors, having finally accepted the legitimacy and permanence of Catholicism, found it convenient to place various social tasks and functions in clerical hands. The mid-nineteenth century also saw the beginnings of mass education and literacy, phenomena in which the church played a large part and which enabled it to extend its influence. Finally, economic conditions improved in both places after the middle of the century, making more funds available for investment in religion.

One indicator of the influence of the church in society is the ratio of priests to population. Data exist on this subject for both Ireland and Quebec, and although they are not exactly comparable, if only because they were collected in different years, the trends that they suggest are broadly similar. In Ireland there was one priest for every 2,100 Catholics in 1800, but only one for every 3,000 in 1840, suggesting that the church was not keeping pace with the very rapid growth of the population. In 1850, however, there was one for every 2,100; by 1870 the ratio was one for every 1,250. Thereafter it seems to have stabilized; more than a century later, in 1981, there was one priest for every 978 Catholics.[82] The period from 1840 to 1870 is that in which the influence of the church grew rapidly.

The Quebec data suggest a similar trend, although they also indicate, somewhat surprisingly, that French Canada was always more abundantly supplied with priests relative to its population than Ireland. In 1759, the year that Quebec fell to the British, there was apparently one priest for every 350 French Canadians, but by 1780 there was only one for every 750, and by 1830 only one for every 1,834. Here too the church was not keeping pace with rapid population growth in the early nineteenth century. However, in 1850 there was one priest for every 1,080 French Canadians, and in 1880 one for every 510. Thereafter the ratio roughly stabilized: one for every 652 in 1910, one for 567 in 1930, and one for 520 in 1970.[83] Here too the middle decades, roughly corresponding to the reigns of Pius IX and Bishop Bourget, are the period in which the influence of the church grew rapidly.

Education, as noted above, was an area of increasing importance in the nineteenth century and one in which the church assumed a dominant role. In Ireland a system of "national schools" was established in 1831. It was supervised by a seven-member board representing the three major churches and including both the Catholic and Protestant archbishops of Dublin. The Catholic bishops were divided in their response to this measure, but in the long term it proved beneficial to Irish Catholicism.[84] Although the schools were originally supposed to be non-denominational, with the students segregated only for religious education by their respective clergy, three-quarters of the schools were under clerical control by 1850.[85] Residential segregation and the fact that most rural villages outside Ulster were almost entirely Catholic, as well as the tendency of more affluent Protestants to send their children to private schools, made most of the national schools denominational, usually Catholic, in practice, and this fact was officially accepted after 1870.

In Lower Canada a statute in 1824 authorized Catholic parishes to establish parish schools and to spend up to a quarter of their revenue for that purpose. Lord Durham, in his report, lamented that the colonial state had done little to educate the people of Lower Canada.[86] Legislation in 1846 established separate Protestant and Catholic school boards for Montreal and Quebec City and boards representing the majority religion (Protestant in most of the Eastern Townships, Catholic almost everywhere else) throughout the smaller towns and rural areas of Canada East. The Protestant or Catholic religious minority in any area could petition for the establishment of a separate board. Thus all schools were denominational, both in theory and in practice, and provided religious education. The Catholic ones of course enrolled the vast majority of the pupils, as in Ireland. This denomination system of education would endure in Quebec for more than a century and a half.

One important difference between Catholic education in Ireland and Quebec should be noted, for it had an impact on nationalism and politics over the long term. In Ireland, where the indigenous language had begun to die out before mass education was established, the Catholic schools made no effort to preserve it. Education was conducted in English and therefore accelerated the decline of the Irish language. In Lower Canada, where the conquest was more recent, the French language had not declined and was used by practically all French Canadians when mass education began. Despite Lord Durham's intentions, Catholic schools educated French Canadians in French, and the survival of the language and of the faith came to be viewed as interdependent.

Catholicism influenced society in other ways as well. For example, in Ireland the temperance campaign started by Father Theobald Mathew in 1838 was a phenomenal success, causing more than half the population to take the teetotal pledge by 1842 and possibly serving as a model for O'Connell's Repeal Association. A similar, although less successful, temperance campaign was launched in Montreal by Bishop Bourget in 1841. These campaigns foreshadowed the Catholic revival that followed soon afterwards. Roy Foster's words, although written about Ireland, are equally applicable to French Canada: "From the 1850s religious societies proliferated; devotional aids and new devotions became the norm."[87]

It was also in the nineteenth century that the church began to exercise a significant influence on the distinct but overlapping spheres of nationalism and electoral politics. O'Connell built his political machine around the Catholic parishes, as we have noted, and the close association between Catholicism and Irish nationalism continued through the nineteenth century and beyond. In Canada the ideology of *la survivance*, which increasingly

acquired religious overtones, developed after, and in response to, the defeat
of secular anticlerical and non-sectarian nationalism in 1837–38 and the
imposition of the Union Act. Significantly, complaints about clerical inter-
ference and intimidation affecting the outcome of elections began to be
heard in Ireland after O'Connell turned to electoral politics in 1832.[88] In
Canada East they begin to be heard after 1850, when the party system polarized between Bleus and Rouges. By the 1870s defeated Rouge candidates
were almost routinely contesting electoral outcomes in the courts.

By the 1850s the dominant position of the Catholic Church in civil society
was firmly established in both Ireland and Canada East, just as the two countries were entering the age of commercial agriculture and industrial enterprise, of railways, mass literacy, and democratic politics. Over the next half
century their paths would diverge in important ways, with different consequences for their respective forms of nationalism. In the next chapter some
of these developments will be explored.

CHAPTER FIVE

The Politics of Home Rule and Federalism

From the 1850s until the end of the nineteenth century, dramatic developments transformed both Ireland and French Canada, paving the way for the different paths that they would follow in the twentieth century. Although parallels and comparisons between the two societies in this period are still possible and useful, the similarities are less apparent and the contrasts more obvious than in earlier periods. With hindsight at least, the transformations that were taking place in the two societies seem to have been moving them inexorably in different directions: towards independence and partition in the Irish case but towards a continuing pursuit of *la survivance* within a federal framework in the case of Quebec. In both cases the political, economic, and social transformations were to a large extent externally imposed, for both Ireland and Quebec were small and relatively powerless entities within much larger systems of relationships: the British Empire, the North Atlantic trading economy, and the universal Roman Catholic Church. Yet the ways in which those larger institutions shaped the transformations of both Ireland and Quebec were influenced to some extent by domestic situations and patterns of forces within the two societies, as well as by the actions of particular leaders.

Ireland's population continued to decline in every decade, despite a respectable rate of natural increase, with a net loss of over two million people between 1851 and 1901. By 1901 the population of Ireland had fallen to slightly less than four and a half million, the approximate level at which it would remain for the next seventy years. The reason for the losses in the second half of the nineteenth century was that almost four million people emigrated from Ireland between 1851 and 1901, or almost as many as were still living in the country at the latter date. In some years more people emigrated from Ireland than died there. At least after 1876, and probably before, the great majority of emigrants went to the United States; Great Britain took most·of the remainder. With the decline of the St Lawrence timber trade and the replacement of sail by steam, Canada ceased to be a significant destination for Irish emigrants, except in 1882 and 1883, when it attracted almost a tenth of the total number.[1]

Ireland's inability to retain its people reflected the most significant fact about Irish society in those years: it remained a predominantly rural and agricultural country at a time when the United Kingdom, of which it was ostensibly part, was the industrial workshop of the world. John Stuart Mill referred to this contrast when in 1866 he said that English people could not understand Ireland because England had a unique history while Ireland was more typical of the human experience.[2] Michael Hechter, an American political sociologist, has argued that the separation of most of Ireland from the United Kingdom in 1922 can be explained by the pattern of uneven development in the United Kingdom, which made Ireland an underdeveloped rural periphery within an industrial state.[3] The percentage of Ireland's population living in towns of two thousand or more inhabitants increased gradually, from 17 per cent in 1851 to 31 per cent in 1901.[4] However, most Irish people, particularly if they were Catholics, still lived on the land, and the land, even after the famine, was quite densely populated. Manufacturing in Ireland grew more slowly than in Great Britain throughout this period.

Data on the principal cities of Ireland indicate another significant fact: the uneven development of the country and the fact that urban and industrial development was concentrated in a small area of the extreme northeast, which shared in Great Britain's industrial revolution while the rest of Ireland for the most part did not. Dublin's population was virtually stable from 1851, when it totalled 246,679, to 1891 when it was only 245,001. In the last decade of the century it increased modestly to reach a level of 290,638. Limerick and Cork both had fewer inhabitants in 1901 than they had a half century earlier. However, Belfast, which was Ireland's main industrial centre by the 1860s, increased very rapidly in size. Its population grew from 97,784 in 1851 to 255,950 in 1891, when it surpassed Dublin for the first time, and 349,180 at the beginning of the new century.[5] Belfast by this time was not only a mainly Protestant city but one of the leading industrial centres of the United Kingdom: an anomaly in a mainly rural and Catholic Ireland. Economics reinforced the impact of religion to prevent Protestant Belfast from sharing in the development of Irish nationalism.

Changes in fiscal policy during the 1850s harmonized Irish taxation with that imposed on residents of Great Britain, who had previously paid somewhat higher rates. These changes, as well as the continuing decline in Ireland's population, meant that taxation in Ireland increased substantially on a per capita basis, while in Great Britain, where population was increasing, it remained stable.[6] Per capita income in Ireland apparently rose from about two-fifths of the British level in 1848 to about three-fifths early in the twentieth century.[7] However, when the declining population is taken into account, Ireland's share of British national income declined.

Most of Ireland, and especially Catholic Ireland, remained rural; Protestants were much more likely than Catholics to live in cities. Furthermore, most of the land on which the population depended for its livelihood was owned by a very small number of landlords. In 1876 half the country was owned by fewer than eight hundred people and almost a quarter of it by non-residents.[8] By the late nineteenth century many landlords were Catholics; Daniel O'Connell, for example, had inherited a substantial estate from his uncle. Most land, however, was still owned by descendants of the Protestants who had taken ownership of most of the country in the days of Cromwell and William of Orange. Many of these people played important roles in British politics during the Victorian era and spent little time in Ireland. Most of their tenants, except in parts of Ulster, were Catholics. These facts placed the question of land reform at the centre of Irish (and British) politics in the later decades of the nineteenth century. They also ensured that the question of land reform would become closely associated with Irish Catholic nationalism.

In other respects Ireland was modernizing. Most of the major centres were connected with one another, or at least with Dublin or Belfast, by railways during this period. The mileage of railway track in Ireland rose from 65 in 1842 to about 2,000 in 1872.[9] Banks, newspapers, and postal service also became part of everyday life. The level of literacy, already high by contemporary standards in 1845, when almost half the population could read, continued to increase with the development of the national school system, whose origins were discussed in the preceding chapter. By 1881 three out of four adults could read, although the proportion was lower in Connacht than in the other provinces.[10] There was also progress in secondary education, particularly for Catholics. The number of Catholic secondary school students doubled between 1871 and 1901, despite the declining population, while the number of Protestant students remained stable.[11]

During this period the (Anglican) Church of Ireland was disestablished. The census of 1861, the first accurate count of Irish religious affiliations, revealed that less than 12 per cent of Ireland's population identified with that church, a finding that surprised many Protestants.[12] The Liberals, led by William E. Gladstone, fought and won the British election of 1868 on the issue of disestablishment, which was popular with English Methodists and Scottish Presbyterians as well as Irish Catholics. The necessary legislation was adopted a year later, despite the disapproval of Queen Victoria and the opposition of the Conservative Party. As Gladstone explained in the House of Commons, the established church was a symbol of Protestant ascendancy, and "so long as that Establishment lives, painful and bitter memories of ascendancy can never be effaced."[13] An unanticipated effect of the measure was to end any serious basis for disagreement between Irish Anglicans and Irish Presbyterians, placing them on an equal footing and facilitating their consolidation into a Protestant bloc opposed to Irish nationalism.

Within the Irish Catholic Church the religious revival that had begun earlier in the century continued, although Archbishop Cullen's effort to have one of Dublin's two Anglican cathedrals transferred to the Catholic Church after disestablishment was not successful. Cullen was a monarchist and a conservative, but some of the younger archbishops who became prominent after his death in 1878 were much more sympathetic to Irish nationalism and to land reform. These included Archbishops Walsh of Dublin, Croke of Cashel, and Logue of Armagh.

In the province of Quebec, which Canada East officially became in 1867, social and economic development followed a somewhat different pattern. The size of the population nearly doubled, from 890,261 in 1851 to 1,648,898 in 1901. While it stood in sharp contrast to Ireland's demographic decline in the same period, this rate of growth was actually slower than that experienced by Lower Canada in the first half of the nineteenth century or by the province of Quebec in the first half of the twentieth, despite a very high rate of natural increase. Like Ireland, Quebec (and Canada as a whole) lost many of its people to the United States in the second half of the nineteenth century. Since most of Quebec's people lived close to the border with the United States and since several railways crossed the border, emigration was much cheaper and easier than it was in Ireland. Furthermore, emigrants living in the United States could easily return to Quebec from time to time to visit relatives. For the whole half-century the net loss of population to the United States suffered by the province of Quebec is estimated at about 580,000, a number more than one-third as large as the number of persons living in Quebec in 1901.[14]

These losses would probably have been much greater had not Quebec made some progress in urbanization and industrialization during that half-century. Its industrial output in 1901 was ten times as high as it had been forty years earlier.[15] The percentage of the population living in towns with populations of more than 1,500 increased from 15 per cent in 1851 to 36 per cent in 1901, a somewhat higher rate of growth in urbanization than Ireland experienced.[16]

Perhaps more importantly, urbanization and industrialization were less uneven in a spatial sense than was true in Ireland, and they involved the French Canadian and Catholic majority to a much greater extent than the Ulster-centred industrialization and urbanization of Ireland involved Irish Catholics.

The data on population growth in particular centres provide an interesting comparison with the Irish data for the same period. No town in Quebec suffered the demographic decline experienced by Cork and Limerick, and a number of new towns were established. Quebec City grew quite modestly by North American standards, from 42,052 in 1851 to 68,840 half a century later, but even this growth contrasted with the stagnation of Dublin. (Most of Quebec City's increase actually occurred in the decade 1861–71, during which it regained its position as the seat of government.) Montreal, which was the leading industrial centre in all of British North America, grew even more rapidly than Belfast: from 57,715 in 1851 to 267,730 in 1901. Furthermore, Montreal and Quebec City, which were about half English-speaking at the earlier date, became increasingly French as they grew, in contrast to Belfast, which became increasingly Protestant. French Canadians who left the land were much more likely to find non-agricultural jobs in their own country than Irish Catholics who did so.

Quebec nonetheless remained a largely rural and agricultural society, with 39 per cent of its labour force in agriculture in 1891; this was a lower percentage than that of Ireland and even slightly lower than that of Canada as a whole.[17] However, Quebec's rural problems were much less acute than those of Ireland and were not of a character to bring about violent protest. The system of seigneurial tenure, never particularly onerous, had become increasingly irrelevant by the time it was abolished in 1854. Its abolition, by what had become a general consensus, was politically easy and left rural French Canada as a society of small landowners, a situation that Ireland achieved, with great difficulty, only after a further half-century of struggle. Furthermore, while the supply of land in Ireland was obviously finite, Quebec was still opening new land for development throughout the nineteenth century. This process, known in Quebec as colonization, expanded the area occupied by French Canadian farmers into virgin territories: the Laurentian hills northwest of Montreal, the area around Lac Saint-Jean, north of Quebec City, and the Abitibi region in the far northwest. The Catholic Church encouraged colonization, although recent research has suggested that its influence over the process was less important than was traditionally assumed.[18] French Canadians also began to move at last into the Eastern Townships. By 1901 only two of the eleven counties in that part of the province were still predominantly English-speaking, although all of them had been so in the 1840s and six of them as recently as the 1880s.[19]

Quebec modernized in other ways as well. The two short lines of railway, totalling about twenty-five miles, that Canada East possessed in 1847 grew into a comprehensive network that reached all the inhabited regions of Quebec and connected the province with other parts of North America to the south, east, and west. By the end of the century Montreal was the railway centre of Canada and the headquarters of both the major Canadian railway systems. The level of literacy, which had been lower in Canada East than in Ireland at mid-century, improved until more than 80 per cent of the people in Quebec were literate at the end. It should again be noted that French Canadians in Quebec became literate in their own language, French, in contrast to the Irish, whose indigenous language was for all practical purposes replaced by English.

The Catholic Church in Quebec, as in Ireland, continued to grow in influence, but it experienced conflict between the ultramontane faction, centred around Bishop Bourget, and a more liberal faction centred around Archbishop Elzéar-Alexandre Taschereau of Quebec City, who became Canada's first cardinal in 1886. Although the factions did not really differ in their views on Quebec's status within Canada and the British Empire, their conflict influenced political life by dividing the Bleu party into ultramontane and moderate factions. The ultramontanes, who published a political manifesto known as "La Programme catholique" in 1871, were known as *castors*. (The beaver, because of its association with the fur trade, was a symbol of French Canadian nationalism.) They gained influence within the Bleu party after the death of its moderate leader, George-Étienne Cartier, in 1873.

In summary, these contrasting developments may suggest some of the reasons why the paths of Ireland and Quebec diverged after 1900, with Ireland winning independence at the cost of partition while Quebec remained an occasionally dissatisfied province within a federation. French Canadian nationalism certainly existed, as will be seen, but the pressure for political change did not build to the same level that it attained in Ireland. Apart from the socio-economic explanations for the contrast, it is surely significant that French Canadians achieved, with little effort, an important political change that gave them significantly more autonomy in 1867, while Ireland failed repeatedly to achieve the same result. These events will be discussed in the pages that follow.

THE REBIRTH OF IRISH REPUBLICANISM

One effect of the famine that had lasting consequences for the North Atlantic world was that it provoked a massive emigration of Irish Catholics to North America. (Previous to the famine, most of the Irish people who crossed the

Atlantic had been Protestants, mainly from Ulster.) Almost a million people made the journey from Ireland to North America between 1847 and 1851.[20] These were the peak years, for fairly obvious reasons, but the emigrant traffic remained heavy until 1914. Particularly in the 1840s and 1850s, many landed in Canada, particularly at the city of Quebec, since the passage to Quebec was shorter and cheaper than to ports in the United States. However, the greater prosperity south of the border, the demand for soldiers during the American Civil War, and the political influence of the Orange lodges in Canada caused many, perhaps most, Catholic Irish in Canada to move on to the United States. The result of these massive migrations of people was a large and increasingly influential population of Irish Catholic Americans, mainly located in the large cities, such as Boston, New York, Philadelphia, Chicago, and San Francisco. While initially the target of ethnic and religious prejudice, particularly in Puritan Massachusetts, they became increasingly integrated into American life after the Civil War, in which Irish soldiers played a notable part. However, they continued to identify with the Ireland from which they had come and to support the cause of Irish nationalism morally and, as they increasingly prospered in their new country, financially. As transatlantic shipping improved in the age of steam and steel, people and ideas could circulate freely between the American diaspora and the growing nationalist movement at home. Such contacts may have been one reason why republican sentiments developed in Ireland after the famine, since the American Irish took a republican regime for granted.

The farcical rising, if such it could be called, of 1848 and the British government's mild response to it had done nothing to promote the cause of Irish republicanism. The decade that followed this event was one of relative prosperity in Ireland, as emigration reduced the pressure of population on the land and as Irish commercial agriculture helped to meet the needs of the rapidly growing British market. However, on St Patrick's Day 1858 a small group of radicals led by James Stephens, a veteran of 1848, met in Dublin to form the Irish Republican Brotherhood. Although it achieved little in the short run, it proved to be the most formidable organization dedicated to Irish independence since the United Irishmen of 1798. It was also remarkably durable, to the point that one can say it never really died. In Irish (and Canadian) history this organization is usually known by the name that was adopted by its American branch, the Fenians.

The Fenian movement was a phenomenon distinct from Ireland's tradition of rural violence against landlords and their property. In fact, it was more urban than rural, at least originally. Another difference was that while the violent agrarian protest groups that had flourished since the early 1700s lacked any clear political ideology or political goals, the Fenians were explicitly republican and dedicated to the pursuit of Irish independence. They declared in 1868 that "the right of Ireland to self-government and independent nationhood is inherent and inalienable." At the same time they insisted that they had no animosity towards the British people, but only towards British rule in Ireland.[21] Their proclamation, issued in 1867 and addressed to "The Irish People of the World," called for "a Republic based on universal suffrage, which shall secure to all the intrinsic value of their labour," as well as "absolute liberty of conscience, and complete separation of Church and State."[22] (This was two years before the disestablishment of the Church of Ireland.) Fenians took an oath pledging their allegiance to the organization and to the Irish Republic, which was optimistically declared in 1859 to be "virtually established."[23]

The proclamation of 1867 also asserted, "The soil of Ireland, at present in the possession of an oligarchy, belongs to us, the Irish people, and to us it must be restored." However, an analysis of the social background of a sample of IRB members suggests that theirs was primarily a movement of the non-agricultural working class and, to some extent, the lower middle class in the small towns and villages of Ireland. Only about a tenth of the members seem to have been farm labourers or tenant farmers. On the other hand, practically none were drawn from the middle and upper classes.[24] The Fenians included very few Protestants, in contrast to earlier manifestations of radical Irish nationalism, despite the Fenian commitment to absolute liberty of conscience. R.V. Comerford, in his study of the Fenians, suggests that they were reacting against economic, social, and cultural change that was disrupting the patterns of village life, rather than against the landlord system as such. They seem to have provided an outlet for the frustrations of young men with few prospects in a society that was controlled by landlords, priests, and policemen.

Political republicanism and agrarian protest, which had erupted simultaneously in 1798, thus continued on their separate paths. The Fenians in the 1860s failed to ignite the discontent of the tenant farmers or to mobilize them behind the project of independence. Nonetheless, the IRB was a formidable movement, with perhaps 50,000 members in Ireland at its peak in the late 1860s. It was quite well organized, with a supreme council and a network of clandestine cells that extended over much of Ireland. It alarmed the authorities by seeking to infiltrate the British army, which recruited many of its soldiers in Ireland.[25] From 1863 to 1865 the IRB published a newspaper, the *Irish People*. It also had a substantial transatlantic wing, many of whose members were Irish-born veterans of the American Civil War. After the war ended, some of these veterans returned to Ireland and were active in the IRB there. Those who remained in North America conceived a plan to invade

Canada, hoping that this attack on the overseas empire would somehow weaken the British grip on Ireland. Although the idea appears improbable in retrospect, the movement was strong enough to mount a series of attacks across the border between the United States and Canada. At Ridgeway, near the Niagara River, they won a victory over the Canadian militia in June 1866, but they subsequently withdrew into the United States. Michael Davitt later argued that these Canadian adventures were irrelevant to Ireland and fatally damaged the prospects of the Fenian movement.[26] Ironically, they strengthened the British Empire in one way, by encouraging its North American colonies to unite as a federation in 1867.

Apart from its appeal to the Irish diaspora, Fenianism seems to have had no international connections, but it bore some resemblance to secret societies in Italy and other parts of Europe at about the same time. As a secret society and one that was alleged to have anticlerical tendencies, the IRB faced the steadfast hostility of the Catholic Church. Although the IRB oath referred to "Almighty God," some of the Fenians had unorthodox religious views or none at all. Archbishop Cullen, a political conservative and a monarchist, declared from the beginning that secret societies were incompatible with Catholicism and compared the Fenians with freemasons and communists.[27] In 1869, after he had become the first Irish cardinal, the Irish bishops formally asked Pope Pius IX to condemn the Fenian movement. Prime Minister Gladstone made a similar request, and the pope issued his condemnation in 1870.[28] However, by this time the Fenians had virtually ceased to be a serious threat.

The British authorities did not wait for an uprising to occur before they cracked down on the Fenians. The *Irish People* office was raided and closed down in 1865, after two years of publication. Regiments infiltrated by the IRB were transferred out of Ireland, and some soldiers suspected of Fenianism were discharged. Habeas corpus was suspended in Ireland for three years, beginning in 1866, and in Canada by the Canadian government for a shorter period. When the long-awaited rising finally occurred, on 5 March 1867, it was suppressed without difficulty, partly because a shipment of weapons from Fenians in the United States was delayed at sea.[29] Later in the year a failed attempt to rescue some Fenian prisoners in England led to the death of a policeman and the execution of three Fenians, who were subsequently known as the Manchester Martyrs. The executions, which contrasted with British leniency in 1848, won the Fenians great sympathy in Ireland, but the organization was no longer capable, if it ever had been, of a serious insurrection. The IRB lived on as a clandestine organization, conducted a number of acts of terrorism in Great Britain, and became involved in the movement for land reform in Ireland. It was also instrumental in

forming the Gaelic Athletic Association, which was founded in 1884 to pop-
ularize traditional Irish sports and discourage games imported from England. Although the Fenian movement failed in its original purpose, its
memory added to the lore and legend of Irish nationalism, and the dormant
IRB would resurface in 1916.

CANADIAN CONFEDERATION AND THE
PROVINCE OF QUEBEC

In Canada the political order established by the Union Act and legitimized
by the achievements of Baldwin and LaFontaine proved to be of short duration. Its breakdown came not because of the French Canadians but because
the rapidly growing western section of the province increasingly resented
the equality of representation that had been included in the Union Act for
its own protection, at a time when Canada East still had more than half the
population. The Reform or Liberal party in Canada West, led by the influential
editor George Brown, began to agitate for "representation by population." In
1854, soon after Canada West surpassed Canada East in population, Westminster amended the Union Act to remove the provision whereby a move in
that direction required a two-thirds majority in the Legislative Assembly.[30]
This important amendment was included in a measure to make the Legislative Council elected rather than appointed, and its significance was totally
overlooked in the debate at Westminster.[31] The provision eliminating the
two-thirds majority requirement was not even mentioned by the Duke of
Newcastle when he commenced the debate on second reading in the House
of Lords. Frederick Peel, who steered the bill through the House of Commons, mentioned it in a way that totally obscured its real significance.[32]

   This amendment to the Union Act, however, made it only a matter of time
before representation by population would be adopted, since the English-speaking members from Canada East would probably choose ethnic
over regional solidarity. On the other hand, "rep by pop" in a united province would be intolerable to the French Canadians, whose share of the total
population was only about one-third and falling. The prospect revived the
French Canadian fear of assimilation, which had declined somewhat during
the 1840s.

   The revival of two completely separate Canadian colonies, as in 1791, was
deemed undesirable for economic reasons; so only two alternative solutions
were politically possible. The simpler of these was a sort of federalism
whereby Canada East and Canada West would each have a local government
and parliament, while a central government, based on representation by
population, would look after their common interests. The alternative was a

scheme which the British had considered from time to time since 1837 and which had been recommended as a long-term goal by Lord Durham: a larger federation including the small colonies on the Atlantic seaboard as well as Canada.[33] Initially, this option was more popular in Britain than in Canada itself, but it gradually gained Canadian support through the efforts of the Conservative leader in Canada West, John A, Macdonald.

In 1864 Brown, Macdonald, and the French Canadian Bleu leader, George-Étienne Cartier, formed a coalition government dedicated to the second option. Thomas D'Arcy McGee, a former member of Young Ireland who had become a monarchist and was now the spokesman for Montreal's Irish community, was a member of this government and one of the most eloquent promoters of British North American federal union. (He would be assassinated, apparently by a Fenian, less than a year after it was achieved.) Meeting with delegates from the Maritime colonies at Quebec City, the coalition partners drafted the Quebec Resolutions as the basis for a federal constitution to be adopted as an act of parliament at Westminster. In Canada West, support for the resolutions was almost unanimous, since the goal of representation by population took priority over everything else. In Canada East the stage was set for a major debate over the future of French Canada. Not for the last time, French Canadians were seriously divided on the question of how best to ensure the survival and well-being of their nationality. Most would have been satisfied with the status quo, but they differed on what should replace it since it no longer seemed likely to endure.

The debate reinforced the polarization that already existed in French Canadian politics between Bleu and Rouge. Neither party could claim a monopoly on French Canadian nationalism, both were dedicated to *la survivance* after their own fashion, and both took the British connection for granted. What little support there might have been for more radical options – independence or annexation by the United States – had disappeared with the outbreak of the American Civil War. Both parties also recognized the inevitability of representation by population and agreed that the restoration of Lower Canada, with its own government and legislature, was therefore essential. (The more democratic Rouges actually agreed with the principle of "rep by pop," for which the Bleus had no enthusiasm whatsoever.) The difference between the two parties was over means, rather than ends.

Cartier, leader of the Bleus since 1856, was the heir of the LaFontaine tradition. As noted in previous chapters, he had fought with the Patriotes at Saint-Denis, been condemned to death in absentia, and helped to found the Société Saint-Jean-Baptiste after his pardon and return from exile. However, he had evolved into a moderate conservative and an anglophile, a lawyer with close ties to the business community and to the Catholic clergy, particularly the Sulpician order, who were the largest landowners on the island of Montreal. Cartier argued that the Quebec Resolutions would satisfy French Canada's needs by re-establishing the old Lower Canada with its own government and legislature, responsible for education, social services, civil law, municipal institutions, and public lands and resources. The addition of the small Maritime provinces to Canada's English-speaking population was a modest price to pay in return, since all the matters related to French Canada's distinct interests and character would fall under provincial jurisdiction. Cartier distinguished between political nationality, shared by all British North Americans, and ethnic nationality, shared by the French Canadians, claiming that federal institutions permitted both to find expression. He also emphasized the threat of invasion by the United States and suggested that the defence of British North America would be facilitated by federation.[34]

The Rouges, led by Antoine-Aimé Dorion, had not been invited to join the coalition. They were no longer as radical as in the days of Papineau, although the Catholic Church still viewed them with considerable distrust. They would have preferred the alternative scheme of a two-province federation, including only Canada East and Canada West, which had also been the original preference of George Brown and his party. Supporters of limited government and low taxes, the Rouges opposed building the Intercolonial Railway, which the Maritime provinces demanded, much as the Patriotes before 1837 had opposed lavish expenditure on public works to benefit the merchants of Montreal. They argued that the sphere of autonomy granted to the provinces by the Quebec Resolutions was too narrow and would not prevent the central government from interfering in virtually every aspect of Lower Canada's internal affairs. Reflecting their pro-American traditions, they were also less worried than Cartier was by the alleged threat from the United States.[35]

A very narrow majority of French Canada's representatives voted for the Quebec Resolutions in the Legislative Assembly: 27 out of 49 members whose ethnic origin was French and 25 out of 49 members who represented mainly French-speaking electorates.[36] This choice was endorsed, somewhat more decisively, by the electorate in the federal and provincial elections two years later. Doubts would persist, and would be encouraged by some French Canadian nationalists, as to whether the will of French Canada had been freely expressed. There is no doubt that the Catholic bishops supported the project of Confederation, with the possible exception of Bishop Bourget, who had his own differences with Cartier and the Sulpicians. The position taken by the bishops possibly reflected their suspicion of the Rouges and their anti-Americanism as much as the merits of the scheme itself.[37] Clerical pressure may have been influential in the federal and provincial elections of 1867, particularly since the secret ballot was not yet in use. A pastoral letter signed by all the bishops except Bourget and circulated before the elections proclaimed that it was henceforth the duty of all Catholics to support the new federal state. However, there is little reason to suppose that the alternative of a two-province federation was a realistic possibility. Certainly, the establishment of representation by population in an undivided Province of Canada would have been a disaster for both French Canada and the church; so the bishops probably chose the best option available.

The support of the British government and parliament was obviously essential to transform Canada into a federation. Both British parties endorsed the project, and their preference for a federation that included the Maritimes over one that did not may have been decisive. The main reason for this preference, it seems, was their growing distrust and envy of the United States and their consequent desire to create a counterweight to it in North America.[38]

Discussions of the Canadian project among British politicians gave relatively little attention to the French Canadians, who appeared to have settled down under responsible government and were no longer viewed as a threat to the stability of the empire. Fading memories of the French Revolution and the fact that France was an ally during the Crimean War may also have contributed to this more benign view.[39] Its less-positive side was that the French Canadian desire for autonomy within the empire could be underestimated, a fact that became evident at the London Conference during the winter of 1866–67.

The British political elite had never really liked the idea of federalism, which they associated with the American democracy that they despised. The governor general of Canada, Lord Monck, an Irish Protestant landlord, was of the same opinion. At the last moment Monck and the colonial secretary, Lord Carnarvon, suggested establishing a much more centralized regime than the one outlined in the Quebec Resolutions, with the province of Quebec having a status little different from that of Scotland in the United Kingdom.[40] This clandestine and totally unexpected initiative, which would subsequently, and unfairly, be blamed on John A. Macdonald, was successfully opposed by Cartier and his French Canadian colleague Hector Langevin. The British reluctantly abandoned their idea when they realized that French Canadians would never accept it. During the parliamentary debate on the British North America bill a few months later, Lord John Russell, leader of the opposition and until recently prime minister, expressed regret that the bill provided for a federal rather than a legislative union.[41] We have already encountered Lord John during the Canadian crisis of 1837 and also during the Irish famine; this was to be his last intervention in Canadian politics.

The province of Quebec nonetheless obtained, when the British North America Act became law in 1867, the sort of "home rule" that Ireland would unsuccessfully seek for half a century. After that date a mainly French Canadian government responsible to a mainly French Canadian legislature imposed taxes, administered justice, managed the natural resources of the province, and enjoyed exclusive jurisdiction over a variety of areas that included education, health, municipal institutions, public works within the province, and the vague but elastic category of "property and civil rights." The federal constitution that guaranteed these powers could not be amended by the government of Canada but only by Westminster. Although the federal government of Canada could disallow provincial acts, this power was used against Quebec only six times, the last instance being in 1910.[42]

The new regime lessened, although it never totally ended, the traditional French Canadian fears of assimilation by the English majority. It satisfied most of the demands of moderate French Canadian nationalists, thus inhibiting, for a time at least, the development of more radical forms of nationalism. It also reinforced the influence of the Catholic Church, which could decisively influence the outcome of provincial elections and to which the province promptly delegated almost complete control over education and social services. In return, the church used its considerable influence to support the legitimacy of the federal regime. The advent of Canadian federalism thus reinforced the alliance between church and state in Quebec and the moderate and conservative character of French Canadian nationalism. Ireland's experience in this regard would be very different.

THE LAND QUESTION IN IRISH POLITICS

With the formation of Canada's federation in 1867, Quebec disappeared from the agenda of British politics. Henceforth it was the responsibility of the Canadian federal government in Ottawa and of its own government in Quebec City. Except perhaps in time of war, Quebec also had little reason to be concerned with the politics or policies of the United Kingdom. Ireland and Great Britain, however, remained locked in their fatal embrace far into the twentieth century and were still not entirely disentangled from each other at the beginning of the twenty-first. After the disestablishment of the Church of Ireland in 1869, two important Irish questions remained to preoccupy British politicians: land reform and home rule. The first problem was eventually resolved, after several efforts, in 1903. The second was never resolved and thus led to the revolutionary crisis of 1916–21. The nature of that crisis, as will be shown in the next chapter, was influenced by the solution of the first question as much as by the non-solution of the second.

The two Irish problems were distinct but at times related. Some of the British hoped, and some of the Irish feared, that land reform would make home rule unnecessary, but they were wrong. The two major British parties tended to have different attitudes towards the relationship between Irish nationalism and economic reform. Conservatives regarded Ireland as an integral part of the United Kingdom and its problems as essentially economic and social, which led them to believe that nationalism could be "killed with kindness" by emphasizing social and economic reforms.[43] Liberals regarded it as a separate country, in fact if not in form, and its problems as essentially ethnic, religious, and constitutional. There was some evidence for both interpretations, but on the whole the Liberals were closer to the truth. As Nicholas Mansergh has argued, Conservatives and Marxists, sharing the same rather bleak view of human nature, both have a tendency to overestimate the importance of economics and class while they underestimate the importance of nationalism.[44]

Land reform was nonetheless an issue that had lurked beneath the surface of Irish politics for generations. Ireland was not unusual in being a country of landlords and tenants, but for historical reasons the landlord system lacked the legitimacy in Ireland that it enjoyed in most parts of Europe, including England. As Philip Bull writes, "An institution which had been so recently implanted by conquest could not, ultimately, avoid debate about its nature and function."[45] The question of land tenure was related to nationalism because everyone knew that the existing pattern of land ownership in Ireland was essentially the result of conquest and colonization. It was related to religion because landlords were still usually Protestant, and tenants, outside Ulster, usually Catholic. Neither politicians nor the Catholic clergy could evade the issue of land reform once it appeared on the agenda.

Like much else in Irish history, the virtues and defects of the landlords have been the subject of controversy between nationalist and revisionist historians.[46] Given the circumstances outlined above, as well as the traumatic experience of the famine, they would probably have been resented by most Irish tenants whatever their merits. Related to the circumstances of conquest was the fact that Ireland, unlike Quebec, had been forced to adopt English common law notions of land tenure and property rights that were alien to its own traditions.[47] English law made the property rights of the landlord absolute, in contrast to the seigneurial system that prevailed in Lower Canada until the 1850s. Rents were set by the landlord, and livestock or crops could be seized from tenants who did not pay. As a last resort, tenants could be evicted for failure to pay or for any other reason, as many were before and during the famine years. Tenants could not sell their rights of occupancy and received no payment for any improvements they might have made to the land if they left or were evicted.

After the Act of Union came into effect in 1801, the abolition of the Irish parliament removed one reason for owners of Irish land to remain in and identify with the country. Many moved to England, where there was still a parliament in which to sit, and lost interest in improving their estates, becoming passive and essentially useless absentee rentiers. Their departure and their habits of conspicuous consumption also caused a considerable outflow of wealth from Ireland to England. Some estates were leased at low rates to middlemen, who sublet them at higher rates to tenants. In some cases there were several layers of middlemen between the absentee landlord and the tenant who worked the land, a system that obviously made rents higher.[48] Legislation to limit this practice, however, was adopted in 1827, and after the famine middlemen were of little importance.[49]

The situation in Ulster was somewhat different from elsewhere. A large proportion of Ulster tenants were Protestants, the descendants of English or Scottish settlers who had been imported by the undertakers or who had migrated independently in the seventeenth century. The Scottish settlers brought with them a different pattern of landlord-tenant relations, not embodied in legislation but generally observed in practice, which was known as "Ulster custom." This gave tenants greater security of tenure and provided some compensation if the lease was transferred from one tenant to another. A bill to extend this system across the whole country was introduced at Westminster in 1835 but not adopted. Daniel O'Connell, a landlord himself, favoured this proposal and continued to advocate it until the end of his life.[50]

The famine simplified the balance of forces by eliminating some of the weaker and less-successful landlords at the same time as it drastically reduced the number of landless labourers and the number of farms that were too small to be economically viable. The result was an improvement in the economic situation of those who survived, and the decade after the famine was one of the most peaceful and prosperous in Irish history, but it left rural Ireland politically and economically polarized between landlords and tenants, with more than half of the latter farming fifteen acres or more.[51] In 1847 a deputation of the Catholic bishops of Ireland presented an address to the lord lieutenant requesting "an equitable arrangement of the relations between landlords and tenants."[52] Two years later the Encumbered Estates Act made it easier for landlords burdened by debt to sell their estates; it did nothing for the tenants but established the principle of government intervention in the Irish land question, despite the popularity of laissez-faire principles at the time. In the 1860s the Fenians ended a decade of British complacency about Ireland and helped to draw more attention to the agrarian problem, even though they were, at least originally, an urban movement more interested in national independence than in the land question itself. From 1870 until 1903 the Irish land question was almost continuously one of the major issues in British politics.

Prime Minister Gladstone's first Land Act, adopted a year after the disestablishment of the Church of Ireland, gave the force of law to the Ulster custom where it existed.[53] It also required landlords to compensate tenants for improvements and also for "disturbance" (i.e., eviction) if they were evicted for any reason other than nonpayment of rent. The question of what constituted a "fair rent" was not addressed. Designed to stabilize the landlord system rather than to replace it, the measure did not satisfy the tenants, who demanded the "three Fs": fixity of tenure, fair rents, and free sale. In effect, what they wanted was similar to the sharing of property rights that *censitaires* in Lower Canada had enjoyed under the old system of seigneurial tenure. Few Irish landlords were willing, or felt they could afford, to contemplate this option.

In 1877 the harvest was disastrous, and simultaneously agricultural prices fell; the long depression in the global economy that had begun four years earlier finally reached Ireland, and the three decades of prosperity that had followed the famine came to an end. Conditions failed to improve over the next two years, and incidents of violent protest became much more numerous, especially in a belt of counties running up the middle of Ireland from Tipperary to Leitrim.[54] In 1879 two Fenian veterans, Michael Davitt and John Devoy, launched what was called the "New Departure" in an effort to revive the Fenian movement and extend it into the rural areas. Davitt, an admirer of James Fintan Lalor's writings, believed in collective ownership of land, but most of the tenants wished to become the individual owners of the land they farmed. However, differences over the ultimate end did not matter in the short term, since the purpose of the New Departure was to demonstrate that land reform was impossible under British rule and thus to build support for Irish independence.

The successful linkage between the two causes of land reform and home rule for Ireland was largely the work of Charles Stewart Parnell, the most important Irish leader in the second half of the nineteenth century and one who almost rivalled the charismatic appeal that O'Connell had enjoyed in the first half.[55] Parnell was a graduate of Cambridge University and a Protestant landlord who owned a substantial estate in County Wicklow, just south of Dublin. Although he shared the lifestyle of the British upper class, he was fundamentally hostile to them. His mother was American, and his grandfather, an American admiral, had fought against the British in the War of 1812. The American Civil War, which took place when he was in his teens, is said to have awakened Parnell's interest in politics. He became leader of the Irish Parliamentary Party in 1880, a year after the death of its first leader, Isaac Butt.

Parnell soon became so popular that he was known as "the uncrowned king of Ireland." By steering a middle course between radical land reformers and Fenians, on the one hand, and old-fashioned home rulers, on the other, Parnell succeeded in linking the cause of home rule, previously regarded as a conservative alternative to the more radical aspirations of the Fenians, with the more popular cause of land reform, at a time when the rural tenants were being mobilized as never before. He joined with Devoy and Davitt to form the Irish Land League, which used a combination of violence and moral pressure to achieve its goals. (The word "boycott" commemorates the surname of an English land agent who was one of the targets of this campaign in 1880.) The league's goal was to end the landlord system, not to reform it. Within a year it had 200,000 members in Ireland and 200,000 in North America.[56] It was particularly active in Connacht, a province that had not previously been renowned for either political or social activism.[57] The league also gained substantial support from parish priests in the areas where it was active. Like their counterparts in Quebec, some of whom were promoting the colonization of Quebec's outlying regions as an alternative to emigration, the Irish clergy feared that those forced to emigrate might lose their faith. Land reform would keep more of them on the land, slowing the depopulation of rural Ireland, which had gone on since the famine.[58] Mystical ideas about the moral superiority of rural life were gaining ground in many parts of the world, including Ireland and Quebec, in response to industrialization. Historians disagree about how much, if at all, such ideas influenced the Land League.[59] In any event, nationalism, religion, and a social conscience reinforced one another, and all suggested support for the tenants' cause.

Prime Minister Gladstone, back in office after 1880, still hoped to reform the landlord system. His response to the Land League in 1881 was another land act that enacted the "three Fs" and established a Land Commission to adjudicate the level of rents. The commission could also make loans of up to 75 per cent of the purchase price to tenants wishing to purchase their holdings. Parnell attacked the measure as inadequate and was arrested, under the Coercion Act then in force, for his efforts to obstruct its implementation. The number of agrarian crimes, or "outrages," as the British called them, reached an all-time peak of 4,439 that year, more than in the whole decade of the 1870s.[60] In the "Kilmainham treaty" of 1882, named after the

Dublin prison where he was held, Parnell agreed to support the act and use his influence to discourage violence and illegality, in return for which he was released. By 1883 the number of outrages declined sharply, and minor improvements to the legislation followed over the next few years.

While Gladstone, and probably Parnell, still hoped to reform the landlord system, many tenants were now determined to abolish the landlords and become the owners of the land. Gladstone's government drafted a scheme to redistribute land, with compensation for the landlords, in 1886. It was dropped because many Liberal members of Parliament, committed to economical government, disliked the idea of paying public funds to compensate rich landowners. Gladstone henceforth made home rule the first priority of his Irish policy, and it was left to the Conservatives to implement the idea of land purchase and redistribution, which their leader, Lord Salisbury, had suggested as early as 1882.[61] The Conservatives combined a rigid resistance to home rule with a belief that social and economic reform could turn the Irish away from nationalism. Since most Irish landlords supported their party, particularly after Gladstone took up the cause of home rule, they demanded full payment of rents and opposed any effort to regulate them, but they had no objection to buying out landlords at the taxpayers', or the tenants', expense. In fact, many landlords, tired of the endless turmoil in Ireland, were ready for a solution along those lines.

Meanwhile the number of tenants evicted from their land had risen sharply in the 1880s, and there seemed little immediate prospect of reform. In response to these conditions, some of Parnell's followers, although not Parnell himself, in 1886 launched the "Plan of Campaign," whereby tenants paid a rent they considered fair rather than the amount set by the landlord. If the lower sum was refused, it went into a fund used to compensate the victims of eviction. This campaign won the support of two out of four Catholic archbishops, Walsh of Dublin and Logue of Armagh, but was nonetheless condemned by Pope Leo XIII in 1888.[62] The Irish bishops defied the pope and unanimously issued a statement two months later proclaiming support for the "most pressing grievances" of Irish tenants and warning of "consequences the most disastrous" if Parliament failed to address them.[63]

In 1891 Lord Salisbury's government provided some funds for the purchase of land and established a Congested Districts Board to facilitate the regrouping of small holdings in the western counties of Ireland into more viable farms, largely at the taxpayers' expense. This proved to be only the precursor of another Conservative measure twelve years later, which was based on the recommendations of a conference of landlord and tenant representatives. The Wyndham Act, as it was called, provided generous funding for the purchase of entire estates by the government and their redistribution among the tenants, with the cost to be gradually paid back over a period of many years by the new owners. This measure eventually transformed Ireland into a country of small proprietors, no less nationalistic than before but socially and economically conservative. If the Conservatives hoped thereby to reconcile Catholic Ireland to its position within the United Kingdom, they failed in the attempt, but the Wyndham Act ensured that the Irish war of independence, when it came, would be a conservative revolution culminating in the establishment of a stable democracy.

THE STRUGGLE FOR IRISH HOME RULE

Irish home rule, or the restoration of an Irish parliament without independence, proved to be unattainable, in contrast to land reform. Whether and for how long Ireland would have been satisfied with a measure providing about the same degree of autonomy as Quebec enjoyed after 1867 is a question that can never be answered conclusively. It can be said, however, that the long and unsuccessful struggle for home rule had a profound impact on both Irish nationalism and British politics.

Tom Garvin has characterized Irish electoral politics in the 1860s as a competition between the Conservatives, who were the party of the landlords, and the Liberals, who were the party of the priests.[64] The campaign for home rule, which ended the two-party system in Ireland, had somewhat ironic origins. Isaac Butt, a Protestant and Conservative barrister who had opposed O'Connell's campaign for repeal, became more sympathetic to Irish nationalism after defending a number of political prisoners in court, including the Manchester Martyrs. He formed the home rule Association in 1870. Initially, many of the members were Protestants and Conservatives who disapproved of Gladstone's reforms, particularly the disestablishment of the Church of Ireland and the Land Act of 1870.[65] In 1874 the association became a political party and won more than half the Irish ridings, mainly at the expense of the Liberals, in the first British general election conducted with a secret ballot. All the ridings it won had predominantly Catholic electorates, but the Catholic Church at this stage held aloof. Only three out of twenty-nine bishops were home rulers in 1874.[66] Archbishop Cullen was actively hostile, but clerical support for the party increased after Cullen's death and as the Liberals ceased to be a viable alternative in Irish ridings.

In the House of Commons, Butt moved that the house resolve itself into a committee of the whole to consider the parliamentary relations between Great Britain and Ireland. In his speech he indicated that he favoured "a federal arrangement" whereby an Irish parliament would deal with Irish questions while Ireland would send members to Westminster to consider questions that concerned the empire as a whole. Irish members would abstain from voting when Westminster considered exclusively English or Scottish questions. He called the Act of Union "a dark spot in the history of England" and criticized English government in Ireland for violating "every principle of the English constitution," but said that the Irish people were essentially conservative and would have no interest in separating from the United Kingdom if they were given home rule.[67] Fifty Irish members voted for Butt's motion, thirty-three opposed it, including twenty-three from Ulster, and nineteen did not vote.[68]

The home rule party's character changed radically over the next few years as a more militant faction emerged within it, led by Parnell. After Parnell became its leader in 1880, the party also won the almost unanimous support of the Catholic clergy, who were becoming increasingly nationalist and populist in the 1880s, following the death of Archbishop Cullen. Patrick O'Farrell has suggested that the decade during which Parnell led the party was the only period in which home rule really captured the imagination of the Irish people.[69]

Whether Parnell really looked forward to a complete separation of Ireland from the British Empire was never entirely clear. In a debate on the Land Bill in 1881, he said that the British administration should be driven out of Ireland "bag and baggage," the same phrase that Prime Minister Gladstone had recently used about the Ottoman Turks in the Balkans.[70] Speaking at Cork a few years later, in words that would later be engraved on his monument in Dublin, Parnell said that Ireland would settle for nothing less than the restoration of Grattan's parliament, but that "no man has the right to fix the boundary to the march of a nation. No man has the right to say to his country: 'Thus far shalt thou go and no further.'"[71] However, Parnell was less radical than most of the Fenians. He hoped that when the land question was settled, landlords like himself would "take their place as the leaders of the Irish nation," much as they had done in the days of Henry Grattan.[72] He believed that the abolition of landlordism would bring national unity to Ireland, in the same way that the abolition of slavery had brought unity to the United States. Apparently he failed to understand that the main obstacle to Irish unity in his time was the industrial complex of Belfast, rather than the moribund landlord system. John Redmond, Parnell's follower and eventual successor, was exactly right when he told the House of Commons in 1893: "There is not an Ulster question. There may be a Belfast question."[73]

Apart from linking the issues of nationalism and land reform, Parnell's other achievement was to transform a loose collection of political notables into a disciplined and organized mass party, largely funded by Irish American sympathizers. It was the first such party in British politics. Candidates had to sign a pledge that they would resign from Parliament if they were found to have violated party discipline. At a time when British members of Parliament received no salary from the state, the Irish Parliamentary Party was unique in paying stipends to its members, using funds provided by its Irish American supporters. This practice opened the possibility of a political career to persons outside the landlord and professional classes. One consequence was that by 1885 all the party's members of Parliament, apart from Parnell himself, were Catholics.

The election of 1885 was the first in which about half of Irish adult males could vote, thanks to the extension of the rural franchise by Gladstone's Reform Act. The Irish electorate increased from 222,018 persons to 737,965.[74] Parnell's party swept Ireland, leaving the Liberals with no Irish seats and the Conservatives with sixteen Ulster seats (out of a possible thirty-three) plus the member elected by graduates of Trinity College.[75] Although Parnell had abandoned his alliance with the Liberals prior to the election and had actually urged Irish voters in English and Scottish ridings to support the Conservatives so as to prevent a decisive Liberal victory, the eventual result was another Liberal government headed by Gladstone, dependent on Parnell's support, and pledged to introduce home rule. Parnell was henceforth tied to the alliance with the Liberals, since the Conservative opposition to home rule was uncompromising. This dependence on the Liberals would ultimately be his downfall.

Gladstone took office in January 1886. In February the Irish bishops formally declared their support for home rule.[76] In April Gladstone introduced his bill, which was partly based on a "rough sketch" submitted by Parnell.[77] Gladstone also examined the British North America Act before drafting his own measure, which echoed the language of the BNA Act by empowering the "Irish Legislative Body" to "make laws for the peace, order and good government of Ireland." However, Gladstone's bill would have given Ireland a status more like that of a Canadian province than of Canada itself. The Irish Legislative Body (the decision not to use the term "parliament" is significant) was explicitly excluded from legislating about militia and defence, trade, navigation, quarantine, postal service, lighthouses, coinage, weights and measures, copyrights and patents, and customs tariffs and excise, all of which were within the jurisdiction of the Canadian parliament. It was also prohibited from taking any action that would favour one religion over another.[78] In return for having a partly elected legislative body with these very limited powers, residents of Ireland would lose their right to elect members to Westminster, where decisions regarding all of the above matters would continue to be made. This was a major difference between Gladstone's bill and what Isaac Butt had suggested a dozen years earlier. Gladstone's bill also differed from Parnell's "rough sketch" in that the latter had envisaged allowing Ireland to impose its own customs tariffs and excise taxes. Under the Gladstone bill, Ireland would receive the customs revenue collected at its ports, but in return it would have to make a contribution to the expenses of foreign policy and defence.

The debate over home rule attracted considerable interest in Quebec, which remembered Daniel O'Connell's support for the French Canadians and Parnell's visit to Montreal on one of his fundraising trips to North America in 1880. The Societé Saint-Jean-Baptiste de Montréal adopted a resolution in favour of home rule and sent it to Gladstone, who replied with a letter.[79] The Legislative Assembly of Quebec unanimously voted, on the motion of two Irish Canadian members, to congratulate Gladstone for introducing the home rule bill.[80]

Speaking in defence of his bill, Gladstone scarcely mentioned federalism but noted the experience of Norway and Sweden, as well as of Austria and Hungary, sharing allegiance to the same crown but with separate parliaments. He said that Ireland could not expect to have both a parliament of its own and representation at Westminster, since in his view it was not possible to distinguish imperial questions from those that were strictly English. Also, he stated that the customs union between England and Ireland was essential.[81] Parnell, in reply, pointed out some problems with the bill, which had not yet been printed, but said that with suitable changes, it would be "cheerfully accepted" by the Irish people and their representatives.[82]

In other quarters the response was considerably less moderate. Joseph Chamberlain, who resigned from Gladstone's government over the issue, complained that Ireland was being given the same status as Canada but that it would continue to receive financial support from the United Kingdom, neither of which statements was true. He said that "separation pure and simple" would be preferable to Gladstone's bill. He went on to remark, rather ominously, that Ireland consisted of two nations, the Protestants of Ulster being one.[83] This theme was pursued a few days later by the young Conservative Randolph Churchill, who also said that Gladstone's bill was the same as repeal.[84] Churchill believed that the Conservative Party should "play the Orange card" against Gladstone and the Liberals. Subsequently he did so by going to Belfast, where in a fiery speech he proclaimed, "Ulster will fight, and Ulster will be right."[85] Churchill's visit marked the real beginning of the Ulster insurgency that would eventually lead to the partition of Ireland. Two things about this development should be emphasized: it began as a partisan Conservative movement, not a religious one, and it was directed against a bill that would have made Ireland an autonomous region within the United

Kingdom, not a sovereign state. Subsequent claims that the partitionist movement in Ulster was inspired by loyalty to the Protestant religion and to the British crown were based on falsehood.

A.V. Dicey, a Liberal and the leading academic authority on British public law, hastily published a tract entitled *England's Case against Home Rule,* which combined its author's hostility towards anything resembling federalism with invidious and bigoted comments about the Irish people and the Catholic Church. Dicey argued that Ireland was incapable of governing itself because of its class and religious divisions. Home rule would not satisfy the Irish and would inconvenience the English. Colonies populated by English settlers could safely be given autonomy within the empire, but Ireland, because it was "remote in sentiment" from England, could not. Dicey was not sure whether Ireland was a nation, or perhaps he was reluctant to admit that it was, but he was convinced that "home rule is the half-way house to Separation."[86]

Speaking again on second reading, Parnell promised that Ireland would accept the bill as "a final settlement of the question," even though he admitted that it gave Ireland much less than the restoration of Grattan's parliament. He attempted to reassure the Protestants by promising them that the Catholic Church would not control education in Ulster. He suggested that the real division in Ireland was between the poor western counties and the more prosperous eastern counties, not between north and south. Separating Ulster from Ireland would not separate the two religious groups, who were mingled in both north and south, and any attempt to exclude Protestants would deprive Ireland of "a most valuable element."[87] In the roll call later that day, the bill was defeated by a margin of thirty votes, with a number of dissident Liberals voting against it. Despite all the talk of "Ulster," more members from that province voted for the measure than against it. Only one Irish county, Antrim, failed to provide at least one vote in favour of the bill.[88] Parliament was dissolved, and in the ensuing election British voters rejected both Gladstone and home rule.

Gladstone would try again after he returned to office for the fourth and last time in 1892, but by that time Parnell was no longer the leader of the Irish Parliamentary Party, and the party itself had divided. Parnell had been intimate for some time with Katherine O'Shea, the English wife of a former Irish Party MP. The husband tolerated the arrangement, which was quite widely known in political circles, for several years, but in December 1889 he unexpectedly instituted divorce proceedings, citing his wife's relationship with Parnell. When the uncontested divorce was granted in November 1890, Gladstone indicated that the Liberals would do nothing for Ireland as long as Parnell remained leader of the party. Two weeks later the Catholic clergy also advised Parnell to resign.[89] Parnell, who neither shared nor understood the peculiar attitudes of the British about sexual immorality in high places, attempted to retain his leadership, but to no avail. The Irish Party split into a minority faction that remained loyal to Parnell and a larger group that renounced him. Parnell died in October 1891, a few months after his marriage to Katherine O'Shea.

Less than a year later Gladstone returned to office as prime minister for the fourth and last time and began to prepare a second home rule bill. This bill, introduced in 1893, was an improvement over the first, largely because Gladstone benefited from the advice of Edward Blake, the former leader of the Liberal Party of Canada.[90] Blake, a Protestant whose parents had emigrated from Ireland to Upper Canada shortly before he was born, had retired from Canadian politics and was elected as an Irish Party MP in the British general election of 1892. He was a brilliant lawyer and undoubtedly the leading authority on federal constitutions in the British Isles. Blake advised Gladstone prior to the introduction of the second home rule bill, as Parnell had advised him prior to the first.

The bill introduced in 1893 returned to Isaac Butt's idea of retaining Irish representation at Westminster, with the stipulation that Irish members would vote only on questions pertaining to the United Kingdom as a whole and not those related to the internal affairs of England. It also differed from the 1886 version in that the Irish legislature (the awkward term "Legislative Body" was abandoned) would be divided into an upper and lower house, rather than being a mixture of appointed and elected members sitting in one chamber. The financial provisions were simpler than before in that both the Irish contribution to imperial expenses and the remittance of customs revenue to Ireland were eliminated.[91] Ireland's status within the United Kingdom would thus have been almost identical with Quebec's status within the Canadian federation.

Gladstone opened the debate with a speech emphasizing that the status quo in Ireland could only be maintained by coercion, which the Conservatives seemed to favour. He noted that Ireland had once been a united nation and attributed Protestant opposition to home rule to those who had used the Orange lodges to stir up "the demon of religious animosity."[92] He also suggested that if home rule was not accepted, there would be a growing demand for Irish independence. In his speech on second reading, he accused opponents of the bill of believing that the Irish were inferior, and he suggested that granting home rule to Ireland was a logical implication of England's progress towards democratic self-government since 1832.[93]

Blake, who was participating in a Westminster debate for the first time, spoke on both first and second reading, using both occasions to oppose the idea of excluding Ulster from home rule. In his second speech he replied to an Ulster Protestant Conservative member's allegations that Quebec, under its version of home rule was corrupt and dominated by the Catholic clergy and that its educational system was inadequate. Blake suggested in reply that Quebec's anglophone Protestants had "shown their wisdom" by accepting the establishment of an autonomous province of Quebec and had been treated generously and liberally by the French Canadians ever since. He also defended Quebec's educational system and pointed out that the Protestant minority there controlled their own schools. He expressed the hope that the United Kingdom as a whole might develop into a federation similar to that of Canada, with home rule for Ireland as the first step.[94]

Unlike its predecessor, Gladstone's second home rule bill was accepted by a majority in the House of Commons. However, it was rejected in the House of Lords after only two days of debate by the overwhelming majority of 419 to 41. The Liberals remained in office for two more years, but home rule disappeared from the agenda of British politics for twenty years, until after the power of the House of Lords to veto legislation had been curtailed.

The fall of Parnell, the fragmentation of his party, and the seemingly conclusive rejection of home rule had a shattering effect on Irish political nationalism. Electoral politics seemed to have lost their relevance. Irish nationalists abandoned politics and turned to a largely non-political cultural nationalism, much as many French Canadians had done for a time after Lord Durham's report. Conor Cruise O'Brien has suggested that in the absence of the scandal that ended Parnell's career, a united Ireland would have become a dominion within the British Commonwealth, like Canada or Australia.[95] A perhaps equally plausible scenario is that if the House of Lords had accepted home rule in 1893, Ireland would have remained within the United Kingdom indefinitely as a self-governing but not fully sovereign province.

Why did Quebec achieve self-government in 1867 while Ireland was denied it in 1886 and 1893? There seem to be a number of reasons. First, Ireland had been governed since 1801 as an integral, although not fully integrated, part of the British state, and any change in its status seemed to call into question the unwritten constitution of that state and to threaten its overall stability, at a time when the extension of the franchise and the advance of democratic and radical ideas in both Great Britain and Ireland had already made the governing class uneasy. The uncertainty in British minds about whether Irish members should or should not continue to sit at Westminster after home rule was symptomatic of this concern. Blake's suggestion that all of the United Kingdom might be transformed into a federation, an idea that Gladstone had suggested during his Midlothian campaign in 1879, probably reinforced some of this anxiety.[96] In contrast, Quebec was a colony, or part of a colony, located on another continent and only tenuously attached to the United Kingdom. Constitutional experiments there did not have the same implications.

Second, Ireland's proximity to the United Kingdom, as well as the recollection that both Spain and France had sent expeditionary forces there in the past, persuaded some British people that a change in its status would have implications for British security. In this regard also, Quebec benefited from its geographical situation. Even Joseph Chamberlain, who raised the issue of national security in the debate on the second home rule bill, conceded that Ireland would have been given self-government already had it been located on another continent.

Third, most of the Protestants in northeastern Ireland were determined to resist home rule and were able to enlist support for their cause among British Conservatives. Memories of religious conflict in the seventeenth century, the bigotry stirred up by the Orange lodges, the Catholic flavour that Irish nationalism had acquired in the era of Daniel O'Connell, and the distinct economic interests of industrialized Belfast all contributed to their determination. The hatred of British Conservatives for Gladstone and their fear of becoming a permanent minority party after his extension of the franchise in 1884 led the Conservative Party to seek allies among the diehard elements in Belfast. Canada also had its Orange lodges, and the Anglophones of Quebec had not really been as supportive of Confederation as Edward Blake suggested they were. However, Quebec had no history of violent, as opposed to rhetorical, religious conflict, it did not have the pronounced pattern of uneven economic development that divided Belfast from the rest of Ireland, and its anglophone minority could have no influence on British party politics.

QUEBEC AS A CANADIAN PROVINCE, 1867–1892

With the adoption of the British North America Act in 1867, Quebec became a province in a quasi-independent Canadian federation of which it comprised about one-third of the population. In the institutions of the central government it was represented roughly in proportion to its numbers. Its own provincial institutions were predominantly staffed by French Canadians, although there were constitutional requirements guaranteeing the representation of the anglophone minority in both houses of the legislature. By convention, the provincial treasurer was almost always an anglophone, a custom that lasted until 1944. Both the Canadian and Quebec governments were officially bilingual, although in practice, in the early years, the English language was used more in Quebec City than the French language was used in Ottawa.

French Canadian nationalism after 1867 became somewhat more political than it had been in the United Province and more focused on the territory and institutions of the province of Quebec. French Canadian supporters of Confederation expected Quebec to be the primary guardian and the political expression of the French Canadian ethnic and cultural nationality, a view that was also soon adopted by their opponents. The central government and the dominion of Canada as a whole were viewed somewhat more abstractly as a partnership between the French Canadians in Quebec and the English (or at least non-French) Canadians, who predominated in all of the other provinces. The relations between the two levels of government and the degree of influence that French Canadians exercised over and within the central government were the primary indicators of how well the partnership was working. As long as it worked reasonably well, virtually all French Canadians accepted the monarchy and their tenuous connection with a remote and somewhat abstract British Empire. Their clergy and cultural elites, although perhaps not the common people, viewed that empire as much less threatening to their language, religion, and way of life than the boisterous republic to the south.

Since the Rouge party was handicapped by the disapproval of the Catholic Church, the Bleu party dominated Quebec politics for most of the three decades after Confederation. The Conservative Party, of which the Bleus were a part, enjoyed an equally lengthy, although more precarious, predominance in federal politics, thanks in large part to its support in Quebec. The same party organizations normally contested both federal and provincial elections, so that politics at the two levels were closely related. For the first five years it was even possible for the same individual to sit in both the federal House of Commons and the provincial Legislative Assembly, a practice known as the double mandate. With most of the public spending and patronage at the federal level, federal politicians tended to dominate their provincial counterparts, who usually hoped to achieve a federal appointment, judicial or otherwise, after leaving office. The federal power of disallowance, although rarely used against Quebec, and the federal appointment of the lieutenant-governor, who exercised the powers of a constitutional monarch in the provincial capital, gave the federal government some influence over Quebec's legislation. On the other hand, this federal influence was counterbalanced by the dependence of federal parties on provincial support during elections. Largely because they functioned in French, a language that few politicians outside Quebec could understand, the Quebec wings of the federal parties were largely self-governing, as long as they demonstrated the public solidarity required by a system of responsible government. In effect, the old British practice of indirect rule had been inherited by the Canadian federal government.

Particularly when the Bleus held office in Quebec and the Conservatives in Ottawa, as was usually the case, federal-provincial relations were mundane and largely concerned with public finance.[97] The transformation of the old Province of Canada into two new provinces plus a federal government made the distribution of debts and assets extremely complex and led to a three-cornered controversy that dragged on for decades. An arbitration in 1870, which displeased Quebec, and another one in the early 1890s, which Quebec liked somewhat better, attempted to resolve the problem, which was lubricated to some extent by periodic increases in federal grants to the provinces.

Since only the federal government could impose excise duties and customs tariffs, the main sources of revenue, Quebec at first depended largely on federal subsidies and such minor sources of income as liquor licences and permits to cut timber on public lands. Gradually it developed other sources of income, such as a tax on the profits of corporations, which the Judicial Committee of the Privy Council upheld in 1887. However, its financial needs were exacerbated by an ambitious program of railway building in the 1870s. The project was complete by 1879, but the province was heavily in debt, and the financial results of the railways were disappointing. Requests to the federal government for assistance were only partially successful and were soon replaced by efforts to sell the railways to one or other of the two major privately owned systems, the Canadian Pacific and the Grand Trunk. These efforts succeeded in 1882, but the proceeds did not cover what Quebec had invested in the railways, and the search for "better terms" from Ottawa continued, with mixed results.

An episode that raised political passions to a considerably higher level resulted from the existence of a Liberal government in Ottawa between 1873 and 1878. Nearing the end of its term, that government appointed a prominent Rouge, Luc Letellier, as lieutenant-governor of Quebec. About a year later Letellier dismissed the Bleu government of the province, claiming that it was implicated in a scandal connected with the construction of the railways, and appointed another Rouge, Henri Joly, as premier. Soon afterwards the Conservatives returned to office in Ottawa, and their Quebec members demanded that Letellier in turn be dismissed. The Conservative prime minister of Canada, John A. Macdonald, was reluctant to do so, since he had publicly stated on an earlier occasion that a lieutenant-governor should enjoy security of tenure for a fixed term, but he eventually bowed to the pressure from his Bleu supporters. Meanwhile both parties had sent delegations to Westminster in an effort to draw the British government into the controversy. Both sides met the colonial secretary, and the Rouges, although they lost the battle itself, enjoyed the compensation of a cordial meeting with the leader of the opposition, Mr Gladstone.

On this occasion, not for the last time, both Quebec parties claimed to be the true representatives of the province's interests and of the French Canadian nationality. The Bleus argued that Quebec's autonomy was violated when the lieutenant-governor, a federal appointee, dismissed the duly elected government of the province. The Rouges replied that Quebec's autonomy was violated when the federal government dismissed the duly appointed lieutenant-governor, the formal head of the province. There was no rational or impartial way of choosing between these allegations; what is more significant is that everyone thought Quebec's autonomy had been violated, whoever was to blame.

In the early 1880s a conservative French Canadian nationalist, T.J.J. Loranger, published a series of letters on the theory and practice of Canadian federalism, which were then collected into a book.[99] Loranger argued that English Canadians and French Canadians were two distinct nationalities with conflicting interests and that the power exercised by the federal government over the provinces, and specifically over Quebec, was a threat to the interests of the French Canadians. He also invented what was later to be called the "compact theory," according to which the federal government had been created by the provinces and derived all its authority from them, an idea borrowed from the theories of John C. Calhoun and other antebellum southern writers about the constitution of the United States. Loranger's conclusion was that no extension of federal power was valid unless the provincial governments unanimously gave their consent and also that any extension of provincial power unanimously desired by the provincial governments must be given to them.

Tensions between the two levels of government increased sharply when Honoré Mercier became premier of Quebec in January 1887. Mercier had begun as a Bleu but had left the party in 1866 because he opposed Confederation. He then became a Rouge, but he was more nationalistic, and a more devout Catholic, than most members of that party. He never seems to have accepted Confederation as other than a painful necessity. His ultimate objective, like that of his contemporary Parnell, remains somewhat obscure, but there can be little doubt that the idea of an independent Quebec attracted him emotionally, even if it did not seem to lie within the realm of practical politics during his lifetime.

Mercier agreed with Papineau's view that the French Canadians should form a single party, rather than dividing their strength between two parties. His first efforts to form such a party in the early 1870s were unsuccessful. In 1883 he became leader of the Rouges and attacked the Bleu government of Quebec for its subservience to the federal Conservative government and its inability to improve the financial situation of the province. In the Legislative

Assembly he introduced resolutions denouncing what he viewed as federal intrusions into fields reserved for the provinces, but they were defeated by the Bleu majority.[100] His opportunity came in 1885 when Macdonald's government executed Louis Riel, a French-speaking Métis who had led an insurrection on the western prairies. A number of Bleus, particularly from the *castor* faction, broke with their party over this issue, and Mercier was able to lure them into his party, which was renamed Le Parti national.

The subsequent election, which brought Mercier and his party to power, is conventionally attributed to popular indignation over the death of Riel. While such sentiment certainly existed and while Mercier did his best to keep it alive, the detailed study of the election by Robert Cox suggests that this was not the whole story.[101] (If it had been, there would have been a noticeable shift of Quebec votes away from the Bleus at the federal level in 1887, which there was not.) It seems, rather, that Mercier benefited from social change. His party appealed to a more modern kind of popular nationalism than its opponents, and it won its victory in areas where economic development was relatively advanced and traditional elites, the remnants of the old seigneurial element, were giving way to middle-class populists like Mercier himself. As it happened, these were essentially the same areas where the Patriotes had enjoyed their greatest support half a century earlier, particularly the Richelieu valley and the area south of Montreal.

Mercier was a more convinced nationalist and a more effective politician than any of his predecessors since 1867. His party was also the first that had no ties to either of the federal parties. John A. Macdonald, alarmed at the thought of "that discreditable person M. Mercier" forming a government, advised the lieutenant-governor to "do what you properly and constitutionally could to prevent such a calamity falling on Quebec."[102] However, there was no doubt that Mercier's followers had won a majority of seats in the Legislative Assembly, so Macdonald had to live with the consequences.

Mercier's first major initiative in office was to convene an intergovernmental conference on the twentieth anniversary of Confederation in order to publicize all his grievances against both the theory and the practice of Canadian federalism. The federal government refused to take part, as did the governments of British Columbia and Prince Edward Island, both headed by allies of Macdonald. Five provincial premiers, including Mercier, attended the conference and adopted twenty-two resolutions, of which eighteen called for amendments to the British North America Act. The conference itself and many of the resolutions were based on Loranger's theory that the federal state derived all of its authority from the provinces, whose governments were therefore the ultimate arbiters of its fate. This concept would increasingly become the dominant opinion in Quebec, but it was always much less popular in the other provinces.

Three measures adopted by the Quebec legislature in the following year provoked major controversy.[103] The first provided for the compulsory retirement of Quebec debentures that paid interest at 5 per cent and their replacement by new ones that paid 4 per cent. Macdonald regarded this as "simply confiscation" and lamented that few Canadians, English or French, would share his indignation, since most of the bondholders lived in the United Kingdom. He tried to persuade the British government to disallow the measure, but was told that disallowance of provincial statutes was the Canadian government's responsibility. As an alternative strategy, the Canadian representative in London, at the suggestion of the colonial secretary, organized a petition by the bondholders asking the Canadian government to disallow the act. Macdonald, however, feared the political consequences in Quebec of disallowing a measure that would save the province money. In the end Mercier backed down, amending his act to make conversion to the new debentures voluntary.

The second measure, the District Magistrates Act, established a new court with provincially appointed judges, ostensibly to relieve the burden on the Superior Court, whose judges were federally appointed. Macdonald promptly disallowed the act, although privately he blamed his own ministers from Quebec, and their endless arguments over judicial patronage, for the fact that the Quebec Superior Court was too understaffed to handle the volume of litigation in the province. In 1889 Mercier introduced a slightly amended version of the District Magistrates Act, and Macdonald disallowed it again.

The third measure, the Jesuit Estates Act, was the least objectionable to the federal government but was so bitterly resented by Canadian Protestant opinion that it caused a major political crisis. It concerned land owned by the Jesuits in Lower Canada and confiscated by the Crown after the original Jesuit order had been dissolved in 1774. The order had since been revived and wanted compensation for its property, but the secular clergy thought that any compensation should be paid to the dioceses in which the land was situated. Mercier, who had been educated at a Jesuit college, proposed a compromise between these positions which had the approval of the Vatican. A grant of $400,000 would be paid partly to the dioceses and partly to the Jesuits, while 15 per cent of it would be paid to the Protestant school commissions in an effort to placate Quebec's Protestant minority. This harmless measure caused an uproar in English-speaking Canada, largely orchestrated by the Orange lodges and some of the Protestant clergy, who demanded that the act be disallowed. Macdonald, whose government depended on

Orange support in Ontario and on ultramontane support in Quebec, was faced with a painful dilemma but adhered to his general policy of not using the power of disallowance for sectarian purposes. Eight of his Ontario MPs, led by an Irish Canadian Protestant named Dalton McCarthy, publicly repudiated the government. The act was allowed to stand, but the precarious relationship between English-speaking Canada and French-speaking Quebec was severely damaged.

Mercier's party was re-elected with an increased majority in 1890, suggesting that his nationalism and his spirited defence of Quebec's autonomy found favour with the French Canadian people. However, the following year he was dismissed by the lieutenant-governor, becoming the second and last premier of Quebec to suffer this fate. Like the earlier dismissal, this one was ostensibly at least in response to a scandal over the construction of railways. In an odd sort of poetic justice, Charles Boucher de Boucherville, the Bleu premier dismissed by Letellier in 1878, was reappointed in succession to Mercier. Mercier's party disintegrated, and the Bleus, with the advantage of incumbency, were returned in the next election.

Mercier, like Parnell, did not long survive the disgrace that had brought him down. He suffered from diabetes, a disease for which there was no treatment at that time, and died less than three years after his dismissal. In the brief time that remained to him, he devoted much of his remaining energy to the numerous French Canadian emigrants living in the United States, whose cause he had espoused throughout his political career. He spent several months in the United States in 1893, visiting the French Canadian communities and urging them to resist the American melting pot. This interest, as well as his unhappiness with Canadian federalism, unfortunately led Mercier to take up a more dubious cause: the annexation of Canada by the United States.[104] Like Papineau before him, he found that few French Canadians who wanted to preserve their language and culture were willing to jump from the Canadian frying pan into the American fire. Presumably, most of those who were willing to do so had already crossed the border on their own.

THE DEPOLITICIZATION OF NATIONALISM

The almost simultaneous disasters that ended the leadership of Parnell and Mercier seemed to close off the possibilities of the kind of political nationalism that they represented, at least for the time being. In 1895 the nationalist Archbishop Croke lamented that the Irish people were "shamefully apathetic" towards home rule.[105] Neither home rule for Ireland nor greater autonomy for Quebec seemed likely to be achieved in the near future, if at

all. With those goals apparently out of reach, nationalism became less territorially bounded and less concerned with politics and the state. More precisely, the abrupt decline in the prospects of political and territorial
nationalism directed more attention to other kinds of nationalism and
other goals that had already begun to develop for various reasons. By the
turn of the century, opposition to the political and territorial status quo had
apparently declined in both Ireland and Quebec, but nationalism had not
so much disappeared as it had turned its energies in other directions.

In his book on cultural nationalism in Ireland, John Hutchinson suggests
a broad definition of cultural nationalism and an explanation for it that
seem to fit both cases reasonably well.[106] He sees cultural nationalism as
independent of political nationalism and having a different purpose. Cultural nationalists seek to create a moral and intellectual vision of community
for an organic group defined by some cultural characteristic, rather than a
political order or a state for a group of persons sharing a particular territory.
They tend to be suspicious of, or at least indifferent to, the state and politics.
Cultural nationalism, according to Hutchinson, arises in response to a crisis
of identity and purpose within the educated intelligentsia of a society
disturbed by the impact of modernization.

Cultural nationalism was not completely new or unprecedented in the
nineteenth century, in Ireland or elsewhere, according to Hutchinson's
account. However, the form of cultural nationalism that had the greatest
impact on Ireland, based on the belief that every nation must have a distinct
language and that every distinct linguistic group is a nation, is a nineteenth-century invention. Certainly, nothing of the kind ever occurred to
Wolfe Tone, let alone to Thomas Jefferson. Furthermore, this kind of
nationalism came later to Ireland than to many other parts of Europe. Neither O'Connell nor Parnell had any interest in preserving the Irish language, although O'Connell could speak it. Neither imposed any cultural
criteria as definitions of Irishness, although the relationship of their nationalism with other causes – Catholic emancipation for O'Connell and land
reform for Parnell – tended to limit the inclusiveness of their appeals.

The growing interest in cultural issues during the 1890s was a form of
escapism, a retreat from politics. Certainly, it did nothing to advance the
cause of Irish independence. The Irish language had been declining for a
long time, and by the 1890s it was making its last stand in remote areas of
western Ireland that were largely beyond the reach of railways, urbanization,
or mass communications. Fewer than one-sixth of the population of Ireland
could speak it at all, and unilingual Irish speakers numbered only 66,140 in
1891, considerably less than 2 per cent of the population.[107] Its extinction

seemed only a matter of time until the movement to revive it at the eleventh hour began.

Although Thomas Davis had wanted to preserve the Irish language half a century earlier, the Gaelic League, founded in 1893, was the first serious movement dedicated to this objective. The league's leading personalities, Eoin MacNeill and Douglas Hyde, were English-speaking intellectuals. Most of its members belonged to the middle class and were themselves more fluent in English than in Irish. One of its principal activities, in fact, was organizing classes to teach its members the language that they were trying to restore. It also campaigned to give Irish names to streets, places, and geographical features and to include Irish in the educational curriculum at all levels. Like most Irish nationalist movements, it gained considerable support among parish priests, although the Catholic Church as an institution had never made any effort to preserve the language. It also appealed to some Protestants, including its first president, Douglas Hyde, who naively hoped that cultural nationalism could transcend the religious differences that were dividing Ireland.

Cultural nationalism of the older kind, which romanticized aspects of Ireland's traditional culture and way of life while not insisting on the use of the Irish language, continued to have its supporters, such as the great Anglo-Irish poet William Butler Yeats, who wrote in English. Both kinds of cultural nationalism sought to reduce English influences on Irish cultural life and to emphasize elements of traditional culture that predated the conquest. Cultural nationalism, in Ireland as elsewhere, also idealized the rural life and viewed most aspects of modernity with suspicion. In practice, it tended to become associated with Catholicism, even though much of the traditional culture that it extolled was pre-Christian and pagan and had always been viewed by the church with very mixed feelings. The alliance between cultural nationalism and Catholicism was natural since the church predated the conquest, resisted British influences in its own way, and had its own reservations about urbanization and modernity. An article in the *Irish Ecclesiastical Record* in 1891 asserted that most contemporary English literature was "dangerous to faith or morals," while Irish literature was pure.[108]

Cultural nationalism attracted some middle-class Protestants, such as Hyde and Yeats, outside Ulster. But it attracted very few Protestants in Ulster, where the Protestants, particularly the Presbyterians, were mainly urban and industrial and self-consciously British, and tended to view traditional and rural Ireland with disdain. Very few Ulster Protestants had any desire to learn a language that was alien to them and that their ancestors had succeeded in almost banishing from the province. Overall, and despite

Hyde's hopes, cultural nationalism, and specifically the language revival, reinforced the already serious division between the mainly urban and mainly Protestant northeastern enclave and the rest of the country.

In its formative years, and in fact, well into the twentieth century, the Gaelic League was resolutely non-political. It had no interest in home rule, which seemed to be a lost cause in any event, or in independence. Its gradual infiltration and takeover by the IRB was a much later development that severely damaged the organization and led to Hyde's resignation as president in 1915. During its years of greatest success, it was an alternative to political nationalism rather than a reinforcement of it. It also won some victories for its cause under British rule, particularly in 1908, when Irish was made a compulsory matriculation subject in the newly established National University of Ireland. However, cultural and political nationalism converged during the First World War, in the last days of the British regime. The league's program of reviving the Irish language would be pursued by the independent Irish state after 1922, with great effort but very limited success.

Quebec's cultural nationalism in the 1890s was somewhat different from the Irish version, although both versions idealized the rural life, opposed modern secular mass culture, and looked back nostalgically to a past before the arrival of the English. The French language, unlike Irish, was in no danger of disappearing, and there was no need for a movement to revive it. There was thus more emphasis on religion than on language in Quebec as the basis of national identity. Yet Quebec's kind of cultural nationalism in that decade, like its Irish counterpart, was promoted by the intelligentsia, and it also owed something to popular disillusionment and frustration with politics and to the fall of a nationalist hero, as well as to cultural insecurity and social change.

For most French Canadians who supported Confederation in 1867, the principal reason for doing so was the establishment of a semi-sovereign French and Catholic province of Quebec in the territory that had been their national homeland since the seventeenth century. As time went on, however, it became apparent that the equation between the French Canadian nationality and the province of Quebec was faulty in two respects. The population of Quebec was not entirely French Canadian, and the French population of the newly extended Canada was not located only in Quebec.

The existence of an English-speaking and largely Protestant minority in Lower Canada, comprising about one-fifth of the population, had of course been apparent long before 1867. What was perhaps less apparent, to both English-speaking and French-speaking Lower Canadians, was the political influence that minority would continue to exercise in the province of Quebec after 1867. This influence was partly the function of the minority's relative affluence and economic power and partly of the fact that the minority, being less divided by ideology than the French, could hold the balance of power between Rouges and Bleus. Its influence was both reflected in and reinforced by certain provisions of the British North America Act.

English, along with French, was an official language of the province, its legislature, and its courts, according to section 133. All Quebec statutes had to be published in English as well as in French. The province's public service also functioned in both languages, with English being extensively used in the departments concerned with economics and finance. The provincial treasurer was always an anglophone. The autonomy of the Protestant school system, which functioned entirely in English, was entrenched in section 93, which also gave the federal government the power to intervene in support of the minority's educational rights if necessary. Counties that were predominantly English-speaking according to the census of 1861 were guaranteed their existing representation in the Legislative Assembly by section 80. Members of the appointed Legislative Council had to own property in specified territorial districts, according to section 72, a provision designed to ensure that the English-speaking minority would be represented. Quebec's representatives in the Canadian Senate had to represent the same districts, according to section 23 (6). The privileges, formal and informal, enjoyed by the minority were resented by French-speaking Quebecers.[109] They made the minority a force in Quebec politics that even a nationalist such as Mercier had to take into account. Controversies over Louis Riel, the Jesuit estates, and other matters revealed how widely the opinions of English-speaking Quebecers differed from those of their French-speaking neighbours. As the historian A.I. Silver suggests, "the decades after Confederation saw an increasing frustration in Quebec, as people realized that the highly autonomous French-Catholic province they had been promised in 1867 was, in fact, far more English and Protestant than they liked."[110]

The relationship between Quebec and French Canada was made even more ambiguous by a circumstance of which people in Quebec were scarcely aware in 1867: the existence of French-speaking minorities in the other provinces and territories of Canada. These totalled about 153,000 persons in 1871, the year of the first census after Confederation, and their numbers more than doubled over the next thirty years, growing much faster than the French-speaking population of Quebec itself. Prior to 1867 the minorities had little contact with Lower Canada; this was particularly true of the Acadians in the Maritime provinces, who regarded themselves as a people entirely distinct from the French Canadians. Contact increased after 1867, however. More significantly, Quebec was made aware of the minorities by a series of controversies regarding minority rights with respect to religion, language, and culture. The abolition of tax-supported Catholic schools in New Brunswick in 1871 aroused concern in Quebec, even though most of the Catholics affected were not French. A similar initiative by Prince Edward Island six years later received much less attention. In both cases the federal government refused to intervene on behalf of the Catholics.

The execution of Louis Riel in 1885, which became a genuine *cause célèbre*, probably marked the real beginning of Quebec's interest in the French-speaking minorities.[111] Riel had lived for some time in Quebec and was considered a defender of French Canadian rights, largely because his provisional government at Fort Garry had forced an unwilling federal government to establish the bilingual province of Manitoba in 1870. His execution, the first for a political offence in almost half a century, polarized Canadian opinion between English and French and seemed to demonstrate the political power of an anti-French, anti-Catholic majority, particularly in Ontario. The controversy over the Jesuit Estates Act soon afterwards reinforced this impression.

Meanwhile, the western prairies, which French explorers had reached in the early 1700s, were being taken over by English-speaking settlers who arrived on the new transcontinental railway. By the time of Louis Riel's death, the province that he had founded, Manitoba, was overwhelmingly English-speaking and Protestant. A few years later it abolished both the tax-supported Catholic school system and the official status of the French language. There was far more concern about these events in Quebec than there had been about Catholic schools in the Maritime provinces in the 1870s. The federal government made a half-hearted effort to intervene on behalf of Manitoba's Catholic schools, but proved unable to rally its own supporters or to coerce the province into changing its policy. Nothing at all was done to preserve the status of the French language.

Quebec's growing interest in the French-speaking minorities and its inability to help them stimulated French Canadian ethnic and cultural nationalism, much as the Canada Union Act had done half a century before. Of what use was an autonomous province of Quebec, itself held captive by its anglophone minority, to protect French Canadians if increasing numbers of French Canadians lived in other parts of Canada or, for that matter, in the United States? The dismissal of Mercier and Quebec's return to the more mundane pattern of politics that had preceded Mercier also seemed to demonstrate the futility and corruption of political life in general. French Canadians came to view the state as a somewhat disreputable institution, suitable for dispensing petty patronage and repairing the roads but not for deciding about more elevated matters such as culture and education, which were better left to the control of the church.[112] Quebec had abolished its ministry of education in 1875, when ultramontane sentiment was at its height. An effort to revive it in 1897–99 was abandoned on account of clerical pressure and direct intervention by the Vatican. Few people appeared to be greatly disturbed by this outcome.

Insofar as French Canadian nationalism remained political, it was divided and weakened by uncertainty about its geographical parameters: Quebec or French Canada or, for that matter, French North America? The original French words of what is now the Canadian national anthem, composed a generation before the insipid (and totally unrelated) English lyrics, testify to this late nineteenth-century ambivalence. The words mention ancestors, the fleur-de-lys, the Cross, a history of brilliant exploits, the Catholic faith, and the protection of our firesides and our rights, but the song is called "O Canada!" not "O Quebec!"

A few persons, such as the American-born ultramontane journalist J.P. Tardivel, focused their attention exclusively on Quebec and believed that it should seek independence. Tardivel's futuristic novel *Pour la patrie*, published in 1895 and ostensibly taking place half a century later, describes how a Macdonald-like prime minister, encouraged by Satan and the freemasons, plots to destroy Quebec by transforming Canada into a legislative union after the disintegration of the British Empire. A heroic French Canadian politician from Quebec braves assorted misfortunes, including two assassination attempts and the deaths of his wife and daughter, to foil the plot, which he does with the aid of divine intervention. At the end of the book the hero has retired to a life of prayer and contemplation, while Quebec is on the road to independence.

This was the disillusioned view of a small minority, however. More typical of the times was the view that French Canadians, whose ancestors had founded Canada, should not abandon their Canadian identity. Canada began to be seen as a partnership between English and French, two nationalities mingled on the same territory, in which the French minorities outside Quebec should enjoy the same rights and the same vitality as the English-speaking minority within Quebec. While English-speaking Canadians showed a discouraging reluctance to view the country in such terms, the vision was given some plausibility by the higher birth rate of the French-speaking population, the increasing size of the French-speaking minorities outside Quebec, and the advent of a French Canadian from Quebec, Wilfrid Laurier, as prime minister of Canada in 1896.

A final reason why Quebec-centred political nationalism failed to make much headway was the belief that Quebec was safer as a province within a dominion of the British Empire than it would be as an independent and vulnerable neighbour of the United States. This view was particularly strong among the Catholic clergy, although it was by no means confined to them. Even in 1867 Quebec had worried more about the American threat than the other provinces. The rapid growth and increasing ethnic diversity of the United States, its liberal individualism, its efforts to assimilate its immigrant minorities, and its absence of tax-supported Catholic education all caused it to be viewed with suspicion as a potential threat to the survival of Catholic French Canada. It seemed safer to retain the protection afforded by the BNA Act and the British tradition of indirect rule, particularly as the interpretations of Canada's federal constitution by the Judicial Committee of the Privy Council gave occasional comfort to supporters of provincial autonomy.

CHAPTER SIX

How Ireland Became Independent and Quebec Did Not

In the early 1920s most of Ireland separated from the United Kingdom to form what for most practical purposes was a sovereign state. At the same time six northeastern counties, in four of which Protestants comprised more than half the population, were detached from the new Irish state to form a Protestant-dominated mini-state that exercised devolved powers within the United Kingdom. These dramatic events, which few would have foreseen twenty or even ten years earlier, contrast with the absence of formal political or constitutional change in Quebec during the same period of time. Having traced the parallel evolution of nationalism in two societies to the end of the nineteenth century, we must now explore why it had such radically different outcomes in the early part of the twentieth. Why did Ireland successfully pursue the path of separation from the political unit to which it belonged, while in Quebec this did not even become a serious possibility? The question is particularly interesting in that the Irish policy of British Conservative governments between 1895 and 1905 was based on a strategy of "killing nationalism with kindness," designed to prevent precisely this eventuality.

The two decades that culminated in the independence and partition of Ireland were periods of rapid cultural, social, and economic change in both Ireland and Quebec. Reforms to local government in 1898 deprived the traditional Protestant landlord elite of most of their remaining political influence in rural Ireland. The Land Purchase Act of 1903, also called the Wyndham Act, was a decisive step in transforming Ireland from a country of landlords and tenants to one of small proprietors. Its effect was reinforced by further legislation in 1907, which provided land for evicted tenants, and in 1909, which provided more generous funding for the purchase and sub-division of estates under the Wyndham Act.[1] These measures did not under-mine Irish nationalism, as some had hoped and others had feared. In fact, they probably stimulated it by making farmers, the main clientele of Irish nationalist politics, more secure and independent, while the surviving ves-tiges of Ascendancy privilege and social status lost their economic underpin-nings and began to seem irrelevant and absurd, like the privileges enjoyed by French aristocrats in 1789. However, the end of the landlord system exposed conflicts of interest between tenants who succeeded in becoming proprietors and those, including their younger sons and younger brothers, who did not, as well as between farmers and graziers. This led to the so-called ranch war between 1906 and 1909, in which cattle herds were sto-len, scattered, or occasionally killed, a form of protest that was condemned by the Catholic Church. In the last analysis, the problem was that there was not enough land in Ireland to provide everybody with a decent standard of living, despite the massive decline in population since the famine. Industri-alization, which might have provided an alternative for people unable to make a living on the land, was still virtually limited to the Belfast enclave, where Protestants monopolized the best industrial jobs.

Nevertheless, Ireland also experienced the rapid growth of a Catholic middle class and of Catholic influence in public administration, journal-ism, and the professions, although not to any noticeable degree in busi-ness.[2] The railways, the banks, and the few large industrial enterprises, such as breweries and distilleries, remained in Protestant hands. But Cath-olics comprised about half the judges and civil servants by the time inde-pendence was achieved, with most of the progress in this regard being made during the Liberal governments of 1892–95 or after the Liberals returned to office in 1905.[3] There were also increasing numbers of Catho-lic doctors and lawyers, although the number of Protestants in those pro-fessions was still disproportionate to their share of the population. The Irish Universities Act of 1908 established the National University of Ire-land, influenced but not dominated by the Catholic Church and serving mainly Catholic students, with campuses at Dublin, Cork, and Galway. (Cultural nationalists succeeded in having the Irish language included as a compulsory subject of matriculation in this university, even though the Catholic Church opposed the idea.) The growing numbers of young edu-cated Catholics, whose opportunities were still restricted to some extent by the disproportionate influence of Protestants in government, business, and the professions, found an outlet to some extent in teaching, journalism, and radical politics. Their situation was similar to that of their counterparts in Germany, Italy, or Hungary a few decades earlier and in Egypt, India, or Indochina a few decades later. Many of them turned naturally to various varieties of nationalism as solutions to their problems. The traditional predominance of Trinity College graduates among the nationalist intelligentsia finally ended in the last years of British rule.

At the same time as the society and economy of rural Ireland was transformed by land reform, Quebec was undergoing rapid urbanization and industrialization. The percentage of its population living in urban areas increased sharply from 36.1 in 1901 to 51.8 in 1921. The latter figure represented a level of urbanization that Ireland, including the six northern counties, would not achieve until forty years later and that the twenty-six-county Irish state would not achieve until fifty years later. By 1910, value added by manufacturing in Quebec was more than double the value of agricultural production. The typical French Canadian in Quebec was an urban worker, not a farmer. Although many remained on the land, the median size of a Quebec farm by 1921 was almost a hundred acres, an unimaginable figure in Ireland.[4]

French Canadians provided most of the labour force for Quebec's developing industries, but most of those industries were owned and managed by English-speaking people. French Canadian entrepreneurship, never very robust after the Conquest, suffered relative decline in the early decades of the twentieth century. Small enterprises were being swallowed up by larger ones all over North America, and the larger enterprises were not owned by French Canadians.[5] Quebec, like the rest of Canada, was also becoming increasingly dependent on foreign direct investment, particularly from the United States, to develop its manufacturing industries and its mineral resources. The consequence was a large number of branch plants that were parts of enterprises owned, based, and largely managed outside Quebec's borders. Here too, needless to say, English was the language of management. After the turn of the century, the economic policies of provincial governments in Quebec increasingly relied on foreign direct investment in industry and emphasized measures to attract it, rather than the traditional nineteenth-century emphasis on railway building and colonization to develop new agricultural land.[6]

This change in policy and the declining importance of French Canadian entrepreneurship led to a growing perception that French Canadians were "hewers of wood and drawers of water," a biblical phrase that has long fascinated the Canadian imagination, in an economy that was owned, managed, and enjoyed by people who were not French Canadian. Just as Ireland was escaping, through land reform, from its traditional situation where the property-owning class was distinguished by ethnicity and religion from those who did the physical labour, that same situation was being reinforced and exacerbated in Quebec by industrialization. Because of the ethnic and religious distinctions between classes, the political response to the situation in Quebec tended to take the form of ethnic nationalism, sometimes with a religious flavour, rather than the socialism and syndicalism that flourished in countries where there was no ethnic or religious distinction between workers and their employers. However, it was not so much the workers themselves as the middle class, and to some extent the Catholic clergy, who were attracted by this nationalism.

Quebec's French Canadian middle class in the early twentieth century were in a somewhat different situation from the Catholic middle class of Ireland since they had enjoyed access to political patronage, the professions, and post-secondary education for a much longer period, extending well back into the nineteenth century. However, they also experienced a sense of social and economic exclusion, owing to the domination of business and industry by anglophones, and a sense of alienation from big business and its values, as well as from English Canadian society. While social prestige in English-speaking Canada, including the anglophone community of Montreal, was mainly based on wealth, in French Canada it was more based on education and culture, religious piety, or the ability to trace one's ancestry back to the seventeenth-century colonization of the province.[7] A few French Canadians were wealthy enough to mix with English Canadian economic and social elites on more or less equal terms, and French Canadian judges or politicians could also mingle with their English-speaking counterparts. For the much larger number of French Canadians who were educated and ambitious but effectively barred from the highest levels of society in their own province of Quebec, to say nothing of Canada as a whole, ethnic nationalism provided an outlet for their frustrations. André Siegfried, a French social scientist who published a book about Canada in 1906 after several visits to that country, described the struggle for control between English-speaking and French-speaking Canadians as "open warfare ... the bitterness of which it is useless to seek to disguise." He went on to suggest, "The two races have no more love for each other than they had at the beginning, and it is easy to see that we are face to face with one of those deep and lasting antipathies against which all efforts of conciliators are in vain."[8]

Both Ireland and Quebec were part of the British Empire, and as such, they were affected by the growing militarism, imperialism, and Anglo-Saxon chauvinism in that empire, which was fully shared by their indigenous minorities of British ethnic origin. This development parallelled similar developments in other parts of the world, including to some extent the United States. All the major powers were becoming militarist and expansionist by the turn of the century, and doctrines of racial and cultural superiority that attempted to justify such behaviour became increasingly popular. Those of British ethnic origin who shared such sentiments tended to view not only non-Europeans but Irish Catholics and French Canadians as inferior and untrustworthy. Their contempt inevitably affected the way in which the targets of their sentiments viewed them in return.

The age of imperialism also brought external issues and problems onto the agenda of Irish and Canadian politics, producing new subjects of disagreement between peoples who already viewed one another with distrust. The British Empire fought a relatively minor war against the Boers of South Africa around the turn of the century and a far more destructive one against Germany and its allies beginning in 1914. War and preparation for war helped to stimulate nationalism and political change in both Ireland and Quebec, but the consequences in the end were far more dramatic in Ireland. Sympathy with the Boers and opposition to what was accurately viewed as an imperialist war against a small nationality fighting for self-determination were widespread in both Catholic Ireland and French-speaking Quebec. The Boer War thus played an important part in stimulating political nationalism, perhaps particularly because the Protestant minorities in both Ireland and Quebec enthusiastically supported the British cause.

During the years between the Boer War and the First World War, nationalism in both Ireland and Quebec became increasingly political, although it did not abandon its concern with cultural issues. Anti-militarism and anti-imperialism became important components of both Irish and French Canadian nationalism as the British Empire, and the world, drifted towards the larger war of 1914. In Quebec this tendency was reinforced by a major political controversy over Canada's contribution to the naval defence of the empire, which had a dramatic, although temporary, impact on electoral politics. In both Ireland and Quebec the imposition of military conscription during the First World War was a decisive event. In Ireland it stimulated the final, and successful, push for political independence. In Quebec it precipitated a serious political crisis and led to the open discussion of independence by influential politicians for the first time since the days of the Patriotes.

A final spur to the intensification of nationalism, although it is hard to say how much effect it would have had in the absence of other circumstances, was the commemoration of historic anniversaries. As noted in chapter 3, the centennial of the rising of 1798 was the occasion for a major celebration in Catholic and nationalist Ireland, although the occasion was sadly ignored by the Presbyterians in the northeast, whose ancestors had played an important part in the original events. Five years later the centennial of Robert Emmet's insurrection was also celebrated in Ireland, but on a smaller scale. Coinciding with the Boer War, these commemorations, particularly the first, were a major stimulus to the resurgence of Irish political nationalism, including the revival of the Irish Republican Brotherhood and the reunification of the Irish Parliamentary Party. Admittedly they were not without controversy among the different strands and factions of Irish nationalism, which chose to emphasize different aspects of the events being commemorated, but their overall effect on the nationalist movement was positive. They also served as a nationalist counterpoise to the celebration by unionists of the sixtieth year of Queen Victoria's reign in 1897.[9]

In Quebec, interest in the commemoration of historical persons and events also increased during this era. Celebration of French Canada's founders was stimulated by the discovery in 1877 of the grave of its first bishop, François de Montmorency Laval, who had died in 1708. Perhaps in part because of this event, the number of statues of historical figures in the public spaces of the province increased from only 3 in the 1880s to 177 by the early 1920s.[10] The 300th anniversary of the founding of Quebec City was extensively commemorated in 1908 and helped to stimulate pride in the long struggle to maintain the French language and culture in North America. Laurier's government joined in the festivities by issuing commemorative postage stamps and inviting Prince George, soon to be King George v, for a royal visit.

An anniversary two years later, however, was of much more lasting significance in the development of Quebec nationalism. It commemorated the 250th anniversary of the death of Adam Dollard des Ormeaux, a young French officer ambushed by Iroquois in the Ottawa valley, whose self-sacrifice supposedly saved the French colony on the St Lawrence from destruction. Ironically, an English-speaking Canadian editor seems to have been the first to suggest the commemoration, and there was some effort at the outset to give it a bicultural flavour.[11] However, English-speaking Canadians took little interest. The cult of Dollard became an exclusively French Canadian enterprise, largely through the efforts of Lionel Groulx, a priest and historian who after the First World War replaced Henri Bourassa as the principal intellectual leader of French Canadian nationalism.[12] Eventually the statutory holiday in May, which for English-speaking Canada was the celebration of Queen Victoria's birthday, was officially designated the Fête de Dollard in Quebec. It retained that designation until 2002, when, as described in chapter 3, the day was redesignated the Fête des Patriotes.

The imperial flavour given to the tercentenary celebrations in Quebec City, including a royal visit, reflected the influence of the governor general, Earl Grey, and was not without controversy. Bourassa was so offended by it that he decided to stay outside Canada during the celebrations.[13] The nationalist newspaper *La Verité*, edited by J.P. Tardivel, complained that the tercentenary had been turned into a British imperial spectacle.[14] British royalty as a symbol of imperialism was even more controversial in Ireland. A visit by Queen Victoria to that country during the Boer War and visits by her son and heir, Edward VII, in 1903, 1904, and 1907 were resented by many Irish nationalists, who rejoiced at the cool reception given to the royal visitors. Even the very moderate Irish Parliamentary Party formally and unanimously resolved to take no part in the celebration of the coronation of Edward VII in 1902 or that of George V in 1911.[15] If feelings were somewhat less intense in Quebec, it was probably in part because Quebec, unlike Ireland, had suffered no harm at the hands of the British for more than sixty years. Its resentment and its fear of assimilation were directed more against English-speaking Canada and the United States than against Great Britain. Many French Canadians still regarded the British connection, which the monarchy symbolized, as a defence against the more immediate threat of Americanization, something with which Irish nationalists were not concerned. However, the First World War and conscription would subsequently stimulate anti-British sentiments in Quebec, as they did with far more important consequences in Ireland.

In both Ireland and Quebec the growth of an increasingly radical nationalism was a subtext to the more mundane developments of electoral politics, where significant changes in the 1890s were followed by a period of superficial stability after the turn of the century. Conventional parties, which dominated electoral politics, and the very moderate form of nationalism to which they gave expression failed to satisfy the aspirations and concerns of increasing numbers of more radical nationalists. They faced competition from new personalities and organizations that appeared more responsive to the changing climate of opinion.

As noted in the previous chapter, the Irish Parliamentary Party, often called the Nationalist Party, had been shattered by the controversy over Parnell's resignation. For a time it was replaced by two successor parties: a faction, headed by John Redmond, that had supported Parnell until the end and a larger group, led after 1896 by the former agrarian radical John Dillon, that had urged Parnell's resignation. The issue between the factions was not Parnell, whom they both admired, but the extent to which Irish nationalism depended on an alliance with the British Liberals, who had insisted on Parnell's departure. Both factions faced internal differences of opinion over land reform, relations with the Catholic Church, and various other matters. In 1900 they reunited under the leadership of Redmond, a Catholic lawyer from Wexford who was effective in parliamentary debate but less so on the hustings. Dillon, a more natural populist politician, was his most influential lieutenant. The newly reunited party soon gained control over the United Irish League, a movement for agrarian reform founded by William S. O'Brien in 1898, which had played an important part in bringing the factions together. (O'Brien himself, however, left the party in 1903 to found a new movement.) The Nationalist Party was also supported by the Ancient Order of Hibernians, a fraternal organization founded in New York in 1836 (and still active there at the time of writing), which spread to Ireland and after 1900 became an important vehicle for the political aspirations of Ulster Catholics under the leadership of Joseph Devlin.

Backed by this impressive array of organizational forces, the Nationalist Party dominated Ireland's representation at Westminster as completely as Parnell's party had done two decades earlier, but it no longer seemed to dominate events. The party ceased to be a movement dedicated to a cause and became a political machine whose elected members spent most of their time in London and whose local organizations were devoted mainly to winning elections. It was apparently content to wait for home rule rather than trying seriously to bring it about and, after the Liberals returned to office in 1905, to support the government and help distribute the patronage that it received in return. Redmond had originally led the pro-Parnell faction, which favoured a truly independent party, but the party under his leadership after 1905 became little more than an appendage to the Liberals. Although a Catholic, he entirely lacked Parnell's hostility to the British. He was married to an English woman and after 1900 spent most of his time in London. As Geraldine Plunkett, whose family played a prominent part in the struggle for Irish independence, reminisced many years later, "It seemed incredible to some of us younger people that the loyalty to Redmond continued, but he had seemed different once."[16]

Redmond clearly lacked the zeal and personal magnetism of Parnell, but there were several other reasons why the Nationalist Party failed to arouse excitement after 1900. It did not identify itself with the cultural and linguistic nationalism represented by the Gaelic League in the way that Parnell had identified his party with the cause of land reform. Its relations with the Catholic Church were less intimate than they had been in the 1880s. It faced additional difficulties after 1903 because the success of land reform opened new conflicts between farmers and cattle ranchers, as described above, and since both groups were part of the Nationalist Party's clientele, it could not make a clear choice between them. A final difficulty was the goal of home rule itself, which was ostensibly the party's raison d'être. While the Conservatives ruled at Westminster, most Irish people thought that it was impossible, and after the Liberals returned in 1905, many thought that it was inevitable; but in both cases many questioned whether it would resolve Ireland's numerous problems. This ambivalence created an opportunity for people to propose more radical solutions.

The Liberals did not make home rule a priority as soon as they returned to office, no doubt because they remembered the damage it had done to the party's popularity in England under Gladstone. Instead, in 1907 they proposed a measure called the Irish Council Bill, which would have provided a very limited degree of administrative devolution. The measure was widely criticized in Ireland and appeared to satisfy nobody, while the Catholic Church feared that it would weaken clerical control over education; so it was abandoned by the government.

In 1912 the Liberals finally introduced a home rule bill. It differed from Gladstone's bill of 1893 in a number of details, the most important being that Ireland would have only forty-two representatives at Westminster, in contrast to the eighty provided in Gladstone's bill.[17] It was finally adopted in 1914, over the objection of the House of Lords, which had recently lost its power to veto legislation. However, implementation was delayed until after the war, and by that time other considerations had intervened, as will be shown below.

In Quebec the fall of Honoré Mercier was followed by a short period of Conservative (Bleu) government, but in 1897 the Rouges, usually known by this time as Liberals, returned to office in Quebec City for what proved to be an uninterrupted term of thirty-nine years. Thanks in part to Mercier, the party had moderated or suppressed its traditional anticlericalism, although the Catholic Church continued to view it with some misgivings. An abortive effort in 1897–99 to revive Quebec's ministry of education might have lessened, although it would not have eliminated, clerical influence in the schools. It was abandoned largely through the influence of the church. After that episode, the Quebec Liberals tended to avoid controversy or radical innovation as much as possible, so that they became increasingly difficult to distinguish from the moderate wing of the Quebec Conservatives.

Electoral politics in Quebec, unlike those in Ireland, were conducted at two levels, and electoral developments at the federal level had an important impact on French Canadian nationalism. A French Canadian from Quebec, Wilfrid Laurier, had succeeded Edward Blake as leader of the Liberal Party of Canada in 1887. Laurier had opposed Confederation as a Rouge in 1867 but had long since been reconciled to it. Although he vigorously opposed the execution of Louis Riel, he rejected the ethnic nationalism of Mercier, whose notoriety among English-speaking Canadians was an asset to Laurier's Conservative opponents. Laurier also distanced himself from the radical anticlericalism of old-style Rouges, defining himself as a Gladstonian Liberal in the English tradition, rather than a counterpart of the French and

Italian liberals condemned by the Catholic Church.[18] In 1896, following the deaths of Macdonald and Mercier, Laurier led his party to victory, becoming the first French-speaking prime minister of Canada. He favoured a compromise with the Liberal government of Manitoba, which had abolished tax-supported Catholic schools, rather than using the coercive powers that the federal government theoretically possessed on behalf of Manitoba Catholics. Most of the Catholic clergy in Quebec urged Catholics to vote against him in 1896, but the secret ballot, the novelty of a French Canadian leading a federal party, and Laurier's argument that respect for provincial autonomy would serve French Canada's interests in the long run combined to give him 49 of the 65 Quebec ridings and a majority of Quebec's popular vote, despite clerical disapproval. In the rest of Canada he won only 69 seats out of 148, but it was enough for an overall majority in the House of Commons.

Laurier's victory in 1896 was in part an expression of French Canadian nationalism, but as prime minister of Canada for the next fifteen years and leader of the Liberal Party until his death, he had to defer to the sentiments of the English-speaking majority, which was becoming increasingly chauvinistic and aggressively "British" in sentiment. He distressed many of his French Canadian supporters by agreeing to a limited Canadian participation in the Boer War, even though the British Liberal Party, which Laurier so greatly admired, was opposing the war from the opposition benches at Westminster. A few years later Laurier decided not to include constitutional guarantees for the status of the French language in the bills that created the new provinces of Saskatchewan and Alberta, although he did provoke the resignation of an important ministerial colleague (from Manitoba) by including guarantees for Catholic education. Even those guarantees had to be watered down because of agitation by the Orange lodges, which were influential in English-speaking Canada because of the massive Protestant Irish immigration during the nineteenth century. Saskatchewan was where Louis Riel had led his rebellion only twenty years earlier. In 1910 Laurier, under pressure from the British government to contribute to the naval defence of the empire, offended anti-militarist sentiment in Quebec by introducing a bill to establish a Canadian navy. This decision lost him considerable support in Quebec in the election of 1911, but his party's more serious losses in English-speaking Canada, which rejected his proposal for freer trade with the United States, would have ended his term in office in any event. Thus Laurier's moderation and tendency to compromise with his opponents, like the similar qualities of John Redmond, gave credence to the arguments of nationalists who charged that he had lost touch with the sentiments of his own people and could no longer be relied upon to represent their interests as a national community.

NEW FORMS OF NATIONALISM

One of the earliest and most influential proponents of the new wave of Irish nationalism was Arthur Griffith, a printer and the grandson of an Ulster Protestant who had converted to Catholicism. Griffith was active in the Gaelic League and other nationalist organizations in the 1890s and seems to have belonged for a time to the IRB, although neither the date when he joined it or the date when he resigned is precisely known.[19] In 1899, at the age of twenty-eight, Griffith, with his friend William Rooney, founded a weekly newspaper called the *United Irishman*. When Rooney died two years later, Griffith became the sole editor. Its name was taken from the paper that John Mitchel had edited in 1847. Griffith greatly admired Mitchel and wrote a laudatory preface to a new edition of the *Jail Journal*. In 1900 he founded a nationalist organization, Cumann na nGaedheal, perhaps in response to the election of John Redmond, whom he despised, as leader of the Nationalists. In 1903 Griffith founded a new organization with the specific purpose of arousing opposition to the visit of King Edward VII. Two years later he changed the name of his newspaper to *Sinn Fein*. (The expression, usually translated as "ourselves," had been used as a slogan by the Gaelic League.) In 1907 Cumann na nGaedheal merged with the Dungannon clubs, a nationalist organization founded by Bulmer Hobson two years earlier, to form the Sinn Fein League. Sinn Fein ran candidates for municipal office in Dublin, where it enjoyed its strongest support, but its one pre-war attempt to challenge the Nationalists in a parliamentary by-election was unsuccessful. Griffith believed, in any event, that Irish representation at Westminster was useless and that the Nationalists should refuse to occupy their seats. He was eventually overtaken by people with even more radical views, but Griffith in the first decade of the twentieth century was the most articulate spokesman for a radical alternative to the increasingly perfunctory nationalism of Redmond's party. His writings, like those of his hero Mitchel, were abrasive, opinionated, controversial, sometimes outrageous, but never dull.

Griffith's political thought is difficult to classify. He clearly disliked the British and their royal family and regarded home rule and the parliamentary Nationalists with disdain, but he does not seem to have been committed to an Irish republic until 1917, if ever. In 1904 he published his most celebrated work, *The Resurrection of Hungary*, which suggested the Austro-Hungarian dual monarchy as a model for the relationship between England and Ireland. In it he argued that the Hungarians had won virtual independence under the Habsburg crown by refusing to accept the half measure of "home rule" and by a policy that he called "passive resistance." This included a refusal to take their seats in the imperial parliament until the Austrians met their demands. He also noted that the Hungarians had retained and, according to Griffith, revived their language. Griffith recommended that Ireland follow the same strategy as Hungary had done, and he regretted that Ireland's political leaders had never been equal to the task. He ignored the fact that Hungary and Austria were about the same size, and seemed confident that the British could be made to accept an equal partnership with a country only one-tenth as large as their own in population.

Griffith was a cultural nationalist who supported the restoration of the Irish language as "a work in which every one of us should help," but he opposed making knowledge of the language a "test of patriotism."[20] He denounced the use of English as a medium of instruction in schools attended by Irish-speaking children. One of his editorials called the Liberal government "mean and dishonest" because it had not fully carried out a promise to restore funding for Irish-language education.[21] In 1908 Sinn Fein opposed any new tax to support the National University until such time as the university agreed to make the Irish language a compulsory subject.[22] Griffith criticized the rector of University College Dublin, a Jesuit, for not supporting compulsory Irish. Not long afterwards, *Sinn Fein* printed a harsh attack on the Irish Catholic bishops over the same issue, which went on to accuse the church of exerting its power for more than a hundred years to destroy the Irish language.[23]

Griffith rejected free trade, which he blamed for the famine and emigration that had reduced Ireland's population by almost half. He recommended that Ireland adopt the mercantilist and protectionist policies of Friedrich List. In one editorial he called List "the greatest of political economists" and argued that List had taught France, Germany, and the United States how to resist British industrial hegemony.[24] (He did not mention List's view that small countries such as Ireland should be absorbed by their larger neighbours.) Griffith urged Irish consumers to avoid foreign products and buy products manufactured in Ireland. He called for Irish municipal councils to take over ownership of the railways, which were owned by British investors, and warned of the danger of relying on British capital to develop Ireland's mineral resources. He believed that policies of economic nationalism would enable Ireland to support a much larger population.

Griffith's newspapers gave considerable attention to international affairs, with particular focus on anti-colonial struggles in the British Empire and any other difficulties that the British experienced. He also welcomed the Mexican and, less enthusiastically, the Chinese revolutions. In 1904 he had described France as, "with all her faults, the noblest Power in the world'"[25] but his writings became increasingly sympathetic to Germany after that country became Britain's main rival. One editorial praised the "courage and wisdom" of Kaiser Wilhelm for opposing German politicians who wanted to reduce military spending. Only a year after he denounced British direct investment in Irish mining enterprises, Griffith wrote that German capital would be welcome, provided that Irish or Irish American capital was not available.[26]

Griffith and Sinn Fein were non-sectarian and frequently anticlerical. He insisted that Irish Protestants were part of the Irish nation and would make an essential contribution to it after independence. He wrote about the unionists of Ulster more in sorrow than in anger, warning them that they were being duped by the English Conservatives and that their true interests lay with Ireland. Unfortunately, his tolerance did not extend to Ireland's very small Jewish community or to Jews in general. In fact, his anti-Semitism was repulsive even by the rather elastic standards of his time. Among other absurdities, Jews were accused in the *United Irishman* of slandering the French army (a reference to the Dreyfus case), starting the Boer War, and exploiting Irish consumers. Another editorial warned that "the Anglo-Jew news agencies" would portray Queen Victoria's visit to Ireland as a success, even if it was not.[27] Griffith's comments on persons of African descent, for whom he routinely used a word that is nowadays considered unprintable, were about on a par, morally and intellectually, with his views about the Jewish question.[28]

During the years when Griffith was editing *Sinn Fein*, the Irish Republican Brotherhood began to revive and also to increase its influence within the Gaelic Athletic Association and the Gaelic League, as well as with the Dungannon clubs.[29] It also seems to have become active in agitation against landlords and graziers in Connacht.[30] In Dublin its most important activist was Tom Clarke, an old Fenian who had served fifteen years in a British prison for his involvement in a bombing plot in the 1880s. After returning from the United States in November 1907 following a long absence from Ireland, Clarke settled in Dublin and opened a tobacco store that became a centre of revolutionary activity. In 1910 he and Sean MacDermott founded a monthly newspaper called *Irish Freedom* to publicize the IRB position. An editorial in the first issue explained that the paper stood for "the complete and total separation of Ireland from England," and the editors described themselves as "Irish separatists and republicans."[31]

Irish Freedom agreed with *Sinn Fein* on a number of questions, including contempt for the parliamentary Nationalists and suspicion of the British Liberals. It blamed the Nationalists for neglecting the northern Protestants and insisted that an effort must be made to reconcile that minority with Irish nationalism since "a national settlement from which Ulster is excluded would not be worth having."[32] On the question of the Irish language, *Irish Freedom* was just as militant as Griffith's paper. It urged the Irish people to become "language bigots" and "aggressive language propagandists." Another article asserted, "The whole thought of the Nation must go into the fight for the predominance of the Irish language in Ireland."[33] Like *Sinn Fein*, *Irish Freedom* was also sympathetic to Germany in that country's rivalry with Great Britain. Both papers were edited in Dublin, and both contained surprisingly few articles and editorials about rural and agricultural questions, considering the nature of the Irish economy at that time. Both Sinn Fein and the IRB supported the enfranchisement of women, in contrast to the Irish Parliamentary Party. Perhaps in part because of this, women would play an important part in the Irish revolution and in the electoral victory of Sinn Fein in 1918. The feminism associated with Irish nationalism also attracted some female supporters from the Protestant elite, of which Maud Gonne and Constance Gore-Booth Markievicz are the best-known examples.

In other respects there were differences between the two papers. *Irish Freedom* was totally free of the anti-Semitic and racist comments that appeared in Griffith's publications. It was apparently less interested in economic nationalism and protective tariffs. It was also somewhat more sympathetic to labour and the working class, although on one occasion it complained that labour spoke too much about its rights and not enough about its duty to stand by the Irish nation. *Sinn Fein* was generally critical of socialism and regarded politics based on class as detrimental to national unity.

Although Ireland was mainly a rural and agricultural country, the urban working class was beginning to make its appearance on the national stage in the years prior to the First World War, a phenomenon which complicated the task of nationalists and which many of them seemed to view with mixed feelings. The Irish Transport and General Workers' Union was established in 1908 by James Larkin, and five years later an attempt by Dublin employers to break this union led to a strike that involved 20,000 workers. Neither Sinn Fein nor the IRB took a very clear position on the strike, which they seemed to regard as a distraction from the national struggle, and the strikers were defeated.

The most serious attempt to combine Irish nationalism with working-class politics and socialism was that of James Connolly, who was born in Scotland to Irish emigrant parents and first went to Ireland as a teenaged soldier in the British army. After leaving the army, he edited a socialist newspaper between 1896 and 1903 and unsuccessfully tried to establish a socialist party. He then lived for seven years in the United States. On his return he became a labour organizer in Belfast and Cork and helped to organize the Irish Labour Party. Later, in Dublin, he formed the Irish Citizen Army, which was involved in the Dublin lockout and strike of 1913. He was a convinced supporter of Irish independence but had no use for middle-class nationalists who disregarded the needs and wants of ordinary Irish people. Despite Connolly's efforts, nationalism and socialism failed to form a successful combination in Ireland, partly because rural Ireland had become a country of small proprietors and partly because of sectarianism. The Protestant working class in Belfast, the industrial centre of Ireland, thought of themselves as Protestants first and workers second. Both Ulster unionism and Irish nationalism, which proved to be much stronger than socialism, developed a predominantly conservative orientation.

Another important nationalist who attracted attention in the years just before the war was Patrick Pearse. He was born to a middle-class family in Dublin, who lived on the street that is now named after him. Although of English descent on his father's side (the family name was spelled "Pierce" until 1892, when Patrick was thirteen years old), he was a very devout Catholic and a convinced cultural nationalist, active in the Gaelic League and initially more interested in the Irish language than in politics. He was politically moderate enough, or naive enough, to support the ill-fated Irish Council Bill in 1907. The following year Pearse founded St Enda's School to teach Irish language and culture and to implement his own philosophy of education, which was remarkably progressive for his time. An advertisement for the new school in *Sinn Fein* described it as "an Irish Ireland school for Catholic boys."[34] Although he seems to have been an excellent teacher, the school hovered on the brink of financial disaster, particularly after 1910, when he moved it to a rather remote location on the southern edge of Dublin. In 1911 he met Clarke and became associated with the IRB, but it did not formally accept him as a member until 1913. He seems to have been converted to a belief in the need for violent insurrection by the long delay in introducing and passing the home rule bill. Most of his memorable speeches and writings on politics date from 1913–16, the last three years of his life.

Pearse viewed Irish history as a long struggle for self-determination and independence against England. He described the nation as "not a mere agglomeration of individuals, but a living, organic thing, with a body and a soul; twofold in nature, like man, yet one." Despite this mystical language, he went on to say, "One loves the freedom of men because one loves men. There is therefore a deep humanism in every true Nationalist."[35] In one of his last articles he insisted on universal suffrage, for women as well as men, and respect for individual rights, committments that would reappear in his proclamation of the Irish Republic at Easter 1916.

Pearse believed that the Irish had always been "separatist" at heart and that leaders who were willing to settle for less than independence, such as

Grattan, O'Connell, and Redmond, had been repudiated by their followers. His heroes were Wolfe Tone, at whose grave he gave a memorable oration in 1913, Robert Emmet, James Lalor, John Mitchel, and Charles Stewart Parnell. Tone seems to have impressed him most as both a leader and a political thinker. Pearse described him as "the greatest of Irish men" and asserted, "To his teaching we owe it that there is such a thing as Irish nationalism."[36] He particularly admired Tone's repudiation of sectarianism and his support for democracy and republicanism. Although he denied that he was a socialist or a syndicalist, Pearse had a strong social conscience and a sympathy for people who had to struggle to put bread on the table. He saw ordinary people as the hope of Ireland and doubted that the wealthy classes could be counted upon to support the national cause. His combination of devout Catholicism with left-of-centre politics, unusual in his time, anticipated the Catholic left that developed in France during the 1940s.

Despite the revival of the IRB after 1907 and the growing impatience of nationalists, it was the bitter opponents of Irish nationalism who did the most to bring violence back into Irish politics. Randolph Churchill may have been speaking rhetorically in 1886 when he predicted that "Ulster will fight," but by 1914 the diehard unionists of Ulster were actually engaged in what his son, Winston Churchill, described as "a treasonable conspiracy."[37] Secret military preparations had begun even before the third home rule bill was introduced. In January 1913 the various unionist paramilitary groups coalesced into the Ulster Volunteer Force, which soon numbered about 100,000 men and was led by retired British army officers. In March 1914 sixty British officers at the Curragh camp in County Kildare resigned their commissions to avoid participating in any possible action by the government against the UVF. A month later the UVF successfully imported from Germany a shipment of 24,600 rifles and three million rounds of ammunition. Frightened by this show of force, the government began to retreat from its committment to home rule.

Nationalists, led by the Gaelic League activist and history professor Eoin MacNeill, responded to the rise of the UVF by forming the Irish Volunteers in November 1913, an initiative that was welcomed by both Sinn Fein and the IRB, although not at first by the parliamentary Nationalists. In terms of military experience and armament, the Irish Volunteers were hardly a match for the UVF. In addition to basic military training and drilling, they published a weekly newspaper, the *Irish Volunteer,* which first appeared in February 1914. John Redmond asked that his party be given two representatives on the Volunteer executive and half the seats on the larger organizing committee. MacNeill, who wanted the Volunteers to represent as broad as possible a spectrum of Irish nationalist opinion, agreed to these requests in

May 1914.[38] The number of Volunteers increased as a result to about 160,000, although the force was still inferior to its unionist counterpart in training and armaments. After the UVF imported its German weaponry, the Irish Volunteers sent a delegation to Germany in May for the same purpose but was only able to buy 1,500 rifles. This rather pathetic arsenal was landed in two consignments, the second of which, intended as a publicity stunt, arrived in broad daylight at Howth, near Dublin, on 26 August. The police fired into the crowd that had come to welcome the private yacht carrying the rifles, and three persons were killed. The British Empire was by this time at war with Germany, and Ireland was on the brink of civil war.

The development of nationalism in Quebec from the Boer War to the First World War had a much less dramatic conclusion, but in certain ways it parallelled the Irish experience. In French-speaking Quebec, as in Catholic Ireland, a succession of international and domestic events led to a growing belief that the elected representatives of the community and the party to which they belonged were unable or unwilling to represent the community's interests and to speak on its behalf.

The most important French Canadian nationalist thinker of this period was Henri Bourassa, a grandson of Louis-Joseph Papineau.[39] Bourassa was first elected to the federal parliament as a Liberal in 1896. He was initially a favourite of Laurier, who became prime minister at the same time as Bourassa entered the House of Commons, but his disenchantment with his leader began three years later when Laurier agreed to Canadian participation in the Boer War. Bourassa resigned his seat in protest, was re-elected by acclamation, and delivered a three-hour speech explaining his position on the war on 13 March 1900. This speech was the beginning of a career as nationalist writer and orator that would last for more than half a century.

Bourassa, like Laurier, sometimes claimed to be a liberal in the Gladstonian tradition. In contrast to his freethinking grandfather, he was also a very devout Catholic, with an ultramontane tendency that increased as grew older. He loved French Canada because it was Catholic, and his nationalism and his religious faith were inseparable. He tended to be conservative on social issues, including the right of women to vote, which he never accepted. This resistance to the emancipation of women was characteristic of early twentieth-century Quebec, where women did not win the right to vote until 1940, and was in significant contrast to the precocious feminism of the Irish revolution.

Bourassa was an anti-imperialist. He distinguished between England, which he admired because of its liberal tradition, and the British Empire, of which he disapproved. At a time when imperialist sentiments were rising in English-speaking Canada, he recognized that imperialism meant militarism and the domination of one people over others. He also took a deep interest in the Irish struggle for home rule and later for independence, as well as for the revival of the Irish language, appreciating the parallels between Ireland and French Canada.[40] Bourassa was never a Quebec separatist. His nationalism was oriented towards French Canada as a whole and not exclusively towards the province of Quebec, which is probably why he chose to run for the federal parliament rather than Quebec's Legislative Assembly. He believed in a Canada that was an equal partnership of what he called the two founding races, British and French; a Canada in which the English and French languages, and the Protestant and Catholic religions, could coexist from coast to coast; and a Canada that was fully autonomous vis-à-vis the United Kingdom. At the same time he believed that Quebec, where most French Canadians lived, must have more autonomy vis-à-vis the federal government.

An important aspect of Bourassa's nationalism, and a major difference between him and his famous grandfather, was his deeply rooted antipathy to the United States. American economic and cultural influence over Canada was increasing noticeably in the first decade of the twentieth century, and it already inspired some concern among English-speaking Canadians, but few if any deplored the trend with as much conviction as Bourassa. He saw American mass culture as a threat to French Canada's way of life, its language, and its religion. His criticisms of American cultural influences were often remarkably similar to those which Irish cultural nationalists directed against contemporary British culture and the British media. Bourassa was also among the first Canadians to express concern about the consequences of American direct investment. A generation earlier, these views might have made Bourassa a Conservative in Canadian politics and a Bleu in Quebec politics, but by the end of the nineteenth century the Conservative Party was increasingly influenced by imperialism and Anglo-Saxon chauvinism, to the embarrassment of its rather feeble Quebec wing. He thus became a Liberal, for the time being, but he was never really comfortable with that allegiance.

Bourassa's views about the English-French partnership in Canada and his views about the United States were interdependent. To English-speaking Canadians who shared his concerns about Americanization, he pointed out that the best way to reinforce Canada's distinct identity was to encourage and support the French language, not only in Quebec but throughout the country. He also warned them that their anti-Catholic and anti-French sentiments risked driving French Canadians into the arms of the United States, although he himself was "more British and less American than the majority of my fellow-citizens."[41] As well, Bourassa disapproved of the growing immigration from Europe and the United States to Canada, particularly to the western provinces and territories. More accurately than most of his contemporaries, he perceived that this demographic influx would make English Canada less English, more American, and in the long run more likely to view French Canada as merely a minority ethnic group rather than one of two founding peoples. Recognizing the fragility of the distinction between English-speaking Canadians and Americans, he believed that French Canada needed English Canadian nationalism as much as English Canada needed French Canadian nationalism to survive.

Bourassa's dilemma, and that of his people, was that Canada was precariously balanced between the British Empire and the United States. If English-speaking Canadians identified fully with either of those larger communities, Canada would cease to exist as a meaningful entity and French Canada's language and culture would be placed in grave danger. Yet English-speaking Canadians, with shallow roots in their own soil and little in the way of a distinctive culture, had difficulty maintaining their balance between American and British influences. Bourassa's pleas that they should try harder to do so usually fell on deaf ears.

Bourassa considered leaving the Liberal Party after his disagreement with it over the Boer War, but in the end he decided not to form a third party. Instead he and four other young men from Quebec in 1903 formed a non-partisan advocacy group, La Ligue nationaliste.[42] As a result of this venture, they came to be known as Nationalists. The other four founders were Olivar Asselin, who became president of the Societé Saint-Jean-Baptiste a few years later, Jules Fournier, Omer Héroux, and Armand Lavergne. Héroux was the son-in-law of J.P. Tardivel, the ultramontane journalist and author of *Pour la patrie*. Lavergne, ostensibly the son of Wilfrid Laurier's former law partner in Arthabaska, was widely believed to be the illegitimate son of Laurier himself, a plausible rumour that has never been either proved or disproved. He was elected to the House of Commons as a Liberal in 1904.

The Nationalist program was based on three principles: the largest possible autonomy for Canada within the British Empire, the largest possible autonomy for the provinces within Canada, and "an exclusively Canadian policy of economic and intellectual development," to be implemented by both levels of government. More specific demands in the program included opposition to any schemes for imperial federation, no participation by Canada in imperialist wars, appointment of judges by the provinces, a ban on government subsidies to private enterprise, and more patriotic education in the schools. None of these ideas was exclusively French Canadian in character, and the program avoided reference to the divisive subjects of language and religion. However, in practice the Nationalists remained an exclusively French Canadian movement, with Bourassa and Lavergne as their only representatives in the federal parliament.

The failure of the Ligue nationaliste to attract any interest in English-speaking Canada, as well as the rancorous debate over the religious clauses in the acts creating Saskatchewan and Alberta, probably contributed to decisions by Bourassa and Lavergne to abandon the federal arena and turn their attention to provincial politics in Quebec. This represented a new direction for Bourassa, who had once advised Lavergne that "we have to come to terms on a common position with sympathetic English Canadians, who are more numerous, moreover, than you believe they are."[43] Laurier offered Bourassa a position in his cabinet, but the offer was refused. Both Bourassa and Lavergne resigned from Parliament to run in the provincial general election of 1908. Both were elected under the Nationalist banner and cooperated with the Conservative opposition in the Legislative Assembly, rather than with Quebec's Liberal government. As a two-member opposition party, they emphasized such issues as support for colonization of Quebec's frontier regions and public control of hydroelectricity.

An apparently more viable alternative to Bourassa's pan-Canadian nationalism was the growth of a more exclusively Quebec-based nationalism among students, priests, and intellectuals. This movement was stimulated by discouragement and frustration over the apparent decline of Quebec's and French Canada's influence in Canada as a whole. One reason for this growing pessimism was the rapid demographic and economic growth of western Canada, which some observers erroneously predicted would soon contain more than half Canada's population and which was apparently destined to become almost entirely English-speaking. Inspired by Tardivel, this type of Quebec nationalism had a strongly religious flavour, but it also featured a renewed emphasis on the French language and the importance of protecting it. Perhaps its most important intellectual figure was the distinguished historian Father Lionel Groulx, whom we have already encountered in connection with the cult of Dollard.

Henri Bourassa served only one term in the Quebec legislature, and from 1910 onwards most of his energies were devoted to the daily newspaper *Le Devoir*, which he founded in that year and continued to edit until 1932. He was also drawn back into the federal arena by the controversy over naval defence. Laurier introduced his bill to create a Canadian navy on 12 January 1910, just two days after *Le Devoir* published its first issue. English-speaking Conservatives argued that Canada should instead make a financial contribution to the British navy, an option that Laurier had rejected when the British government proposed it in 1907. French-speaking Conservatives in Quebec rejected both options, and in 1911 they broke with their party to run a virtually separate campaign under the Nationalist banner, which was organized by Bourassa in the western half of the province and by Lavergne in the eastern half. They won twenty-one of the French-speaking ridings, mainly in northern and eastern Quebec, but failed to hold the balance of power, since the Conservatives won a decisive majority in English-speaking Canada, particularly Ontario, at the same time. The Nationalists supported the new Conservative prime minister, Robert Borden, but their influence in his government was minimal. Their leader, Frederick Monk, resigned from the government after a year in office in response to Borden's policy on the naval question.

For the first time since the days of LaFontaine, the future of the French language in Canada was becoming a source of concern, largely because of the unprecedented levels of immigration that Canada experienced under Laurier's government. The French Canadian share of Canada's population declined from 31 to 28 percent in the first decade of the century, and those French Canadians who lived outside Quebec, more than a fifth of the total number, faced increasing difficulties in retaining their language. In 1905 Bourassa argued that it was just as reasonable to make French an official language in Alberta and Saskatchewan as it was to have English as an official language in Quebec, but few English-speaking Canadians agreed with him.[44] A year later Lavergne introduced a bill in the House of Commons that would have required the use of French on currency and postage stamps, but it was not adopted.[45] Bourassa and Lavergne also drew attention to the unequal status of the two languages in the federal public service, but to no avail. The two Nationalists had more success in the Quebec Legislative Assembly, where on the second attempt, in 1910, they persuaded the provincial Liberals to support a bill requiring railway, telegraph, telephone, and shipping companies to use French as well as English for written communications with the public. A similar bill the year before had been objected to by the government as impractical and unconstitutional.[46] That such a law was even needed in a province where four-fifths of the population used French as their first language indicated the extent to which Quebec's economy was controlled by the English-speaking minority.

A congress of the French language was held at Quebec City in June 1912 and attended by most of the notables of French-speaking Canada, as well as delegations from the French-speaking minorities in the United States. Laurier put in an appearance, and Bourassa delivered a lengthy address on "the French language and the future of our race," in which he warned that a people could not retain its national character if it lost its language and proclaimed that French had the right to exist as a public language throughout Canada. He also reminded his listeners, and by implication the English-speaking Canadians, that the French language was a barrier against the Americanization of Canada.[47]

Less than a year after the congress, a new pressure group was formed in Montreal, La Ligue des droits du français. This was largely the project of a Jesuit priest, Louis-Joseph Archambault, who had earlier written a series of articles in *Le Devoir* on the situation of the French language in Montreal. The group's manifesto, written by Father Archambault, warned of a growing tendency to use English instead of French in everyday life, which it blamed on the indifference and complacency of French-speaking Quebecers. It promised measures to encourage the use of French in business and commerce and implicitly threatened to boycott business enterprises that insisted on using only English.[48]

The most serious threat to the French language, however, was in Ontario, where the provincial government in 1912 introduced Regulation 17, prohibiting the use of French as a language of instruction in the schools and confining the teaching of French as a second language to a maximum of one hour a day. More than half the French-speaking Canadians outside of Quebec lived in Ontario, where they comprised about 8 per cent of the population. Most of Ontario's French-speaking children were enrolled in the Catholic schools guaranteed by the British North America Act. To the disappointment of French Canadians, the Catholic bishops of Ontario, most of whom were of Irish ancestry, supported the government's position. Bourassa contrasted the Ontario government's efforts to suppress the French language with the British government's increasing acceptance of the Irish language.

Regulation 17 remained a major French Canadian grievance throughout the First World War, when the threat, and then the reality, of conscription brought intercultural relations in Canada to the boiling point. The controversy eventually involved the Vatican, which issued an encyclical in 1918 calling on Franco-Ontarians to obey the law but to try to bring about as favourable an interpretation of it as possible. This did not satisfy Bourassa, who in a major speech, later published as a pamphlet, argued that the French language was the guardian of the Catholic faith in French Canada and that the loss of one would place the other in peril.[49] After years of defeats and disappointments, many French Canadians were angry and disappointed with their situation by this time. However, their discontents did not have nearly as dramatic a result as those in Ireland, to which we now return.

THE IRISH WAR OF INDEPENDENCE

The outbreak of the First World War in 1914 caused the British government to postpone the implementation of home rule until the end of the war, a further concession to the unionists of Belfast. It also widened the gap between John Redmond's parliamentary party, on the one hand, and the more radical nationalists represented by Sinn Fein and the IRB, on the other. Redmond acquiesced in the postponement of home rule, immediately announced his party's support for the war effort, and urged Irishmen to enlist in the British forces. In contrast, *Sinn Fein* opposed both the postponement of home rule and the recruitment of Irish soldiers, but could not resist adding that the latter was understandable because, although Ireland's population had been cut in half under British rule, "there is more fighting material in the remnant than in England's industrial hordes."[50] The first wartime issue of *Irish Freedom* proclaimed in a banner headline that "Germany is not Ireland's Enemy." Its editorial denounced Redmond as "Judas" for his support of recruiting.[51] After enduring a few more months of such commentary, the government shut down both papers in December 1914.

The Irish Volunteers, in whose ranks both parliamentary and radical nationalists were represented, could achieve no consensus about the war. In its first comment on the subject, the *Irish Volunteer* suggested that "the rogues have fallen out" and the conflict among the European powers might provide an opportunity for Ireland, as it had done in 1798. A week later it expressed admiration for Belgium's resistance to the German invasion, suggested that neutrality for Ireland was not possible, and recommended supporting the British cause if Ireland received fair treatment. Two weeks after that, however, the paper urged its readers not to be fooled by British propaganda into thinking that Ireland had any reason to oppose Germany. "England's war is not our war, except insofar as it offers Ireland a unique opportunity to achieve freedom."[52] In September the Volunteers split. The vast majority, who supported Redmond and the war effort, broke away and became the National Volunteers. A much smaller group of less than 3,000 that favoured Irish neutrality, led by Eoin MacNeill, remained in the Irish Volunteers. This organization quickly fell under the influence of the IRB, to which a large proportion of its members already belonged.[53]

The recruitment of soldiers in Ireland was reasonably successful, and three Irish divisions were formed, one representing Ulster Protestants and the remaining two being predominantly, although not entirely, Catholic. Overall, about 206,000 men from Ireland served in the British army, of whom about 30,000 were killed.[54] The formation of a coalition government at Westminster in May 1915, which included the leader of the diehard Irish unionists, Edward Carson, caused concern that conscription might be imposed, as some Conservatives were already demanding. The Irish Parliamentary Party issued a statement opposing conscription, and Redmond warned the prime minister that "the enforcement of conscription in Ireland is an impossibility."[55] Conscription was not actually introduced in Britain until May 1916, a year after the coalition was formed. When it was brought in, Ireland was initially exempted, but the exemption was later removed.

An attempt to enlist Irish soldiers to fight against the British failed ignominiously. The source of this initiative was Sir Roger Casement, an Irish Protestant who had been active in the Gaelic League and who had been knighted for service to the Crown. Casement joined the Volunteers in November 1913, soon after his retirement from the British public service, at the suggestion of Eoin MacNeill. When the war broke out, he went to Germany by way of New York, hoping to persuade the German government to issue a pro-Irish statement and thus discourage British recruiting in Ireland. While there, he conceived the idea of forming an Irish brigade from Irish prisoners of war, which would attempt to liberate Ireland or possibly other parts of the British Empire, with German help. The German government agreed to this plan in December 1914 but did not seem to take it seriously, perhaps understandably since Casement was able to raise only 136 recruits among the Irish soldiers held in Germany.[56] The Germans also refused to commit any of their own forces to an Irish expedition. Casement became disillusioned and eventually decided that the Germans were as bad as the British, if not worse.[57]

Meanwhile planning for an insurrection within Ireland by the IRB and the Irish Volunteers had begun in 1914, or, at the latest, 1915. Although the British would mistakenly refer to the insurrectionists later on as "Sinn Fein," Arthur Griffith, who had resigned from the IRB by 1910 at the latest, had no interest in violent rebellion, and his party was not involved in any way. Joseph Plunkett, a prominent member of the IRB, prepared a "plan of campaign" estimating how much support and how much opposition to the rising could be expected in each county.[58] Plunkett also visited Germany in 1915 and met with Casement. Tom Clarke, Patrick Pearse, Joseph Plunkett, Sean MacDermott, and Eamonn Ceannt comprised the Military Council of the IRB, which decided in 1915 to launch a rising before the end of the war. The poet Thomas McDonagh was added to the council in 1916, as was James Connolly, who had been planning independently for a working-class rising by his Irish Citizen Army, which was completely separate from the Volunteers. He was persuaded to join the main effort instead.[59] By 1916 the Irish Volunteers had increased their numbers to about 15,000.[60]

The rising was scheduled for Easter of 1916. A shipment of weapons from Germany was arranged but failed to arrive; the German captain scuttled his ship when intercepted by the British. Eoin MacNeill, although still head of the Irish Volunteers, did not even know that the Military Council existed and was not informed of the planned rising until a few days before it occurred. When Pearse finally confessed to him that a rising was imminent, MacNeill tried to prevent it from taking place.[61] So did Roger Casement, who concluded that without a German expeditionary force, the rising had no chance of success. He persuaded the Germans to send him to Ireland by submarine, hoping that his capture by the British, which he knew would lead to his execution, would prevent the useless sacrifice of Irish lives.[62]

Much has been written about the Easter rising of 1916, which was arguably the most important event in Irish history since the conquest, and only the briefest outline of events can be given here.[63] It began on Easter Monday, 24 April, a day behind schedule, with the reading of a proclamation, written by Pearse and signed by all seven members of the Military Council, who described themselves as the Provisional Government of the Irish Republic. (Eoin MacNeill was asked to sign it but refused, since he disapproved of the rising.) The proclamation proclaimed the right of the Irish nation, including all Irish men and women regardless of religion, to national self-determination and independence, as well as its commitment to liberal and democratic principles. After the lapse of almost a century, it reads remarkably well, apart from a gratuitous reference to "gallant allies in Europe," which was more than the Germans deserved, given their halfhearted and useless efforts on Ireland's behalf.

The rebels seized several buildings in Dublin, including the General Post Office on Sackville Street (now O'Connell Street), which served as their headquarters. Despite some feeble preparations in the supposedly discontented hinterlands of western Ireland, the only serious engagement outside Dublin was at Ashbourne in County Meath, about twelve miles from the GPO. The British had some knowledge that a rising was being planned but seem to have been surprised by its timing. However, they had substantial forces in Ireland and were able to reinforce them with more troops from Great Britain. By the fourth day of the rising, they had at least 18,000 soldiers in Dublin alone.[64] Much of downtown Dublin was in ruins from British artillery fire. Connolly, who had served as military commander-in-chief during the rising, was seriously wounded by a sniper. The rebel headquarters had to be moved from the GPO to a shop around the corner. On Saturday, 29 April, Pearse, a humane and gentle man, ordered the surrender of all rebel forces to prevent further civilian casualties, a decision of which Clarke apparently disapproved. About 450 people, British and Irish, had died in six days of fighting. British courts martial imposed ninety death sentences by firing squad, of which fifteen were carried out within two weeks of the surrender, including all seven members of the Military Council. The victims included Pearse's younger brother Willie, whose execution caused particular outrage since he had played a fairly minor part in the rising. Roger Casement was hanged in London a few months later after a civil trial for treason.

The main questions still debated about the Easter rising are whether it was intended to be successful, how the Irish people felt about it, and whether it was justified. The three questions are in a sense related. Popular sympathy (or its absence) was obviously one factor influencing the chances of success. As for justification, the constitution of the IRB prohibited a rebellion until such time as it was supported by the Irish people. In Catholic doctrine also, some prospect of success is a necessary, although not sufficient, condition for a morally justified insurrection. The separate decisions by Casement and MacNeill to prevent the rising if possible were both motivated by the view that it was doomed to failure if it took place.

It appears that Clarke and perhaps Connolly thought originally that an insurrection would have some realistic chance of success, although by the morning of Easter Monday this must have seemed questionable even to them. (In her memoirs, Clarke's widow blamed Eoin MacNeill for the fiasco, a view that she attributed to Clarke himself.)[65] Pearse may have seen it more as a suicidal gesture of self-sacrifice, a paradoxical position since he was the only practising and devout Catholic of the three, although not the only one on the Military Council. W.B. Yeats's poem "The Rose Tree" makes the point through an imaginary dialogue between Pearse and Connolly. The tree is a metaphor for Irish nationalism, which has "withered." Connolly says that it will revive if it is watered, but Pearse replies that only "our own red blood" can bring it back to life.[66]

As for popular sentiment, most accounts agree that only a small minority of Irish nationalists in 1914, or even 1916, had any interest in a violent insurrection or, indeed, any serious commitment to a republic. Redmond's pro-British party had won five by-elections between August 1914 and April 1916 and had lost none. Most Irish men and women would probably have been content with home rule and most probably believed British promises that it would be granted after the war, which is not to say that they were necessarily correct in that assumption. Accounts of hostile demonstrations against the rebels during and after the rising are sometimes cited in support of the view that their cause was not popular. On the other hand, more careful studies suggest that there were demonstrations of sympathy as well, and that most of those who showed hostility were either affluent Protestants (a substantial minority in Dublin at that time) or the relatives of soldiers in the British army.[67] Certainly, opinion turned rapidly against the British after the executions, which were thus counterproductive from a British point of view, as such reprisals usually are.

The argument that the rising was not morally justified was presented by Father Francis Shaw in his posthumous article "The Canon of Irish History: A Challenge," which has already been cited in chapter 3. Shaw argued that the United Kingdom was a democracy in 1916, that Ireland was reasonably well governed, and that therefore an insurrection was not justified. He was particularly critical of Pearse for attempting to combine revolutionary nationalism with Catholicism, a combination that Shaw described as "unorthodox." According to Shaw, most Irish people in 1916 were not anti-British, supported the war against Germany, and had faith that independence could be achieved incrementally and peacefully, presumably following the Canadian model.

It is perhaps presumptuous for a non-Irish writer to enter a debate that still continues. However, the argument against the rising seems to depend on a number of assumptions, about Irish public opinion and the likely course of British policy after the war, that cannot be proven. One could also respond with the observation that, even if British policy was as benign as the argument suggests, "good government is no substitute for self-government." Finally, Father Shaw ignores the seditious Ulster unionist resistance to home rule, which had cast doubt on the future of that project and which had driven moderates such as Pearse to contemplate violence out of desperation, It seems likely, although not certain, that without the Easter rising or something like it, Ireland would have remained indefinitely part of the United Kingdom, with or without home rule. This does not answer the question, but if it was worth several million human lives, including those of over 900,000 British subjects, to restore the independence of Belgium, which the British alleged to be their motive for entering the war against Germany, 450 lives for the independence of Ireland seems a very low price in comparison. One might also suggest that, without the rising, Ireland would not have been exempted from conscription from 1916 to 1918 and that many Irishmen would have died on the battlefields as a result.

While the Easter rising was a failure in the short term, its effect was to consolidate and radicalize the forces of Irish nationalism. The Irish Parliamentary Party, which had unanimously declared on 9 May 1916 that "the people of Ireland have had no hesitation in condemning the rising in Dublin," was the first casualty.[68] Between February and August 1917 it lost four by-elections to radical candidates who had served time in British detention and who were running under the label of Sinn Fein, although only the last of them, W.T. Cosgrave, had been formally endorsed by that party. The first of the four winners was Count George Plunkett, the father of Joseph Plunkett, in Roscommon. He was followed by Joe McGuiness in Longford South,

Eamon de Valera in Clare, and Cosgrave in Kilkenny. Both de Valera and Cosgrave had been sentenced to death for their parts in the Easter rising, but the sentences had not been carried out. All four of the winners refused to take their seats at Westminster. In October, three months after his victory in the Clare by-election, de Valera informed Arthur Griffith that he intended to challenge him for the presidency of Sinn Fein. Griffith gracefully withdrew and agreed to nominate de Valera as his successor, while Plunkett, the only other candidate, also withdrew. Soon afterwards de Valera was acclaimed leader of the party at a convention attended by more than 1,700 delegates, representing more than a thousand Sinn Fein branches throughout the country. The convention also formally committed Sinn Fein to the Irish republic that had been proclaimed on Easter Monday 1916, despite the reluctance of Arthur Griffith.[69]

Three by-elections early in 1918, however, suggested that support for Sinn Fein might have peaked. Two of these were in Ulster, where Joseph Devlin's well-organized mass movement, the Ancient Order of Hibernians, continued to support the old parliamentary party rather than Sinn Fein. The third was to replace the deceased John Redmond in Waterford. Fortunately for Sinn Fein, the British again demonstrated their talent for defeating themselves. (They had already displayed it by the executions in 1916 and again by the fatal force-feeding of Thomas Ashe, a republican prisoner on hunger strike at Dublin's Mountjoy prison, in September 1917.) In April 1918, within weeks of Redmond's death, the British government, now predominantly Conservative although headed by the Liberal leader David Lloyd George, introduced a Military Service Bill, which authorized the extension of conscription to Ireland. Although it was accompanied by yet another promise of home rule after the war, this measure caused universal outrage in Catholic Ireland.

The renewed threat of conscription finally ended the uneasy alliance that Pitt, Peel, and Gladstone had constructed between the British regime and the Catholic bishops of Ireland. Up to this point most bishops had opposed "separatism" and Sinn Fein, relying on the British promise of home rule. They had opposed the Easter rising, although, as in 1798, a few priests had supported the rebels on that occasion. (The bishop of Limerick refused to discipline republican priests when asked to do so by the British army commander who put down the rising, General Maxwell.)[70] However, the threat of conscription in 1918 created a consensus against British rule that forged an alliance between Sinn Fein and the church. The bishops condemned conscription and proclaimed that Catholics had a right to resist it.

The end of the war in November 1918 was immediately followed by a general election campaign, the first in eight years. Lloyd George sealed the fate of the Irish Parliamentary Party by stating that home rule was not immediately feasible, presumably a reference to the situation in Ulster. It was the first British election with nearly universal suffrage, including votes for women over the age of thirty. As in 1885, the enlargement of the franchise contributed to rise of a new party in Ireland and the eclipse of an old one. Sinn Fein won every Irish seat outside Ulster except for Waterford city (held by Redmond's son), the largely Protestant Dublin suburb of Rathmines, and the seat representing graduates of Trinity College. Many of the seventy-two Sinn Fein members were elected by acclamation. In the ridings where there was a contest, Sinn Fein won 46.9 per cent of the vote, the old parliamentary party 21.7 per cent, and the unionists, mainly concentrated in Ulster, 28.5 per cent.[71]

The Sinn Fein members were pledged to work for an independent Irish republic, to accept nothing less than "complete separation from England," and to abstain from attending "the English Parliament."[72] Their refusal to take their seats effectively ended southern Ireland's representation at Westminster 117 years after the Act of Union. The minority of successful Sinn Fein candidates who were not in jail or otherwise unavailable constituted themselves into an Irish parliament, Dáil Éireann, which met at the Mansion House, the official residence of Dublin's mayor, in January 1919. They issued a declaration of independence – distinctly inferior in literary quality to Pearse's proclamation – and elected Eamon de Valera president of the republic. The first meeting was conducted entirely in Irish, but subsequent meetings were bilingual. There were eight further meetings between April and October 1919 and then none until June 1920.

Guerilla warfare against the British began on 21 January 1919; the fact that the first incident was on the same day that the Dáil met for the first time appears to be a coincidence. British efforts to suppress the Irish Volunteers, particularly in Munster, led to a spontaneous and apparently unexpected outbreak of violence. British reprisals could not suppress it and in fact made it worse. This was a classic situation for insurgency: politically weak central government, rugged terrain, and a movement of disaffected young men whose knowledge of the rural society and population far exceeded that of the government.[73]

The guerrilla fighters, usually known after January 1919 as the Irish Republican Army, fought under the brilliant leadership of Michael Collins, a twenty-eight-year-old former postal clerk who had played a modest part in the Easter rising. In contrast to most Irish nationalist leaders, Collins was what in Quebec would be called *pure laine*. His ancestry was 100 per cent Celtic Irish. Although he had no formal military training, he proved to be one of the great military leaders of the twentieth century, the inventor of modern guerrilla warfare. The main targets of IRA attacks were the barracks and personnel of the Irish constabulary, which gradually ceased to be an effective presence outside the major cities. The British were reluctant to use their regular army in a conflict that they did not recognize as a war; instead they formed an irregular force of war veterans known as the Black and Tans, whose atrocities against civilians and their property did much to discredit the British cause.

The Irish war of independence, as it came to be called, was more a series of assassinations and small-scale ambushes than a war in the classic sense.[74] The largest "battle," at Cross Barry, County Cork, on 19 March 1921, involved between sixteen and thirty deaths, of whom only six were IRA Most of the fighting, if such it could be called, was in the province of Munster, the southwestern part of the country. However, the bloodiest single day of the war was in Dublin on 21 November 1920, when the IRA assassinated fourteen British officers and the British retaliated by killing twelve civilians at a Gaelic football match in Croke Park. This episode was known as "Bloody Sunday" until that sombre title was claimed by another British atrocity in Ireland, more than half a century later. Overall, the war of independence cost about fourteen hundred lives, British and Irish, or fewer than two lives for every day that it lasted.

During the war of independence the British regime gradually disintegrated in most of Ireland, particularly in Munster, where the IRA was strongest.[75] A new unofficial Irish state, with its own police, courts, and local government, gradually emerged while the war was still in progress. It and the IRA were largely independent of the Dáil, which met only intermittently. Sinn Fein had even less influence. Its leader, de Valera, spent most of the war of independence in the United States, which was his native country, raising money and trying to win American support for Ireland's independence.

While the war continued in the south, Ireland was partitioned, a possibility that had been discussed at Westminster as early as 1912.[76] Edward Carson, the Dublin lawyer who led the unionist resistance to home rule, hoped to keep all of Ireland within the United Kingdom. As this became increasingly unlikely, the idea of partition emerged as a second-best solution, particularly appealing to Presbyterians, 96 per cent of whom lived in Ulster, and to Belfast business interests. Various proposals for partition were discussed, sometimes involving all nine counties of Ulster, sometimes the six that had the smallest proportions of Catholics, and sometimes only the four that had Protestant majorities. A four-county partition, but excluding the mainly Catholic city of Derry from mainly Protestant County Londonderry, would have been the fairest solution, if there had to be partition at all. However, Ulster's unionists eventually received six counties, retaining Fermanagh and

Tyrone, where Catholics slightly outnumbered Protestants, but writing off Donegal, Cavan, and Monaghan, where Protestants were only about a fifth of the population. This solution gave the unionists the largest possible area in which the overall Protestant minority would not be precarious. Neither the Catholic Church nor the Church of Ireland liked the idea of partition, which would leave 430,000 Catholics in the partitioned area and 250,000 Anglicans in home rule Ireland.[77] John Redmond and his party had reluctantly agreed to it in 1916 as part of the price for home rule.

The tragedy of partition was a consequence of the timing of Irish independence. Had independence been achieved, with French help, in 1798, there would have been no partition of Ireland. On the other hand, if independence had been delayed until the end of the twentieth century, there would probably have been no partition either. With independence coming when it did, partition was probably inevitable. Its roots lay in the association that O'Connell had created between Catholicism and Irish nationalism, the fusion of Ulster Anglicans and Presbyterians into a conservative Protestant unionist bloc through the efforts of Henry Cooke, the mobilization of Ulster Protestants against Gladstone by the British Conservatives in the 1880s, and the uneven development that created the Belfast industrial complex in a rural and agricultural country.

In 1920 Westminster adopted the Government of Ireland Act, which established two home rule parliaments, one for the six counties and the other for the rest of the country. This was an ironic outcome for Ulster unionists, who had not originally wanted to have a local parliament at all. Elections were held for both parliaments in May 1921. Sinn Fein won every seat in the southern parliament by acclamation, apart from four seats representing Trinity College. This group of members became the second Dáil, replacing the one elected in 1918. Unionists won a comfortable majority in the six-county parliament. Having secured their northern bastion, the British were ready to cut their losses in the south. The Irish had also had enough of the war, in which a decisive victory still evaded them. A series of peace initiatives took place, and a truce finally went into effect in June 1921.

In July of that year the British offered a compromise between home rule and independence, whereby Ireland would assume a share of the British national debt and be denied the power to impose tariffs against British goods. De Valera rejected this offer, but talks resumed in London in September. As de Valera chose not to take part, the Irish delegation was headed by Griffith, now minister for foreign affairs, and Collins, who was minister for finance. The British still refused to accept an Irish republic. They also wanted to limit the fiscal autonomy of the Irish state, to prevent it from having a navy, and to retain the right to use several ports in southern Ireland for their own navy.

The precise boundaries and status of "Ulster," as well as its institutional links, if any, with the Irish state provided additional issues to complicate the negotiations. However, agreement was eventually reached whereby Ireland would retain the Crown but would have complete fiscal autonomy, including tariffs, and the same "dominion status" as Canada. Britain would retain use of the ports, but Ireland could have its own navy, provided it included no submarines. The six-county partitionist state would remain, but its boundary might be "adjusted" later on by a commission representing both sides, with an impartial chairman. The Anglo-Irish treaty embodying these compromises was signed on 6 December 1921, but still had to be approved by both the British parliament and the Dáil.[78] When it was brought back to Dublin, President de Valera refused to accept it, as did the minister of defence, Cathal Brugha, and the minister of home affairs, Austin Stack.[79] All three of these men had fought in 1916 and the latter two were hardline, intransigeant republicans, but de Valera's opposition was more unexpected.

The debate on the treaty in the Dáil is of unusual interest, not only for the insights it provides into Irish nationalism but because of the generally high quality of the speeches on both sides. The issue bitterly divided the government, the Dáil, and the country, laying the foundation for a brief but tragic civil war and, subsequently, for the two-party system that still exists in Ireland. In Tim Pat Coogan's words, "The big battalions – the Church, business, the bigger farmers, the press and most of the senior army officers – were on the side of the Treaty. However, the power of the antis was not negligible."[80] The truth of the last statement was demonstrated when the Dáil accepted the treaty by the narrow margin of 64 to 57.

The chief objection of the treaty's opponents was the abandonment of the republic in favour of dominion status and the oath of allegiance to the British crown that would be required as a result of this concession. For many members, this was a moral issue on which no compromise was possible; they had sworn a sacred oath to the republic for which other people had given their lives in 1916, and to violate it was incompatible with their religious convictions and their sense of honour. The point was made most eloquently by Kathleen Daly Clarke, the widow of Tom Clarke, and by Margaret Pearse, the mother of Patrick and Willie Pearse. Mrs Clarke described the treaty as "a surrender of all our national ideals" and added, "I took an oath to the Irish republic, solemnly, reverently, meaning every word. I will never go back on that."[81] Mrs Pearse, who described her eldest son as "a follower and a disciple" of Tom Clarke, said that Patrick Pearse would never have accepted the treaty, which she described as "a Home Rule bill" rather than independence. In her opinion it would be perjury to break the oath she had taken to Dáil Éireann.[82]

The monarchy and the oath were also unacceptable to de Valera, who had earlier proposed a formula for Ireland to be a republic within the Commonwealth, virtually identical to the formula that the British would accept in the case of India a generation later. He referred to this formula as "external association." De Valera could accept the king as head of the Commonwealth but not as head of state, which was essentially the position that the Dáil Éireann had unanimously accepted only eleven days before the signing of the treaty.[83] He predicted that the treaty would bring neither harmony within Ireland nor friendly relations between Ireland and Britain, which could only be based on equality between the two countries. Describing the treaty as "the most ignoble document that could be signed," he asserted, "The Irish people would not want me to save them materially at the expense of their national honour."[84] Austin Stack rejected the comparison between Ireland and Canada as dominions. Canada, he said, was an offshoot of Britain and naturally felt affection for that country, but the Irish were a distinct nationality and did not.[85] Cathal Brugha's speech was chiefly notable for his personal attack on Michael Collins, whose popularity in the army he resented.[86]

Arthur Griffith, who had favoured a dual monarchy at the beginning of his political career and who had not taken part in the Easter rising, seemed to have no difficulty accepting the treaty. He described the difference between republic and dominion as a "quibble of words" that was not worth "one young Irishman's life" and said the oath of allegiance was meaningless since the king would only be the symbol of the Irish state. He insisted at some length that the treaty was compatible with "the ideals of Thomas Davis," but he did not mention his other hero, John Mitchel. In what was perhaps the decisive argument, he asserted, "We have done the best we could for Ireland."[87]

Collins, "the man who won the war," as Griffith described him, had surprised many of his admirers by accepting the treaty. He had privately opposed accepting the oath of allegiance only three days before signing the treaty.[88] His decision to support the treaty was obviously based more on military necessity than real enthusiasm. Having outlined the military situation in secret session, he was content to remind the public session of the Dáil, "We had not beaten the enemy out of our country by force of arms." Referring to the treaty, he said, "In my opinion it gives us freedom, not the ultimate freedom that all nations desire and develop to, but the freedom to achieve it."[89] He pointed out that Canada had evolved towards virtual independence since 1867, whatever its formal constitution might say. The main merit of the treaty, according to Collins, was that it would remove the British forces from most of Ireland. Ireland would then be able to work to restore its economic and cultural independence.

William T. Cosgrave, the minister for local government, also defended the treaty by emphasizing Canada's de facto independence. He pointed out that Sinn Fein had not originally been committed to a republican form of government. Cosgrave also suggested that dominion status might make it easier to persuade northern unionists, whom he described as "great citizens of this country even though they differ from us," to join in a united Ireland.[90] He said he would prefer a dominion of Ireland that was united to a republican Ireland that excluded six counties.

How are we to interpret this debate and, by implication, the civil war and the party system that both grew out of it? To begin with, it should be emphasized that it was not about partition. Although some speakers on both sides mentioned partition, it was not a dominant theme in the debate, probably because both sides had accepted it as an unpleasant, although possibly temporary, necessity. The central issue was clearly the contrast between dominion status and a republic. Most recent commentators on the issue seem to agree with Griffith that this was a "quibble of words" and to dismiss de Valera's arguments as either frivolous or hypocritical. But this is hindsight. No one could have known for sure at the time that the treaty would bring what Collins called "the freedom to achieve it." The view of some anti-treaty speakers that Canada's virtual independence under the Crown was only possible because of its geographical situation was equally credible, if not more so. Furthermore, if the difference between a dominion and a republic was trivial, why did the British insist on it, even to the point of threatening to renew the Anglo-Irish war if the treaty was rejected? The Irish civil war was certainly a tragedy, but the British, not the republicans, should be blamed for it. Certainly, de Valera should not be blamed, since republicans such as Brugha and Stack, as well as many of the IRA commanders in the field, would have rejected the treaty even if de Valera had supported it. The British could have prevented the civil war by agreeing in 1921 to what they would accept in the case of India a generation later. Having provoked a dangerous polarization in Ireland by refusing to concede more than the status of a British dominion, they then made bloodshed inevitable in 1922 by discouraging Collins's efforts to arrive at a compromise with de Valera and the republicans.[91] Finally, they rejected Collins's draft of a constitution for the Irish Free State on the grounds that it was incompatible with the treaty, a rejection that "guaranteed that Civil War would be the inevitable result for Ireland."[92] The blood that was shed in the civil war, as in the earlier war of independence, is primarily their responsibility.

An interesting, but not persuasive, interpretation of the debate over the treaty is provided by Jeffrey Prager in his book *Building Democracy in Ireland*. Prager views the debate over the treaty as a confrontation between two "ideal types" of Irish nationalism: an individualistic, forward-looking, and liberal "Irish enlightenment" tradition, exemplified by Wolfe Tone, and a collectivist, backward-looking, "Gaelic-Romantic tradition," which he says is exemplified by the Fenians. He associates the pro-treaty side with the first and the anti-treaty side with the second, apart from Collins and de Valera, who both wanted to prevent a confrontation and who, according to Prager, both ended up on the opposite sides from where they logically belonged.

Prager is right to emphasize the ambivalence of the two main opponents, Collins and de Valera, but in other respects his interpretation seems over-simplified at best. His view of the Fenians as looking backward to a rural and Gaelic past is misleading; Thomas Davis might better have been cited in that connection. One also suspects that Wolfe Tone, had he lived in 1921, would have opposed the treaty. Contrary to what Prager suggests, those who derive their political ideals from the American and French Revolutions should logically insist on a republic, while romantics looking back to the rural and Gaelic traditions of antiquity could just as logically swear allegiance to a king. It is interesting that many pro-treaty speakers referred to the importance of preserving the Irish language, while far fewer anti-treaty speakers did so: the opposite of what Prager's interpretation would suggest.[93] As an alternative interpretation, it could be argued that most of those who were primarily political nationalists, and therefore interested in political forms and institutions, opposed the treaty, while most of those who were primarily cultural nationalists supported the treaty. This interpretation still leaves Collins on the opposite side of the treaty debate from where one would expect to find him, but his support for the treaty surprised many of his contemporaries as well. It surely owed more to his realistic understanding of Ireland's military weakness than to real conviction. The ambivalence of de Valera also fits this interpretation, for he was perhaps equally committed to political and to cultural nationalism.

As a further, although not decisive, argument against Prager's view, it is interesting to note that some of the most prominent opponents of the treaty were of mixed origins. De Valera's father was Spanish, and de Valera himself was born in New York. Cathal Brugha's actual birth name was Charles Burgess, and his father was English. Constance Markiewicz (birth name Constance Gore-Booth) was a daughter of the Anglo-Irish Ascendancy. Erskine Childers, who had been secretary to the Irish delegation in London but refused to accept the treaty, was an Englishman with only tenuous connections to Ireland, although he had been skipper of the yacht that landed the Volunteers' rifles at Howth in 1914.

An entirely different, and simpler, explanation for the polarization over the treaty seems to fit the facts better than Prager's, although no explana-

tion can account for the choice of every single individual on an issue that
was both complex and emotional. The more a person had to lose from the
continuation of warfare, the more likely he or she was to support the treaty.
Most of the rising Catholic middle class and most of the new property owners who had benefited from the Wyndham Act were thus pro-treaty. Those
who had already lost what they cared most about, such as Margaret Pearse
and Kathleen Clarke, or those who had nothing to lose, such as the proper-
tyless young men in the flying columns of the IRA, were less inclined to support the treaty or the Free State that arose out of the treaty. Although the
Irish civil war was not an ideological or class conflict in the usual European
sense, it had more to do with self-interest than with cultural differences.

THE CONSCRIPTION CRISIS AND QUEBEC NATIONALISM

The beginning of the First World War found French-speaking Quebec, and
French-speaking Canada more generally, in a somewhat disturbed state of
opinion. Ontario's Regulation 17, which seemed to violate the French
Canadian understanding of Confederation as a compact between two cultural communities and to threaten the French outside Quebec with extinction, was particularly resented. The controversy over naval defence, which
had ended with the adoption of Laurier's policy after the Liberal majority in
the appointed Senate refused to approve a financial contribution to the
British navy, had exacerbated the anti-imperialist sentiments already stimulated by the Boer War. The rapid growth of population and the shifting
demographic balance in the western provinces, the anti-Catholic sentiments
of many English-speaking Canadians, and the growing cultural influence of
the United States created other anxieties.

Nonetheless, when war broke out and France was invaded by the Germans, Quebec was initially sympathetic to the Allied cause. Crowds in Montreal and Quebec City sang the French national anthem. Laurier, as leader
of the opposition, offered unconditional support to the war effort. Even
Bourassa suggested at first in *Le Devoir* that Canada should offer some support to Britain and France. On 23 September 1914, several weeks after the
war had begun, the Catholic bishops of Quebec issued a pastoral letter
endorsing the war effort and approving the policy of sending Canadian
troops overseas to participate in it. A week after this event, the government
authorized an entirely French Canadian regiment, the Royal 22nd.

Arrangements had already begun for a massive expansion of the virtually
non-existent Canadian army. A large training camp had hastily been constructed at Valcartier, near Quebec City, a site selected because of its prox-

imity to the port. The first Canadian contingent of some 30,000 men sailed for England in early October 1914. After further training, it was sent into battle about six months later. However, a substantial majority of the soldiers in this contingent had been born in the British Isles, even though only about one-sixth of all the men of military age in Canada had been born there. Only about 1,200 of the contingent, or 4 per cent, were French Canadians, although French Canadians outnumbered British immigrants in the population of Canada by almost two to one.[94] This first contingent established a pattern that continued throughout the war: British immigrants were the most enthusiastic about the war and the most likely to enlist, native-born English-speaking Canadians distinctly less so, and French Canadians least of all. During the whole war just over half the "Canadian" soldiers who served in France and Belgium were British immigrants, and French Canadians were significantly under-represented among the remainder. However, it was the under-representation of French Canadians and of the province of Quebec that attracted the most attention and the most criticism in English-speaking Canada. British immigrants were mingled with the general population, particularly in the western provinces, where they were particularly numerous, and their disproportionate contribution to the high rates of enlistment in English-speaking Canada was not widely appreciated, then or later.

French Canadian enthusiasm for the war effort, such as it was, declined for a number of reasons as the war continued. The refusal of Ontario's Conservative government to repeal Regulation 17, which was incorporated in a new school act in 1915, was deeply resented. It also reflected badly on the Conservative federal government, which owed its electoral victory in 1911 to Ontario voters and which refused to use its power of disallowance. The Quebec Legislative Assembly unanimously adopted a motion urging the Ontario government to reconsider.[95] A petition by the Catholic bishops of Quebec requesting disallowance was ignored. *Le Devoir* kept the issue alive in 1916 by running almost daily commentaries on the situation; in fact, it received more coverage than the war. Quebec adopted a measure in that year allowing the province's school boards to give financial aid to French-language education in Ontario. Largely because of this issue, Bourassa turned against the war, suggesting that Regulation 17 cast doubt on the moral superiority of the Allies over their opponents.

There were also causes for disaffection in the army. No French Canadians held prominent positions in the government, which had difficulty communicating with or understanding the French-speaking population. The minister of militia and defence for the first two years of the war, Sam Hughes, was an Ontario Orangeman who showed little sensitivity to French Canadian feelings. French Canadians who volunteered for the army were often assigned to English-speaking units whose officers knew no French, even though a few French Canadian battalions existed. There were serious allegations of discrimination against French Canadians in the army. Nationalists became increasingly hostile to the war. Armand Lavergne, an officer in the militia, was offered the command of a French Canadian battalion but refused to enlist. Olivar Asselin, on the other hand, supported the war and enlisted in the army, but even he criticized the pastoral letter of September 1914 for implying that Catholics had an obligation to do so.[96] In 1916 a French Canadian lieutenant colonel was court-martialled for advising his own men to desert after their battalion was assigned to garrison duty in Bermuda instead of being sent to France.[97] Laurier, as leader of the opposition in Ottawa, tried to encourage enlistment, but with little result.

By the second half of 1916, enlistments were declining sharply in English-speaking Canada as well, and the possibility of conscription, which had just been introduced in Great Britain, began to be widely discussed. A year earlier a rumour that it was being considered had caused a riot in Montreal. The government formed a National Service Board to take an inventory of manpower, and in January 1917 all men of military age had to register. A last voluntary recruiting drive in Quebec raised only ninety-two men in a province of more than two million people.[98] According to the government's data, only 4.5 per cent of the soldiers serving overseas were French Canadians, a proportion equal to about one-sixth of their share of the population. Laurier and other Liberal politicians from Quebec questioned the accuracy of the statistics, however.[99]

In April 1917 the United States entered the war, eliminating the possibility that deserters and draft evaders could escape to a neutral country. A month later the Canadian government finally announced that it would introduce conscription, and a bill to that effect was adopted by Parliament in July. Prime Minister Robert Borden asked Laurier to join him in a coalition government, such as had already been formed in the United Kingdom, but Laurier opposed conscription on principle, even though he approved of the war. He also knew that French Canadian opinion would never accept conscription. If he had supported it, a new nationalist party would probably have replaced the Liberals in Quebec, consigning them to the same fate as Redmond's party in Ireland.

There was practically no French Canadian support for conscription. As in Ireland, the Catholic clergy were solidly against it. The government's refusal to exempt Catholic lay brothers and students studying for the priesthood from conscription was particularly resented and was denounced by Cardinal Bégin, the archbishop of Quebec.[100] Mass meetings in Quebec, addressed by

Lavergne and other nationalist leaders, protested against conscription by breaking windows and firing blank cartridges. A previously unknown Montrealer, Elie Lalumière, claimed that five hundred men under his command were drilling to resist conscription by force. He was arrested in August after being implicated in the bombing of the suburban home of an ultra-imperialist newspaper publisher, Lord Atholstan.[101]

Conscription polarized the country between English and French as never before. In Mason Wade's words, "English Canadians, regardless of political affiliation, were loud in their lip service to conscription, if not much more willing in fact to accept it than the French Canadians, who in overwhelming majority were opposed to it."[102] Prominent editors and politicians accused French Canadians of disloyalty and treason. The Liberal Party divided more or less along ethnic lines, with most of its English-speaking members of Parliament joining a coalition with Borden's Conservatives. Laurier, with his mainly French-speaking followers, continued to lead the opposition, and the two sides squared off for an election in December 1917. The government elected only three members in Quebec, all in English-speaking constituencies, and won less than a quarter of the popular vote there. Elsewhere in Canada it outpolled the opposition by almost 2 to 1 and took 150 out of 170 seats.

A few days after the election, a Liberal member of the Quebec Legislative Assembly, Joseph-Napoléon Francoeur, tabled a motion stating that Quebec "would be disposed to accept the breaking of the Confederation Pact of 1867 if, in the opinion of the other provinces, it is believed that she is an obstacle to the union, progress, and development of Canada." Francoeur had represented the county of Lotbinière, southwest of Quebec City, for six years without attracting much attention. Despite the notoriety of his motion, he would go on to a lengthy political career as speaker of the assembly, minister of public works, federal member for the same county, and eventually a federally appointed judge. There is no evidence to suggest that he was ever a committed separatist. The phrasing of his motion indicates that it was written more in sorrow than in anger. It also implies a curious assumption that "the other provinces" should decide whether Quebec would stay or leave, rather than Quebec itself or the federal government.

The Francoeur motion was debated for two days in January 1918.[103] Francoeur introduced it by explaining that it was not a protest against the results of the federal election but against anti-Quebec statements made by English-speaking Canadians over several years. He affirmed his loyalty to the British crown but stated that French Canadians in Quebec wanted to retain their own language, religion, and institutions. The Conservative leader in the assembly, Arthur Sauvé, replied to Francoeur by denouncing the motion as dangerous and separation as contrary to Quebec's interests. He added that only the federal parliament, with the consent of the imperial government in London, had the power to dissolve the federation. Premier Lomer Gouin, a son-in-law of Honoré Mercier, intervened on the second day of the debate. He said that Quebec had freely accepted Confederation, that federalism was the only possible form of government for Canada and Quebec, and that separation would be harmful to Quebec in several ways. He also asked, "Enfin dans quelle position serait les nôtres en dehors du Québec?" suggesting that the French-speaking minorities in other provinces would be lost if Quebec abandoned them. The motion was not put to a vote, and Francoeur indicated that he merely wanted the spirit of the British North America Act to be respected and that he was satisfied to have provoked a debate on the issue.

Attempts to enforce the Military Service Act soon led to violence in Quebec City. On 29 March, Good Friday, the arrest of a young man for evading conscription provoked a riot in the course of which a police station was burned and the offices of two newspapers ransacked, as well as the local office of the National Service Board. Lavergne was asked by the authorities to help disperse the crowd, but his words, whether intentionally or not, failed to have the desired effect. A battalion of soldiers was sent from Toronto to restore order, rather tactlessly since there were French-speaking troops in the vicinity. When they encountered sniper fire from the crowd, the soldiers opened fire, killing four civilians. Habeas corpus was suspended, and there were fifty-eight arrests. Order was not restored until early Tuesday morning.[104] Quebec's Easter disturbance of 1918 hardly deserved comparison with the one in Dublin two years before, if only because it was unplanned and entirely spontaneous, but it was the closest the province had come to civil war in eighty years.

The Quebec City riot proved to be the high point of tension over conscription, although passive resistance to it continued for the remaining seven months of the war and many potential soldiers were hidden in rural areas of Quebec. Laurier died three months after the armistice, Borden retired a year later, and the coalition government in Ottawa gradually disintegrated. Its remnants were swept out of office by the voters on 6 December 1921, the same day that the Anglo-Irish treaty was signed in London. Laurier's stand on conscription had saved Quebec for the Liberals, who dominated that province in the 1920s as never before. No new nationalist party emerged to take their place in either federal or provincial politics, although both Bourassa and Lavergne returned to federal politics after the war.

The First World War, however, was clearly significant in the development of nationalism in Quebec, as well as in Ireland, even though its effects in

Quebec were obviously much less dramatic. In Ireland, where a potentially revolutionary situation was already smouldering beneath a tranquil surface, the war pushed the country over the edge. In Quebec, where there was significant discontent but no organized movement for political or social change, the war raised the level of ethnic tension and animosity, but the status quo was not seriously threatened.

In accounting for the contrast, therefore, we must look primarily at the differences between Quebec and Ireland in terms of underlying circumstances that predated the war. First, Quebec had enjoyed a form of "home rule" since 1867, while Ireland had been repeatedly denied it in 1886, 1893, and 1914. Second, Quebec, with more than a quarter of Canada's population, had significant influence in Canadian politics at the federal level, while Ireland, particularly Catholic Ireland, had very limited influence in the politics of the United Kingdom, partly because of its small and declining share of the population. A third difference was that Ireland's rural overpopulation and the landlord system had led to a tradition of clandestine organization and agrarian and political violence which continued even after the problems that had given rise to it were well on the way to solution. A fourth was that the English-speaking minority in Quebec, although they often disagreed with their French-speaking neighbours, did not feel threatened by Quebec's status as a province and were too interdependent with French-speaking Quebec to contemplate seceding from it. They provided no counterpart to the violence and fanaticism of the Ulster Protestants, against which Catholic Irish separatism arose as a natural reaction. Fifth, the identity of French Canadians in Quebec was not entirely bounded by the territory of the province, since French Canadians in other parts of Canada were viewed as part of the ethnic nation, a fact that diminished the attractiveness of secession. And sixth, many French Canadians, like Bourassa, saw the political status quo, even if less than ideal, as a barrier against the greater threat to their language and culture from the United States. For all of these reasons, Quebec was neither ready to contemplate fundamental change in its political status nor organized to bring it about, and the unhappiness over conscription was easily contained within the framework of conventional politics.

CHAPTER SEVEN

The Triumph of Conservative Nationalism

The Anglo-Irish treaty was approved by the Dáil, and by the British parliament in January 1922. As provided in the treaty, a Provisional Government of the Irish Free State was elected by the Dáil members from southern Ireland, with Arthur Griffith as president of the council and Michael Collins as minister of finance. British troops were withdrawn from the twenty-six counties over which the Free State exercised jurisdiction. A constitution was approved by the Dáil in October and came into effect on 6 December 1922, the first anniversary of the signing of the treaty. After these events Ireland, apart from the six counties in the northeast, was a virtually independent state enjoying the same status as Canada within the British Commonwealth; it soon became a member of the League of Nations. The Irish civil war, between the Free State government and republican opponents of the treaty, was fought in 1922–23 and took a greater toll in human life (possibly four thousand dead) than the war of independence had done, even though it lasted for only about a year.[1] The Free State won the civil war, but its legitimacy remained precarious since a substantial minority of the population had opposed the treaty. Its problems were exacerbated in some ways, although paradoxically simplified in others, by the partition of the country, which deprived it of what was then its largest city, Belfast, and its industrial heartland in the northeast. Ireland for several decades after 1922 experienced severe economic difficulties and continued to suffer the loss of its people through emigration, so that there was virtually no net increase in the size of the population for half a century.

Quebec, by contrast, was spared these traumatic events and circumstances. The excitement over conscription quickly subsided after the armistice of November 1918, and politics quickly returned to normal. Quebec continued, of course, to exercise the powers of a province within the Canadian federation, giving it roughly the degree of autonomy that Ireland might have enjoyed under home rule, had that project ever come to fruition. It also continued on the path of peaceful evolution that it had followed since 1867. In contrast to Ireland, it experienced respectable rates of economic growth during most of the decades that followed. Emigration to the United States was relatively low, in relation to the size of the population, compared to what it had been before the war.[2] Quebec's population, which had almost doubled between 1871 and 1921, almost doubled again between 1921 and 1956. Living standards lagged behind most parts of North America but were certainly very high by European standards.

In spite of these obvious differences, there were similarities in the situations faced by Ireland and Quebec after the First World War and in their responses to internal and external problems. Despite formal differences in status, both were relatively small and dependent communities exposed to the political, economic, social, and cultural influences of the larger North Atlantic world to which they belonged. Both sought to maximize their political autonomy and economic well-being while protecting what was viewed as a distinct way of life and cultural heritage against external influences that were not always easy to resist. These three objectives – autonomy, material well-being, and cultural preservation – essentially defined the agenda of nationalism, and of politics more generally, in the two societies.

From the 1920s through the 1950s, both Ireland and Quebec were affected by ideological trends and currents of political opinion in the outside world, which influenced the way that problems were perceived and created new alignments and cleavages, superimposed on those that arose out of strictly domestic circumstances and historical memories. However, both were and remained essentially conservative societies during those years, in which existing social relationships were stable and largely taken for granted. Ideologies of the extreme right had relatively little influence, and those of the extreme left even less. Conservatism was rooted in a firm alliance between the Catholic Church and the political authorities, underscored by political and economic ties that anchored Ireland and Quebec within the North Atlantic world. Both had unresolved problems and nationalist aspirations, but those aspirations were usually not pursued in ways that threatened the status quo.

In Ireland, Catholic economic and social teachings found expression in Articles 41 and 45 of the constitution adopted in 1937. The Jesuit order formed a committee of five to advise the government on the drafting of this constitution, although the extent to which the committee actually influenced the text is disputable.[3] Article 41, entitled "The Family," identified that institution as "the natural primary and fundamental unit group of Society and as a moral institution possessing inalienable and imprescriptible rights, antecedent and superior to all positive law." The same article prohibited divorce and expressed a preference for women's place in the home, rather than in the labour force. Article 45, entitled "Directive principles of social policy," called for a social order based on "justice and charity," emphasized the right of everyone to a decent standard of living, and referred to the need for the state to protect the public against "unjust exploitation" by private enterprise. It also warned of the dangers of excessive concentrations of wealth and economic power, in both the rural and industrial sectors.

Similar ideas were promoted by the church and its various orders in Quebec during the same era, although there was no opportunity to entrench them in a constitution. The Catholic hierarchy in Quebec successfully resisted the establishment of a ministry of education (until 1965) and even compulsory school attendance (until 1943) on the grounds that the state should not interfere in matters that properly fell under the authority of the family. Women were not allowed to vote in Quebec's provincial elections until the 1940s, despite the fact that the federal government had given them the right to vote in federal elections more than two decades earlier. A divorce could not be obtained within Quebec through the courts, although it was possible to get one by having a private bill adopted by the federal parliament in Ottawa.

Of course, neither the conservatism of these two societies nor of the Catholic Church itself should be overestimated. British and Anglo-Canadian Protestant disdain for the "priest-ridden" and supposedly backward societies of Ireland and Quebec has a long and unsavoury history, quite apart from the fact that it was often a case of the pot calling the kettle black. Both Britain and English-speaking Canada in the first half of the twentieth century were in some ways more dedicated to conservative social values than the United States, and both often took pride in being so, a fact that makes their expressions of disdain for Ireland and Quebec all the more curious. The Catholic Church itself also contained liberal and progressive tendencies, particularly in Quebec after 1945, when the ideas of progressive French Catholics such as Emmanuel Mounier and Jacques Maritain were influential.[4] The faculty of social sciences at Université Laval, led by the Dominican Georges-Henri Lévesque, was in some ways the seedbed of what came to be called Quebec's Quiet Revolution.

However, the view that Quebec before 1960 was conservative, backward, and subservient to clerical authority was also expressed, occasionally before

1960 and very frequently thereafter, by French-speaking Quebecers them-selves.[5] In fact, it became fashionable in retrospect to describe the era of Pre-mier Maurice Duplessis (1936–59) as "la grande noirceur" (the great darkness). According to this perspective, Quebec was a traditional society whose social and political development had been retarded in relation to the rest of North America, forcing it to make up lost ground through a process of radical change and reform in the 1960s, a process that came to be known as the Quiet Revolution.

Inevitably, there was a reaction against this perspective, and by the 1990s a revisionist interpretation of "la grande noirceur" seemed to be gaining ground rapidly. Revisionists pointed out that Quebec during that period had been mainly urban and industrialized with a capitalist economy largely based on foreign direct investment. In the view of one sociologist who helped to for-mulate the revisionist interpretation, it was a modern and liberal society in the full sense of the term.[6] While it was conservative in the North American sense, it was far from traditional in its values or way of life. As for the Catholic Church, it had not been the dominant social force, according to revisionists, but only one of several influential social forces that formed a power bloc in a society that was essentially capitalist and liberal. The kind of conservatism espoused by clerics was good for business and convenient for the state. A close analysis of clerical discourse from the era was cited as evidence that the church had really abandoned the ultramontane ideas of the nineteenth cen-tury and accepted the independent role of the state, although it still favoured some limits on the state's intervention in civil society.[7]

Should similar qualifications be made to the conventional picture of a conservative Ireland in the same era? Admittedly, the Irish Free State, after partition, was less urban, less industrial, and more homogeneous in terms of religion than Quebec was or than a united Ireland would have been. After 1939 it was also more isolated from external influences than Quebec was, because of its neutrality during the Second World War. However, Ireland had been extensively modernized in the last years of British rule, experienc-ing almost universal education and literacy, the beginnings of a welfare state, the rise of labour unions, and the development of large-scale capitalist enterprises.[8] By 1922, it was a long way from being a traditional society.

In terms of politics and political institutions, Ireland and Quebec in the four decades after the First World War were certainly not backward in rela-tion to most of the world. One similarity between them that is often taken for granted, but should not be, is that both were liberal democracies. Que-bec, along with the rest of Canada, Australia, the United States, France, and Switzerland, had been among the earliest countries to complete the transition to this form of government. Ireland's achievement of democratic stability in the 1920s was perhaps more surprising, given the traumatic experiences of a war for independence followed by a civil war. Although a considerable number of new liberal democratic polities were established after the First World War, most of them proved to be fragile and of short duration, particularly after the onset of the Great Depression in the 1930s. Ireland was one of the exceptions. Students of Irish political history have tried to explain this achievement of democratic stability in different ways, as will be examined below. A brief sketch of the relevant political history, beginning with the civil war, will be useful to introduce the discussion.

The provisional government agreed in February 1922 that the election of a new Dáil would be postponed for three months and the new constitution published beforehand. In March a convention of the Irish Republican Army, which had grown enormously in numbers since the truce of the previous year, voted to reject the treaty. A month later the IRA defied the authority of the provisional government by occupying the Four Courts, the principal seat of justice in downtown Dublin. Efforts to avert war through some kind of compromise were made by Michael Collins, Eamon de Valera, and the archbishop of Dublin, who met in a conference at the initiative of Dublin's lord mayor.[9] In May Collins and de Valera agreed that Sinn Fein would run a slate including both pro-treaty and anti-treaty candidates. This "pact," as it was known, was greatly resented by the British, who feared that it would give anti-treaty politicians too much influence, but their fears proved to be unjustified. The new constitution, after its first draft had been modified in response to British objections, was published on 16 June. The election held on the same day returned 36 anti-treaty Sinn Fein candidates, 58 pro-treaty Sinn Fein, 17 members of the Labour Party, which implicitly supported the treaty, and 17 others, most of whom supported the treaty.[10] In districts where there was an alternative to the combined Sinn Fein slate, about 40 per cent of the voters rejected it.[11]

Twelve days after the election, under British pressure, the Free State army attacked the republicans besieged in the Four Courts, beginning the civil war. De Valera assumed nominal leadership, although not effective control, over the anti-treaty forces. Griffith died suddenly in August, and Collins was assassinated ten days later, not far from his birthplace in County Cork. Collins had predicted, when he signed the treaty, that he might lose his life as a result. How Ireland's history would have unfolded had he lived is a question that can never be answered with certainty.[12] Most would agree, however, that his death was a tragic loss to the new state, at the time when his leadership was most needed.

Leadership of the provisional government thus passed to William Cosgrave and his right-hand man, Kevin O'Higgins, who pursued the war with exceptional ferocity, executing seventy-seven Irish patriots between November and May, more than the British had done in a hundred and twenty years since the Act of Union. O'Higgins, a young conservative representative of the Catholic middle class, had not been involved in the rising of 1916 and was a very different type of leader from Collins. Free State forces had gained control of all the major cities in the twenty-six counties by the time Collins died, but guerrilla warfare continued. In October the Catholic bishops condemned the irregular forces fighting against the government as murderers. In May 1923 the irregulars laid down their arms, and the civil war was at an end.

Another election followed, the first to be conducted under the new constitution, in which proportional representation was used. The anti-treaty or republican candidates, led by de Valera, ran under the banner of Sinn Fein, while the pro-government forces formed a new party called Cumann na nGaedheal, or "party of the Irish." Sinn Fein won 27.4 per cent of the vote, mainly in Connacht and the western counties of Munster, but its members refused to take their seats, since to do so would involve swearing the oath of allegiance to the Crown. Cumann na nGaedheal won 39.0 per cent of the vote, virtually the same percentage that the pro-treaty wing of Sinn Fein had won a year earlier. The Labour Party, which claimed descent from James Connolly but was in practice even less radical than its British namesake, won 10.6 per cent.[13] Cosgrave's government continued in office until 1932, surviving an army mutiny in 1924, the collapse of its hopes to regain at least a part of the six counties, and the assassination of O'Higgins in 1927.

Meanwhile Eamon de Valera, having failed to persuade Sinn Fein to modify its rigid policy of abstention from Free State politics, resigned as its leader in 1926 and formed a new party known as Fianna Fail, or "soldiers of destiny." Fianna Fail announced that its aims were a united Irish republic, restoration of the Irish language, equal opportunity for all, land reform, and economic self-sufficiency.[14] Despite its military-sounding name, it was in practice a moderately left-of-centre, slightly anticlerical, mildly populist party committed to peaceful and constitutional politics. It differed from the conservative Cumann na nGaedheal in much the same way that Canadian Liberals differed from Canadian Conservatives.

De Valera hoped that the oath of allegiance could be modified or abolished so as to facilitate his party's participation in the Dáil. Instead, following the assassination of O'Higgins, the Cosgrave government introduced a bill requiring all candidates to promise in advance that they would take the oath if elected. Fianna Fail then decided that the oath was merely an empty formality – essentially what Griffith had argued during the debate on the treaty – and agreed to participate in the 1927 elections on those terms. After that election, Fianna Fail was the second strongest party in the Dáil, and after the election of 1932, it was the strongest. De Valera formed a government that lasted without interruption until 1948; he again headed the government from June 1951 until June 1954 and from March 1957 until his retirement from active party politics in June 1959, at which time he became the ceremonial head of state. De Valera and Fianna Fail after 1932 secured the political neutrality of the Catholic Church, which had favoured Cumann na nGaedheal in the 1920s as a logical consequence of its pro-treaty position during the civil war.

Sinn Fein survived as a minor party after de Valera and his followers abandoned it in 1926, but it was of little importance in electoral politics. A much more formidable, and seemingly irrepressible, manifestation of intransigent republicanism was the Irish Republican Army, which had survived its defeat in the civil war. The IRA became increasingly left-wing and even pro-Soviet after the formation of Fianna Fail.[15] Although the extreme left wing eventually split off, the IRA was banned by de Valera's government in 1936 as a threat to national security, but it lived on as a clandestine and illegal organization. It launched a terrorist campaign in Britain, beginning in 1939, with the aim of bringing about the withdrawal of British forces from the six counties. This campaign continued throughout the Second World War and included contacts with Admiral Canaris's intelligence bureau in Germany.[16] In order to protect Ireland's neutrality, de Valera was forced to take draconian measures, including internments and six executions, against the IRA. By 1945, Ireland's minister of justice, Gerald Boland, announced (prematurely) that the IRA was defunct.[17] Three years later the IRA issued a general order that prohibited aggressive actions against the twenty-six-county state.[18]

Meanwhile a more visible but less formidable counterpart to the IRA had emerged and briefly flourished at the other end of the political spectrum. Ostensibly in response to the threat of the IRA, but also because they distrusted de Valera, some elements of Cumann na nGaedheal formed a quasi-fascist private militia soon after Fianna Fail took office in 1932. Known officially as the Army Comrades' Association and unofficially as the Blueshirts, the organization was headed after 1933 by Eoin O'Duffy, who had been commissioner of the national police force until his dismissal by de Valera.[19] The Blueshirts joined with the Centre Party and Cumann na nGaedheal to form Fine Gael, of which O'Duffy was briefly the leader. The Fianna Fail government banned uniformed private militias in 1934, but the Blueshirts were not formally disbanded until after the IRA was banned in 1936.[20] O'Duffy later led a contingent to fight for General Franco's insurgents in the Spanish Civil War. Some members of the IRA fought in the same war on the republican side, making Ireland one of the very few countries with combatants on both sides.

Despite these disturbances, the peaceful transition of power in 1932 and the fact that the change of government was not used as an opportunity to settle any scores arising from the civil war indicated that Ireland had established a stable democratic regime. This was an unusual achievement in the context of the 1930s, the more so because the two principal parties in the state had fought on opposite sides of a civil war only a decade earlier. Since the alignments of the civil war are still reflected in the modern Irish party system, it is perhaps not surprising that Irish scholars differ as to which side deserves most of the credit for Ireland's democratic stability. Tom Garvin gives most of the credit to Cosgrave and Cumann na nGaedheal, while John M. Regan and Bill Kissane give most of it to de Valera and Fianna Fail. Garvin views the anti-treaty IRA as the greatest potential threat to Irish democracy and endorses the stern measures by which it was suppressed.[21] Regan, as the title of his book *The Irish Counter-Revolution* suggests, emphasizes the right-wing and authoritarian characteristics of Cumann na nGaedheal as a potential threat to democracy.[22] Kissane, who tends to agree with Regan on this point, suggests that the regime did not become truly legitimate and effective until the 1930s, when de Valera and Fianna Fail succeeded in gradually transforming it into a republic.[23] Jeffrey Prager, the American scholar whose interpretation of the treaty debate was cited in chapter 6, seems to divide the credit more evenly between the two sides; although his sympathies are pro-treaty, he gives de Valera credit for his conversion to constitutional politics between 1926 and 1972, and he views the democratic order that resulted from this change of orientation as a synthesis of the two traditions.[24]

Whichever party one supports, some explanatory variables influencing the success of Irish democracy can perhaps be agreed upon. First, Ireland had a fairly long tradition of peaceful, democratic, and popular mobilization, going back at least to Daniel O'Connell. Second, British institutions, including the courts, local government, and the public service, provided some training in the operation of a democratic state, even though Britain itself was not really democratic before 1918. Third, land reform made rural Ireland a country of small peasant landowners, who became the primary support base for Fianna Fail, and other reforms, particularly in the field of education, had created a substantial middle class in the cities, the primary support base for Cumann na nGaedheal. Neither class wanted fundamental social change after 1922. An Ireland of landlords and tenants, in which most wealth and status belonged to an ethnic and class minority, could probably never have established a democratic party system.

It should also be noted that the civil war, as Kissane rightly argues, was not really a clash between two distinct and incompatible political cultures. It has become customary for Irish scholars to compare their country's civil war with the one that took place a few years earlier in Finland, a country with about the same population, and to point out that the Finnish civil war killed about 25,000 persons, while estimates of the death toll in the Irish civil war are much lower.[25] Yet the two civil wars were actually very different. The civil war in Finland, like later civil wars in Spain, China, Greece, and Vietnam, was between Reds and Whites, ideological and class adversaries who believed that they had virtually nothing in common with their opponents. The Irish civil war, in contrast, was more of a family quarrel between people who in many cases knew one another, who had recently fought together on the same side against the British, and who realized they had much in common. The ideological gap between Arthur Griffith and Cathal Brugha was probably less than that between Alexander Hamilton and Thomas Jefferson. Between Michael Collins and Eamon de Valera it was virtually non-existent. It is significant that even Kathleen Daly Clarke, a republican who remained a member of Sinn Fein after de Valera left it to form Fianna Fail, was shocked and upset in 1925 when an Irish American sympathizer referred to Collins as a traitor. She rebuked the man and said that she had disagreed with Collins, but still respected his memory.[26] It was this mutual tolerance and respect, as well as the absence of fundamental differences between adversaries, that made a peaceful transition such as that of 1932 and the establishment of a stable democratic regime possible. That is the real explanation for the success of Irish democracy.

The most significant, although short-lived, challenge to Ireland's two-party system was Clann na Poblachta (party of the republic), which was founded in 1946 and received 13.2 per cent of the vote in the general election of 1948. Its formation was partly a response to de Valera's repressive measures against the IRA during the wartime "emergency." Led by Sean MacBride, a prominent republican who had abandoned the IRA for constitutional politics in 1937, Clann na Poblachta provided a more radical republican alternative to the largely rhetorical nationalism of Fianna Fail. Its existence contributed to that party's defeat in 1946 after sixteen years in office. After joining in a rather incongruous coalition with the highly conservative and somewhat pro-British Fine Gael party, Clann na Poblachta won only 4.1 per cent of the vote in 1951, although it lingered on for several more elections.

In Quebec the controversy over conscription and Laurier's decision to oppose it reinforced the predominance of the Liberal Party in both federal and provincial politics, which dated from the 1890s. Laurier's death in 1919 made little difference in this regard. The Liberals won every Quebec riding in the federal election of 1921, the first and last time that any party ever achieved this feat. They continued to win overwhelming majorities of Quebec's federal seats until 1958, apart from the election of 1930, when they managed a respectable but not overwhelming majority of 40 seats out of 65. Until the Second World War, references to "conscription" and "imperialism" featured prominently in Liberal election campaigns at the federal and even at the provincial level. Although the federal party after Laurier's death had a unilingual English-speaking leader from Ontario, William Lyon Mackenzie King, its support in the province was maintained by King's Quebec lieutenants, who normally held the office of minister of justice in Ottawa when he was prime minister. Lomer Gouin, who had been premier of the province during the First World War, served as Quebec lieutenant from 1921 until 1924, when he was succeeded by Ernest Lapointe. After Lapointe's death in 1941, he was replaced by Louis St Laurent, who eventually succeeded Mackenzie King as leader of the party and prime minister of Canada in 1948.

At the provincial level, where Louis-Alexandre Taschereau succeeded Gouin in 1920, the Liberals faced little effective opposition for the next fifteen years. The Liberal Party by this time had entirely shed the image of radicalism that seemed to handicap it in its earlier days. It provided essentially conservative government and tended to leave economic initiatives to private enterprise and social policy to the Catholic Church. An important consequence was that the church abandoned its traditional suspicion of Liberals and became politically neutral. With the state devoting most of its energies to roads, local government, and the administration of justice, the ideological content was largely emptied out of provincial politics, leaving little space for a more conservative party. The small number of Conservatives in the Legislative Assembly were disproportionately drawn from constituencies with a large English-speaking population, where the stigmas of imperialism and conscription were not major handicaps.

In the 1930s, however, Quebec politics became more competitive, at the same time as Ireland was demonstrating its ability to manage a peaceful transition between two parties. The provincial Conservatives attempted to broaden the appeal of their party in 1929 by electing Camilien Houde as its leader. Houde, a populist and nationalist of working-class background, had been elected mayor of Montreal a year earlier. He remained mayor for most of the next quarter-century, but his venture into provincial politics was less successful, and he soon gave way to a more conventional and more astute Conservative leader, Maurice Duplessis. Duplessis had solidly Conservative credentials; his father had been a Bleu member of the Legislative Assembly around the turn of the century. He was a lawyer in Trois-Rivières, a medium-sized city that had been a Bleu stronghold since the days of its ultramontane and pro-Confederation bishop Louis-François Laflèche. In 1933 the Conservative Party adopted a mildly progressive program, partly inspired by the social thought of the Catholic Church. It thus hoped to outflank the Liberals on the left, although Duplessis himself was at least as conservative as Taschereau.

At about the same time, tensions within the Liberal Party caused a relatively progressive faction led by Paul Gouin, the son of Lomer Gouin, to secede from the party and form a new party called Action libérale nationale.[27] Its program, like that of the Conservatives, was partly inspired by Catholic social thought, although with a strong dose of French Canadian nationalism. Prior to the provincial election of 1935, Duplessis agreed to an alliance with Gouin whereby the Conservatives would nominate the anti-government candidate in one-third of the ridings, while Action libérale nationale would do so in the other two-thirds. If the opposition was successful, Duplessis would lead the government, but Gouin would select two-thirds of the ministers. This coalition was known as the Union nationale. In the election that followed, the Liberals retained only a bare majority of 48 out of 90 constituencies, while the ALN elected 26 of its 60 candidates and the Conservatives 16 out of 30. The Liberals remained in office, but Taschereau stepped down in favour of a younger and more progressive colleague, Adélard Godbout, in June 1936. Gouin, who doubted Duplessis's commitment to the coalition's progressive program, unexpectedly withdrew from the Union nationale, taking only 4 of the elected members with him. Duplessis then transformed the Union nationale from a coalition into a united party under his leadership, which won a majority in a second election. The Conservative Party as such ceased to exist. Duplessis was premier from 1936 to 1939 and again from 1944 to his death in 1959.

As Gouin had predicted, Duplessis in office was truer to his Conservative roots than to the progressive platform of his new party. In effect, the Union nationale replaced the old Conservative Party with an equally conservative party that was freed from the stigma of conscription and whose label recalled the nationalism of Honoré Mercier. This shift made Quebec politics after 1935 more competitive than it had been since the 1890s. The Liberals after 1936 were somewhat further to the left than the Union nationale, which was somewhat more nationalist than the Liberals. However, as in Ireland and in Canadian politics at the federal level, the ideological differences between the two major parties were not particularly pronounced; nor did their supporters differ sharply in terms of class or socio-economic status. The Catholic Church, which had taken a generally neutral position in party politics in the days of Gouin and Taschereau, tended to favour the Union nationale in the era of Duplessis.

In office from 1936 to 1939, Duplessis made little effort to implement the program on which he had been elected. In late 1939 he sought a fresh mandate, claiming that the emergency powers exercised by the federal government since the outbreak of the Second World War placed Quebec's autonomy in peril. The Quebec ministers in the federal Liberal government, proclaiming themselves as Quebec's only defence against conscription for overseas service, responded by threatening to resign if Duplessis was returned to office. Duplessis was defeated, and Adélard Godbout formed a Liberal government in Quebec. It proved to be more progressive than its predecessor by giving women the vote and making education compulsory, reforms that had been taken for granted everywhere else in North America for many years.

The pressure of public opinion in English-speaking Canada, particularly after June 1940, drove the federal government towards conscription for overseas service, despite Mackenzie King's sincere wish to avoid it. In 1940 conscription for home defence was authorized, and Camilien Houde was jailed for advising French Canadians not to register. Two years later a plebiscite on conscription for overseas service revealed overwhelming opposition to it in Quebec and support for it elsewhere. Parliament adopted a bill giving the government the power to impose conscription for overseas service as a last resort or, as the prime minister put it, "Not necessarily conscription but conscription if necessary."[28] (Eventually he decided that it was necessary, but not until November 1944.)

These events led to the formation in 1942 of a new nationalist, although not separatist, party, the Bloc populaire canadien, which grew out of the organization formed to mobilize anti-conscription voters for the plebiscite.[29] Its federal wing was led by Maxime Raymond, a member of Parliament who had resigned from the Liberal Party over conscription, and its provincial wing by a young intellectual, André Laurendeau. Henri Bourassa supported the Bloc but did not actually join it. The Bloc resembled Ireland's Clann na Poblachta in combining idealistic nationalism, disillusionment with the old parties, and a populist program that catered to both economic and political grievances. Both parties originated as responses to events during the Second World War: conscription in Canada and de Valera's draconian measures against the IRA in Ireland. Many of the Bloc's members had previously belonged to Action libérale nationale, and they resented the betrayal of that movement's promise by Duplessis. Others were active in nationalist organizations such as the Societé Saint-Jean-Baptiste. Like several previous manifestations of both Irish and French Canadian nationalism, the Bloc had considerable support among the Catholic clergy, although not among the bishops. Because it opposed the war against Germany, it attracted a certain number of anti-Semites and crypto-fascists, but it would be unfair to attribute such tendencies to the party as a whole.

The Bloc took 15.2 per cent of the vote in the Quebec election of 1944, which was won by Duplessis's Union nationale, and elected four members. In the federal election a year later it took 12.8 per cent of the Quebec vote and elected only two members.[30] Even before the elections, it was torn by conflicts over strategy that reflected the mixed origins of the party. The older and more conservative members believed that it should concentrate on federal politics and the struggle against imperialism and conscription, conceding the nationalist vote at the provincial level to the Union nationale. The younger and more radical members, such as Laurendeau, wanted to reform Quebec politics and viewed the conservative Duplessis, with his largely rhetorical nationalism, as their primary opponent. Like its Irish counterpart, Clann na Poblachta, the Bloc declined almost as rapidly as it had arisen, and by 1948 it ceased to exist. The Union nationale would govern Quebec until 1960.

Ireland and Quebec differed from most other democracies in the first half of the twentieth century in that both failed to develop a significant socialist or social democratic party. Ireland's small Labour Party has already been mentioned; after showing surprising strength in the "pact" election of 1922, it subsided into virtual irrelevance. In Quebec the political left was virtually non-existent, even though the province was significantly more industrialized and urbanized than the Irish Free State. It could be argued that the absence of a left-wing party in both Ireland and Quebec, as well as in the United States, partly occurred because democratic mobilization of the mass electorate preceded either industrialization or the spread of socialist ideas.[31] This theory fails, however, to account for the somewhat greater success of the political left in English-speaking Canada and its much greater success in Australia and New Zealand.

Several factors seem to have contributed to the weakness of the left in both Ireland and Quebec. First, most rural families owned land and were thus conservatively inclined; the effect of this factor in Quebec was magnified by the overrepresentation of rural voters in the Legislative Assembly. Second, the organizational and ideological strength of the Catholic Church, with its well-known hostility to socialism and its association with popular nationalism, was a serious obstacle to the left. In Quebec, for example, the Catholic bishops as late as 1934 urged Catholics not to vote for Canada's mildly social democratic party, which had just been established.[32] (This attitude of course paralleled their predecessors' hostility to liberalism about two generations earlier.) On a more intellectual level, Catholic social doctrine, especially the notion of corporatism, provided a more congenial and familiar alternative to Marxism in societies where virtually all education was provided and most intellectual activity was regulated or influenced by the church. A fourth explanation might be the strength of nationalism and its ability to deflect resentment away from dominant classes towards external enemies, or at least towards the relatively affluent Anglo-Protestant and Jewish minorities in Dublin and Montreal. Many nationalists in both countries agreed with Arthur Griffith's view that class politics were at best irrelevant and at worst a dangerous source of division within the national community. Finally, both de Valera and Duplessis, although they differed in other ways, were adept in combining populist anti-elitism with largely rhetorical nationalism, a combination that acted as a placebo and a substitute for left-wing politics in the 1930s and afterwards.

POLITICAL NATIONALISM: THE SEARCH FOR AUTONOMY

Although both Ireland and Quebec after the First World War were basically conservative societies in which few people sought radical social or economic change, there were still collective national aspirations that remained unfulfilled. Both Ireland and Quebec remained politically dependent in certain ways, and both perceived external threats, actual or potential, to such autonomy as they possessed. In both cases, too, political subordination to external centres of Anglo-Protestant power both reinforced and was reinforced by the disproportionate economic power enjoyed by internal Anglo-Protestant minorities. Irish and Quebec governments sought to protect, and at times increase, their political autonomy in both practical and symbolic ways. From time to time they also sought to protect and increase their economic autonomy, as will be discussed subsequently. However, economic nationalism might raise more delicate and dangerous issues of internal power relationships and social change, and since it would probably imply higher taxes and require greater administrative capabilities than these societies possessed, it was pursued more cautiously and less systematically in these basically conservative societies than political nationalism, which promised easier gains with less risk of upheaval.

The Anglo-Irish treaty had left the Irish Free State with the status of a British dominion at a time when the implications of that status were ambiguous and in a process of evolution. Prior to the First World War, Canada and the other dominions had been generally and accurately regarded as no more than self-governing British colonies, but their unexpected military achievements during the war had been rewarded with membership in the League of Nations, albeit under a formula that noted their continuing status as part of the British Empire. By 1922 they were beginning to regard themselves, and to act, as virtually sovereign states. They were still something less than that in theory, however, and to some extent in practice.

The constitution of the Irish Free State, despite modifications to the first draft that were insisted upon by the British, went somewhat beyond the degree of formal autonomy that the other dominions had attained at that time. The celebrated oath of allegiance required by the treaty, to which de Valera took such exception, was worded to imply that the king was only a symbol of the Irish constitution and not really head of state. The powers of the governor general were carefully circumscribed, and the Irish government was consulted about his appointment. Australia did not have a native-born governor general until 1930 and Canada not until 1952, but the first governor general of Ireland was an elderly and somewhat controversial right-wing Irish politician, Timothy Healy, who had been a leading anti-Parnellite in 1891. Dublin wits referred to the viceregal residence in Phoenix Park as "Uncle Tim's cabin."

Over the next ten years the Cosgrave government, with occasional support from South Africa and Canada, led the way towards a redefinition of dominion status, which culminated in the Statute of Westminster in 1931.[33] The British objected, at times strenuously, to virtually every step in this direction, but there was little they could do to prevent it. In 1923 Ireland, which was not yet a member of the League of Nations, applied to join the organization, but with the stipulation that it would do so as sovereign state and not as a dominion. Its application was accepted. In the following year it applied to register the Anglo-Irish treaty at the headquarters of the league under a provision in the League Covenant requiring all international treaties between member states to be so registered. The British protested that, in their view, it was not a truly international treaty between sovereign states, but to no avail. Also in 1924 Ireland appointed an ambassador to Washington, which Canada had announced its intention to do in 1920 but did not actually do until 1927. Ireland also began to issue its own passports in 1924. At the imperial conference two years later it insisted, with support from Canada and South Africa, that the dominions be recognized as equal in status to the United Kingdom, united with it only by common allegiance to the Crown, and that the governor general cease to be the channel of communication between British and dominion governments. The final declaration of the conference accepted these principles.

The only constitutional issue about which the Cosgrave government failed to achieve satisfaction concerned the practice of appeals to the Judicial Committee of the Privy Council. The British had insisted on the continuation of these appeals in 1921, largely to protect the property and civil rights, as they saw it, of the still influential and relatively affluent Protestant and unionist minority in southern Ireland. They could never be persuaded to agree to the abolition of appeals. However, in 1933 the de Valera government abolished appeals unilaterally, and the British, already in dispute with Ireland over issues they considered more important, accepted a *fait accompli.*

One of de Valera's first acts on taking office in 1932 was the abolition of the oath of allegiance, a violation of the Anglo-Irish treaty that contributed to provoking economic reprisals from the British. Later he took advantage of the confusion caused by the abdication of King Edward VIII to abolish the constitutional provisions relating to the office of governor general in December 1936.[34] However, the Executive Authority (External Relations) Act, adopted at the same time, stipulated that external relations would still be conducted in the king's name.

This move was but the prelude to the drafting of a completely new constitution, which was approved in a referendum on 1 July 1937 by a less than overwhelming 56.5 per cent of the valid votes cast.[35] Among other changes, the new constitution abolished the term "Irish Free State" and replaced the governor general with an elected president. Douglas Hyde, the former president of the Gaelic League, was elected the first president of Ireland in 1938. Parliamentary responsible government was retained, however. The head of government, or prime minister, referred to in the old constitution as "president of the council" in imitation of the French *president du conseil,* was henceforth known as the "taoiseach." External relations continued to be conducted in the king's name until 1949, but Ireland's neutrality in the Second World War demonstrated that this had little significance. The de Valera constitution satisfied most but not all republicans. The dozen or so diehard survivors of the unreconciled anti-treatyites in the second Dáil formally transferred their authority in 1938 to the Army Council of the IRA, which henceforth considered itself the legal government of Ireland, both north and south.

Of even greater practical significance than the constitution was the new Anglo-Irish treaty signed in April 1938, which was perhaps the greatest triumph of de Valera's career. It resolved the two major economic disputes between Britain and Ireland, relating to trade and annuities, which will be discussed below. It also terminated the right of the Royal Navy to use three Irish ports, as provided for in the original treaty. Control of the ports made it easier for Ireland under de Valera's leadership to maintain its neutrality throughout the Second World War, despite persistent British and later American pressure to become a belligerent. Hope of persuading Ireland to enter the war may have contributed to a British decision not to impose conscription in the six counties, to the chagrin of unionists.[36] Although the policy of neutrality was supported by both major parties, probably only de Valera would have had the fortitude and political skill to pursue it successfully to the end. By doing so, he conclusively demonstrated that Ireland was a fully sovereign state, although neutrality did not prevent Ireland from tacitly assisting the British war effort in a number of ways. To his credit, he did not jump on the Allied bandwagon in the last months of the war, as did Turkey and Argentina. The price of his integrity, however, was that Ireland was not admitted to the United Nations until 1955.

The final step in confirming Ireland's formal sovereignty was the Republic of Ireland Act, which in 1949 ended the state's tenuous links with both Crown and Commonwealth by repealing the Executive Authority (External Relations) Act of 1936. The act was the unexpected initiative of the coalition government headed by John Costello, who had been a compromise choice to lead an unstable coalition of right-wing Fine Gael and republican Clann na Poblachta. (Fine Gael's actual leader, Richard Mulcahy, was unacceptable to his coalition partners because of his role in winning the civil war.)[37] Costello had rather bizarrely announced his intention to leave the Commonwealth while on a state visit to Canada in September 1948. De Valera supported the Republic of Ireland Act at the time, asserting in the Dáil, "We are merely giving a name to what already exists – that is, a republican state."[38] Eleven years later, however, he told a British historian that Costello had made a mistake in withdrawing from the Commonwealth, since India had been allowed to remain in the organization as a republic.[39] In 1965 the British government tried to persuade Ireland to re-enter the Commonwealth, but without success.[40]

One effect of the constitutional changes in 1937 and 1949 was to redefine the agenda, or at least the emphasis, of the non-constitutional republican opposition to the regime. It was obvious to most people after 1949 that the state was a republic. However, from the standpoint of its republican opponents in the IRA and Sinn Fein, it was still not <u>the</u> republic that had been proclaimed in 1916 and reaffirmed in 1919 because it did not include the six counties of Northern Ireland. Furthermore, it was becoming increasingly obvious that the state was making no serious effort to regain the six counties. Republicans henceforth relied primarily on this argument to deny the legitimacy of the state. Its apparent acceptance of partition indicated to them that it was not truly independent of British control in fact, even though it appeared to be so in form. Left-wing republicans also considered that partition reinforced conservative and sectarian tendencies in the south as well as in the north. They believed that in an undivided Ireland, class politics would take priority over religious divisions.

One does not have to accept all these arguments to concede that the most serious failure of mainstream Irish nationalism after 1922 was its complete inability to undo the partition of the country which had taken place in 1920. It is hard to avoid the conclusion that Irish policy on this issue lacked both consistency and logic, as well as singleness of purpose, although in fairness it must be added that there was no obvious or easy solution to the problem. Logically, the only options were to try to undermine the partitionist six-county state by hostile means, to try to lure the unionists into a united Ireland by making concessions to their point of view, or to accept partition as a *fait accompli*. All three were tried at various times. Perhaps only the last of these options was realistic, but there was understandably great reluctance to say so. During the treaty negotiations in 1921 the Irish delegation had been persuaded to accept the right of the six-county state established the year before to opt out of the Free State, at least for the time being. In return for this concession, Article 12 of the treaty provided for a Boundary Commission, which would readjust the boundary "in accordance with the wishes of the inhabitants." According to one widely accepted account, David Lloyd George persuaded Michael Collins that the Boundary Commission would award so much territory to the Free State as to make the partitionist state unviable.[41] (Since it was still a part of the United Kingdom, its size was totally irrelevant to its viability, an obvious fact that neither Collins nor the Ulster unionists appeared to understand.) Somewhat more realistically, the Irish negotiating team seem to have assumed that the Boundary Commission would at least award the counties of Tyrone and Fermanagh, both of which had decisive but not overwhelming Catholic majorities, to the Free State. Lloyd George gave this belief some credibility by stating in the House of Commons, eight days after signing the treaty, "There is no doubt – certainly since the Act of 1920 – that the majority of people of two counties prefer being with their Southern neighbours to being in the Northern Parliament."[42]

During the treaty debate in the Dáil, as noted above, there were surprisingly few references to the problem of partition. Some pro-treaty speakers held out vague hopes that the unionists could be lured into a united Ireland, and that acceptance of dominion status rather than a republic would make this scenario more likely. In January and March 1922 two agreements between Michael Collins and the unionist leader, James Craig, attempted to normalize relations between the two parts of the island. The agreements broke down, however, because of sectarian violence in Belfast, of which Catholics were the main, although not the only, victims, and for which the Craig regime bore much of the responsibility.[43]

The Irish civil war and the death of Collins, who apparently cared more about the northern Catholics than did most southern politicians, distracted

the attention of the Free State from the problems of the six counties. However, it continued until 1925 to pay the salaries of Catholic teachers in the
six counties who refused to accept remuneration from the partitionist
regime, a practice that suggests it may not have entirely written off the six
counties. (On the other hand, it might be noted that Quebec governments
have at times subsidized French Canadian education and culture in other
Canadian provinces, without questioning the legitimacy or the boundaries
of those provinces.) Even if partition itself may have been implicitly
accepted by the Free State as inevitable, there was a continuing hope of at
least regaining Tyrone and Fermanagh, which one internal cabinet document described as "the key issue."[44] To add to the confusion, Kevin
O'Higgins outlined a plan in 1924 to restore at least a semblance of Irish
unity, with separate parliaments for north and south but a single governor
general and some common institutions, in return for which the northern
regime might be given more territory.[45]

The Boundary Commission was finally established in 1923, with Eoin
MacNeill, who was originally from County Antrim, as the Free State representative and a South African judge as the supposedly neutral chairman. In a
memo to MacNeill, Cosgrave urged a drastic reduction in the size of Northern Ireland, with Derry city and a large part of Armagh, as well as Tyrone and
Fermanagh, being transferred to the Free State.[46] The commission's majority report, which MacNeill refused to sign, was a major disappointment since
it recommended only minor changes to the boundary, with territory being
transferred in both directions. The Free State would have gained small portions of Tyrone, Fermanagh, and Armagh, but would have lost two portions
of Donegal.[47] Rather than accepting this award, Cosgrave went to London
and negotiated a revision of the treaty whereby the boundaries of the
six-county state would remain unchanged, the Boundary Commission
would be abolished, and the Free State would be relieved of some financial
obligations. Claiming that this agreement demonstrated "a new spirit of cordial co-operation and friendship," he suggested that it was time to "put this
barren question of the Boundary behind us once and for all."[48]

The agreement marked the end of serious efforts to reunify Ireland, or
even to assist northern nationalists against the partitionist and sectarian
regime in the six counties, although lip service continued to be paid to the
cause for many years. It is fair to ask whether any major southern politician
holding office after the death of Michael Collins was seriously interested in
pursuing the issue, with all its uncertainties and inconveniences. A united
Ireland with a minority of 900,000 pro-British Ulster Protestants would have
been difficult to govern, particularly if its government remained committed
to policies of political, economic, and cultural nationalism for which most

Ulster Protestants had little or no sympathy. On the other hand, the abandonment of such policies in the slim hope of enticing Ulster Protestants into a united Ireland was not an attractive option either, partly because the policies were the result of sincere conviction and partly because there was no certainty, or even much probability, that Ulster Protestants would respond.

Soon after Fianna Fail took office, de Valera suggested that the only hope for reunification was "to use such freedom as we can secure to get for the people in this part of Ireland such conditions as will make the people in the other part of Ireland wish to belong to this part."[49] Yet his protectionist economic policies, his commitment to restoring the Irish language, and his efforts to weaken the tenuous constitutional ties between Ireland and Britain did not seem calculated to attract northern unionists into a united Ireland under his leadership. The weakness of southern Ireland's economy, even though it was partly the consequence of partition, did nothing to make the prospect of reunification more tempting to the people of the six counties. In 1933 and again in 1936 the Dáil debated motions by an opposition member to the effect that the Fianna Fail government was not doing enough to bring about reunification, but the critics had no practical remedy to offer.

The constitution of 1937 affirmed in Article 2, "The national territory consists of the whole island of Ireland, its islands and the territorial seas," although Article 3 implicitly admitted that, "Pending the re-integration of the national territory," its laws only applied in the twenty-six counties. However, several articles of the constitution suggesting the influence of Catholic social doctrine, as well as an explicit reference to the "special position" of the Catholic Church, were criticized for placing additional obstacles in the way of reunification, even though the contributions of the Protestant and Jewish minorities were also recognized in the constitution.

De Valera suggested in 1938 that the six counties could retain a "local Parliament with its local powers" in a united Ireland, but no response to this offer was forthcoming.[50]

In 1945 nationalists in the six counties founded an Anti-Partition League, which also attracted support in southern Ireland and in Great Britain. Its efforts to keep the issue alive continued for about nine years. Frustration with the division of Ireland also contributed to the formation of Clann na Poblachta a year later, and thus to the defeat of de Valera's government in 1948. After Fianna Fail lost office, de Valera and another prominent member of his former government, Frank Aiken, began their own anti-partition campaign, which took them on a global tour to the United States, New Zealand, Australia, and India.[51] Shortly afterwards, the Costello government's Republic of Ireland Act made the goal of reunification even more elusive. Catholics in Northern Ireland were shocked by the measure, which they viewed as a sign that the politicians of the south had rejected or abandoned any hope of reunification.[52] The British responded to Ireland's severing of its last ties with the Crown by adopting their own Ireland Act, which affirmed their commitment not to abandon the six counties without the consent of the parliament of Northern Ireland.[53]

In 1954 an independent member of the Dáil introduced a motion proposing legislation to allow elected representatives of the six counties to sit in the Dáil. He lamented that "we are gradually drifting further away from our people in the six occupied territories."[54] Sean MacBride, who had been minister for external affairs in the first Costello government but was now in opposition to the second, supported the motion, pointing out with good reason, "In the past thirty years we have taken no positive action towards bringing about the unification of our country."[55] However, the motion was lost, with both the government and the major opposition party, Fianna Fail, voting against it.

By the late 1950s opposition to partition had apparently receded from the realm of practical politics in southern Ireland. Although the United Nations, after Ireland finally became a member state, was used as a platform to affirm the Dublin government's continuing opposition to partition, this gesture contributed nothing to a solution and had little impact on world opinion, particularly as it took place only days after the Suez crisis and the anti-communist insurrection in Hungary.[56] Only the clandestine and illegal IRA and the surviving rump of Sinn Fein, which had virtually been taken over by the IRA in 1948, continued to take any serious interest in the issue of Irish reunification.[57] Even de Valera failed to mention partition in his last speech as party leader to a Fianna Fail convention in 1958. After a dismal decade of demographic and economic decline that contrasted painfully with optimism and growth in virtually every other country of the Western world, the Irish people had more immediate problems on their minds.[58] The northern question would dramatically return to their attention a decade later, however.

Quebec's pursuit of political and economic autonomy during the decades after the First World War, like that of Ireland, met with a mixture of success and failure. Ireland's main task was to turn a state of virtual, but not quite complete, independence within an empire that was evolving towards greater decentralization into one of formal and complete independence. Quebec's main task was to strengthen its position as a province within an evolving federation whose central government, like that of other federations at the same time, was becoming more active in social, economic, and fiscal policy. Quebec could and did seek the aid of other provinces, just as Ireland could and did seek the aid of other dominions, even if their allies in each case shared their objectives only in part.

Quebec's nationalism continued to operate at two levels, since its influence in Canadian federal politics was by no means negligible. The federal Liberal Party, in office for all but five years between 1921 and 1957, owed much of its electoral success to the extreme weakness of the Conservative Party in Quebec. The large contingent of Quebec members comprised at least a third, and at times almost half, of the Liberal Party's strength in the House of Commons. Canada's pursuit of greater autonomy for itself within the Commonwealth during the 1920s and its support for Irish initiatives in that regard were among the consequences of the presence of those Quebec members in Ottawa. Another consequence was Canada's reluctance to incur international commitments, especially of a military nature. Still another was the reluctance of Canadian federal governments, at least until the 1940s, to involve themselves in fields of policy traditionally left to the provinces. Issues of this kind and especially the threat of conscription being imposed again (as it eventually was) during the Second World War kept a part of Quebec's attention focused on federal politics. There was thus understandable resentment in the province when a redistribution of parliamentary representation that would have taken into account Quebec's increased share of the population was postponed, for no very good reason, during the war, with the result that the election of 1945 was fought on the old boundaries. Since the postponement required an amendment of the British North America Act by Westminster, Premier Godbout sent a petition to Winston Churchill in an unsuccessful effort to prevent it.[59]

Quebec's main political concern, however, was still provincial autonomy. As the only government in which French Canadians predominated, the province of Quebec seemed to be the essential guarantee of national and cultural survival. Any threat to its freedom of action was seen as a threat to French Canadian survival, even though many French Canadians, more than one-fifth of the total number in 1921, lived in other provinces. Despite the failure of the Francoeur motion to attract much support, the trauma of the conscription crisis had reinforced the tendency of Quebec to turn inwards and rely on its own resources. Symptomatic of this orientation was the eclipse of the kind of bicultural, pan-Canadian nationalism that Henri Bourassa had promoted before the war. Bourassa had returned to the Canadian House of Commons as an independent member between 1925 and 1935, but he was no longer the acknowledged pre-eminent spokesman for French Canadian nationalism after the First World War. His pan-Canadian orientation and the priority that he increasingly gave to his religious faith over nationalism were no longer fashionable. In 1932 he even lost control of Le Devoir, which for the next fifteen years, under the direction of Georges Pelletier, espoused a narrow and intolerant right-wing ethnic nationalism.[60]

Le Devoir during those years also catered to anti-Semitism, which the rapid growth of Montreal's Jewish community since the turn of the century had unfortunately brought to the surface.[61] Bourassa's old comrade Armand Lavergne, meanwhile, had rejoined the federal Conservative Party. He served as deputy speaker of the House of Commons in Ottawa from 1930, when the Conservatives won a majority, until his death in 1935.

Henri Bourassa's place as the intellectual leader of French Canadian nationalism was taken by a priest-historian ten years his junior, Father Lionel Groulx. The intellectual influence of Groulx, who lived until 1967, extended over several generations, and it is appropriate, although in some circles controversial, that a principal station on Montreal's urban transit system bears his name. The movement known as Action française, which he founded and led in the 1920s, will be discussed later in this chapter. He influenced the Bloc populaire, which has already been discussed, and to some extent even the Parti québécois, which was founded a year after his death. Although he never clearly committed himself to the view that Quebec should seek independence, Groulx apparently had little interest in the rest of Canada, apart from its French-speaking minorities. In a comment on the fiftieth anniversary of Confederation, which coincided with the conscription crisis of 1917, he wrote that it was sad to recall the naive optimism which French Canadians had felt about it in 1867 and which now seemed like an illusion. Although the founders of the federal state had had good intentions, according to Groulx, English Canadians had never respected the rights of French Canadians or the idea of a partnership between two nations. Ten years later Groulx wrote that Confederation was still fragile because French Canadians did not really support it; they could not be expected to do so until their rights were respected all over the country. In 1936 he urged French Canadians to work for a French state within Confederation if possible or outside of it if necessary.

Since this seemed a remote prospect in the interwar period, Quebec concentrated on protecting its provincial rights and reinforcing its freedom from external influences. It suffered a serious reverse in 1927 when the Judicial Committee of the Privy Council defined the boundary between Quebec and Newfoundland, which was then a British dominion separate from Canada. Newfoundland had long claimed a vaguely defined "coast of Labrador" on the mainland, which was generally assumed to be merely a narrow strip along the seaboard. The Judicial Committee, however, defined Labrador as a roughly triangular area of about 115,000 square miles, parts of which were 500 miles inland and most of which had been claimed by Quebec. Quebec never accepted the validity of this decision, and its official maps continued to show Labrador as part of its own territory. Like Ireland's claim to sovereignty over the six counties, Quebec's claim to Labrador could not be exercised in practice. However, the issue cast a shadow over Quebec's relations with its northeastern neighbour, even after Newfoundland became a Canadian province in 1949.

Quebec also had to defend its traditional understanding of provincial autonomy. The Canadian federal government, like other governments at the time, was becoming active in fields of public policy that it had largely ignored before the First World War, some of which clearly fell under provincial jurisdiction, while others had not been explicitly mentioned in the British North America Act. It was also beginning to tap new sources of revenue, rather than relying almost entirely on excise taxes and customs tariffs as it had done traditionally, to supply its financial needs. Soon after taking office in 1920, Premier Taschereau of Quebec criticized the imposition of a federal income tax, which had begun in 1917 but continued after the end of the war. He also criticized federal efforts to make policy with regard to agriculture and colonization, education and training, welfare, housing, and highways, particularly through the use of conditional grants.[62] In 1927 his government refused to participate in a federal plan to provide means-tested old-age pensions through a conditional grant to the provinces, taking the view that the plan was probably unconstitutional and in any event contrary to the social philosophy of Quebec, which emphasized the responsibility of the extended family to support its elderly members. In the same year Taschereau challenged the constitutionality of the federal Aeronautics Act, which had been adopted in 1919. He considered that air transport within the boundaries of a province fell under the provincial authority over property and civil rights. On similar grounds, he also challenged another federal statute, the Radiotelegraph Act of 1927.[63] The Judicial Committee of the Privy Council, although it had struck down a number of important federal statutes in the 1920s and would do so again in the 1930s, ruled in separate decisions that aeronautics and broadcasting fell entirely under federal jurisdiction. Both decisions asserted that the new technologies related to the peace, order, and good government of Canada, and not to the provincial responsibility for property and civil rights.

It was the gradual development of what came to be called the welfare state, however, that seemed to pose the greatest threat to Quebec's traditional understanding of the distribution of authority between the two levels of government, and more generally to its traditional understanding of the relations between the state and civil society. Even as late as 1948, Premier Maurice Duplessis expressed the predominant view held by Quebec's political and clerical elites when he asserted that "state paternalism infallibly paralyzes fruitful and necessary initiative and, in the end, invokes the ruin of individuals and peoples."[64] Although he agreed to accept the conditional grant for old-age pensions soon after taking office, he was not receptive to new federal initiatives in related fields. A federal effort to establish unemployment insurance had been struck down by the Judicial Committee of the Privy Council in 1937, as a result of which the federal government sought to have the British North America Act amended so as to add unemployment insurance to the list of federal jurisdictions. Doing so required action by the British parliament at Westminster at Canada's request, but it was considered politically hazardous to make the request without the prior approval of the provinces. Duplessis refused to agree, but Adélard Godbout, after the Liberals defeated Duplessis's Union nationale in 1939, gave his consent soon afterwards, and the amendment was adopted in 1940. Even Godbout, however, was displeased when the federal government argued that its new responsibility for unemployment insurance also authorized it to attack the causes of unemployment by subsidizing occupational training.[65]

Duplessis returned to office in 1944, just as the federal government was planning a post-war expansion of the welfare state, based on the unprecedented levels of fiscal centralization achieved during the Second World War. Until his death in 1959, he waged a series of battles against the proposals of a federal government that he claimed was "insidiously socialistic."[66] He argued that the new program of federal family allowances, which disproportionately benefited Quebec residents because of the province's higher than average birth rate, interfered with provincial jurisdiction over the family, education, and civil rights.[67] The federal government continued its program nonetheless, and its authority to do so was eventually upheld by the Supreme Court of Canada. When the federal government relied on conditional grants to the provinces or grants to provincially funded institutions, rather than direct grants to individuals, Duplessis was more successful in interfering with its plans. He refused to participate in a cost-shared scheme for a trans-Canada highway, which the federal government began in 1949, and in one for universal hospital insurance, which it introduced in 1957. He also opposed federal grants to universities, which were offered from 1951 onwards, as an intrusion in a provincial field of jurisdiction. Eventually he forced Quebec's universities to refuse the grants. The suggestion for federal grants to universities had come from a federal royal commission chaired by Vincent Massey, soon to become Canada's first native-born governor general. The Massey Commission recommended that the federal government involve itself more in the intellectual and cultural life of the country, partly in order to protect Canada from the cultural influences of the United States.

English-speaking Canada's growing sense of nationalism vis-à-vis Great Britain and the United States was beginning to create an obstacle to the aspirations of Quebec's nationalism, and vice-versa. This was a somewhat ironic outcome, since Bourassa, and occasionally even Groulx, had lamented the absence of nationalist sentiments among English-speaking Canadians. During the Second World War, the federal government began the process of abolishing appeals to the Judicial Committee of the Privy Council, partly to escape from the Judicial Committee's narrow definition of federal jurisdiction and partly on the same nationalistic grounds that had led Ireland to do so earlier. Despite its decision on the Labrador boundary, the Judicial Committee was popular in Quebec for the same reason that it was unpopular in English-speaking Canada: its tradition of defending provincial autonomy against the federal government. Appeals were ended in 1949, and the Supreme Court of Canada became supreme in fact as well as in name. Duplessis, claiming that the Supreme Court was biased in favour of federal supremacy, compared it to the leaning tower of Pisa, which always leans in the same direction.[68]

In another manifestation of Canadian nationalism the same year, the federal government persuaded the British parliament to amend the British North America Act so that henceforth Canada's parliament could amend certain parts of the act on its own, without the involvement of either Westminster or the provinces. The federal government also opened discussions with the provinces over a possible amending formula that would not require Westminster's participation in any future amendments. Duplessis objected unsuccessfully to the unilateral assertion of amending power and insisted, citing Honoré Mercier, that Confederation was a pact whose terms could not be altered without Quebec's approval.[69] Prime Minister St Laurent, a Quebecer of mixed French and Irish ancestry and a distinguished constitutional lawyer, proclaimed that the veto was a myth and that from a juridical standpoint, "Le Québec est une province comme les autres." The federal-provincial discussions were inconclusive.

In 1951 the federal government decided to replace its program of means-tested old-age pensions with a much more costly universal scheme. Since this would be funded with a special tax, it required a constitutional amendment by Westminster, unlike family allowances, which were funded out of general revenue. Duplessis gave his consent, but only on condition that the amendment would make pensions a concurrent jurisdiction, with provincial legislation having paramountcy over federal. Having asserted the principle, he was content to let the federal government have its program.

Perhaps the most serious of Quebec's conflicts with the federal government in the 1950s was over taxation.[70] Since 1942, all provinces had left the field of personal income tax to the federal government, which had originally insisted that this was necessary to finance the war effort. Provinces that agreed for a five-year period to "rent" their taxing powers to the federal government received a subsidy; those that did not sign a rental agreement (i.e., Quebec) were promised that their residents could credit provincial tax paid against their federal liability, up to a maximum of 5 per cent. In 1954 Quebec broke ranks by imposing income tax at a rate equal to 15 per cent of the federal tax. The preamble to the statute imposing the tax asserted that the Canadian constitution gave the provinces "priority in the field of direct taxation" and that it would be "unfair and harmful" to continue depriving the province of revenue from taxing incomes.[71] The federal government backed down and compromised by increasing the credit for provincial tax paid to 10 per cent, an offer that was extended to the other provinces after 1957. Within a few years the tax rental system was replaced by "tax sharing," with the provinces imposing their own income taxes and the federal government gradually reducing its rates of taxation to give them a larger share.

In 1953, in the midst of his controversies with the federal government over taxation and spending, Duplessis established the Royal Commission on Constitutional Problems, usually known as the Tremblay Commission. Its report, issued three years later, argued that the profound cultural differences between French and English Canada, which were based on religion and history as well as language, made a centralized government both unacceptable and impossible. The purpose of Canadian federalism should be to allow the two great cultural communities to flourish independently, while pursuing a limited range of common interests through the federal state. Skating rather lightly over the problem that French Canada did not exactly correspond with the province of Quebec, it proposed a decentralized form of federalism in which the federal government would abstain from direct taxation and from intervention in social and cultural policy. Unemployment insurance and other social insurance or welfare programs should be run by the provinces, and the richer provinces should make equalization payments to the poorer ones, as in post-war German federalism, rather than the poorer provinces being subsidized by the federal government. There would be a Council of the Provinces to coordinate policies in areas of provincial jurisdiction and a secretariat to organize federal-provincial conferences. The provinces should also be given the right to borrow from the central bank. The Tremblay report described this program as a return to the original spirit of the British North America Act.

The Tremblay proposals were never implemented, and in fact were not seriously pursued by Duplessis or his government. A few years earlier, however, he had taken an important symbolic step to affirm Quebec's identity as a distinct nation by adopting an official flag. The blue and white flag combined a cross, symbolizing Quebec's Catholic faith and heritage, with the fleur-de-lys, symbol of pre-revolutionary France, and was a modified version of a flag designed in 1902 by a Catholic priest, Father Elphège Filiatrault.[72] It was made official by order-in-council in January 1948, an initiative applauded by both the Liberal opposition leader, Adélard Godbout, and the leader of the Bloc populaire, André Laurendeau.[73] Canada itself did not adopt an official flag until seventeen years later.

ECONOMIC NATIONALISM: THE UNCERTAIN
PURSUIT

The achievement of political self-government did not end Ireland's economic dependence on Britain, let alone its other economic problems. Disentangling two economies that had been one state since the beginning of the nineteenth century was not easy, and Ireland's geographical situation as well as its weakness and relative poverty limited its options. In the 1920s the Cosgrave government rejected Arthur Griffith's philosophy of economic nationalism, even though most of the party rank and file supported protectionist policies.[74] Instead, it pursued a policy of low tariffs and specialization in agricultural exports to Britain. This pleased the ranchers and relatively prosperous commercial farmers, most of whom supported Cumann na nGaedheal, as well as the Protestant and formerly unionist businessmen of Dublin who supported Cosgrave's party for lack of a more acceptable alternative. About five-sixths of the Free State's exports went to Britain and about two-thirds of its imports came from that country throughout the decade, making Ireland a classic instance of what would later be referred to as neo-colonialism.[75]

In the 1930s Ireland, like most other countries at the time, moved towards more protectionist policies in response to the economic crisis. This tendency was reinforced when Fianna Fail, whose program committed it to pursuing self-sufficiency, took office in 1932 and raised tariffs substantially. It was rather ironic that Arthur Griffith's opponents in the civil war should have been the ones to implement his economic policies, which his own followers had ignored after his death. However, the contrast reflected Fianna Fail's greater hostility to Britain and its electoral base among voters who had less of a direct economic stake in the British connection. Fianna Fail's economic policies were also influenced by the social and economic teachings of the Catholic Church, since it was trying to win the political support, or at least political neutrality, of that institution and to live down its reputation as being made up of radical republicans who had instigated the civil war.

The Fianna Fail government in 1932 decided to end the payment of interest to the British treasury on the annuities by which Ireland, under the terms of the Anglo-Irish treaty, was still paying back the cost of buying out the landlords under the Wyndham Act of 1903. This decision provoked the so-called economic war in which both sides increased their tariffs, causing a sharp decline in trade between them. The percentage of Ireland's declining exports that went to Britain did not really change, since the economic crisis and the trend to protectionism around the world had reduced exports to other markets. There was, however, some diversification in its sources of imports. The "economic war" was ended by the new Anglo-Irish treaty of 1938, under which Ireland agreed to a one-time payment of £10 million sterling in return for the cancellation of annuities worth several times as much, a surprisingly favourable settlement.[76] Thereafter trade between the two neighbours gradually recovered. Ireland's neutrality in the Second World War did not prevent substantial trade with Britain, whose war effort it thus indirectly assisted. By the early 1950s Britain still absorbed about three-quarters of Ireland's exports and provided about half its imports.

Excessive British ownership in the Irish economy was also a concern. Soon after taking office in 1932, the Fianna Fail government introduced the Control of Manufactures Act, which provided that any foreign direct investment in Irish industry would require a licence from the government. The minister who introduced the measure, Sean Lemass, apologized that it was "too moderate." Explaining its purpose, he warned that foreign firms would try to get over the tariff wall by establishing branch plants in Ireland, which would make the Irish "hewers of wood and drawers of water" in their own country.[77] (As noted in an earlier chapter, this biblical expression was also used by Henri Bourassa.) Two years later he introduced amendments to strengthen the legislation, noting that geographical proximity and the common use of the English language facilitated British control of the Irish economy.[78] By 1937, however, Lemass was losing faith in the effectiveness of the Control of Manufactures Act. Somewhat later he worried about the contradiction between protective tariffs, which encouraged foreign branch plants, and restrictive policies towards foreign direct investment, which discouraged them. One possible escape from the contradiction, if British direct investment was not wanted for political reasons, was to encourage direct investment from other sources of capital. This might also contribute to a diversification of Ireland's external trade. In 1953 Lemass visited the United States and Canada to promote both North American direct investment in Irish industry and Irish exports to North America.[79] Ireland's economic problems continued, and its poverty in relation to Britain, or even to the six counties, increased. Emigration in the 1950s, almost entirely to Britain, was the highest for any decade since the 1890s.

Lacking jurisdiction over trade and tariffs, Quebec could not pursue the protectionist economic policies that de Valera's governments followed in Ireland, although Canada as a whole maintained a relatively high level of tariff protection for its manufacturing industries, many of which were in Quebec. Probably Quebec's lack of jurisdiction in this regard was beneficial to its economy, which flourished in close association with the rest of Canada, and increasingly with the United States, while the Irish economy stagnated under the protectionist and inward-looking policies of Fianna Fail. Although Quebec probably had some constitutional authority to regulate foreign direct investment, its governments of both parties made no effort to do so. Instead, they pursued an open-door policy that contributed to a rapid growth of American ownership and control in Quebec's economy, particularly after 1945. Duplessis, in particular, actively solicited American capital and enjoyed excellent relations with the English-speaking business elite, both Canadian and American. In his 1944 election campaign, he used the slogan "Maîtres chez nous," which Lionel Groulx had originated, but there is little to suggest that Duplessis took it seriously. His post-war government commissioned a study on the feasibility of establishing a steel mill in Quebec but suppressed the study when the project was indeed found to be feasible.

Despite, or perhaps because of, the laissez-faire policies pursued by both the Liberals under Taschereau and the Union nationale under Duplessis, there was much discussion in intellectual circles of alternative approaches to managing the economy.[80] This was in contrast to the situation before about 1920, when French Canadians had hardly ever discussed such matters. Many of the economic ideas and proposals discussed in Quebec, like those of Fianna Fail in Ireland, were directly or indirectly inspired by Catholic social thought, particularly the encyclicals Rerum Novarum, published in 1891, and Quadrigesimo Anno, which, as its title suggests, appeared forty years later. These encyclicals taught that, although the centralized state was potentially dangerous and Marxist socialism was anathema, economic laissez-faire was not an acceptable alternative. Society should be based on harmony and cooperation, not on class conflict or the relentless competition of the free market. People were entitled to economic security and reasonable living standards, and the state had an obligation to help them in pursuing these objectives. Rather than relying entirely on the state, however, people should form natural associations based on functional interests, which would collaborate with one another and be incorporated into economic policy-making through representative institutions. This concept, known as corporatism, had supposedly been implemented by dictatorships in Portugal and Italy, regimes that received at least a qualified endorsement in Quadrigesimo Anno. Corporatism greatly attracted Quebec's intelligentsia for about a quarter of a century after that encyclical appeared. Montreal's municipal council between 1940 and 1960, like the Irish senate after 1937, was partly based on corporatist principles of representation.

Ideas of this kind, collectivist and mildly interventionist but not socialist, were espoused by the few trained French Canadian economists, such as Esdras Minville and François-Albert Angers. They found their way, in a rather diluted form, into the programs of Action libérale nationale, the Union nationale, and the Bloc populaire canadien. More specific economic proposals favoured by Quebec nationalists included support for colonization and rural electrification, easy credit for farmers and small business proprietors, attacks on the "trusts," which were controlled by English-speaking Canadians or Americans, control of foreign direct investment, more active involvement by the provincial government in the development of natural resources, and measures to encourage the purchase of locally produced goods and services. Tariffs were not discussed, since they obviously fell under federal jurisdiction.

One interesting parallel between the economic ideas of Irish and Quebec nationalism was a common fascination with the subject of hydroelectricity. Both Ireland and Quebec lacked coal, which had been the basis of British and American economic success, but both hoped that the new technology of hydroelectric power would serve as a substitute. Michael Collins was an early proponent of developing the hydroelectric resources of the Shannon River as a state-owned enterprise.[81] Between 1925 and 1929 this feat was actually accomplished by the Cosgrave government with technical assistance from Germany, making electricity available in much of rural Ireland for the first time. The major generating station was opened with an impressive ceremony, including a prayer by the bishop of Killaloe, just as the depression of the 1930s began.[82] It was an important symbol of economic progress and emancipation for the newly independent state, at a time when there was little good economic news in Ireland or anywhere else.

In Quebec, hydroelectric development by private enterprise, mainly English Canadian or American, had begun before the First World War. By the 1930s the allegedly high rates charged by "the electricity trust" were often criticized by nationalists and economic reformers of various kinds. The program of Action libérale nationale, and later of the Union nationale, pledged that rural electrification would be encouraged, that hydroelectric resources not already developed would be administered by the province, and that a gradual nationalization of existing hydroelectric facilities would be considered. Duplessis made no effort to implement these promises between 1936 and 1939, but the Godbout government in 1944 nationalized the Montreal Light Heat and Power company to create Hydro-Québec, a provincial enterprise that served Montreal and its environs but not the hinterlands of the province.[83] Duplessis's government encouraged rural electrification after the Second World War, but relied on private enterprise to generate most of the power. The idea that the province should play a more direct role nonetheless remained popular. The link between hydro-electricity and the politics of nationalism would be finally consummated in the 1960s.

CULTURAL NATIONALISM: THE SEARCH FOR IDENTITY

In the minds of many nationalists, the political and economic goals of Irish and Quebec nationalism were subordinate to a higher purpose: the protection of a distinct language, culture, and way of life, which was the real justification for the nationalist enterprise. Politics and economics were means rather than ends; the end was cultural survival. Since cultural influences tending to erode the distinctiveness of the national community were strong and always present, cultural nationalists had to be continuously on guard against the danger. If the Irish became indistinguishable from the British, or if French Canadians became indistinguishable from other Canadians or North Americans, nationalism, according to this view, would have failed in its purpose, even if the people were prosperous and the state was free of external control.

Apart from the practical difficulties of implementing it, cultural nationalism in Ireland and Quebec faced the problem that it was exclusive in two senses. First, it tended, like similar movements elsewhere, to inspire the enthusiasm mainly of the well-educated and relatively affluent middle class, whose influence over their society it would tend to reinforce insofar as it was successful. Poorer and less-educated people were inclined to welcome the popular and mass culture emanating from Britain and the United States, insofar as they gave any thought to such matters. Second, cultural nationalism tended to exclude those who did not fully share the cultural characteristics used to define the nation, or did not share them at all. In Ireland this category included the small but influential Protestant minority in the south and the Protestant majority in the six counties of the north, without whose consent reunification of Ireland was unlikely to be possible. In Quebec it included the substantial English-speaking minority, as well as growing numbers of immigrants from continental Europe. How could these peoples accept a nationalist project that excluded them, and what were the implications if they did not?

Catholicism played a large part in defining the national identity of Ireland and the provincial identity of Quebec, although this was a somewhat delicate issue because of the non-Catholic minorities in both places. The Catholic Church enjoyed a quasi-official status in both Ireland and Quebec, including an explicit mention in the Irish constitution of 1937, with Catholic symbols, prayers, and clergy much in evidence on official occasions. When Douglas Hyde, the first president of Ireland and a Protestant, died in 1949, none of Ireland's Catholic politicians could attend his funeral in the Protestant cathedral. It was said that the only Catholics who dared to do so were the non-believing writer Austin Clarke and the French ambassador.[84] Heads of government in both Ireland and Quebec took care to remain on good terms with the Catholic bishops and rarely took major policy initiatives of which they disapproved.[85] When Duplessis's government announced its intention to establish a ministry of youth in 1946, Cardinal Villeneuve expressed concern and advised Duplessis that the new ministry must not be involved in education.[86] The report of Quebec's Tremblay Commission placed great emphasis on Catholicism as a component of Quebec's distinct culture. In Ireland clerical power seemed to be demonstrated by the "mother and child" controversy of 1951, in which Noel Browne, the minister of health in Costello's government, was forced to resign after the Catholic bishops condemned his scheme to provide free medical care to mothers and their children.[87] However, some studies of the episode question this interpretation.[88] The more tactful and astute Fianna Fail government was able to establish a similar scheme a few years later.

Perhaps the strongest affinity between the Catholic Church and the conservative nationalism of both Ireland and Quebec was their common distaste for the secularism, materialism, individualism, and hedonism conveyed by Anglo-American mass culture and their common desire to shield their societies from its influence. This was the real truth behind Henri Bourassa's argument that the (French) language was the guardian of the faith. The link between Catholicism and nationalism should not, however, be overemphasized. There was a latent tension between a universal church and the idea of nationalism which caused the devoutly religious Henri Bourassa to have increasing misgivings about nationalism in the interwar years, particularly after extreme nationalism was condemned by Pope Pius XI. Some of the Catholic clergy were extremely nationalistic in both Ireland and Quebec, but others were less so. Some nationalists were devout, but others were less so. A Protestant such as Douglas Hyde could still be an Irish nationalist.

The relationship between language and cultural identity was less ambiguous. Nationalists since the nineteenth century have tended to emphasize language as an attribute of nationality. Thus cultural nationalism in Ireland tended to focus on the goal of reviving the Irish language, just as in Quebec it emphasized the need to protect the French language. Mainly this emphasis was because the Irish language and the culture that it embodied were genuinely valued, but for many Irish nationalists there were two other motives. First, a distinctive language was considered a necessary badge of nationhood, like an army or a flag, and the proof that independence had been worth fighting for.[89] Second, the language might serve as a barrier against ideological and cultural influences that were considered objectionable Some measures to revive the language had been taken even before the war of independence, and by 1921 a quarter of all schoolchildren were studying Irish in school.[90] However, English was clearly the dominant language in all parts of the country, except for some rural districts, mainly in the far west, whose most obvious characteristics were poverty and isolation. While almost everyone in Ireland could speak English, only a small minority spoke Irish, and the proportion that spoke it well or often was even smaller. Even the cultural nationalists who were most preoccupied with preserving the Irish language had learned it in adulthood as a second language and were more fluent in English.

Despite these facts, and despite the many other problems confronting the new state, the restoration of Irish was given a high priority from the outset. It was one issue that united the two sides in the civil war, when so much else divided them. Article 4 of the constitution of the Free State proclaimed in 1922 that Irish was the national language, although English was equally recognized as a second official language. Article 8 of the 1937 constitution modified this formula slightly by proclaiming Irish the national language and the first official language, while English was only the second official language. The concessions to English reflected practical reality, as quickly became apparent; even debates in the Dáil were conducted mainly in English. In 1923 the chief justice of Ireland ruled that an Irish affidavit presented as evidence in court must be accompanied by an English translation. The Gaelic League protested, but as Kevin O'Higgins pointed out when the matter was debated in the Dáil, its letter of protest was also accompanied by an English translation! O'Higgins defended the chief justice, but another member described the episode as "a certain slight and slur cast on the position of Irish as the National language."[91] Even that member, however, admitted that he did not expect Irish to replace English as the dominant language within his lifetime.

Despite the member's pessimism, or his frankness, many Irish nationalists genuinely hoped and even expected that Irish could be made the normal working language of Ireland, just as French was the normal working language of France and German of Germany. As a minister of education told the Dáil in 1937, "We are not out to teach Irish as a literary subject in the schools; we are out to make Irish the living, spoken language of this country."[92] This aspiration ignored the fact that most Irish people had more or less voluntarily accepted English a century earlier, as well as the proximity and power of England, a country whose population was about ten times that of Ireland, not to mention the close ties of many Irish families with the United States.

Efforts to revive and encourage the language proceeded on three main fronts: education, public administration, and assistance to those parts of the country where Irish was still the predominant language. In the field of education, including primary, secondary, and post-secondary levels, some progress in promoting Irish as a subject of study had already been made in the last years of British rule. After 1922, efforts were devoted to using Irish as a medium of instruction for teaching other subjects, although the lack of suitable textbooks and the limited Irish-language facility of many teachers created serious obstacles. In a Dáil debate on the subject fifteen years later, a member with teaching experience claimed that schoolchildren spent a quarter of their time learning in Irish, but that results had not been encouraging; many parents were complaining that their children were not learning enough or not learning it well when they were taught in Irish.[93]

In the public administration some steps were taken almost immediately after independence, such as requiring the registration of all births, marriages, and deaths to be recorded in Irish only. After 1925 virtually all positions in the public service required a knowledge of Irish as a condition of entry. Three years later knowledge of the language was made a requirement for admission to the bar. However, the public service, like the Dáil and the courts, continued to do most of its business in English. The head of the public service warned against imposing Irish more rapidly or more coercively than public opinion was willing to accept it. In 1934 the Fianna Fail government was reduced to approving a recommendation that a sign reminding officials to speak Irish be displayed in every government office. In 1945 it required a test in spoken Irish as a condition of promotion within the public service, but those who had been hired before 1925 were exempted.[94]

A commission was appointed in 1925 to define the boundaries of the areas, known collectively as the Gaeltacht, where Irish still seemed to be the predominant language. These received various kinds of special assistance, but measures to improve their standard of living tended also to increase the use of English, while their populations continued to be thinned by out-migration. A government memo in 1929 directed that, "as far as practicable," officials in the Gaeltacht should use Irish to communicate with Irish-speaking members of the public.[95] Seventeen years later Eamon de Valera told the Dáil that his government was still trying to implement this policy, but he implied that it was not fully succeeding. When Richard Mulcahy, the leader of Fine Gael, charged that the Gaeltacht areas were dwindling and the use of Irish within them was declining, de Valera admitted that this was so.[96] By 1958, when a Commission on the Restoration of the Irish Language was appointed, it appeared that this national goal had made no real progress since independence.

Language, meaning French, was also an important badge and symbol of nationality in Quebec, as the previous chapter has discussed. Henri Bourassa had associated language, faith, and patriotism in his speech and pamphlet entitled *La langue gardienne de la foi* and in other speeches and writings. However, the position of the French language in Quebec was so much stronger than that of the Irish language in Ireland that it sometimes tended to be taken for granted. In 1931, for example, well over half the population of Quebec could speak only French, while fewer than one person out of seven could speak only English. The demographic position of French in Quebec and Canada even improved somewhat after the First World War, mainly because of declining rates of immigration. Persons with French as their mother tongue increased from 26.7 per cent of Canada's population in 1921 to 29.0 per cent in 1951. In Quebec the increase was from 79.3 to 82.5 per cent over the same period of time. It was perhaps also significant that Ontario modified its infamous Regulation 17 to restore French-language education in 1927. Some persons, including Lionel Groulx, even believed that French was destined to become the predominant language in eastern and central Canada, although obviously not in the western provinces.[97]

The French language was still overwhelmingly outnumbered in North America, however, and the desire to retain and strengthen it remained as strong as ever. In 1920 Groulx was instrumental in forming a nationalist organization known as Action française, which never acquired a mass membership but was reasonably influential for several years.[98] Action française grew out of the old Ligue des droits du français, in which Groulx had also been active, and the protection of the French language was one of its major preoccupations. Like its French namesake, founded a few years earlier by Charles Maurras, it had serious doubts about democracy and called for the leadership of a "chef." It disappeared soon after Maurras and his movement were condemned by the pope in 1928.

In the 1920s Action française campaigned for more bilingualism in Canada and for more (French) unilingualism in Quebec. The reference to unilingualism did not imply an attack on the right of the English-speaking minority in Quebec to use their own language. The point was to counter the argument, frequently heard at that time, that all French Canadians must learn English if they wished to achieve economic success. Nationalists feared that if this argument were generally accepted, their language might suffer the fate of the Irish language in the nineteenth century. Since Quebec's government and most of its civil society already functioned in French, campaigns to promote the language mainly targeted the private sector of the economy, which was still disproportionately controlled by the English-speaking minority and was not always sensitive to the linguistic concerns of French Canadians. The ethnic division of labour and the inferior economic position of the French were the realities behind the concern about linguistic questions. A sociological study in 1938 found that the Montreal Board of Trade, the organization representing big business in a city that was about two-thirds French Canadian, had only 206 French Canadians among its 1,566 members.[99]

A French language movement with a somewhat different purpose from that of Action française was the Ordre de Jacques Cartier, which was founded in Ottawa in the 1920s to assist French Canadians who felt themselves discriminated against in the federal public service. Probably in response to the rigid rules barring political activity by federal employees, it was a clandestine and somewhat mysterious organization, a fact that caused rumours to proliferate about its true nature and purpose. In 1944 the recently appointed chairman of Hydro-Québec, a veteran anticlerical and left-leaning Liberal politician named Télesphore-Damien Bouchard, caused a sensation when he publicly accused the Catholic clergy of supporting the OJC, which he claimed was promoting separatism and fascism. Bouchard was forced to resign after Premier Godbout and most other prominent Quebec politicians defended the organization and disassociated themselves from his views.[100]

Despite their willingness to defend the OJC, Quebec politicians actually took little interest in linguistic questions until the 1960s, perhaps because they saw no need for concern and more likely because they feared frightening away private investment. Premier Taschereau's government was actively hostile to Action française. The Duplessis government appeared to have little interest in cultural matters, and its only serious effort on behalf of the French language was a bill in 1937 entitled "A law respecting the interpretation of the laws of the province." The bill provided that in the event of any dispute over the interpretation of Quebec statutes, including the Civil Code, the Municipal Code, and the Code of Civil Procedure, the French text and not the English text would be considered authoritative. The English-speaking minority in Quebec did not welcome this measure, and a year after its adoption it was repealed on the ostensible grounds that it "may give rise to friction and problems difficult of solution, which it is expedient to avoid."[101] Duplessis's only other linguistic initiative was to decree in 1958 that his ministers must answer parliamentary questions in French, even when the question was asked in English by an English-speaking member.[102]

Some nationalists, including Lionel Groulx, argued that the preservation of the French language and culture in North America called for "a French state." Groulx promised the second Congrès de la langue française in 1937, "Notre État nous l'aurons."[103] He suggested on that occasion that this state could be achieved within Confederation. When others used his expression, it was not always clear whether they meant a state within or outside the Canadian federation, or whether it would consist only of Quebec or would include those parts of Ontario and New Brunswick adjacent to Quebec that were predominantly French-speaking. Interest in separatism, such as it was, had subsided for a decade after the debate on the Francoeur motion, but it revived again during the economic crisis of the 1930s. It was given a further impetus by disappointment over the fate of Action libérale nationale and disillusionment with the conservative and largely rhetorical nationalism of Duplessis. Another stimulus to dreams of independence was the centennial of the Patriote rebellion of 1837–38, which had a somewhat similar effect in Quebec to that of the centennial of 1798 in Ireland.

The revival of separatist or quasi-separatist nationalism was encouraged by *La Nation,* a right-wing and at times pro-fascist periodical published in Quebec City during the 1930s.[104] A frequent contributor to its columns, Dostaler O'Leary, published a volume in 1937 with the title *Séparatisme: Doctrine constructive.* (It was perhaps appropriate that a French Canadian with an Irish family name should introduce the Irish word "separatism" into the discourse of Quebec politics, although there was nothing Irish about O'Leary's political philosophy.) O'Leary did not begin to make the case for an independent French state until well into the second half of his book, which began with his reflections on French Canadian history and continued with a discussion of his political ideas. He asserted the need for a French state that was Catholic and corporatist. He said that parliamentary democracy was outmoded, praised the censorship of newspapers in fascist Italy, and called Benito Mussolini the greatest political genius of the century. He used an offensive word for Jews in a passage discussing Canada's immigration policy. Elsewhere in the book he referred to Léon Blum, the head of France's popular-front government, as "Ce juif sans patrie" and accused him of handing over France to the "Asiatic vultures" of the Kremlin. O'Leary called communism the logical conclusion of liberalism, but asserted, somewhat inconsistently, that liberal democracy was only a facade to conceal the power of big business.[105]

Canada, according to O'Leary, was an artificial entity, even more than Belgium, which also had two languages but at least had a common religion. Canada could only become a nation by assimilating the French Canadians, and Henri Bourassa's support for federalism was therefore utopian and misguided. Quebec, on the other hand, had all the attributes of a nation, and the existence of francophone minorities in other parts of Canada was no reason to reject the idea of independence. An independent Quebec would continue to attract foreign capital because of its natural resources, O'Leary argued, although elsewhere in the book he suggested that the resource industries would probably be nationalized. The French Quebec state would be willing to keep the British monarch as its ceremonial head of state and its link with the British Empire. The English-speaking minority would be treated fairly and would continue to have their Protestant schools. Even "Israelites" would be "tolerated," although a quota would be used to limit their participation in the professions. French Canadians in other parts of North America would be encouraged to "repatriate" themselves to Quebec.[106]

Some of O'Leary's political views were bizarre even for 1937, and they became distinctly unfashionable two or three years later. When a serious movement for the independence of Quebec developed a generation after he published his book, its adherents were understandably reluctant to claim him as a precursor, and most of them would have been shocked by the book if they had read it. However, his book was the first to give extended consideration to the idea of a sovereign Quebec, and some of his arguments were not without merit. He had planted a seed that would flourish long afterwards, independently of the unfortunate associations that he gave to it.

For the moment, however, O'Leary was a voice crying in the wilderness. Mainstream nationalism was not separatist in the 1930s, or for a long time afterwards. A far more significant and representative contributor to nationalist thought in the Duplessis era and for almost a decade afterwards was André Laurendeau, the young intellectual who headed the provincial wing of the Bloc populaire in the 1940s.[107] After the Bloc disintegrated, he became associate editor and then editor of Le Devoir, restoring that newspaper to its former position as the intellectual voice of a humane and civilized French Canadian nationalism. While disapproving of Duplessis for his conservatism, Laurendeau supported the premier's struggle to maintain provincial autonomy.[108] Laurendeau never became a separatist, although he took the ideas of the independence movement seriously. He was more of a liberal than Groulx and more of a Quebec (as opposed to Canadian) nationalist than Bourassa, but he built on the intellectual foundations of their thought. Like Bourassa, he hoped that English-speaking and French-speaking Canadians could collaborate to protect their two cultures against assimilation by the United States. As Louis Balthazar has suggested, Laurendeau was a bridge between the old pre-war nationalism from which he sprang and the neo-nationalism of the 1960s, which he lived just long enough to see.[109]

Laurendeau is perhaps the most representative of Quebec's political thinkers because he never resolved the ambiguous relationship between French Canada and Quebec. To put it another way, he could not choose between a French Canadian ethnic and cultural nationalism that implicitly included the minorities outside Quebec and excluded the minorities within and a Quebec nationalism that drew a boundary around the province. He tried to resolve the problem by advocating a bilingual Canada that would be an equal partnership of the two nations, including a Quebec that would exercise more powers than the other provinces. Like Bourassa, he was a highly cultured man who cared deeply about his French cultural heritage. Although he lacked (or rather lost) Bourassa's religious faith, he acknowledged Catholicism as an important part of that heritage. He was also a reformer, as Bourassa could be from time to time, who disliked political corruption and the dishonesty and pettiness that political life displayed at its worst, in Quebec and elsewhere. Yet he kept his faith in democracy and believed that the state could be used to protect and promote the cultural heritage that he loved, as well as to improve the lives of French Canadians, who were still, in his time, economically and socially disadvantaged in relation to their fellow citizens of British ancestry. Paul Gouin and Maurice Duplessis had briefly raised hopes that this could happen, only to disappoint their supporters. The hopes lived on, but their realization would have to await another day.

CHAPTER EIGHT

Things Fall Apart

William Butler Yeats wrote the poem from which the title of this chapter is taken in response to the Russian Revolution, but the poem was often quoted in the 1960s, a decade of turbulence and upheaval in much of the world. Most of Africa was released from British, French, or Belgian colonial rule at the beginning of the decade, a development that, among other consequences, led to the deaths of ten Irish soldiers serving with the United Nations in the Congo. John F. Kennedy, Robert Kennedy, and Martin Luther King Jr were assassinated. Afro-Americans rebelled against the institutionalized racism of the southern states, and the federal government at last took measures to protect their civil rights. The war in Vietnam took an appalling toll of human life and was still in progress as the decade ended. The Greek army overturned its country's fragile democracy and imposed a military dictatorship. Czechoslovakia was invaded and occupied by its "allies" in the Warsaw Pact. Mexican students were massacred by the Mexican army as their country played host to the Olympic Games. In France the Fifth Republic was threatened by a military insurrection at the beginning of the decade and a wave of student demonstrations that almost brought down the regime in 1968. China was convulsed by the Cultural Revolution.

It was also a decade of dramatic change and upheaval in Quebec and in Ireland, both north and south. Eamon de Valera resigned as taoiseach and leader of Fianna Fail in June 1959, to assume the largely ceremonial position of president of the republic. Less than three months later Premier Maurice Duplessis died in office. To these almost simultaneous transitions, both of which seemed to end a long era of conservative stability, should be added another that took place with similar results four years later, when Lord Brookeborough (Sir Basil Brooke) retired after twenty years as prime minister of Northern Ireland, to be replaced by Terence O'Neill. All three events were followed by significant and largely unexpected periods of political, social, and economic change. The changes in southern Ireland following de Valera's resignation, while certainly important, were the least dramatic and the least disruptive of the three; the constitutional regime that he himself had done more than any other person to establish proved stable and resilient enough to absorb them. In contrast, the changes in Northern Ireland following Brooke's retirement were the most dramatic and disruptive, unleashing a generation of civil violence that killed more than three thousand persons by 1992 and destroyed the viability of a regime that dated from 1920, as well as spilling over the border into southern Ireland in the early 1970s. The changes in Quebec following Duplessis's death, which are known there as the Quiet Revolution, occupy an intermediate position between the relative stability of southern Ireland and the violent upheaval in the six counties. Deaths from political violence in Quebec were very few, and the regime – that is, the Canadian federation established in 1867 – did not collapse. However, the legitimacy of that regime in Quebec was seriously reduced, and a credible movement for the independence of Quebec emerged and gained extensive support. For a period of about ten years, Quebec even had its own local version of the Irish Republican Army, although it proved to be weaker and much less durable than its Irish counterpart.

Bearing these differences in mind, we can usefully compare the three sets of events with one another, and also perhaps with the earlier events that led to the formation of the Irish Free State, as described in Chapter 6. In each case, changes and reforms took place. In Northern Ireland and in Quebec the changes and reforms led to demands for more, demands that the existing regime could not easily provide. They also led to a resurgence of nationalism among Catholics in Northern Ireland (where they comprised a significant and growing minority) and among francophones in Quebec (where they comprised a substantial majority), culminating in demands for a change in the regime. These in turn caused anxiety and resentment among Protestants in the six counties and anglophones in Quebec, who saw themselves as threatened by these developments. On the other hand, neither Catholics in the rest of Ireland (where they comprised the overwhelming majority) nor francophones in the rest of Canada (where they comprised only a small minority) were directly involved in these events, which they viewed from afar as sympathetic spectators. Nonetheless, they were affected by them in a number of ways.

The situation in which improvements in the status of a group lead to demands for more improvements, demands that cannot be satisfied without more fundamental change, has been called a revolution of rising expectations. Ireland in the decades before the First World War, with improvements in land tenure, education, local government, and the franchise, as well as the rise of a Catholic middle class and the decline of the Protestant landowning class, fits this model quite well. It can also be applied to Northern Ireland after 1963 and to Quebec after 1959, or perhaps even a slightly earlier date.[1] In the case of southern Ireland after 1959 we can see some changes and reforms that partly parallel those which Quebec experienced almost simultaneously, but no revolution of rising expectations, and no resurgence of nationalism, seems to have taken place. Apparently the conditions that produced these consequences in Northern Ireland and in Quebec were not present, or were present to a much lesser extent, in southern Ireland, a point to which we will return. Insofar as there was a threat to the Irish regime (and arguably there was, for a brief period in the 1970s), it was a spillover from events in the six counties, rather than a product of events within the state, and thus a reminder that the "border" in Ireland is not really an international border in the usual sense.

QUEBEC'S QUIET REVOLUTION

In Quebec, as in much of the Western world, the decade of the 1950s was one of rapid economic and demographic growth. The province's population increased by 30 per cent during the decade, while that of Montreal (including its suburbs) increased by more than 50 per cent in the same period. With rapid industrial growth, largely driven by foreign direct investment, added to very low inflation and virtually full employment, Quebec entered the age of mass consumption. Automobiles, hot running water, oil-fired central heating, and electric stoves and refrigerators all became a part of everyday life for a majority of the population.

An innovation that was probably more significant for the future of Quebec than any of these devices was television. A federal government agency, Radio-Canada, began producing and broadcasting television programs in French in 1952. The government monopoly of television broadcasting ended in 1958, and two years later the first privately owned and operated French-language channel began broadcasting. By 1960 almost 90 per cent of all homes in Quebec had a television receiver, a significantly higher percentage than in Canada as a whole.[2] The studios of Radio-Canada in Montreal became the centre of French-speaking Quebec's cultural life and its primary source of information and communication during the 1950s. One effect was to break down the barriers of localism, making francophone Quebec a single network of communication, information, and ideas. Another was to reinforce the boundary between French-speaking Quebec and the rest of Canada, not to mention the rest of North America. Although Radio-Canada was a federal agency, its programs were produced in Quebec by residents of Quebec, reflected Quebec perspectives and preoccupations, and in the early days of the medium were viewed only in Quebec. The extension of French-language broadcasting to other parts of Canada did not occur until much later and was largely a response to what the federal government perceived by that time as the growing threat of separatist Quebec nationalism. English-speaking Canadians, including those in Quebec, had their own television networks, but they also had access to television channels and programs from the United States, to which they quickly became addicted. French-speaking Quebecers, however, preferred their own locally produced programs in their own language. Louis Balthazar has rightly emphasized the importance of television in making Quebec a national community.[3]

In spite of material progress and social change, some aspects of life in Quebec changed less rapidly in the 1950s. The government of Maurice Duplessis, first elected in 1936 and returned to office after a brief intermission in 1944, waged a rearguard battle against the development of the interventionist welfare state at the federal level, but was handicapped by its own lack of an effective merit-based public service. One reason for this lack was the Union nationale's reliance on the distribution of patronage, one of several political practices associated with that party that began to seem anachronistic and anomalous in a rapidly changing society. Tentative efforts at civil service reform by the wartime Liberal government had been shelved as soon as Duplessis returned to office in 1944. Another reason why administrative reform was not a priority was a traditional skepticism in Quebec regarding the efficacy, and even the honesty, of the state. This attitude had led to a tradition of leaving economic matters largely to private enterprise and social matters largely to the Catholic Church, insofar as they did not fall under the federal government's jurisdiction.[4] Thus Quebec continued to lack a ministry of education, although the inadequacy of the educational system was increasingly criticized during the 1950s. While neglecting some of its responsibilities, the provincial government contented itself with using private bills and discretionary spending to reward its actual or potential supporters and occasionally to punish its opponents. For example, counties that had the temerity to elect a member of the Liberal opposition received only a bare minimum of public expenditure, as Duplessis frankly confessed on more than one occasion.[5]

The Union nationale's effective political machine won four consecutive elections between 1944 and 1956, a feat that has not since been duplicated in Quebec. Among the growing intelligentsia, the middle class, and some of the lower clergy, however, opposition to it gradually developed during the 1950s. Radio-Canada, which as a federal agency could attack the provincial government with impunity, was an important vehicle of opposition to the Union nationale. A pamphlet by two priests denouncing corrupt electoral practices caused a sensation in 1956 and was later expanded into a book which appeared in time for the next election. Organized labour, particularly the Catholic unions, became increasingly hostile after the government supported the employers in two celebrated strikes, one involving asbestos miners in 1949 and another involving copper miners nine years later. Radical nationalists argued that, beneath a veneer of rhetorical nationalism, Duplessis was allowing foreign capital to exploit the province's natural resources and its relatively cheap labour on highly favourable terms, while French Canadians remained "hewers of wood and drawers of water" in the only province where they comprised a majority of the population. Writing in *Le Devoir*, André Laurendeau even compared Duplessis to the puppet rulers allegedly found in certain African colonies, who kept the natives quiet while European settlers pulled the strings and dominated the economy.[6]

The historian Michael Behiels has suggested that there were two distinct, although overlapping, currents of opinion in the opposition to Duplessis during the post-war years.[7] Those critics who were primarily individualist liberals despised the conservatism and anti-intellectualism of the Union nationale, its corrupt and dishonest electoral practices, and the stifling atmosphere of social and political conformity that it, and its clerical allies, imposed on the province. They were cosmopolitans with little sympathy for French Canadian nationalism, although some of them agreed with Duplessis's view that the federal government should not meddle in areas of provincial jurisdiction. The person who was destined to become the most famous of this group, Pierre Elliott Trudeau, summed up their sentiments in the comment "Open the borders! This people is dying of asphyxiation." Behiels calls this group the *citélibrists*, after the intellectual magazine *Cité libre*, which was one of their principal platforms in the 1950s.

The other group of critics were critical of Duplessis's nationalism on the grounds that it did not go far enough. They resented what they saw as Quebec's subordinate position within a predominantly English-speaking Canada, whose central government operated almost entirely in English and had little sensitivity to French Canada's distinct culture and way of life. They resented even more the anglophone domination of Quebec's economy and the privileged status of its English-speaking minority. They were less critical of French Canadian society than the *citélibrists* and more inclined to attribute its problems to external sources. Many of their concerns had been voiced by Action française in the 1920s, by Action libérale nationale in the 1930s, and by the Bloc populaire in the 1940s. Le Devoir was the principal medium for propagating their ideas. Behiels calls this group the neo-nationalists.

Two relationships whose origins lay in the era of British colonialism continued to shape the peculiar character of Quebec society in the 1950s: the relationship between church and state and the relationship between the English-speaking minority and the French-speaking majority of Quebec's population. The *citélibrists* tended to be more preoccupied with the first, and the neo-nationalists with the second. As the decade drew to a close, both relationships were increasingly unstable, threatened by new forces and circumstances that were making them obsolescent.

For reasons explained in earlier chapters, the Catholic Church occupied an unusually prominent role in Quebec society, as it did in Ireland. Catholics were about 90 per cent of the population, and in the 1950s virtually all of them practised their faith. A network of Catholic associations of various kinds provided most of the framework for civil society. In the 1950s the total number of priests, nuns, and monks in Quebec exceeded the number of persons employed by the provincial government. By general consent and long-standing practice, the church performed most of the functions that were ostensibly under the jurisdiction of the province: organizing, operating, and staffing the schools, colleges, universities, hospitals, orphanages, and asylums that served the vast majority of Quebec's population. As an urbanized and industrialized society needed more of the services provided by such institutions, more and more clerical energies were diverted from strictly spiritual matters into managing what the sociologist Hubert Guindon termed the church's "bureaucratic empires."[8] These institutions made the church's role in society conspicuous and pervasive, but concealed its inflexibility, its vulnerability to the intrusion of new ideas, and its increasing dependence on the provincial government.

At one time Quebec's Catholic institutions had required no funding from the state, but by the 1950s they had become much more expensive to operate and were increasingly dependent on it. Despite Duplessis's insistence on balancing the budget and the general preference for low taxes and limited government, per capita spending by the Quebec government more than tripled in real terms between 1945 and 1960. The proportion of this spending devoted to education, health, and welfare increased from just over a third to almost half.[9] Most of this money was channelled through Catholic institutions before it reached the general public. Knowing the dependence of the institutions on his largesse, Duplessis, although a devout Catholic himself, boasted privately that "the bishops eat out of my hand."[10] Partly to preserve this state of affairs and partly out of a sincere belief in provincial autonomy, he refused to allow any federal funds to reach the "bureaucratic empires," whether in the form of university grants or the federal cost-sharing of universal hospital insurance that was offered to all provinces in 1957. On the other hand, his arbitrary and unpredictable allocations of funds, rational in terms of the Union nationale's electoral strategy but not conducive to rational planning by the recipients, was increasingly resented.

When Duplessis died in 1959, he was succeeded by his chosen heir apparent, Paul Sauvé, whose father, Arthur Sauvé, had led Quebec's Conservative Party from 1916 to 1927. Paul Sauvé was expected to provide more spending, less capricious budgeting, and a more flexible approach to federal-provincial relations.[11] He had shown signs of meeting these expectations when he died suddenly after less than four months in office. He was succeeded by a much less impressive politician, Antonio Barrette, who rapidly dissipated the hopes that Sauvé's arrival in power had encouraged. Whether Sauvé could have combined the modernization of the Quebec state and of the Union nationale with a reinforcement and improvement of their traditionally close relationship with the church will never be known. Even before 1959 some dissident voices had begun to question the hegemonic role of the church in Quebec society, as well as its relationship with a conservative party that did not always live up to Christian ideals as they were understood in the post-war world. Some of the dissidents could be heard and seen on Radio-Canada. Others wrote in *Le Devoir* or in *Cité libre*, which had first appeared in 1950 and was inspired by the liberal Catholicism of postwar France. In 1960 a book that harshly criticized Quebec's church-controlled educational system, and by implication much of its traditional culture, was published under the pseudonym of "Frère Untel."[12] It became an instant best-seller. The author was soon revealed to be a lay brother named Jean-Paul Desbiens, who was dismissed from his teaching position and sent to Rome for a period of study and reflection. His ideas could not be dismissed as easily, however. When clerical authority and power in Quebec suddenly and unexpectedly disintegrated in the 1960s, it would become apparent how fragile they had really been.

The decline of clerical power and of the Catholic Church's "bureaucratic empires" would have important implications for non-Catholics, because the church's insistence on controlling Catholic civil society and its resistance to the rise of a bureaucratic state had shielded them from contact with the Catholic majority and allowed them to develop their own practically autonomous civil society on the territory of Quebec.[13] Clerical power, anglophone economic power, and the federal state (the successor to British colonial rule) had supported one another in Quebec like the three legs of a tripod. When one leg collapsed, the other two were placed in a precarious position. The economic power and wealth of Quebec's English-speaking minority, like the temporal power of the church, had deep roots in the province's history; it was still conspicuous as Quebec moved into the second half of the twentieth century. An ethnic division of labour, which some attributed to the lasting impact of the British conquest and others to the deficiencies of French Canadian culture and education, left French Canadians with below average incomes in every Canadian province, including Quebec. According to the 1961 census, males of British Isles ethnic origins in Quebec had average incomes more than 50 per cent greater than males of French ethnic origin. French-ethnic-origin men who could speak English as a second language had incomes considerably higher than those who could not, although not nearly as high as men of British Isles origin. However, men of British Isles origin who could speak French as a second language actually earned slightly less than those who were unilingual – in a province where French was the language of the overwhelming majority. In the Montreal metropolitan area, 38.9 per cent of British non-Catholics were in professional, technical, or managerial occupations, compared with 25.4 per cent of "British" (mainly Irish) Catholics and only 16.6 per cent of the French. Even those French Canadians who practised professions such as engineering, architecture, and medicine had lower incomes than British Canadians in Quebec who had the same occupations.[14]

The data on economic power, as opposed to wealth, were even more striking. Measured by value added, only 15.4 per cent of manufacturing industry in Quebec in 1961 was owned by francophone Canadians, who comprised more than 80 per cent of the population. Ownership of the remainder was divided almost evenly between anglophone Canadians and foreign-controlled enterprises. Measured by employment, the francophone share was somewhat higher, at 21.8 per cent, the anglophone Canadian share also somewhat higher, and the foreign-controlled share considerably lower. The only sectors of the Quebec economy in which most of the labour force worked for francophone-controlled enterprises were agriculture, services, retail trade, and, by a very slight majority of 50.7 per cent, construction, an industry that depended heavily on government contracts.[15] In the downtown core of Montreal, where the head offices of major enterprises were concentrated, there was little visible or audible evidence that one was in a mainly French-speaking city or province, apart from the occasional Catholic church. Immediately up the hill from this area, in the "square mile" where the anglophone economic elite had lived in the not-too-distant past, there was even less. Instead, one encountered four department stores with British names and largely unilingual anglophone personnel, an internationally renowned English-language university, the offices of English-speaking doctors and dentists, and an assortment of Protestant churches.

French-speaking Quebecers had understood and quietly resented the economic power and wealth of the anglophone minority for many years, without being able to do much about it. In the 1950s the resentment was expressed mainly in the editorial pages of *Le Devoir* and in the seminar rooms at the French-language Université de Montréal, particularly its department of history. Other evidence, for those who cared to see, was a major riot in March 1955 that was touched off when Quebec's greatest athlete, the hockey player Maurice Richard, was suspended for the duration of the playoffs by the English-speaking commissioner of the league. Few recognized the political significance of that event at the time, however.

Even fewer seemed to recognize that by 1960 the power and wealth of the anglophone minority rested on foundations that were gradually being undermined. The transcontinental economy based on railways, protective tariffs, and staple exports to the British market, of which Montreal had been the centre before the Second World War, was rapidly ceasing to exist. Toronto had already replaced Montreal as the financial and commercial centre of Canada and the principal destination for immigrants, although it was still somewhat smaller in population. With most of Canada's exports going to the United States and most of its capital inflow coming from that country, Montreal's seaport and its traditional ties with British capital were diminishing assets. The best and the brightest of Quebec's anglophone minority were gradually departing for Ontario or the United States in search of better opportunities. The old Anglo-Montreal elite no longer had the real economic importance to match their status and their privileges. By the time Montreal sank to the status of a regional city in the northeastern corner of North America, its bilingual French Canadian middle class or their children would be ready to take control of its economy.

On 22 June 1960 the Union nationale, led by Antonio Barrette, was narrowly defeated in a general election by the Liberal Party, led by Jean Lesage. Less than two weeks later, Lesage was sworn in as the head of a Liberal government.[16] The new premier, a handsome bilingual lawyer who had already been a minister in the federal government, was a moderately conservative reformer not very different in substance from the recently deceased Paul Sauvé. He was surrounded, however, by some quite different people from those in the Union nationale. His predecessor as Liberal leader, who became attorney general, was Georges-Émile Lapalme, a nationalist in the style of André Laurendeau and a reformer who had transformed the Liberal Party from a traditional patronage-based machine into the kind of party that

Paul Gouin had envisaged in the 1930s. An even more significant figure, as it turned out, was a former war correspondent and recent host of a current events program on television, René Lévesque, whose nationalist instincts had been awakened by the federal government's indifference to a lengthy and bitter producers' strike at Radio-Canada a year earlier.[17] Lévesque became minister of hydraulic resources or, more precisely, hydroelectricity. As noted in an earlier chapter, this subject already loomed large in the economic aspirations of Quebec nationalism.

During its first two years in office, the new government devoted itself to reforming the public service, eliminating some of the unseemly practices associated with the Union nationale machine, and implementing some of the Liberal Party's campaign promises, such as free secondary education and participation in the federal-provincial hospital insurance program, which Duplessis had declined to join. It began the process of building a modern secular and bureaucratic state to replace the Catholic Church's "bureaucratic empires." These initiatives did not at first lead to conflict with the federal government or with the anglophone minority in Quebec, and there was little obvious indication that Quebec was entering an era of radical nationalism. It was in this period that the expression "Quiet Revolution" was first used and that the Duplessis era began to be referred to as "la grande noirceur." The liberal and individualistic ideas of the *citélibrists* seemed to have triumphed over obscurantism and reaction, just as Pope John XXIII was shaking the Catholic Church out of its conservatism and preparing the ground for Vatican II. There were some early signs, however, that the growing tendency to question authority and tradition in Quebec might lead in some unexpected directions. One such was the sudden rise of the Créditiste movement, whose leader, an automobile salesman named Réal Caouette, used television to propagate a populist message mingled with the inflationary economic theories of Major C.H. Douglas. In the federal election of June 1962 this previously unknown movement won twenty-six Quebec ridings, mainly in the same hinterland areas that had decided the outcome of the provincial election two years earlier.

Soon after this event, the resurgence of nationalism in Quebec became obvious. It was precipitated at least in part by René Lévesque's determination to nationalize the hydroelectric companies, a project that the Union nationale had promised to carry out almost three decades earlier. Although public ownership of electricity already existed in several Canadian provinces, it lacked the significance elsewhere that it had in Quebec, where it would mean a substantial transfer of economic power from the anglophone minority to a predominantly francophone state. During a weekend retreat at Lac l'Épaule, near Quebec City, the Lesage government decided to proceed with nationalization, but not before seeking a fresh mandate from the voters. Lesage told a party gathering, "The era of economic colonialism will be definitely dead, even forgotten," once the government was returned to office.[18] The ensuing election campaign in the fall of 1962 was fought by the Liberals on the slogan "Maîtres chez nous," a phrase coined years previously by Lionel Groulx and also used by Duplessis in 1944. The Liberals won two-thirds of the seats in the Legislative Assembly. The campaign both revealed and reinforced the growing nationalism of French-speaking Quebecers, particularly the well-educated urban middle class.

Following its electoral triumph, the Lesage government purchased the power companies with funds borrowed in the United States. Hydro-Québec, when it absorbed the new acquisitions, became the first large industrial enterprise in North America that operated in French and employed mainly French-speaking personnel. The government now had the electoral mandate to proceed with other controversial plans, such as the establishment of a ministry of education, to which Quebec's two Catholic archbishops gave reluctant consent. It also found itself pushed by the climate of nationalist fervour that it had helped to create into a series of confrontations with the federal government, which proved to be relatively accommodating after April 1963 under the leadership of Lester Pearson. Pearson appointed a Royal Commission on Bilingualism and Biculturalism, with André Laurendeau as co-chair, to investigate how Quebec's aspirations could be accommodated within Canadian federalism. He also met frequently with provincial leaders in an effort to make the existing federal system more flexible. Quebec's share of income tax revenue was substantially increased, and it was allowed to "opt out" of certain shared-cost programs while receiving additional tax revenue in lieu of federal grants. Nonetheless, the friction between Quebec and the federal government was such that the Quebec Liberal Party seceded from its federal namesake in 1964, becoming a completely separate organization. The federal party continued to operate within Quebec, where it had substantial support, for the purpose of electing members to Canada's parliament.

The most serious conflict was over pensions, a field of divided responsibility in the constitution. Both governments were determined to establish universal contributory pension plans under their own control; an important motive in Quebec's case was the desire to create a capital fund that could be used to encourage francophone-controlled enterprise and develop the province's economy. The confrontation was so serious that a respected member of the Ottawa press gallery, Blair Fraser, told René Lévesque that it could mean "the end of Confederation."[19] Eventually the federal government retreated, allowing Quebec to establish its own pension plan while the federal plan operated in other parts of Canada.[20] This was a significant step towards conceding that Quebec, as the homeland of a distinct people, merited a status different from that of the other provinces. However, Quebec eventually discovered that English-speaking Canada was reluctant to entrench recognition of that view in the formal constitution.

Canadian governments had been trying for several years to devise an acceptable procedure for amending the British North America Act so as to eliminate the necessity of seeking amendments from the British parliament at Westminster. The Pearson government, like its Conservative predecessor, proposed a formula that would require the unanimous consent of all provinces to remove provincial powers and rights, but would allow other changes with the consent of two-thirds of the provinces comprising at least half Canada's population. Lesage initially was inclined to accept this formula, but many nationalists argued that it was too rigid in regard to changes that Quebec might want or not rigid enough in regard to changes that Quebec might not want. The wording of the document was, perhaps deliberately, obscure enough to make both concerns equally plausible. In January 1966 Lesage informed Pearson that because of the "inquietude" in Quebec, his government would "postpone indefinitely" its consideration of the formula.[21]

Lesage, like his contemporary André Laurendeau, was a transitional figure between the old French Canadian nationalism and the new Quebec nationalism which his government was helping to create. His own vision of Canada was similar to that of the Tremblay Commission: a bilingual and bicultural Canada including a Quebec that would have more powers and responsibilities than the other provinces, but also including francophone minorities elsewhere that would benefit from a strong Quebec and in which Quebec would continue to take an interest. He knew that "Quebec" and "French Canada" were not precisely synonymous, but like earlier nationalists, he saw no need to choose one over the other. He also saw no need to discard an identification with Canada as a whole, in which he sincerely believed. He sometimes argued, as Henri Bourassa had done, that Canada's two nationalisms could assist each other in resisting cultural assimilation to the United States.[22] By 1963 the Lesage vision of a new role for Quebec within Canadian federalism, sometimes known as "statut particulier," or special status, was widely supported in Quebec, and the old idea that strict adherence to the "compact" of 1867 would meet its needs had been virtually abandoned. When Lesage attempted to promote the new vision on a tour of English-speaking Canada in 1965, however, he met with a cold reception.

In Quebec itself some persons were already moving beyond the Lesage vision of reformed federalism in a more radical direction. André Laurendeau, an astute observer, was convinced as early as the spring of 1964 that René Lévesque was a separatist. A year later, according to Laurendeau's diary, Lévesque admitted privately that he was. Laurendeau himself confessed in his diary that he was tempted by separatism on occasion, particularly when his royal commission encountered the attitudes of English-speaking Canadians towards Quebec.[23] However, he never actually became a supporter of independence for Quebec.[24]

The idea of a "French state," whatever it meant, had never entirely died, but its few proponents, prior to the 1960s, had tended to look backwards to the Catholic and conservative non-territorial French Canadian cultural nationalism of the past. They were skeptical about liberal democracy, and their ideas about the state remained wedded to the vision of Portuguese-style corporatism. Alliance laurentienne, a group formed in 1957, represented this point of view; it attracted relatively little attention, then or later.[25]

In 1960, however, a new kind of separatist nationalism began to emerge with the formation of a group called Rassemblement pour l'indépendance nationale. Its founders were young, university-educated men and women, several of whom had belonged to Alliance laurentienne.[26] The RIN, however, tried to distance itself from traditional French Canadian nationalism. Its nationalism was secular and, in principle at least, not ethnically exclusive. Proclaiming that French Canadians were a colonized people and that their homeland was Quebec, it favoured a secular, democratic, and independent republic of Quebec with French as its only official language, but at first it avoided more specific committments so as to attract as wide a spectrum of nationalist opinion as possible. It decided, after some debate, not to include a reference to God in its constitution, after being assured by a friendly cleric that this decision would not prevent devout Catholics from joining.[27] Its first program, adopted in 1962, called for a number of liberal reforms, to many of which Lesage's government was also committed. By March 1963, when the RIN decided to become a political party, its original twenty members had increased in number to about two thousand.

The best-known member of the RIN, until his expulsion in 1963, was a biochemist named Marcel Chaput. In 1961, following his resignation from the federal public service, where he had been reprimanded for his political views, he published a book called Pourquoi je suis separatiste. This led, somewhat ironically, to his expulsion from the Ordre de Jacques Cartier.[28] The book sold widely and was even translated into English. Chaput's later expulsion from the RIN, of which he had been among the founders, was occasioned by the fact that he had organized a rival group, the Parti républicain du Québec, apparently because he considered the RIN program too liberal.

Not long after the RIN became a political party, another separatist party was formed, the Ralliement national. While the RIN was urban, secular, and leaned increasingly to the left, the Ralliement was more socially conservative and based in the rural hinterlands of Quebec. Its leader, Gilles Grégoire, had been one of the Créditistes elected to the federal parliament in 1962, but had become disillusioned by Caouette's hostility to separatism and exclusive preoccupation with the federal level of government. While the RIN was made up of polycentric nationalists, proclaiming their solidarity with other colonized peoples, the Ralliement seemed to have little interest in the world beyond Quebec's borders.

Perhaps the most unusual manifestation of Quebec's new nationalism was the Rhinoceros Party, which claimed a rhinoceros in the Granby Zoo as its "honourary president." Founded in 1965 by Jacques Ferron, a doctor and writer who was active in the RIN, it ridiculed Canadian federal politics by running satirical campaigns in federal general elections for the next twenty-five years, commenting on the issues of the day with such observations as "If the good Lord had wanted us to use the metric system, he only would have had ten disciples." In 1980 two Rhinoceros candidates actually came second in their Montreal ridings.[29]

In contrast to the conservative Chaput and to the Ralliement, some of the younger Quebec nationalists were beginning to espouse Marxist socialism. Raoul Roy founded Action socialiste pour l'indépendance du Québec in 1960, the precursor of many such movements. As the Catholic Church lost its ideological hegemony in Quebec, the traditional taboo against Marxist ideas disappeared. The failure of Lesage's middle-class Quiet Revolution to eliminate poverty in Quebec and Pearson's decision to accept American nuclear weapons for the Canadian armed forces were additional radicalizing influences, as was, later in the decade, the war in Vietnam. Marxism was also fashionable in the 1960s for the same reasons that fascism had been in the 1930s: it promised revolutionary vigour and an escape from the stale compromises of parliamentary politics, it opposed Anglo-American hegemony in the world, it flattered the self-esteem of intellectuals who craved appreciation for their talents, and it seemed to be the wave of the future. Unlike fascists, however, Marxists have a fatal propensity for arguing among themselves about obscure points of doctrine. The result was a multiplicity of small Marxist sects, all of them equally powerless. Towards the end of its life, however, the RIN adopted a vaguely socialist program.

Quebec, and especially Montreal, became famous in the 1960s for political demonstrations, most of which expressed a mixture of ethnic nationalism and economic radicalism, with Quebec's relatively affluent anglophone minority often the target. The first major instance was in 1962, after the

Scottish-born president of Canadian National Railways arrogantly stated that no French Canadians could be found with the educational qualifications to be vice-presidents of that federal crown corporation. (It was later revealed that he had never graduated from a university himself.) A future premier of Quebec, Bernard Landry, was among the students who demonstrated outside the railway's headquarters. Among the more notable later demonstrations were those against Air Canada (which had refused to buy French aircraft) in 1964, against the visit of Queen Elizabeth to Quebec City in the same year, against Italian immigrants who wanted their children educated in English in 1968, against the taxi monopoly at the airport later that year, against McGill University in 1969, and against a bill guaranteeing parents the right to educate their children in English, also in 1969. Montreal finally adopted a by-law allowing it to ban such demonstrations, which was upheld by the Supreme Court of Canada.

A few individuals, some of whom had been active in the RIN or in Raoul Roy's ASIQ, turned to revolutionary violence. In February 1963 they coalesced into the Front de libération du Québec and began a series of bombings, using dynamite stolen from construction sites. When a train carrying Prime Minister John Diefenbaker narrowly escaped being derailed by one of their first efforts, Diefenbaker reportedly asked, "Is this Ireland?"[30] FLQ actions over the next few months killed a night watchman at a Canadian armed forces recruiting centre, maimed a soldier who was attempting to disarm a bomb placed in a mailbox, and demolished the statue of General Wolfe on the Plains of Abraham. The following year, FLQ members killed two persons while robbing a store that sold firearms, and there were a number of other robberies. Robberies and attempted bombings continued, with railways and military installations as frequent targets of the bombs, and in 1966 there were two more fatalities, one of whom was an FLQ member killed by his own bomb. The movement then seemed to be dormant for about two years, but in the fall of 1968 it revived spectacularly, with incidents occurring almost every week, culminating in a gigantic bomb that injured twenty-seven persons at the Montreal Stock Exchange in February 1969.[31]

Meanwhile there had been important developments in the field of electoral politics. In 1966 both the RIN and the Ralliement participated in Quebec's general election, although neither ran a full slate of candidates. They elected no members but won between them almost 10 per cent of the vote. The intervention of the RIN may have cost the Liberals the election, since the Liberals lost ten ridings where the RIN vote exceeded the margin between the winning candidate and the defeated Liberal incumbent. However, the Liberals also suffered from a rural backlash against high taxes, educational reforms, and the elimination of local patronage. The Union nationale, led by Daniel Johnson (a French Canadian despite his name), won a narrow majority of the seats and returned to office. Johnson had earlier demonstrated his nationalist credentials by publishing a short book in which he argued that unless Canada was reorganized into a federation of two equal nations, English and French, Quebec would have to seek independence. Although the first of these options was obviously his preference, he made it clear that the British North America Act was no longer acceptable.[32] This position was in sharp contrast to the traditional nationalist view of his mentor Duplessis, who had complained that the federal government was violating the terms of the BNA Act but never questioned the act itself. The Union nationale slogan in the election of 1966 was "A young party for a young nation."

Johnson was less successful in persuading the federal government to compromise with Quebec's demands than Lesage had been, partly because the federal Liberals regarded Lesage as a political ally and Johnson as an opponent. Increasing federal rigidity also reflected the growing influence in Ottawa of Pierre Elliott Trudeau, the law professor and former editor of *Cité libre* who had become a federal politician in 1965 to combat what he viewed as the excesses of Quebec nationalism. Trudeau had welcomed the Quiet Revolution but became disillusioned after 1962 with its growing nationalism, which he considered a threat to both freedom and order, the two things that he prized the most. His attitude towards the "separatists," a word he used with such contempt that supporters of Quebec independence eventually stopped using it themselves, resembled the attitude of Kevin O'Higgins, the Irish minister of justice in the 1920s, towards Irish republicans.[33] Trudeau's emergence as a federal politician, and as prime minister of Canada after April 1968, indicated a parting of the ways between the *citélibrists* and the neo-nationalists and the winding down of the Quiet Revolution. Henceforth Quebec would be polarized on the issue of federalism versus nationalism, rather than that of conservatism versus reform.

Daniel Johnson had seized the banner of Quebec nationalism, but he did not hold it for long. René Lévesque, whose growing dissatisfaction with Canadian federalism had become increasingly obvious, was no longer inhibited by cabinet solidarity after the defeat of the Lesage government. In 1967, following discussions with colleagues and friends, he unveiled a proposal for "sovereignty-association" as a compromise between Johnson's options of equality or complete independence.[34] Lévesque proposed an independent sovereign state of Quebec that would form a common market and, at least for a trial period of five years, a monetary union with the rest of Canada. (Many of the people with whom Lévesque discussed his idea doubted that the monetary union which he favoured was feasible; the five-year trial was a concession to their point of view.) Common institutions – a central bank, a council of ministers, and periodic joint meetings of parliamentary delegations – would manage the shared interests of the two partners. The idea of sovereignty-association had some resemblance to the Hungarian scenario that Arthur Griffith had outlined for Ireland and Great Britain in 1904. Lévesque suggested that it would give Quebec all the advantages of independence and would also be acceptable to the rest of Canada, which would be freed of the inconvenience of trying to accommodate a dissatisfied Quebec within its federal system. Special status, he argued, had neither of these advantages.

Like the RIN, but unlike Lesage, Johnson, or Laurendeau, Lévesque was prepared to abandon the French-speaking minorities outside Quebec in order to secure the sovereignty of Quebec itself. His desire to maintain an association with the rest of Canada was motivated by economic and geopolitical, rather than cultural, considerations. His proposal was thus an important milestone in the transition from traditional French Canadian cultural nationalism to a more territorially defined and state-centred but also inclusive Quebec nationalism. It was a sign of the times: French-speaking people in Quebec were beginning to refer to themselves as "Québécois," a term that had hardly ever been used before the 1960s. A few weeks after Lévesque released his proposal, the Estates General of French Canada, a congress organized by the Fédération des Societés Saint-Jean-Baptiste, adopted a resolution proclaiming that Quebec was the homeland of the French Canadian nation and as such had the right of self-determination. Most of the delegates from Quebec voted for this resolution, and most of those from the French Canadian minorities elsewhere opposed it.[35]

Lévesque tried to have his proposal for sovereignty-association endorsed by the Quebec Liberal Party at the party's convention in October 1967. After failing in this endeavour, he resigned from the party and formed the Mouvement souveraineté-association. A year later the MSA, which was essentially a movement of the educated urban middle class, united with the rural and populist Ralliement national to form the Parti québécois. Lévesque was elected party leader and Gilles Grégoire deputy leader. Lévesque refused to negotiate a merger with the RIN, disliking its increasing anglophobia and its penchant for disorderly demonstrations.[36] However, the RIN soon afterwards dissolved and advised its members to join the Parti québécois. Most did, becoming in effect the party's left wing and a source of considerable distress to their new leader over the next few years.

By the time the next Quebec general election took place in April 1970, Lesage had retired, Johnson had died, and the Créditiste party, already in decline at the federal level, had belatedly entered the provincial arena. The Liberals won a majority of the seats under their new leader, Robert Bourassa, a young economist who had participated in the early discussions of sovereignty-association but had withdrawn from them because he regarded the proposed monetary union as unworkable.[37] The Union nationale fell to third place in terms of votes, although it retained seventeen seats in the malapportioned legislature. It ceased henceforth to be a serious contender for office, as its middle-class nationalist supporters defected to the Parti québécois and its conservative supporters rallied around the Liberals, while much of its rural electorate went to the Créditistes. The Parti québécois won almost a quarter of the vote but only seven seats, all but one of them in Montreal. Lévesque, running in the ethnically mixed Montreal riding that he had won three times as a Liberal, lost his own seat and had to lead his party from outside the assembly for the next six and a half years. Although his party avoided ethnic exclusiveness and had a few supporters in the anglophone and immigrant communities, most members of those communities viewed it with deep distrust.

Quebec nationalism had aroused interest on the part of the French government as early as the summer of 1967, when President Charles de Gaulle ended a speech from the balcony of the Montreal city hall with the nationalist slogan "Vive le Québec libre!" The speech offended the Canadian federal government but caused great excitement among Quebec nationalists.[38] While the slogan shouted from the balcony may have been spontaneous, the president's explicit endorsement of an independent Quebec at a press conference a few months later certainly was not. Relations between Canada and France became distinctly cool and remained so after de Gaulle's resignation. It was probably soon after the 1970 election in Quebec that the French government, now headed by President Georges Pompidou, made a substantial offer of financial support to the Parti québécois. The offer was refused at the insistence of René Lévesque, and a member of the party who was visiting France delivered the rejection to the Quai d'Orsay in a sealed envelope. The Canadian government, whose police force had already been investigating possible French ties with the separatist movement for several months, apparently learned that the offer had been made but not that it had been refused.[39]

French intervention was not the only Quebec-related problem that occupied the attention of the security forces that year. FLQ activity continued in and around Montreal, with the usual bombings and thefts of explosives. In February and June of 1970 the local police uncovered two FLQ plans to kidnap foreign diplomats, the consuls of Israel and the United States being the intended victims.[40] In October the FLQ actually did kidnap the British trade commissioner in Montreal, precipitating one of the major crises in Canadian history. A few days later another FLQ cell kidnapped Pierre Laporte, Quebec's minister of labour and immigration. Trudeau responded to the kidnappings by sending army units to Montreal at the request of Premier Bourassa and Mayor Jean Drapeau. He refused FLQ demands for the release of "political prisoners" and the naming of informers, but agreed to another request that the FLQ manifesto be broadcast on Radio-Canada. The manifesto, which basically argued that both the federal and provincial governments were controlled by Canadian and American big business, was favourably received by at least some of those who heard it for the first time. Soon afterwards Trudeau invoked emergency powers under the War Measures Act, a statute adopted at the beginning of the First World War, which allowed persons to be arrested and held without specific charges being laid against them. More than 450 persons were arrested on suspicion of some involvement with the FLQ, although it is doubtful that the Front ever had that many members. Laporte was killed by his captors, who announced his death in a communiqué that contemptuously referred to him as the "minister of unemployment and assimilation."[41] The trade commissioner was rescued as part of a deal with the authorities whereby his kidnappers were exiled to Cuba. The federal police force began a systematic campaign to destroy the FLQ by almost any means, legal or otherwise, a task that they accomplished for all practical purposes by 1973.[42]

The October Crisis, as it came to be called, was a temporary setback for the Parti québécois and a major victory for its principal opponent, Trudeau. Lévesque, in particular, was shocked and saddened by the actions of the FLQ, especially the death of Laporte, and many of the party's members had been arrested during the crisis. The general public was shocked by the murder of Laporte, an event so unprecedented in Quebec that the FLQ lost most of the sympathy it had gained through the reading of the manifesto. Opinion shifted noticeably but temporarily to the right and towards support for the federal government. In the longer term the increasingly conspicuous association between conservatism, federalism, and the two Liberal governments may have benefited the Parti québécois by persuading most of the leaders of organized labour in Quebec to support it. The party's ideological orientation had been rather unclear at the outset, but it positioned itself in the early 1970s as a moderately social democratic party and as the true heir to the legacy of Jean Lesage and the Quiet Revolution. By doing so, it probably contributed to a marked improvement in the social climate of Quebec, and a noticeable decline after about 1973 in the number of disorderly demonstrations. (The destruction of the FLQ, and a gradual reduction in the economic disparity between anglophones and francophones in Quebec were also contributing factors.)

For whatever reason, the party's share of the popular vote increased to 30 per cent in the Quebec election of 1973, which left it as the only alternative to the victorious Liberals. Part of the reason for the improvement may have been that the party had now committed itself to holding a referendum before it would attempt to bring about the sovereignty of Quebec. This idea was intended to reassure the voters that they would not be committing themselves to separation from Canada, with all its potential risks, by voting for the party. The fact that such reassurance was needed hardly suggested that most Quebecers regarded Canadian federalism as intolerable, and the party was implicitly conceding that they did not. The referendum strategy had another implication that was not fully appreciated at the time. By giving everyone in Quebec the right to participate in the decision on sovereignty-association, the party was implicitly discarding an ethnic or cultural definition of the nation that it claimed to represent in favour of an inclusive civic type of nationalism. It was also setting itself a difficult task in winning such a referendum, since the anglophones and other minorities would vote almost unanimously against the party's option.

By 1976 the Parti québécois had further refined its referendum strategy by pledging to hold one referendum before beginning negotiations with the Canadian government and a second to ratify the result. It emphasized that the election would merely choose a government for Quebec and that the decision on sovereignty-association would be deferred until later. The Bourassa government had lost popularity because of a series of scandals and conflicts of interest that were symptomatic of its increasingly close ties with big business. The final straw was Trudeau's capitulation to the demands of the air traffic controllers' union, which had insisted that all air-to-ground communication over Quebec be in the English language. This seemed to belie the federal leader's proclaimed support for the equality of the two languages in Canada. In the election that followed on 15 November 1976, the Parti québécois won almost two-thirds of the seats in what had been known since 1969 as the Quebec National Assembly. Apart from the predominantly anglophone districts in West Montreal, its support was quite evenly spread across the province. Although its share of the popular vote was only 41 per cent, this number indicated that almost exactly half of francophone Quebecers had voted for the party, since it was apparent that hardly any non-francophones had done so.

The Quiet Revolution in Quebec thus led to a significant increase in the strength and influence of nationalism, as well as a change in its character. Historically, as we have seen, political nationalism since 1867 had taken the form of defending Quebec's autonomy and resisting what were viewed as centralizing initiatives by the Canadian federal government, but had rarely contemplated a radical revision of constitutional arrangements, let alone independence. After the Quiet Revolution this kind of resistance continued, but it was supplemented and then to a large extent replaced by the more ambitious project of constructing a modern secular and democratic state on the territory of Quebec. This project, which particularly appealed to the educated middle class and to people who worked in the public sector, somewhat resembled the goal of the Patriotes in 1837–38. In its new manifestation it was deemed to require political independence or at the very least a complete restructuring of the Quebec-Canada relationship. The Parti québécois, arising out of what had been the more progressive wing of the old Liberal Party but subsequently incorporating other elements such as radical students, discontented rural residents, and sections of the working class, became the vehicle of this new kind of political nationalism.

There was an even more radical change in the character of cultural nationalism. Traditionally, cultural nationalism, which became particularly strong after the defeat of political nationalism in 1837–38, had promoted a French Canadian nation defined in terms of its Catholic faith, French ethnicity, and historical roots in pre-conquest settlement but lacking clear geographical boundaries. The primary goals of this cultural nationalism had been to secure recognition of the French Canadian nation as one of two equal partners in the Canadian state and to protect the interests of francophones and Catholics from coast to coast.

Although some representatives of this kind of cultural nationalism, such as Lionel Groulx, continued in theory to be admired after 1960, their hopes and objectives, as well as their Catholic faith, were increasingly discarded. The new kind of nationalism that emerged in Quebec was secular and largely indifferent to religion. It also tended, at least implicitly, to exclude the francophone minorities outside Quebec from its imagined community. The Quiet Revolution caused Quebec to look inwards and reinforced the importance of the Quebec "state" as the instrument of collective purpose. Quebec redefined itself after 1960, as France had redefined itself after 1789. Its people began to call themselves "Québécois" and to define their identity in terms of Quebec's particular institutions. The francophone minorities outside Quebec did not share in this defining experience and were not directly affected by it. Increasingly, they became, in effect, a separate people, "French Canadians," a label that in Quebec was beginning to seem old-fashioned.

Yet a sense of ethnic identity did not disappear in Quebec with the coming of the Quiet Revolution. One of the goals of the new nationalism was to overturn the traditional ethnic division of labour in the province and, by doing so, to reduce the disproportionate wealth, power, influence, and status of Quebec's anglophone minority. Some animosity towards anglophones had always existed, particularly in Montreal, where the two language communities rubbed shoulders, even if it was not quite as pervasive in Quebec as William Johnson has suggested in his rather pessimistic study of the subject.[43] It was understandable that it existed, given the conspicuous economic disparity between the two communities and the casual arrogance of many anglophones. Action libérale nationale and the Bloc populaire had given voice to it after a fashion. However, it had been relatively inconspicuous, and certainly ineffectual, until the 1960s. The "Maîtres chez nous" election campaign of 1962 and the subsequent nationalization of the power companies was a turning point. From that moment onwards, the sense of collective empowerment through a modernized provincial state, the declining vitality of the old anglophone economic elite, and the rapidly growing number of young educated francophones who felt their mobility blocked by anglophone economic power brought suppressed resentment into the open. The Liberals had unleashed sentiments which they did not particularly welcome and which they could neither control nor satisfy.

To some extent, these sentiments found expression, as noted above, in a growing number of public demonstrations and riots. There were also increasing demands for measures to protect the French language and to restrict the prominence of the English language in public life. Traditionally, it had been accepted that most European immigrants who came to Quebec speaking other languages would learn English, educate their children in English, and be absorbed into the anglophone community, which was able thus to compensate for its lower birth rate and its losses through migration to other parts of Canada. After the 1960s, francophones in Quebec no longer accepted this assumption, particularly as their traditional advantage of a higher birth rate was rapidly disappearing with secularization and the changing status of women. Fears were expressed that Montreal might become a predominantly English-speaking city if measures were not taken to reinforce the status of the French language.

Following the report of a provincial royal commission on the status of the French language (not to be confused with the federal royal commission on bilingualism and biculturalism), the Bourassa government tried to defuse the issue with the Official Language Act of 1974, or Bill 22. This fairly innocuous measure prohibited English-language education for children (i.e., the children of immigrants) who could not demonstrate fluency in English, required a French-language test for entry into the professions, and, at least in theory, required firms receiving government contracts to conduct their internal operations in French. Anglophone Quebecers were outraged, but

Bill 22 proved to be only the prelude to more stringent language legislation introduced by the Parti québécois in 1977.[44]

IRELAND AFTER DE VALERA: ANOTHER QUIET REVOLUTION?

Eamon de Valera retired as taoiseach and as leader of Fianna Fail in June 1959, a few days before he assumed the less-demanding and largely ceremonial office of president of the Republic of Ireland. He had governed the state for most of the preceding three decades by the same methods that Taschereau and Duplessis had perfected in Quebec: rhetorical nationalism and social conservatism, deference to the wishes of the Catholic Church combined with respect for religious minorities, and the distribution of patronage and infrastructural spending, particularly in rural areas, through a highly effective grassroots political machine. From the time it first took office in 1932 until sixty years later, Fianna Fail never received less than 40 per cent of the first preference votes, while its principal rival never reached that threshold and was usually far below it.

De Valera had many achievements to his credit, including the creation of Fianna Fail itself, the republican constitution of 1937, the return of the ports that had been held by the Royal Navy after independence, and the preservation of both Ireland's neutrality and its democracy during the difficult years of the Second World War. However, his last years as head of the government would come to be viewed in retrospect, like those of his contemporary Duplessis, as a great darkness. Ireland in the 1950s was isolated from the rest of the world as a result of its wartime neutrality, its withdrawal from the Commonwealth, its refusal to join the North Atlantic alliance, and its inability for several years to enter the United Nations. It seemed trapped in a stifling social conservatism, partly because so many of its young people emigrated to Great Britain or elsewhere. The population of the state was slightly smaller when de Valera retired as head of the government than it had been when he founded his party. The problem of partition was unsolved, and perhaps insoluble. The Irish language, which de Valera cherished, continued to decline. Most of all, the economy was stagnating and the gap between Irish and British living standards was growing, a fact that was naturally the main cause of emigration. According to Joseph Lee and Gearóid Ó Tuathaigh in their retrospective account of de Valera's era, "By the late fifties the very viability of a sovereign Irish state was being widely questioned."[45]

De Valera was succeeded by his deputy leader (*tanaiste* in Irish), Sean Lemass, who was nearly sixty years old and had participated as a teenager in the rising of 1916. Lemass had been a founding member of Fianna Fail and had famously referred to it, when it operated under the Free State constitution, as "a slightly constitutional party."[46] As discussed in the preceding chapter, he was responsible for the protectionist policy towards foreign direct investment that Ireland adopted in the 1930s, but he began to have doubts about it subsequently. Somewhat later he was attracted by the economic ideas of John Maynard Keynes and William Beveridge. Although regarded as the heir apparent by de Valera, he was in some ways a more modern leader than his predecessor; in this regard, their relationship resembled that between Maurice Duplessis and Paul Sauvé. As a Dubliner, Lemass also did not share de Valera's romantic enthusiasm for the rural way of life.

The sorry state of the economy was obviously the first priority when Lemass took over. The groundwork for a new economic strategy had already been laid by T.K. Whitaker, the permanent head of the Department of Finance, in a report entitled simply "Economic Development," which he completed more than a year before Lemass succeeded de Valera. The report became the basis of a white paper, the *Programme for Economic Expansion*, published in November 1958. Whitaker recommended a policy of free, or at least freer, trade, emphasis on export-oriented agriculture, encouragement of foreign direct investment, and a shift of priority in public spending towards economic development. The white paper, in deference to political realities, was slightly less market-oriented than the original document. It also suggested a target of 2 per cent a year for economic growth.[47] (It speaks volumes about Ireland in 1958 that such a modest target – indeed, the very idea of setting a target – was considered radical.)

Since Lemass's ideas were already moving in the same direction, the Whitaker report became the basis for his government's economic policies. Ireland applied for admission to the European Community (now the European Union) simultaneously with the British application in 1961. When the British application was vetoed by President de Gaulle, however, the Irish application also ended. Lemass settled for a free trade agreement between Ireland and the United Kingdom, which was signed in December 1965. The agreement was to be phased in over a ten-year period, but was eventually overtaken by the entry of both countries into the European Community in 1973. To counterbalance the greater intimacy with Britain, Lemass also pursued closer relations with the United States. Ireland's contribution to United Nations peacekeeping in the Congo and its general support for American foreign policy contributed to this end. President John F. Kennedy enjoyed a highly successful visit to Ireland in July 1963, and Lemass reciprocated by visiting the United States in October. During the Kennedy visit, *Time* magazine devoted its cover and a laudatory lead story to Lemass and to the changes taking place in Ireland under his government.

The economic policies of Whitaker and Lemass caused the value of Ireland's external trade to more than double during the 1960s, but its heavy dependence on the British market did not diminish significantly until after it entered the European Community. GDP per capita rose faster in the state than in the United Kingdom after 1960 and finally overtook that country in 1996, an outcome that would have seemed inconceivable in 1960.[48] One immediate result of the trend was a very sharp decline in emigration as economic prospects and opportunities in Ireland improved. Net emigration from the state per thousand inhabitants fell from 14.8 in 1956–61 to 5.7 in 1961–66 and only 3.7 in 1966–71. The latter was the lowest rate since the foundation of the Free State and a lower rate than Northern Ireland experienced in the same period.[49]

Educational reform was also a priority for the Lemass government, although financial constraints and the attitude of the Catholic Church posed more serious obstacles to reform in Ireland than they did in Quebec at the same period of time. Nonetheless, comprehensive secondary schools were established in some rural areas, and many one-room and two-room rural schools were closed and replaced by larger schools with better facilities. Free secondary education was promised by the minister of education just before Lemass's retirement and finally implemented in 1967 under his successor, Jack Lynch. (Quebec had made secondary education free in 1960, and Northern Ireland in 1947.)

A more gradual and subtle change in Ireland after 1959 was a declining commitment to the goal of reviving Irish as a working everyday language, although the Irish language continued to be cherished as a cultural heritage. De Valera had been a lifelong enthusiast for reviving the language, and Richard Mulcahy, the Fine Gael leader, who also retired in 1959, was equally if not more so. Their successors as party leaders, James Dillon and Lemass, were much less committed.[50] Lemass could speak only a few words of Irish, but Dillon's call for an end to compulsory Irish during the election campaign of 1961 led Lemass and Fianna Fail to stake out a position as the defenders of the language as an essential part of Ireland's cultural heritage and to denounce Dillon's suggestion as "irresponsible."[51] Nonetheless, Lemass admitted in 1964 that "in practice English will remain the general vernacular," a comment for which he received some criticism.[52] After 1968 most positions in the public service were advertised in English only. As a result of an initiative by the Fine Gael government in 1973, a pass in Irish was no longer required after that date to graduate from secondary school or to enter the public service, although secondary students were still required to study the subject and it was still required to enter the National University.

Lemass also began a cautious opening to the north which included, for the first time, tacit acceptance of the term "Northern Ireland" rather than "the six counties" as a description of the partitionist state. This rapprochement was facilitated by the retirement of Lord Brookeborough from the leadership of the northern state in 1963 and his replacement by the more modern and flexible Terence O'Neill. At O'Neill's invitation, Lemass visited Belfast in January 1965. On his return he told the Dáil that he believed in "practical co-operation" between the two states in Ireland and was happy to discover that O'Neill shared this belief. He described his visit as "the beginning of a process which has considerable potentialities for good," While reiterating his wish that partition should be ended eventually, Lemass declined the suggestion that ending partition was the sole responsibility of the British government and said that "the primary aim must be to eliminate the barriers of suspicion and animosity which have divided the Irish people in the past so that unity can be founded on tolerance and goodwill."[53] This proved easier said than done, but free trade with the United Kingdom removed another kind of barrier between the two parts of Ireland. Lemass's successor, Jack Lynch, visited O'Neill in Belfast in December 1967.

The fiftieth anniversary of the Easter rising was commemorated a few months before Lemass retired and in the midst of de Valera's campaign for a second term as president. A private citizen, who confessed his identity years later, celebrated in his own way, a few weeks before the anniversary, by blowing up the Nelson monument on O'Connell Street.[54] The less-dramatic official commemoration in Dublin was resented by many northern unionists. Lemass tried to minimize the damage by excluding radical republicans such as Kathleen Clarke from the ceremonies, and the state railways, at his request, suspended passenger service across the border to discourage the celebrations from spilling over into the six counties.[55] De Valera's speech at the GPO on the anniversary avoided any mention of partition and was largely devoted to the subject of reviving the Irish language, a goal to which he was still devoted.[56] Lemass was present for the occasion but did not speak.

Shortly before his retirement as taoiseach, Lemass established an all-party parliamentary committee on the constitution, on which he himself served after stepping down from the leadership of the government. One of the changes that it recommended in 1967 was to replace Article 3, which proclaimed jurisdiction over the entire island, with a new article whereby the Irish nation would proclaim "its firm will that its territory be reunited in harmony and brotherly affection between all Irishmen."[57] (The cultural conservatism of post-independence Ireland is suggested by the failure to mention Irishwomen, in contrast to Pearse's proclamation of 1916, which had explicitly done so.) The idea was dropped because of opposition within Fianna Fail.

Lemass's record of innovation and reform between 1959 and his retirement in 1966 deserves comparison with Jean Lesage's Quiet Revolution, which occurred simultaneously. However, some important differences between the two situations must be noted. The sharp decline in the influence of the Catholic Church which Quebec experienced in the 1960s did not occur in Ireland until two decades later.[58] This delay may reflect the fact that Ireland was a much more rural and less affluent, and thus more traditional, society than Quebec. In 1961 only 46.1 per cent of the population in the state lived in towns of 1,500 or more persons.[59] This proportion was below the level of urbanization that Quebec had achieved half a century before, in the year that Wilfrid Laurier's government was defeated. Television broadcasting in Ireland did not begin until the end of 1961, almost a decade after it began in Quebec. As late as 1970, only about half of Irish homes had a television receiver, a proportion comparable to Quebec in the mid-1950s. Even in 1980 the ratio of television licences to homes in Ireland was apparently only about two to three.[60] The decline of organized religion in both Ireland and Quebec seems to have occurred only after access to television became almost universal.

These contrasts might seem to explain another contrast that is particularly relevant to the theme of this book, namely, the fact that southern Ireland did not experience a resurgence of nationalism in the 1960s, while Quebec did. Some observers of Quebec, particularly those who are somewhat hostile to nationalism, have suggested that the increased intensity of nationalism and the development of the independence movement were substitutes for a declining religious faith. While there may be some truth in this assertion, it would lead one to predict, erroneously, that southern Ireland should have experienced a similar resurgence of nationalism in the 1980s, when it finally experienced the secularization that Quebec had in the 1960s. Moreover, it fails to explain the fact that Ireland between 1912 and 1922 experienced a resurgence of nationalism without having experienced secularization or a loss of religious faith. Both these outcomes suggest that in fact there is no clear relationship between secularization and nationalism.

Other explanatory factors must be sought to explain the contrast between southern Ireland and Quebec in the years after 1959. First, as already noted, Ireland had stagnated economically in the 1950s while Quebec had flourished. Economic and demographic growth gave Quebec the self-confidence and optimism needed to pursue a nationalist project at a time when these were conspicuously lacking in Ireland. A second contrast concerns political status. Ireland was already a sovereign state, recognized as such by the entire world. Quebec was only a province in a federation, and federalism imposed some obvious constraints on its freedom of action. These constraints were resented by nationalists precisely because Quebec was a dynamic and afflu-ent society with the potential of becoming a viable sovereign state. This fact was particularly apparent in the 1960s, when so many Asian, African, and Caribbean countries with social and economic capabilities inferior to those of Quebec were becoming viable sovereign states.

A final contrast between the Quebec of Lesage and the Ireland of Lemass concerns their most significant minorities: the anglophones of Quebec and the Protestants of southern Ireland, both of which were in a sense relics of former British rule. In Quebec, as noted above, the anglophones still visibly dominated and controlled the economy in the 1960s and held a dispropor-tionate share of the managerial and professional positions in the private sec-tor. Their prominence was particularly apparent in Montreal, and it is thus understandable that the resurgence of nationalism and the independence movement began there. Resentment against this privileged minority led many to conclude that secession from a predominantly anglophone Can-ada, or at least a much looser relationship with it, would contribute to the economic emancipation of French Canadians in Quebec.

In southern Ireland the minority was not nearly as important. Protestants were less than 5 per cent of the state's population in 1961, while in the same year anglophones were 13 per cent of Quebec's population, and an even larger percentage if immigrants who had adopted English as their working language were included. More significantly, the southern Irish economy was not dominated by Protestants in the 1960s as it had largely been fifty years earlier. The Protestant minority within the state had already become weak and harmless by the time Lemass took office.[61] There were still some traces of the old Protestant elite, and some prominent firms, such as the Guinness brewery, were still controlled by Protestants, but the economic influence of Protestants was rapidly declining, a trend that was probably accelerated by the new openness to foreign direct investment under Lemass. The *Irish Times* newspaper, which had been the voice of southern unionism before independence and remained a Protestant institution until the 1950s, aban-doned its sectarian character during the Lemass era. The days when the southern suburbs of Dublin and the more affluent neighbourhoods on the south side of Dublin itself were Protestant strongholds had long passed. Middle-class Dublin Catholics had no reason to believe in the 1960s, as mid-dle-class Montreal francophones still did, that their accent or background were barriers to social and economic mobility.

Thus in significant ways the Quebec of the 1960s, despite its urbanization and affluence, resembled the Ireland of half a century earlier more than it resembled southern Ireland in the 1960s. A political status that provided less autonomy than the country felt capable of exercising, a rising middle class within the ethnocultural majority that faced continuing barriers to its mobility, an economically dominant minority that regarded itself as part of the majority in a larger political entity and was thus hostile to any change in the political status of the subordinate unit – all these circumstances were conducive to the rise of separatist nationalism. They did not exist in southern Ireland in the 1960s, where the analogous problems had already been solved. Northern Ireland, however, was another story. It was the spillover of developments in the six counties across the border that restored the national question to the centre of Irish politics in the 1970s.

NORTHERN IRELAND: FROM CIVIL RIGHTS TO CIVIL WAR

The six-county state of Northern Ireland had been established in 1920 as "a Protestant state for a Protestant people." Its boundaries, as we noted in chapter 6, corresponded to no historical, geographical, or sociological reality; they simply enclosed the largest possible area that the unionists could detach from Ireland without including enough nationalists to place their own majority status in potential danger. As finally drawn, they included a compact area east of the Bann River that was industrialized and overwhelmingly Protestant, as well as a much larger area to the west that was largely rural and about half Catholic. The result was an entity that contained roughly equal numbers of Anglicans, Presbyterians, and Catholics, with the first two groups forming a Protestant power bloc. Northern Ireland – or rather, its Protestant majority – enjoyed the home rule that its founders had earlier denied to the rest of Ireland. In practice, this arrangement gave them the best of both worlds: virtually complete self-government combined with massive subsidization by the British taxpayer, including, after 1945, all the benefits of the post-war welfare state.

To symbolize Protestant power and the anticipated permanence of this artificial state, a gigantic white marble parliament building was constructed on a hilltop east of Belfast, a structure out of all proportion to the needs of a semi-sovereign province with less than one and a half million inhabitants. Power at Stormont, as the parliament was known, was monopolized by the Unionist Party, affiliated with the Conservative Party in Great Britain, whose candidates ran unopposed in most constituencies. The party in turn was controlled by a power elite of Presbyterian businessmen, mostly in Belfast, and Anglican landlords, who were distributed more widely through the truncated province. Most Catholics who bothered to vote supported the almost equally conservative Nationalist Party, a surviving remnant of the party that John Redmond and his northern lieutenant, Joe Devlin, had led before the First World War. The Nationalists, however, were handicapped by the abolition in 1929 of proportional representation, which had originally been provided for in both Irish states, north and south, to protect the religious minorities. (In southern Ireland it still exists.) After 1932 the Nationalists usually abstained from attending the Stormont parliament, leaving their opponents in complete control.

Despite their virtually unchallenged power, the Unionists persistently regarded themselves as under siege from "disloyal" elements. This belief became the pretext for systematic discrimination against Catholics in employment, public housing, and the distribution of patronage, the gerrymandering of electoral boundaries, and a variety of repressive laws. The most notorious of these, the Special Powers Act of 1922, had originally been designed as "emergency" legislation but was made permanent in 1933. A statute passed in 1954, during a resurgence of IRA activity directed against partition, prohibited the display of the Irish flag, even on private property.[62] Catholics emigrated in large numbers and thus remained about one-third of the population, despite having a higher birth rate than their Protestant neighbours.

In the post-war world after 1945 this structure of power and privilege had to adapt to the British welfare state, which distributed benefits without regard to religious affiliation and contributed to the gradual growth of an educated Catholic middle class. In the short term the welfare state may have reconciled some Catholics to British rule, but in the long term it had a different effect. One writer has suggested that the "eleven plus" examination, which allowed selected working-class children to qualify for entrance to university, was the main cause of Northern Ireland's "Troubles," which began two decades later.[63] Catholics first began to attend Queen's University in significant numbers in the 1950s. (By the early 1990s they would comprise more than half the students.) However, their rising expectations were not matched by the opportunities available to them in the Protestant-dominated state. The economy of Northern Ireland, like that of southern Ireland, stagnated in the 1950s, while the rest of Europe experienced a post-war boom. Unemployment was high. The province's traditional industries, linen and shipbuilding, were in decline, and the Protestant (largely Presbyterian) business elite was declining with them. Economic changes were undermining the basis of its power much as economic changes were beginning to undermine the anglophone elite of Montreal.[64]

Terence O'Neill, who became prime minister in 1963, was a product of the same Anglican landlord class as his predecessor, Lord Brookeborough.

His attitude towards Catholics was patronizing at best, but he recognized the need for change and believed that if the Catholics were treated better, they would learn to "live like Protestants."[65] Like Lemass in the south, he tried to revive the economy through foreign direct investment and transborder cooperation. He also sought to give the regime a more ecumenical flavour by reaching out to the Catholic minority with symbolic gestures, despite resistance by some of the diehards in his own party. When Pope John XXIII died, O'Neill sent a message of condolences to the Vatican and ordered flags lowered to half-mast. Catholic schools began to receive subsidies from the Northern Ireland state, which the clergy had earlier refused to accept. O'Neill also visited Dublin in January 1968, returning the earlier visits to Belfast by Sean Lemass and Jack Lynch. In response to O'Neill's intiatives, the Nationalist Party agreed for the first time in 1965 to play the role of official opposition in the Northern Ireland parliament. On the other hand, there was a backlash from some Protestants, including Ian Paisley, a minister of the gospel in a minor Presbyterian sect who first became prominent during the British general election of 1964.[66] Intercommunal violence, in abeyance since before the Second World War, was renewed with the killing of four Catholics by a Protestant paramilitary group, the Ulster Volunteer Force, in June 1966. The group was theoretically outlawed after this incident, but no one was actually arrested for belonging to it until seven years later.

O'Neill's initiatives contributed to a revolution of rising expectations among the Catholics, who had grudgingly begun to accept the northern state as a *fait accompli* after 1949 but were not resigned to their subordinate economic and social status. Discontent was particularly strong in the mainly Catholic city of Derry, separated from the rest of the six counties by the River Foyle, which had suffered economically from the closing of its main railway line and its British naval base and had been disappointed by the government's refusal to give it a university.[67] As in Quebec, the climate of change in the Catholic Church unleashed by Pope John XXIII spilled over into the political arena. The election in 1964 of Harold Wilson, a British prime minister considered sympathetic to Ireland, also had an impact. The unfulfilled dream of a thirty-two-county republic had also been reawakened by the bicentennial of Wolfe Tone's birth in 1963 and the fiftieth anniversary of the Easter rising in 1966. In January 1967 the Northern Ireland Civil Rights Assocation (NICRA) was formed. Some of those who took this initiative were republicans who viewed a civil rights campaign as an opportunity to undermine the six-county state, or at least to demonstrate that it was incapable of reform.[68] Others were liberals who were not primarily interested in ending partition but were inspired by the work of Martin Luther King Jr in the American South. It was an apt analogy because Northern Ireland's home rule had led to discriminatory and repressive practices that would not have been tolerated in Great Britain, just as American federalism and "states' rights" had permitted similar practices in the southern states that would not have been tolerated in other regions of the United States.[69]

A survey conducted by Richard Rose in 1968, just before the beginning of what came to be called "the Troubles," indicated the conflict of national loyalties in Northern Ireland and the tenuous legitimacy of the regime. Of Catholic respondents, 76 per cent considered their national identity to be Irish, while only 15 per cent considered it to be British. On the other hand, only 20 per cent of Protestant respondents considered themselves Irish, while 39 per cent chose a British identity. Almost as many Protestants, 32 per cent, described their national identity as "Ulster," an option chosen by only 5 per cent of the Catholics. Among Catholics, 74 per cent believed that Catholics were discriminated against in Northern Ireland, an opinion shared by only 18 per cent of Protestants. Some 68 per cent of Protestants, but only 33 per cent of Catholics said that they approved of the existing constitution of Northern Ireland. A somewhat more encouraging finding was that majorities in both communities thought relations between them had improved since "five years ago," that is, since O'Neill became prime minister.[70]

Almost half a century after partition, Irish Catholics in Northern Ireland inevitably had a somewhat different perspective from those who lived south of the border. In some ways the contrast resembled that between French Canadians outside Quebec and French Canadians (or, as they increasingly styled themselves, Québécois) in Quebec after the Quiet Revolution. According to Marianne Elliott, "The declaration of a republic by the Irish Government in 1949 was a shock, a token of southern rejection."[71] Britain's response to this event, the Ireland Act of 1949, seemed to make a reversal of partition highly unlikely. At the same time, the benefits of the British welfare state and the obvious economic difficulties south of the border tended to make the continuation of partition relatively more attractive to northern Catholics than it had been and to increase its legitimacy. On the other hand, the continuing sectarianism and discrimination that Catholics suffered at the hands of Stormont caused understandable resentment in the 1960s, a time when peoples all over the world were questioning the status quo and demanding recognition of their "rights." Disillusioned with the southern state and unable to fully accept, or be accepted by, the northern state, northern Catholics, like French Canadians outside Quebec, tended to define their identity in a way that emphasized culture and religion rather than political nationalism.[72] Protestant unionists, rather than the British state, were the main focus of their resentment.[73] The British, particularly under Harold Wilson's Labour government, were viewed more favourably than the unionists of Stormont, in the same way that most French Canadians outside Quebec view the bilingual federal government as more sympathetic than the governments of the provinces in which they live.

In 1968 NICRA began to hold marches for civil rights, imitating Dr King's technique. In October a NICRA march in Derry, a predominantly Catholic city but one that had historic significance for Protestants, was brutally broken up by the police, sparking a series of communal disturbances. O'Neill's response was to announce measures designed to end discrimination against Catholics.[74] His decision to hold a public inquiry into the incident led to the resignation of Brian Faulkner, his hardline minister of commerce, in January 1969. Another NICRA march, from Belfast to Derry, took place at the beginning of the new year and was met with further violence. In April a Queen's University student who was active in the civil rights movement, Bernadette Devlin, was unexpectedly elected to the Westminster parliament for mid-Ulster in a by-election. She was a critic of traditional Irish nationalism, an admirer of James Connolly, and one of the founders of a new left group known as People's Democracy, which had gained considerable influence over NICRA. More a socialist than a nationalist, she sought, as Connolly had done, to unite the working class across the sectarian barrier. As she wrote in her memoirs, "I had realized that the essential problem was not to unite the country, but to unite the people."[75]

A few days after the mid-Ulster by-election, the Protestant paramilitary Ulster Volunteer Force conducted a series of bombings in Belfast that were erroneously blamed on the IRA. O'Neill resigned soon afterwards and was succeeded by James Chichester-Clark. Serious rioting that summer led the new prime minister to request intervention by the British army, even though Northern Ireland's constitution gave it responsibility for its own internal security. On 12 August, nationalists attacked the annual loyalist parade in Derry, which commemorated the successful resistance of that city to a siege by King James II in 1689. This incident led to three days of rioting, which were called, with some exaggeration, the Battle of the Bogside. On 14 August the Wilson government agreed to Chichester-Clark's request for military assistance, and army units were sent to Belfast and Derry in aid of the civil power. At first they were welcomed by most Catholics as likely to be more impartial peacekeepers than the Protestant-dominated Royal Ulster Constabulary. Ironically, as Bernadette Devlin noted soon afterwards in her memoirs, unionists gave the troops a much more cool reception.[76]

The civil strife in Northern Ireland helped to revive and also to transform the Irish Republican Army and the closely associated Sinn Fein party. The

IRA had abandoned its conspicuously unsuccessful military campaign against the six-county state early in 1962. By the late 1960s the Marxist leadership of Sinn Fein contemplated abandoning its traditional policy of refusing to participate in parliamentary politics, and it also wished to place more emphasis on social and economic issues and less on nationalism. Despite, or perhaps because of, this change of emphasis, the Department of Justice in Dublin continued to regard the IRA as a threat. A memo from the minister to Lynch in March 1969 recommended that the Irish government try to split the IRA and Sinn Fein by encouraging their non-Marxist elements to reject the leadership.[77] Such a split actually occurred in December at the army convention in Belfast and a month later at the Sinn Fein convention in Dublin. The dissidents formed new organizations known as the Provisional IRA and Provisional Sinn Fein, which had more in common with the republicans of half a century earlier than with the Marxists. Many of them were devout Catholics, and their first priority was overthrowing the partitionist state in the six counties. The split was encouraged, although probably not caused, by elements in Fianna Fail who hoped that the Provisionals would lead the struggle against partition in the north while curbing IRA activity south of the border.[78] The Marxists were left in control of the "Official" IRA and Sinn Fein, which gradually dwindled away to insignificance in Northern Ireland. (South of the border, the Officials survived for a while as a radical left-wing party, known as the Workers' Party after 1982, which elected several members to the Dáil in the 1980s. Most of its deputies broke away in 1992 to form a new party called the Democratic Left, which merged with the Labour Party in 1999.)

Meanwhile, the Provisionals pursued the traditional Sinn Fein policy of refusing to take their seats in Dublin, Belfast, or Westminster if they were elected, a policy that the old Marxist leadership had wished to abandon. Catholic voters in Northern Ireland thus had a choice between abstentionist republicanism and the "green Toryism" of the old Nationalist Party, which had suffered a severe setback in the Northern Ireland election of 1969. In the Catholic ghettoes of Belfast, Provisional Sinn Fein was a working-class movement whose support was more a protest against poverty and deprivation than an expression of ideological republicanism.[79] In the outlying parts of the province, its support was more broadly based, with a considerable middle-class element, and its appeal relied more on hostility to partition.[80]

To provide a less-violent and controversial alternative to the Provisionals, a new Social Democratic and Labour Party was formed in August 1970, at the suggestion of John Hume, a civil rights activist in Derry who had been elected to Stormont the year before. Although committed to Irish unity in the long run, it placed more emphasis on civil rights in the short term and totally rejected violence. A few years after its formation, it proposed a new treaty that would give Britain and Ireland joint sovereignty over the six counties.[81] Like Sinn Fein and People's Democracy, it was officially non-sectarian but in practice could make no inroads among Protestant voters, just as the Parti québécois could make none among anglophone voters in Quebec. SDLP members participated in both the Stormont and Westminster parliaments. Both the British and Irish governments, when they began jointly to seek a peaceful solution in Northern Ireland, would rely heavily on this party for assistance and tacitly supported it in return.

The brief Catholic honeymoon with the British army ended at Easter 1970, when the local army commander authorized an Orange parade through the Catholic neighbourhood of Ballymurphy and then intervened on the side of the Orangemen in the disturbances that resulted.[82] In June that year the Wilson government was defeated in the British general election, and Edward Heath formed a Conservative government. Given the ties between Heath's party and the Ulster unionists, Irish Catholics had reason to view the new government with distrust. Soon after the election the British army began to harass the local population in the Catholic ghettos of West Belfast or to turn a blind eye when loyalist paramilitaries did so. The Provisional IRA gained popularity and new recruits in the ghettos by defending them against these attacks.[83] It began a systematic campaign against the security forces and against the partitionist state, reminiscent of the Irish war of independence half a century earlier. The first death of a British soldier as a result of this campaign was in February 1971. Two months later, and with less justification, the Provisionals began to set bombs that killed civilians at random, imitating the tactics of their loyalist counterparts.

In March 1971 Chichester-Clark was replaced by Brian Faulkner, the hardline Presbyterian who had earlier resigned from O'Neill's cabinet but had returned to serve under Chichester-Clark. In August the Faulkner government suddenly imposed a policy of interning, without trial, persons suspected of belonging to the IRA. In an action reminiscent of Pierre Trudeau's offensive against the FLQ less than a year earlier, 342 northern Catholics were interned within twenty-four hours. Because the British lacked reliable intelligence about their adversaries, fewer than a hundred of those arrested were actually members of the IRA.[84] De Valera had used internment as a weapon against the IRA in the south on more than one occasion, but the new policy was bitterly resented by northern nationalists, particularly because no action was taken against loyalist paramilitary groups. The SDLP announced that it would abstain from further participation in Northern Ireland's institutions in protest, and it called on all Catholics to do likewise. Some of its members, including John Hume, had already withdrawn from Stormont in July to protest the government's failure to hold an inquiry into the shooting of two civilians in Derry by British soldiers.[85]

The policy of internment led to a massive escalation of violence in Northern Ireland. It stimulated a further growth in support for the Provisionals in working-class Catholic areas of West Belfast, which suffered from extremely high levels of unemployment as well as the unwelcome attentions of the British soldiers and the loyalist paramilitaries. In 1970 there had been only 29 deaths in Northern Ireland related to political and sectarian strife, but in 1971 there were 180, of which the great majority occurred in the last twenty weeks of the year, after internment was introduced. In 1972, which proved to be the worst year of the Troubles, there were 497 deaths.[86] January of that year was marked by Bloody Sunday (the second event to be given that name in Irish history), when 14 unarmed civilian demonstrators were shot and killed by British paratroopers in Derry. Whether this was a spontaneous action by the soldiers involved or a deliberate effort to destroy the civil rights movement was still in dispute, and the subject of an official inquiry, more than thirty years later.

Northern Ireland was now out of control, and the British government had to recognize that the experiment of 1920 had failed. In March, less than two months after Bloody Sunday, it suspended home rule and closed down the Stormont parliament, pending further developments. Instead of a prime minister chosen from Stormont, Northern Ireland would be directly ruled by a secretary of state who sat in the British cabinet and was responsible to Westminster. The long search began for a more viable regime that would be based on power-sharing between Northern Ireland's two communities. Much blood remained to be shed, however, before the search ended. A total of 3,677 people, more than half of whom were civilians, would be killed as a result of political violence in Northern Ireland in the years 1969 through 2001.[87] (Relative to population, this toll, while horrifying by western European standards, was lower when averaged over the thirty-three-year period than the "normal" homicide rate in the southern region of the United States.) The IRA was responsible for about half the deaths, but the majority of its victims were soldiers or policemen, and many of the others were IRA members suspected of being informers. Most of the persons killed by the security forces were members of the IRA. The more than 1,000 persons killed by loyalist paramilitaries were almost entirely civilians.[88] Between them, the security forces and the loyalists killed more civilians over a twenty-year period than did the IRA.[89] More than 60 per cent of all the civilians killed during the Troubles were Catholics.[90] In addition to the killings, between August 1969 and February 1973 between 30,000 and 60,000 persons, about four-fifths of whom were Catholics, were expelled from their homes in parts of Belfast or fled to escape the paramilitaries and the army.[91]

The five years from 1972 through 1976 were the worst period of the Troubles in terms of loss of life, accounting for almost half the total number of deaths. The military campaign of the Provisional IRA was, however, interrupted by three ceasefires: in the early summer of 1972, around the Christmas and New Year holidays in 1974–75, and for a longer period beginning in February 1975. During the first and last of these ceasefires, secret discussions took place between the IRA and the British authorities.[92] The policy of internment, which had helped to provoke the violence in the first place, ended in December 1975, but 1976 proved to be one of the worst years of violence ever recorded. In addition to the main struggle against the British and the loyalist paramilitaries, the Provisionals were engaged in sporadic hostilities against the Official IRA, which was still trying to regain the ground it had lost since the emergence of the newer organization. The Provisional IRA campaign during these years was a failure in every sense: it did not convince the British to withdraw from Northern Ireland, and it alienated much of the sympathy that the Provisionals had originally enjoyed both north and south of the border. The violent campaign was also repeatedly condemned by the Catholic Church. It was apparent by the end of 1976 that the Provisionals were no match for the British army in a military sense. At the same time their political allies, Sinn Fein, lagged far behind the SDLP in popularity. The SDLP established itself as the first choice of northern Catholics in the local council elections of 1973, a result confirmed by the election of a new assembly later that year. It had the support of the Catholic Church and of both major parties in the Irish state south of the border.

Long before the imposition of direct rule, southern Ireland had been drawn into the events in the six counties. Although Irish governments had made little or no practical effort to reunify the country since 1925, a sentimental commitment to reunification survived. Even the violent IRA campaign against partition in 1954–57, although opposed by the de Valera government, received some public sympathy south of the border.[93] In a 1968 poll only 20 per cent of persons in southern Ireland thought reunification should not take place without the consent of a majority of Northern Ireland's population.[94] Belfast with its environs was a somewhat alien and unfamiliar place to most people in the south, but the same could not be said of the part of Northern Ireland west of the Bann, which was religiously and economically more similar to the south. Derry was a particularly sore point; it was a far more Catholic town in 1968 than it had been at the time of partition, although Catholics had been a majority of its population even then. Its geographical position on the extreme western edge of Northern Ireland, with its natural hinterland across the border in Donegal, also underlined its anomalous status. The Irish army made preparations to intervene in Derry to protect the Catholics there in August 1969, but abandoned the idea when the British army arrived instead. Neil Blaney, the minister of defence, had thought that moving the Irish army into Derry might lead to intervention by the United Nations. Most of his colleagues considered the move too risky. Some residents of Derry were, however, allowed to join reserve units of the Irish army in Donegal to receive military training.[95]

Jack Lynch, who succeeded Sean Lemass as taoiseach in 1966, had been a reluctant candidate for the Fianna Fail leadership but had been persuaded to run by Lemass himself. He never fully won the loyalty of Fianna Fail's more nationalist wing, which included Blaney and Kevin Boland as well as his eventual successor (and Lemass's son-in-law), Charles Haughey. These ministers and other party members of like mind urged a more aggressive policy in support of northern nationalists than the cautious Lynch was prepared to tolerate. The Department of Finance, of which Haughey was the minister, secretly subsidized a republican newspaper in the north, as well as a secret meeting between northern nationalists and an Irish army officer which took place south of the border.[96] Some of its funds may have reached the Provisional IRA in 1970.[97] Gerry Fitt, the leader of the SDLP, complained to an Irish civil servant that Irish government money was being used in the north for violent purposes.[98] There was an obvious tension between this kind of intervention on behalf of northern nationalists and the policy of rapprochement between the two governments that had been begun by Lemass and continued by Lynch. Another concern for the Irish government was that too much zeal on behalf of northern nationalists might imperil Ireland's hopes of entering the European Community alongside the United Kingdom.

In the summer of 1969 General Charles de Gaulle visited Ireland for a long vacation following his resignation as president of France. The Irish government gave a banquet in his honour at which the general proposed a toast to a united Ireland, perhaps hoping to repeat his success in stimulating Quebec nationalism two years earlier. However, his microphone failed to function properly as he made the toast, and the incident was not widely reported.[99]

Lynch pursued a carefully ambiguous strategy after the Troubles in Northern Ireland began. He seems to have ignored a suggestion by Haughey that all ministers should be asked to prepare contingency plans for dealing with the reunification of the country and its impact on their departments.[100] On the other hand, Lynch's speech in response to the Battle of the Bogside, which was drafted by the entire cabinet, criticized the deployment

of British troops and seemed to threaten the possibility of military intervention. The Irish army in fact was too weak to have intervened with any chance
of success; it went no further than to establish field hospitals in Donegal to
assist refugees from the fighting in Derry who might flee across the border.
Speaking a month later at Tralee, a city with a reputation for republicanism,
Lynch said that while "the overwhelming majority" of Irish people wanted
reunification, his government had "no intention of using force to realise this
desire." He also noted his government's acceptance, "as a practical matter," of
the existence of the northern regime and the many fruitful contacts
between the two governments in recent years.[101] This speech was drafted by
T.K. Whitaker, the architect of the new economic strategy under Lemass.[102]
Whitaker had advised Lynch in November 1968 that the policy of cooperation
with the northern regime should be continued and that efforts to force the
issue of reunification would be counterproductive.[103] Lynch reportedly told
some nationalists from Derry in 1970 that Ireland could not afford to take
over the six counties since it could not hope to match British expenditures
on the province; he hoped that it might be able to do so in about ten years.[104]

    As an immediate and largely symbolic response to the situation in Derry,
Ireland brought the situation in Northern Ireland before the Security Council of the United Nations for the first time. (Previous Irish speeches on the
subject had been in the General Assembly.) The British representative tried
to prevent any discussion of the situation by arguing that it fell under domestic jurisdiction but eventually agreed to a proposal by Finland that the Security Council at least hear the Irish case "as a matter of courtesy." Patrick
Hillery, the Irish minister of external affairs, correctly noted that the British
had not objected to relations between the Greeks and Turks in Cyprus being
discussed by the council, although that was more clearly a matter of domestic jurisdiction. He called for a United Nations peacekeeping force, like the
one that existed in Cyprus, to replace the British troops in Derry and Belfast,
which the residents of those cities had only accepted as "the lesser of two
evils." The British representative then repeated his argument about domestic jurisdiction.[105] Given the British veto and British influence over several of
the other members, the failure of the Security Council to accomplish
anything was a foregone conclusion.

    In a parliamentary debate on the northern situation in October, Lynch
repeated his commitment to pursue reunification only by peaceful means
and said that the first step was to ensure equal rights for the Catholics of
Northern Ireland and harmony between them and the Protestants. Fine
Gael leader Liam Cosgrave, whose father had headed the Free State's first
government from 1922 to 1932, took essentially the same position.
Brendan Corish, leader of the Labour Party, was more critical of the Fianna

Fail government, saying that it had not used its contacts with the north to promote civil rights. He also blamed the Irish people more generally for tolerating partition for half a century and not devoting enough effort to maintaining social ties across the border.[106] Dr Garret FitzGerald, who would succeed Cosgrave as leader of Fine Gael several years later, went further.[107] He asserted that the southern Irish had taken no real interest in the north since partition and had even tended to look down upon it, an attitude that he called dishonest and hypocritical. Furthermore, some policies of the southern state, such as excessive censorship, deference to the Catholic Church in social policy, and requiring a knowledge of the Irish language for jobs in the public service, had reinforced partition by making the state less attractive to northern Protestants. FitzGerald blamed the "unscrupulous" unionists above all for manipulating "the poor ordinary working people of Northern Ireland" through a strategy of divide and rule, but he also posed a challenge to southern politicians and to the people: either accept that the northern Protestants were Irish and make some concessions to their point of view or else admit that they wanted the country to remain partitioned.[108]

Nationalists in the north had requested military assistance from the south after the Battle of the Bogside but officially had received none. Official documents released thirty years later suggested, however, that Lynch's government had agreed to supply arms at one point after discussions with northern nationalists.[109] In May 1970 Lynch dismissed two of his ministers, Charles Haughey and Neil Blaney, for allegedly conspiring to import weapons into Ireland for use in the six counties. Another minister, Kevin Boland, resigned from the government to show his solidarity with Haughey and Blaney. Haughey was placed on trial for his involvement in this affair in October but was acquitted of all charges, after which he called upon Lynch to resign.[110] Blaney was eventually expelled from Fianna Fail, and Boland left it to form his own party. Haughey, a much more skilful and effective politician, retained his standing in Fianna Fail and eventually succeeded Lynch as its leader in 1979.

The arms crisis, as it was known, was symptomatic of the growing influence of northern events on southern politics and vice versa. Another symptom was popular support in the south for Provisional Sinn Fein and the Provisional IRA, which operated on both sides of a border whose legitimacy they did not recognize. In June 1970 the Provisionals organized their own ceremony at Wolfe Tone's grave for the first time and drew an audience of about five thousand. A year later they attracted fourteen thousand to the annual commemoration.[111]

Lynch, however, continued his policy of pursuing the cooperation with the northern authorities that Lemass had begun and giving priority to civil rights, while making occasional public statements that expressed a long-term aspiration for Irish unity. This policy harmonized in practice with that of the SDLP, a party whose formation in 1970 was encouraged by the Irish government. But Lynch had more difficulty in making this conciliatory policy appear credible after the Heath government took office in Britain than before. In May 1971 Heath refused permission for the construction of a transmitter that would allow Irish television programs to be watched throughout Northern Ireland, citing "important political considerations" as a reason.[112] The introduction of internment later that year and the fact that numerous republicans but no loyalist paramilitaries were interned placed further strains on the relationship and made Lynch's task no easier. When the British requested that he also introduce a policy of internment, as de Valera had done of his own volition more than once, Lynch refused. The British continued to put pressure on him to act more vigorously against the IRA. In December 1971, following the assassination of a unionist politician, the British ambassador in Dublin sent a note of protest to the taoiseach, while Faulkner accused the Irish government of complicity. Lynch replied publicly that violence was caused by the denial of civil rights to northern Catholics and should not be blamed on the Irish government.[113]

Another problem was British military incursions over the border, either by ground forces or aircraft. According to Irish estimates, there had been thirty of these by the end of August 1971, slightly more than two years after British troops arrived in Northern Ireland, and there were ten more by the end of October.[114] The British insisted that all the violations of the border had been accidental and ignored protests from the Irish government. By late 1971 British-Irish intergovernmental relations had reached their lowest point since the signing of the treaty half a century before. Harold Wilson, now leader of the opposition, called for the reunification of Ireland within fifteen years, but Prime Minister Heath appeared totally rigid and hostile, suggesting that he would not support it even if a majority in Northern Ireland wanted it.[115]

A bitter debate in the Dáil on 20–21 October 1971 revealed that Lynch was caught in the middle. The nationalist wing of his own party argued that the partition was illegitimate and unacceptable and that Lynch was not doing enough to end it. On the other hand, he was attacked by Fine Gael and the Labour Party for not doing enough to appease the northern Protestants.[116] Neither group of opponents could really provide a convincing explanation of how their preferred strategy would improve matters, and it was obvious that there could be no consensus on either strategy in any event. As a gesture to northern Protestants, a referendum was held in which an overwhelming majority in the twenty-six counties voted on 7 December

1972 to delete the section of the Irish constitution referring to the "special position" of the Catholic Church. This decision had no visible effect on unionist attitudes.

Bloody Sunday, almost a year prior to this event, had produced a rare moment of consensus among the major parties in the Irish state. Lynch called it "the saddest occasion on which I have ever addressed this House" and declared a day of national mourning. He also recalled the Irish ambassador from London and demanded the withdrawal of British troops from Northern Ireland. Cosgrave said that the cause of the massacre was partition, which he called a "mistake" by the British, and asserted that "the British have learned nothing by their experience." Corish referred to "the murderous and unprovoked attack by the British army on a peaceful march and meeting."[117] A mob in Dublin sacked and burned the British embassy. Lynch deplored the action in a statement to the Dáil, but his biographer suggests that he tacitly allowed it to happen and that it had a cathartic effect on Irish opinion.[118]

Late in 1972 there were a number of bombings south of the border, attributed to the IRA. Legislation was adopted making it easier to convict persons of belonging to an illegal organization on hearsay evidence. At the general election of 1973, Fianna Fail was defeated, although its popular vote did not decline, because of a pre-election agreement between Fine Gael and the Labour Party. Lynch resigned, and a coalition government between the other two parties took office under the leadership of Liam Cosgrave. The coalition partners were united by a strong distaste for republicanism, particularly on the part of Cosgrave and the Labour Party's most prominent personality, the writer and former diplomat Conor Cruise O'Brien. (Some observers wondered why O'Brien, who had worked hard as United Nations representative to prevent a neo-colonialist partition of the Congo, was prepared to let the neo-colonialist partition of Ireland continue indefinitely.) Their government brought in additional repressive legislation and cooperated with the British against the IRA. The coalition's four years in office were marked by an escalation of violence south of the border. In March 1974 the IRA murdered a Protestant Fine Gael senator, Billy Fox. Two months later loyalist bombs caused numerous fatalities in Dublin and Monaghan. The following year the IRA kidnapped a Dutch businessman. Cosgrave, like Pierre Trudeau in 1970, refused to negotiate with the kidnappers, and the hostage was released. In 1976 an IRA car bomb killed the British ambassador and his secretary on a country road near Dublin.

The situation in Northern Ireland after 1968 exposed some of the contradictions in Irish nationalism and had a complex impact on Irish opinion south of the border. It reminded people in the south of a situation that they had preferred to ignore for almost half a century. It exposed the failure of Irish governments over that period either to end partition by making meaningful concessions to Protestant and unionist concerns about the ideology of Irish nationalism or to overturn partition by militant action on behalf of the northern nationalists. Above all, it was a reminder of Irish weakness in relation to both the economic and military power of Great Britain and the determination of the unionists to defend their northeastern enclave, exactly the situation that had brought about partition in the first place.

The immediate reaction to the deteriorating situation in the north, with its killings, internments, expulsions of Catholics from their homes, and destruction of property, was an expression of sympathy for the northern nationalists and of indignation directed against the British. In the longer term, though, it may have weakened southern opposition to partition by making the north and its problems seem increasingly unattractive.[119] As northern violence increasingly spilled over into the south after the imposition of direct rule, there seems to have been a growing wish on the part of southern Irish opinion to keep the north at arm's length. The situation would not go away, however, and Irish governments would increasingly be drawn into efforts to find a solution.

CHAPTER NINE

The Search for Accommodation

The rise of the independence movement in Quebec and the Troubles in Northern Ireland were dramatic developments in two small provinces of the peaceful and prosperous North Atlantic world that had seemed at least superficially stable for many years. Although there were many differences between them, both situations can be viewed as expressions of resurgent nationalism on the part of peoples who, for different reasons, had been denied the normal means of collective self-expression through a national state. Both can also be attributed to the frustration of rising expectations that had been created by social and economic changes during the decades that followed the Second World War. With the benefit of hindsight, neither development seems particularly surprising or mysterious. At the time they occurred, however, neither was widely anticipated.

Both sets of events unfolded within and around political structures that were not well adapted to dealing with them and in a complicated context of conflicting interests, demands, and perspectives. Both situations were to a large extent internal struggles for space and power among neighbours doomed to coexist in close proximity on the same territory: anglophones and francophones in Quebec, unionists and nationalists in Northern Ireland. Both also had an external dimension, related to the lack of consensus over states and borders. As a result, they involved the interests and attracted the attention of states and governments outside the area directly concerned: the Canadian federal government and the various provincial governments in the case of Quebec and the British and Irish governments in the case of Northern Ireland. As the hegemonic power in the North Atlantic world, the government of the United States was also at least an interested spectator to both conflicts.

As events unfolded, in ways that were often unexpected even by those directly involved, observers who were less directly involved responded with surprise, bewilderment, and sometimes apprehension. Anglophone Canadians, who had shared a state with French Canadians for more than a century while barely noticing their existence, let alone learning their language, had a tendency to ask, "What does Quebec want?" a question that Quebec viewed occasionally with amusement, more often with irritation.[1] British people, viewing Ireland through a similar screen of ignorance, were inclined to regard the six Irish counties attached to their ostensibly "United" Kingdom as a bizarre place whose natives had an incomprehensible penchant for settling theological controversies with bombs and bullets. (The prominence of Ian Paisley and his singular ability to attract attention encouraged the non-Irish media to portray the situation in those terms.) Neither the Ottawa River nor the Irish Sea is particularly wide, but at times they almost seemed like the spaces between different planets.

These parallels should not of course obscure the differences between the two situations. The situation of francophones in Quebec before the Quiet Revolution was unquestionably better than that of Irish Catholics in Northern Ireland before the Troubles, and the reaction against the status quo was correspondingly less dramatic. Quebec francophones were a politically influential, even though economically disadvantaged, majority in their partially self-governing province and a relatively large and influential minority in Canada as a whole. Northern Irish Catholics were a large but oppressed minority in the six counties and an insignificant one in the United Kingdom. Peaceful change was possible in Quebec, anti-nationalist violence was non-existent, and the nationalist violence of the FLQ was therefore minimal, enjoyed little support, and was easily contained by the authorities. Both Quebec francophones and Northern Irish Catholics eventually divided into two parties representing more moderate and more radical versions of nationalism, but the more "radical" party in Quebec, the Parti québecois, perhaps had more in common with Northern Ireland's SDLP than it had with the Provisional IRA and Sinn Fein.

QUEBEC AND THE QUEST FOR SOVEREIGNTY

As discussed in the previous chapter, discontent with Quebec's status under the Canadian constitution had become apparent during the 1960s, even before the formation of the Parti québecois. From 1963 to 1965 the Canadian federal government, led by Lester Pearson, attempted to reduce the discontent by allowing Quebec somewhat greater autonomy in practice, but without formal constitutional change, and by appointing the Royal Commission on Bilingualism and Biculturalism, of which André Laurendeau was co-chair.

After January 1966, when Pierre Elliott Trudeau was appointed parliamentary secretary to the prime minister, and especially after April 1968, when Trudeau became prime minister himself, a different federal strategy emerged. Trudeau was an individualist liberal and an admirer of the nineteenth-century liberal Catholic philosopher Lord Acton, who had praised multinational states and had opposed the view that there should be a sovereign state for every nation. Trudeau himself distrusted Quebec nationalism and any form of collectivism. He became disillusioned with the Quiet Revolution, which he had helped to bring about, because he felt it had betrayed his liberal expectations by reinforcing the power of the Quebec state and attempting to use that state as the instrument of an ethnic group seeking redress of its grievances. In Trudeau's view, a just state was one that served the interests of all its people impartially and not just of the ethnic group that happened to comprise the majority within its borders. He sincerely believed that a nationalist sovereign state of Quebec would not be liberal and would not benefit the majority of francophones in Quebec. He also believed that the independence movement in Quebec was merely a cloak for the self-interest of the nationalist intelligentsia, whose politics he denounced with derision and scorn. Furthermore, although he had championed provincial autonomy in his writings as late as 1961, he had become convinced a few years later that any constitutional concessions to Quebec's desire for enhanced status would merely pave the way for more demands and eventually lead to complete independence.[2]

Trudeau argued that the only way to prevent Quebec from seeking independence was to persuade francophones in Quebec that their language could be protected and their access to individual opportunity enhanced without making the province more autonomous. He believed that they could be so persuaded by making the Canadian federal state bilingual in form and in fact, by reinforcing the French-speaking minorities outside Quebec, and by giving francophones more prominent positions in the federal government and the public service. They would then, according to the scenario, transfer their loyalty from Quebec to Canada, and Quebec nationalism would die a natural death. Moderate nationalists such as Laurendeau and Lesage, not to mention Henri Bourassa in an earlier generation, had favoured combining a more bilingual Canada with a more autonomous Quebec. Trudeau insisted that Quebec must choose either one or the other, and he was determined that a more bilingual Canada would be the eventual choice.

Trudeau's analysis and his proposals were understandably controversial in francophone Quebec, but they were greeted with relief and enthusiasm by other Canadians, who had become increasingly distressed by the resurgence of Quebec nationalism. Now an able, articulate French Canadian from Quebec was promising them that they need not feel guilty about opposing Quebec nationalism, and that their nightmares could be ended with a few simple reforms. This response helped Trudeau and his Liberal Party to win a convincing mandate in the federal election of June 1968.

His task was made easier by the fact that André Laurendeau had died suddenly just before Trudeau became prime minister. As a result of his death, the Royal Commission on Bilingualism and Biculturalism never produced the constitutional proposals that Laurendeau had apparently envisaged.[3] The report it did produce, in several volumes between 1965 and 1969, emphasized Trudeau's own priorities: strengthening the francophone minorities outside Quebec and increasing the francophone presence in the federal government and administration. Trudeau proceeded to do precisely that, notably through the Official Languages Act of 1969 and through a determined effort to recruit more francophones for the public service. His government also tried to assist the economy of Quebec, where unemployment was higher and incomes lower than in most of Canada, by encouraging both public and private investment in the province through a newly created Department of Regional Economic Expansion, headed by Trudeau's friend the former labour union leader Jean Marchand.

Demands for formal constitutional change, however, could not be totally dismissed, since the government of Ontario, the largest province, had joined Quebec in insisting that they be discussed and had hosted an interprovincial conference for that purpose in 1967. Just before his retirement, Pearson had reluctantly convened an intergovernmental conference on the subject, the first of many over the next twenty-five years. Trudeau, however, argued that constitutional change did not necessarily need to include more powers for Quebec or for the provincial governments in general. Instead, he emphasized a different set of priorities: constitutional entrenchment of bilingualism, a judicially enforceable charter of human rights binding on both levels of government, and an end to the embarrassing situation whereby constitutional amendments still had to be made by Westminster at Canada's request.[4] A document embodying these ideas, known as the Victoria Charter, was presented to the provinces in 1971. Quebec's Liberal premier, Robert Bourassa, under pressure from the nationalist intelligentsia and his own advisers, rejected it on the grounds that it did not provide enough additional powers for Quebec. Subsequently, some other provincial governments began to join Quebec in demanding additional legislative powers for themselves. Trudeau placed the constitution on the back burner, where it remained for four years, but in 1975–76 he reopened the file. Discussions with Quebec's premier, Robert Bourassa, led to a slightly revised Victoria Charter, including a clause that would specify "preservation and the full development of the French language and the culture based on it" as a fundamental purpose of Canadian federalism.[5] However, Quebec and certain other provinces insisted on changes in the distribution of powers before they would discuss an amending formula.

Quebec continued to give Trudeau's Liberals a large majority of its seats in federal elections, where there was no nationalist alternative to vote for. At the same time, support for the Parti québécois, to which Trudeau's ideas were anathema, continued to increase in provincial elections. Perhaps this apparently inconsistent voting behaviour reflected ambivalence. More likely, Quebec was indicating that it wanted the best of both worlds: more influence over Canada with Trudeau and more sovereignty for Quebec with René Lévesque. But that proved easier said than done.

A study of voting in the Quebec elections of 1970 and 1973 indicates the social and electoral base of the Parti québécois during the years of its early growth and development. Virtually all who voted for the party had French as their mother tongue. They were also disproportionately likely to be young and well-educated. Professionals and semi-professionals were the most likely occupational category to support the party, while business proprietors or managers and farmers were the least. The white-collar lower middle class and the blue-collar working class were equally likely to support the party. Francophones who lived in the Montreal urban area, where the competition for jobs and status against anglophones and immigrants was particularly intense, were more likely to vote for the party than those who lived elsewhere in the province. Those who thought that recent changes in Quebec had not been fast enough were overwhelmingly inclined to vote for the party.[6]

The electoral victory of the Parti québécois in November 1976 produced a euphoric mood in much of French-speaking Quebec. Lévesque told a huge crowd of well-wishers that night that he had never felt so proud to be a Quebecer. Happy nationalists drove through the streets of Montreal honking their car horns and waving flags, like hockey fans celebrating yet another championship for the Montreal Canadiens. Many assumed that independence was just around the corner. At the very least, the momentum of the Quiet Revolution, which had languished for almost a decade, would resume under the new government. The anglophone minority, on the other hand, reacted with shock and dismay. More than 100,000 of them, or about one-eighth of the total number, would flee the province over the next four years.

The new government's first priority, however, was not independence but legislation to protect the French language. The Bourassa government's Official Language Act of 1974 had been intended as a reasonable compromise between conflicting demands but had failed to produce consensus. Nationalists considered it inadequate, while anglophones and immigrants, who traditionally supported Bourassa's party, considered it excessive. The latter sentiment had contributed to Bourassa's defeat in the 1976 election, since many anglophones and immigrants voted for minor parties or for a temporarily revived Union nationale.

Having virtually no anglophone or immigrant supporters to lose, the Lévesque government could afford to be more radical and to act more quickly. A white paper on language policy was introduced in April 1977, followed by a bill less than four weeks later. Bill 1, which occupied the first place on the order paper of the National Assembly, was entitled the Charter of the French Language. Two features of it attracted particular criticism: a preamble implying that only those whose mother tongue was French were true Quebecers and a "notwithstanding" clause that gave the provisions of the bill priority over Quebec's charter of human rights and freedoms in the event of any conflict between the two. A revised version, known as Bill 101, which eliminated both of these controversial features, was introduced in July.

The provisions of the Charter of the French Language, a much longer document than the Official Language Act, which it was intended to replace, touched upon virtually every aspect of public life in Quebec. Only the French text of statutes and judicial decisions would be considered official. Litigation involving corporations and other artificial entities as parties had to be conducted in French, unless all the litigants agreed to the use of English. Collective agreements and arbitration awards in industrial disputes had to be in French. No one could be dismissed, suspended, or demoted from his or her job on the grounds of inability to speak English. Businesses had to publish their catalogues, brochures, and flyers in French, and advertising signs had to be in French only, unless they advertised goods or services of interest only to a particular ethnic group. All firms with fifty or more employees would have to apply for and receive a certificate of "francisation," demonstrating that their internal affairs were conducted in French. Children could receive an English-language education only if an older sibling or one of their parents had received an English-language education in Quebec. Those who migrated to Quebec, even from another Canadian province, after the bill came into effect would thus be denied this privilege. Four administrative agencies were established: an office of the French language to draft regulations, a council of the French language to advise the government on policy, a surveillance commission to find and prosecute violations of the law, and a commission to invent French replacements for the English names of localities and geographical features. (Some renaming actually did take place over the next few years, but less than in Ireland after 1922. Many towns, cities, and counties, particularly in the Eastern Townships, retained their English names.)

The minister who introduced the bill, Camille Laurin, was a psychiatrist who attributed the emotional problems experienced by many of his patients to francophone Quebec's status as an internal colony of anglophone Canada. Only through decolonization, according to his analysis, could Quebec became "normal," a word that occupied a prominent place in the lexicon of the Parti québécois. In his speech on second reading, Dr Laurin explained that the bill was necessary to overcome the privileges unjustly enjoyed by the anglophone minority in Quebec, privileges that he attributed to the legacy of colonialism. Speaking to those who deplored the coercive nature of some of its provisions, he said that dominant groups always benefit when the state fails to act and that formal "rights" enjoyed by such groups must be examined critically with regard to the distribution of economic assets that make them possible. Citing, without attribution, a nineteenth-century French monarchist writer, the Comte de Montalembert, Dr Laurin stated that in such circumstances it is true to say that it is liberty that oppresses and the law that liberates. In conclusion he predicted that the bill would prepare Quebec to be "a French country," able, by virtue of its cultural specificity, to make its own contribution to the international community.[7]

Although the Lévesque government introduced a significant amount of new legislation during its first term in office, the Charter of the French Language proved to be its most lasting and important legacy to Quebec. The provisions eliminating bilingualism in statutes and in the courts were promptly struck down by the Supreme Court of Canada, since they violated section 133 of the British North America Act.[8] Subsequent judicial decisions, after the Canadian Charter of Rights and Freedoms was adopted in 1982, led to modification of the provisions dealing with access to English-language education and with commercial signs. However, most of the Charter of the French Language survived. Despite some grumbling by anglophones, it eventually established a fairly stable and peaceful equilibrium between the two main linguistic communities in Quebec, with French as the clearly dominant language but with the English language continuing to play an important role.

Within a few years after Bill 101 was adopted, the gap in incomes between anglophones and francophones within Quebec had virtually disappeared. The percentage of anglophones in Quebec who could speak French increased dramatically, but there was also a more modest increase in the percentage of Quebec francophones who could speak English. Two decades after Bill 101 was adopted, the anglophones of Quebec were a gradually dwindling, occasionally complaining, but generally comfortable and well-treated minority, not unlike the southern Irish Protestants in the age of de Valera. Intermarriage between anglophones and francophones had become commonplace. While some anglophones were nostalgic for what they considered happier times, most were making the best of their circumstances.[9]

Bill 101 contributed to a process that was already underway before it existed: the embourgeoisement of Quebec nationalism. By the mid-1970s, Quebec nationalists were becoming older and more affluent than they had been during the Quiet Revolution, and they had more to lose than before from economic uncertainty, disorder, and violence. The FLQ and the RIN had disappeared, and the angry demonstrations and protests of the 1960s and early 1970s were largely a thing of the past. Quebec's labour unions, after a brief flirtation with Marxism in the early 1970s, had adopted a generally corporatist orientation and at least implicitly accepted the economic status quo. They were pleased with the changes to the labour code that the Lévesque government adopted early in its term. Their preference for harmony and collaboration between classes was shared by the Parti québécois itself. The party's left wing, mainly concentrated in Montreal, was distrusted by Premier Lévesque and had little influence on his government's policies. The government's most dramatic economic initiatives were to nationalize a failing regional airline and a portion of the asbestos mining industry, initiatives that resembled those taken by other Canadian provinces at about the same time. Its major statement on economic policy emphasized the importance of the private sector.[10] As if to illustrate its reconciliation with conservative nationalism, it even unveiled a long-forgotten statue of Maurice Duplessis, which had been commissioned by his immediate successor but then hidden in a storage room by the Liberals for nearly two decades.

In a televised speech nine days after the Parti québécois was elected, Prime Minister Trudeau stated that it had not won a mandate to separate Quebec from Canada and that the people of Quebec had no wish to renounce the Canadian part of their identity. He promised to cooperate with the new government as it performed its responsibilities under the constitution and expressed confidence that Canada would remain intact by voluntary consent and not by the use of force, which he rejected as an option.[11] In 1978 he again unveiled plans to modify the Canadian constitution, suggesting changes in federal institutions and hinting that concessions to the provinces of the kind he had earlier opposed might follow. However, the project soon bogged down in the face of discordant demands from the various provincial governments, particularly the western provinces, whose self-confidence had been reinforced by the growing global demand for their oil and natural gas. In May 1979 Trudeau's party was defeated in the federal election, and the opposition Conservatives, who had practically no support in Quebec, formed a minority government led by Joe Clark.

The Quebec government finally announced its referendum strategy in the same year, having achieved most of its other objectives. It published a white paper setting out its case for what it called sovereignty-association.[12] It also adopted legislation to govern the conduct of the referendum by which the people of Quebec would vote for or against the project. This legislation provided that all expenditure, publicity, and fundraising during the campaign must be tightly controlled by two committees, one for supporters of the option and the other for opponents. In practice these committees would be dominated by Quebec's two major political parties, the Parti québécois and the Liberal Party of Quebec.

The white paper traced the history of Quebec from its origins, with particular attention to the period since 1867. It portrayed the province's experience with federalism as essentially one of defeats, humiliations, gradually declining influence over the rest of Canada, and increasing federal intrusions into provincial fields of jurisdiction. It alleged that reform of the system to meet Quebec's needs had been proved impossible after fifteen years of effort, and the only escape from the impasse was a completely new relationship between Quebec and Canada. The paper then outlined the proposal of sovereignty-association in considerable detail, including the controversial idea of a common currency on which Lévesque had insisted, even though many doubted that it was workable. After citing evidence that the rest of Canada would be willing to negotiate a new relationship following a successful referendum in Quebec, the document ended with an encouraging portrayal of the future Quebec. This included promises that a sovereign Quebec would both respect the rights of its anglophones and other minorities and provide "support and solidarity" to francophone minorities in the other provinces.

The last decisions to be made were the wording of the question that would appear on the ballot and the date when the referendum would take place. The question was drafted in December 1979 and the date was finally set for 20 May 1980. The question was long and complex. In its English-language version, it read as follows:

The Government of Quebec has made public its proposal to negotiate a new agreement with the rest of Canada, based on the equality of nations;

This agreement would enable Quebec to acquire the exclusive power to make its laws, levy its taxes, and establish relations abroad – in other words sovereignty –

and at the same time, to maintain with Canada an economic association including a common currency;

Any change in political status resulting from these negotiations will be submitted to the people through a referendum. On these terms do you agree to give the Government of Quebec the mandate to negotiate the proposed agreement between Quebec and Canada?[13]

If read carefully, this was what was known as a "soft" question. A vote in favour of it was not even a commitment to sovereignty-association, let alone to full independence, but merely an expression of support for negotiations between Quebec and Canada. The real decision, if any, would be made in the second referendum, which was promised after the negotiations. The two-referendum strategy, known as *étapisme*, was the invention of Claude Morin, the minister responsible for intergovernmental affairs and a former civil servant who had advised Premier Bourassa at the time of the Victoria Charter negotiations. Although criticized as excessively cautious by some of the party's left wing, it seemed to offer a reasonable chance that the electorate would respond favourably. Nor is there any reason to doubt the sincerity of Morin in advocating it, even though he was later revealed to have been acting as an informant for the Royal Canadian Mounted Police during his years in the Quebec government.

Supporters of sovereignty-association had been encouraged by the electoral defeat and anticipated retirement of Trudeau and his replacement by a prime minister with little support in Quebec who proposed to abstain from direct intervention in the referendum campaign. Unfortunately for the Parti québécois, the Clark government lost a parliamentary vote on its budget in December 1979 and then lost the subsequent election. Trudeau returned to office in March 1980, just in time to participate directly, and perhaps decisively, in the campaign. He accused members of the Quebec government of trying to make separation from Canada more palatable by promising to couple it with association, when they could not guarantee that association would ever take place. He contrasted them unfavourably with the separatists of the 1960s, who at least had been honest enough to indicate what they wanted and brave enough to take the risk of complete independence.

Trudeau's most important speech during the campaign was delivered in Montreal, just a few days before the referendum. In it he accused the Parti québécois of ethnic intolerance, citing an ill-considered comment by René Lévesque, who had suggested that Trudeau's middle name and partly Scottish origin might explain his hostility to Quebec nationalism. Having thus placed his opponents on the defensive, Trudeau went on to promise that a vote against the referendum question would not be interpreted as support for the status quo but as a mandate for the reform of the Canadian constitution.[14] Probably much of his audience interpreted this as a promise of decentralized federalism and more legislative powers for Quebec, which most of Quebec's provincial politicians had been demanding for twenty years. However, Trudeau did not explicitly promise this, and it is difficult to accuse him of deliberate deception, since his own constitutional priorities – a new amending formula and a charter of rights – had been on record for almost as long.

At the end of March, polls conducted for the Quebec government showed a very slight majority in support of the yes option, but thereafter they showed a steady decline. The actual referendum, in which 85.6 per cent of the eligible voters participated, was a crushing defeat for the government: 40 per cent in favour and 60 per cent against. It was not even possible to argue on the basis of these results that a majority of francophone voters had supported the yes option. Only the isolated northern part of the province, which had few social or economic ties with the rest of Canada, and a few strongly nationalist districts in and around Montreal had voted for sovereignty-association. The percentage in favour was almost identical with the percentage that had supported the Parti québécois in 1976: enough to win a first-past-the-post election against a divided opposition but not enough to win a referendum in which there were only two options, yes or no.

Trudeau's promise of change – his kind of change – proved to be no idle boast. Soon after the referendum, he announced plans to resume constitutional discussions with the provinces. In September he terminated the discussions, which had demonstrated that no consensus was possible, and announced that the federal government would unilaterally request the changes it wanted from the British parliament. The main features of the federal proposals were a charter of rights and freedoms, including a guarantee of minority language educational rights (for anglophones in Quebec and for francophones elsewhere) that was contrary to the provisions of Quebec's Charter of the French Language, and an amending formula that would give Quebec a veto over changes that affected it. If eight of the provinces suggested an alternative amending formula within two years, the people of Canada would be asked to choose between the two formulas in a referendum.[15] Quebec's immediate neighbours, Ontario and New Brunswick, were the only two provinces whose governments supported this initiative.

More than a year of complicated manoeuvres followed before Westminster adopted a modified version of Trudeau's proposals, which by virtue of last-minute concessions managed to win the support of every provincial government except that of Quebec. In the course of these events, Quebec nationalism suffered another major, and largely self-inflicted, defeat on top of that which it had already suffered in the referendum. Lévesque initially formed an alliance with the seven other provinces that opposed Trudeau's proposals, unwisely agreeing in return to abandon Quebec's traditional insistence that any new amending formula give it a veto. Quebec voters appeared to endorse his strategy by unexpectedly re-electing his government with an increased majority in April 1981. The Parti québecois won almost 300,000 more votes in this election than its option had attracted in the referendum less than a year earlier. The vote for the provincial Liberals, most of whom also disapproved of Trudeau's unilateral initiative, fell short of the number that had voted against sovereignty-association in the referendum by more than half a million. This result may conceivably have been influenced by disillusionment with either the substance or the procedure of Trudeau's initiative. It was not a vote for sovereignty-association, since Lévesque had promised not to raise the issue during his second term if re-elected.

Westminster's reluctance to adopt the federal government's constitutional proposals in the face of so much provincial opposition, Margaret Thatcher's lack of rapport with Trudeau, and a ruling by the Supreme Court of Canada that there was a constitutional convention requiring provincial consent for major constitutional changes[16] eventually brought Trudeau back to the negotiating table in the fall of 1981. At this point Lévesque alarmed his allies in the other provinces by appearing to accept a suggestion by Trudeau that a referendum be held on the Charter of Rights and Freedoms, which would certainly have been endorsed by the electorate in anglophone Canada and probably also in Quebec.[17] This second miscalculation by Lévesque gave his allies an excuse to negotiate, behind his back, a compromise with Trudeau that modified the proposals to meet their concerns but did not respond to Quebec's major objections. In one respect the revised package of reforms was even worse for Quebec than Trudeau's original version, since its amending formula did not give Quebec a veto over most kinds of amendments. Quebec subsequently requested a judicial ruling as to whether it had ever had a veto, a question that the Supreme Court of Canada answered in the negative.[18]

There was little overt response by the people of Quebec to this series of defeats. Demonstrations in the streets were no longer in fashion. The Lévesque government, apparently bereft of new ideas, turned sharply to the right after its second electoral victory. By the early 1980s some observers were arguing, not for the first or last time, that Quebec nationalism itself was moribund.[19] But the bitterness of those who had lost is suggested by Yves

Beauchemin's novel *Le Matou,* a bleak portrayal of post-referendum Montreal. In the book a naive young couple, perhaps representing the people of Quebec, are deceived by the federal government, cheated by an anglophone businessman, and pursued by a sinister character with disreputable right-wing antecedents. The couple rescue an abused child from his prostitute mother, who lives on Gilford Street. Few readers would have needed to be reminded that the headquarters of the Quebec Liberal Party were on the same street.

Despite the apparent decline of Quebec nationalism, the two issues that had driven it, the Canadian constitution and language policy, would both re-emerge by the end of the decade. Trudeau finally retired in 1984, his work done. A few months later his federal Liberals were swept out of office by a resurgent Conservative Party, which was now led by an anglophone Quebecer of Irish ancestry, Brian Mulroney. Mulroney had supported Trudeau's constitutional initiative in 1980, but in a campaign speech written for him by his personal friend Lucien Bouchard, a member of the Parti québecois, Mulroney promised four years later to modify the constitution again so that Quebec could accept it "with honour and enthusiasm."[20] Almost simultaneously with this speech, the Supreme Court of Canada struck down the provision in the Charter of the French Language restricting access to English schools, basing its decision on Trudeau's Charter of Rights and Freedoms.[21] For only the second time in the twentieth century, the Conservatives won more Quebec votes in a federal general election than the Liberals, most of whose surviving Quebec members were in ridings with large anglophone or immigrant populations.

René Lévesque publicly welcomed both Mulroney's speech and his victory in the election, saying that the Liberals had been disastrous for Quebec.[22] He later announced that Quebec would resume attendance at federal-provincial conferences, which it had ceased to attend after the constitution was modified without its consent. Lévesque also declared that pursuing Mulroney's offer of constitutional reform was "un beau risque," thus implicitly abandoning the goal of sovereignty-association.[23] This position provoked a rebellion by his more nationalist ministers, several of whom resigned from the cabinet and from the party. Lévesque was soon forced to retire, and his successor, who agreed with him about Mulroney and the constitution, was defeated in the election that followed. Robert Bourassa returned to office at the head of a Liberal government to undertake the "beau risque" of negotiating a new constitutional agreement with Mulroney. In May 1986 a conciliatory speech by Bourassa's minister of intergovernmental affairs, indicating that Quebec's new government accepted the Charter of Rights and Freedoms and would demand only five changes in other parts of the constitution in return for its consent, paved the way for serious negotiations.[24]

The result a year later was what came to be called the Meech Lake Accord. In contrast to Trudeau's initiative, it was not announced to the public until all the provincial premiers had agreed to it. The accord gave Quebec its five demands: a declaration that the courts would interpret the constitution in a manner that recognized Quebec as "a distinct society," a constitutional veto, a role in selecting judges for the Supreme Court of Canada, a slight restriction on the federal power to spend in areas of provincial jurisdiction, and the constitutional entrenchment of an existing agreement that gave Quebec a role in selecting immigrants. It also gave the provinces, including Quebec, the power to nominate prospective members of the appointed Canadian senate. The accord had to be approved by all ten provincial legislatures within three years, but this requirement was erroneously assumed to be merely a formality. It became problematical, however, over the next few months, when Pierre Trudeau came out of retirement to campaign against the Meech Lake Accord, which he described as a cowardly and unnecessary surrender to Quebec nationalism.[25]

Meanwhile the subject of language legislation, apparently settled in 1977, returned to haunt the Bourassa government. Quebec anglophones, many of whom owned retail stores or other small businesses, particularly resented the provision in the Charter of the French Language requiring that commercial signs be in French only. Efforts to overturn it by litigation were given a new impetus by Trudeau's Charter of Rights and Freedoms, which guaranteed freedom of expression. Bourassa promised to change the law during the election campaign of 1985, but he began to backpedal when he realized how much this promise offended Quebec nationalists. When the Court of Appeal ruled against the ban on bilingual signs in 1986, some anglophone businesses were vandalized. And when the Supreme Court of Canada upheld that ruling two years later, it provoked one of the largest nationalist demonstrations since the 1960s. Bourassa introduced new legislation that continued to ban bilingual signs on the outsides of buildings, making use of the notwithstanding clause which had been added to Trudeau's charter in the final round of negotiations with the premiers.[26] Following his decision, support for the Meech Lake Accord declined sharply in English-speaking Canada, with the "distinct society" clause in particular being viewed with suspicion. The premier of one province delayed plans to submit the accord to his legislature. Soon afterwards another province elected a new legislature, which reversed the approval given by its predecessor. There was also a backlash within Quebec, where three anglophone ministers resigned from Bourassa's government. Some disgruntled anglophones formed the Equality Party, whose name reflected their view that the English language should enjoy equal status with the French language in Quebec. In 1989 the party won four seats in the Quebec National Assembly.

As the three-year deadline approached, the Meech Lake Accord was in crisis. In an effort to save it, Mulroney appointed a parliamentary committee, headed by Jean Charest, to modify it by watering down its concessions to Quebec nationalism. In protest, several Quebec members of Parliament with nationalist antecedents resigned from the Conservative Party, including Mulroney's friend Lucien Bouchard, who was serving as minister of the environment. The dissidents formed a new party called the Bloc québécois, loosely allied with the Parti québécois.[27] It was the first Quebec nationalist party to be represented in the federal parliament since the disappearance of the Bloc populaire more than forty years earlier. Furthermore, the changes that had provoked this development were not enough to save the Meech Lake Accord, which expired in June 1990 after two provincial legislatures still withheld their consent.

Although, or perhaps because, many Quebec nationalists thought the Meech Lake Accord had been insufficient, its rejection by anglophone Canada was viewed as a humiliation and an insult to Quebec. The demise of Meech Lake also revived memories of the constitutional changes imposed on Quebec without its consent a few years earlier, which Meech Lake had been intended to rectify. If anglophone Canada was so rigidly attached to the existing constitution that it refused to make even minor changes for Quebec's benefit, what hope was there for any lasting accommodation between the two nations? Only 34 per cent of Quebeckers polled had supported sovereignty-association in 1985 and 40 per cent in 1989, but in 1990 the number rose to 60 per cent. If the poll referred to "independence" rather than "sovereignty-association," the increase over the same period was from 15 to 34 to 46 per cent. In 1991 sovereignty-association was still supported by 58 per cent and independence by 44 per cent.[28]

Premier Bourassa, a lover of compromise and moderation but also a committed federalist, acted shrewdly to keep the situation under control. Suggesting that Quebec should consider all possible options for its future relationship with Canada, he allowed his Liberal Party to establish a committee on constitutional reform and the National Assembly to establish a committee on "the political and constitutional future of Quebec," jointly chaired by nominees of both major parties and with representation from business, labour, and other sectors of society as well as the political parties. Early in 1991 the Liberal committee, headed by Jean Allaire, presented its report, which advocated an extremely radical decentralization of Canadian federalism, apparently in an effort to shock anglophone Canada into a realization that the resurgence of Quebec nationalism required serious action on its part.[29] The Allaire report was discussed at the Liberal Party's convention that year but not actually adopted. A few party members who supported it left the Liberals to form a new party known as Action démocratique du Québec. The all-party committee of the National Assembly, known as the Bélanger-Campeau Commission, could predictably reach no consensus on whether Quebec should remain part of Canada or become a sovereign state. It recommended that another referendum on sovereignty be held in 1992, but that if Canada produced an acceptable offer of constitutional change before the referendum date, voters could be asked to vote on the offer rather than on sovereignty.[30] The National Assembly approved this recommendation soon afterwards.

This outcome led the Mulroney government and the other provinces to come up with another offer. Bourassa at first refrained from participating in the new round of constitutional discussions, but he entered them at the last moment and declared that the new offer was satisfactory enough to be submitted to the voters in a referendum. Known as the Charlottetown Accord, it included some of the substance of Meech Lake but also a variety of other provisions, including self-government for aboriginal peoples throughout Canada. The "distinct society" clause was placed within a so-called Canada clause that also affirmed the equality of the ten provinces, a notion that was anathema to Quebec nationalists. The Parti québécois, now led by Jacques Parizeau, understandably viewed the Charlottetown Accord as a step backwards from Meech Lake, which it had considered barely adequate. Trudeau, for reasons that were less obvious, also opposed the new accord.

On 26 October 1992 Quebec held its referendum on the Charlottetown Accord. The federal government conducted a simultaneous referendum on the same question in other parts of Canada. Voters in both Quebec and anglophone Canada rejected the accord, with only 42.4 per cent favouring it in Quebec and a somewhat higher percentage in the rest of Canada.[31] Only the three smallest provinces, the Northwest Territories, and Quebec's anglophone minority endorsed the document. Mulroney and Bourassa retired soon afterwards, and their respective parties were defeated in subsequent elections. Two years after the Charlottetown referendum, the Parti québécois was in office under Parizeau, who had been Lévesque's minister of finance and had resigned in 1984 because Lévesque responded favourably to Mulroney's offer of a new constitutional compromise. The new federal prime minister was Jean Chrétien, a Quebecer who had been Trudeau's minister of justice and a principal architect of the constitutional changes adopted without Quebec's consent in 1981–82. The stage thus appeared set for a re-enactment of the referendum of 1980.

Parizeau had the reputation of being a more rigid and uncompromising supporter of independence than Lévesque. He had not fully agreed with the strategy of *étapisme* or with Lévesque's insistence on coupling sovereignty with "association."[32] In contrast to Lévesque, he made sovereignty the first order of business after taking office. He rejected the *étapisme* of 1980 in favour of a more direct approach, hoping that the continuing resentment over Meech Lake and the popularity that new governments usually enjoy could produce a decisive mandate for sovereignty early in his term. The first bill introduced by his government, in December 1994, was "An Act respecting the future of Quebec." The bill declared that Quebec was already sovereign, but that sovereignty would take effect only after a referendum approved it. It authorized the government to conclude an economic association with Canada if possible, although sovereignty would not depend on this. However, use of the Canadian dollar, rather than an independent Quebec currency, was still envisaged after sovereignty was achieved. Public hearings were held throughout the province, as provided in the bill, to stimulate support for sovereignty, but they appeared to attract little interest. Polls suggested that support in 1995 was still at a high level but slightly below the peak attained after the demise of the Meech Lake Accord.[33]

In contrast to the situation in 1980, the Parti québécois now had to consider its independent ally in the federal parliament, the Bloc québécois, headed by Lucien Bouchard. That party had won a majority of Quebec's ridings in 1993, attracting most of the Quebec voters who had supported Mulroney's Conservatives in the 1980s. Bouchard believed that the referendum should not be held immediately and that it should propose a political as well as an economic partnership with Canada.[34] Action démocratique, the party of moderate nationalists that had been formed when the Liberals failed to endorse the Allaire report, adopted a similar position. When the commission reporting on the results of the public hearings also recommended proposing a political partnership with Canada, Parizeau agreed to do so. On 12 June 1995 the leaders of the three nationalist parties signed an agreement to conduct the referendum campaign jointly. In September Parizeau announced that the referendum would take place on 30 October. The question, briefer than the one used in 1980, was as follows: "Do you agree that Quebec should become sovereign, after having made a formal offer to Canada for a new economic and political partnership, within the scope of the bill respecting the future of Quebec and of the agreement signed on June 12, 1995?"[35] Unlike the question used in 1980, this one suggested that Quebec would become sovereign whether or not Canada agreed to a partnership. Polls conducted in September and October showed opinion very evenly divided, with no assurance that sovereignty would be endorsed by the voters. In early October, less than four weeks before the referendum, Parizeau formally surrendered the leadership of the campaign to the more popular Lucien Bouchard, although he remained the premier of Quebec.

The campaign noticeably lacked the passion and excitement of 1980. Nationalists argued that Quebec was now less dependent on Canada, because of the Canada–United States Free Trade Agreement, which had been signed in 1988. They expressed confidence that Quebec would continue to enjoy free trade with the United States, whether or not it was part of Canada. On the other hand, they insisted that Quebecers could still retain their Canadian citizenship and passports, if they wished, after sovereignty was achieved and could continue to use the Canadian dollar. In place of the anti-colonial nationalist rhetoric of earlier times, supporters of sovereignty in 1995 emphasized the burden of Canada's rapidly growing national debt (although admitting that Quebec would probably have to assume a share of it), the fiscal and administrative advantages of having only one level of government, and the fact that Quebec's trade with the United States was growing more rapidly than its trade with the rest of Canada. These were hardly arguments that aroused passionate feelings. Chrétien also chose to conduct a low-key campaign and made no promises of constitutional reform. However, he warned that there was no automatic right to secede from Canada on the basis of a referendum and indicated that he would not view a very narrow majority in favour of sovereignty as a mandate to proceed with it. His government also encouraged a massive pro-federalist rally in Montreal three days before the vote, which was attended by thousands of Canadians from outside Quebec.

The rate of participation in the referendum was more than 90 per cent, an all-time record. The result could not have been much closer: 49.43 per cent in favour of sovereignty and 50.57 per cent against.[36] Outside the ethnically mixed neighbourhoods of Montreal, the Eastern Townships, and the ridings along the Ottawa River, where many voters worked for the federal government, the pro-sovereignty vote predominated throughout the province, but it was not enough to secure the elusive majority. Premier Parizeau, visibly shaken by the results, conceded defeat on television. He then shocked many viewers by observing that a majority of francophone Quebecers had voted for sovereignty and that they had been denied their choice by "money and ethnic votes." Several months earlier he had accepted the resignation of an adviser, former RIN leader Pierre Bourgault, who had publicly predicted that such an outcome would produce "a dangerous situation."[37] Yet there was no violence following the referendum; nationalists accepted their defeat calmly and gracefully. The day after the referendum

Parizeau announced that he would resign as premier; he was succeeded soon afterwards by Lucien Bouchard.

The response of Quebec's anglophones, whose votes had decided the outcome and who had every reason to celebrate, was less graceful than that of the nationalists. When support for sovereignty appeared to be growing in the early 1990s, some prominent members of their community had suggested that if Quebec voted for sovereignty, it should be partitioned, like Ireland in 1920, to ensure that predominantly anglophone and federalist parts of the province remained in Canada. Sometimes they alleged, falsely, that northern territories annexed by Quebec in 1898 and 1912 were not really part of the province and should be automatically detached from it in the event of independence. Surprisingly, support for this nightmare scenario appeared to increase, rather than subsiding, in the aftermath of the referendum. Two major conferences on partition were held in Montreal in the winter of 1996, and a public opinion poll showed a majority of Quebec anglophones in favour of it.[38]

Prime Minister Chrétien had been criticized for not intervening as actively in the campaign as Trudeau had done in 1980, but he made up for his inactivity soon afterwards. He announced plans to transfer control over labour training to Quebec by administrative agreement, introduced a bill indicating that the federal government would recognize a Quebec veto over constitutional change, sponsored a parliamentary resolution recognizing Quebec as a "distinct society," and recruited a prominent Quebec political scientist, Stéphane Dion, as his minister of intergovernmental affairs, with the specific task of leading the battle against Quebec nationalism.

Chrétien's government also sought a ruling from the Supreme Court of Canada on the conditions, if any, under which Quebec could legally secede. A disillusioned former nationalist lawyer, Guy Bertrand, had already commenced litigation on this issue, arguing that the referendum violated his civil rights by threatening to deprive him of his Canadian citizenship. After the referendum, the federal government took over the file and submitted the case to the Supreme Court in September 1996, asking whether either constitutional or international law supported Quebec's right to secede. Two years later the court handed down its judgment, asserting that a referendum would have no legally binding effect but that Canada "could not be indifferent" to the will of "a clear majority" of Quebecers. Secession would require a number of constitutional amendments, and any negotiations on the issue would have to take into account the interests of other provinces, of Canada as a whole, and of Quebec's minorities. As for international law, it was irrelevant, because the right of self-determination applied only to oppressed or colonized peoples, not to provinces in a democratic federation.[39]

Believing itself to be vindicated by this opinion, the federal government introduced what it called the Clarity Act, which became law in 2000. This measure declared that Canada would only agree to negotiate the secession of Quebec if secession were endorsed by a "clear" majority in answer to a "clear" question, with the House of Commons to decide at its own discretion whether these criteria had been met. Even then negotiations would have to involve the other provincial governments and would have to satisfy Canadian concerns about boundaries, assets and liabilities, and minority rights, including those of aboriginal peoples. Quebec promptly responded by adopting Bill 99, "An Act respecting the exercise of the fundamental rights and prerogatives of the Quebec people and the Quebec state." This measure declared that Quebec was a "people" entitled to exercise the right of self-determination, but it carefully avoided defining the Quebec people in ethnic or cultural terms. It further declared that the Quebec people had a right to decide their future by a majority of "fifty per cent of the valid votes cast plus one" and that Quebec's boundaries could not be altered without the consent of the National Assembly and the Quebec government.

Despite the brave words, Bill 99 did not seem to attract much interest or enthusiasm in Quebec, even though a poll suggested that most Quebec francophones disapproved of the Clarity Act.[40] Support for sovereignty-association rose slightly to almost 50 per cent in the year following the introduction of the Clarity Act and Bill 99, but after another year passed, it had returned to its previous level of just over 40 per cent.[41] Perhaps more significantly, the percentage of Quebecers who expected Quebec to be independent within ten years continued a precipitous decline. Six months after the 1995 referendum 62 per cent of those polled had expected independence within ten years, but by January 2001 only 20 per cent expected independence within ten years.[42] Premier Bouchard, apparently sharing their pessimism, retired in discouragement soon afterwards. His successor, Bernard Landry, indicated that there would not be another referendum until he was reasonably sure of a successful outcome. In 2003 the Quebec Liberals returned to office under the leadership of Jean Charest, the former federal MP whose efforts to make the Meech Lake Accord more palatable to anglophone Canada in 1990 had led to Bouchard's resignation from the Mulroney government.

Although the Parti québécois was now out of office, the Bloc québécois, which had appeared to be in decline, enjoyed an unexpected resurgence a year later. Jean Chrétien rather unwillingly retired as prime minister of Canada and was replaced by his former minister of finance, Paul Martin, an anglophone businessman who resided in Montreal, although he was originally from Ontario. At about the same time the Progressive Conservative

Party, which had retained at least a vestigial presence in Quebec even after Mulroney's departure, was absorbed by the western-based Canadian Alliance Party, which had no organization and virtually no support in Quebec. Liberal popularity was weakened, particularly in Quebec, by allegations of corruption and misuse of public funds in the context of the Chrétien government's post-referendum campaign against the Quebec sovereignty movement. These allegations, collectively known as the sponsorship scandal, were the subject of a public inquiry after the federal election of June 2004, in which the Bloc won 54 of Quebec's 75 ridings, sweeping the entire province apart from the Ottawa Valley and the ethnically mixed neighbourhoods of Montreal. Martin's government remained in office, but without a majority of seats in the House of Commons. In keeping with the usual Canadian practice, he did not form a coalition with any of the opposition parties, preferring to seek their support on an ad hoc basis; so his government seemed likely to be weak and unstable for some time. In Quebec the Charest government also suffered a decline in popularity because of some of its controversial policies, and it lost two seats in by-elections in September. However, the Parti Québécois was simultaneously weakened by internal dissatisfaction with the leadership of former premier Bernard Landry, as well as controversy over the appropriate strategy for pursuing independence.

Four decades after the Quiet Revolution, the socio-economic status of the francophone majority within Quebec had been radically improved in relation to the once-dominant anglophone minority. But Quebec appeared no closer to independence than ever, and it was becoming clear that anglophone Canada would never allow Quebec any formal recognition of special status within a restructured federalism. Although Martin was willing to accept a modest degree of "asymmetrical federalism," meaning federal-provincial agreements on specific subjects that treated Quebec somewhat differently from the other provinces, even this was anathema to a large segment of Anglo-Canadian opinion. Since the days of the Quiet Revolution, Quebec's share of Canada's population had fallen from 28.8 to 24.1 per cent. The percentage of all Canadians, including those in Quebec, whose mother tongue was French had fallen even more sharply, from 28.1 to 22.7 per cent.[43] The search for accommodation had apparently ended, but not on Quebec's terms.

NORTHERN IRELAND: THE STRUGGLE FOR EQUALITY

In Northern Ireland, as in Quebec, the search for a new constitutional order more in harmony with nationalist aspirations than the old one proved to be lengthy, frustrating, and, by the early years of the twenty-first century, still inconclusive. Like the independence of Quebec, the reunification of Ireland seemed lost in a future that never came any closer. Just as most Quebec nationalists seemed prepared in practice to settle for a restructuring of the Canadian federation as a binational state, most Irish nationalists seemed prepared in practice to settle for a restructuring of Northern Ireland as a consociational democracy. Yet even those more modest goals proved to be surprisingly elusive.

The first, and apparently premature, effort to establish a consociational power-sharing regime in Northern Ireland took place in 1973, not long after the Heath government had brought the province under the direct rule of Westminster. It will be recalled that a new assembly was elected in that year, using a form of proportional representation, to replace the now-defunct Stormont parliament. It was at this election that the SDLP emerged as the most significant nationalist party in the six counties, partly because Sinn Fein refused to take part in the election.

The British intent, set out in a white paper issued prior to the election, had been to bring about a "power-sharing" executive – or, in other words, a coalition of unionists and nationalists – that would be responsible to the new assembly. This idea appealed to moderate nationalists, who were increasingly alienated by the IRA campaign of violence and saw power-sharing as an alternative.[44] However, the project bitterly divided the Ulster Unionist Party, with a bare majority supporting the decision of their leader, Brian Faulkner, to accept a sharing of power with the SDLP The dissidents, led by Harry West, were sustained in their opposition by forces outside the party: the populist and fundamentalist movement led by Ian Paisley and the loyalist para-militaries. The Democratic Unionist Party, which Paisley had founded in 1971, gained support from its opposition to the white paper and became a serious competitor to the Ulster Unionist Party. Unionist opponents of power-sharing argued that it would lead inexorably to the reunification of Ireland and the end of the British connection. Faulkner nonetheless persisted, and in November 1973 a power-sharing executive of thirteen members was formed, with him as leader and Gerry Fitt of the SDLP as his deputy. It could count on a rather slender majority in the assembly, including the middle-of-the-road Alliance Party, which held two seats on the executive and eight in the assembly.

Less than a month later a meeting took place at Sunningdale, in England, between Prime Minister Edward Heath, Taoiseach Liam Cosgrave, and Brian Faulkner as head of the Northern Ireland executive. The three leaders agreed that the status of Northern Ireland would not be changed without the consent of the majority of its people, although they noted that the Irish government and the SDLP favoured reunification of Ireland as an ultimate goal. They also agreed to establish a Council of Ireland representing the two Irish states, north and south, to deal with problems of mutual concern. The Irish government and the Northern Ireland executive agreed to cooperate in prosecuting violent crimes committed anywhere on the island. The British government promised to devolve responsibilities for policing and other matters to the Northern Ireland executive and to end the practice of internment as soon as the security situation made it feasible to do so. Britain also promised to introduce legislation, as soon as the executive began to function, to restore the powers taken from Northern Ireland by the imposition of direct rule.[45]

This carefully nuanced agreement was a significant compromise, even though the Unionists and the SDLP differed somewhat in their interpretation of what it implied. However, the power-sharing experiment proved to be stillborn, in large part because Faulkner could not persuade his party to accept the Council of Ireland. In January 1974 he was forced to resign as party leader in favour of Harry West, although he remained the head of the power-sharing executive. In May the Ulster Workers' Council, which was a mainly Protestant body because Catholics were still excluded from most unionized and highly paid industrial jobs, called a general strike in an effort to bring down the executive. Two days later bombs set by loyalist paramilitaries killed thirty-four people in Dublin and Monaghan, in the most violent incident in the state since the civil war. The British government, again headed by Harold Wilson since the general election in February, admitted defeat and restored direct rule, bringing the first experiment in power-sharing to an end.

By the late 1970s a number of circumstances had changed in both Ireland and Britain. Towards the end of 1976, the Provisional IRA, which had been faring badly in its sanguinary war against the British forces, began to be drastically reorganized. It was divided into northern and southern commands, with the northern command responsible for the five counties immediately south of the border as well as the six north of the border.[46] Its large operational units, which had been easily penetrated by British informers, were dissolved and replaced by small cells or "active service units" with only a few members.[47] Although they made the Provisional IRA more effective, these reforms were accompanied by a reduction in its violence: it had killed an average of 144 persons per year from 1972 through 1976, but it averaged only 51 per year from 1977 through 1994, when its war virtually ended.[48] The reorganization was largely the work of Gerry Adams, a Belfast republican who was emerging as a leading figure both in the IRA, of which he was allegedly chief of staff for a brief period in 1977–78, and in Sinn Fein, of which he was president from 1983 onwards. More of a politician than a soldier, Adams was apparently not personally involved in violent acts, although he was interned for lengthy periods.[49] Years later he wrote in his autobiography that the use of force was only a last resort and that armed struggle should not be "romanticized."[50] In the late 1970s he appears to have become convinced that the British could not be driven out of Ireland by force. He may have already been planning to wind down the war and also to end Sinn Fein's policy of abstention from constitutional politics in both north and south. Eventually he would do both of these things, at some risk to himself, much as Michael Collins in 1921 and Eamon de Valera in 1926 had made the transition from guerrilla warfare to peaceful politics.

At about the same time as the changes in the IRA were taking place, Fianna Fail swept back into office south of the border. In the election of 1977 the party, still led by Jack Lynch, won more than 50 per cent of the first preference votes for the first (and last) time since 1938. It also won 84 seats in the Dáil, an all-time record.[51] Charles Haughey became a minister again in the new government, having lived down his dismissal seven years earlier. In December 1979 he replaced Lynch as taoiseach and party leader, suggesting that the more nationalist wing of Fianna Fail was again in the ascendant. Haughey's elevation to the leadership occurred in the same year that a strong British nationalist, Margaret Thatcher, became prime minister of her country. Also in 1979, both the major constitutional parties in Northern Ireland experienced changes in leadership. Gerry Fitt resigned as leader of the SDLP after the party's executive rejected a British invitation to participate in a conference that would seek a purely internal solution to the problem of Northern Ireland. The executive insisted that any solution must have an "Irish dimension" and that the Dublin government must be involved.[52] Fitt, who complained that the party was becoming too nationalist, was subsequently given a life peerage by the Thatcher government. He was succeeded as leader of the SDLP by John Hume. At about the same time, James Molyneaux replaced Harry West as leader of the Ulster Unionist Party.

Although the IRA could apparently not win its war, neither could the British army. In other words, the military struggle had become a stalemate. In August 1979 eighteen British soldiers were killed in a successful IRA operation in County Down, on the same day that Lord Mountbatten, a prominent member of the British royal family, was assassinated while vacationing in County Sligo. Even before these events the British had admitted, publicly and privately, that the effectiveness of the IRA had greatly increased because of the recent changes in its structure.[53] Overall, in the years 1977 through 1982 the British army suffered more than twice as many deaths as the republican paramilitaries: 122 British casualties and only 52 for the republicans.[54]

Whether because of the military stalemate, changes in leadership, or both, the British and Irish governments increasingly began to deal directly with each other, ignoring the unionists of Northern Ireland as irrelevant. Two meetings between Haughey and Thatcher in 1980 appeared successful, but when Haughey subsequently implied that Thatcher had agreed to consider the option of moving towards Irish unity, she was forced to deny any such intent, and their relationship deteriorated. Haughey's support for Argentina in the Falklands War of 1982 certainly did not help matters.

At this point the political situation was transformed by the revival of hunger striking, a technique that had been used to good effect during the Irish war of independence. Conditions in the prison of Long Kesh, where republican prisoners were confined, had grown increasingly deplorable and were condemned by Cardinal Tomas O'Fiaich, the Catholic primate of all Ireland, after he visited the prison.[55] The hunger strikes began after other forms of protest had failed to secure recognition of "political" status for the prisoners, which would have included the right to wear civilian clothes rather than a prison uniform. Adams and other republicans outside the prison were not in favour of hunger strikes, and their concerns seemed to be vindicated when the first hunger strike, in 1980, ended ignominiously after two months.[56] However, a second group of hunger strikers in the following year proved to be made of sterner stuff. They persisted until ten of them died: seven members of the IRA and three of a radical splinter group, the Irish National Liberation Army. While the hunger strike was in progress, one of the ten, Bobby Sands of the IRA, was elected to the British House of Commons for Fermanagh–South Tyrone in a by-election, defeating Harry West. Four weeks after his election, Sands was the first hunger striker to die, on 5 May 1981. The "crime" for which he had been imprisoned was possession of a firearm.

One immediate result of the hunger strikes was an escalation of republican violence. The IRA extended its bombing campaign to the "mainland" of Great Britain, and the much smaller INLA was responsible for fifty-three deaths in the years 1981 through 1983.[57] A more important consequence was political. The ten dead men became martyrs in the cause of Irish nationalism, perhaps the most important since 1916. Their self-sacrifice made them international, as well as national, celebrities. Thatcher's insensitive response to their deaths reinforced their moral victory and the public relations disaster for the British. Support for republicanism increased sharply. When a new Northern Ireland assembly was elected in 1982, Sinn Fein ran a slate of candidates, including Gerry Adams and his alleged successor as IRA chief of staff, Martin McGuiness. In four elections between 1982 and 1985 Sinn Fein averaged about 40 per cent of the Catholic vote.[58] It became a serious political force in its own right and not merely an appendage of the IRA, particularly after Adams became its president in 1983. In the same year that he became president of Sinn Fein, Adams was elected to the British House of Commons for West Belfast, defeating Gerry Fitt. British and southern Irish politicians grew increasingly fearful that Sinn Fein would surpass the SDLP in popular support, a concern that led them to redouble their efforts to find a political solution to the problem of Northern Ireland.[59]

South of the border, Haughey and Fianna Fail lost office to a coalition government headed by Garret FitzGerald. Although perhaps just as hostile to republicanism as the Cosgrave coalition a decade earlier, the FitzGerald coalition was more subtle and effective in its methods. It convened the New Ireland Forum in 1983 to define a new agenda for moderate Irish nationalism, All the major southern parties participated in the forum, as did the SDLP. The forum's report, published in the following year, endorsed the view to which Hume and FitzGerald were already committed: the division of Ireland was not primarily the result of British machinations, but instead reflected the separate collective identity of the northern unionists, whose concerns would therefore have to be met in order to reunite the country. Even Fianna Fail accepted this position at least implicitly by accepting the report. Although Haughey in his opening remarks blamed British policy over the years for partition, he also said that "we do not see unity in terms of the people of the North being absorbed into or annexed by the Republic. It is instead a question of building the new Ireland with their help and participation."[60] The New Ireland Forum report suggested three possible solutions for the problem of Northern Ireland: a unitary Irish state, a federal Irish state, or joint British and Irish responsibility for the six counties.[61] Although Thatcher rather brusquely commented that all three options were "out" or, in other words, not acceptable to her government, the search for accommodation continued, in more than one way.

The forum report, at Haughey's insistence, stated that a unitary state was the most desirable option. De Valera had offered the unionists a sort of federalism in 1938, but Haughey considered that this was no longer desirable because Ireland was "too small to need or support elaborate tiers of government."[62] The federal option had also been discarded by the Provisional IRA in 1979 and by Sinn Fein in 1982, although both had been formally committed to it since 1972.[63] Apart from its possible use as a way of reassuring the unionists, federalism had a natural appeal, as it does in other countries, to thinly populated rural areas that resented metropolitan domination and would benefit from a more decentralized form of government. The declining popularity of a federal solution probably reflected the growing influence of urban and metropolitan interests in both republican and mainstream politics.

A small but significant step towards the third option, a sharing of reponsibility for the six counties between Dublin and London, was taken by the Anglo-Irish agreement that FitzGerald and Thatcher signed on 15 November 1985.[64] The agreement established an Anglo-Irish Intergovernmental Conference, which could meet at either ministerial or official level, as a framework within which they could work together to resolve Northern Ireland's problems. Both governments committed themselves to respect and accommodate "the rights and identities of the two traditions which exist in Northern Ireland." The Irish government formally accepted the principle that reunification could take place only with the consent of the majority of people in the six counties, but in return it was given at least a consultative role in the government of the province. The British government agreed to facilitate reunification if a majority of the people of Northern Ireland ever expressed a desire for it.

Most sources consider that the Anglo-Irish agreement was motivated primarily by a shared concern about the growing influence of Sinn Fein, which had done well in local council elections earlier that year, and by the desire by both the Dublin and London governments to preserve the SDLP as the major voice of northern nationalism. The agreement was bitterly resented by unionists, however. All fifteen of the Ulster Unionist members of the British House of Commons resigned in protest, provoking a series of by-elections to fill their seats. The Belfast city council adjourned for several months in protest, there was a unionist general strike for one day in March, and the Ulster Unionist Party formally severed its ties with the Conservative Party. There was also an escalation of loyalist rioting and violence. None of this activity succeeded in overturning the agreement, in contrast to what had happened after the protests against Sunningdale more than a decade earlier.[65]

A more serious threat to the agreement seemed to be the opposition of Fianna Fail, most of which refused to support it. A Fianna Fail member of the Dáil who did support it, Mary Harney, was expelled from the party and soon afterwards helped to form a new party, the Progressive Democrats, of which she subsequently became leader.[66] Haughey and a future taoiseach, Bertie Ahern, argued in the Dáil that the agreement was unconstitutional because it recognized British sovereignty over the six counties, contrary to the claim in Articles 2 and 3 of the constitution that Irish sovereignty extended over the whole island. They contended that the agreement surrendered this claim but gave Ireland little of substance in return. The council would not be a decision-making body and would only give the Irish government the power to make suggestions, a power that it already possessed. Ahern said that the coalition government had "wantonly squandered our deepest aspirations" and quoted Parnell's statement that no one could put a stop to the march of a nation, a statement that he said had met "a sad and untimely end at the hands of this government."[67] Nonetheless, the Anglo-Irish Intergovernmental Conference continued to function after Haughey returned to office as taoiseach in March 1987. Ahern would eventually agree, years later, to the deletion of Articles 2 and 3 from the constitution as part of the Good Friday Agreement, which replaced the Anglo-Irish Agreement of 1985.

In the mid-1980s the IRA still had some hopes of expelling the British from Ireland by force. Its traditional reliance on American sources for weapons had been largely replaced by a new relationship with the government of Libya, which resented the British government's support for American initiatives against that North African state. Several shipments of weapons from Libya reached the IRA during this period, and these new armaments inspired republican hopes of a major offensive that would break the British will to continue, much as the Tet Offensive of 1968 had caused the United States to abandon its search for victory in Vietnam. However, the interception of a shipload of weapons by the French navy in October 1987 ended these hopes, and the military stalemate continued.[68] This episode may have helped to persuade republicans that they would have to seek a compromise by peaceful means.

Although the Anglo-Irish Agreement had been motivated by a desire to reduce the growing influence of Sinn Fein, it was followed by several years during which Sinn Fein increasingly became an accepted participant in constitutional politics and in what came to be called the peace process. In 1986 Sinn Fein renounced its traditional policy of boycotting the Dáil, an initiative that Adams had favoured as early as 1983. Some dissidents who disagreed with the new policy left Sinn Fein and formed a splinter group known as Republican Sinn Fein. In 1987 Sinn Fein published a "scenario for peace" which suggested that a British declaration of intent to withdraw from Ireland should be followed by the election of an all-Ireland constituent assembly. The new constitution envisaged by Sinn Fein would guarantee the rights of northern Protestants, including provision for divorce and access to contraception, which was still illegal in the south. British withdrawal would follow after the new constitution was in place.[69]

In 1988 Sinn Fein and the SDLP made a serious effort to develop a common nationalist position on the future of Northern Ireland. The two leaders, Gerry Adams and John Hume, met secretly in January, apparently at the suggestion of Father Alec Reid, a well-known priest in West Belfast.[70] At the first meeting Adams and Hume exchanged documents setting out the respective views of their parties. Further meetings between delegations headed by Adams and Hume followed in March, May, June, and August, and more documents were exchanged.[71] Although some common ground was discovered, the SDLP refused to acknowledge the legitimacy of the violent struggle being waged by the IRA. The SDLP was also inclined to accept at face value British assurances of neutrality in the Northern Ireland conflict and to view the conflict as one between two communities, unionist/Protestant and nationalist/Catholic, both of which had deep roots in Irish soil. Sinn Fein, on the other hand, viewed the conflict as essentially an anti-colonial struggle against British rule and believed that the unionists would accept their destiny within a united Ireland once they lost the assurance of British support. The SDLP was prepared to accept a power-sharing regime in the six counties as at least an interim solution, although it hoped that Irish reunification would come some day when the unionists had lost their fear of Catholic domination. Sinn Fein still insisted that there could be no substitute for a united Ireland, although it was willing to guarantee minority rights. It argued that the sectarian and socially conservative tendencies of the southern state were the consequence, rather than the cause, of partition and that a united Ireland would be secular and pluralist, like the Ireland envisaged by Wolfe Tone in 1798. The dialogue between the two nationalist parties broke down over these issues. When it resumed in the 1990s, Sinn Fein had moved much closer to the SDLP position, rather than vice versa. The talks in 1988, although unsuccessful in the short term, were an essential and decisive step towards the peace process, but there were other steps as well.

Secret contacts between the British government and Gerry Adams apparently began as early as 1986, also through the efforts of Father Alec Reid. The enterprise was facilitated by the fact that Cardinal O'Fiaich, a cleric more sympathetic to republicanism than most, was the Catholic primate of all Ireland in the 1980s.[72] Using Reid as an intermediary, Adams allegedly posed some questions about British intentions to Tom King, the secretary of state for Northern Ireland in the Thatcher government. King's reply stated that Britain had no selfish interests in Northern Ireland and would be happy to facilitate any solution agreed upon by the various parties there, including Sinn Fein, if the IRA abandoned its violent campaign.[73] Over the next few years Adams very gradually distanced Sinn Fein from the violent campaign, which nonetheless continued both in Northern Ireland and, increasingly, in England. He did not inform the Army Council of the IRA about his contacts with the British. (The British had also established their own contacts with the Army Council, separate from their dialogue with Adams.) Perhaps in response to the continuing violence, electoral support was shifting from Sinn Fein to the SDLP, which captured Adams's West Belfast constituency in the British general election of 1992. This trend presumably gave Adams an incentive to continue his dialogue with the British and with Hume and to seek an end to the armed struggle.

Margaret Thatcher was replaced by John Major in November 1990, and Albert Reynolds succeeded Charles Haughey as taoiseach early in 1992. The new leaders appeared more committed than their predecessors to pursuing the peace process, and they established a good relationship. In December 1993 they signed the Downing Street Declaration, partly based on ideas suggested by Hume and indirectly by Adams. It ingeniously combined the nationalist idea of self-determination for Ireland with the unionist insistence on consent by the majority in the north to any change in status. The British government agreed that the people of Ireland should "exercise their right of self-determination on the basis of consent, freely and concurrently given, North and South, to bring about a united Ireland, if that is their wish." The Irish government agreed that "the democratic right of self-determination by the people of Ireland as a whole must be achieved and exercised with and subject to the agreement and consent of the majority of the people of Northern Ireland." Reynolds also promised to re-examine any aspects of the Irish state that might appear threatening to unionists.[74] Pursuant to this promise, the prohibition of divorce was deleted from the Irish constitution two years later, after a very narrow majority in a referendum voted to do so.

Almost a year prior to the Downing Street Declaration, a new factor had entered the equation with the inauguration of Bill Clinton as president of the United States. Before his presidency, there had never been a great deal of substance to support the widespread Irish belief that the United States, and not only its Irish Catholic minority, was a friend of Irish nationalism. Clinton, however, made the peace process in Northern Ireland a major priority of his administration. He visited Ireland three times during his presidency, in November 1995, September 1998, and December 2000. Early in 1994 he granted a visa to Gerry Adams, who had earlier been denied permission to visit the United States, and began to push all parties towards a settlement of their differences. In March the IRA announced a three-day ceasefire, and in August it proclaimed a "complete cessation" of its campaign. Adams was allowed to visit the United States for a second time. Reynolds welcomed the ceasefire, but Major was initially more skeptical. The loyalists responded in October with a ceasefire of their own. Clinton announced an aid package for Northern Ireland and appointed George Mitchell, a former majority leader in the United States Senate, as a special envoy to the province. The fact that the British government accepted and even welcomed Clinton's intervention was a tacit but clear admission that Northern Ireland was not a matter of "domestic jurisdiction," as the British had traditionally pretended it was.

Late in 1994 the Reynolds government in Dublin fell after the Labour Party, its coalition partner for almost two years, refused to agree to a judicial appointment favoured by the taoiseach. A new coalition government of Fine Gael and Labour, with John Bruton as taoiseach, was formed without an election. Although Bruton had earlier expressed disapproval of John Hume's dialogue with Gerry Adams, he himself shook hands with Adams shortly after taking office. Contrary to what some had feared, there was no change in the Irish government's policy towards the peace process.

The same could not be said for the British government. Tom King had secretly promised Adams years before that Sinn Fein could enter all-party discussions on the future of Northern Ireland once the IRA abandoned its violent struggle, but the British now demanded a new condition in addition to the ceasefire that had already taken place: a "decommissioning," or in other words, destruction, of weapons held by the IRA Although urged by Reynolds, Bruton, and Hume not to persist in this demand, the British did so for more than a year, preventing any further progress. They were perhaps encouraged to take this position by the rise of a new Ulster Unionist Party leader, David Trimble, who succeeded Molyneaux in September 1995. Trimble, a Presbyterian from County Armagh, was considered one of the hard-liners in his party and had reinforced his reputation as such by walking hand in hand with Ian Paisley at an Orange parade only two months before winning the leadership.[75] However, he was eventually to prove somewhat more flexible than he seemed.

In January 1996 the three-member international committee headed by Senator Mitchell suggested that the demand for decommissioning prior to negotiations was unrealistic and recommended that decommissioning and negotiations should take place in parallel. British intransigence finally provoked the IRA to end its ceasefire with the highly destructive bombing of Canary Wharf, a major commercial development in London, in February. Interparty talks on the future of Northern Ireland began in June under the chairmanship of George Mitchell, but with Sinn Fein barred from participation. Ian Paisley's Democratic Unionist Party did participate, although it was suspicious both of the process and of Mitchell. Loyalist violence in connection with the celebration of the Battle of the Boyne on 12 July was the worst in many years, including two deaths and much destruction of property.

There was little or no further progress in the peace process until the spring of 1997, when the British Labour Party won a general election and formed a government headed by Tony Blair. Both Gerry Adams and Martin McGuinness were elected to the House of Commons, as were three members of the SDLP, the largest number of Irish nationalists elected to that house since before partition. Blair reopened contacts with Sinn Fein, which had been broken off by Major. He also showed his good intentions by apologizing for British policy during the famine of the 1840s.[76] Soon afterwards a general election in Ireland brought Fianna Fail back to power under Bertie Ahern, in a coalition with the neo-liberal Progressive Democrats, now headed by Mary Harney. The new British and Irish governments agreed that decommissioning of IRA weapons was not a prerequisite for participation by Sinn Fein in the negotiations, but a renewal of the ceasefire obviously was. The IRA soon declared a new ceasefire. David Trimble and his party agreed to continue participating in talks, which would now include Sinn Fein, but Ian Paisley and his Democratic Unionists withdrew from any further participation in the peace process. Sinn Fein accepted Mitchell's conditions for participation in the negotiations, even though the IRA expressed some misgivings. A commission headed by John de Chastelain, a retired Canadian general, was set up to supervise the decommissioning of IRA weapons.

The last months of negotiations were among the most difficult. Both loyalist and republican violence continued to some extent, Sinn Fein and a minor loyalist party were temporarily suspended from the negotiations, and Trimble faced increasing unrest within his own party. Sinn Fein pretended up to the last minute to oppose the main ideas in the agreement that was emerging.[77] Nonetheless, Trimble and Adams appeared together at the British embassy in Washington in March 1998. On 10 April, Good Friday, an agreement was finally concluded between the British and Irish governments, the Ulster Unionists, the SDLP, and Sinn Fein.[78] All sides had made concessions and the agreement remained precarious, but it was done.

The agreement imposed significant modifications on three political systems: the United Kingdom, the twenty-six-county Irish state, and the six-county state of Northern Ireland. The United Kingdom promised to repeal the Government of Ireland Act of 1920. Northern Ireland would remain part of the United Kingdom until a majority of its people voting in a poll decided otherwise, but the secretary of state for Northern Ireland could order a referendum for that purpose at any time, unless one had already been held less than seven years previously, and was obligated to do so if it appeared likely that a majority would express the wish to be united with the rest of Ireland.

The Irish state agreed to amend its constitution to remove Articles 2 and 3, which stated a claim to the whole island although acknowledging that the state's authority de facto extended only to the twenty-six counties. In their place, new articles would affirm the entitlement of anyone born anywhere in Ireland to be part of the Irish nation, as well as the will of the Irish nation "to unite all the people who share the territory of the island of Ireland, in all the diversity of their identities and traditions, recognising that a united Ireland shall be brought about only by peaceful means with the consent of a majority of the people, democratically expressed, in both jurisdictions in the island."

For northern Ireland itself, the agreement prescribed a new regime based on the principles of consociational democracy. There would be an assembly of 108 members elected from the eighteen existing Westminster constituencies by the single transferable vote method of proportional representation. Committee chairs, committee membership, and ministerial portfolios would be allocated in proportion to party strengths, so that all significant parties would share in power. Cross-community (unionist and nationalist) support would be required for all "key decisions," including election of the speaker, the first minister, and the deputy first minister, standing orders, and budgetary allocations. The assembly would be the prime source of authority for all devolved responsibilities and could be given other responsibilities later, including policing, which was recognized as a sensitive issue requiring further study, given the fact that the existing Royal Ulster Constabulary lacked legitimacy among nationalists. An independent commission on policing would be established to recommend future arrangements that would be more likely to have cross-community support. (Christopher Patten, the last governor of Hong Kong, was subsequently appointed to head this commission.) Executive authority over Northern Ireland would be exercised by an executive committee comprising a first minister, a deputy first minister, and up to ten other ministers drawn proportionately from the nominees of the different parties. Ministers would be required to take a pledge of office committing them to use only peaceful and democratic means and to serve all the people of Northern Ireland equally and without discrimination. They could be removed from office by the assembly, acting on a cross-community basis, if they failed to live up to these obligations.

Additional institutions were established involving the three political entities affected by the agreement. A north-south ministerial council would be required to meet in plenary sessions twice a year, with delegations headed by the first minister and the taoiseach. It would also meet more frequently in sectoral formats, with north and south each represented by the appropriate minister. The council would exchange information, discuss and consult on matters of common interest, and try to agree on common policies to be implemented either separately in the two Irish jurisdictions or on an all-island basis through institutions to be set up later.

The agreement also provided for a British-Irish intergovernmental conference representing primarily the governments in Dublin and London, which would meet as required either at summit level or at the level of appropriate ministers and officials. It would try to promote bilateral cooperation on all matters of mutual interest, including security matters, and would also provide a forum for the Irish government to make suggestions regarding Northern Ireland. Relevant executive members of the Northern Ireland regime would also be involved.

Speaking in the Dáil eleven days later, Bertie Ahern suggested that the proposed changes to the Irish constitution pursuant to the agreement reflected "modern, progressive republican thought that is truly pluralist and keeps faith with the inclusive tradition of Irish nationalism stemming from Wolfe Tone and the United Irishmen."[79] The ruling council of the Ulster Unionist Party promptly endorsed the agreement, although 28 per cent of the Unionist councillors voted against it. It was also endorsed in May by conventions of both the IRA and Sinn Fein, with Sinn Fein thus agreeing to discard its traditional policy of refusing to participate in any Northern Ireland assembly.[80] (Sinn Fein members elected to Westminster, however, still refuse to take their seats or to swear allegiance to the queen.) In simultaneous referenda in May 1998, the Good Friday Agreement was approved by the electorates both south and north of the border. The vote in favour was an overwhelming 94.4 per cent of those voting south of the border.[81] Exit polls in Northern Ireland, where 71.1 per cent of those voting were in favour, suggested that Catholics had given the same overwhelming support to the agreement there as voters in the twenty-six counties, while Protestants had given it a bare majority of either 55 or 51 per cent, depending on which exit poll was the more accurate.[82]

The assembly was elected in June. The SDLP proved to be the most popular party, with 22.0 per cent of the first preference votes, while the Ulster Unionist Party came second with 21.3, followed by Ian Paisley's anti-agreement Democratic Unionist Party with 18.1 and Sinn Fein with 17.6, by far the best showing for that party in Northern Ireland since partition. The Alliance Party, representing middle-class liberals from both communities, received 6.5 per cent of first preferences. Owing to the distribution of second preferences, the allocation of seats put the Ulster Unionist Party in first place with twenty-eight, followed by the SDLP with twenty-four, the Democratic Unionists with twenty, Sinn Fein with eighteen, the Alliance Party with six, and the Women's Coalition with two. Other unionist candidates, most of them opposed to the agreement, took the remaining ten seats.[83] The assembly met in July and elected David Trimble first minister; the DUP voted against him and Sinn Fein abstained. Seamus Mallon of the SDLP was named deputy first minister since John Hume declined at the last moment to be a candidate, even though he remained leader of the party. In December Trimble and Hume, but not Gerry Adams, were jointly awarded the Nobel Peace Prize for 1998.

Implementation of the agreement proved to be a very lengthy and difficult process. Dissidents on both sides, loyalist and republican, responded with lethal violence at a level not seen since 1994, including a car bomb at Omagh in August 1998 with which the so-called Real IRA killed twenty-nine people. (Omagh is a nationalist town; a similar atrocity in a loyalist town might have ended the already tenuous unionist support for the peace process.) The summer "marching season," when Protestants commemorate the war between King William and King James, produced an annual escalation of violent protest and intercommunal strife. However, the real problem was the same issue of "decommissioning" that had threatened to derail the peace process prior to Good Friday. The IRA seemed in no hurry to dispose of its weapons, even if it was not using them, partly because it was dissatisfied with the rate of progress in establishing new and more impartial policing arrangements as recommended by the Patten report. Trimble, urged on by a large section of his party, cited the lack of progress on decommissioning as evidence that Sinn Fein had not really renounced violent means of struggle and was thus not eligible to participate in the executive under the terms of the Good Friday Agreement. He insisted that decommissioning must be well underway before the executive could begin to function. Prime Minister Blair and his secretary of state for Northern Ireland, Mo Mowlam, were prepared to give Sinn Fein the benefit of the doubt but had no effective way of putting pressure on the first minister designate. The Patten report, which proposed transforming the Royal Ulster Constabulary into a non-sectarian police force with a new name, caused further unrest among unionists.

In September 1999 George Mitchell returned to Northern Ireland, at the request of the Irish and British governments, to sort out the situation; Mo Mowlam was replaced by a new secretary of state, Peter Mandelson, who was more acceptable to the unionists; and the peace process was underway once more. The IRA agreed to appoint a representative to the de Chastelain commission. The Ulster Unionist ruling council agreed to allow the formation of an executive on the understanding that decommissioning would begin soon. In November the executive was formed, with the Democratic Unionists and Sinn Fein each represented by two ministers, while the Ulster Unionists and the SDLP each had three, in addition to the first minister and deputy first minister. Sinn Fein ministers took the two major spending departments, education and health, while SDLP members took finance, higher education, and agriculture.[84] This executive functioned for only two months before it was suspended by Mandelson and direct rule restored. The north-south council and the British-Irish intergovernmental conference continued to function during this and later periods of suspension.

During the four-month suspension of the assembly and executive, Trimble successfully survived a challenge to his leadership of his party. The IRA issued a statement on decommissioning that was accepted by a very narrow majority of the Ulster Unionist council as sufficient grounds to resume power-sharing with Sinn Fein. At the end of May 2000 the executive was again restored, although the Democratic Unionists participated with obvious reluctance. In the British general election a year later, the Democrat Unionists and Sinn Fein made gains in electoral support at the expense of the Ulster Unionists and the SDLP. John Hume retired from the leadership of the SDLP in favour of Mark Durkan. In July 2001 Trimble again resigned as first minister. In October 2001 the IRA finally agreed to begin decommissioning, perhaps influenced by the election of a less-sympathetic administration in Washington and by the American hostility to "terrorism" after September 11. Gerry Adams subsequently admitted that September 11 had been a factor, and he described the decision to begin disarming as an act of patriotism that was "painful" in a context of continuing loyalist violence.[85] (Of the twenty-eight deaths caused by political violence in 2000 and 2001, eighteen were attributed to loyalists and only ten to republicans.)[86] General de Chastelain confirmed that a significant act of decommissioning had taken place. Trimble agreed to serve again as first minister but was only elected through the support of two members of the Alliance Party and one of the Women's Coalition, who agreed temporarily to redesignate themselves as "unionist" so that Trimble would have enough "unionist" votes in the assembly to meet the criterion of sufficient support in both communities. The power-sharing executive resumed functioning, with Mark Durkan of the SDLP replacing Seamus Mallon as deputy first minister. A further act of decommissioning of IRA weapons, involving a substantial number of firearms, took place in April 2002. Yet almost as soon as the IRA made this concession, the unionists began to demand more. In July the minister of education, Martin McGuinness of Sinn Fein, predicted that the executive would not last until the elections scheduled for the following May.[87]

Although both Sinn Fein and the SDLP appeared comfortable with the power-sharing institutions, it was apparent that many unionists were not. In March 2002 David Trimble unexpectedly made a bizarre statement describing southern Ireland as a "pathetic sectarian state," a remark that was condemned by the Anglican archbishop of Dublin and by a spokesman for the Presbyterian church, as well as by the leaders of most of Ireland's political parties, north and south.[88] The broader context of Trimble's outburst was one of growing unionist discontent and growing loyalist violence, in response to the visible evidence of declining Protestant influence and power in Northern Ireland. A psychologist working in Belfast was quoted as saying that the unionist community showed signs of suspicion, aggression, and withdrawal, and that it needed to be reassured.[89] In November 2001 the Royal Ulster Constabulary was replaced by the non-sectarian Police Service of Northern Ireland. In June 2002 a Sinn Fein member, Alex Maskey, was elected lord mayor of Belfast, a city that had been a Protestant and unionist bastion for generations. The census of 2001, whose results were not published until December 2002, revealed that Catholics had reached 44 per cent of the population in Northern Ireland as a whole, as compared with 35 per cent in the last census before the Troubles. In Belfast there was virtual parity in numbers between Protestants and Catholics in 2001, although Catholics had comprised only 27.5 per cent of the population forty years earlier.[90] A poll conducted in 2001 showed that only 25 per cent of Protestants, compared with 33 per cent of Catholics, thought relations between the two communities had improved over the last five years. Both communities were less inclined to think so than they had been in 1996, when a similar poll was conducted, but the gap between their respective perceptions had grown over the five-year period.[91]

The re-election in 2001 of the Blair government, which was viewed by unionists as too tolerant of Irish nationalism, reinforced unionist anxiety about the future of Northern Ireland. The result of this anxiety was to make it more difficult for Trimble to maintain a stable majority in his community and in his party in support of power-sharing. To remain credible, he had to sound almost as uncompromising as Ian Paisley, with whom he competed for the support of the unionist electorate. His efforts to appease the extreme elements in his own community did not satisfy them and yet offended those nationalists, in both north and south, with whom he had to collaborate if power-sharing was to work. The frequent suspensions, threats, and ultimatums exasperated not only Sinn Fein, which was their ostensible target, but also the SDLP, the Alliance Party, and the Irish government.

Throughout the spring and summer of 2002, Trimble and other unionists frequently asserted that the IRA had not really abandoned its armed struggle and that Sinn Fein, which they regarded as merely an appendage of the IRA, should therefore be considered ineligible to participate in the power-sharing executive. They demanded more concrete evidence that the IRA had, in effect, ceased to exist, failing which they would withdraw from the executive and force a return to direct rule from London. In October 2002 they finally carried out this threat, citing as their pretext a report that an IRA agent within the Northern Ireland Office in London had been secretly collecting confidential information. The DUP, which had never believed that Sinn Fein should be included in the executive, expressed satisfaction that Trimble had come round to its point of view. In a joint statement, Blair and Ahern said that they were "deeply saddened" and still committed to power-sharing, but that devolved government could not work given the "breakdown of trust" that had occurred.[92]

For the next six months the British, Irish, and American governments sought a statement from the IRA, through the intermediary of Gerry Adams, that would satisfy Trimble's criteria and allow power-sharing to resume. Logically, it is impossible to prove that a secret organization has ceased to exist, which in effect was what Trimble was demanding. Whatever Adams or the IRA said, Trimble had no great incentive to admit that he was satisfied. A poll early in 2003 showed that almost half of Northern Ireland's Protestants (but very few of its Catholics) preferred British direct rule to devolution.[93] The election of a new assembly in Northern Ireland was scheduled for 29 May 2003, almost five years after the election of the first power-sharing assembly, which had been able to function only during about half the time it had existed. The two largest parties in the old assembly, the Ulster Unionists and the SDLP, had good reason to fear losses of support to their rivals, the DUP and Sinn Fein. Sinn Fein had outpolled the SDLP in the Westminster election of 2001, when it elected four of its candidates, and had shown its vitality south of the border in the Irish general election of 2002, when it elected five members to the Dáil, including two in Dublin, its best showing since 1927. There was a good possibility that the DUP and Sinn Fein would be the two largest parties in a new Northern Ireland assembly if the 2003 election took place on schedule. Faced with this possibility, Trimble urged the British government to postpone the election if the IRA failed to respond to his demands, arguing that there was no point in electing an assembly if an executive could not be formed. The idea of postponing the election until 2004 had first been suggested by one of Trimble's advisers, Professor Paul Bew, prior to the imposition of direct rule in October.[94]

By April 2003 it seemed unlikely that direct rule would be ended before the election, but it was still generally taken for granted that the election would take place. On the 13th, Gerry Adams and Martin McGuinness delivered a statement said to be from the IRA to the British and Irish governments, although the text of the statement was not revealed at that time. Two weeks later, after Blair had requested clarification of the IRA statement, Adams made a speech declaring his confidence that "the IRA statement is a statement of completely peaceful intent."[95] Both the British and Irish governments responded favourably to the speech, but the Ulster Unionist Party expressed "disappointment." Some republican activists and Sinn Fein voters in Belfast were reported to believe that Adams and the IRA had made more than enough concessions.[96] At the last possible moment, only four weeks before the anticipated date of the May election, the Blair government announced that the IRA statement of good intentions was inadequate and postponed the election *sine die*. This unexpected action, on the last possible day before the election writs were issued, was condemned by the SDLP, the DUP, Sinn Fein, and even the Conservative opposition at Westminster. Mark Durkan, of the SDLP, said that he was satisfied with the IRA assurances. In Dublin the taoiseach issued a statement saying that he disagreed with the British decision but that the partnership between the British and Irish governments in pursuit of peace would continue. The two governments issued a joint declaration promising further steps to implement the Good Friday Agreement but also warning, "Paramilitarism and sectarian violence, therefore, must be brought to an end, from whichever part of the community they come."[97]

Trimble remained under pressure from diehard unionists both within and outside his party, but in September the Ulster Unionist council rejected a challenge to his leadership by Jeffrey Donaldson, who subsequently defected to Ian Paisley's Democratic Unionist Party. Trimble was at least temporarily in a strong enough position to begin negotiations with Gerry Adams in an effort to resolve the impasse. Soon afterwards the IRA demobilized a substantial part of its arsenal of weapons, a gesture to which the British government responded by announcing that the long-awaited election of a new assembly would take place on 26 November 2003, six months behind schedule.

The election resulted in major gains for Sinn Fein at the expense of the SDLP, and for Paisley's DUP at the expense of various unionist splinter groups. Although Trimble's party lost only one seat and it slightly increased its share of the first preference votes, the election left it with fewer seats and fewer votes than the DUP and thus constituted a defeat, for all practical purposes. Furthermore, several members elected under the Ulster Unionist banner were dissidents who shared the DUP's opposition to the Good Friday Agreement. Thus the outcome long feared by both the British and Irish governments had come to pass: Sinn Fein and the DUP had replaced the SDLP and the Ulster Unionist Party as the main political expressions of nationalism and unionism respectively.

Although both Sinn Fein and the DUP had been frequently stigmatized, especially by the non-Irish media, as "hard-liners" and "extremists," and although both, in contrast to their "moderate" rivals, drew most of their support from the working class, the analogy between them was flawed. Sinn Fein was firmly and enthusiastically committed to the Good Friday Agreement, which had enabled it to make major electoral gains both north and south of the border. The DUP, on the other hand, had never accepted the agreement. Following the election, Paisley triumphantly announced that the Good Friday Agreement was dead, an interpretation that was given some credence by subsequent events. As the largest unionist party in the newly elected assembly and the largest party overall, the DUP was entitled to name the first minister in a restored executive, but such an executive could not be formed under the terms of the Good Friday Agreement since the DUP refused to share power with Sinn Fein. Until this impasse was resolved, if it ever could be, there was little point in convening the assembly, which therefore did not meet. The situation after the election thus continued much as before, with the British ruling the six counties directly, a state of affairs that the DUP apparently preferred to the implementation of the Good Friday Agreement. Paisley argued, as Trimble had done before the election, that power-sharing could not be restored until the IRA ceased to exist. Sinn Fein responded that the IRA had refrained from overt violence for almost a decade and that it was the victim of a double standard, since a number of loyalist paramilitary organizations also continued to exist.

A conference at Leeds Castle in September, attended by Blair, Ahern, Adams, and Paisley, produced no agreement but some indications of flexibility on the part of both Paisley and Sinn Fein. Later in the month Paisley travelled to Dublin for an unprecedented meeting with Bertie Ahern, although he still refused to negotiate directly with Sinn Fein. Deadline for the conclusion of an agreement between the DUP and Sinn Fein were set, overtaken, and replaced by new deadlines. By mid-November the IRA had apparently agreed to complete disarmament before the end of the year, supervised by General de Chastelain and observed by representatives of the Catholic and Protestant clergy. Paisley insisted that disarmament by the IRA must have a visual aspect, meaning that photographs of it would be published. At the end of the month he went further by asserting in a speech at Ballymena, County Antrim, that the IRA "needs to be humiliated" and must "wear sackcloth and ashes," words that cast understandable doubt on his interest in reaching a settlement.[98] Blair and Ahern announced that they were still hopeful and unveiled a hypothetical timetable for the restoration of Northern Ireland's institutions in the new year. In September 2005, two months after the IRA had ordered all its units to disarm, General de Chastelain confirmed that all IRA wepons had been put "beyond use."[99]

CONCLUSION

The parallels between Quebec's peaceful Quiet Revolution and the Troubles, which cost several thousand lives in Northern Ireland, may appear far-fetched, but both resulted from rising expectations among a population who felt themselves economically, socially, and politically disadvantaged in a territory that they regarded as their own. Individual demands for an escape from economic and social disadvantages spilled over into collective demands for a change in political status or, in other words, nationalism. In both cases, however, the disadvantaged groups, francophones in Quebec and Catholics in Northern Ireland, had more success in overcoming their problems of economic disadvantage and social discrimination than they did in changing the political status of the territorial entity in which they lived.

Admittedly, there was never a firm consensus in favour of either the independence of Quebec or the reunification of Ireland; so it is perhaps not surprising that neither goal has been achieved. The perceived economic advantages of remaining part of Canada or the United Kingdom, fear of the unknown, and misgivings about other aspects of the political agenda promoted by those who advocated the change all contributed to this absence of consensus. Most francophones in Quebec, even those who did not totally reject independence, were realistically prepared to settle for something less, such as special status for Quebec within the Canadian federation. Most nationalists in Northern Ireland, including most republicans by 1998, were also realistically prepared to settle for something less than immediate reunification, such as power-sharing between the two communities in the six-county state. Yet even settling for less proved to be surprisingly difficult.

Extending the parallel, one can compare the Meech Lake Accord, which represented a very minimal degree of special status for Quebec, with the Good Friday Agreement, which represented the option of consociational power-sharing for Northern Ireland. Neither was entirely new, for special status had been widely discussed since the days of Jean Lesage, and the Good Friday Agreement had been foreshadowed by the British white paper of 1973 and the Sunningdale agreement that followed. Both Meech Lake and the Good Friday Agreement were constructed in the course of prolonged negotiations that were ultimately, and unexpectedly, successful. Yet it was at the point of success that their problems really began. Anglophone Canada turned against Meech Lake, to which all the provincial premiers had consented, and eventually defeated it, just in time for the three-year deadline, with the legislatures of two small provinces serving in effect as proxies for the opinions of most English-speaking Canadians. The Protestants or unionists of Northern Ireland turned against the Good Friday Agreement, about which they had been far from unanimous to begin with, and provoked repeated crises that led to the reimposition of direct rule. Seven years after the Good Friday Agreement was signed, Northern Ireland's institutions were in suspension and the future of power-sharing looked increasingly problematic.

CHAPTER TEN

Retrospect and Prospect

Viewed comparatively, the history of nationalism in Ireland and Quebec suggests both questions and answers. This study began with the assumption that two relatively small, predominantly Catholic, North Atlantic societies colonized by the British might be expected to display common features in their response to colonization and in their struggle to maintain their national identities. While the parallels between these two cases of nationalism are interesting and significant, their respective destinies, as we have seen, have not been identical. Québécois (or French Canadian) nationalism, as Louis Balthazar pointed out in his classic book on the subject, has been unusually limited in its aims and moderate in its methods. Only twice, according to Balthazar, did it attain a high level of intensity, and then only for brief periods: from 1837 to 1838 and again from 1976 to 1980.[1] To these instances we may add another one subsequent to the writing of his book: the period from the collapse of the Meech Lake Accord in 1990 to the referendum of 1995. All these episodes, as Balthazar suggests of the first two, were marked by the creation of "great political projects" which divided, rather than uniting, the population and which eventually failed, leaving the nation weaker and less confident than before. For the rest of its history, the flame of Quebec's nationalism has usually burned low, even if it has never been extinguished. It is not surprising that Quebec is often compared with Scotland, the other modern North Atlantic nation that seems content to exist indefinitely without a sovereign state of its own.

Irish nationalism, despite the efforts of revisionist historians in recent years to deny its significance, presents quite a different picture. While it is now fashionable to consider the traditional image of eight hundred years of struggle as an oversimplification at best, that image retains considerable validity. No doubt the intensity of Irish nationalism has varied over time, no doubt its ideological content has changed, sometimes radically, and no doubt it has at times been divisive. However, it is difficult to deny that the idea of Irish nationhood has shown an impressive ability to mobilize large numbers of people, often at the risk of their lives, over a very long period of time – not perhaps the continuous eight hundred years of legend but at least very frequently throughout the second half of that period. It is also striking how the idea of Irish national identity has persisted among members of the Irish or Irish-descended diaspora in the United States, Canada, Australia, and elsewhere, even when they are simultaneously loyal citizens of their new homelands, as most of them are. In contrast, practically all the millions of persons in other parts of North America whose ancestors were French Canadians from Quebec seem to have lost any meaningful affinity with, or interest in, Quebec and its national identity within a generation or two after migration.

This contrast in the intensity and persistence of nationalism is perhaps related to another contrast that requires attention: namely, the strikingly different levels of political violence over the years in the two societies. In Quebec, political violence has been almost absent, except in 1837–38 and, to a very limited extent, during the decade after 1963, when the FLQ was active. In Ireland it has been far more significant, although not uniquely so; viewed in global context, Quebec's peacefulness seems the aberration and Ireland's lack of it the norm, rather than vice versa. Furthermore, even the worst episodes of Irish political violence in modern times have been very small in scale in relation to events elsewhere; Cambodia in the 1970s and Rwanda in the 1990s are only two of the many that come to mind. Nonetheless, it cannot be denied that violence has played a significant role in Irish nationalist politics from 1798, through the struggles for land reform, the Fenians, the Easter rising, the war of independence, the civil war, and the troubles in Northern Ireland since 1968.

Since there is no scientifically valid reason to presume that some ethnic groups are more predisposed to nationalism or to violence than others, the explanation for the contrast between Ireland and Quebec in this regard must be found in circumstances. David Laitin has suggested an explanation for the greater levels of violence in some nationalist movements in an article that compares a number of European cases, particularly the non-violent nationalism of Catalonia and the more violent nationalism of the Basques.[2] He suggests that a "dense" rural social structure, with a large number of social membership groups, is a necessary condition for widespread political violence. This would seem to fit rural Ireland, with its history of secret societies, much better than rural Quebec, where a lower density of population and the lure of industrial jobs in the cities may have inhibited the development of associations. Laitin further argues that a tendency towards political violence, once established, is reinforced by what he calls "tipping" (the tendency of people to imitate behaviour that seems to be becoming more widespread) and by the perception that violent protest is having some effect.

In a comparative analysis of Northern Ireland and other "settlement frontiers," Frank Wright suggests that violence develops when there is conflict between two ethnic groups, settlers and natives, mingled on the same territory in close proximity to one another.[3] It is perhaps interesting in this regard that County Armagh, where the two ethno-religious communities are roughly equal in size, has been more notorious for political violence than any other Irish county from the 1790s, when the Orange Order was formed there, until the 1980s, when the British army had great difficulty in keeping this nominally occupied county under control. In Quebec, with its low population density, abundance of land, and a relatively small anglophone population that was largely concentrated in the cities or in a previously unpopulated frontier area (the Eastern Townships), there was much less potential for this kind of violence than in Ireland.

Ireland's nationalism became more intense and more violent than Quebec's because its experience of conquest and colonization was more traumatic, more violent, and more conducive to ethnic conflict over territory. The English conquerors of Ireland, in part because they were fearful that it might fall into the wrong hands and threaten their own security, subdued the country with unusual ferocity, particularly, but not only, during the rule of Oliver Cromwell. Except perhaps for a brief period at the end of the eighteenth century, Ireland was denied any meaningful self-government under English or British rule. The Catholic religion, professed by most of its inhabitants, was persecuted, and a Protestant state church on the English model was established for three centuries. The indigenous language was suppressed. Alien laws related to property were forcibly imposed on a people whose traditional approach to such matters was entirely different. Most of the land was taken from the inhabitants and distributed among the invaders, reducing the indigenous people to the status of tenants or labourers. The northeastern part of the country was systematically colonized with an alien population, so that the indigenous people became a minority in that part of Ireland. The Protestant settler minority (or majority, as they were in the northeast) dug in to protect their privileges, which included virtually absolute control over the country's industrial centre, to the point where in

1914 they threatened armed defiance of a British government that had promised home rule to Ireland. Again it must be emphasized that this northeastern unionist resistance to political change was originally directed against home rule bills that would have made Ireland an autonomous region within the United Kingdom, not a sovereign state.

In these circumstances, an intense and violent response to British rule, and to unionist provocation, on the part of the Irish people was almost inevitable. Habits of violence acquired during the struggles over land could easily be applied to other purposes, and the fairly recent memories of class oppression and religious discrimination added fuel to the flames. Given the right circumstances, which the First World War provided, Irish nationalists were numerous enough and determined enough to extricate most of their country from British rule, although not perhaps from British influence, albeit at the terrible cost of partition. Furthermore, the cynical and unjustifiable nature of the partition and the obvious illegitimacy of the sectarian Protestant state that was established by the threat of force in the six counties created the likelihood of a second wave of revolutionary nationalist violence, given the right circumstances, which were actually present in the 1960s.

In contrast to the Irish experience, the conquest of Quebec was relatively benign and had a relatively superficial impact on the country. The conquest itself, although it involved a few battles, was less of a conquest in the usual sense than a negotiated transfer of sovereignty between two European kingdoms. Geographical remoteness from Great Britain and the small size of the indigenous population lessened British concerns over security and made the British willing to concede at least a limited degree of self-government to French Canadians. The Catholic religion of the inhabitants was allowed to flourish, in part for the same reasons and in part because the conquest occurred at a time when the intensity of western Europe's religious conflicts had already passed its peak. The seigneurial system of land tenure, which was not particularly oppressive, and the civil law were left intact after the colony changed hands, as were existing patterns of landownership. The suppression of the French language, although occasionally contemplated by Lord Durham and others, was never seriously pursued; the people eventually were allowed to become literate in French, not in English. Systematic colonization was confined to areas where few French Canadians had settled, first the Eastern Townships and then the western frontier that became the province of Upper Canada or Ontario. There was enough land, and enough economic growth, in British North America to alleviate the conflict over land between different groups of settlers. British rule and the invidious sense of being a conquered people were not particularly pleasant for French Canadians in Quebec, but they were mild enough that the nationalist response to them was also relatively mild and peaceful. The British North America Act provided Quebec with the sort of "home rule" that Ireland was denied. Quebec was thus very slow to develop a movement for political independence, and when such a movement did emerge, it was overwhelmingly peaceful and constitutional in its orientation.

Colonial rule was thus established and maintained in quite different circumstances in our two societies, with lastingly different consequences for their political cultures and their subsequent development. The effects of these formative circumstances were then influenced by subsequent events, some of which were common to the two societies, such as the First World War, while others were unique to one, such as the Irish famine of 1845–47. There were parallel events, such as the aborted revolutions of 1798 and 1837–38, but also contrasting events, such as the achievement of provincial home rule by Quebec in 1867 and its denial to Ireland in 1886 and 1893. A very important variable in this regard was the contrast between the Protestants of northeastern Ireland and the anglophones of Quebec. It must be remembered that the activities of Craig and Carson and their followers in 1913–14 provided the precedent, the excuse, and to some extent even the inspiration for nationalist Ireland's subsequent move towards revolutionary violence. Quebec's anglophones generally opposed the "home rule" that Quebec gained in 1867, but they were too heterogeneous in ethnicity and religion to form a solid bloc against it, too recently arrived to have a deep attachment to the land that they occupied, and too easily able to move elsewhere in Canada to consider defending their position within Quebec by force.

It is tempting to devise counterfactual scenarios for both Ireland and Quebec. Suppose that the rebellions of 1798 and 1837–38 had succeeded in ending British rule. Would the resulting republics have been as politically and economically successful as the United States of America, as unsuccessful as Haiti, or somewhere in between those two extreme cases? (A prominent Irish academic once told the writer, only half in jest, that Wolfe Tone's Ireland might have been "a cooler and greener Haiti.") Would the republics of Ireland and Quebec have overcome their ethnic and religious cleavages to become pluralistic, non-sectarian, and liberal societies on the Jeffersonian model, as the revolutionaries hoped, or would the forces of division have proved too strong? Would Quebec have merely exchanged British for American rule, as the conservative (and anti-American) Canadian historian Donald Creighton has argued?

Suppose, as an alternative scenario, that Quebec had failed to achieve a form of provincial home rule in 1867 or that Ireland had achieved home rule in 1886 or 1893. Would a French Canada submerged within a predominantly British and Protestant Canadian unitary state have developed a serious independence movement by the early twentieth century, as Ireland actually did? If so, would the First World War have given that independence movement an opportunity to win at least a qualified and incomplete sort of independence, as Ireland actually did? Alternatively, would an Ireland granted home rule by Gladstone's government have been content with that degree of autonomy for several generations? Given suitable guarantees in a written constitution, would Ulster Protestants have eventually realized, as Quebec Protestants and other anglophones actually did, that a limited degree of home rule posed no real threat to their interests? Might they even have accepted dominion status for a united Ireland if the province of Ulster, where they predominated, had been given the same degree of autonomy within a federal Ireland that the province of Quebec was given within a federal Canada?

An almost infinite number of counterfactual scenarios can be imagined by anyone wishing to construct alternative histories for Ireland, Quebec, or any other country. The questions posed by such scenarios can never be conclusively answered, since history took a different course. "The moving finger writes, and, having writ, moves on: nor all thy piety nor wit shall lure it back to cancel half a line, nor all thy tears wash out a word of it." But the scenarios can serve a heuristic purpose. At the very least, they can warn us against the errors of Karl Marx, who told his friend Engels in November 1867 that he had previously thought the independence of Ireland was impossible and now thought it was inevitable.[4] Marx was wrong both times, as many less-distinguished pundits, contemplating the future of Quebec, have been more recently. Historical events are neither inevitable nor impossible until they have happened or failed to happen. Only with hindsight do they appear so.

The last word will not be written for a long time, if ever; so in a sense a book such as this one can have no "conclusion." In assessing the achievements and prospects of nationalism in Ireland and Quebec, or anywhere else, one can only make tentative judgments that will perhaps be in need of revision before the book is published. What follows should be read with that caveat in mind.

In one sense, as anyone who reads, hears, or watches the international news must know, Ireland and Quebec at the beginning of the twenty-first century are two of the world's most fortunate societies. Both are prosperous and stable. Both have maintained their distinct cultures and identities to a large extent, insofar as this is possible for small and open societies in a world of mass media, mass migration, and multinational enterprise. Most of their people enjoy levels of material affluence, freedom, security, education, health, and longevity that would be the envy of their own great-grandparents, not to mention the majority of the people now living outside of the North Atlantic world. The socio-economic advantages that were once enjoyed by previously privileged minorities, the Protestants of Ireland (both north and south) and the anglophones of Quebec, have virtually disappeared, along with most other legacies of colonialism. Ireland's population has increased by almost one-third since 1961, dramatically reversing more than a century of demographic decline. While affluence has brought some political corruption in Ireland, as happened a few decades earlier in Quebec, most would consider this a relatively small price to pay for its benefits.

Both Ireland and Quebec have also achieved some success in implementing the cultural goals of nationalism, although the results, particularly in the Irish case, have fallen short of nationalist aspirations. The hopes of some Irish nationalists that Irish would replace English as the working language of the new state could probably not have been achieved in any conceivable circumstances, given the overwhelming predominance of English in Ireland by the end of the nineteenth century. The Gaeltacht areas, defined as those areas within the state where Irish rather than English is the everyday spoken language of most of the population, have continued to shrink, and in 1996 the total Irish-speaking population of those areas was only 61,035. Furthermore, fewer than half the people in the officially Gaeltacht areas actually used Irish as an everyday language, according to the census of 1996. It will probably be necessary to concede within the next two decades that a Gaeltacht no longer exists in any meaningful sense.

Nonetheless, Irish as a second language continues to flourish, and there are signs that it is enjoying a revival. In 1996 no less than 43.5 per cent of the Irish state's population claimed the ability to speak Irish, as compared with only 32.5 per cent five years earlier and only 19.3 per cent in 1926, the date of the first census after independence. More than two-thirds of persons between the ages of ten and nineteen claimed the ability to speak Irish, which is a compulsory subject in all schools, and more than half those between the ages of twenty and twenty-four. The Irish-language television channel is watched by an average of 335,000 persons each day.[5] Even in the six counties of Northern Ireland, where the language received no official encouragement between 1920 and 1998, 22 per cent of the Catholic population claimed the ability to speak Irish in the census of 2001, although only 1 per cent of the Protestants did so. The Good Friday Agreement promises measures to promote the Irish language in Northern Ireland. In the south, the Fianna Fail government in 2003 introduced an Official Language Bill, apparently modelled after Canada's Official Languages Act, which gives citizens the right to deal with any state agency or government department in Irish, obliges all state agencies and departments to provide "higher quality services" in Irish, and provides for an Irish language commissioner or ombudsman to oversee the implementation of the legislation.[6]

In Quebec, although nationalists continue to express concern about the survival of the French language, there can be little doubt that its position has been significantly strengthened since the Quiet Revolution. (Its situation in other provinces of Canada, where it is largely confined to scattered rural enclaves analogous to Ireland's Gaeltacht, is another story.) The percentage of Quebec residents claiming the ability to speak French has steadily increased in recent years and reached the level of 94.6 per cent in the census of 2001, as compared with 87.3 per cent in 1961 and 92.5 per cent in 1981. Most of the increase is the result of greater knowledge of French among Quebec's anglophone and immigrant minorities, who have had to adapt to an increasingly francophone environment since the Charter of the French Language was adopted in 1977. A series of agreements with the federal government have enabled Quebec to select its own immigrants and to assume responsibility for integrating them into the province after their arrival. In 2001 a report by the Estates General on the situation and future of the French language in Quebec, a body appointed by the government of Quebec, concluded, "Bill 101 has enabled Quebec to make considerable progress in enhancing the status and attractiveness of the French language. Over 90% of young immigrants attend French-language schools. French is generally present in commerce and signs and its use is growing in businesses. Quebecers have acquired a form of security because French, the official, common language, has become more a part of everyday life."[7]

These are important achievements, but in a larger sense the nationalist projects of both Ireland and Quebec remain unfulfilled and the dreams of nationalists in both countries have been disappointed, at least for the present. Neither Québécois nor Irish nationalism has resulted in the creation of a nation-state in the full sense, something that is taken for granted by most other Western peoples. Quebec, although it enjoys a significant degree of autonomy within the Canadian state, remains merely one of ten provinces in a federation. Ireland, although most of it is under the jurisdiction of a sovereign state, still has six counties under British occupation, and in those six counties, as recent events have shown, the entire population can be disenfranchised at the whim of a British prime minister.

A generation ago it seemed neither inevitable nor particularly likely that these outcomes would be in place at the beginning of the twenty-first century. As noted in the previous chapter, some Irish nationalists, both north and south, believed after 1968 that the civil rights movement in the six counties might be the prelude to the reunification of their country. The collapse of the Stormont regime, the imposition of direct rule, and the escalation of violence to a level that British public opinion seemed unlikely to tolerate all gave credence to these hopes in the early 1970s. There were indications at that time that some British policy-makers were at least considering the possibility of withdrawal from the six counties, and that some Irish policy-makers in the southern state were prepared to assume responsibility for governing the six counties if the opportunity was offered. The Sunningdale agreement and the Anglo-Irish Agreement more than a decade later certainly convinced many unionists that the British were about to abandon their partitionist state and accept the reunification of Ireland.

Quebec nationalists were also hopeful, and their opponents discouraged, from the mid-1960s until the referendum of 1980 and again from 1990 until 1995. The emergence of the FLQ, the RIN, and later the Parti québécois during the 1960s, the discontent encountered by the Royal Commission on Bilingualism and Biculturalism during its public hearings in Quebec, and the frequent riots, strikes, and demonstrations in the province all suggested that the legitimacy of the Canadian federal state among francophones in Quebec had been fatally undermined. President de Gaulle's support for the Quebec independence movement during his last years in office gave that movement additional credibility. The electoral victory of the Parti québécois in 1976 was as much of a shock to Canadian federalists and to Quebec's anglophone minority as the Sunningdale agreement was to Northern Ireland's unionists. Yet the Canadian federal state, like the union between Great Britain and Northern Ireland, proved to be more durable than either its supporters or its opponents anticipated.

As was suggested earlier with reference to Karl Marx and the Irish question, no one who studies politics should make categorical predictions that particular events will or will not happen. Circumstances can change very quickly, and what seems unlikely at one point in time may actually happen a few years later. Few anticipated the reunification of Germany, the collapse of the Soviet Union, or the end of apartheid in South Africa even five years before those events took place. With that caveat in mind, however, it is legitimate to pose the question of what prospect there is for the reunification of Ireland or for the independence of Quebec. At the time of writing, neither event seems likely to happen in the near future, if ever.

Irish republicans still maintain, at least in their public pronouncements, that reunification will occur in the not too distant future. Martin McGuinness of Sinn Fein, Northern Ireland's minister of education, predicted in 2002 that reunification was "inevitable" and that it would probably happen in time for the centennial of the Easter rising in 2016.[8] The Good Friday Agreement, as we have seen, makes reunification theoretically possible if a majority of Northern Ireland's voters ever wish it to happen, but both electoral and census data suggest that unionists are still at least 56 per cent of the population, and the opposition of unionists to the unification of Ireland seems as rigid as ever. The increase in the relative weight of the Catholic/ nationalist population between 1961 and 2001 was significant, and the median age of the Catholic population is also lower than that of the Protestants. On the other hand, the proportion of Catholics (44 per cent) recorded by the 2001 census fell short of some nationalist expectations, and there is still a small but significant group of Catholics who support the British connection, however odd that may seem. Failing any erosion of northern Protestant opposition to the reunification of Ireland, the Catholic share of the population would have to reach about 55 per cent for it to happen, an eventuality that is unlikely to occur at least for several decades.

An additional reason to discount the possibility of reunification is the apparent apathy of most of the population in southern Ireland. Only in the border counties of Cavan, Monaghan, and Donegal, all of which are part of the historic province of Ulster, does the prospect of reunification appear to inspire much enthusiasm or even interest. The apathy of the southern population is apparently shared by southern politicians. Apart from those affiliated with Sinn Fein, which is still a minor, albeit growing, political force south of the border, they rarely discuss reunification during their electoral campaigns and do not seem to attach a high priority to it. In this, as we have seen, they are at least consistent with the attitudes and behaviour of most of their predecessors over the last eighty years. There are probably several reasons for this apathy, related to both politics and economics. In a reunified Ireland, Sinn Fein would be a fairly significant party and the SDLP might join with the Irish Labour Party, developments that would drastically reduce the influence of both of the southern state's major parties, Fianna Fail and Fine Gael. The post-reunification behaviour of Protestant voters is unpredictable, although Fine Gael would probably attract more of them than Fianna Fail. In addition to these political uncertainties, diehard loyalist resistance to reunification by a segment of the Protestant population might create a serious problem of security for the reunified state. The Irish state would also find it burdensome, despite the recent prosperity of the twenty-six counties, to match the relatively high level of public expenditure that Northern Ireland has experienced since the imposition of direct rule in 1972. Although the south surpassed the north in terms of incomes and living standards by about 1995, public expenditure per capita in the six counties is about 50 per cent higher than it is in the southern Irish state.[9] This high level of expenditure is heavily subsidized by taxpayers in Great Britain. Given the relatively large size of Northern Ireland's population (about 40 per cent of the southern state's population, or about 28 per cent of the whole island's), the six counties could not be absorbed as easily into the southern Irish state as Newfoundland, with about one-fortieth of Canada's population, was absorbed into Canada in 1949. The reunification of Germany, which has been unexpectedly difficult in economic and fiscal terms, provides a better parallel to what could be expected.

Given these facts, it is perhaps surprising that most, although not all, republicans in Northern Ireland accept the Good Friday Agreement, which appears to bring reunification no closer than did the very similar Sunningdale agreement of 1973, which republicans opposed. The reasons for this change of position seem to be a recognition that the military war against partition could not be won; a belief that IRA violence was discrediting, rather than advancing, the republican cause; and a growing appreciation that Protestant Ulster unionism, whatever its historical origins may have been, is a political force in its own right and not just a smokescreen for British machinations. In addition, most left-wing Irish republicans, including those who are practising Catholics, are sincere in their rejection of sectarianism and their desire to substitute the politics of class for the politics of religious affiliation. In the long term they apparently believe that by participating in a power-sharing arrangement in Northern Ireland, rather than fighting for reunification, they can reach out to working-class Protestants, with the result that working-class Protestant hostility to reunification will eventually decline and disappear. This is a belief that does republicans credit, however naive and unrealistic it may seem in the short to medium term.

It is sometimes argued that the process of European integration, which has dramatically lessened the Irish state's traditional dependence on Great Britain as a trading partner, could also contribute to the reunification of Ireland by making the border less significant. The European Union itself treats Ireland as a single economic region, despite the fact that Britain, and therefore the six counties, has not yet joined the common European currency, which came into existence in 2001. Southern Ireland voted overwhelmingly to join Europe in 1972, with 83 per cent of votes cast in favour, although it is not clear how much the issue of partition contributed to this result. Northern Ireland was more evenly divided in the British referendum on joining Europe, with Ian Paisley's Democratic Unionist Party leading the opposition, but it has since become more supportive of European integration.[10] On the other hand, Sinn Fein, both north and south of the border, has emerged as Ireland's leading opponent of European integration, a stance that casts some doubt on the thesis that European integration is conducive to Irish reunification. At the end of the twentieth century, Eamon de Valera's granddaughter Sile de Valera, who was then a minister in the Irish government and a leading member of Fianna Fail's more republican faction, also expressed disquiet about the impact of European integration on Ireland's national identity and independence.[11] Voters in the Irish state rejected the Treaty of Nice by a narrow margin in 2001 but approved it a year later in a second referendum. The link between European integration and Irish unity remains unproven. One could argue just as credibly that European integration, by eliminating some of the disadvantages of parti- tion, has contributed to popular apathy about partition itself and has thus made the political reunification of Ireland less likely.

If we turn to Quebec, it appears that supporters of an independent Que- bec face as many obstacles in the twenty-first century as do supporters of a thirty-two-county Irish republic. In fact, unlike the Irish republicans, who can perhaps draw some comfort from the results of the recent census in the six counties, Quebec nationalists have little reason to be encouraged even by demographic trends. Although the anglophone minority in Quebec is gradually declining, it is being replaced by an influx of immigrants who, even if they become fluent in French, continue to reject the option of an independent Quebec by overwhelming majorities. As will be discussed below, this is a problem to which Quebec nationalists have devoted consid- erable attention in recent years, and it has helped to promote a redefinition of Quebec nationalism that is still in progress.

Yet Jacques Parizeau's notorious comment about "ethnic votes" defeating the 1995 referendum, while arithmetically accurate, begs the question of why francophone voters were so evenly divided, even after the failure of efforts to give Quebec more recognition in the Canadian constitution, that a relatively small number of "ethnic" voters could tip the balance against inde- pendence. As suggested above, there are historical reasons why Quebec's nationalism has rarely, if ever, attained the intensity of Irish nationalism. An important consequence of this history, and also of more recent develop- ments, is that Quebec's national identity, while relatively strong, is not exclu- sive. For most people in Quebec, identification with the Quebec nation still coexists with a somewhat weaker and more diffuse but not insignificant identification with Canada as a whole. A poll conducted in October 2001, for example, found that 85 per cent of the Quebec sample, obviously includ- ing many supporters of the Parti québécois, admitted to having some sense of Canadian identity, even though only 20 per cent of the sample gave it pri- ority over their Quebec identity. A third of the sample considered their Que- bec and Canadian identities of equal importance, a somewhat higher proportion than had done so in a similar poll eight months earlier.[12] These data may be contrasted with those of a Northern Ireland survey at about the same time, in which only 12 per cent of Catholics indicated acceptance of "British" as part of their identity.[13]

As we have seen in earlier chapters, this residual attachment to the idea of Canada has characterized French Canadian ethnic nationalism from the earliest times. For Henri Bourassa and André Laurendeau, among others, it ruled out the option of supporting an independent Quebec, even when they were most tempted to do so. The fact that Canada is the name of an actual state in which francophones comprise less than a quarter of the population is not really the issue, for the idea of Canada was invented before the British arrived. The effort since the Quiet Revolution to create a civic nationalism focused exclusively on Quebec has not been entirely successful. Furthermore, Canadian federal governments, particularly when the Liberals are in office, have enthusiastically followed the advice that Pierre Trudeau gave them in 1964, more than a year before he himself entered federal politics: "One way of offsetting the appeal of separatism is by investing tremendous amounts of time, energy, and money in nationalism *at the federal level*. A national image must be created that will have such an appeal as to make any image of a separatist group unattractive ... In short the whole of the citizenry must be made to feel that it is only within the framework of the federal state that their language, culture, institutions, sacred traditions, and standard of living can be protected from external attack and internal strife."[14] Although often denounced and ridiculed by Quebec nationalists, such efforts have been systematically pursued by the federal government since then and appear to have had some effect.

As in Ireland, the impact of continental economic integration on nationalist aspirations is an issue that has received some attention in Quebec. Canada signed a free trade agreement with the United States in 1998, which was replaced a few years later by a trilateral agreement including Mexico, the North American Free Trade Agreement, or NAFTA. Although no referendum was held on either agreement, free trade with the United States was the issue that dominated the federal general election of 1988, in which Quebec gave the Mulroney government, and thus by implication the free trade initiative, a decisive margin of support. Quebec's Liberal government supported free trade with the United States, as did the Parti québécois, which was then out of office. There was significant opposition to free trade, however, from farm and labour organizations, which are traditionally sympathetic to the Parti québécois.

In abandoning its farm and labour allies to take a different position from theirs on this important issue, the Parti québécois was not acting out of character, for it has generally displayed little or none of the anti-Americanism of earlier nationalists such as Bourassa, Groulx, and Laurendeau. One could argue that its position is congruent with the pro-Americanism of the Patriotes in 1837–38, albeit in a very different context. However, the real reason it supported continental free trade was the belief that North American free trade would lessen Quebec's economic dependence on the rest of Canada, much as European free trade lessened Ireland's dependence on Great Britain. The outcome of the 1980 referendum on sovereignty-association had been influenced by the uncertainty, deliberately promoted by Canadian politicians, as to whether Canada would actually agree to a sovereignty-association arrangement, or even free trade, with a sovereign Quebec. Free trade with the United States, a much larger market than Canada, would make an agreement with Canada less essential and increase Quebec's bargaining power in any negotiation about the terms of separation. It would also make Quebec voters less likely to be influenced by fears that sovereignty would have a damaging effect on Quebec's trade and standard of living. These arguments particularly appealed to Jacques Parizeau, the leader of the Parti québécois from 1988 to 1995, who had never been fully convinced that an "association" with Canada after independence was either feasible or desirable.[15]

The argument that North American economic integration makes the independence of Quebec more likely seemed to be partially vindicated by the much closer result of the 1995 referendum, after a campaign in which economic anxieties played a relatively small part, as compared with that of 1980. By 1995 Quebec's trade with the United States exceeded its trade with the rest of Canada, which had not been the case in 1980. Some voters in 1995 may have been convinced by the argument that NAFTA would guarantee the living standards of an independent Quebec, regardless of Canada's attitude. Federalists argued, however, that a Quebec which was no longer part of the Canadian state would not automatically continue to enjoy the benefits of NAFTA, at least not unless Canada, the United States, and Mexico all agreed that it should do so. It is also possible, paradoxically, that an independent Quebec adhering to NAFTA would be more constrained by the treaty than is the actual province, since the legal constraints which NAFTA imposes on the actions of governments apply to sovereign member states and not, or at least not directly and explicitly, to their sub-national units.

When the Parti québécois was first established, it was generally assumed that an electoral victory by the party would automatically result in independence. After the adoption of the strategy of *étapisme* in the early 1970s, it was assumed that a majority vote for independence in a referendum would automatically lead to that result. Following the Supreme Court's decision on the legality of secession in 1998 and following the Clarity Act adopted by the Canadian parliament in 2000, even this outcome can apparently no longer be taken for granted. Even if the federal government and parliament agreed that the referendum question and the outcome were sufficiently clear, the negotiations that followed would be exceptionally complex, would involve other provincial governments, aboriginal groups, and possibly representatives of Quebec's minorities, and could conceivably drag on for several years. Faced with these difficulties, is even the leadership of the Parti québécois itself seriously committed to the goal of independence? Following the disappointment of 1995, the party's two subsequent leaders, Lucien Bouchard and Bernard Landry, displayed little inclination to hold another referendum, at least until such time as a successful outcome could be guaranteed. Both leaders faced accusations by party militants that they were no longer genuinely committed to the cause or even, in Bouchard's case, that he never really had been. Although a split in the party has been avoided, this unhappiness at the grassroots may have contributed to the relatively ineffective campaign that ended with its electoral defeat in April 2003, despite a flourishing economy and a quite commendable record in office. However, the general public, in contrast to party militants, seems quite apathetic about independence at the time of writing. It is possible to imagine a scenario in which the commitment of the Parti québécois to independence would become purely rhetorical and theoretical, like the commitment of Fianna Fail to the reunification of Ireland. Alternatively, the Parti québécois might explicitly accept a modification of Quebec's relationship with the rest of Canada that fell short of independence, at least in the short to medium term, although rationalizing its decision by maintaining that the short-term objective would lead to independence in the longer term. This course of action has been proposed in a much-discussed book by a former adviser to Premier Bouchard.[16] The parallel that comes to mind is Sinn Fein's acceptance of the Good Friday Agreement in place of its previous insistence on the reunification of Ireland.

Neither Irish nationalism nor Quebec nationalism has ever been a monolithic force, and within both nationalist camps there have always been differences of opinion about means and even about ends. In Ireland the legacy of 1798 was a republican tradition, based on the universalist ideals of the French Revolution, which manifested itself in opposition to British rule, even symbolically, over any part of the island of Ireland and a willingness to use violence, if necessary, to end it. Yet that tradition coexisted, and to some extent overlapped with, another tradition of Irish nationalism which focused more on cultural self-preservation, cared less about ideology, and was relatively pragmatic about political arrangements. In practice, even some prominent republicans – Collins in 1921, de Valera in 1927, Sean McBride in 1937, and Gerry Adams in 1998 – proved willing to accept a less-than-ideal political solution to Ireland's problems, although a residual faction of intransigents always remained.

In Quebec, despite 1837–38, the republican tradition was too weak to produce a similar polarization, at least until recent times. Yet after the Quiet Revolution a somewhat similar division developed between those nationalists who insisted on a fully sovereign state of Quebec and those other nationalists who were prepared to accept some continuing political association with Canada, if Quebec's national identity and right to self-determination would only be recognized. In theory at least, this difference of opinion became the basis for the distinction between Quebec's two major political parties, at the provincial and eventually at the federal level. Yet the distinction was less absolute than it seemed, with prominent "separatists" such as René Lévesque and Lucien Bouchard at times drifting closer to the second alternative and prominent "federalists" such as Daniel Johnson and Jean Allaire at times drifting closer to the first.

If a united Ireland and a sovereign Quebec remain elusive, does it really matter? Irish republicans traditionally blamed partition for the sectarianism and social conservatism of the southern Irish state, as well as its dismal economic performance, but those characteristics, which the state unquestionably exhibited in the early decades of its existence, are far less evident in the secular, liberal, and prosperous Ireland of today. Even the entity known as Northern Ireland has virtually lost its sectarian character in recent years, although its boundary is both geographically and culturally irrational and the formal symbols of British sovereignty remain. As Fionnuala O'Connor wrote more than a decade ago, "The overall picture is of a confident Catholic group, young and growing very rapidly, faced with nervous and retreating Protestants: a middle class in the making watching another in flight."[17] The parallel with Quebec in the 1970s is irresistible. Partition did not prevent Belfast from having a Sinn Fein lord mayor in 2002–3; nor has it prevented a northern Catholic, Mary McAleese, from being elected president of Ireland in 1997. The accusation that partition tore the economic heart out of the country, while true at the time, has little relevance now that Belfast's industrial complex has vanished. The Irish "border," thanks to European integration, can be crossed today as easily as the borders between Canadian provinces or between American states. Travellers on the trains that link Dublin and Belfast several times a day are hardly aware of its existence. Many Irish institutions, from the churches to the Gaelic Athletic Association to the Political Studies Association of Ireland, function as though the border did not exist.

Much the same can be said about the impact of Canadian federalism on Quebec. Quebec still lacks an army or a seat at the United Nations, but it exercises powers and responsibilities that other Canadian provinces do not, such as collecting its own income tax, administering its own contributory pension plan, and selecting its own immigrants. To most Canadians from other provinces, it seems almost as much a foreign country as does the United States, or as Ireland seems to visitors from England. Quebec's federally appointed lieutenant-governor is as invisible today as the governor general of the Irish Free State was from 1932 to 1937, if not more so. The speech from the throne has been replaced by the premier's "inaugural address" to the National Assembly. On balance, the province of Quebec probably exercises at least as much meaningful "sovereignty" within Canada as do the smaller member states within the European Union at its current stage of evolution. What more could Quebec gain by being formally sovereign? An independent Quebec would not be more liberal or democratic than the status quo, as the Patriotes could legitimately argue in 1837. It would not even give francophones more control over the economy, as the RIN could quite credibly argue in the 1960s. At most, the French language would be a little more secure, but even that is problematic.

In both Ireland and Quebec the increasingly ambiguous nature of borders and boundaries seems to be making old grievances less painful and less relevant than before. Traditionally, nationalism thrived on a justified sense of being victimized by the more powerful nations with which Ireland and Quebec were closely associated, but that sense of victimhood increasingly lacks credibility today. Understandably and for excellent reasons, it lasted longest among the Catholics of Northern Ireland, but even there it will decline, barring the unlikely event of a complete and definitive breakdown of the peace process.

What, then, is the future of nationalism in Ireland and Quebec? It is often pointed out that Irish nationalism became a powerful force because the "British" national identity created by the British state after 1707 was unable to include the Irish, or at least the Catholic Irish, in the way that it quite successfully, although not completely, incorporated the identities of the Scottish and the Welsh. In a somewhat similar way, the British North American or "Canadian" identity created by the Canadian state after 1867 was not as successful in including the francophones of Quebec as it was in incorporating, for example, Nova Scotians or British Columbians, even though its failure was not as complete as that of the British in Ireland. In response to British and British North American nationalism, the Irish nationalist and French Canadian/Quebec nationalist identities were created out of the elements – religion, language, culture, and history – that did not fit easily into the British or British North American mould. Irish and French Canadian nationalism drew its strength in part from economic grievances and from a sense of social exclusion, but also from the belief that the religion, language, culture, and history that distinguished the Irish or French Canadian people from their neighbours were worth preserving and could only be preserved by some form of collective self-government and separateness, given their incongruity with the British or British North American values of the dominant group.

Undoubtedly, the desire to protect and promote the cultural heritage of a previously dominated and oppressed group has given nationalism much of its strength and vitality in both countries, as it has in many other parts of the world, and has accounted for much of its ability to mobilize popular enthusiasm on its behalf. Nor is there anything wrong with the desire of a national group to protect and promote its own cultural heritage on its own territory, particularly when that heritage appears to be threatened with destruction. However, the disadvantage of cultural nationalism is that it arouses little or no interest on the part of minorities who may be present on the territory, and who do not share the culture in question. In fact, it may even repel them. In other words, nationalism that promotes the cultural heritage and values of a particular group will fail to be inclusive of all the people on the territory that it claims as its own, just as British or British North American nationalism failed to be inclusive of Irish Catholics or French Canadians in the first place.

In the last analysis, the failure of both Irish and Quebec nationalism to achieve their political and territorial goals can be attributed largely to this problem. After the Act of Union, as we have seen, Irish nationalism became increasingly associated with Catholicism, particularly because of the British failure to implement Catholic emancipation for a generation after the union was achieved. In the latter part of the nineteenth century, Irish nationalism also became associated with the effort to preserve and restore the Irish language, as well as other elements of the cultural heritage, such as Gaelic football and hurling. The result was to define the nation in a way that most of the Protestant minority could not easily identify with, although there were some individual exceptions, and to exclude most of that minority from the potential support base of Irish nationalism. Unionists could and did argue that if Irish Catholics had the right to secede from the United Kingdom, northeastern Protestants had the right to secede from Ireland. Largely as a result, the country was partitioned, and as we have seen, the somewhat arbitrary partition line drawn in 1920 and the determination of northern unionists to maintain it have proved remarkably resistant to change.

Something of the same sort happened in Canada East (Quebec) after 1841. French Canadian ethnic nationalism was stimulated by the apparent threat to the French language from Lord Durham's report, and it also became closely associated with the Catholic Church, which filled the vacuum left by the defeat of the Patriotes in 1837–38. The tendency to define the nation in ethnocultural rather than territorial terms was encouraged by the abolition of Lower Canada's Legislative Assembly and the replacement of Lower Canada by a larger political unit in which French Canadians were a minority. The anglophone minority, reinforced by the other immigrant groups that arrived subsequently, could not identify with this kind of nationalism and generally opposed, although not very strenuously, the re-establishment of a predominantly francophone province in 1867. Thereafter they became instinctively supportive of the federal government and hostile to any increase in the autonomy of the province, which they viewed as an entity devoted to exclusively French Canadian interests. In provincial politics they generally opted for whichever was perceived as the less nationalistic of the two major parties. In recent times virtually all anglophones and the great majority of immigrants have refused to support the Parti québécois. Although some immigrants, particularly those from Latin America, have voted for the party in elections, even they almost unanimously rejected its option of a sovereign Quebec in the referendums of 1980 and 1995. This overwhelming refusal of minorities in Quebec even to consider a sovereign Quebec as an acceptable option is as baffling and frustrating to Quebec nationalists as the refusal of northern Protestants to consider a united Ireland is to Irish republicans. Yet since the main argument for an independent Quebec has always been based, quite understandably, on the need to protect the French language and the culture associated with it from assimilation, there is no obvious reason why anglophones and immigrants should be expected to prefer an independent Quebec to Canadian federalism.

The Quiet Revolution was largely an assertion of French Canadian ethnic nationalism, even though its effect was to build a Weberian bureaucratic state on the territory of Quebec that treated everyone equally, regardless of ethnicity or religion. Since then, French Canadian ethnic and Catholic nationalism has been replaced, at least in theory, by a more secular and inclusive civic nationalism focused on the territory and political institutions of Quebec. Nationalism has in fact become entirely secular as the power and influence of the Catholic Church in Quebec have dramatically declined. But Quebec nationalism is still closely associated with cultural grievances and concern over the future of the French language, which Balthazar suggests has been the constant factor in its history.[18] The result is that most persons who are not of French ancestry and mother tongue continue to view it with suspicion or at best with indifference. Like Sinn Fein, the Parti québécois is inclusive and non-sectarian in principle, but remarkably homogeneous in practice. In recent elections only about 5 per cent of its candidates have been of non-French origin, and the percentage of successful candidates who were of non-French origin has been even lower.

Since the referendum of 1995, there has been considerable soul-searching among Quebec nationalists about the issue of inclusiveness and the presumed contrast between ethnic and civic nationalism. Premier Parizeau's bitter comment that "ethnic votes" had prevented the outcome that most francophone Quebecers desired was widely viewed as an embarrassing indication that his party had by no means completed the transition to a more inclusive kind of nationalism. A few years later the issue was reignited when Yves Michaud, a veteran separatist who was seeking the Parti québécois nomination in a by-election, criticized the voters in a predominantly Jewish Montreal suburb for their overwhelming federalist vote in the referendum and described them as "immigrants," even though most of them were actually born in Quebec. Lucien Bouchard, who was then the leader of the party, sought to limit the damage by declaring that Michaud would not be an acceptable candidate.[19] Books have been written alleging that the Parti québécois, despite its professions, has not in practice been inclusive of Quebec's minorities and has not fully freed itself from the legacy of old-style French Canadian ethnic nationalism.[20] According to the critics, this orientation not only makes it more difficult to win a majority in any referendum on sovereignty but undermines the moral case for demanding sovereignty. If French Canadians in Quebec are a nation, then how can Quebec as a whole be a nation? If Quebec as a whole is not a nation, how can it claim the right of national self-determination? More to the point, how can nationalists who base their case for a sovereign Quebec on French Canadian ethnic nationalism argue that aboriginal nations in Quebec's northern hinterlands, or perhaps even anglophones in the mainly non-French western half of Montreal, do not have the right to secede from Quebec, if Quebec has the right to secede from Canada?

Since its first referendum defeat in 1980, the Parti québécois has repeatedly assured Quebec's anglophone minority that their contribution to the province is valued and that a sovereign Quebec would guarantee their access to education and health care in their own language. These overtures have apparently not softened the minority's hostile attitude towards the party. Since the anglophone minority is gradually declining and is now outnumbered by residents of Quebec whose mother tongue is neither English nor French, the Parti québécois has devoted even more attention to the latter group, who are a growing force in Quebec politics. Apart from the fact that their pro-federalist sympathies create a serious obstacle to winning any referendum on sovereignty, the existence of the growing immigrant and "ethnic" communities in Montreal has forced a reconsideration of the whole nature of Quebec nationalism.

Historically, as we have seen, the predominant form of nationalism in Quebec after 1841 was French Canadian ethnic nationalism. Although the "pure laine" ethnic origin of the francophone population was a myth, it was generally assumed that immigrants, even if they were Catholics, neither could nor should be absorbed into that population. Even the growing popularity in the 1960s of the label "Québécois" did not really change this attitude, because "Québécois" at first was merely a new label for the ethnic group of French Canadians in Quebec, a label that was no more inclusive and even excluded French Canadian minorities in other provinces. Minorities were seen as being in Quebec but not really of it, with the predictable consequence that they regarded themselves as (hyphenated) Canadians but not really as Quebecers. Until after the Quiet Revolution, the Catholic school boards in Quebec actually discouraged immigrants from educating their children in French, in ironic contrast to the policies that would be adopted by the Quebec state a few years later. Most immigrants and minorities therefore gravitated towards Quebec's English-speaking community, where they replaced anglophones who had migrated to other parts of Canada and, in effect, maintained the relative strength of the anglophone community within Quebec, despite the higher birth rate of the francophone population.

By the 1970s nationalists realized that, given continuing high levels of immigration, this policy placed the predominance of the French language at risk in Montreal, where most of the immigrants settled. The result was the new policy of not only encouraging but even requiring immigrants to send their children to French schools. Somewhat later, it became apparent that Quebec would need a high level of immigration to maintain a rate of population growth similar to that of Canada as a whole. But what kind of society would Quebec become if it relied on immigrants to renew its population, and what implications did that situation have for the meaning and content of its nationalism? To old-fashioned ethnic nationalists, the declining birth rate seemed to pose an unpalatable choice between a Quebec that would dwindle in size and a Quebec that would lose its French identity. Civic nationalists tried to develop a third option.

The gradual and still by no means complete transition from ethnic to civic nationalism after the Quiet Revolution was thus the result of several converging circumstances. In part it reflected the growth of a bureaucratic state in Quebec, the aspiration to make that state a sovereign entity, and the implicit recognition that the scattered francophone minorities in other parts of Canada, who had not shared in the Quiet Revolution, could not realistically be included in the evolving nation; which was rooted in the soil of Quebec. But in part it also implied a recognition that those who were not "pure laine" must be included in that nation for it to be a viable project. Yet if Quebec as an entity had no distinct and homogeneous culture and heritage to protect, what would be the rationale for its pursuit of sovereignty?

The government headed by René Lévesque gave serious thought to this question and to the place of minorities in Quebec society more generally, despite the faux pas that it committed in 1977 by incorporating an ethnically exclusive definition of the Quebec people in the first version of its Charter of the French Language. After April 1981 Quebec's ministry of immigration was known as the ministry of cultural communities and immigration, "cultural communities" henceforth being the officially designated label for ethnic and linguistic minorities in Quebec. In the same year the government produced an "action plan" to integrate the minorities into Quebec society while encouraging their distinct cultural contributions to it.[21] This document began the process of developing a policy known as "interculturalism" in contrast to, and partially in response to, the official "multiculturalism" of the Canadian federal state. While Canadian "multiculturalism" implies a national "identity" completely devoid of content and an obsessive celebration of "diversity" for its own sake, the Quebec model envisages the convergence of minority cultures towards a common identity based on the use of French as a common public language and on a shared participation in Quebec's distinctive institutions and way of life, particularly as they have evolved since the Quiet Revolution.[22] This seems the only way to make Quebec nationalism sufficiently inclusive to appear respectable in the modern world. It may also be the only way to assert a credible claim for national self-determination without provoking counterclaims from Quebec's minorities that would threaten the integrity of its territorial boundaries.

Bill 99, the Quebec government's response to the federal government's so-called Clarity Act in 2000, attempted to define the Quebec "people," whose right of national self-determination it proclaimed, in terms that were entirely civic and non-ethnic. Introduced by the minister of intergovernmental affairs, Joseph Facal, himself an immigrant from Uruguay, Bill 99 emphasized Quebec's institutions as the basis of its identity and did not even mention the French language or culture. Instead it declared that "the Quebec people possesses specific characteristics and a deep-rooted historical continuity in a territory over which it exercises its rights through a modern national state, having a government, a national assembly and impartial and independent courts of justice." The bill also proclaimed that the National Assembly derived its legitimacy from the Quebec people and that the Quebec people "is free to take charge of its own destiny, determine its political status and pursue its economic, social and cultural development." It is not entirely clear from this formulation whether the "people" is considered to have created the institutions or vice-versa. Yet it must be conceded that the same ambiguity applies to other civic nationalisms, including particularly that of the United States of America.

These debates are by no means irrelevant to the situation of Ireland as it enters the twenty-first century. As we have seen, the Irish state has already abandoned its constitutional recognition of the "special position" of the Catholic Church in an effort to appear more inclusive. Since the Good Friday Agreement, it has modified Articles 2 and 3 of the Irish constitution so that the state's traditional claim to the national territory is qualified and conditional on the achievement of concurrent majorities for reunification in the two "jurisdictions" on the island. Furthermore, Article 3 in its new version refers to "all the people who share the territory of the island of Ireland, in all the diversity of their identities and traditions." On the other hand, Article 2 retains a trace of ethnic nationalism by proclaiming that "the Irish nation cherishes a special affinity with people of Irish ancestry living abroad who share its cultural identity and heritage." This is in contrast to Quebec, which seems to have largely abandoned any formal commitment to its traditional "affinity" with francophones of French Canadian ancestry in other parts of North America.

The most important problem of defining Irish identity is still unquestionably the status of nearly a million unionists in the northeast. Officially, the Irish state at last recognizes that if they are really part of the Irish nation, the Irish identity must be redefined to include them, however difficult and complicated that process may be. Yet a second problem, with which Quebec has a longer experience, is beginning to impinge on the Irish consciousness. That problem is the need to incorporate immigrant and ethnic communities of diverse origins into Irish society and the Irish nation. Ireland has become a rich country, and like other rich countries, in Europe as well as in North America and the South Pacific, it has become attractive to immigrants at the same time as its own birth rate has declined sharply. Millions of its own people once left it to escape from poverty, but Ireland now receives thousands of newcomers who have left their own countries for the same reason. While not yet as cosmopolitan as London, Paris, or Montreal, Dublin is becoming a city of increasing diversity in race, language, and culture. The Irish state and, by and large, the Irish people are responding to this unaccustomed situation in a spirit of liberal tolerance. No organized anti-immigrant movement has appeared as in France, Italy, or Germany. Yet hard questions about the nature and meaning of Irish identity will arise when net immigration, rather than natural increase, becomes the main source of population growth, as has already happened in Canada and Quebec. The newcomers will adapt easily to Irish laws and political institutions, but what of Irish culture? As they develop political power through the ballot box, for how long will they accept the compulsory teaching of the Irish language in school? How deeply will they care about Wolfe Tone or Patrick Pearse? Will their children play Gaelic football, or will they prefer soccer, which is played in the lands from which their parents came? Will they even speak English with Irish accents? Anxiety over such questions was indicated in June 2004 when the Irish government proposed, and the voters overwhelmingly approved in a referendum, a constitutional amendment depriving children born in Ireland to foreign parents of their automatic right of citizenship. It is interesting, however, that Sinn Fein, which favours an inclusive civic nationalism, opposed the amendment. Sinn Fein and the SDLP both expressed concern that the amendment might be contrary to the Good Friday Agreement, which guarantees Irish citizenship to any child born on the island of Ireland.

As both Ireland and Quebec come to terms with their increasingly ambiguous identities, the fundamental dilemma of modern nationalism is becoming apparent. Ethnocultural nationalism has the emotional power to mobilize people for political purposes and can inspire them to sacrifice their time, their money, and even their life and liberty for the cause of national self-determination. As long as the national group does not have a sovereign state of its own, it can pursue its collective interests without raising awkward questions about territorial boundaries. However, ethnic nationalism is an awkward basis on which to construct a territorial state because the populations of territorial states, with very few exceptions, are unavoidably diverse in ethnicity and culture. If the state is constructed on a basis of ethnocultural nationalism, it can only deal with minorities by marginalizing them, subordinating them, or excluding them. The argument of national self-determination may be turned against it by territorially based minorities such as the aboriginal nations in Quebec or the unionists in Ireland. Immigrant groups usually lack a distinct territorial base and therefore cannot threaten to secede. If the national identity is defined in a way that they find insufficiently inclusive, however, they can make other demands, such as separate schools or official status for their languages, that risk making the ethno-national state ungovernable.

Inclusive civic nationalism may be more conducive to the peace, order, and good government of an established state, as its defenders argue, but it is not conducive to political mobilization. To be sufficiently inclusive to accommodate everyone, the national identity may have to be watered down to a lowest common denominator that fails to generate any enthusiasm or commitment. Precisely because it is so lacking in substantive content, civic nationalism usually lacks the emotional appeal that would lead anyone to die for it or even to sacrifice much disposable income or leisure time on its

behalf. The dramatic decline in the emotional intensity of Quebec nationalism over the last thirty years and the loss of the idealism and enthusiasm that
characterized the Parti québécois in its formative years bear witness to the
problem. So, perhaps, does the growing apathy towards the national question in southern Ireland, which has led some observers to characterize it as a
post-nationalist society.[23] The relatively intense, although non-ethnic,
nationalism of the United States may be an exception to the rule, but it is a
unique phenomenon that cannot be replicated elsewhere. American
nationalism (a term that Americans themselves hardly ever use to describe
it) has an ideological and, to some extent, even a religious character: the
conviction of most Americans that freedom is a divine gift, that their political institutions are uniquely conducive to freedom, and that their country is,
as Abraham Lincoln called it, the last best hope of earth. In its heyday under
Stalin, the Soviet Union may have had, for some of its people, a similar sense
of ideological mission, although old-fashioned Russian ethnic nationalism
was probably just as powerful, or more so, even then. For small nations such
as Ireland and Quebec, however, the dilemma remains: a purely ethnic
nationalism is too exclusive to serve as the basis of a just and stable order, but
a purely civic nationalism, if one can call it that, is too insipid to inspire any
sense of communitarian solidarity.

Will nationalism itself be discarded, as Pierre Trudeau suggested in one
of his more utopian moments, and relegated to history's dustbin along with
the divine right of kings?[24] In the cases of Ireland and Quebec, at least, it
would seem inadvisable to throw out the baby with the bathwater. It would
be regrettable for the nationalism of either Ireland or Quebec to disappear,
for both of these small nations have an appealing quality to those who know
them; both have important cultural, as well as political, achievements to
their credit; and both, although heavily influenced by powerful neighbours,
add a welcome element of diversity to the North Atlantic region of the
world. The world needs more distinct nations to flourish, not fewer, as economic globalization and mass migration continue to erode traditional
boundaries and ways of life. Only the nation-state can inspire the commitment that induces free people to pay taxes for the support of programs and
policies that benefit their neighbours. Nationalism also meets important
human psychological needs for tradition, solidarity, and identity. Although
it is not the only force capable of meeting such needs, it appears to be the
most consistently successful in modern times, with the possible exception of
religion. Who would even care about the Olympic Games or about World
Cup soccer were it not for nationalism?

No one can predict with certainty whether Ireland will be politically
reunited after almost a century of partition or whether Quebec will become

a sovereign state. Whether or not these things occur, both Ireland and Quebec will have to coexist with larger neighbours with which they have been intimately associated for long periods of time and to which many of their own inhabitants will remain emotionally attached to some degree. In any event, it is to be hoped that both Ireland and Quebec will survive as politically and culturally distinct national societies; whatever their political and constitutional arrangements may be. It is to be hoped also that both will continue to strike a middle course between xenophobic intolerance and the mindless glorification of "diversity" for its own sake that has become an official cult in anglophone Canada today.[25] But the future, as always, is hidden from our view.

Notes

CHAPTER ONE

1 Hobsbawm, *Nations and Nationalism since 1780*, 12.
2 Quoted in Ryerson, *French Canada*, 171.
3 McCrone, *The Sociology of Nationalism*, 99–100.
4 A lengthy extract from Renan's lecture, with an English translation, was reprinted as a full-page advertisement in the *Globe and Mail*, 28 October 1995. I have substituted my own translation of the French text for the one provided in the advertisement.
5 Gellner, *Nations and Nationalism*, 7.
6 Anderson, *Imagined Communities*, 15–16.
7 Connor, *Ethnic Nationalism*, xi.
8 Gellner, *Nations and Nationalism*, 1.
9 Smith, *Theories of Nationalism*, 171.
10 Hechter, *Containing Nationalism*, 7–8.
11 Kedourie, *Nationalism*, 9.
12 Connor, *Ethnic Nationalism*, xi.
13 Balthazar, *Bilan du nationalisme au Québec*, 19 (my translation).
14 Smith, *Nationalism and Modernism*, 46.
15 Hastings, *The Construction of Nationhood*, 2–4.
16 Greenfeld, *Nationalism*.
17 Lipset, *The First New Nation*.
18 Anderson, *Imagined Communities*, 49.
19 Hutchinson, *The Dynamics of Cultural Nationalism;* the quotation is from 9.
20 Smith, *Theories of Nationalism*, 158–60.

21 *Irish Times*, 11 November 2004.

22 Smith, *Nationalism and Modernism*, 125–7.

23 Kohn, *The Idea of Nationalism*, 329–34.

24 Connor, *Ethnic Nationalism*, 99.

25 See, for example, the chapters by Dominique Arel and David Miller in Gagnon and Tully, *Multinational Democracies*.

26 Two prominent exceptions may be cited: Keating, *Nations against the State*; See, *First World Nationalisms*.

27 Büthe, "Taking Temporality Seriously."

28 Pierson, "Increasing Returns, Path Dependence, and the Study of Politics."

29 Anderson, *Imagined Communities*, 17–19.

30 S. Dion, "The Dynamic of Secessions."

31 See, for example, *Écrits du Canada français*, particularly the introductory article by Patrick Gormally: "L'étrange parallèle: Québec-Irlande."

32 O'Farrell, "Irish Families in Ancient Quebec Records." The article is a reprint of a lecture given in Montreal in 1872.

33 Ferron, *Le salut de l'Irlande*.

34 Moore, *The Revolution Script*.

35 See its pamphlet *Pour mieux comprendre le drame irlandais*.

36 Comité Québec-Irlande, *Bernadette Devlin à Montreal*.

CHAPTER TWO

1 Golway, *For the Cause of Liberty*, 9–10.

2 Connolly, *The Oxford Companion to Irish History*, 330.

3 Macmillan, *State, Society and Authority in Ireland*, 27.

4 Beckett, *The Making of Modern Ireland, 1603–1923*, 14.

5 Ibid., 16–17.

6 Golway, *For the Cause of Liberty*, 13.

7 Connolly, *The Oxford Companion to Irish History*, 457–8.

8 Moody et al., *A New History of Ireland*, 3: 103–7.

9 G.A. Hayes-McCoy in ibid., 135.

10 Foster, *Modern Ireland*, 59–78, provides a useful description of the plantation of Ulster.

11 Tanner, *Ireland's Holy Wars*, 10.

12 Beckett, *The Making of Modern Ireland*, 1603–1923, 48–9.

13 Foster, *Modern Ireland*, 115.

14 Connolly, *The Oxford Companion to Irish History*, 323.

15 Foster, *Modern Ireland*, 85, gives the figure of two thousand, but some estimates are higher.

16 Connolly, *The Oxford Companion to Irish History*, 158.

17 Beckett, *The Making of Modern Ireland, 1603–1923*, 109.

18 Foster, *Modern Ireland*, 103.

19 Ibid., 115–16.
20 Estimate taken from Miquelon, *The First Canada: to 1791*, 79.
21 Vaughan and Fitzpatrick, *Irish Historical Statistics*, 1–2, gives rough estimates as far back as 1672.
22 Miquelon, *The First Canada: to 1791*, 57–9.
23 Bouchard, *Genèse des nations et cultures du Nouveau Monde*, 85.
24 A useful account of the hostilities that followed, on which the next four paragraphs are largely based, is Eccles, *France in America*, 178–208.
25 Ibid., 188–9.
26 The text of the treaty is reproduced in Kennedy, *Documents on the Canadian Constitution, 1759–1915*, 14–18.
27 Chinneide, "The Gaelic Contribution to Irish Nationalism."
28 There is a vast literature on this controversy. A useful introduction to the debate is Boyce and O'Day, *The Making of Modern Irish History*, especially the introductory chapter.
29 The two principal interpretations are discussed in Rudin, *Making History in Twentieth Century Quebec*, 93–128 and 129–70.
30 Maurice Séguin provides a succinct expression of this view in his *L'idée d'indépendance au Québec*, 10–13.
31 Ouellet, *Economic and Social History of Quebec, 1760–1850*, is perhaps the best-known example of this interpretation. See particularly the preface to the English edition, xi–xiv.
32 Foster, *Modern Ireland*, 14.
33 Ibid., 77.
34 Beckett, *The Making of Modern Ireland, 1603–1923*, 47–8.
35 Moody et al., *A New History of Ireland*, 3: 223.
36 Ibid.
37 Ibid., 196–206.
38 Elliott, *The Catholics of Ulster*, cites this figure at 101, although she says most of them perished from exposure to the elements rather than being deliberately killed. Foster, *Modern Ireland*, 85, gives a "speculative" estimate of 2,000 deaths.
39 Foster, *Modern Ireland*, 115.
40 J.G. Simms in Moody et al., *A New History of Ireland*, 3: 487.
41 Foster, *Modern Ireland*, 14.
42 Beckett, *The Making of Modern Ireland, 1603–1923*, 161.
43 Foster, *Modern Ireland*, 157.
44 Ouellet, *Economic and Social History of Quebec, 1760–1850*, 149.
45 *Parliamentary History* 17 (1771–74): 1368.
46 Rudin, *The Forgotten Quebecers*, 28. Ouellet, *Economic and Social History of Quebec, 1760–1850*, discusses the widely varying contemporary estimates at 149–50.
47 Rudin, *The Forgotten Quebecers*, 28.
48 Séguin, *La "nation canadienne" et l'agriculture (1760–1850)*, 202–3.

49 Colley, *Britons: Forging the Nation, 1707–1837*.

50 Boyce, *Nationalism in Ireland*, 54–6.

51 Golway, *For the Cause of Liberty*, 39. This author estimates the Presbyterians at 15 per cent of the population and the Church of Ireland at 10 per cent in the eighteenth century, but other sources suggest they were about equal in numbers.

52 Beckett, *The Making of Modern Ireland, 1603–1923*, 150–2; Tanner, *Ireland's Holy Wars*, 161–2.

53 Connolly, *The Oxford Companion to Irish History*, 438, provides a useful summary of the Penal Laws.

54 Foster, *Modern Ireland*, 154.

55 Connolly, *The Oxford Companion to Irish History*, 438.

56 O'Farrell, *Ireland's English Question*, 51–2.

57 Connolly, *The Oxford Companion to Irish History*, 544–5.

58 Ibid., 543.

59 Beckett, *The Making of Modern Ireland, 1603–1923*, 156–7; Foster, *Modern Ireland*, 161–3.

60 Foster, *Modern Ireland*, discusses "the Ascendancy mind" at 167–94.

61 Ibid., 30. Leinster, one of the four traditional provinces of Ireland, includes Dublin and twelve counties, an area somewhat larger than the Pale.

62 Quoted in Crowley, *The Politics of Language in Ireland, 1366–1922*, 60.

63 Hyde, *A Literary History of Ireland*, 622.

64 Foster, *Modern Ireland*, 222–5.

65 Guindon, "The Crown, the Catholic Church, and the French-Canadian People: The Historical Roots of Quebec Nationalism," in his *Quebec Society*, 94–111.

66 Burt, *The Old Province of Quebec*, 124–6.

67 The text of the royal proclamation is in Kennedy, *Documents on the Canadian Constitution, 1759–1915*, 18–21.

68 Neatby, *Quebec*, 25.

69 Burt, *The Old Province of Quebec*, 81–3.

70 Lemieux, *Histoire du catholicisme québécois*, 2, tome 1: 18–26.

71 Ibid., 48–9.

72 Ibid., 26–7.

73 Lawson, *The Imperial Challenge*, 75–6.

74 Neatby, *The Quebec Act*, 15.

75 Ibid., 23–4.

76 Burt, *The Old Province of Quebec*, 153–4.

77 Wade, *The French Canadians, 1760–1945*, 35.

78 Séguin, *La "nation canadienne" et l'agriculture (1760–1850)*, 151–2.

79 Burt, *The Old Province of Quebec*, 42, 90.

80 Lawson, *The Imperial Challenge*, 108.

81 The text is reproduced in Kennedy, *Documents on the Canadian Constitution, 1759–1915*, 132–6.

82 *Parliamentary History* 17 (1771–74): 1358–9, 1389–90, 1391, 1402.
83 Ibid., 1363, 1400.
84 *Parliamentary History* 19 (1777–78): 1127–30.
85 Connolly, *The Oxford Companion to Irish History*, 77–8.
86 The text appears in Lamonde and Corbo, *Le rouge et le bleu*, 42–3.
87 Lanctôt, *Canada and the American Revolution, 1774–1783*, 62–75.
88 Ibid., 91, 116.
89 Lemieux, *Histoire du catholicisme québécois*, 2, tome 1: 32.
90 Wade, *The French Canadians, 1760–1945*, 73.
91 Lanctôt, *Canada and the American Revolution, 1774–1783*, 175, 187–9.
92 The text of the Constitutional Act is in Kennedy, *Documents on the Canadian Constitution, 1759–1915*, 207–20.
93 Ouellet, *Lower Canada, 1791–1840*, 22.
94 Wade, *The French Canadians, 1760–1945*, 94–6.
95 *Parliamentary History* 29 (1791–92): 105–13.
96 Ibid., 655–8.
97 Foster, *Modern Ireland*, 260.
98 Beckett, *The Making of Modern Ireland, 1603–1923*, 207.
99 Connolly, *The Oxford Companion to Irish History*, 581.
100 Beckett, *The Making of Modern Ireland, 1603–1923*, 217–18.
101 Ward, *The Irish Constitutional Tradition*, 22.
102 Kee, *The Green Flag*, 32–4.
103 "Grattan's parliament" is discussed in Foster, *Modern Ireland*, 251–5, and more briefly in Golway, *For the Cause of Liberty*, 53–5.
104 Connolly, *The Oxford Companion to Irish History*, 78.
105 Quoted in Wade, *The French Canadians, 1760–1945*, 56.

CHAPTER THREE

1 Connell, "The Population of Ireland in the Eighteenth Century." Connell estimates the population in 1791 as 4,753,000, but notes that contemporary estimates were considerably lower.
2 Ó Gráda, *Ireland*, 29–32.
3 *Parliamentary History*, 34 (1798–1800): 237.
4 Beckett, in *The Making of Modern Ireland, 1603–1923*, 181, suggests that only Ulster had a significant middle class and that it was almost exclusively Protestant. However, he concedes at 196 that a Catholic middle class was beginning to develop. Foster, in *Modern Ireland*, 204–5, asserts that there was a significant Catholic urban middle class in Ireland as a whole.
5 S.J. Connolly, "Eighteenth Century Ireland," in Boyce and O'Day, *The Making of Modern Irish History*, 15–33.
6 Pakenham, *The Year of Liberty*, 137–8.
7 Golway, *For the Cause of Liberty*, 90.

8 Bouchard, *Genèse des nations et cultures du Nouveau Monde*, 97.

9 Population estimates are based on the graph in Ouellet, *Economic and Social History of Quebec, 1760–1850*, 659.

10 Ouellet, *Lower Canada, 1791–1840*, 24–6.

11 G. Bernier and D. Salée, "Les Patriotes, la question nationale et les rébellions de 1837–1838 au Bas-Canada," in Sarra-Bournet, *Les nationalismes au Québec du XIXe au XXIe siècle*, 25–36.

12 Ouellet, *Economic and Social History of Quebec, 1760–1850*, 339.

13 Séguin, *La "nation canadienne" et l'agriculture (1760–1850)*, 80.

14 Ouellet, *Lower Canada, 1791–1840*, 279–80.

15 Greer, *The Patriots and the People*, 50.

16 O'Connell, "The American Revolution and Ireland."

17 Woods, "Ireland and the French Revolution."

18 Tillyard, *Citizen Lord*, 131.

19 Elliott, *Partners in Revolution*, xv.

20 Knox, *Rebels and Informers*, 120–3.

21 Golway, *For the Cause of Liberty*, 66.

22 Tillyard, *Citizen Lord*, 32, 77–9, 102.

23 Ibid., 178.

24 Tone, *The Autobiography*, 36.

25 Ibid., 36–7.

26 Elliott, *Partners in Revolution*, 38–9.

27 Knox, *Rebels and Informers*, 9.

28 Syndergaard, "The Fitzwilliam Crisis and Irish Nationalism."

29 Golway, *For the Cause of Liberty*, 65.

30 Connolly, *The Oxford Companion to Irish History*, 601.

31 Greenwood, *Legacies of Fear*.

32 This estimate and the one in the next paragraph are from Rudin, *The Forgotten Quebecers*, 28.

33 Wade, *The French Canadians, 1760–1945*, 94. In Ireland only three counties endured this treatment at the hands of the English: Offaly, Laois, and Derry.

34 Ouellet, *Lower Canada, 1791–1840*, 64, 69.

35 Ibid., 61–2.

36 Lemieux, *Histoire du Catholicisme québécois*, 2, tome 1: 42.

37 Ibid., 48–9.

38 Filteau, *Histoire des Patriotes*, 101.

39 Ibid., 144.

40 A complete translation may be found in Kennedy, *Documents of the Canadian Constitution, 1759–1915*, 366–87.

41 Rumilly, *Histoire de la Societé Saint-Jean-Baptiste de Montréal*, 16–17.

42 *Parliamentary Debates*, 3rd series, 36: 1324.

43 Creighton, *The Empire of the St. Lawrence*, 297–8.

44 Smith, *Theories of Nationalism*, 158–60.

45 Knox, *Rebels and Informers*, 79–81, 184–7.

46 Tone, *The Autobiography*, 86–8.

47 Elliott, *Partners in Revolution*, 53–7.

48 Knox, *Rebels and Informers*, 235–41.

49 L.G. Harvey, "La Révolution américaine et les Patriotes, 1830–1837," in Sarra-Bournet, *Les nationalismes au Québec du XXIe au XXIe siècle*, 15–24.

50 Filteau, *Histoire des Patriotes*, 125.

51 Library and Archives Canada, Papineau family papers, MG 24, B2, vol. 2, 2134–46, handwritten petition dated 15 March 1836.

52 Filteau, *Histoire des Patriotes*, 211.

53 Foster, *Modern Ireland*, 275–7.

54 Gahan, *Rebellion!* 8 (map).

55 Pakenham, *The Year of Liberty*, 131.

56 Gahan, *Rebellion!* 97–103.

57 Pakenham, *The Year of Liberty*, 171–3, 183, 217, 226.

58 Gahan, *Rebellion!* 110–24.

59 Ibid., 124–6.

60 Ouellet, *Lower Canada, 1791–1840*, 285–93.

61 Ryerson, *Unequal Union*, 56–7.

62 Greer, *The Patriots and the People*, 226. Ouellet, *Lower Canada, 1791–1840*, estimates the crowd at 4,000.

63 The text appears in Lamonde and Corbo, *Le rouge et le bleu*, 109–16.

64 Library and Archives Canada, "Les événements de 1837 et 1838," MG 8, A25, reel M-8266, item no. 4025.

65 Creighton, "The Economic Background of the Rebellions of 1837," in his *Towards the Discovery of Canada*, 103–21, at 120.

66 The remarkable extent and significance of British support for the Americans is discussed in Phillips, *The Cousins' Wars*, 233–68. Phillips emphasizes the continuity between the English resistance to the Stuarts in the seventeenth century and the American struggle in the eighteenth.

67 The quotation is from a dispatch written by Lord Durham on 8 August 1838 and printed in Canada, Public Archives, *Report ... for the Year 1923*, 318.

68 See Tone's comments in *The Autobiography*, 55, 63–4, 215–16, 255–6, 264–5.

69 Fernand Ouellet, "Papineau, Louis-Joseph," in *Dictionary of Canadian Biography*, 10: 564–78, at 571.

70 Filteau, *Histoire des Patriotes*, 327, 336, 362.

71 Pakenham, *The Year of Liberty*, 125, 147.

72 Lemieux, *Histoire du Catholicisme québécois*, 2, tome 1: 384–9.

73 Library and Archives Canada, "Les événements de 1837 et 1838," MG 8, A25, reel M-8264, item no. 101.

74 Pakenham, *The Year of Liberty*, 224.

75 Clark, *Movements of Political Protest in Canada, 1640–1840*, 324–6, 456.

76 This is not to say that all rural protest movements become violent. For a possible explanation of why some rural-based nationalist movements are more violent than others, see Laitin, "National Revivals and Violence." Laitin's theory is discussed in chapter 10 of the present work.

77 Nairn, *Faces of Nationalism*, 91.

78 Knox, *Rebels and Informers*, 114–15.

79 Greer, *The Patriots and the People*, 239–57.

80 Ibid., 168–88.

81 Pakenham, *The Year of Liberty*, 342.

82 *Parliamentary History* 33 (1797–98): 1516–23.

83 National Library of Ireland, Wolfe Tone papers: MS 36094/3 contains the correspondence; Tone's request to be shot by a firing squad is in MS 36094/4.

84 Library and Archives Canada, LaFontaine papers, MG 24, B14, vol. 24, folder 62 (copy of ordinance listing the names). Both Ouellet, *Lower Canada, 1791–1840*, and Ryerson, *Unequal Union*, erroneously give the number of death sentences as twelve.

85 Ryerson, *Unequal Union*, 80–1.

86 The text of the Union Act is in Kennedy, *Documents of the Canadian Constitution, 1759–1915*, 536–50.

87 *Parliamentary History* 34 (1798–1800): 254–89.

88 Geoghegan, *The Irish Act of Union*, 87.

89 Ibid., 163–9, 189.

90 *Parliamentary Debates*, 3rd series, 40: 7–42, 65–80.

91 Ibid., 223–9.

92 Filteau, *Histoire des Patriotes*, 294.

93 *Parliamentary Debates*, 3rd series, 54: 748–50.

94 Collins, *Who Fears to Speak of '98?* 9–10, 17–24.

95 Costigan, "Romantic Nationalism."

96 Collins, *Who Fears to Speak of '98?* 54.

97 O'Keefe, "The 1898 Efforts to Celebrate the United Irishmen."

98 O'Keefe, "Who Fears to Speak of '98?"

99 O'Keefe, "The 1898 Efforts to Celebrate the United Irishmen," 73.

100 Elliott, *Wolfe Tone*, 415–16.

101 Collins, *Who Fears to Speak of '98?* 57–65.

102 Shaw, "The Canon of Irish History," 129.

103 Foster, "Remembering 1798," in his *The Irish Story*, 211–34.

104 Dáil Éireann, *Debates*, 489: 1439–40 (3 July 1998).

105 Rumilly, *Histoire de la Société Saint-Jean-Baptiste de Montréal*, 78–9.

106 Groulx, "Louis-Joseph Papineau," in his *Notre maître, le passé*, 189–211, at 207.

107 Filteau, *Histoire des Patriotes*, 120–2.

108 Canada, *House of Commons Debates*, session 1938, 115 (2 February 1938).

109 Parti québécois, "La lettre du parti," 28 November 2002.

110 *Globe and Mail*, 19 May 2003.

CHAPTER FOUR

1 Foster, *Modern Ireland*, 283.
2 Beckett, *The Making of Modern Ireland, 1603–1923*, 280–1.
3 Foster, *Modern Ireland*, 291.
4 Brian Girvin, "Making Nations: O'Connell, Religion, and the Creation of Political Identity," in O'Connell, *Daniel O'Connell*, 13–34, at 25.
5 Boyce, *Nationalism in Ireland*, 132.
6 Beckett, *The Making of Modern Ireland, 1603–1923*, 287–8.
7 Durham, *The Report*, 48.
8 Ibid., 17.
9 Ibid., 221–2.
10 Martin, *Britain and the Origins of Canadian Confederation, 1837–67*, 48.
11 Hoppen, *Elections, Politics and Society in Ireland, 1832–1885*, 103.
12 Woodham-Smith, *The Great Hunger*, 36.
13 Agrarian violence in this period is described in Foster, *Modern Ireland*, 292–4, and in Connolly, *The Oxford Companion to Irish History*, 5–6.
14 Vaughan and Fitzpatrick, *Irish Historical Statistics*, 259–61.
15 Ó Gráda, *Ireland*, 348.
16 Foster, *Modern Ireland*, 321, 342.
17 Useful accounts are Woodham-Smith, *The Great Hunger*, and Donnelly, *The Great Irish Potato Famine*.
18 Woodham-Smith, *The Great Hunger*, 296.
19 Donnelly, *The Great Irish Potato Famine*, 171.
20 Vaughan and Fitzpatrick, *Irish Historical Statistics*, 15–16.
21 Woodham-Smith, *The Great Hunger*, 407.
22 Quoted in Wade, *The French Canadians, 1760–1945*, 257.
23 Séguin, *La "nation canadienne" et l'agriculture (1760–1850)*, 162.
24 Ibid., 155–6, 164–6.
25 Ibid., 239.
26 Étienne Parent, "The Importance of Studying Political Economy," in Forbes, *Canadian Political Thought*, 43–55.
27 Linteau et al., *Histoire du Québec contemporain*, 1:151.
28 The quotation is from Thornley's historical introduction to Chubb, *The Government and Politics of Ireland*, 18.
29 Garvin, *The Evolution of Irish Nationalist Politics*, 46.
30 O'Ferrall, *Daniel O'Connell*, 30–9.
31 Ibid., 7.
32 *Parliamentary Debates*, 2nd series, 20: 727–80.
33 *Parliamentary Debates*, 2nd series, 21: 47.
34 Beckett, *The Making of Modern Ireland, 1603–1923*, 301.
35 National Library of Ireland, Daniel O'Connell papers, ms. 17721.
36 Macintyre, *The Liberator*, 74.

37 *Parliamentary Debates*, 3rd series, 23: 271–86.

38 Cahill, "Irish Catholicism and English Toryism."

39 Macintyre, *The Liberator*, 157.

40 Ibid., 211–25.

41 Ibid., 127–8.

42 Gallagher, "Socialism and the Nationalist Tradition in Ireland, 1798–1918," 71.

43 Cahill, "Some Nineteenth-Century Roots of the Ulster Problem, 1829–1848."

44 Cleland, *History of the Presbyterian Church in Ireland*, 228, 248.

45 O'Ferrall, *Daniel O'Connell*, 86–7.

46 McBride, *Scripture Politics*, 215.

47 Tanner, *Ireland's Holy Wars*, 200–2.

48 Garvin, "O'Connell and the Making of Irish Political Culture," in O'Connell, *Daniel O'Connell*, 7–12.

49 A list of meetings with the estimated attendance at each appears in O'Day and Stevenson, *Irish Historical Documents since 1800*, 61. The source of the estimates is not given.

50 Cahill, "Some Eighteenth-Century Roots of the Ulster Problem, 1829–1848," 71–5.

51 Cronin, "'The Country Did Not Turn Out.'"

52 The contrast between the two kinds of nationalism is discussed in Costigan, "Romantic Nationalism."

53 Beckett, *The Making of Modern Ireland, 1603–1923*, 333.

54 Hutchinson, *The Dynamics of Cultural Nationalism*, 97.

55 Thomas O. Davis, "Our National Language" in his *Literary and Historical Essays*, 173–82. The collection, first published in 1846, is a selection of Davis's writings in the *Nation*.

56 "Memorials of Wexford" in Davis, *Literary and Historical Essays*, 104–7.

57 "Influences of Education" in Davis, *Literary and Historical Essays*, 246–52.

58 National Library of Ireland, Daniel O'Connell papers, ms. 22480, original draft of letter from O'Connell to the Repeal Association, 8 November 1844.

59 Lalor, *Collected Writings*.

60 John Mitchel, "Letter to the Protestant Farmers, Labourers and Artisans of Northern Ireland," in *Writings of John Mitchel*, 18–24.

61 Quoted in Gwynn, *Young Ireland and 1848*, 76.

62 Vaughan and Fitzpatrick, *Irish Historical Statistics*, 260.

63 This aspect of Mitchel's thought is unconvincingly defended by Arthur Griffith, the founder of Sinn Fein, in his preface to Mitchel, *Jail Journal*, xiv.

64 Tanner, *Ireland's Holy Wars*, 119.

65 Hoppen, *Elections, Politics and Society in Ireland, 1832–1885*. 17–8.

66 Kelly, *La petite loterie*, 181–5.

67 Balthazar, *Bilan du nationalisme au Québec*, 73.

68 The evolution of Parent's thought is examined by J.Y. Theriault in his "Étienne Parent: Les deux nations et la fin de l'histoire," in Sarra-Bournet, *Les nationalismes au Québec du XIXe au XXIe siècle*, 37–56.

69 Wade, *The French Canadians, 1760–1945*, 285.

70 Ibid., 288–9.

71 Quoted in Theriault, "Étienne Parent: Les deux nations et la fin de l'histoire," in Sarra-Bournet, *Les nationalismes au Québec du XIXe au XXIe siècle*, 50.

72 Rumilly, *Histoire de la Societé Saint-Jean-Baptiste de Montréal*, 47–8, 51–3.

73 National Archives of Canada, LaFontaine papers, MG 24, B14, microfilm reel M-860, LaFontaine to Gosford, 19 November and 4 December 1837.

74 Ibid., vol. 24, folder 62.

75 Quoted in Wade, *The French Canadians, 1760–1945*, 256.

76 An excerpt from the speech appears in Bélanger et al., *Les grands débats parlementaires, 1792–1992*, 57.

77 The text of the act that made French an official language is in Kennedy, *Documents of the Canadian Constitution, 1759–1815*, 591–2.

78 Parliamentary Debates, 3rd series, 100: 509–10.

79 Monet, *The Last Cannon Shot*, 119, 363–7.

80 Bernard, *Les rouges*, 53, 61.

81 Excerpts from both speeches are in Bélanger et al., *Les grands débats parlementaires, 1792–1992*, 15–17. LaFontaine's entire speech is in Lamonde and Corbo, *Le rouge et le bleu*, 154–65.

82 Larkin, "The Devotional Revolution in Ireland, 1850–75." The figure for 1981 is from Inglis, *Moral Monopoly*, 46.

83 Hamelin, "Évolution numérique séculaire du clergé catholique dans le Québec," table at 225.

84 Tanner, *Ireland's Holy Wars*, 239–40.

85 Akenson, *Small Differences*, 119–22.

86 Durham, *The Report*, 96.

87 Foster, *Modern Ireland*, 342.

88 Macintyre, *The Liberator*, 111.

CHAPTER FIVE

1 Vaughan and Fitzpatrick, *Irish Historical Statistics*, 259–65.

2 Quoted in Mansergh, *The Irish Question, 1840–1921*, 316.

3 Hechter, *Internal Colonialism*.

4 Vaughan and Fitzpatrick, *Irish Historical Statistics*, 27.

5 Ibid., 5–17.

6 Beckett, *The Making of Modern Ireland, 1603–1923*, 363.

7 Ó Gráda, *Ireland*, 242.

8 Foster, *Modern Ireland*, 375.

9 Lee, *The Modernisation of Irish Society*, 1848–1918, 13.

10 Hoppen, *Elections, Politics and Society in Ireland, 1832–1885, 457.*

11 Hutchinson, *The Dynamics of Cultural Nationalism,* 260.

12 Boyce, *The Irish Question and British Politics, 1868–1996,* 6.

13 *Hansard's Parliamentary Debates,* 3rd series, 194: 414.

14 Linteau et al., *Histoire du Québec contemporain,* 1:42.

15 Ibid., 143.

16 Ibid., 151.

17 Stevenson, *Ex Uno Plures,* 27.

18 Bouchard, *Genèse des nations et cultures du Nouveau Monde,* 142.

19 Joy, *Languages in Conflict,* 28.

20 Vaughan and Fitzpatrick, *Irish Historical Statistics,* 260.

21 "Message from the Supreme Council of the Irish Republic to the Irish People," reprinted in *Irish Historical Studies* 19, no. 75 (March 1975), 299–302.

22 O'Day and Stevenson, *Irish Historical Documents since 1800,* 76–7.

23 Ibid., 74.

24 Comerford, "Patriotism as Pastime."

25 Golway, *For the Cause of Liberty,* 134.

26 Davitt, *Speech Delivered … in Defence of the Land League,* 55.

27 McCartney, "The Church and Fenianism."

28 Rafferty, "The Catholic Bishops and Revolutionary Violence in Ireland."

29 Golway, *For the Cause of Liberty,* 147.

30 Martin, *Britain and the Origins of Canadian Confederation, 1837–67,* 48–9.

31 The text of the measure is in Kennedy, *Documents of the Canadian Constitution, 1759–1915,* 592–4.

32 *Hansard's Parliamentary Debates,* 3rd series, 134: 159–65, and 135: 1319–26.

33 Martin, *Britain and the Origins of Canadian Confederation, 1837–67,* 81–116, discusses the origins and growth of British interest in this project.

34 Cartier's major speech on the subject is in *Parliamentary Debates on the Subject of the Confederation of the British North American Provinces,* 53–62.

35 Dorion's major speech in reply to Cartier's arguments is in ibid., 245–69.

36 Bernard, *Les rouges,* 265. Some English-speaking members represented French electorates and vice versa.

37 Bellevance, *Le Québec et la Confédération,* 76–80.

38 Martin, *Britain and the Origins of Canadian Confederation, 1837–67,* 173–81.

39 Ibid., 163–5.

40 Saywell, "Backstage at London, 1864–1867."

41 *Hansard's Parliamentary Debates,* 3rd series, 185: 579.

42 La Forest, *Disallowance and Reservation of Provincial Legislation,* appendix A.

43 O'Farrell, *Ireland's English Question,* 208.

44 Mansergh, *The Irish Question, 1840–1921,* 123.

45 Bull, *Land, Politics and Nationalism,* 43.

46 For a revisionist interpretation, see Solow, *The Land Question and the Irish Economy, 1870–1903.*

47 Bull, *Land, Politics and Nationalism*, 49–52.
48 Christianson, "Landlords and Land Tenure in Ireland, 1790–1830."
49 O'Neill, "The Irish Land Question, 1830–1850."
50 Ibid.
51 Table showing the growing percentage of large farms in Foster, *Modern Ireland*, 336.
52 O'Neill, "The Irish Land Question, 1830–1850," 335.
53 All the land acts are listed and summarized in Bull, *Land, Politics and Nationalism*, 193–207.
54 Hoppen, *Elections, Politics and Society in Ireland, 1832–1885*, 369–78.
55 A useful brief biography is Bew, *Charles Stewart Parnell.*
56 Golway, *For the Cause of Liberty*, 163.
57 Hoppen, *Elections, Politics and Society in Ireland, 1832–1885*, table on 480.
58 O'Farrell, *Ireland's English Question*, 176–8.
59 See the contrasting views of O'Farrell, *Ireland's English Question*, 170–1, and Lee, *The Modernisation of Irish Society, 1848–1918*, 97.
60 A table showing the number of incidents by year appears in O'Day and Stevenson, *Irish Historical Documents since 1800*, 74.
61 Bull, *Land, Politics and Nationalism*, 108–9.
62 Tanner, *Ireland's Holy Wars*, 257–8.
63 Anon., "Resolutions of the Irish Bishops on the Irish Land Question."
64 Garvin, *The Evolution of Irish Nationalist Politics*, 58.
65 O'Farrell, *Ireland's English Question*, 161–2.
66 O'Day, *Irish home rule*, 1867–1921, 43.
67 *Hansard's Parliamentary Debates*, 3rd series, 220: 700–17.
68 The roll call appears in ibid., 966–9.
69 O'Farrell, *Ireland's English Question*, 167.
70 *Hansard's Parliamentary Debates*, 3rd series, 261: 896.
71 The relevant paragraph of the speech is in O'Day and Stevenson, *Irish Historical Documents since 1800*, 105
72 *Hansard's Parliamentary Debates*, 3rd series, 261: 897.
73 *Parliamentary Debates*, 4th series, 11: 242–3.
74 O'Day, *Irish Home Rule, 1867–1921*, 93.
75 Ibid., 106.
76 O'Brien, *Parnell and His Party, 1880–90*, 184.
77 Ward, *The Irish Constitutional Tradition*, 61. The document itself is reproduced in O'Day, *Irish Home Rule, 1867–1921*, 317–19.
78 The portion of the bill defining the legislative powers of the Irish body is reproduced in O'Day, *Irish Home Rule, 1867–1921*, 319–20.
79 Rumilly, *Histoire de la Societé Saint-Jean-Baptiste de Montréal*, 143.
80 Quebec, Legislative Assembly, *Débats*, 1886, 355–411.
81 *Hansard's Parliamentary Debates*, 3rd series, 304: 1046, 1047, 1057, 1058.
82 Ibid., 1124–34.
83 Ibid., 1194, 1199, 1200.

84 Ibid., 1327–9, 1333.
85 Quoted in Buckland, *Ulster Unionism and the Origins of Northern Ireland, 1886 to 1922*, 10.
86 Dicey, *England's Case against Home Rule*, 287.
87 *Hansard's Parliamentary Debates*, 3rd series, 306: 1174–5, 1176–8, 1179–80.
88 The roll call is in ibid., 1240–5.
89 Magnus, *Gladstone*, 385–94.
90 Banks, *Edward Blake, Irish Nationalist*, 44–52.
91 The most significant portions of the bill are reproduced in O'Day, *Irish Home Rule, 1867–1921*, 322–4.
92 *Parliamentary Debates*, 4th series, 8: 1247.
93 Ibid., 10: 1603, 1619–20.
94 Ibid., 414, 415, 417–18, 418–19, 420–2, 422–3.
95 O'Brien, *Parnell and His Party, 1880–90*, 349.
96 The Midlothian speech is quoted in Magnus, *Gladstone*, 262.
97 A fairly detailed account of Quebec's relations with the federal government in the early years may be found in Stevenson, *Ex Uno Plures*, 77–105.
98 Ibid., 268.
99 Loranger, *Letters upon the Interpretation of the Federal Constitution known as the B.N.A. Act*.
100 Rumilly, *Honoré Mercier et son temps*, 1: 217.
101 Cox, "The Quebec Provincial General Election of 1886."
102 Library and Archives Canada, Macdonald papers; MG 26, A, vol. 527, Macdonald to Masson, 8 December 1886.
103 Stevenson, *Ex Uno Plures*, describes these measures in greater detail at 100–5.
104 Rumilly, *Honoré Mercier et son temps*, 2: 359–71.
105 Quoted in O'Day, *Irish Home Rule, 1867–1921*, 174.
106 Hutchinson, *The Dynamics of Cultural Nationalism*, 8–47.
107 Hyde, *A Literary History of Ireland*, 630.
108 McNeill, "Why and How the Irish Language Is to Be Preserved," 1104.
109 Silver, *The French Canadian Idea of Confederation, 1864–1900*, 55–6, 125–30.
110 Ibid., 219.
111 Ibid., 171, 179, 187.
112 Heintzman, "The Political Culture of Quebec, 1840–1960."

CHAPTER SIX

1 The main terms of these measures are summarized in Bull, *Land, Politics and Nationalism*, 199–200.
2 This phenomenon is discussed in Peseta, *Before the Revolution*, and Garvin, *Nationalist Revolutionaries in Ireland, 1858–1928*, 33–56.

3 McBride, *The Greening of Dublin Castle*, 31–6, 43–7.

4 Linteau et al., *Histoire du Québec contemporain*, 1: 151, 410, 374, 431, 439.

5 Ibid., 423–4.

6 Ibid., 448–9.

7 Gagnon and Hamelin, *Histoire du catholicisme québécois*, 1: 34.

8 Siegfried, *The Race Question in Canada*, 15, 85.

9 O'Keefe, "The 1898 Efforts to Celebrate the United Irishmen."

10 Rudin, *Founding Fathers*, 4.

11 Wade, *The French Canadians, 1760–1945*, 576–7.

12 The birth of the Dollard cult is discussed in Rudin, *Founding Fathers*, 228–30.

13 Ibid., 166.

14 Nelles, *The Art of Nation-Building*, 122–40.

15 National Library of Ireland, ms. 12080 and 12081, minutes of the Irish Parliamentary Party, 17 June 1902 and 21 February 1911.

16 Plunkett, "The Irish Party," 33.

17 The main provisions of the bill are reproduced in O'Day, *Irish Home Rule, 1867–1921*, 322–4.

18 See Laurier's speech on "Political Liberalism," delivered to a not very sympathetic audience of Catholic clergy in 1877, a translation of which appears in Forbes, *Canadian Political Thought*, 134–51.

19 Younger, *Arthur Griffith*, 17, 41–2.

20 *United Irishman 1* (4 March 1899).

21 *Sinn Fein 5* (2 June 1906).

22 *Sinn Fein 131* (7 November 1908).

23 *Sinn Fein 135* (5 December 1908) and 139 (2 January 1909).

24 *Sinn Fein 44* (2 March 1907).

25 Griffith, *The Resurrection of Hungary*, 40.

26 *Sinn Fein 40* (2 February 1907) and 74 (5 October 1907).

27 *United Irishman 56* (24 March 1900).

28 *United Irishman 130* (24 August 1901), 138 (19 October 1901), 271 (7 May 1904).

29 Some information about the IRB in this period may be found in Dillon, "Irish Republican Brotherhood." The author of this article, Geraldine Dillon, is the same person as Geraldine Plunkett, cited in note 16.

30 See the police report of a conversation with an informant in Sligo, 21 November 1907, in Public Record Office, class CO904/23, 73–74 (National Library of Ireland, microfilm P8174).

31 *Irish Freedom 1* (November 1910).

32 *Irish Freedom 2* (December 1910).

33 *Irish Freedom 13* (November 1911), 31 (June 1913).

34 *Sinn Fein 122* (5 September 1908).

35 "The Spiritual Nation" in Pearse, *Political Writings and Speeches*, 299–329, at 305, 326.

36 "Theobald Wolfe Tone," in Pearse, *Political Writings and Speeches*, 53–63, at 54, 56.

37 "The Ulster Situation," in James, *Churchill Speaks*, 263–73, at 269.

38 National Library of Ireland, Redmond Papers, ms. 15204, Redmond to MacNeill, 16 May 1914, MacNeill to Redmond, 23 May 1914.

39 A representative selection of Bourassa's political thought appears in Levitt, *Henri Bourassa on Imperialism and Bi-culturalism.*

40 Bourassa, *Ireland and Canada.*

41 Bourassa, *The Spectre of Annexation and the Real Danger of National Disintegration*, 18.

42 This episode is the subject of Levitt, *Henri Bourassa and the Golden Calf.* The program of the league is printed as an appendix at 147–50.

43 Library and Archives Canada, Lavergne papers, MG 27 II, E12, vol. 1 (microfilm reel H–1756), Bourassa to Lavergne, 12 January 1902. The original reads, "Nous devons necessairement nous entendre sur un terrain commun avec les Canadiens-anglais de bonne volonté, plus nombreux d'ailleurs que vous ne le croyez."

44 Canada, *House of Commons Debates*, 30 June 1905, 8589–90.

45 Wade, *The French Canadians, 1760–1945*, 550.

46 Excerpts from the debate appear in Bélanger et al., *Les grands débats parlementaires, 1792–1992*, 432–6.

47 A lengthy summary appears in Wade, *The French Canadians, 1760–1945*, 621–3.

48 The manifesto is reproduced in Bouthillier and Meynaud, *Le choc des langues au Québec, 1760–1970*, 358–60.

49 Bourassa, *La langue, gardienne de la foi.*

50 *Sinn Fein* 428 (5 September 1914).

51 *Irish Freedom* 47 (September 1914).

52 *Irish Volunteer* 1, no. 27 (8 August 1914), no. 28 (15 August 1914), no. 30 (29 August 1914).

53 "Open Letter to the Irish Volunteers," 24 September 1914, signed by MacNeill and several known members of the IRB, explains the reasons for the split. It can be found in University College Dublin Archives, O'Rahilly papers, P102/344.

54 Connolly, *The Oxford Companion to Irish History*, 196.

55 National Library of Ireland, Redmond papers, ms. 15169 (4), Redmond to Asquith, 15 November 1915.

56 A list of the recruits is in National Library of Ireland, Casement papers, ms. 13085 (6).

57 Casement's diary for March-April 1916, indicating his growing distaste for the Germans, is in National Library of Ireland, McHugh papers, ms. 13740.

58 A copy is in National Library of Ireland, Casement papers, ms. 13085 (5).

59 National Library of Ireland, Hobson papers, ms. 28904, and McCullough Papers, ms. 31653, contain recollections of these events. For another first-hand account, see O'Donoghue, "Plans for the 1916 Rising."

60 Connolly, *The Oxford Companion to Irish History*, 270.

61 MacNeill's reminiscences are in Martin, "Eoin MacNeill on the Rising."

62 This seems to be implication of the entries in Casement's diary for 2 April and 6 April 1916 (National Library of Ireland, McHugh papers, ms. 31740, 39 and 64–5).

63 Two useful full-length studies are Caulfield, *The Easter Rebellion*, and Foy and Barton, *The Easter Rising.*

64 Foy and Barton, *The Easter Rising*, 221.

65 Clarke, *Revolutionary Woman*, 75–6, 94.

66 Yeats, *Collected Works*, 1: 185.

67 Foy and Barton, *The Easter Rising*, 203–8.

68 National Library of Ireland, ms. 12082, Irish Parliamentary Party, minute books, 1910–18, 9 May 1916.

69 Coogan, *Eamon de Valera*, 95–6.

70 Press accounts of this episode are in National Library of Ireland, Martin papers, ms. 32695/1, 24–5 and 76–8.

71 Laffan, *The Resurrection of Ireland*, 166–8.

72 A copy of the pledge is in National Library of Ireland, O'Kelly papers, ms. 8469 (6).

73 For a discussion of these conditions, supported by empirical data, see Fearon and Laitin, "Ethnicity, Insurgency, and Civil War."

74 Information in this paragraph is from Hopkinson, *The Irish War of Independence.*

75 Fitzpatrick, *Politics and Irish Life, 1913–1921,* discusses this process with a focus on County Clare, the most Catholic of Ireland's thirty-two counties.

76 A useful and balanced account of the relevant history is Laffan, *The Partition of Ireland, 1911–1925.* See also Bew, *Ideology and the Irish Question.*

77 Tanner, *Ireland's Holy Wars*, 284, 288.

78 The definitive account of the treaty negotiations is Pakenham, *Peace by Ordeal.* The text of the treaty is in O'Day and Stevenson, *Irish Historical Documents since 1800*, 174–9.

79 National Archives of Ireland, Dáil Éireann, Ministry and Cabinet Minutes, vol. 3, 184 (8 December 1921).

80 Coogan, *Eamon de Valera*, 295.

81 *(Official Report) Debate on the Treaty between Great Britain and Ireland,* 141.

82 Ibid., 221–2.

83 National Archives of Ireland, Dáil Éireann, Ministry and Cabinet Minutes, vol. 3, 168 (25 November 1921).

84 *(Official Report) Debate on the Treaty between Great Britain and Ireland,* 24–5.

85 Ibid., 27.

86 Ibid., 326–7.

87 Ibid., 21–3.

88 National Archives of Ireland, Dáil Éireann, Ministry and Cabinet Minutes, vol. 3, 177 (3 December 1921).

89 Ibid., 32.
90 Ibid., 107.
91 See the message by Winston Churchill to Collins quoted in Costello, *The Irish Revolution and Its Aftermath, 1916–1923*, 299.
92 Ibid., 302.
93 For pro-treaty references to preserving the language, see *(Official Report) Debate on the Treaty between Great Britain and Ireland*, 140, 177, 179, 193, 218, 224, 241, 313.
94 Armstrong, *The Crisis of Quebec, 1914–18*, 81–2.
95 Bélanger et al., *Les grands débats parlementaires, 1792–1992*, 435–6.
96 Armstrong, *The Crisis of Quebec, 1914–18*, 107–8, 114–16.
97 Ibid., 130.
98 Ibid., 166.
99 Wade, *The French Canadians, 1760–1945*, 744.
100 Armstrong, *The Crisis of Quebec, 1914–18*, 181, 189, 194–5.
101 Wade, *The French Canadians, 1760–1945*, 747.
102 Ibid., 751.
103 Excerpts from the debate appear in Bélanger et al., *Les grands débats parlementaires, 1792–1992*, 25–27, from which the quotations in this and the previous paragraph are drawn.
104 Wade, *The French Canadians, 1760–1945*, 764–5.

CHAPTER SEVEN

1 Lee, *Ireland, 1912–1985*, 69, cites this figure but describes it as "possibly exaggerated." There is a surprising absence of precision in all the estimates.
2 Linteau et al., *Histoire du Québec contemporain*, 1: 42.
3 See Faughnan, "The Jesuits and the Drafting of the Irish Constitution of 1937," and Keogh, "The Jesuits and the 1937 Constitution."
4 Jean Gould, "La genèse catholique d'une modernisation bureaucratique," in Kelly, *Les idées mènent le Québec*, 145–74.
5 See, for example, the influential essay by Pierre Elliott Trudeau, "Some Obstacles to Democracy in Quebec," first published in 1958 and reprinted in his *Federalism and the French Canadians*, 103–23.
6 Jacques Beauchemin, "Conservatisme et traditionalisme dans le Québec duplessiste: Aux origines d'une confusion conceptuelle," in Gagnon and Sarra-Bournet, *Duplessis*, 33–54, at 50.
7 Bourque, Duchastel, and Beauchemin, *La société libérale duplessiste, 1944–1960*, 251–309.
8 Lee, *The Modernisation of Irish Society, 1848–1918*.
9 National Archives of Ireland, Dáil Éireann, Ministry and Cabinet Minutes, vol. 4, 125 (10 April 1922).

10 Coakley and Gallagher, *Politics in the Republic of Ireland*, 368 (appendix 2c).

11 Gallagher, "The Pact General Election of 1922."

12 For speculation on this point, see Mackay, *Michael Collins*, 301–3.

13 Electoral data from Coakley and Gallagher, *Politics in the Republic of Ireland*, 367 (appendix 2b).

14 Press release, 17 April 1926, in O'Day and Stevenson, *Irish Historical Documents since 1800*, 187–8.

15 Bell, *The Secret Army*, 65, 79, 81.

16 Ibid., 157–8, 183–6.

17 Ibid., 235.

18 English, *Armed Struggle*, 71.

19 The Blueshirts are described in Regan, *The Irish Counter-Revolution, 1921–1936*, 324–40.

20 Finnegan, "The Blueshirts of Ireland during the 1930s."

21 Garvin, *1922*.

22 Regan, *The Irish Counter-Revolution, 1921–1936*.

23 Kissane, *Explaining Irish Democracy*, 165–94.

24 Prager, *Building Democracy in Ireland*, 194–215.

25 The comparison with Finland appears in Garvin, *1922*, 28; Lee, *Ireland, 1912–1985*, 69; and Litton, *The Irish Civil War*, 132.

26 Clarke, *Revolutionary Woman*, 205.

27 The standard source on this party is Dirks, *The Failure of L'Action libérale nationale*.

28 Quoted in Wade, *The French Canadians, 1760–1945*, 951. The effect of the Second World War on Quebec is described in considerable detail at 916–1101.

29 The standard source on the Bloc is Comeau, *Le Bloc populaire*.

30 Linteau et al., *Histoire du Québec contemporain*, 2: 140–1.

31 Tom Garvin makes this argument for Ireland (and the United States) in *The Evolution of Irish Nationalist Politics*, 5.

32 Wade, *The French Canadians, 1760–1945*, 827.

33 Harkness, *The Restless Dominion*.

34 Ward, *The Irish Constitutional Tradition*, 229.

35 Coakley and Gallagher, *Politics in the Republic of Ireland*, 372 (appendix 2h).

36 Bowman, *De Valera and the Ulster Question, 1917–1973*, 244–6.

37 Lee, *Ireland, 1912–1985*, 299.

38 Dáil Éireann, *Debates*, 113: 410 (24 November 1948).

39 National Library of Ireland, ms. 33047: "Confidential Account by Sir John Wheeler-Bennett of His Interview with President de Valera in October 1959."

40 National Archives of Ireland, Department of the Taoiseach, file 97/6/422, dispatch dated 5 July 1965.

41 Pakenham, *Peace by Ordeal*, 220–2.

42 *Parliamentary Debates*, 149: 40 (14 December 1921).

43 Elliott, *The Catholics of Ulster*, 374–5.

44 National Archives of Ireland, Department of the Taoiseach, file S26, "Views of the man in the street," 25 (25 March 1922).

45 University College Dublin Archives, MacNeill papers, file LA1/F/292.(29 September 1924).

46 Ibid., file LA1/H/110 (no date).

47 See map in Duffy, *The Macmillan Atlas of Irish History*, 117.

48 Dáil Éireann, *Debates*, 13: 1306 (7 December 1925).

49 Ibid., 46: 192 (1 March 1933).

50 "Press Interview on Partition, 13 October 1938," in Moynihan, *Speeches and Statements by Eamon de Valera, 1917–73*.

51 Coogan, *Eamon de Valera*, 638–40.

52 Elliott, *The Catholics of Ulster*, 398.

53 United Kingdom, Statutes, 12–13 George VI, chapter 41.

54 Dáil Éireann, *Debates*, 147: 162 (28 October 1954).

55 Ibid., 209 (28 October 1954).

56 See the speeches by Liam Cosgrave in United Nations, *General Assembly Official Records*, session 11, 576th plenary session (13 November 1956) and 603rd plenary session (30 November 1956).

57 Feeney, *Sinn Fein*, 188–9, 195–6.

58 Ibid., 224–5.

59 Genest, *Godbout*, 253.

60 Oliver, *The Passionate Debate*, 34–5.

61 Ibid., 186–7.

62 Quebec, Ministère des affaires intergouvernementales, *Quebec's Traditional Stands on the Division of Powers, 1900–1976*, 13, 31, 41, 75, 87, 93, 111.

63 Saywell, *The Lawmakers*, 193, 196.

64 York University Archives, Duplessis papers, microfilm reel 3, New Year's Day message by Premier Duplessis, 1 January 1948.

65 Genest, *Godbout*, 158–61, 246–8.

66 York University Archives, Duplessis papers, microfilm reel 1, Duplessis to J.W. McConnell, 18 June 1946. McConnell was the proprietor of the *Montreal Star* and one of the most influential members of the anglophone business elite.

67 Archives nationales du Québec, 85–05–002, Conseil executif, Cabinet du premier ministre, Correspondance de Maurice Duplessis, Duplessis to Mackenzie King, 31 January 1945.

68 Quoted in Rumilly, *Maurice Duplessis et son temps*, 2: 543.

69 Archives nationales du Québec, 85–05–002, Conseil executif, Cabinet du premier ministre, Correspondance de Maurice Duplessis, Duplessis to St. Laurent, 21 September 1949.

70 A useful account is in Black, *Duplessis*, 411–46.

71 Quebec, Statutes, 2–3 Elizabeth II, chapter 17.

72 Parti québécois, *La lettre du parti*, 10 January 2003.

73 *Le Devoir*, 22 January 1948, 12.

74 Regan, *The Irish Counter-Revolution, 1921–1936*, 262.

75 Calculated from trade data in *Statesman's Yearbook*, various years.

76 Lee, *Ireland, 1912–1985*, 211–14.

77 Dáil Éireann, *Debates*, 42: 1233–6. (14 June 1932).

78 Ibid., 53: 1251–8.

79 Horgan, *Sean Lemass*, 91, 112. 116, 146, 156.

80 Oliver, *The Passionate Debate*, is the definitive source on this topic.

81 Collins, *The Path to Freedom*, 117–18.

82 Somerville-Large, *Irish Voices*, 119.

53 Genest, *Godbout*, 263–6.

84 Somerville-Large, *Irish Voices*, 253.

85 Maurice Duplessis's relations with the church are discussed in Black, *Duplessis*, 497–549. De Valera's are discussed in Coogan, *Eamon de Valera*, 647–73. The role of the Catholic Church in Irish politics in this period is discussed in Tanner, *Ireland's Holy Wars*, 294–311, 335–52.

86 York University Archives, Duplessis papers, microfilm reel 1, Villeneuve to Duplessis, 18 January 1946.

87 Lee, *Ireland, 1912–1985*, 313–21.

88 For example, McKee, "Church-State Relations and the Development of Irish Health Policy."

89 O'Callaghan, "Language, Nationality and Cultural Identity in the Irish Free State, 1922–7."

90 Hindley, *The Death of the Irish Language*, 24.

91 Dáil Éireann, *Debates*, 2: 2328 (20 March 1923).

92 Ibid., 65: 448 (17 February 1937).

93 Ibid., 436–41 (17 February 1937).

94 O'Hullachain, *The Irish and Irish*, 86, 92, 88, 96–7, 100.

95 Ibid., 92–3.

96 Dáil Éireann, *Debates*, 99: 1512, 1294, 1507–8 (20 February 1946).

97 Trofimenkoff, *Action française*, 97.

98 Trofimenkoff, ibid., discusses the rise and fall of this organization.

99 Jamieson, "French and English in the Institutional Structure of Montreal," 157–64.

100 Wade, *The French Canadians, 1760–1945*, 996–1009.

101 Quebec, Statutes, 1 George VI, chapter 13, and 2 George VI, chapter 22.

102 LaTerreur, *Les tribulations des conservateurs au Québec*, 172.

103 Monière, *André Laurendeau et le destin d'un peuple*, 117.

104 Oliver, *The Passionate Debate*, 137–45.

105 O'Leary, *Séparatisme*, 107, 85, 174, 89, 122, 101, 113–14.

106 Ibid., 139–41, 131, 135–8, 163, 193, 196, 204–8.

107 Monière, *André Laurendeau et le destin d'un peuple*, is the fullest account of Laurendeau's life. See also Horton, *André Laurendeau*.

108 See, for example, Laurendeau's article "Il faut restaurer le fédéralisme," in *Le Devoir*, 4 May 1951.

109 Louis Balthazar, "André Laurendeau, un artiste du nationalisme," in Comeau and Beaudry, *André Laurendeau*, 169.

CHAPTER EIGHT

1 The relevance of this concept to Northern Ireland is discussed in McGarry and O'Leary, *Explaining Northern Ireland*, 257–8.

2 Linteau et al., *Histoire du Québec contemporain*, 2: 365.

3 Balthazar, *Bilan de nationalisme au Québec*, 120–2.

4 Heintzman, "The Political Culture of Quebec, 1840–1960."

5 Quinn, *The Union nationale*, 137.

6 Laurendeau, "La théorie du roi nègre," *Le Devoir*, 4 July 1958.

7 Behiels, *Prelude to Quebec's Quiet Revolution*.

8 Guindon, "The Social Evolution of Quebec Reconsidered," in his *Quebec Society*, 3–26. This essay, first published in 1960, remains the most brilliant analysis of the background to the Quiet Revolution.

9 Latouche, "La vrai nature de ... la Révolution tranquille."

10 Black, *Duplessis*, 512.

11 Guindon, "The Social Evolution of Quebec Reconsidered," in his *Quebec Society*, 23.

12 Desbiens, *Les insolences du frère Untel.*

13 Stevenson, *Community Besieged*, 32–3, 84–5.

14 Data in this paragraph are from Canada, Royal Commission on Bilingualism and Biculturalism, *Report*, 3: 18, 21, 44, 65–7.

15 Ibid., 54, 56.

16 The indispensable source on Lesage and his government is Thomson, *Jean Lesage and the Quiet Revolution*.

17 See René Lévesque, "Au coeur du probleme: Radio-Canada est une fiction! La réalité s'appelle CBC," *Le Devoir*, 7 March 1959.

18 Archives nationales du Québec, Jean Lesage papers, P688, S3, SS1/3, NO. 232.

19 Quoted in "Point de mire sur René Lévesque" (a series of radio programs broadcast on Radio-Canada in 2002), episode 4. The title of the series is taken from the title of the television program that Lévesque hosted in the late 1950s.

20 For an account of the episode, see Thomson, *Jean Lesage and the Quiet Revolution*, 373–89.

21 Archives nationales du Québec, Jean Lesage papers, P688, S3, SS4, NO. 34, Lesage to Pearson, 20 January 1966.

22 Ibid., ss1/3. The speeches gathered here are a useful source on Lesage's view of Quebec and Canada. See particularly NO. 360 and NO. 372, both delivered to francophone audiences during Lesage's tour of western Canada in 1965.

23 Laurendeau, *The Diary*, 78, 90, 142.

24 Monière, *André Laurendeau et le destin d'un peuple*, 276–7.

25 Balthazar, *Bilan du nationalisme au Québec*, 107.

26 A complete list of the founders appears in Allemagne, *Le RIN et les débuts du mouvement indépendantiste québécois*, 137. This book, whose author was the first president of the RIN, is an indispensable source.

27 Ibid., 52–3.

28 Ibid., 18.

29 Ferron is mentioned in Reid, *The Shouting Signpainters*, 222–3, 247–8. Reid's book is an excellent insider's account of the revolutionary nationalism of the 1960s.

30 Fournier, *flq*, 31.

31 A chronological list of incidents attributed to the FLQ appears in Pelletier, *The October Crisis*, 197–205.

32 Johnson, *Égalité ou indépendance*.

33 See Trudeau's collection of essays *Federalism and the French Canadians*, especially 151–81 and 204–12.

34 Lévesque, *Option Québec*.

35 Roy, *Le choix d'un pays*, 111–21.

36 For Lévesque's views on the RIN, see his memoirs, *Attendez que je me rappelle*, 270–1.

37 Fraser, *PQ*, 41–2.

38 Bosher, *The Gaullist Attack on Canada, 1967–1997*, 38–49.

39 Pierre Duchesne, "Les dossiers secrets de Parizeau," *L'Actualité*, 15 May 2001, 21–4.

40 George Bain, "The Makings of a Crisis," in Rotstein, *Power Corrupted*, 3–14.

41 Pelletier, *The October Crisis*, 242.

42 Fournier, *FLQ*, 275–333.

43 Johnson, *Anglophobie Made in Québec*.

44 Bill 22 is discussed in Stevenson, *Community Besieged*, 114–25.

45 Lee and Ó Tuathaigh, *The Age of de Valera*, 165.

46 Horgan, *Sean Lemass*, 55.

47 Ibid., 174–7.

48 Coakley and Gallagher, *Politics in the Republic of Ireland*, 39.

49 Vaughan and Fitzpatrick, *Irish Historical Statistics*, 266–8.

50 Lemass's record on this issue is discussed in Horgan, *Sean Lemass*, 301–10.

51 National Archives of Ireland, Department of the Taoiseach, General Registered Files, s13180, D/61, typescript of election speech, 20 September 1961.

52 Ibid., D/95, typescript of address to Fianna Fail Ard Fheis, 17 November 1964.

53 Dáil Éireann, *Parliamentary Debates*, 214: 1–5 (10 February 1965).

54 *Irish Times*, 22 January 2003. The newspaper reported that this person, Mr Liam Sutcliffe, admired the "millennium spire" that has been erected on the site of the former Nelson monument.

55 Horgan, *Sean Lemass*, 283–5.

56 "Ireland Commemorates the Rising," *Irish Times*, 11 April 1966. The full text of President de Valera's speech was printed adjacent to this story.

57 Bowman, *De Valera and the Ulster Question, 1917–1973*, 323–5.

58 This seems to be the conclusion of both Inglis, *Moral Monopoly*, and Kenny, *Goodbye to Catholic Ireland*.

59 Vaughan and Fitzpatrick, *Irish Historical Statistics*, 27.

60 Coakley and Gallagher, *Politics in the Republic of Ireland*, 40.

61 On the decline of the Dublin Protestants, see Tanner, *Ireland's Holy Wars*, 418–20.

62 Hennessey, *A History of Northern Ireland, 1920–1996*, 115–16.

63 Moloney, *A Secret History of the IRA*, 45.

64 For an analysis of this trend, see Probert, *Beyond Orange and Green*.

65 Quoted in Hennessy, *A History of Northern Ireland, 1920–1996*, 162.

66 Rose, *Governing without Consensus*, 100–1.

67 Elliott, *The Catholics of Ulster*, 409.

68 English, *Armed Struggle*, 85–92.

69 Rose, *Governing without Consensus*, discusses the American analogy at 462–73.

70 The results of the questionnaire appear as an appendix in ibid., 474–510.

71 Elliott, *The Catholics of Ulster*, 126.

72 Ibid., 450–7.

73 O'Connor, *In Search of a State*, 196.

74 Elliott, *The Catholics of Ulster*, 414–15.

75 Devlin, *The Price of My Soul*, 119. Her admiration for Connolly is expressed at 87–8.

76 Ibid., 204.

77 National Archives of Ireland, Department of Justice files, 2000/36/3, memorandum from minister of justice for government in relation to the IRA, 18 March 1969.

78 Dwyer, *Nice Fellow*, 201–2; Collins, *The Power Game*, 93. However, this interpretation is disputed by Feeney, *Sinn Fein*, 252–3.

79 O'Connor, *In Search of a State*, 126.

80 Ibid., 72.

81 Social Democratic and Labour Party, *Towards a New Ireland*.

82 Moloney, *A Secret History of the IRA*, 86–7.

83 Ibid., 89–92.

84 English, *Armed Struggle*, 139–40.

85 Hennessey, *A History of Northern Ireland, 1920–1996*, 192, 195.

86 Data from McKittrick and McVea, *Making Sense of the Troubles*, 327 (table).

87 Ibid.

88 Hennessey, *A History of Northern Ireland, 1920–1996*, 250.

89 McGarry and O'Leary, *Explaining Northern Ireland*, 86. Their data cover civilian deaths only and are similar, but not precisely identical, to those in Hennessey, *A History of Northern Ireland, 1920–1996*.

90 McKittrick and McVea, *Making Sense of the Troubles*, 327.

91 O'Connor, *In Search of a State*, 160–1.

92 Moloney, *A Secret History of the IRA*, 246.

93 Bowman, *De Valera and the Ulster Question, 1917–1973*, 288.

94 Lee, *Ireland, 1912–1985*, 478.

95 Dwyer, *Nice Fellow, 179–81*, 185–6.

96 Ibid., 197–9.

97 O'Brien, *The Arms Trial*, 96.

98 National Archives of Ireland, Department of the Taoiseach, General Registered Files, 2001/8/15, report of conversation with Fitt, 4 January 1971.

99 Dwyer, *Nice Fellow*, 174.

100 National Archives of Ireland, Department of the Taoiseach, General Registered Files, 2000/6/660, Haughey to Lynch, 25 September 1969.

101 The text of the speech is printed in Lynch, *Speeches and Statements, August 1969-October 1971*, 9–12.

102 Collins, *The Power Game*, 43–4, 67.

103 National Archives of Ireland, Department of the Taoiseach, General Registered Files, 2001/8/1, Whitaker to Lynch, 11 November 1968.

104 Dwyer, *Nice Fellow*, 212.

105 United Nations, *Security Council Official Records*, 1503rd meeting, 20 August 1969.

106 Dáil Éireann, *Parliamentary Debates*, 241: 1399–431 (22 October 1969).

107 Ibid., 1497–536 (22–23 October 1969).

108 Ibid., 1533, 1536 (23 October 1969).

109 A program broadcast on RTÉ television in 2001 cited official documents to suggest that Lynch's government had agreed to supply weapons after discussions with northern nationalists and that trucks loaded with weapons actually drove to Dundalk, close to the border (*Irish Times*, 13 December 2001).

110 O'Brien, *The Arms Trial*, is the most complete account of this episode.

111 Moloney, *A Secret History of the IRA*, 96.

112 National Archives of Ireland, Department of the Taoiseach, General Registered Files, file 2002/8/424, Heath to Lynch, 10 May 1971.

113 Dáil Éireann, *Parliamentary Debates*, 257: 2345–6 (16 December 1971).

114 Details are in National Archives of Ireland, Department of the Taoiseach, General Registered Files, file 2002/8/417, covering the period August-November 1971.

115 Dwyer, *Nice Fellow*, 278–9.
116 Dáil Éireann, *Parliamentary Debates*, vol. 256. The speeches by Neil Blaney at 141–62 and by Garrett Fitzgerald at 162–84 starkly illustrate the breakdown of consensus on the issue.
117 Ibid., 258: 824–30 (1 February 1972).
118 Dwyer, *Nice Fellow*, 284.
119 Lee, *Ireland, 1912–1985*, 478, notes that opposition to reunification without the consent of the north rose in southern Ireland from 20 per cent in 1968 to over 60 per cent a decade later.

CHAPTER NINE

1 For an attempt to answer the question, see Bernard, *What Does Quebec Want?*
2 Trudeau, *Federalism and the French Canadians*, provides a good sampling of his political writings prior to becoming prime minister. The essay defending provincial autonomy in 1961 is at 124–50.
3 The general introduction to the report, known as "the blue pages" because it is printed on blue paper, is believed to represent Laurendeau's preliminary thoughts about this question. It appears in Canada, Royal Commission on Bilingualism and Biculturalism, *Report*, book 1, xxi–lii.
4 Trudeau, *Federalism and the French Canadians*, 3–60.
5 Quoted in Saywell, *Canadian Annual Review of Politics and Public Affairs, 1976*, 43.
6 Hamilton and Pinard, "The Bases of Parti Québécois Support in Recent Quebec Elections."
7 Quebec, National Assembly, *Débats*, 1977, 2184–93. This speech deserves careful study by anyone seeking to understand Quebec nationalism.
8 *A.G. Quebec v. Blaikie et al.* [1979] 2 S.C.R. 1016.
9 Stevenson, *Community Besieged*, 281–310. Data on linguistic abilities are at 305.
10 *Bâtir le Québec.*
11 Canada, Office of the Prime Minister, Press Release, 24 November 1976.
12 *Québec–Canada: A New Deal.*
13 Quoted in Fraser, *PQ*, 207.
14 Ibid., 226–8.
15 *The Canadian Constitution 1980.*
16 *Reference re. Amendment of the Constitution of Canada* [1981] 1 S.C.R. 753.
17 Fraser, *PQ*, 295–6. For Lévesque's own account of this event see his memoirs, *Attendez que je me rappelle*, 443–6.
18 *Quebec Veto Reference* [1982] 2 S.C.R. 793.
19 For example, Clift, *Le déclin du nationalisme au Québec.*
20 Martin, *The Antagonist*, 97, 101.
21 *A.G. Quebec v. Quebec Protestant School Boards* [1984] 2 S.C.R. 66.

22 Archives nationales du Québec, Executive Council, official records, Conferences de presse de M. René Lévesque, 5 September 1984.
23 Fraser, *PQ,* 359.
24 The text of the speech is in Leslie, *Rebuilding the Relationship,* 39–47.
25 Trudeau published his comments in the *Toronto Star,* 27 May 1987.
26 A detailed account of this episode is in Stevenson, *Community Besieged,* 186–94.
27 The party's origins are discussed in Cornellier, *The Bloc,* 18–31.
28 Bernier, Lemieux, and Pinard, *Un combat inachevé,* 47, 50.
29 *A Quebec Free to Choose.*
30 Quebec, Commission on the Political and Constitutional Future of Quebec, *Report.*
31 Results by province and territory are shown in Russell, *Constitutional Odyssey,* 227. The support of Quebec anglophones for the accord can be inferred from the geographical distribution of the vote in Quebec.
32 Richard, *Jacques Parizeau,* 181–3, 186–7.
33 Bernier, Lemieux, and Pinard, *Un combat inachevé,* 47.
34 Martin, *The Antagonist,* 277–9.
35 The question appears as an annex to the final version of Bill 1, "An Act respecting the future of Quebec."
36 *Gazette* (Montreal), 31 October 1995.
37 *Globe and Mail,* 19 January 1995.
38 Stevenson, *Community Besieged,* 225–9.
39 *Reference re. Secession of Quebec,* [1998] 2 S.C.R. 217.
40 *Globe and Mail,* 23 December 1999.
41 *Globe and Mail,* 26 October 2001.
42 *Toronto Star,* 2 February 2001.
43 Data from Census of Canada, 1961 and 2001.
44 Moloney, *A Secret History of the I.R.A.,* 127–9.
45 The text of the agreement is in O'Day and Stevenson, *Irish Historical Documents since 1800,* 227–32.
46 Moloney, *A Secret History of the I.R.A.,* 159–60.
47 Ibid., 174.
48 Calculated from data in McKittrick and McVea, *Making Sense of the Troubles,* 329.
49 Moloney, *A Secret History of the I.R.A.,* 88.
50 Adams, *Before the Dawn,* 170–1.
51 Coakley and Gallagher, *Politics in the Republic of Ireland,* 367–8.
52 Social Democratic and Labour Party, *A Brief History of the SDLP on Its 30th Anniversary.*
53 Moloney, *A Secret History of the I.R.A.,* 171, 173–4.
54 Calculated from data in McKittrick and McVea, *Making Sense of the Troubles,* 327.

55 Ibid., 140.

56 Moloney, *A Secret History of the I.R.A.*, 206–7.

57 McKittrick and McVea, *Making Sense of the Troubles*, 329.

58 Moloney, *A Secret History of the I.R.A.*, 240–1.

59 McKittrick and McVea, *Making Sense of the Troubles*, 158.

60 Mansergh, *The Spirit of the Nation*, 753–4.

61 Hennessey, *A History of Northern Ireland, 1920–1996*, 268–9.

62 Mansergh, *The Spirit of the Nation*, 755.

63 Moloney, *A Secret History of the I.R.A.*, 180–3.

64 The text is in O'Day and Stevenson, *Irish Historical Documents since 1800*, 240–6.

65 McKittrick and McVea, *Making Sense of the Troubles*, 163–6.

66 Collins, *The Power Game*, 167–8.

67 Dáil Éireann, *Debates*, 361: 2864–5 (20 November 1985).

68 The Libyan connection and the "Tet Offensive" scenario are discussed in Moloney, *A Secret History of the I.R.A.*, 3–33.

69 Sinn Fein, *A Scenario for Peace*.

70 The Sinn Fein documents refer to an "anonymous third party." He is identified as Father Reid in English, *Armed Struggle*, 264.

71 An outline of the dialogue and the texts of all the documents exchanged have been printed as *The Sinn Fein/SDLP Talks, January–September 1988*. The main Sinn Fein position paper, presented on St Patrick's Day 1988, has also been published separately under the title *Towards a Strategy for Peace*.

72 Moloney, *A Secret History of the I.R.A.*, 225–33.

73 The text of the British reply is in ibid., 251–3.

74 The full text of the Downing Street Declaration appears as an appendix in McGarry and O'Leary, *Explaining Northern Ireland*, 408–13.

75 McKittrick and McVea, *Making Sense of the Troubles*, 205–6.

76 *Globe and Mail*, 3 June 1997.

77 Moloney, *A Secret History of the I.R.A.*, 485.

78 The text of the agreement as released by the Northern Ireland Office of the British government was found at its Web site, www.nio.gov.uk/agreement.htm; the summary in the next few paragraphs is based on this text.

79 Dáil Éireann, *Debates*, 489: 1029 (21 April 1998).

80 Moloney, *A Secret History of the I.R.A.*, 480–1.

81 Coakley and Gallagher, *Politics in the Republic of Ireland*, 372.

82 Wilson, *Agreeing to Disagree?* 133–4.

83 Data on the results in votes and seats are taken from ibid., 138.

84 A list of ministers, their affiliations, and their portfolios appears ibid., 75.

85 *Gazette* (Montreal), 3 November 2001. Adams was on a fundraising visit to North America at the time.

86 Data from McKittrick and McVea, *Making Sense of the Troubles*, 329.

87 *Irish Times,* 22 July 2002.
88 *Irish Times,* 12 March 2002.
89 *Irish Times,* 15 January 2002.
90 Data from www.nisra.gov.uk/Census.
91 *Irish Times,* 9 July 2002.
92 *Irish Times,* 15 October 2002.
93 *Irish Times,* 21 February 2003.
94 *Irish Times,* 2 October 2002.
95 *Irish Times,* 28 April 2003.
96 *Irish Times,* 1 May 2003.
97 *Irish Times,* 2 May 2003.
98 *Irish Times,* 30 November 2004.
99 *Irish Times,* 26 September 2005.

CHAPTER TEN

1 Balthazar, *Bilan du nationalisme au Québec,* 209–10.
2 Laitin, "National Revivals and Violence."
3 Wright, *Northern Ireland.*
4 Marx, *Political Writings,* 3: 158.
5 *Local Ireland Almanac and Book of Facts, 2000,* 393–4.
6 *Irish Times,* 27 May 2003.
7 Commission des États généraux sur la situation et l'avenir de la langue française aux Québec, *French, a Language for Everyone,* 3.
8 *Irish Times,* 3 April 2002.
9 Calculated from data in *Local Ireland Almanac and Book of Facts, 2000,* 225–6.
10 Goodman, *Single Europe, Single Ireland?* 87, 107–8.
11 *Irish Times,* 19 September 2000.
12 *Globe and Mail,* 27 October 2001.
13 Gilland and Kennedy, "Data Yearbook 2002," 99.
14 Trudeau, *Federalism and the French Canadians,* 193. The quotation is from a paper called "Federalism, Nationalism, and Reason," which Trudeau read to an academic conference in June 1964.
15 Parizeau's views on North American free trade are discussed in Richard, *Jacques Parizeau,* 217–21.
16 Lisée, *Sortie de secours.*
17 O'Connor, *In Search of a State,* 190.
18 Balthazar, *Bilan du nationalisme au Québec,* 210.
19 "Doing the Right Thing" (editorial), *Gazette* (Montreal), 15 December 2000.
20 For example, Brulé, *PQ-de-sac;* Bariteau, *Québec: 18 septembre 2001.*
21 *Autant de façons d'être Québécois.*
22 For a useful explanation of the concept see Alain-G. Gagnon and Raffeale Iacovino, "Framing Citizenship Status in an Age of Polyethnicity: Quebec's

Model of Interculturalism," in Telford and Lazar, *Canadian Political Culture(s) in Transition*, 313–42.

23 For example, Kearney, *Post-Nationalist Ireland.*

24 Trudeau, *Federalism and the French Canadians,* 196.

25 Readers who find this an unduly harsh assessment are referred to the *Globe and Mail,* 7 June 2003; the whole issue was devoted to this theme.

Bibliography

ARCHIVAL SOURCES

ARCHIVES NATIONALES DU QUÉBEC
Conseil executif, official records
Jean Lesage papers

LIBRARY AND ARCHIVES CANADA
"Les événements de 1837 et 1838" (microfilm of originals held by Archives
nationales du Québec) (MG 8, A25)
Louis-Hippolyte Lafontaine papers (MG 24, B14)
Armand Lavergne papers (MG 27, IIE12)
Sir John A. Macdonald papers (MG 26, A)
Honoré Mercier papers (MG 27, IF1)
Wolfred Nelson papers (MG 24, B34)
Papineau family papers (MG 24, B2)

NATIONAL ARCHIVES OF IRELAND
Dáil Éireann, Ministry and Cabinet Minutes
Department of Justice files
Department of the Taoiseach, General Registered Files
Jack Lynch papers

NATIONAL LIBRARY OF IRELAND
"The British in Ireland" papers (microfilm of originals in Public Records Office,
London)

Roger Casement papers
Maire Comerford papers
Timothy Harrington papers
Bulmer Hobson papers
Irish Parliamentary Party, minute books
James Fintan Lalor papers
McCullough papers
Thomas MacDonagh papers
Joseph McGarrity papers
McHugh papers
Kathleen McKenna Napoli papers
Eoin MacNeill papers
Martin papers
Daniel O'Connell papers
Sean T. O'Kelly papers
Patrick Pearse papers
John Redmond papers
Theobald Wolfe Tone papers

UNIVERSITY COLLEGE DUBLIN ARCHIVES
Frank Aiken papers
Michael Collins papers
Desmond Fitzgerald papers
Eoin MacNeill papers
Mary MacSwiney papers
Richard Mulcahy papers
O'Rahilly papers

YORK UNIVERSITY ARCHIVES
Maurice Duplessis papers (microfilm of originals held by Conrad Black or the
    University of Windsor Archives)

PUBLISHED SOURCES

Anon. "Important Resolutions of the Irish Bishops on Coercion, the Land Bill and
    the Education Question." *Irish Ecclesiastical Record*, 3rd series, 8 (1887): 477–8.
– "Resolutions of the Irish Bishops on the Irish Land Question." *Irish Ecclesiastical
    Record*, 3rd series, 9 (1888): 670–2.
Acton, John E.E. Dalberg, Baron. "Nationality." In *The History of Freedom and Other
    Essays*, 270–300. London: Macmillan, 1922.
Adams, Gerry. *Before the Dawn: An Autobiography.* New York: William Morrow, 1996.
– *Free Ireland: Towards a Lasting Peace.* Dingle: Brandon, 1999.

– *Hope and History: Making Peace in Ireland,* Dingle: Brandon, 2003.

Akenson, Donald H. *God's Peoples: Covenant and Land in South Africa, Israel, and Ulster.* Montreal: McGill-Queen's University Press, 1992.

– *Small Differences: Irish Catholics and Irish Protestants: An International Perspective, 1815–1922.* Kingston: McGill-Queen's University Press, 1987.

Akenson, Donald H., and J.F. Fallin "The Irish Civil War and the Drafting of the Free State Constitution." *Eire/Ireland* 5, no. 1 (Spring 1970): 10–26; no. 2 (Summer 1970): 42–93; no. 4 (Winter 1970): 28–30.

Allemagne, André d'. *Le RIN et les débuts du mouvement indépendantiste québécois.* Outremont: Editions l'Étincelle, 1974.

Alter, Peter. "Symbols of Irish Nationalism." *Studia Hibernica* 14 (1974): 104–23.

Alvey, David. "Thomas Davis, the Conservation of a Tradition." *Studies* 85 (1996): 37–42.

Anderson, Benedict. *Imagined Communities: Reflections on the Origin and Spread of Nationalism.* London: Verso, 1983.

Angers, François-Albert. "Mesure de l'influence du chanoine Lionel Groulx sur son milieu." *Revue d'histoire de l'Amérique française* 32 (1978–79): 357–84.

– "Nationalisme et vie économique." *Revue d'histoire de l'Amérique française* 22 (1968–69): 589–615.

Aquin, Hubert. *Prochain Épisode.* Toronto: McClelland and Stewart, 1967.

Archer, J.R. "Necessary Ambiguity: Nationalism and Myth in Ireland." *Eire/Ireland* 19, no. 2 (Summer 1984): 23–37.

Archibald, Clinton. *Un Québec corporatiste?* Hull: Éditions Asticou, 1983.

Ardagh, John. *Ireland and the Irish.* London: Hamish Hamilton, 1994.

Arès, Richard, SJ. *Nos grandes options politiques et constitutionelles.* Montréal: Éditions Bellarmin, 1972.

Armstrong, Elizabeth. *The Crisis of Québec, 1914–18.* New York: Columbia University Press, 1937.

Arthur, Paul. "Three Years of the Anglo-Irish Agreement." *Irish Political Studies* 4 (1989): 105–9.

Autant de façons d'être québécois: Plan d'action du gouvernement à l'intention des communautés culturelles. Québec, 1981.

Baker, Susan. "Nationalist Ideology and the Industrial Policy of Fianna Fail: The Evidence of the Irish Press (1955–1972)." *Irish Political Studies* 1 (1986): 57–66.

Balthazar, Louis. *Bilan du nationalisme au Québec.* Montréal: L'Hexagone, 1986.

Banks, Margaret A. *Edward Blake, Irish Nationalist: A Canadian Statesman in Irish Politics, 1892–1907.* Toronto: University of Toronto Press, 1957.

Barbeau, Raymond. *Le Québec, est-il une colonie?* Montréal: Éditions de l'homme, 1962.

Bariteau, Claude. *Québec: 18 septembre 2001.* Montréal: Editions Québec/Amérique, 1998.

Barrington, Donal. "Uniting Ireland." *Studies* 46 (1957): 379–402.

Bâtir le Québec: Énoncé de politique économique. Quebec: Éditeur officiel du Québec, 1979.

Bauer, Julien. *Les minorités au Québec.* Montréal: Boréal, 1994.

Beckett, J.C. *The Making of Modern Ireland, 1603–1923.* New York: Alfred A. Knopf, 1966.

Behiels, Michael. "The Bloc populaire canadien: Anatomy of Failure, 1942–1947." *Journal of Canadian Studies* 18, no. 4 (Winter 1983–84): 45–74.

– "The Bloc populaire canadien and the Origins of French-Canadian Neo-nationalism, 1942–8." *Canadian Historical Review* 63 (1982): 487–512.

– *Prelude to Quebec's Quiet Revolution.* Kingston and Montreal: McGill-Queen's University Press, 1985.

Belanger, André-J., et Vincent Lemieux. "Le nationalisme et les partis politiques." *Revue d'histoire de l'Amérique française* 22 (1968–69): 539–66.

Bélanger, Réal, et al. *Les grands débats parlementaires, 1792–1992.* Sainte-Foy: Les Presses de l'Université Laval, 1994.

Bélanger, Yves, and Michel Levesque. *René Levesque: L'homme, la nation, la democratie.* Sillery: Les Presses de l'Université du Québec, 1992.

Bell, J. Bowyer. *The Secret Army: The IRA.* Rev. ed. Dublin: Academy Press, 1983.

Bellevance, Marcel. *Le Québec et la Confédération: Un choix libre?* Sillery: Les Éditions du Septentrion, 1991.

– "La rébellion de 1837 et les modèles théoriques de l'émergence de la nation et du nationalisme." *Revue d'histoire de l'Amérique française* 53 (2000): 367–400.

Bergeron, Gérard, and Rejean Pelletier. *L'état du Québec en devenir.* Montréal: Boréal Express, 1980.

Berlatsky, Joel. "Roots of Conflict in Ireland: Colonial Attitudes in the Age of the Penal Laws." *Eire/Ireland* 18, no. 4 (Winter 1983): 40–56.

Berman, David, et al. "The Theology of the IRA." *Studies* 72 (1983): 137–44.

Bernard, André. *What Does Quebec Want?* Toronto: Lorimer, 1978.

Bernard, Jean-Paul. *Les rouges: Liberalisme, nationalisme et anticlericalisme au milieu du XIXe siecle.* Montréal: Les Presses de l'Université du Québec, 1971.

Bernier, Gérald, et Daniel Salée. "Les insurrections de 1837–1838 au Québec: Remarques critiques et théoriques en marge de l'historiographie." *Canadian Review of Studies in Nationalism* 13 (1986): 13–29.

Bernier, Robert, Vincent Lemieux, and Maurice Pinard. *Un combat inachevé.* Sainte-Foy: Presses de l'Université du Québec, 1997.

Bernstein, George L. "Liberals, the Irish Famine, and the Role of the State." *Irish Historical Studies* 29 (1995): 513–36.

Bew, Paul. *Charles Stewart Parnell.* Dublin: Gill and Macmillan, 1980.

– *Conflict and Conciliation in Ireland, 1890–1910.* Oxford: Clarendon Press, 1987.

– *Ideology and the Irish Question.* Oxford: Clarendon Press, 1994.

Bew, Paul, Peter Gibbon, and Henry Patterson. *Northern Ireland, 1921–1996: Political Forces and Social Classes.* London: Serif, 1996.

Birrell, Augustine. *Things Past Redress.* London: Faber and Faber, 1937.

Blacam, Aodh de. "Some Thoughts on Partition." *Studies* 23 (1934): 561–76.

Black, Conrad. *Duplessis*. Toronto: McClelland and Stewart, 1977.

Blais, André, and Richard Nadeau. "To Be or Not to Be Sovereignist: Quebeckers' Perennial Dilemma." *Canadian Public Policy* 18 (1992): 89–103.

Blythe, Ernest. "The Significance of the Irish Language for the Future of our Nation." *University Review* 2, no. 2 (1958): 3–21.

Boisman, Gerard, et al. *Espace régional et nation: Pour un nouveau débat sur le Québec.* Montréal: Boréal, 1983.

Boismenu, Gerard. *Le duplessisme: Politique économique et rapports de force, 1944–1960.* Montréal: Presses de l'Université de Montréal, 1981.

– "Perspectives on Quebec-Canada Relations in the 1990s: Is the Reconciliation of Ethnicity, Nationality and Citizenship Possible?" *Canadian Review of Studies in Nationalism* 23 (1996): 99–109.

Bolduc, Denis, and Pierre Fortin. "Les francophones sont-ils plus 'xenophobes' que les anglophones au Québec? Une analyse quantitative exploratoire." *Canadian Ethnic Studies* 22, no. 2 (1990): 54–77.

Bonenfant, Jean-Charles. *The French Canadians and the Birth of Confederation.* Ottawa: Canadian Historical Association, 1966.

Bosher, J.F. *The Gaullist Attack on Canada, 1967–1997.* Montreal and Kingston: McGill-Queen's University Press, 1999.

Bouchard, Gérard. *Genèse des nations et cultures du Nouveau Monde.* Montréal: Boréal, 2001.

– *La nation québécoise au futur et au passé.* Montréal: VLB, 1999.

Bouchard, Lucien. *Un nouveau parti pour l'étape décisive.* Saint-Laurent: Fides, 1993.

Bourassa, Henri. *Ireland and Canada: An Address Delivered in Hamilton, Ontario, on St. Patrick's Day 1914.* Montréal: Imprimerie Le Devoir, 1914.

– *La langue, gardienne de la foi.* Montréal: Imprimerie Le Devoir, 1918.

– *The Spectre of Annexation and the Real Danger of National Disintegration.* Montréal: Imprimerie Le Devoir, 1912.

Bourassa, Robert. *Gouverner le Québec.* Montréal: Fides, 1995.

Bourque, Gilles, Jules Duchastel, and Jacques Beauchemin. *La societé libérale duplessiste, 1944–1960.* Montréal: Presses de l'Université de Montréal, 1994.

Bouthillier, Guy, and Jean Meynaud. *Le choc des langues au Québec, 1760–1970.* Montréal: Presses de l'Université de Montréal, 1972.

Bowen, Kurt. *Protestants in a Catholic State.* Kingston: McGill-Queen's University Press, 1983.

Bowman, John. *De Valera and the Ulster Question, 1917–1973.* Oxford: Clarendon Press, 1982.

Boyce, D.G. "British Conservative Opinion on the Ulster Question and the Partition of Ireland, 1912–21." *Irish Historical Studies* 17 (1970): 89–112.

– *The Irish Question and British Politics, 1868–1996.* New York: St. Martin's Press, 1996.

Boyce, George. *Nationalism in Ireland.* Baltimore: Johns Hopkins University Press, 1982.

Boyce, George, and Alan O'Day. *The Making of Modern Irish History*. London: Routledge, 1996.

Boyle, J.W. "The Belfast Protestant Association and the Independent Orange Order, 1901–10." *Irish Historical Studies* 13 (1962): 117–52.

Bradshaw, Brendan. "Nationalism and Historical Scholarship in Modern Ireland." *Irish Historical Studies* 26 (1989): 329–51.

Breton, Raymond. "From Ethnic to Civic Nationalism: English Canada and Quebec." *Ethnic and Racial Studies* 11 (1988): 85–102.

Breuilly, John. *Nationalism and the State*. London: Manchester University Press, 1982.

Bromage, Mary C. "Consolidation of the Irish Revolution, 1921–1922: De Valera's Plan." *University Review* 5, no. 1 (1968): 23–35.

– "Image of Nationhood." *Eire/Ireland* 3, no. 3 (Autumn 1968): 11–26.

Brooks, Stephen, and Brian Tanguay. "Quebec's Caisse de dépôt et placement: Tool of nationalism?" *Canadian Public Administration* 28 (1985): 99–119.

Brulé, Michel. *PQ-de-sac*. Montréal: Les Intouchables, 1997.

– *Québec-Canada anglais: Deux itinéraires/un affrontement*. Montréal: Éditions HMH, 1969.

Buckland, P.J. "The Southern Irish Unionists, the Irish Question, and British Politics, 1906–14." *Irish Historical Studies* 15 (1967) 228–55.

Buckland, Patrick. *Ulster Unionism and the Origins of Northern Ireland, 1886 to 1922*. Dublin: Gill and Macmillan 1973.

Bull, Philip. *Land, Politics and Nationalism: A Study of the Irish Land Question*. Dublin: Gill & Macmillan, 1996.

– "The Significance of the Nationalist Response to the Irish Land Act of 1903." *Irish Historical Studies* 28 (1993): 283–305.

Burns, Robin A. "D'Arcy McGee and the Fenians." *University Review* 4, no. 3 (1967): 260–73.

Burt, Alfred Leroy. *The Old Province of Quebec*. Toronto: McClelland and Stewart, 1968.

Büthe, Tim. "Taking Temporality Seriously: Modeling History and the Use of Narratives as Evidence." *American Political Science Review* 96 (2002): 481–94.

Cahalan, James M. "Michael Davitt: The 'Preacher of Ideas,' 1881–1906." *Eire/Ireland* 11, no. 1 (Spring 1976): 13–33.

Cahill, Gilbert A. "Irish Catholicism and English Toryism." *Review of Politics* 19 (1957): 62–76.

– "Some Nineteenth-Century Roots of the Ulster Problem, 1829–1848." *Irish University Review* 1 (1971): 215–37.

Callanan, Frank. "After Parnell: The Political Consequences of Timothy Michael Healy." *Studies* 80 (1991): 371–6.

Cameron, David. *Nationalism, Self-Determination and the Quebec Question*. Toronto: Macmillan of Canada, 1974.

Canada. *House of Commons Debates*. 1905, 1938. Ottawa.

Canada. Public Archives. *Report of the Public Archives for the Year 1923.* Ottawa: King's Printer, 1924.

Canada. Royal Commission on Bilingualism and Biculturalism. *Report of the Royal Commission on Bilingualism and Biculturalism.* 6 vols. in 5. Ottawa: Queen's Printer, 1967–70.

The Canadian Constitution 1980: Proposed Resolution respecting the Constitution of Canada. Ottawa: Publications Canada 1980.

Cannon, Gordon E. "Consociationalism vs. Control: Canada as a Case Study." *Western Political Quarterly* 35 (1982:) 50–64.

Carroll, Terence. "Owners, Immigrants and Ethnic Conflicts in Fiji and Mauritius." *Ethnic and Racial Studies* 17 (1994): 301–24.

Carty, Anthony. *Was Ireland Conquered?* London: Pluto Press, 1996.

Carty, R.K. *Party and Parish Pump: Electoral Politics in Ireland.* Waterloo, Ont.: Wilfrid Laurier University Press, 1981.

Caulfield, Max. *The Easter Rebellion.* New York: Holt, Rinehart and Winston, 1963

Chaput, Marcel. *Pourquoi je suis séparatiste.* Montréal: Éditions du jour, 1961

Charron, Claude G. *La Partition du Québec.* Montréal: VLB, 1996.

Chennels, David. *The Politics of Nationalism in Canada: Cultural Conflict since 1760.* Toronto: University of Toronto Press, 2001.

Chinneide, Sile ni. "The Gaelic Contribution to Irish Nationalism." *University Review* 2, no. 9 (1960): 67–76.

Christianson, Gale E. "Landlords and Land Tenure in Ireland, 1790–1830." *Eire/Ireland* 9, no. 1 (Spring 1974): 25–58.

Chubb, Basil. *The Government and Politics of Ireland.* Oxford: Oxford University Press, 1970.

Churchill, Winston S. *The Aftermath.* New York: Scribner, 1929.

Clark, S.D. *Movements of Political Protest in Canada, 1640–1840.* Toronto: University of Toronto Press, 1959.

Clark, Sam. "The Social Composition of the Land League." *Irish Historical Studies* 17 (1971): 447–69.

Clarke, Kathleen Daly. *Revolutionary Woman.* Dublin: O'Brien Press, 1991.

Cleland, William. *History of the Presbyterian Church in Ireland.* Toronto: Hart and Co., 1880.

Clery, Arthur E. "Pearse, MacDonough and Plunkett: An Appreciation." *Studies* 6 (1917): 212–21.

Clift, Dominique. *Le déclin du nationalisme au Québec.* Montréal: Libre Expression, 1981.

Coakley, John. "Patrick Pearse and the 'Noble Lie' of Irish Nationalism." *Studies* 72 (1983): 119–36.

Coakley, John, and Michael Gallagher. *Politics in the Republic of Ireland.* 3rd ed. London; New York: Routledge, in association with PSAI Press, 1999.

Cochrane, Feargal. "Progressive or Regressive? The Anglo-Irish Agreement as a Dynamic in the Northern Ireland Polity." *Irish Political Studies* 8 (1993): 1–20.

Coleman, William D. *The Independence Movement in Quebec, 1945–1980.* Toronto: University of Toronto Press, 1984.

Colley, Linda. *Britons: Forging the Nation, 1707–1837.* New Haven and London: Yale University Press, 1992.

Collins, Michael. *The Path to Freedom.* Dublin: Talbot Press, 1922.

Collins, Peter. *Who Fears to Speak of '98? Commemoration and the Continuing Impact of the United Irishmen.* Belfast: Ulster Historical Foundation, 2004.

Collins, Stephen. *The Cosgrave Legacy.* Dublin: Blackwater Press, 1996.

– *The Power Game: Ireland under Fianna Fail.* Dublin: O'Brien Press, 2001.

Comeau, Paul-André. *Le Bloc populaire.* Montréal: Québec-Amérique, 1982.

Comeau, Robert, and Lucille Beaudry. *André Laurendeau: Un intellectuel d'ici.* Sillery: Presses de l'Université du Québec, 1990.

Comeau, Robert, Michel Levesque, and Yves Belanger. *Daniel Johnson: Rêve d'égalité et projet d'indépendance.* Sillery: Presses de l'Université du Québec, 1991.

Comerford, R.V. *The Fenians in Context: Irish Politics and Society, 1848–82.* Dublin: Wolfhound Press, 1998.

– "Patriotism as Pastime: The Appeal of Fenianism in the Mid–1860s." *Irish Historical Studies* 22 (1987): 239–50.

Comité Québec-Irlande. *Bernadette Devlin à Montréal: samedi 31 mars 19:30.* Montréal, 1984.

Commission des États généraux sur la situation et l'avenir de la langue française au Québec. *French, a Language for Everyone: Summary of the Final Report.* Québec, 2001.

Congrès des affaires canadiennes. *Le Canada, expérience ratée ... ou réussie?* Québec: Presses de l'Université Laval, 1962.

Conlogue, Ray. *Impossible Nation: The Longing for Homeland in Canada and Quebec.* Stratford: The Mercury Press, 1996.

Connell, K.H. "The Population of Ireland in the Eighteenth Century." *Economic History Review* 16 no. 2 (1946): 111–24.

Connolly, S.J., ed. *The Oxford Companion to Irish History.* Oxford: Oxford University Press, 1998.

Connor, Walker. *Ethnic Nationalism: The Quest for Understanding.* Princeton: Princeton University Press, 1994.

– "The Politics of Ethnonationalism." *Journal of International Affairs* 27 (1973): 1–21.

Coogan, Tim Pat. *Eamon de Valera: The Man Who Was Ireland.* New York: HarperCollins, 1995.

– *Michael Collins: A Biography.* London: Hutchinson, 1990.

Cook, Ramsay, ed. *French Canadian Nationalism: An Anthology.* Toronto: Macmillan, 1969.

Cornellier, Manon. *The Bloc.* Translated by Robert Chodos, Simon Horn, and Wanda Taylor. Toronto: James Lorimer, 1995.

Costello, Francis. *The Irish Revolution and Its Aftermath, 1916–1923.* Dublin: Irish Academic Press, 2003.

405

Costello, Francis J. "The Irish Representatives to the London Anglo-Irish Conference in 1921: Violators of Their Authority or Victims of Contradictory Instructions?" *Eire/Ireland* 24, no. 2 (Summer 1989): 52–78.
– "The Republican Courts and the Decline of British Policy in Ireland, 1911–1921." *Eire/Ireland* 25, no. 2 (Summer 1990): 36–55.
Costigan, Giovanni. "The Anglo-Irish Conflict, 1919–1922: A War of Independence or Systematized Murder?" *University Review* 5, no. 1 (1968): 64–86.
– "Romantic Nationalism: Ireland and Europe." *Irish University Review* 3 (1973): 141–52.
Coulter, Colin. "The Character of Unionism." *Irish Political Studies* 9 (1994): 1–24.
Cox, Robert W. "The Quebec Provincial Election of 1886." MA thesis, McGill University, 1948.
Cox, W. Harvey. "The Politics of Irish Unification in the Irish Republic." *Parliamentary Affairs* 38 (1985): 437–54.
– "Who Wants a United Ireland?" *Government and Opposition* 20 (1985): 29–47.
Creighton, Donald. *The Empire of the St. Lawrence.* Toronto: Macmillan Co. of Canada, 1980.
– *Towards the Discovery of Canada: Selected Essays.* Toronto: Macmillan of Canada, 1972.
Cronin, Michael. "Defenders of the Nation? The Gaelic Athletic Association and Irish Nationalist Identity." *Irish Political Studies* 11 (1996): 1–19.
Cronin, Sean. "'The Country Did Not Turn Out': The Young Ireland Rising of 1848." *Eire/Ireland* 11, no. 2 (Summer 1976): 3–17.
– "The Making of NATO and the Partition of Ireland." *Eire/Ireland* 20, no. 2 (Summer 1985): 6–18.
– "Nation-Building and the Irish Language Revival Movement." *Eire/Ireland* 13, no. 1 (Spring 1978): 7–14.
Crossman, Virginia. "Emergency Legislation and Agrarian Disorder in Ireland, 1821–41." *Irish Historical Studies* 27 (1991): 309–23.
Crowley, Tony. *The Politics of Language in Ireland, 1366–1922, A Sourcebook.* London and New York: Routledge, 2000.
Curran, Joseph M. "The Consolidation of the Irish Revolution, 1921–23: The Free Staters." *University Review* 5, no. 1 (1968): 36–50.
– "The Decline and Fall of the IRB." *Eire/Ireland* 10, no. 1 (Spring 1975): 14–23.
– "Ireland since 1916." *Eire/Ireland* 1, no. 3 (Autumn 1966): 14–28.
– "Lloyd George and the Irish Settlement, 1921–1922." *Eire/Ireland* 7, no. 2 (Summer 1972): 14–46.
Curtin, Nancy J. "The Transformation of the Society of United Irishmen into a Mass-Based Revolutionary Organization, 1794–6." *Irish Historical Studies* 24 (1985): 463–92.
Cyr, Francois, and Remi Roy. *Éléments d'histoire de la FTQ: La FTQ et la question nationale.* Laval, Qué.: Éditions coopératives A. Saint-Martin, 1981.

Daignault, Richard. *Lesage.* Montréal: Libre expression, 1981.

Dáil Éireann. *Debates.* Vols. 2–489. Dublin.

Daly, Mary E. "The Economic Ideals of Irish Nationalism: Frugal Comfort or Lavish Austerity?" *Eire/Ireland* 29, no. 4 (Winter 1994): 77–100.

Dangerfield, George. "James Joyce, James Connolly, and Irish Nationalism." *Irish University Review* 16 (1986): 5–21.

Davis, Richard P. *Arthur Griffith and Non-violent Sinn Fein.* Dublin: Anvil Books, 1974.

Davis, Thomas O. *Literary and Historical Essays.* Dublin: J. Duffy, 1883.

Davitt, Michael. *Speech Delivered by Michael Davitt in Defence of the Land League.* London: Kegan Paul, 1890.

Delaney, Enda. "State, Politics, and Demography: The Case of Irish Emigration, 1921–71." *Irish Political Studies* 13 (1998): 25–49.

Dennehy, H.E. "Nationalization of the Land." *Irish Ecclesiastical Record,* 3rd series, 11 (1890): 132–47.

Desbiens, J.P. *Les insolences du frère Untel.* Québec: Institut littéraire du Québec, 1960.

Désilets, Andrée. *Hector Louis Langevin, un père de la Confédération canadienne.* Québec: Presses de l'Université Laval, 1969.

Desrosiers, Richard. *Le personnel politique québécois.* Montréal: Éditions du Boréal Express, 1972.

Devlin, Bernadette. *The Price of My Soul.* London: Pan Books, 1969.

Dicey, A.V. *England's Case against Home Rule.* London: Murray, 1886.

Dillon, Geraldine. "Home Rule." *University Review* 2, no. 6 (1959): 40–50.

– "Irish Republican Brotherhood." *University Review* 2, no. 8 (1960): 25–33; no. 9 (1960): 23–36.

– "Legal and Political Position in pre–1916 Ireland." *University Review* 3, no. 1 (1962): 48–67.

– "1914." *University Review* 3, no. 7 (1966): 52–63.

Dion, Léon. *Québec: The Unfinished Revolution.* Montreal and London: McGill-Queen's University Press, 1976.

– *Québec, 1945–2000.* Quebec: Les Presses de l'Université Laval, 1987.

– *La Révolution déroutée 1960–1976.* Montréal: Boréal, 1998.

Dion, Stéphane. "The Dynamic of Secessions: Scenarios after a Pro-Separatist Vote in a Quebec Referendum." *Canadian Journal of Political Science,* 28 (1995), 533–51.

– "Why Is Secession Difficult in Well-Established Democracies? Lessons from Quebec." *British Journal of Political Science* 26 (1996): 269–83.

Dirks, Patricia. *The Failure of L'Action Liberale Nationale.* Montreal: McGill-Queens University Press, 1991.

Donnelly, James S., Jr. *The Great Irish Potato Famine.* Stroud, Gloucestershire: Sutton Publishing, 2001.

– "Propagating the Cause of the United Irishmen." *Studies* 69 (1980): 5–23.

Doyle, John. "Workers and Outlaws: Unionism and Fair Employment in Northern Ireland." *Irish Political Studies* 9 (1994): 41–60.

Doyle, Roddy. *A Star Called Henry*. New York: Viking, 1999.

Duane, Tom. "La trahison des clercs: British Intellectuals and the First Home Rule Crisis." *Irish Historical Studies* 23 (1982): 134–73.

"Dublinensis." "The Land-and Nationhood." *Catholic Bulletin* 21 (1931): 458–84.

Duffy, Sean, ed. *The Macmillan Atlas of Irish History*. New York: Macmillan, 1997.

Dugré, Adelard, and Somerville, Henry. "Henri Bourassa and Canadian Nationalism." *Studies* 7 (1918): 485–508.

Durham, John George Lambton, Earl of. *The Report of the Earl of Durham, Her Majesty's High Commissioner and Governor-General of British North America.* London: Methuen, 1902.

Dwyer, T. Ryle. *Nice Fellow: A Biography of Jack Lynch.* Cork: Mercier Press, 2001.

Eagleton, Terry. "Nationalism and the Case of Ireland." *New Left Review* 234 (March-April 1999): 44–61.

Eccles, W.J. *France in America.* Vancouver: Fitzhenry and Whiteside, 1972.

Edwards, Robert Dudley. "The European and American Background of O'Connell's Nationalism." *Irish Monthly* 75 (1947): 468–73, 509–20; 76 (1948): 31–6, 129–34, 327–31, 512–21.

Elliott, Marianne. *The Catholics of Ulster: A History.* London: Penguin Books, 2002.

– *Partners in Revolution: The United Irishmen and France.* New Haven: Yale University Press, 1982.

– *Wolfe Tone: Prophet of Irish Independence.* New Haven: Yale University Press, 1989.

Ellis, Steven G. "Historiographical Debate: Representations of the Past in Ireland: Whose Past and Whose Present?" *Irish Historical Studies* 27 (1991): 289–308.

English, Richard. *Armed Struggle: The History of the I.R.A.* London: Macmillan 2003.

Esman, Milton J. "Ethnic Politics and Economic Power." *Comparative Politics* 19 (1987): 395–418.

Fahey, Denis. "Nationality and the Supernatural." *Irish Ecclesiastical Record,* 5th series, 21 (January-June 1923): 261–74.

Fanning, J.R. "The Unionist Party and Ireland, 1906–10." *Irish Historical Studies* 15 (1966): 147–71.

Faughnan, Sean. "The Jesuits and the Drafting of the Irish Constitution of 1937." *Irish Historical Studies* 26 (1988): 79–102.

Fearon, James D., and David D. Laitin. "Ethnicity, Insurgency, and Civil War." *American Political Science Review* 97 (2003): 75–90.

Feeney, Brian. *Sinn Fein: A Hundred Turbulent Years.* Dublin: O'Brien Press, 2002.

Ferron, Jacques. *Le salut de l'Irlande.* Montréal: Éditions du Jour, 1970.

Fidler, Richard. *Canada, Adieu? Quebec Debates Its Future.* Lantzville, BC: Oolichan Books, 1991.

Filteau, Gerard. *Histoire des Patriotes.* Montréal: Les Éditions Univers, 1980.

Finnegan, Richard B. "The Blueshirts of Ireland during the 1930s: Fascism Inverted." *Eire/Ireland* 24, no. 2 (Summer 1989): 79–99.

Fitzgerald, Alexis. "Irish Democracy." *University Review* 2, no. 2 (1958): 31–46.

FitzGerald, Garret. *Reflections on the Irish State.* Dublin: Irish Academic Press, 2003.

Fitzpatrick, David. *Politics and Irish Life, 1913–1921: Provincial Experience of War and Revolution.* Dublin: Gill and Macmillan, 1977.

Forbes, H.D., ed. *Canadian Political Thought.* Toronto: Oxford University Press, 1985.

Fortin, Gérald. "Le nationalisme canadien-français et les classes sociales." *Revue d'histoire de l'Amérique française* 22 (1968–69): 525–37.

Foster, R.F. *The Irish Story: Telling Tales and Making It Up in Ireland.* London: Penguin Books 2001.

– *Modern Ireland: 1600–1972.* New York: Penguin Books, 1989.

Foster, Roy. "Interpretations of Parnell." *Studies* 80 (1991): 349–57.

Fournier, Louis. *FLQ: The Anatomy of an Underground Movement.* Toronto: NC Press, 1984.

Fournier, Marcel, et al. *Quebec Society: Critical Issues.* Scarborough: Prentice-Hall, 1997.

Foy, Michael, and Brian Barton. *The Easter Rising.* Phoenix Mill: Sutton Publishing, 1999.

Fraser, Graham. *PQ: René Lévesque and the Parti Québécois in Power.* Toronto: Macmillan of Canada, 1984.

Gagnon, Alain-G., ed. *Québec: État et société.* Montréal: Québec-Amérique, 2003.

Gagnon, Alain-G., and Guy Laforest. "The Future of Federalism: Lessons from Canada and Quebec." *International Journal* 48 (1993): 470–91.

Gagnon, Alain-G., and Guy Lachapelle. "Quebec Confronts Canada: Two Competing Societal Projects Searching for Legitimacy." *Publius: The Journal of Federalism* 26 (1996): 177–91.

Gagnon, Alain-G., and K.Z. Paltiel. "Toward *maîtres chez nous:* The Ascendancy of a Balzacian Bourgeoisie in Quebec." *Queen's Quarterly* 93 (1986): 731–49.

Gagnon, Alain-G., and Michel Sarra-Bournet, eds. *Duplessis: Entre la grande noirceur et la societé libérale.* Montreal: Éditions Québec-Amérique, 1997.

Gagnon, Alain-G., and Tully, James, eds. *Multinational Democracies.* Cambridge and New York: Cambridge University Press, 2001.

Gagnon, Alain-G., and Luc Turgeon. "Managing Diversity in Eighteenth and Nineteenth Century Canada: Quebec's Constitutional Development in Light of the Scottish Experience." *Commonwealth and Comparative Politics* 41, no. 1 (March 2003), 1–23.

Gagnon, Jean, and Nicole Hamelin. *Histoire du catholicisme québécois: Le XXe siècle.* Vol. 1, *1898–1940.* Montréal: Boréal, 1984.

Gahan, Daniel J. *Rebellion! Ireland in 1798.* Dublin: O'Brien Press, 1997.

Gailey, Andrew. *Ireland and the Death of Kindness: The Experience of Constructive Unionism, 1890–1905.* Cork: Cork University Press, 1987.

Gallagher, Frank. *The Indivisible Island.* London: Gollancz, 1957.

Gallagher, Michael. "Do Ulster Unionists Have a Right to Self-determination?" *Irish Political Studies* 5 (1990): 11–30.

- "How Many Nations Are There in Ireland?" *Ethnic and Racial Studies* 18 (1995): 715–39.
- "The Pact General Election of 1922." *Irish Historical Studies* 21 (1979): 404–21.
- "Socialism and the Nationalist Tradition in Ireland, 1798–1918." *Eire/Ireland* 12, no. 2 (Summer 1977): 63–102.

Gallagher, Tom. "Fianna Fail and Partition, 1926–1984." *Eire/Ireland* 20, no. 1 (Spring 1985): 28–57.

Garvin, Tom. "The Anatomy of a Nationalist Revolution: Ireland, 1858–1928." *Comparative Studies in Society and History* 28 (1986): 468–501.
- *The Evolution of Irish Nationalist Politics.* New York: Holmes & Meier, 1981.
- *Nationalist Revolutionaries in Ireland, 1858–1928.* Oxford: Clarendon Press; New York: Oxford University Press, 1988, 1987.
- *1922: The Birth of Irish Democracy.* Dublin: Gill and Macmillan, 1996.
- "The Politics of Language and Literature in Pre-independence Ireland." *Irish Political Studies* 2 (1987): 49–63.
- "Priests and Patriots: Irish Separatism and Fear of the Modern, 1890–1914." *Irish Historical Studies* 25 (1986): 67–81.
- "The Strange Death of Clerical Politics in University College, Dublin." *Irish University Review* 28 (1998–99): 308–14.

Geary, R.C. "The Oneness of Ireland." *Studies* 70 (1981): 17–34.

Gellner, Ernest. *Nations and Nationalism.* Ithaca: Cornell University Press, 1983.

Genest, Jean-Guy. *Godbout.* Sillery: Septentrion, 1996.

Geoghegan, Patrick M. *The Irish Act of Union: A Study in High Politics, 1798–1801.* New York: St. Martin's Press, 1999.

Gibbs, Edward J. "Home Rule in Ireland and Canada." *New Ireland Review* 7 (1897): 145–61.

Gilbert, Arthur N. "Ethnicity and the British Army in Ireland during the American Revolution." *Ethnic and Racial Studies* 1 (1978): 474–83.

Gilland, Karin, and Fiachra Kennedy, eds. "Data Yearbook, 2002." Supplement to *Irish Political Studies*, 17.

Girvin, Brian. "The Divorce Referendum in the Republic, June 1986." *Irish Political Studies* 2 (1987): 93–9.
- "The Irish Divorce Referendum, November 1995." *Irish Political Studies* 11 (1996): 174–81.
- "Political Culture, Political Independence and Economic Success in Ireland." *Irish Political Studies* 12 (1997): 48–77.

Glandon, Virginia E. "The Irish Press and Revolutionary Irish Nationalism." *Eire/Ireland* 16, no. 1 (Spring 1981): 21–33.

Golway, Terry. *For the Cause of Liberty: A Thousand Years of Ireland's Heroes.* New York: Simon and Schuster, 2000.

Goodman, James. *Single Europe, Single Ireland?* Dublin; Portland, Ore.: Irish Academic Press, 2000.

Gormally, Patrick. "L'étrange parallèle: Québec-Irlande." *Écrits du Canada français* 59–61.

Gougeon, Gilles. *A History of Quebec Nationalism.* Toronto: J. Lorimer, 1994.

Greenfeld, Liah. *Nationalism: Five Roads to Modernity.* Cambridge, Mass.: Harvard University Press, 1992.

Greenwood, F. Murray. *Legacies of Fear.* Toronto: Published for the Osgoode Society by University of Toronto Press, 1993.

Greer, Alan. "1837–38: Rebellion Reconsidered." *Canadian Historical Review* 76 (1995): 1–18.

– *The Patriots and the People: The Rebellion of 1837 in Rural Lower Canada.* Toronto: University of Toronto Press, 1993.

– *Peasant, Lord and Merchant: Rural Society in Three Quebec Parishes, 1740–1840.* Toronto: University of Toronto Press, 1985.

Griffin, Anne. *Quebec: The Challenge of Independence.* Rutherford, NJ: Fairleigh Dickinson University Press; London: Associated University Presses, 1984.

Griffith, Arthur. *The Resurrection of Hungary: A Parallel for Ireland.* Dublin: James Duffy and Co., 1904.

Groulx, Lionel. "Un débat parlementaire en 1849." *Revue d'histoire de l'Amérique française* 2 (1948): 375–89.

– "Faillite d'une politique." *Revue d'histoire de l'Amérique française* 2 (1948): 81–96.

– *Notre maître le passé.* 1st series. Montréal: Librairie Granger Frères, 1946.

Guindon, Hubert. *Quebec Society: Tradition, Modernity and Nationhood.* Toronto: University of Toronto Press, 1988.

Guntzel, Ralph P. "The Motivational Sources of Mainstream Quebec Separatist Nationalism: A Reevaluation." *Canadian Review of Studies in Nationalism* 24 (1997): 43–9.

Gwynn, Denis. *Young Ireland and 1848.* Cork: Cork University Press, 1949.

Hamelin, Jean, ed. *Histoire du Québec.* Sainte-Hyacinthe: Edisem, 1976.

Hamelin, L.E. "Évolution numérique séculaire du clergé catholique dans le Québec." *Recherches sociographiques* 2 (1961): 189–241.

Hamilton, Richard, and Maurice Pinard. "The Bases of Parti Québécois Support in Recent Quebec Elections." *Canadian Journal of Political Science* 9 (1976): 3–26.

Handler, Richard. *Nationalism and the Politics of Culture in Quebec.* Madison: University of Wisconsin Press, 1988.

Hansard's Parliamentary Debates. 3d series, vols. 134–306. London.

Harkness, D.W. *The Restless Dominion: The Irish Free State and the British Commonwealth of Nations, 1921–31.* New York: New York University Press 1970

Hart, Peter. *The IRA and Its Enemies: Violence and Community in Cork.* Oxford: Clarendon Press; New York: Oxford University Press, 1998.

Hastings, Adrian. *The Construction of Nationhood: Ethnicity, Religion and Nationalism.* Cambridge, New York: Cambridge University Press, 1997.

Hayes, Michael. "Dáil Éireann and the Irish Civil War." *Studies* 58 (1969): 1–23.

Hechter, Michael. *Containing Nationalism.* New York: Oxford University Press, 2000.

– *Internal Colonialism: The Celtic Fringe in British National Development, 1536–1966.* Berkeley: University of California Press, 1975.
– "Nationalism as Group Solidarity." *Ethnic and Racial Studies* 10 (1987): 415–26.
Heintzman, Ralph. "The Political Culture of Quebec, 1840–1960." *Canadian Journal of Political Science* 16 (1983): 3–59.
– "Political Space and Economic Space: Quebec and the Empire of the St. Lawrence." *Journal of Canadian Studies* 29 (1994): 19–63.
Hennessey, Thomas. *A History of Northern Ireland, 1920–1996.* Dublin: Gill & Macmillan, 1997.
Hennessy, Thomas. "Ulster Unionist Territorial and National Identities, 1886–1893: Province, Island, Kingdom and Empire." *Irish Political Studies* 8 (1993): 21–36.
Hickman, Mary J. "Reconstructing Deconstructing 'Race': British Political Discourses about the Irish in Britain." *Ethnic and Racial Studies* 21 (1998): 288–307.
Hill, Jacqueline R. "The Intelligentsia and Irish Nationalism in the 1840s." *Studia Hibernica* 20 (1980): 73–109.
– "Nationalism and the Catholic Church in the 1840s: Views of Dublin Repealers." *Irish Historical Studies* 19 (1975): 371–95.
Hill, Robert. *Voice of the Vanishing Minority: Robert Sellar and the* Huntingdon Gleaner, *1863–1919.* Montreal: McGill-Queen's University Press, 1998.
Hiller, Harry H. "The Foundations and Politics of Separatism: Canada in Comparative Perspective." *Research in Political Sociology* 3 (1987): 39–60.
Hindley, Reg. *The Death of the Irish Language: A Qualified Obituary.* London and New York: Routledge, 1990.
Hobsbawm, E.J. *Nations and Nationalism since 1780: Programme, Myth, Reality.* Cambridge and New York: Cambridge University Press, 1990.
Holmes, Michael. "Symbols of National Identity and Sport: The Case of the Irish Football Team." *Irish Political Studies* 9 (1994): 81–98.
Hopkinson, Michael. "The Craig-Collins Pacts of 1922: Two Attempted Reforms of the Northern Ireland Government." *Irish Historical Studies* 27 (1990): 145–58.
– *The Irish War of Independence.* Montreal and Kingston: McGill-Queen's University Press, 2002.
Hoppen, K. Theodore. *Elections, Politics and Society in Ireland, 1832–1885.* New York: Oxford University Press, 1984.
Horgan, John. *Sean Lemass: The Enigmatic Patriot.* Dublin: Gill and Macmillan, 1997.
Horton, Donald J. *André Laurendeau: French Canadian Nationalist.* Toronto: Oxford University Press, 1992.
Howe, Stephen. *Ireland and Empire: Colonial Legacies in Irish History and Culture.* Oxford: Oxford University Press, 2000.
Hroch, Miroslav. "From National Movement to the Fully-Formed Nation." *New Left Review* 198 (March/April 1993): 3–20.

Hurst, Michael. "Fenianism in the Context of World History." *University Review* 4, no. 3 (1967): 274–81.

Hutchinson, John. "Cultural Nationalism, Elite Mobility and Nation-Building: Communitarian Politics in Modern Ireland." *British Journal of Sociology* 38 (1987): 482–501.

– *The Dynamics of Cultural Nationalism.* Boston: Allen & Unwin, 1987.

Hyde, Douglas. *A Literary History of Ireland: from earliest times to the present day.* London: T. Fisher Unwin, 1899.

Inglis, Tom. *Moral Monopoly: The Rise and Fall of the Catholic Church in Modern Ireland.* Dublin: University College Dublin Press, 1998.

– "Sacred and Secular in Catholic Ireland." *Studies* 74 (1985): 38–46.

Ivory, Gareth. "Fianna Fail, Constitutional Republicanism, and the Issue of Consent: 1980–1996." *Eire/Ireland* 32, nos. 2 and 3 (Fall and Winter 1997): 93–116.

Jackson, Alvin. *Home Rule: An Irish History.* London: Phoenix, 2004.

Jalland, Patricia. "Irish Home Rule Finance: A Neglected Dimension of the Irish Question, 1910–14." *Irish Historical Studies* 23 (1983): 233–53.

– "United Kingdom Devolution, 1910–14: Political Panacea or Tactical Diversion?" *English Historical Review* 94 (1979): 757–85.

James, Robert Rhodes, ed. *Churchill Speaks: Collected Speeches, 1897–1963.* Leicester: Windward Books, 1981.

Jamieson, Stuart M. "French and English in the Institutional Structure of Montreal: A Study of the Socio-Economic Division of Labor." MA thesis, McGill University, 1938.

Johnson, D.S. "Northern Ireland as a Problem in the Economic War, 1932–1938." *Irish Historical Studies* 22 (1980): 144–61.

Johnson, Daniel. *Egalité ou indépendance.* Montréal: Éditions de l'homme, 1965.

Johnson, William. *Anglophobie Made in Québec.* Montréal: Alain Stanké, 1991.

Jones, Richard. *Community in Crisis.* Toronto: McClelland and Stewart, 1972.

Joy, Richard J. *Languages in Conflict: The Canadian Experience.* Toronto: McClelland and Stewart, 1972.

Kamenka, Eugene, ed. *Nationalism: The Nature and Evolution of an Idea.* Canberra: Australian National University Press, 1973.

Kearney, Richard. *Post-Nationalist Ireland.* New York: Routledge, 1997.

Keating, Michael. *Nations against the State: The New Politics of Nationalism in Quebec, Catalonia, and Scotland.* New York: St. Martin's Press 1996.

Kedourie, Elie. *Nationalism.* New York: Praeger, 1960.

Kee, Robert. *The Green Flag.* London: Quartet Books, 1976.

Kelley, Kevin. *The Longest War: Northern Ireland and the IRA.* London: Zed Books, 1982.

Kelly, James. "The Origins of the Act of Union: An Examination of Unionist Opinion in Britain and Ireland, 1650–1800." *Irish Historical Studies* 25 (1987): 236–63.

Kelly, Stéphane. *La petite loterie: Comment la Couronne a obtenu la collaboration des canadiens français après 1837.* Montréal: Boréal, 1997.
– ed. *Les idées mènent le Québec: Essais sur une sensibilité historique.* Québec: Les Presses de l'Université Laval, 2003.
Kendle, John. *Ireland and the Federal Solution.* Kingston and Montreal: McGill-Queen's University Press, 1989.
Kennedy, W.P.M. *Documents of the Canadian Constitution, 1759–1915.* Toronto: Oxford University Press, 1918.
Kenny, Mary. *Goodbye to Catholic Ireland.* Revised ed., Dublin: New Island Books, 2000.
Keogh, Dermot. "The Jesuits and the 1937 Constitution." *Studies* 78 (1989): 82–95.
Kissane, Bill. *Explaining Irish Democracy.* Dublin: University College Dublin Press, 2002.
– "Majority Rule and the Stabilisation of Democracy in the Irish Free State." *Irish Political Studies* 13 (1998): 1–24.
– "The Not-So Amazing Case of Irish Democracy." *Irish Political Studies* 10 (1995): 43–68.
Knowlton, Steven R. "The Politics of John Mitchel: A Reappraisal." *Eire/Ireland* 22, no. 2 (Summer 1987): 38–55.
Knox, Oliver. *Rebels and Informers: Stirrings of Irish Independence.* London: John Murray, 1997.
Kohn, Hans. *The Idea of Nationalism: A Study in Its Origins and Background.* New York: Collier 1944.
Kostick, Conor, and Lorcan Collins. *The Easter Rising: A Guide to Dublin in 1916.* Dublin: O'Brien, 2000.
Krause, David. "The Conscience of Ireland: Lalor, Davitt, and Sheehy-Skeffington." *Eire/Ireland* 28, no. 1 (Spring 1993): 7–31.
Kumar, Radha. "The Troubled History of Partition." *Foreign Affairs* 76 (1997): 22–34.
Kwavnick, David. "Quebec and the Two Nations Theory: A Re-examination." *Queen's Quarterly* 81 (1974): 357–74.
– "Québécois Nationalism and Canada's National Interest." *Journal of Canadian Studies* 12, no. 2 (Summer 1977): 53–68.
– "The Roots of French-Canadian Discontent." *Canadian Journal of Economics and Political Science* 31 (1965): 509–23.
Lachapelle, Guy, et al. *The Quebec Democracy: Structures, Processes, Policies.* Toronto: McGraw-Hill Ryerson, 1993.
Laczko, Leslie. *Pluralism and Inequality in Quebec.* New York: St. Martin's Press, 1995.
Laffan, Michael. *The Partition of Ireland, 1911–1925.* Dundalk: Dundalgan Press, 1983.
– *The Resurrection of Ireland.* New York: Cambridge University Press, 1999.

La Forest, G.V. *Disallowance and Reservation of Provincial Legislation*. Ottawa: Queen's Printer 1955.

Laitin, David D. "National Revivals and Violence." *European Journal of Sociology* 36 (1995): 3–43.

Lalor, James Fintan. *Collected Writings*. With a biographical note by L. Fogarty. Dublin: Talbot Press, 1947.

Lamonde, Yvan, and Claude Corbo, eds. *Le rouge et le bleu: Une anthologie de la pensée politique au Québec de la Conquête à la Révolution tranquille*. Montréal: Les Presses de l'Université de Montréal, 1999.

Lanctôt, Gustave. *Canada and the American Revolution, 1774–1783*. Toronto: Clarke, Irwin, 1967.

Larkin, Emmet. "Church, State and Nation in Modern Ireland." *American Historical Review* 80 (1975): 1244–76.

– "The Devotional Revolution in Ireland, 1850–75." *American Historical Review* 77 (1972): 625–52.

– "Economic Growth, Capital Investment, and the Roman Catholic Church in Nineteenth-Century Ireland." *American Historical Review* 72 (1967): 852–84.

– "The Fall of Parnell: Personal Tragedy, National Triumph." *Studies* 80 (1991): 358–65.

– "Launching the Counter-Attack: Part II of the Roman Catholic Hierarchy and the Destruction of Parnellism." *Review of Politics* 28 (1966): 359–83.

– "Mounting the Counter-Attack: The Roman Catholic Hierarchy and the Destruction of Parnellism." *Review of Politics* 25 (1963): 157–82.

– "Socialism and Catholicism in Ireland." *Studies* 74 (1985): 66–92.

LaTerreur, Marc. *Les tribulations des conservateurs au Québec*. Quebec: Les Presses de l'Université de Laval, 1973.

Latouche, Daniel. *Canada and Quebec, Past and Future: An Essay*. Toronto: University of Toronto Press, 1986.

—. "La vrai nature de ... la Révolution tranquille." *Canadian Journal of Political Science* 7 (1974): 525–36.

Laurendeau, André. *The Diary of André Laurendeau: Written during the Royal Commission on Bilingualism and Biculturalism, 1964–1967*. With an introd. by Patricia Smart. Toronto: James Lorimer, 1991.

Lawlor, S.M. "Ireland from Truce to Treaty: War or Peace? July to October 1921." *Irish Historical Studies* 22 (1980): 49–64.

Lawson, Philip. *The Imperial Challenge: Quebec and Britain in the Age of the American Revolution*. Montreal: McGill-Queen's University Press, 1990.

Lee, J.J. *Ireland, 1912–1985: Politics and Society*. Cambridge, New York: Cambridge University Press, 1995.

Lee, Joseph. *The Modernisation of Irish Society, 1848–1918*. Dublin: Gill and Macmillan, 1973.

Lee, Joseph, and Gearóid Ó Tuathaigh. *The Age of de Valera*. Dublin: Ward River Press, 1982.

Lemco, Jonathan. *Turmoil in the Peaceable Kingdom.* Toronto: University of Toronto Press, 1994.

Lemieux, Lucien. *Histoire du catholicisme québécois.* Vol. 2, tome 1, *Les années difficiles.* Montréal: Boréal, 1989.

Leslie, Peter M. *Ethnonationalism in a Federal State: The Case of Canada.* Kingston: Institute of Intergovernmental Relations, Queen's University, 1988.

– *Rebuilding the Relationship: Quebec and Its Confederation Partners.* Kingston: Institute of Intergovernmental Relations, 1987.

Létourneau, Jocelyn. *A History for the Future: Rewriting Memory and Identity in Quebec.* Montreal and Kingston: McGill-Queen's University Press, 2004.

Leuprecht, Christian. "The Liberal Contradictions of Québec Nationalism." *Canadian Review of Studies in Nationalism* 29 (2002): 13–26.

Lévesque, René. *Attendez que je me rappelle.* Montréal: Québec/Amérique, 1986.

– *Option Québec.* Montréal: Les Éditions de l'Homme, 1968.

Levine, Marc. *The Reconquest of Montreal.* Philadelphia: Temple University Press, 1990.

Levitt, Joseph. *Henri Bourassa and the Golden Calf.* Ottawa: Les Éditions de l'Université d'Ottawa, 1972.

– *Henri Bourassa on Imperialism and Bi-culturalism 1900–1918.* Toronto: Copp Clark, 1970.

– "La perspective nationaliste d'Henri Bourassa." *Revue d'histoire de l'Amérique française* 22 (1968–69): 569–85.

Lijphart, Arend. "The Framework Document on Northern Ireland and the Theory of Power-Sharing." *Government and Opposition* 31 (1996): 267–74.

Linteau, Paul-André, et al. *Histoire du Québec contemporain.* Vol. 1, *De la Confédération à la Crise.* Montréal: Boréal, 1979.

– *Histoire du Québec contemporain.* Vol. 2, *Le Québec depuis 1930.* Montréal: Boréal, 1986.

Lipset, Seymour Martin. *The First New Nation: The United States in Historical and Comparative Perspective.* New York: Basic Books 1963.

Lisée, Jean-François. *Dans l'oeil de l'aigle: Washington face au Québec.* Montréal: Boréal, 1990.

– *Sortie de secours.* Montréal: Boréal, 2000.

Litton, Helen. *The Irish Civil War: An Illustrated History.* Dublin: Wolfhound Press, 1995.

Lloyd, Trevor. "Partition-within-Partition: The Irish Example." *International Journal* 53 (1998): 505–21.

Local Ireland Almanac and Book of Facts, 2000. Dublin: Local Almanac, 1999.

Loranger, T.J.J. *Letters upon the Interpretation of the Federal Constitution Known as the B.N.A. Act.* Quebec: Morning Chronicle, 1884.

Loughlin, James. "The Irish Protestant Home Rule Association and Nationalist Politics, 1886–93." *Irish Historical Studies* 24 (1985): 341–60.

Lustick, Ian. *State-Building Failure in British Ireland and French Algeria.* Research Series no. 63. Berkeley: Institute of International Studies, University of California, 1985.

Lynch, John. *Speeches and Statements, August 1969-October 1971*. Dublin: Government Information Bureau, 1971.

Lyons, F.S.L. *Culture and Anarchy in Ireland, 1890–1939*. Oxford: Clarendon Press; New York: Oxford University Press, 1979.

McBride, Lawrence W. *The Greening of Dublin Castle: The Transformation of Bureaucratic and Judicial Personnel in Ireland, 1892–1922*. Washington: Catholic University of America Press, 1991.

McCartney, Donal. "The Church and Fenianism." *University Review* 4, no. 3 (winter 1967): 203–15.

McCrone, David. *The Sociology of Nationalism: Tomorrow's Ancestors*. London and New York: Routledge, 1998.

MacDermot, Frank. "A Postscript on Tone." *Studies* 28 (1939): 639–50.

McDowell, R.B. "The Irish Executive in the Nineteenth Century." *Irish Historical Studies* 9 (1955): 264–80.

McGarry, John. "Political Settlements in Northern Ireland and South Africa." *Political Studies* 46 (1998): 853–70.

McGarry, John, and Brendan O'Leary. *Explaining Northern Ireland: Broken Images*. Oxford; Cambridge, Mass.: Blackwell, 1995.

– "Five Fallacies: Northern Ireland and the Liabilities of Liberalism." *Ethnic and Racial Studies* 18 (1995): 837–61.

McInerney, Michael. "Noel Browne: Church and State." *University Review* 5, no. 2 (1968): 171–215.

Macintyre, Angus. *The Liberator: Daniel O'Connell and the Irish Party, 1830–1847*. London: H. Hamilton, 1965.

McIntyre, Anthony. "Modern Irish Republicanism: The Product of British State Strategies." *Irish Political Studies* 10 (1995): 97–121.

Mackay, James. *Michael Collins: A Life*. Edinburgh; London: Mainstream Publishing; N. Pomfret, Vt: Distributed by Trafalgar Square, 1996.

McKee, Eamonn. "Church-State Relations and the Development of Irish Health Policy: The Mother-and-Child Scheme, 1944–53." *Irish Historical Studies* 25 (1986): 159–94.

McKenna, Brian, and Susan Purcell. *Drapeau*. Toronto: Clarke Irwin, 1980.

McKittrick, David, and David McVea. *Making Sense of the Troubles: The Story of the Conflict in Northern Ireland*. New York: New Amsterdam Books, 2002.

Macmillan, Gretchen. *State, Society and Authority in Ireland: The Foundations of the Modern State*. Dublin: Gill and Macmillan, 1993.

McMinn, Richard. "Presbyterianism and Politics in Ulster, 1871–1906." *Studia Hibernica* 21 (1981): 127–46.

McNeill, J. "Why and How the Irish Language Is to Be Preserved." *Irish Ecclesiastical Record* 3rd series, 12 (1891): 1099–108.

MacQueen, Norman. "Eamon de Valera, the Irish Free State, and the League of Nations, 1919–46." *Eire/Ireland* 17, no. 4 (Winter 1982): 110–27.

McRoberts, Kenneth. "Internal Colonialism: The Case of Quebec." *Ethnic and Racial Studies* 2 (1979): 293–318.
– *Misconceiving Canada: The Struggle for National Unity.* Toronto: Oxford University Press, 1997.
– *Quebec: Social Change and Political Crisis.* 3rd ed. Toronto: McClelland and Stewart, 1988.
– "The Sources of Neo-Nationalism in Quebec." *Ethnic and Racial Studies* 7 (1984): 55–85.
McWhinney, Edward. *Quebec and the Constitution, 1960–1978.* Toronto: University of Toronto Press, 1979.
Magnus, Philip. *Gladstone: A Biography.* London: John Murray, 1954.
Mandle, W.F. "The I.R.B. and the Beginnings of the Gaelic Athletic Association." *Irish Historical Studies* 20 (1977): 418–38.
Manning, Helen Taft. *The Revolt of French Canada, 1800–1835: A Chapter in the History of the British Commonwealth.* Toronto: Macmillan of Canada, 1962.
Manning, Maurice. *Irish Political Parties: An Introduction.* Dublin: Gill and Macmillan, 1972.
Mansergh, Martin, ed. *The Spirit of the Nation: The Speeches and Statements of Charles J. Haughey.* Cork and Dublin: Mercier Press, 1986.
Mansergh, Nicholas. *The Irish Question, 1840–1921: A Commentary on Anglo-Irish Relations and on Social and Political Forces in Ireland in the Age of Reform and Revolution.* Toronto: University of Toronto Press, 1975.
Martin, F.X. "Eoin MacNeill on the Rising." *Irish Historical Studies* 12 (1961): 226–71.
Martin, Ged. *Britain and the Origins of Canadian Confederation, 1837–67.* Vancouver: UBC Press, 1995.
Martin, Lawrence. *The Antagonist: Lucien Bouchard and the Politics of Delusion.* Toronto: Viking, 1997.
Martin, Pierre. "Association after Sovereignty? Canadian Views on Economic Association with a Sovereign Quebec." *Canadian Public Policy* 21 (1995): 53–71.
Marx, Karl. *Political Writings.* Vol. 3, *The First International and After.* New York: Random House, 1974.
Mason, David. "Nationalism and the Process of Group Mobilisation: The Case of 'Loyalism' in Northern Ireland Reconsidered." *Ethnic and Racial Studies* 8 (1985): 408–25.
Mathieu, Geneviève. *Qui est Québecois? Synthèse du débat sur la redéfinition de la nation.* Montréal: VLB Éditeur, 2001
Maume, Patrick. "The Ancient Constitution: Arthur Griffith and His Intellectual Legacy to Sinn Fein." *Irish Political Studies* 10 (1995): 123–37.
– *The Long Gestation: Irish Nationalist Life, 1891–1918.* New York: St. Martin's Press, 1999.
Meadwell, Hudson. "Ethnic Nationalism and Collective Choice Theory." *Comparative Political Studies* 22 (1989): 139–54.
– "The Politics of Nationalism in Quebec." *World Politics* 45 (1992–93): 203–41.

Meisel, John, Guy Rocher, and Arthur Silver. *As I Recall: Historical Perspectives.*
    Montreal: The Institute for Research on Public Policy, 1999.
Miller, David W. *Queen's Rebels: Ulster Loyalism in Historical Perspective.* Dublin: Gill
    and Macmillan, 1978.
– "The Roman Catholic Church in Ireland: 1898–1918." *Eire/Ireland* 3, no. 3
    (Autumn 1968): 75–91.
Miquelon, Dale. *The First Canada: to 1791.* Toronto: McGraw-Hill Ryerson, 1994.
Mitchel, John. *Jail Journal.* With a preface by Arthur Griffith. Dublin: M.H. Gill, 1914.
– *Writings of John Mitchel.* Dublin: Republican Publications, 1972.
Mitchell, Paul. "Party Competition in an Ethnic Dual Party System." *Ethnic and
    Racial Studies* 18 (1995): 773–96.
Moloney, Ed. *A Secret History of the I.R.A.* London: Penguin Books, 2002.
Monet, Jacques. *The Last Cannon Shot: A Study of French Canadian Nationalism,
    1837–1850.* Toronto: University of Toronto Press, 1969.
Monière, Denis. *André Laurendeau et le destin d'un peuple.* Montréal:
    Québec-Amérique, 1983.
– *Ideologies in Quebec: The Historical Development.* Toronto: University of Toronto
    Press, 1981.
– *Pour comprendre le nationalisme au Québec et ailleurs.* Montréal: Les Presses de
    l'Université de Montréal, 2001.
Moody, T.W., Martin, F.X., Byrne, F.J. *A New History of Ireland.* Vol. 3, *Early Modern
    Ireland.* Oxford: Clarendon Press, 1976.
Moore, Brian. *The Revolution Script.* New York: Holt, Rinehart and Winston, 1971.
Moran, Sean Farrell. *Patrick Pearse and the Politics of Redemption: The Mind of the
    Easter Rising, 1916.* Washington: Catholic University Press, 1994.
Morin, Claude. *Mes premiers ministres: Lesage, Johnson, Bertrand, Bourassa et Lévesque.*
    Montréal: Boréal, 1991.
Morris, Ewan. "'God Save the King' versus 'The Soldier's Song': The 1929 Trinity
    College National Anthem Dispute and the Politics of the Irish Free State." *Irish
    Historical Studies* 31 (1998): 72–90.
Morton, W.L. "Lord Monck and Nationality in Ireland and Canada." *Studia
    Hibernica* 13 (1973): 77–99.
Moynihan, Maurice, ed. *Speeches and Statements by Eamon de Valera, 1917–73.*
    Dublin: Gill and Macmillan, 1980.
Munck, Ronald. "At the Very Doorstep: Irish Labor and the National Question."
    Eire/Ireland 18, no. 2 (Summer 1983): 36–51.
– "Rethinking Irish Nationalism: The Republican Dimension." *Canadian Review of
    Studies in Nationalism* 14 (1986): 31–48.
Murphy, Brian. *Patrick Pearse and the Lost Republican Ideal.* Dublin: James Duffy, 1991.
Murray, Peter. "Irish Cultural Nationalism in the United Kingdom State: Politics
    and the Gaelic League 1900–18." *Irish Political Studies* 8 (1993): 55–72.
Murray, Vera. *Le Parti québécois: De la fondation à la prise du pouvoir.* Montréal:
    Hurtubise HMH, 1976.

Murray, Vera, and Don Murray. *De Bourassa à Lévesque*. Montréal: Éditions Quinze, 1978.

Nairn, Tom. *Faces of Nationalism: Janus Revisited*. London; New York: Verso, 1997.

Neatby, Blair. *Laurier and a Liberal Quebec*. Toronto: McClelland and Stewart, 1973.

Neatby, H. Blair, and John T. Saywell. "Chapleau and the Conservative Party in Quebec." *Canadian Historical Review* 37 (1956): 1–22.

Neatby, Hilda. *Quebec: The Revolutionary Age, 1760–1791*. Toronto: McClelland and Stewart, 1966.

— ed. *The Quebec Act: Protest and Policy*. Scarborough: Prentice-Hall, 1972

Nelles, H.V. *The Art of Nation-Building: Pageantry and Spectacle at Quebec's Tercentenary*. Toronto: University of Toronto Press, 1999.

O'Bride, Ian. *Scripture Politics: Ulster Presbyterians and Irish Radicalism in the Late Eighteenth Century*. Oxford: Clarendon Press, 1998.

O'Brien, Conor Cruise. *Parnell and His Party, 1880–90*. Oxford: Clarendon Press, 1964.

O'Brien, Justin. *The Arms Trial*. Dublin: Gill and Macmillan 2000.

O'Callaghan, Margaret. *British High Politics and a Nationalist Ireland: Criminality, Land, and the Law under Forster and Balfour*. Cork: Cork University Press, 1994.

– "Language, Nationality and Cultural Identity in the Irish Free State, 1922–7: The *Irish Statesman* and the *Catholic Bulletin* Reappraised." *Irish Historical Studies* 24 (1984): 226–45.

O'Connell, Maurice R. "The American Revolution and Ireland." *Eire/Ireland* 11, no. 3 (Fall 1976): 3–12.

– ed. *Daniel O'Connell: Political Pioneer*. Dublin: Institute of Public Administration, 1991.

O'Connor, Fionnuala. *In Search of a State: Catholics in Northern Ireland*. Belfast: Blackstaff Press, 1993.

O'Day, Alan. *Irish Home Rule, 1867–1921*. Manchester and New York: Manchester University Press, 1998.

O'Day, Alan, and John Stevenson, eds. *Irish Historical Documents since 1800*. Dublin: Gill and Macmillan, 1992.

O'Deirg, Iosold, ed. "Oh! Lord, the Unrest of Soul: The Jail Journal of Michael Collins." *Studia Hibernica* 28 (1994): 7–34.

O'Donoghue, Florence. "Plans for the 1916 Rising." *University Review* 3, no. 1 (1962): 3–21.

O'Donovan, Teresa. "Ulster and Home Rule for Ireland, to 1914." *Eire/Ireland* 18, no. 3 (Fall 1983): 6–22.

O'Duffy, Brendan. "Violence in Northern Ireland, 1969–1994: Sectarian or Ethnonational?" *Ethnic and Racial Studies* 18 (1995): 740–72.

O'Farrell, John. "Irish Families in Ancient Quebec Records." *Eire/Ireland* 2 no. 4 (Winter 1967): 19–35.

O'Farrell, Patrick. *Ireland's English Question: Anglo-Irish Relations, 1534–1970*. New York: Schocken Books, 1971.

O'Ferrall, Fergus. *Daniel O'Connell.* Dublin: Gill and Macmillan, 1981.

(Official Report) Debate on the Treaty between Great Britain and Ireland. Dublin: Talbot Press, 1925.

Ó Gráda, Cormac. *Ireland: A New Economic History, 1780–1939.* Oxford: Clarendon Press; New York: Oxford University Press, 1994.

O'Halloran, Clare. *Partition and the Limits of Irish Nationalism: An Ideology under Stress.* Dublin: Gill and Macmillan, 1987.

O'Hullachain, Father Colman. *The Irish and Irish: A Sociolinguistic Analysis of the Relationship between a People and Their Language.* Dublin: Franciscan Friars, 1994.

O'Keefe, Timothy J. "The 1898 Efforts to Celebrate the United Irishmen: The '98 Centennial." *Eire/Ireland* 23, no. 2 (Summer 1988): 51–73.

– "Who Fears to Speak of '98? The Rhetoric and Rituals of the United Irishmen Centennial, 1898." *Eire/Ireland* 27, no. 3 (Fall 1992): 67–91

O'Leary, Brendan. "Afterword: What Is Framed in the Framework Documents?" *Ethnic and Racial Studies* 18 (1995): 862–72.

– "Introduction: Reflections on a Cold Peace." *Ethnic and Racial Studies* 18 (1995): 695–714.

– "The Limits to Coercive Consociationalism in Northern Ireland." *Political Studies* 37 (1989): 562–88.

O'Leary, Dostaler. *Séparatisme: Doctrine constructive.* Montréal: Les Éditions des Jeunesses patriotes, 1937.

Oliver, Michael. *The Passionate Debate: The Social and Political Ideas of Quebec Nationalism, 1920–1945.* Montreal: Véhicule Press, 1991.

O'Luing, Sean. "Arthur Griffith, 1871–1922: Thoughts on a Centenary." *Studies* 60 (1971): 127–38.

– "Douglas Hyde and the Gaelic League." *Studies* 62 (1973): 123–38.

O'Neil, Daniel J. "The Cult of Self-Sacrifice: the Irish Experience." *Eire/Ireland* 24, no. 4 (Winter 1989): 89–105.

– "Irish Nationalism and Roman Catholicism: The Revolutionary Experience of Patrick Pearse, Horace Plunkett, and James Connolly." *Canadian Review of Studies in Nationalism* 19 (1992): 59–78.

O'Neill, Thomas P. "The Irish Land Question, 1830–1850." *Studies* 44 (1955): 325–36.

Ó'Riagáin, Pádraig. *Language Policy and Social Reproduction: Ireland, 1893–1993.* Oxford: Clarendon Press; New York: Oxford University Press, 1997.

O'Riain, Seamas. "Dail Eireann 1919." *Capuchin Annual* (1969): 323–29.

O'Shiel, Kevin R. "The Problem of Partitioned Ireland." *Studies* 12 (1923): 625–38.

Ouellet, Fernand. *Economic and Social History of Quebec, 1760–1850: Structures and Conjunctures.* Toronto: Gage, 1980.

– *Lower Canada, 1791–1840: Social Change and Nationalism.* Toronto: McClelland and Stewart, 1979.

Pakenham, Frank. *Peace by Ordeal.* London: Sidgwick & Jackson, 1972.

Pakenham, Thomas. *The Year of Liberty: The Story of the Great Irish Rebellion of 1798.* London: Hodder & Stoughton, 1969.

Paquet, Gilles. *Oublier la Révolution tranquille: Pour une nouvelle socialité.* Montréal: Liber, 1999.

Parliamentary Debates. 2nd series, vols. 20–2; 3rd series, vols. 23–100; 4th series, vols. 8–11. London.

Parliamentary Debates on the Subject of the Confederation of the British North American Provinces. Quebec: Hunter, Rose and Co., 1865.

Parliamentary History. Vols. 17–34 (1771–1800).

Parti québécois. *La lettre du parti.* 28 November 2002, 10 January 2003.

– *Le Québec dans un monde nouveau.* Montréal: VLB, 1993.

Paseta, Senia. *Before the Revolution: Nationalism, Social Change, and Ireland's Catholic Elite, 1879–1922.* Cork: Cork University Press, 1999.

Pearse, Padraic. *Political Writings and Speeches.* Dublin: Talbot Press, 1962.

Pelletier, Gérard. *The October Crisis.* Toronto: McClelland and Stewart, 1971.

Phelan, Michael J., SJ. "The Language Question in Canada: A Lesson for the Gael." *Irish Ecclesiastical Record,* 5th series, 12 (July-December 1918): 307–15.

Phillips, Kevin. *The Cousins' Wars: Religion, Politics, and the Triumph of Anglo-America.* New York: Basic Books, 1999.

Pierson, Paul. "Increasing Returns, Path Dependence, and the Study of Politics." *American Political Science Review* 94 (2000): 251–68.

Pinard, Maurice. "The Dramatic Reemergence of the Quebec Independence Movement." *Journal of International Affairs* 45 (1991–92): 471–97.

Pinard, Maurice, and Richard Hamilton. "The Class Bases of the Quebec Independence Movement: Conjectures and Evidence." *Ethnic and Racial Studies* 7 (1984): 19–54.

– "The Parti québécois Comes to Power: An Analysis of the 1976 Quebec Election." *Canadian Journal of Political Science* 11 (1978), 739–75.

Plunkett, Geraldine. "The Irish Party." *University Review* 2, no. 1 (1958): 31–38.

Pouliot, Léon, SJ. "Les évêques du Bas-Canada et le projet d'union (1840)." *Revue d'histoire de l'Amérique française* 8 (1954–55): 157–70.

Power, Charles G. *A Party Politician: The Memoirs of Chubby Power.* Toronto: Macmillan, 1966.

Prager, Jeffrey. *Building Democracy in Ireland: Political Order and Cultural Integration in a Newly Independent Nation.* Cambridge and New York: Cambridge University Press, 1986.

Probert, Belinda. *Beyond Orange and Green: The Political Economy of the Northern Ireland Crisis.* Dublin: Academy Press, 1978.

Purdie, Bob. "Was the Civil Rights Movement a Republican/Communist Conspiracy?" *Irish Political Studies* 3 (1988): 33–41.

Pyne, Peter. "The New Irish State and the Decline of the Republican Sinn Fein Party, 1923–1926." *Eire/Ireland* 11, no. 3 (Fall 1976): 33–65.

Quebec. Commission on the Political and Constitutional Future of Quebec. *Report of the Commission on the Political and Constitutional Future of Quebec.* Quebec: Editeur officiel du Québec, 1991.

– Ministère des affaires intergouvernementales. *Quebec's Traditional Stands on the Division of Powers, 1900–1976.* Quebec, 1978.

– Legislative Assembly/National Assembly. *Débats.* 1886, 1977. Québec.

Québec-Canada: A New Deal. Quebec: Éditeur officiel du Québec, 1979.

A Quebec Free to Choose: Report of the Constitutional Committee of the Quebec Liberal Party. Montreal, 1991.

Quinn, Herbert. *The Union nationale: Québec Nationalism from Duplessis to Lévesque.* 2nd ed. Toronto: University of Toronto Press, 1979.

Rafferty, Oliver J., SJ. "The Catholic Bishops and Revolutionary Violence in Ireland." *Studies* 83 (1994): 30–42.

Ranelagh, John O"Beirne. "The IRB from the Treaty to 1924." *Irish Historical Studies* 20 (1977): 26–39.

Raymond, Raymond James. "Irish Nationalism in the Early Twentieth Century: A Reappraisal." *Canadian Review of Studies in Nationalism* 14 (1987): 19–30.

Regan, John M. *The Irish Counter-Revolution, 1921–1936.* Dublin: Gill and Macmillan, 1999.

– "The Politics of Reaction: The Dynamics of Treatyite Government and Policy, 1922–33." *Irish Historical Studies* 30 (1997): 542–63.

Reid, Malcolm. *The Shouting Signpainters.* Toronto: McClelland and Stewart, 1972.

Reilly, Wayne G. "The Management of Political Violence in Quebec and Northern Ireland: A Comparison." *Terrorism and Political Violence* 6, no. 1 (Spring 1994), 44–61.

Richard, Laurence. *Jacques Parizeau: Un bâtisseur.* Montreal: Les Éditions de l'Homme, 1992.

Rodner, William S. "Leaguers, Covenanters, Moderates: British Support for Ulster, 1913–1914." *Eire/Ireland* 17, no. 3 (Fall 1982): 68–85.

Rose, Richard. *Governing without Consensus: An Irish Perspective.* Boston: Beacon Press, 1971.

Rotstein, Abraham, ed. *Power Corrupted: The October Crisis and the Repression of Quebec.* Toronto: New Press, 1971.

Roy, Jean-Louis. *Le choix d'un peuple: Le débat constitutionnel Québec-Canada, 1960–1976.* Montréal: Leméac, 1978.

Ruane, Joseph, and Jennifer Todd. "Diversity, Division and the Middle Ground in Northern Ireland." *Irish Political Studies* 7 (1992): 73–98.

– *The Dynamics of Conflict in Northern Ireland: Power, Conflict, and Emancipation.* Cambridge and New York: Cambridge University Press, 1996.

Rudin, Ronald. *The Forgotten Quebecers.* Québec: Institut québécois de recherche sur la culture, 1985.

- *Founding Fathers: The Celebration of Champlain and Laval in the Streets of Quebec, 1878–1908.* Toronto: University of Toronto Press, 2003.
- *Making History in Twentieth Century Quebec.* Toronto: University of Toronto Press, 1997.
- "One Model, Two Responses: Quebec, Ireland and the Study of Rural Society." *Canadian Papers in Rural History* 9 (1994): 259–89.
- "Revisionism and the Search for a Normal Society: A Critique of Recent Quebec Historical Writing." *Canadian Historical Review* 73 (1992): 30–61.
Rumilly, Robert. *Histoire de la Société Saint-Jean-Baptiste de Montréal: Des Patriotes au fleurdelisé, 1834–1948.* Montréal: Les Éditions de l'Aurore, 1975.
- *Honoré Mercier et son temps.* 2 vols. Montreal: Fidès, 1975.
Russell, Peter H. *Constitutional Odyssey: Can Canadians Become a Sovereign People?* 2nd ed. Toronto: University of Toronto Press, 1993.
Ryerson, Stanley B. *French Canada.* Toronto: Progress Books, 1980.
- *Unequal Union: Confederation and the Roots of Conflict in the Canadas, 1815–1873.* Toronto: Progress Books, 1968.
Sarra-Bournet, Michel, ed. *Les nationalismes au Québec du XIXe au XXIe siècle.* Québec: Les Presses de l'Université Laval, 2000.
Savage, D.C. "The Origins of the Ulster Unionist Party, 1885–6." *Irish Historical Studies* 12 (1961): 185–208.
Saywell, John T. "Backstage at London, 1864–1867: Constitutionalizing the Distinct Society." *National History* 1: 4 (Summer 2000): 331–46
- *The Lawmakers: Judicial Power and the Shaping of Canadian Federalism.* Toronto: University of Toronto Press, 2002.
- ed. *Canadian Annual Review of Politics and Public Affairs, 1976.* Toronto: University of Toronto Press.
Schmitt, David E. "Catholicism and Democratic Political Development in Ireland." *Eire/Ireland* 9, no. 1 (Spring 1974): 59–72.
Schull, Joseph. *Rebellion: The Rising in French Canada, 1837.* Toronto: Macmillan of Canada, 1971.
Scott, Frank, and Michael Oliver. *Quebec States Her Case: Speeches and Articles from Quebec in the Years of Unrest.* Toronto: Macmillan of Canada, 1964.
Scowen, Reed. *Time to Say Goodbye: The Case for Getting Quebec Out of Canada.* Toronto: McClelland and Stewart, 1999.
See, Katharine O'Sullivan. *First World Nationalisms: Class and Ethnic Politics in Northern Ireland and Quebec.* Chicago: University of Chicago Press, 1986.
Séguin, Maurice. *L'idée d'indépendance au Québec: Genèse et historique.* Trois-Rivières: Boréal Express, 1968.
- *La "nation canadienne" et l'agriculture (1760–1850): Essai d'histoire économique.* Trois-Rivières: Éditions Boréal Express, 1970.
Senior, Hereward. "The Place of Fenianism in the Irish Republican Tradition." *University Review* 4, no. 3 (1967): 250–9.
- "Quebec and the Fenians." *Canadian Historical Review* 48 (1967): 26–44.

Shade, William G. "Strains of Modernization: The Republic of Ireland under
    Lemass and Lynch." *Eire/Ireland* 14, no. 1 (Spring 1979): 26–46.
Shapiro, Daniel M., and Morton Stelcner. "Language and Earnings in Quebec:
    Trends over Twenty Years, 1970–1990." *Canadian Public Policy* 23 (1997): 115–40.
Shaw, Father Francis. "The Canon of Irish History: A Challenge." *Studies* 61
    (1972): 113–53.
Siegfred, André. *The Race Question in Canada.* Toronto: McClelland and Stewart,
    1966.
Silver, A.I. *The French-Canadian Idea of Confederation, 1864–1900.* Toronto:
    University of Toronto Press, 1982.
Sinn Fein. *A Scenario for Peace: A Discussion Paper.* May 1987.
– *Towards a Strategy for Peace.* 1988.
The Sinn Fein/SDLP Talks, January–September 1988. Dublin: Sinn Fein Publicity
    Department, January 1989.
Sinnott, Richard. "The North: Party Images and Party Approaches in the
    Republic." *Irish Political Studies* 1 (1986): 15–31.
Skocpol, Theda. *Social Revolutions in the Modern World.* New York: Cambridge
    University Press, 1994.
Smith, Anthony D. "Culture, Community and Territory: The Politics of Ethnicity
    and Nationalism." *International Affairs* 72 (1996): 445–58.
– *Nationalism and Modernism: A Critical Survey of Recent Theories of Nations and
    Nationalism.* London and New York: Routledge, 1998.
– *Nationalism in the Twentieth Century.* New York: New York University Press, 1979.
– *Theories of Nationalism.* New York: Harper & Row, 1971.
Social Democratic and Labour Party. *A Brief History of the SDLP on Its 30th
    Anniversary.* Belfast, 2000.
– *Towards a New Ireland: Proposals by the Social Democratic and Labour Party.* Belfast,
    1973.
Société Saint-Jean-Baptiste. *Pour mieux comprendre le drame irlandais.* Montréal, n.d.
    [apparently 1981].
Solow, Barbara. *The Land Question and the Irish Economy, 1870–1903.* Cambridge,
    Mass.: Harvard University Press, 1971.
Somerville-Large, Peter. *Irish Voices: Fifty Years of Irish Life, 1916–1966.* London:
    Chatto & Windus, 1999.
Statesman's Yearbook. Various years. London: Macmillan.
Stevenson, Garth. *Community Besieged: The Anglophone Minority and the Politics of
    Quebec.* Montreal: McGill-Queen's University Press, 1999.
– *Ex Uno Plures: Federal-Provincial Relations in Canada, 1867–1896.* Montreal:
    McGill-Queen's University Press, 1993.
Syndergaard, Rex. "The Fitzwilliam Crisis and Irish Nationalism." *Eire/Ireland* 6,
    no. 3 (Fall 1971): 72–82.
Tannam, Etain. "The European Union and Northern Irish politics." *Ethnic and
    Racial Studies* 18 (1995): 797–817.

Tanner, Marcus. *Ireland's Holy Wars: The Struggle for a Nation's Soul, 1500–2000.* New Haven and London: Yale University Press, 2001.

Tardivel, Jules Paul. *Pour la patrie.* Québec: Éditions Hurtubise HMH, 1989.

Telford, Hamish, and Lazar, Harvey, eds. *Canadian Political Culture(s) in Transition.* Montreal and Kingston: McGill-Queen's University Press, 2002.

Tetley, William. "Language and Education Rights in Quebec and Canada." *Law and Contemporary Problems* 45 (1982): 177–219.

Thomson, Dale C. *Jean Lesage and the Quiet Revolution.* Toronto: Macmillan of Canada, 1984.

Thornley, David. *Isaac Butt and Home Rule.* London: MacGibbon & Kee, 1964.

– "Patrick Pearse and the Pearse Family." *Studies* 62 (1973): 332–46.

Tierney, Michael. "Origin and Growth of Modern Irish Nationalism." *Studies* 30 (1941): 321–36.

– "The Revival of the Irish Language." *Studies* 16 (1927): 1–10.

– "Thomas Davis: 1814–1845." *Studies* 34 (1945): 300–10.

Tillyard, Stella. *Citizen Lord: The Life of Edward Fitzgerald, Irish Revolutionary.* New York: Farrar, Straus and Giroux, 1997.

Todd, Jennifer. "Equality, Plurality and Democracy: Justifications of Proposed Constitutional Settlements of the Northern Ireland Conflict." *Ethnic and Racial Studies* 18 (1995): 818–36.

– "Northern Ireland Nationalist Political Culture." *Irish Political Studies* 5 (1990): 31–44.

– "Two Traditions in Unionist Political Culture." *Irish Political Studies* 2 (1987): 1–26.

Tone, Theobald Wolfe. *The Autobiography of Theobald Wolfe Tone.* Abridged and edited by Sean O'Faolain. London: T. Nelson, 1937.

Tovey, Hilary, et al. *Why Irish? Language and Identity in Ireland Today.* Dublin: Bord na Gaeilge, 1989.

Tremblay, Rodrigue. *Indépendance et marché commun Québec-États-unis.* Montréal: Éditions du jour, 1970.

Trofimenkoff, Susan Mann. *Abbé Groulx: Variations on a Nationalist Theme.* Vancouver: Copp Clarke Publishing, 1973.

– *Action française: French-Canadian Nationalism in the Twenties.* Toronto: University of Toronto Press, 1975.

Trudeau, Pierre Elliott. *Federalism and the French Canadians.* Toronto: Macmillan, 1968.

United Nations. *General Assembly Official Records.* 1956.

– *Security Council Official Records.* 1969.

Vadeboncoeur, Pierre. "A Break with Tradition? Political and Cultural Evolution in Quebec." *Queen's Quarterly* 65 (1958): 92–103.

Vallières, Pierre. *Nègres blancs d'Amérique: Autobiographie précoce d'un "terroriste" québécois.* Ottawa: Éditions Parti Pris, 1967.

Vaughan, W.E., and A.J. Fitzpatrick, eds. *Irish Historical Statistics: Population, 1821–1971.* Dublin: Royal Irish Academy, 1978.

Verney, Douglas V. *Three Civilizations, Two Cultures, One State: Canada's Political Traditions.* Durham: Duke University Press, 1986.

Voisine, Nive. *Histoire du Catholicisme québécois.* Montréal: Boréal Express, 1984.

Wade, Mason. *The French Canadians, 1760–1945.* Toronto: Macmillan of Canada, 1956.

Walker, Brian Mercer. "The Irish Electorate, 1868–1915," *Irish Historical Studies* 18 (1973): 359–406.

Walker, Graham. "Propaganda and Conservative Nationalism during the Irish Civil War, 1922–1923." *Eire/Ireland* 22, no. 4 (Winter 1987): 93–117.

Ward, Alan J. "America and the Irish Problem, 1899–1921." *Irish Historical Studies* 16 (1968): 64–90.

– *The Irish Constitutional Tradition: Responsible Government and Modern Ireland, 1782–1992.* Washington: Catholic University of America Press, 1994.

Weaver, R. Kent, ed. *The Collapse of Canada?* Washington: Brookings Institution, 1992.

Whelan, Christopher T. *Values and Social Change in Ireland.* Ireland: Gill and Macmillan, 1994.

Whelan, Noel, and Nicholas Whyte. *The Tallyman's Guide to the Northern Ireland Assembly Elections 2003.* Belfast: Limelight Communications 2003.

Whitaker, Reginald. "Apprehended Insurrection? RCMP Intelligence and the October Crisis." *Queen's Quarterly* 100 (1993): 383–406.

Whyte, J.H. *Church and State in Modern Ireland, 1923–1970.* Dublin: Gill and Macmillan, 1971.

Whyte, John H. "Daniel O'Connell and the Repeal Party." *Irish Historical Studies* 11 (1959): 297–316.

– "How Is the Boundary Maintained between the Two Communities in Northern Ireland?" *Ethnic and Racial Studies* 9 (1986): 219–34.

Wilson, Desmond. *Democracy Denied.* Dublin: Mercier Press, 1997.

Wilson, Robin. *Agreeing to Disagree? A Guide to the Northern Ireland Assembly.* Norwich: The Stationery Office, 2001.

Woehrling, José. "Les aspects juridiques d'une éventuelle sécession du Québec." *Canadian Bar Review* 74 (1995): 293–329.

Woodham-Smith, Cecil. *The Great Hunger: Ireland, 1845–1849.* New York: Harper & Row, 1962.

Woods, C.J. "Ireland and the French Revolution." *Eire/Ireland* 8, no. 2 (Summer 1973): 34–41.

Wright, Frank. *Northern Ireland: A Comparative Analysis.* Dublin: Gill and Macmillan, 1987.

Yeats, W.B. *Collected Works.* Vol. 1, *The Poems.* New York: Scribner, 1989.

Younger, Calton. *Arthur Griffith.* Dublin: Gill and Macmillan, 1981.

Index